Racial Hygiene

Racial Hygiene

Medicine under the Nazis

Robert Proctor

Harvard University Press
Cambridge, Massachusetts
London, England
1988

Copyright © 1988 by the President and Fellows of Harvard College
All rights reserved
Printed in the United States of America
10 9 8 7 6 5 4 3 2 1

This book is printed on acid-free paper, and its binding materials have been chosen for strength and durability.

Library of Congress Cataloging-in-Publication Data
Proctor, Robert, 1954–
  Racial hygiene : medicine under the Nazis / Robert Proctor.
    p.   cm.
  Bibliography: p.
  Includes index.
  ISBN 0-674-74580-9 (alk. paper)
  1. Medicine—Political aspects—Germany. 2. Physicians—Germany—Political activity. 3. National socialism. 4. Antisemitism—Germany. I. Title.
  [DNLM: 1. Ethics, Medical—history—Germany. 2. Eugenics—history—Germany. 3. History of Medicine, 20th Century—Germany. 4. Social Control, Formal—history—Germany.   WZ 70 GG4 P93r]
RA418.3.G3P76 1988
174'.2'0943—dc19
DNLM/DLC   87-31116
for Library of Congress   CIP

For my parents, Neel and Gene

Acknowledgments

A number of friends and colleagues helped inspire this study—among them, Stephen Jay Gould, Ruth Hubbard, Richard Levins, Richard Lewontin, and Everett Mendelsohn, each of whom has explored for many years the political character of science. A grant from the Fulbright-Hays Foundation allowed me to spend a year in Germany in 1980–81, where I began research on this topic. It was in a seminar offered by Gerhard Baader at the Free University of Berlin that I first discovered the efforts of German scholars to shed light on this darker side of the history of science. Through Gerhard Baader I was also able to make contact with other pioneering historians in this field, including Fridolf Kudlien at Kiel, Stephan Leibfried at Bremen, Gunter Mann at Mainz, Karl Heinz Roth in Hamburg, and Florian Tennstedt in Kassel.

In the course of this study I have had the opportunity to share ideas with other scholars working in this field. Garland Allen, John Beatty, Daniel Kevles, Diane Paul, James Sheehan, Florian Tennstedt, Peter Weingart, and Sheila Weiss all offered helpful criticisms of earlier drafts. I would also like to thank the staff of several libraries who helped me track down obscure publications. In West Berlin the librarians of the Preussische Staatsbibliothek and the Freie Universität were very helpful, as were the staffs of the Deutsche Staatsbibliothek in East Berlin and the Bundesarchiv in Koblenz. Daniel Simon at the Berlin Document Center satisfied all my requests to obtain Nazi party records; the staff at the Max Planck Gesellschaft in Dahlem facilitated my access to the archives of several of Germany's leading research bodies. Gunter Mann of the Medizinhistorisches Institut in Mainz allowed me on several occasions to use the rich resources of his institute's library; Stephan Leibfried kindly facilitated my access to papers of the Association of Socialist Physicians. Stanford University's Lane Medical Library contains one of the most complete collections of twentieth-century German medical journals in the world; these, along with the collections of the Hoover Institution, the New York Academy of Medicine, and the Yiddish Scientific Institute, proved to be valuable resources. A two-year postdoctoral Mellon fellowship in the philosophy department at Stanford University provided me the time to prepare a final version of the manuscript.

I should also thank several friends for their insight and humor over the years—Jim Adler, Iain and Gillian Boal, Peter Galison, Mohammed Haghi, Lee Mintz, Geoff Sea, Gordon Wood, and especially Londa Schiebinger.

Contents

Introduction	1
1. The Origins of Racial Hygiene	10
2. "Neutral Racism": The Case of Fritz Lenz	46
3. Political Biology: Doctors in the Nazi Cause	64
4. The Sterilization Law	95
5. The Control of Women	118
6. Anti-Semitism in the German Medical Community	131
7. The Destruction of "Lives Not Worth Living"	177
8. The "Organic Vision" of Nazi Racial Science	223
9. Medical Resistance: The Association of Socialist Physicians	251
10. The Politics of Knowledge	282
Epilogue. Postwar Legacies	298
Appendix A: German Medical Journals under the Nazis	315
Appendix B: University and Research Institutes Devoted to Racial Hygiene	327
Bibliography	330
Notes	338
Index	405

> German scientists are today making world history.
> —Alfred Mjoen, Norway's leading racial hygienist, 1935

Introduction

We have long heard that science helps us to expand our horizons, to cure disease, and to make our lives easier. Especially since World War II, we have seen the increasing use of science to augment industrial production, military strength, and medical excellence. Science in the modern world serves to stimulate production and provides a wellspring for new technologies and inventions.

Most people are also aware, however, that enlightenment and production are not the only functions of science. Particularly in recent years, people have come to recognize that science-based technologies also serve to maintain social order and to facilitate the policing of society. In the 1950s and 1960s, the development of the sciences of counterinsurgency and of riot and crowd control demonstrated that science and science-based technologies could be used for the maintenance or disruption of social order.[1]

Since the 1960s, recognition of the fact that science may be used or abused has given rise to concerns that science be socially responsible. This in turn has coincided with a growing awareness that the kind of science people create has something to do with the social context within which science is formed. In this sense, we may speak of a new appreciation of the politics of science—politics that affects not only how science is used or abused but also what aspects of nature are investigated in the first place. Historians now generally recognize that the logic, the methods, and the social structure of science have varied over time and place, and that the growth of knowledge can no longer be understood simply in terms of the mastery of nature by tools or the application of genius or curiosity to nature. We recognize, in short, that there are circumstances in broader society that structure the interests and priorities of science.

There is also increasing recognition that this dependence of the interests or priorities of science on broader social goals has fostered a rethinking of traditional ideals of academic freedom. J. D. Bernal once observed that science, however free, must be funded. And when we study the effects of neutron flux on semiconductors or the expression of oncogenes in viruses, this may have as much to do with the priorities of a nation's military or medical budget as with any "inherent" interest of some particular part of nature. Nature, after all, is infinitely large and infinitely rich, and scientists must narrow their focus. Scientists may divide among themselves their piece of the pie, but only after others have decided how big that piece will be.

If the structure and priorities of science are part of the broader structure of society, then enlightenment, production, and even social control are not the only functions of science. A fourth function, one that is important in the history of science under the Nazis, is closely tied to social control: this is the function of *apology*. It has long been recognized that if people can be convinced that the social order is a natural order, and that the misery (or abundance) they find around them derives from the will of God or Nature or both, then attention can be diverted from those parts of the social order that are the true source of that misery (or abundance).

The idea that the social order is natural or inevitable, fixed by the will of God or the laws of nature (or, more recently, by the structure of one's genes) is not a new one. According to Roman legend, Menenius Agrippa in the sixth century B.C. was sent to a plebeian camp to quell a rebellion. Agrippa told the plebeians a fable in which the various parts of the body rebel against the stomach. He convinced the unruly mob that the several classes of society are dependent on one another, like the parts of the body, and that it makes no more sense for one part of society to rebel against another than for the stomach to rebel against the heart. Legend has it that Agrippa was thereby able to persuade the crowd that the rebellion should stop and the troublemakers should return quietly to the city.

There are many other examples where lessons concerning human rank and privilege are said to be learned from nature. In the Middle Ages, literary "bestiaries" instructed men and women in vice and virtue through examples of the courageous lion, the crafty fox, and the industrious bee. Metaphors of the city and the body—the "body politic"—justified the ways of the polis in terms of the ways of the natural body. In the nineteenth and twentieth centuries, biology continues to serve as a social weapon, providing a set of tools and arguments that allow either the direct control of populations (through sterilization or biological warfare, for example) or their indirect control by reinforcing particular visions of the proper social order (sociobiology, theories of brain lateralization, and so on).[2]

The various functions of science—enlightenment, production, control, and apology—are interconnected. Knowledge of nature, for example, requires a certain degree of control over nature; hence the progress of science depends on the development of tools and instruments. Development of the tools and instruments of science depends on the progress of industrial or craft production. Continuous and profitable production in turn requires a certain level of social stability; the sciences of social and personal control (economic and behavioral sciences, management and police science, counterinsurgency technologies, and the like) help maintain that stability. Control in turn, at least when people are the object, is most effective when invisible; hence the importance of ideologies in obscuring the nature of that control. Hence also the importance of apologetics designed to demonstrate the naturalness or inevitability of some *status* or *fluxus quo,* that what is, or will be, ought to be.

The following pages explore the place of science, especially biomedical science, under the Nazis, with particular reference to the functions of apology and social control. This departs somewhat from other ways science under the Nazis has been studied. Until recently, most historical and sociological studies have concentrated on the Nazi destruction of science, the expulsion of Jews from the universities, and the corruption of intellectual and liberal values. Each of these is an important aspect of the fate of science under the Nazis. My focus here, however, is not primarily on how the Nazis *corrupted* or *abused* science, but rather on how scientists themselves participated in the construction of Nazi racial policy.

This approach can perhaps be distinguished most clearly when compared with that of Alan Beyerchen's pioneering book, *Scientists under Hitler,*[3] which has played an important role in reopening discussion of Nazi science, especially in the field of what was known as *deutsche Physik.* Beyerchen's book represents one of the more thoroughgoing attempts to wrestle with the problem of science under the Nazis, and his work has inspired others in both Germany and the United States to pursue this further. Beyerchen, however, sees the power relations between science and National Socialism working almost entirely one way: he is primarily interested in how German physicists *responded* to National Socialism, and to what extent the Nazi regime *pressured* scientists into cooperation with the regime. He does not see the scientific community in the years 1933–1945 as responsible in any deep sense for the political events or crimes in this period; rather, he sees the politicization of science as something that emerged *after* World War II, especially as scientists began to reflect on their role in the construction and use of the atomic bomb. Scientists up to this time, according to Beyerchen, were not generally aware of the potential uses or abuses of their skills; they eschewed political power and political responsibility and retreated to the privacy of their laboratories and seminars. Science in this view was largely independent of politics. To be fair, Beyerchen does point out that under the Nazis "a small band of politically active scientists" did try "to inject racial considerations into the content and conduct of physics as a discipline."[4] He considers this primarily an injection of politics into science, however, rather than a movement growing from within science itself.

It is important to distinguish the political nature of science from the political consciousness of scientists; it is also important to distinguish among the various sciences in this regard. It is true that the political *consciousness* of physicists increased in the years following the development of the atomic bomb. But the question of how and in what sense science is political is not simply a question of political consciousness. The development of a discipline may be shaped by political forces, even if its leading agents are unaware of this influence.

This becomes clear when we turn to the case of the German biomedical community. Here, the model of an essentially passive and apolitical scientific community responding to purely external political forces underestimates (a) the extent to which political initiatives arose from within the scientific community itself, and (b) the extent to which medical scientists actively designed and administered key elements of National Socialist racial policy. I do not want to suggest that there was *no* political coercion of medical science in this period. What we shall see, however, is that the coercion often took the form of one part of the scientific community coercing another, rather than a nonscientific political force imposing its will on an apolitical scientific community. If this is true, then the most common way we have been led to see the experience of science under the Nazis is flawed in at least two senses. First, people have generally assumed that science *suffered* under the Nazis. In much of the early literature on science under the Nazis, scholars tended to accept at face value the testimony of emigrés that the Nazis were either hostile to science or supported what today would be called pseudoscience. Joseph Needham, for example, in *The Nazi Attack on International Science,* argued that "German science has been largely destroyed," and illustrated this with the claim that the *Biochemische Zeitschrift* had become "thin" under Nazi rule.[5] It is true that as many as 18 percent of German academics were dismissed from their posts and that the number of students studying at German universities dropped by about one-half from 1933 to 1938. Yet one should not conclude from this that German medical science was entirely or even in large part destroyed under the Nazis. In 1937 more than 25,000 books were published in Germany; nearly a thousand of these were medical books.[6] The overwhelming majority of German medical journals continued publishing uninterruptedly during the first five years of Nazi rule; and more than a dozen new medical journals began publication in this period (see Appendix A). Medical journals published in Germany between 1933 and 1938 fill more than 100 meters of shelf space—more than any other country in the world in this period.

The tacit assumption of Needham's book, and of much other early literature, is that science thrives only under democracy and that democracy in turn benefits from values implicit in the free pursuit of science.[7] A closer look at the history of science under the Nazis indicates that this is not always the case. While certain sciences, such as physics and mathematics, suffered, other sciences, such as psychology, anthropology, human genetics, and various forms of racial science and racial hygiene, actually flourished. A second and related misconception concerns a more general view of the nature of the Nazi regime itself. The popular media, for example, commonly portray the Nazi regime as fanatic, half-crazed criminals conducting their evil plans with as much reason or sense as 1930s television gangsters. This is a false impression for a number of reasons, but primarily because it underestimates the degree to which large numbers of intellectuals, often leaders in their fields, were willing and eager to serve the Nazi regime.

6 Racial Hygiene

Nazi racial science is probably most often associated with the medical experiments performed on so-called lower races. Testimony presented at the Nuremberg and Buchenwald trials documented the involvement of German physicians in a series of brutal and often "terminal" experiments, where prisoners in concentration camps were forced to submit to bone grafts or limb transplants, or were exposed over long periods to severe cold or low pressure, or were forced to drink seawater. These experiments were justified by Nazi doctors on the grounds that the knowledge collected could be used to help save pilots forced to bail out at high altitudes or to crash-land in the icy waters of the North Sea. Evidence presented in the trials revealed the involvement of doctors in a massive program for the extermination of "lives not worth living," including, first, infants with heritable defects, and later, handicapped children and patients of psychiatric institutions, and finally, entire populations of "unwanted races."

The Nazi medical experiments and even the program for the destruction of "lives not worth living" represent only the tip of a much larger iceberg. In fact, the ideological structure we associate with National Socialism was deeply embedded in the philosophy and institutional structure of German biomedical science long before the beginning of the euthanasia program in 1939—and to a certain extent, even before 1933. The published record of the German medical profession makes it clear that many intellectuals cooperated fully in Nazi racial programs, and that many of the social and intellectual foundations for these programs were laid long before the rise of Hitler to power. What I want to argue in addition to this, however (and here I shall be drawing upon a growing body of recent German scholarship on this question) is that biomedical scientists played an active, even leading role in the initiation, administration, and execution of Nazi racial programs. In this sense the case can be made that science (especially biomedical science) under the Nazis cannot simply be seen in terms of a fundamentally "passive" or "apolitical" scientific community responding to purely external political forces; on the contrary, there is strong evidence that scientists actively designed and administered central aspects of National Socialist racial policy.

The structure of this book is as follows. The first chapter traces the rise of what was known as racial hygiene[8] (*Rassenhygiene*) from the social Darwinism of the late nineteenth century to its synthesis with National Socialism at the end of the Weimar period. In the second chapter I explore the conception of race espoused by Fritz Lenz, Germany's most eminent racial hygienist and coauthor of the most important genetics textbook of the interwar years. In the third chapter I document the dual phenomenon of (a) the early and active support of the German medical profession for National Socialism and (b) the eagerness of Nazi philosophers to base their "revolution" on what they considered sound biology and medicine. Nazism, according to many in this period, was simply applied biology. Here I also trace the *Gleichschaltung* (unification and subordination to Nazi ideals) of the German medical profession and the place of racial hygiene within the German biomedical research establishment.

Chapters 1–3 are intended to lay the groundwork for understanding the extent to which the German medical profession found Nazi ideology attractive; Chapters 4–8 detail the participation of the medical profession in Nazi racial practice. Chapter 4 explores the origins and administration of the 1933 Sterilization Law—a law that resulted in the sterilization of more than 1 percent of the entire adult population of Germany. The Sterilization Law (modeled on similar laws in the United States) represents the first major triumph of Nazi racial hygiene. Chapter 5 presents a discussion of Nazi attempts to provide what some called "a solution to the woman question"; here the focus is on the Nazi conception of women as bearers and rearers of children. This chapter also explores the curious confrontation of this ideology with the practical exigencies that emerged with preparations for war.

Chapter 6 discusses attempts to solve "the Jewish question" in Nazi racial science and racial policy. My focus here is on what can be called the medicalization of anti-Semitism: the attempt on the part of doctors to conceive the so-called Jewish problem as a medical problem, one that required a "medical solution." The medicalization of anti-Semitism represents only part of a larger attempt by the German medical profession to medicalize or biologize various forms of social, sexual, political, or racial deviance; Jews, homosexuals, Gypsies, Marxists, and other groups were typecast as "health hazards" to the German population. When the Nazis herded Jews into the ghettos of the occupied East, public health provided the ideological rationale: concentration was justified as "quarantine." Chapter 7 continues this discussion, exploring the participation of physicians in the Nazi pro-

8   Racial Hygiene

gram to destroy "lives not worth living." Here we examine how the Nazi extermination of handicapped children and psychiatric patients in gas chambers outfitted in German hospitals provided a model for the subsequent destruction of Germany's racial and ethnic minorities. We also look at some of the links between the euthanasia operation and plans for a "final solution" to the Jewish question; the chapter concludes with a brief look at some of the medical experiments conducted by physicians in Germany's concentration camps.

The final three chapters discuss certain broader aspects of German racial science and medicine. Chapter 8 explores the "organic" vision of Nazi racial medicine. Many people may be surprised to learn that the Nazis worried about the long-term effects of environmental pollutants and established policies to guard against the toxic effects of substances such as alcohol, tobacco, heavy metals, and asbestos. The Nazis stressed the importance of a diet rich in fruit and fiber and encouraged the consumption of whole-grain bread. Nazi medical philosophers encouraged a return to the practices of the traditional German midwife; these and other practices were defended on the grounds they would improve the quality of "the German germ plasm."

Chapter 9 investigates one of the "paths not taken" by German medical science, examining the structure of medical resistance to the Nazis, with special focus on the activities of the Association of Socialist Physicians (Verein Sozialistischer Ärzte). Here, we see an example of how German medicine might have evolved had the Nazis not come to power. Chapter 10 then considers some of the broader moral and political questions raised by the example of doctors under National Socialism. And in the Epilogue, we look at some of the legacies of racial science in postwar Germany.

I should also introduce a caveat on the method followed in this study. My focus is on the role of physicians in the construction of Nazi racial science and policy. By physicians, I mean those with medical degrees. Many of those we shall be looking at were biologists or anthropologists. The divisions between medicine and biology or anthropology were not always clear in the early part of this century. For most of those pursuing basic biological or racial research, the medical degree was the appropriate path of study. Thus August Weismann, Ernst Haeckel, Wilhelm Weinberg, Wilhelm Schallmayer, Fritz Lenz, Eugen Fischer, and Alfred Ploetz all had medical degrees; Weismann, Weinberg, Lenz, and Ploetz all practiced medicine at one time or another. Biology was simply not a separate profession, as we think of it today. "Racial hygiene" was both a priority of scientific research and a form of medical practice.

I have assumed throughout this study that "science is what scientists do." Not because there is no difference between genuine and spurious science (there is, or at least can be), or because it is necessary to maintain a cool and detached attitude toward such things in order to understand them (it isn't, and one shouldn't). I believe instead that it serves little purpose to continually ask, "But was it science?" We should not allow our judgment of the ethical character of Nazi medical practice to hinge entirely on whether we consider it to have been based on "genuine science." One cannot (or at least should not) radically divide the practice of science from its product; science is, among other things, a social activity, and the politics of those who practice it is part of that science. Furthermore, we miss something if we assume at the outset a fundamental hostility between science and a form of political practice such as National Socialism. This was not how scientists themselves viewed the matter; understanding how this could have come to be is one of the goals of this study.

The purpose of this study is programmatic as well as expository. The broader thesis guiding this book is that movements that shape the policies of nations can also shape the structure and priorities of science. The history of medicine under National Socialism presents a clear and indeed dramatic case; but it may not be as extraordinary as people sometimes think. Politics enters science in ways we are only beginning to understand. If we are to appreciate how this works, then we need to examine more closely the political history and philosophy of science. The following pages explore one example of how politics can shape the practice of science. One should keep in mind, however, that science shaped by politics is not something foreign to science as it is practiced today.

1 | The Origins of Racial Hygiene

> Biology and genetics are the roots, from which the National Socialist world-view has grown.
> —Rudolf Ramm, 1943

Scientific racism is older than one might imagine. As early as 1727 the earl of Boulainvilliers tried to argue that the noblemen of France represented descendants of an original and superior race of long-headed Nordic Franks, whereas the lower estates of French society were descended from subjugated Celtic Gauls. Boulainvilliers' doctrine was intended to support the claims of vested nobility against the critics of noble privilege.[1] Critics of that privilege turned to quite another metaphor to explain the origins of human institutions and character: philosophers championing a new and enlightened liberalism argued that it was nurture, rather than nature, that was responsible for determining a man's standing. Enlightenment enthusiasts invested climate or education with extraordinary powers: Dr. Samuel Smith, seventh president of Princeton College, speculated toward the end of the eighteenth century that Negro pigmentation was the result of "a large freckle" that spread itself over the body after long exposure to the tropical sun. Dr. Benjamin Rush speculated that all babies were born white, and that the distinctive coloration of the Negro arose as a "mild form of leprosy," from which a certain former slave named Henry Moss was said to be undergoing a spontaneous cure.[2]

Early Scientific Racism

In the period of history we call the Enlightenment, many of those who claimed that race was the product of climate or disease also argued that the races of men were equal to one another in dignity or character. Locke, for example, argued that the human mind was at birth a blank slate, or "empty cabinet," and that character was the product of education, or soil, or climate. The Scottish philosopher Lord Monboddo suggested that, with proper training, even certain apes (such as the chimpanzee) might one day be taught to speak and to reason.[3]

Enlightenment "environmentalism" emerged in what many saw as a hopeful period of history. Many imagined that social, sexual, or racial differences separating the various stations of men and women would be soon overcome through proper implementation of social reforms and legislation. In the French Revolution, many aristocratic privileges were overthrown. Jews were granted certain civil liberties, and feminists wrote treatises on "the Rights of Woman." The liberal spirit of *liberté, egalité,* and *fraternité* offered hope that, given equal opportunity and the rule of enlightened laws, the free play of economic markets might soon eradicate social differences and inequalities.

Enlightenment philosophers were not of course willing to grant the privileges of liberty, equality, and fraternity to everyone. John Locke, himself a merchant adventurer in the African slave trade, defended slavery as the natural consequence of relations that ensue from the fighting of a "just war."[4] The American Constitution recognized the legitimacy of slavery and extended the full "rights of man" only to propertied white males. Enlightened European philosophers championed liberty and yet made the enjoyment of liberty contingent upon the practice of "reason," a faculty shared unequally among humans. David Hume, for example, compared the intelligence of the Negro to that of a parrot, and argued that a man of this race could never achieve a status equal to that of the European.[5] Jean-Jacques Rousseau claimed that women were inferior to men in the sphere of reason and therefore did not deserve the same rights as men. Such were the kinds of views that led Samuel Johnson, in the middle of the eighteenth century, to ask, "How is it that we hear the loudest yelps for liberty among the drivers of negroes?"

In the midst of the social changes that shook European and American society at the end of the eighteenth century, scholars looked to experimental science for help in finding something fixed in human nature, qualities that were stable amid the chaos of changing political relations. Joseph Gall's "phrenology" became popular in France and Germany (both Auguste Comte and G. W. F. Hegel appealed to

Gall's theories). Pieter Camper (1722–1789) presented the "facial angle" as the key to comparing humans and lower animals; Anders Retzius (1796–1860) developed the concept of the "cephalic index." In the first half of the nineteenth century, however, the idea of "race" remained in Europe a relatively unimportant category of scholarly discussion. Racial theories were written,[6] but these remained marginal to larger movements within European science and philosophy (positivism, empiricism, romanticism, German idealism, and so forth). In Europe it was not until the second half of the nineteenth century that the problem of race began to receive detailed attention from scholars.

In 1853–1855 Arthur Comte de Gobineau published his pioneering *Essay on the Inequality of the Human Races*. The significance of Gobineau's treatise was that, for the first time, race was cast as the primary moving force of world history.[7] According to Gobineau, "racial vitality" lies at the root of all great transformations in history. Greece flourished because of it; Rome fell for want of it. Gobineau argued that the shift from the Stone Age to the Bronze Age was the result of one race seizing the reins of history from another; racial movement is the root cause of all that is grand in history.

Gobineau's theory was not initially well received in Europe. Tocqueville, for example, in a letter to Gobineau, pointed out that the racial theorist would probably find a better audience for his ideas among the slave-owning planters of the American South.[8]

The significance of Gobineau's theory was not just that he saw the history of the world as a history of racial struggle. Equally important was his contention that his racial history was a *science*. Racial or ethnic prejudice, after all, predates Gobineau by many hundreds of years. Yet prior to the nineteenth century, racial or ethnic prejudice was couched primarily in religious rather than biological or racial terms.

The attempt to cast a theory of race in biological terms was the product, in part, of the growing importance of science in European culture. By the second half of the nineteenth century, the dramatic achievements of the experimental and theoretical sciences had brought a certain prestige to science. Science in the middle decades of the century becomes a major source of military, industrial, and economic strength. As a consequence, one sees a fundamental transformation in the political function of science. Science becomes increasingly a metaphor for the explanation of why things are as they are: people look to science to explain the origin of human character and institutions; science becomes an important part of ideological argumentation and a means of social control.

Examples of this are easy to name. Cesare Lombroso's 1876 *L'uomo delinquente* sought to identify "criminal types" according to head forms and body markings; in America, scholars following in the tradition of Samuel George Morton attempted to prove the intellectual inferiority of Indians, blacks, and women through the size of their skulls.[9] The intent of such sciences was to find evidence for what many already believed—that criminality is inborn, or that the schooling of women will shrink their ovaries,[10] or that the social station of certain groups is natural and inevitable. The use of science for such purposes generally arises in the context of concrete struggles. Prior to 1865, for example, medical men in the American South tried to identify certain "Negro diseases" to prove the inevitability of Negro servitude; Samuel Cartwright thus sought to prove that Negroes "consume less oxygen than white people" and suffer from a host of diseases peculiar to their race, such as "dirt eating" (Cachexia Africana) and "an insane desire to run away" (Drapetomania).[11] Ethnologists and zoologists (such as Samuel George Morton and Louis Agassiz) sought to prove that the various races of men represent the fruits of separate creations ("polygeny"). American "pre-Adamites" even went so far as to claim that the Negro was "a beast of the field" created by God on the fifth day to labor for the ultimate object of God's creation: white human beings.[12]

In many such cases, the appeal to science lent a certain authority to ideological pronouncements. By the mid-nineteenth century, science had become an important metaphor in Anglo-European culture, and people looked to science for the answers to social problems. The science to which one looked, however, was of a very special kind. Science was appealed to, not in the abstract, but only insofar as it could be given a certain interpretation. The kind of "science" that found expression in scientific racism claimed that the empirically real exhausts the ontologically possible, that the way things are is the way things ought to be. Scientific racism was an explanatory program, but it was also a political program, designed to reinforce certain power relations as natural and inevitable.

From Social Darwinism to Racial Hygiene

The publication of Charles Darwin's *Origin of Species* in 1859 represents a watershed in the history of biological determinism in general and scientific racism in particular. Prior to Darwin, it was difficult to argue against the Judeo-Christian conception of the unity of man, based on the single creation of Adam and Eve. Darwin's theory suggested that humans had evolved over hundreds of thousands, even millions of years, and that the races of men had diverged while adapting to the particularities of local conditions.

The impact of Darwin's theory was enormous. Scholars in both Europe and America, excited by the prospect of founding a science of man on biological principles, began to apply the principle of natural selection to the science and ethics of human society. Opinions differed widely, however, over just how Darwin's theory was to be applied. American social Darwinists saw in evolution by natural selection a kind of scientific guarantee of "cosmic optimism," whereby those who survive are (by definition) those who are also most fit; Darwin in this view had demonstrated the moral superiority of industrial capitalism and the competitive entrepreneurial spirit. For American social Darwinists, economic competition was a natural form of social existence, one that would guarantee the success and prosperity of a society evolving gradually by variation and natural selection. Andrew Carnegie's motto was, "All is well since all grows better"; John D. Rockefeller saw in the success of a large business "merely the working out of a law of nature and a law of God."[13]

Social Darwinists in Germany also sought to justify a certain political order by a natural order, but with a somewhat different emphasis. Wilhelm Schallmayer and Alfred Ploetz—two of Germany's leading social Darwinists—were no less enthusiastic about the need to maintain the struggle for existence in social life, but were much less optimistic about whether that struggle could be maintained, given the rise of revolutionary democratic movements (the French Revolution, German Social Democracy) and policies designed to secure minimum standards of welfare in the spheres of medicine and social services.[14] Neither conservative nor progressive German intellectuals at the end of the nineteenth century had much confidence in the automatic or inevitable nature of evolution; Germany had come out short in the struggle for overseas colonies and was in the midst of a political struggle that would polarize German society into far Right and far Left. This may help explain why German social Darwinists rejected the optimistic laissez-faire free-market liberalism so popular in England and America, and stressed instead the need for state intervention to stop what they saw as the beginnings of a supposed "degeneration" of the human species.

The degeneration of the race feared by German social Darwinists was said to have come about for two reasons: first, because medical care for "the weak" had begun to destroy the natural struggle for existence; and second, because the poor and misfits of the world were beginning to multiply faster than the talented and fit.

The German eugenics, or racial hygiene, movement emerged in the late nineteenth century in response to these fears. In 1895, in the founding document of what came to be known as racial hygiene, Alfred Ploetz warned against the various kinds of social "counterselection" (such as bloody war, revolution, welfare for the sick or inferior) that lead to racial degeneration. If only the fit are to survive, Ploetz argued, then such counterselective forces must be avoided. He listed ways this might be achieved. War and revolution should be avoided wherever possible, and support for the poor should be given only to those past child-bearing age. Inbreeding and procreation by the very young or very old should be discouraged, and people should be protected from agents such as alcohol, venereal disease, or anything else that might damage the human germ plasm.[15] But most of all, Ploetz warned against medical care for "the weak," for this allows those individuals to survive and reproduce who otherwise, without the intervention of doctors, would never have survived. (The British social Darwinist John Haycraft wrote in a similar vein that diseases such as tuberculosis, scrofula, and leprosy should actually be considered "our racial friends," because they attacked only those of weak constitution.)[16] Traditional medical care thus helps the individual but endangers the race; Ploetz called for a new kind of hygiene—a racial hygiene (*Rassenhygiene*—Ploetz coined this term) that would consider not just the good of the individual but also the good of the race.

Ploetz sympathized with many of the ideals of other social reformers of his time. He claimed to support many of the policies put forward in the name of "Socialismus"—policies designed to reduce unemployment and to insure against accidents and disease; policies supporting social security in old age, reduced work hours, and the elimination of child labor; policies that favored higher wages, profit sharing, the construction of workers' cooperatives, and so forth. Ploetz expressed sympathy for these policies but also noted that, important as these are, they place an obstacle in the path of "maintaining the quality of the race" insofar as they all, in one way or another, allow the weak elements in society to prosper and to procreate. In such situations, he argued, there is a contradiction between the goals of welfare or charity, on the one hand, and the "brute facts of nature," on the other.[17]

The solution to such a contradiction, according to Ploetz, lies in recognizing alternative ways human breeding might be controlled. If negative qualities of the race could be located and eliminated in the germ cells, then the need for a Darwinian struggle for existence would be eliminated.[18] A kinder and more "humane" form of selection might thereby replace the brutal force of natural selection; indeed, intelligent racial hygiene might eliminate the need for a struggle for existence altogether.

It is important to realize that social Darwinism was not simply the result of any straightforward application of science to society. Others, after all, saw the import of Darwin's message quite differently. Socialists tended to stress the historical *fact* of evolution (that is, that humans are descended from apes); conservatives or liberals tended to stress the *mechanism* of selection (natural selection, the struggle for existence).[19] People generally found in Darwin what they wanted to find. Where Carnegie saw competition, Kropotkin saw cooperation. Where Morgan and Alexander found the glory of God, the American pragmatists found the liberation from teleology. Where Spencer found the necessity of struggle, Bebel found the possibility of symbiosis. The particular version of social Darwinism that found favor among industrial and academic circles was one that harmonized with the interests of those circles. When phrases such as "the struggle for existence" and "the survival of the fittest" became catchwords for the new social Darwinism, this reflected the broader social and economic structure of the times; this is what is meant when we hear that Darwin's theory cannot be understood apart from the Manchester economics of Ricardo and Smith and the dog-eat-dog world of mid-nineteenth-century British capitalism. This was the view of Karl Marx, for example, reflecting on how remarkable it was that

> Darwin recognizes among brutes and plants his English society with its "division of labour," competition, opening up of new markets, "inventions" and Malthusian "struggle for existence." It is Hobbes' *bellum omnium contra omnes,* and it is reminiscent of Hegel in the *Phenomenology,* where bourgeois society figures as "spiritual animal kingdom," while with Darwin the animal kingdom figures as bourgeois society.[20]

It is not surprising, then, that Darwin was used as well by the champions of Germany's rising industrial classes to justify their particular interests.

In 1900 the German arms industrialist Friedrich Alfred Krupp sponsored a prize essay contest on the question: "What can the theory of evolution tell us about domestic political development and legislation of the state?" The prize money of 30,000 reichsmarks drew more than sixty applicants, and the ten winning volumes were published as a veritable encyclopedia of social Darwinism, for which there was no equivalent in any other country.[21]

Wilhelm Schallmayer, winner of the 1900 Krupp contest, joined a host of other writers in calling for ways to "improve the race." The French Count Georges Vacher de Lapouge proposed the breeding of men; Heinrich Driesmans in his *Die Wahlverwandtschaften* envisioned the betterment of the race through careful selection of mates. The Nibelungen poet Wilhelm Jordan in his novel *Zwei Wiegen* postulated a utopia where breeding was a central part of life.[22]

The most sustained efforts toward "improving the biology of the human species," however, were those advanced by Alfred Ploetz. In 1904 Ploetz founded the *Archiv für Rassen- und Gesellschaftsbiologie* (Journal of racial and social biology) to investigate "the principles of the optimal conditions for the maintenance and development of the race."[23] In 1905 Ploetz, together with the psychiatrist Ernst Rüdin, the lawyer Anastasius Nordenholz, and the anthropologist Richard Thurnwald, founded the Society for Racial Hygiene (Gesellschaft für Rassenhygiene) to further the cause of human racial improvement.[24] Those wanting to join the society were asked to promise they would refrain from marriage if they were in any way "unfit." (There is, I should point out, no evidence that anyone in the society ever admitted such a defect.) Membership in the society grew throughout the teens and twenties, as racial hygiene became recognized as a respectable part of German biomedical science. In 1905 there were 32 members in the society; by 1907 this had grown to 100. In 1907 local branches of the society were founded in Berlin and Munich; the Berlin society, headed by Ploetz, Thurnwald, and (later, in 1917) the geneticist Erwin Baur, included "notable scholars, physicians, industrialists, and representatives of other professions."[25] In 1909 Freiburg established a local branch with Fritz Lenz as secretary and Eugen Fischer as chairman; in 1910 Stuttgart established a branch under the leadership of Wilhelm Weinberg (famous for what later became known as the Hardy-Weinberg Law).

In 1907 the Society for Racial Hygiene changed its name to the Internationale Gesellschaft für Rassenhygiene, and in 1910 Sweden's Sällskap för Rashygien became the first foreign affiliate. After World

War I, the society expanded rapidly. In 1922 a Dresden branch was formed (headed by Philalethes Kuhn); this was followed by branches in Kiel, Bremen, and Graz (1923); Württemberg and Vienna (1925); Münster and Osnabrück (1926); Solingen, Barmen-Elberfeldt, Wuppertal, and Lower Silesia (1929); Leverkusen, Vechta-Cloppenburg, Cologne, and the state of Baden (1930). Beginning with only a handful of members before World War I, the Society for Racial Hygiene by 1930 had grown to over 1,300 members in sixteen local branches, with four additional branches in Austria. Regional branches continued to form in the early 1930s. By 1933 new branches had been founded in Westphalia, East Friesland, Görlitz, Erfurt, Upper Silesia, and Holstein. In 1935 Professor Andreas Pratje announced the formation of an Erlangen Society for Racial Hygiene (he stressed the relevance of racial hygiene for "the Jewish question"); this same year the journal *Volk und Rasse* announced the appointment of new leaders for societies in Augsburg, Karlsruhe, Schleswig, Freiburg, and Kaufbeuren. In 1941 the *Anthropologischer Anzeiger* announced the formation of a local branch in Prague, under the leadership of Karl Thums. In 1943 a branch of the society, chaired by Dr. H. Girschek, was formed in Troppau (in the eastern Sudetenland); this was probably the last branch formed.[26]

Two examples may be cited to illustrate the fears of racial hygienists for the degeneration of the race. In her article in the 1912 *Archiv*, Dr. Agnes Bluhm criticized the racial hygiene of modern medical birth assistance. Fewer women, Bluhm wrote, die in childbirth—but this is precisely the danger, for modern medicine allows women to survive and reproduce who, without the intervention of doctors, would never have been able to give birth. Bluhm argued that the incidence of incapacity to give birth (due to narrow pelvis and so forth) was growing in the population (evidenced by the growing numbers of caesarean sections), and even maintained that the labor pains associated with modern childbirth were of recent historical origin. "It is well known," Bluhm wrote, quoting the racial anthropologist Ludwig Woltmann, "that the 'primitive peoples' of the world [*Naturvölker*] give birth without pain." Citing Wilhelm Schallmayer, Bluhm ended her article with a warning to the effect that the more women rely on medical aid to give birth, the more dependent on that help they will become.[27]

Related to this fear of the care for the weak was a growing fear of what Dr. Hermann Siemens (of the Siemens industrial family) called the proletarization of the population: the fear that various inferiors of the world—the poor and the weak, but also the sick and the insane—were beginning to multiply more rapidly than more "gifted" elements of society, by which was usually meant the military, political, and intellectual elite. In his article in the 1916/18 issue of the *Archiv,* "The Proletarization of Our Future Generations—a Danger of Non-Racial Hygienic Population Policy," Siemens cited Galton and Pearson's estimate that the "value" of a man usually stands in inverse proportion to the number of his children. Siemens warned that the poor were outbreeding the rich, and illustrated this with birthrates from rich and poor areas of Vienna, Paris, and Berlin. He also noted that his own illustrious family (of whose genetic excellence he had no doubts) had averaged only 2.8 children per marriage. Siemens warned that unless this rising tide of inferiors was stemmed, "the best of human heredity will be swamped with a mess of inferior types"[28] (see Figures 1 and 2).

Racial hygienists criticized "neo-Malthusians" in the first decade of the twentieth century for their indiscriminate advocacy of birth control. According to the racial hygienists, those advocating free access to birth control failed to recognize the importance of a high birthrate in maintaining a stiff struggle for existence; it was also wrong, they argued, to emphasize the importance of population size per se, without differentiating between valuable and worthless hereditary lines. Alfred Ploetz, in his 1895 *Grundlinien einer Rassenhygiene,* had argued similarly against the indiscriminate distribution of birth control, on the grounds that it tended to be used by the "fitter" elements of a population, leading thereby to the degeneration of the race.[29]

Racial hygienists worried not only about the birthrate of the fit versus the unfit within Germany, but also about the declining birthrate of Germany vis-à-vis other European nations (see Figures 3 and 4). In 1914 Professor Max von Gruber, whom Fritz Lenz called *the* leading racial hygienist in the first two decades of the twentieth century, warned that from 1876 to 1911 the birthrate in Germany had declined from 4.3 births per thousand to only 3.0 per thousand; fecundity in Berlin for married women in this same period had dropped from 240 births per thousand inhabitants to less than 85 per thousand. Gruber attributed this decline to voluntary contraception, on the one hand, and to sterility caused by venereal disease, on the other. Voluntary contraception was in turn the product of the rise of "theoretical and practical individualism" and its most dangerous offshoot: the "so-called women's liberation movement," with its devaluation of motherhood and its emphasis on the employment of women outside the home. This was not an uncommon view at this time: American eugenicists rejected the entire concept of birth control because it was associated, in their view, with an "antibaby strike" on the part of emancipated women.[30]

Curiously, at the same time that racial hygienists warned of a declining population, conservative apologists for the Pan-German League argued that overseas colonies were needed to relieve the "overcrowding" caused by Germany's rapidly growing population.[31] Similar contradictions would persist into the Nazi period. Nazi Interior Minister Wilhelm Frick in 1933 thus found it possible to warn of "race-suicide" (caused by the declining birthrate) in one breath and then to call for the need to acquire *Lebensraum* for Germany's growth, in the next.[32] Such pronouncements make one suspect that population concerns were (then as now) more the product of political interests than of incontrovertible facts.

Was Racial Hygiene Racist?

The concerns of racial hygienists, at least until the 1920s, were different from what one might today imagine. Racial hygienists worried less about the "Jewish question," or the "de-nordification" (*Entnordung*) of the German people,[33] than about the declining birthrate and the growing number of mentally ill in state institutions. They stressed both the importance of population growth for maintaining national strength and the links between "racial fitness" and national efficiency. Alfred Grotjahn linked racial hygiene with the "rationalization of sexual life"; Erwin Baur spoke of the "rational economy in human life."[34] Racial hygienists worried that feminism and World War I had destroyed the family; racial hygiene was proposed as one way to reverse this destruction.[35] The ideology of racial hygiene, at least before the mid-twenties, was in this sense less racialist than nationalist or meritocratic, less concerned with the comparison of one race against another than with discovering principles of improving the human race in general—or at least the Western "cultured races" (*Kulturrassen*).[36]

Alfred Ploetz, for example, in his 1895 founding treatise, made it clear that he did not intend his racial hygiene to be anti-Semitic. Ploetz ranked Jews along with Aryans as two of the world's premier

Figure 1. "The Threat of the Underman." Male criminals have an average of 4.9 children; a criminal marriage, 4.4 children; parents of slow learners, 3.5 children; a "German family," 2.2 children; and a marriage from the educated circles, 1.9 children. From Otto Helmut, *Volk in Gefahr* (Munich, 1937), p. 29.

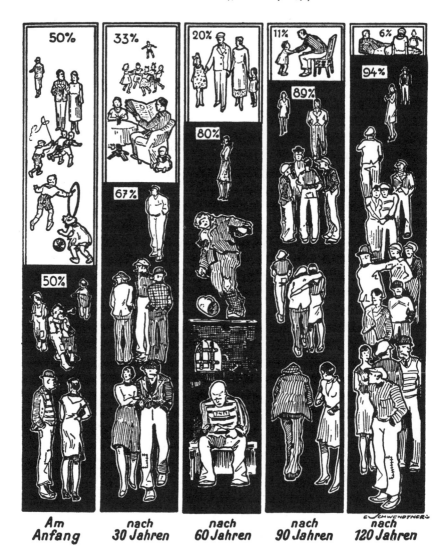

Figure 2. "Degeneration of the Population as a Result of Insufficient Reproduction of Valuable Families." The dark lower portion shows the growing percentage of "criminal families"; the lighter top shows "full-value" families, declining from 50 percent of the population to only 6 percent after 120 years. From Helmut, *Volk in Gefahr*, p. 31.

Figure 3. "Fecundity of European Peoples, Measured in Births per 1,000 Inhabitants in 1934." Note the birthrate of the Ukraine at 34 per 1,000, compared with Germany's 18 per 1,000. From Helmut, *Volk in Gefahr*, p. 35.

Figure 4. "Fertility and Race, the Growth of the Slav in Europe." The proportions of Germanic, Slavic, and Latin "races" in 1810 and 1930 are compared to those anticipated in 1960. From Helmut, *Volk in Gefahr*, p. 33.

cultured races, citing as evidence the cultural and scientific achievements of Jesus, Spinoza, and Marx. He called anti-Semitism a useless ploy (*Schlag ins Wasser*) that would one day disappear, washed away by the rising tide of scientific knowledge and the forces of democracy. (Ploetz did caution, however, that anti-Semitism would disappear more rapidly were it not for the "reactionary nationalist spirit that has recently arisen among the Jews.") He rejected the notion that there are pure races anywhere in the world; the races, Ploetz argued, have been mixing since time immemorial, and European peoples are no more purely Aryan, than Jews are purely Semitic. He also denied that racial mixing is necessarily harmful; he claimed that the interbreeding of individuals belonging to races "not too far apart" was widely recognized as "a means of increasing fitness and as a source of good variations." Ploetz cited the Japanese as an example of a people whose achievements might be traced to racial mixing—the Japanese, according to Ploetz, are not a pure race but rather a mixture of Mongol and Malay. Trying to strike what he considered a prudent balance in the nature-nurture debate, he criticized as one-sided T. H. Buckle and other "socialists" who deny that there are hereditary differences between the rich and the poor; he criticized as equally one-sided, however, those "bourgeois Darwinians" who ignore entirely the effects of the environment and try to trace everything back to heredity.[37]

Others agreed with Ploetz that the goals of racial hygiene should not be restricted to any one people. Hugo Ribbert, for example, listed among the goals of racial hygiene "the prevention and conquest of diseases afflicting the entire human race, diseases from which each of the various races might suffer in similar manner."[38] Wilhelm Schallmayer preferred the term *Rassehygiene* (rather than the plural *Rassenhygiene*) to express the idea that his science concerned itself with the human species *as a whole,* and not just the Nordic race. Schallmayer, winner of the 1900 Krupp Prize and one of the earliest members of the Society for Racial Hygiene (along with Ploetz, Rüdin, and Bluhm), criticized those who followed, cultlike, the Gobineau-inspired visions of Nordic superiority professed by various groups at this time; both Ploetz and Schallmayer warned against letting "vulgar race propaganda" spoil what they saw as the objective and value-free goals of racial science.[39]

Ploetz, Schallmayer, and even Ludwig Woltmann were all, at least until sometime before World War I, cautious advocates of certain forms of progressive social reform. Many racial hygienists supported a kind of state socialism whereby a strong central government would direct social policy toward programs to improve the race. The Society for Racial Hygiene allied itself with a number of groups advocating social reform (for example, the Mutterschutzbund, which racial hygienists admired for its efforts to establish colonies in the countryside where unwed mothers could raise their children). Conversely, many of those today remembered as progressives were attracted by Ploetz's movement to improve the health of the race. Alfred Grotjahn, for example, today considered the father of German social medicine and one of the leading architects of Weimar Germany's progressive health reforms, saw racial hygiene as a legitimate concern of medicine. He was one of those who defended the use of the term *eugenics* (rather than *racial hygiene*) in order to avoid confusion with racist notions of the political-anthropological variety. According to Grotjahn, racial hygiene would provide long-range preventive medicine for the germ plasm of humanity; this would complement both (a) traditional "curative" medical care and (b) concerns for the human physical and social environment provided by public health and social medicine. Racial hygiene—along with social hygiene and personal hygiene—was simply one element in a larger, more comprehensive program of human health care. Grotjahn's views earned him the respect of more devout racial hygienists: he was one of the few social hygienists in the Weimar Republic willing to advocate compulsory sterilization; he also advocated increased powers to commit upward of a million "defective asocials" to psychiatric institutions. After 1933, Nazi racial theorists (such as Lenz, Astel, and Schultze) were able to turn to Grotjahn as an example of a socialist who supported strong measures in the field of racial hygiene.[40]

We now know, from a number of recent studies, that the early racial hygiene movement does not fall cleanly into Left-Right divisions.[41] Many socialists identified eugenics with state planning and the rationalization of the means of production; many thus found the idea of a "planned genetic future" an attractive one. Loren Graham has shown that even as late as 1925, the leading Soviet eugenics journal published translations of articles from the *Archiv für Rassen- und Gesellschaftsbiologie;* the journal also reported favorably on German treatises on racial hygiene, including the works of Fritz Lenz (see Chapter 2).[42] Some of the first sterilizations undertaken on eugenic (that is, nonpunitive) grounds in Germany were performed (illegally) in 1928 by Rainer Fetscher, a physician with socialist sympathies.[43] In 1930 the women's supplement to the Social Democratic party's newspaper, *Vorwärts,* criticized the 1929 Danish sterilization law for not allowing compulsory sterilization of inferiors.[44] And in 1931 the Communist party of Germany expressed support for the sterilization of psychiatric patients under certain circumstances.[45] Paul Weindling has pointed out that between 1931 and 1938 Germany and the Soviet Union shared a joint Institute for Racial Biology established in Moscow on the initiative of the German eugenicists Ludwig Aschoff and Oscar Vogt.[46] A number of historians have concluded from this that racial hygiene (or eugenics), at least in its early stages, cannot be considered a conservative movement but should be seen instead as a progressive movement designed to rationalize and control the reproductive process.[47]

Garland Allen has defined progressivism as "naturalism coupled with a belief in social reform." And in this sense it is certainly fair to call certain aspects of racial hygiene progressive. Racial hygienists saw in genetics and eugenics a set of tools that might help solve social problems. One might even say that National Socialism was itself progressive—if we mean by this that application of science to social problems (in a particularly "biologistic" manner) was an important element in Nazi ideology. If such diverse ideologies are all "progressive," however, one may doubt the value of the term. As Allen and others (such as Nils Roll-Hansen) have pointed out,[48] the value of casting eugenicists as progressives may be dubious, given the fact that some of the strongest critics of eugenics—figures such as Franz Boas, John Dewey, or Georg Lukács—were equally and quintessentially "progressive."

One important point to recognize here is that many of those who considered themselves progressive were in fact quite sympathetic to nativist or protofascist assumptions. Karl Valentin Müller, professor of anthropology at the German University of Prague, is a case in point. Müller belonged to that right-wing faction of the German Social Democratic party (SPD) which found itself increasingly enchanted with racist and nationalist variants of socialism in the course of the 1920s. In his 1927 article "Race and Socialism," Müller rejected the idea that socialism applied equally to all races of the world. Müller maintained that "the goals of the workers' movement extend only to *white* workers: socialism simply cannot mean the same thing for a Chinese and an Indian, for an 'Alpine' Frenchman or a Nordic

Swede." He collected statistics to show that the most highly honored heroes of the socialist movement were generally of "Nordic stock": Müller counted 75–80 percent blonds among the leaders of a textile union, and referred the reader to his findings that 54 percent of all participants at an SPD school for leaders in the workers' movement were blond.[49] The Nazis would later use the works of men like Müller to argue that even socialists (and not just National Socialists) were forced to recognize Nordic supremacy.

It would be a mistake, however, to conclude from the example of certain isolated individuals such as Müller that race played an important role for the Marxist Social Democrats. Neither the Association of Socialist Physicians nor the Association of Social Democratic Doctors supported racial hygiene to anywhere near the degree that Nazi medical groups did. In the final years of the Weimar Republic, physicians writing in the leading socialist doctors' journal *(Der Sozialistische Arzt)* attacked the racial hygiene that was growing in popularity among the Nazis. This contrasts sharply with early Nazi medical publications *(Ziel und Weg; Zur Gesundung)*, in which racial hygiene played a leading role (see also Chapter 9).

In recent years some German historians have tried to drive a wedge between the (generally anti-Semitic) Nordic movement and the non-racist racial hygiene movement supported by medical men.[50] But one must admit that there was significant overlap between the two movements even before World War I. Consider the case of Alfred Ploetz himself. Ploetz was a member of a secret Nordic club called the Mittgartbund; he also organized a secret Nordic division within the Society for Racial Hygiene from the very beginning. It is true that in 1895 he denounced anti-Semitism in his founding treatise on racial hygiene. Part of his evidence for ranking the Jews among the cultured races of the world, however, was that European Jews were "more Aryan than Semitic"; Ploetz cited Lombroso's estimate that only 5 percent of all Jews were "of pure Semitic blood" and claimed that most Jews should actually be classed as Aryan.[51]

In his 1895 treatise Ploetz makes it clear he considers the white man to represent the superior race on earth. He devotes a substantial portion of his book to a comparison of the "aptitudes" of the various races; he begins chapter 3, for example, with the query, "Why is the white man more perfect than the Negro, and the Negro more perfect than the gorilla?" The answer, Ploetz says, is that the Caucasian is better adapted to the different conditions of the earth than is the

Negro; the Negro is in turn better adapted than the gorilla. As evidence, he cites the works of several craniologists and demographers, supposedly demonstrating that the Negro has a smaller skull and a lower birthrate than the white. Ploetz also claims it is a fact "known to every American school child" that the Negro learns more slowly than does the white and that in terms of intelligence, the white is to the Negro as the Negro is to the gorilla. As further evidence of Negro inferiority, he cites studies showing that in 1890 illiteracy was nearly ten times higher among American blacks than among American whites.[52]

Ploetz's Nordic supremacy can also be seen in certain institutional affiliations. In 1907 Ploetz, together with F. Wollny and Fritz Lenz, established a secret Nordic Ring (Ring der Norda—which later became the Bogenclub München), a club whose goals included the cultivation of German racial character through training and sports. The Society for Racial Hygiene also maintained a loose affiliation with the Gobineau Vereinigung, an organization founded in 1894 by Ludwig Schemann to popularize Gobineau's works and ideas. Schemann himself joined the Freiburg branch of the Society for Racial Hygiene, where he was not alone in his support for Gobineau. Fritz Lenz, Germany's premier racial hygienist in the Weimar and Nazi periods, ended his 1917 article "The Rebirth of Ethics" with a celebration of Gobineau's vision of "the German Volk, last bastion of the Nordic race."[53] Lenz, as we shall see, forged an important link between the Nordic movement and the racial hygiene movement: it was in his 1923 textbook (written with Erwin Baur and Eugen Fischer) that we first find mention of the expression "Nordic Ideal" (*der Nordische Gedanke*).

Several years before this, the ideal of Nordic supremacy had been recognized as an integral part of the Society for Racial Hygiene. On March 14, 1909, during discussions at the fifth annual meeting of the society (at Munich's Institute for Hygiene), a lively debate arose over whether membership in the society should be limited to individuals belonging to a particular race. While some argued that membership should be open "even to the yellow race," the consensus was that membership should be limited to those of the "white," or "Nordic," race. The society resolved to include this requirement as section 4 of its new statutes.[54]

One cannot, in other words, draw a sharp line between the Nordic movement and racial hygiene in the early decades of the century.

26   Racial Hygiene

Many of the leading figures in the early Nordic movement were medical doctors. Ludwig Woltmann, editor of the *Politisch-anthropologische Revue* (Germany's leading Nordic-supremacist journal), was himself a doctor, as were many other contributors to the *Revue*. A number of Germany's foremost racial hygienists (Rüdin, Lenz, Fischer, and Schallmayer) wrote for the *Revue;* we also find that the *Revue* included from the very beginning (1902) goals similar to those of the Society for Racial Hygiene, including research into "the conditions required for the maintenance and development of the human species and human society, and the problems of social and racial hygiene."[55]

The early racial hygiene movement was not a monolithic structure but rather a diverse blend of both Left and Right, liberals and reactionaries. By the end of World War I, however, conservative nationalist forces controlled most of the important institutional centers of German racial hygiene; it was this right wing of the racial hygiene movement that was ultimately incorporated into the Nazi medical apparatus. Crucial in this transition from Weimar to Nazi racial hygiene were the activities of one of Germany's leading medical publishers: Julius Friedrich Lehmann (see Figure 5). Beginning even before the war, Lehmann built a reputation for publishing handsomely illustrated medical atlases and texts; it was Lehmann who turned the *Münchener Medizinische Wochenschrift* from a relatively small journal into one of the largest medical weeklies in Germany. (The company once boasted that Lehmann had never allowed Jews to work in any position of power in the journal.)[56] Lehmann published military tracts during World War I; after the war he assumed publication of the *Archiv für Rassen- und Gesellschaftsbiologie* and founded (in 1917) the nationalist *Deutschlands Erneuerung,* the "first German political journal to give the question of race and racial hygiene its deserved and proper place."[57] He was responsible for founding the journal *Volk und Rasse* in 1926 and was also said to have urged the anthropologist Hans F. K. Günther to write his *Rassenkunde des deutschen Volkes.*[58] Lehmann published the Baur-Fischer-Lenz textbook I shall describe at length in Chapter 2; after the triumph of the Nazis, he published the official commentaries to the 1933 Sterilization Law and the 1935 Nuremberg Laws. The Lehmann Verlag may well have published more works in the fields of racial science, racial hygiene, and racial anthropology than all other private publishers combined.[59] By 1940, for example, publication of the various editions

Figure 5. Julius Friedrich Lehmann, Germany's most important publisher of works in the field of racial hygiene. From *Volk und Rasse*, 9 (1934): 369.

Figure 6. Tribute to Alfred Ploetz, the "founder of German racial hygiene." The caption notes the seventieth anniversary of Ploetz's birth on August 22, 1930. Theobald Lang's article is titled "National Socialism as the Political Expression of Our Biological Knowledge." From the *Nationalsozialistische Monatshefte*, 1 (1930).

of Günther's fifteen racialist tracts alone had reached half a million volumes.

Lehmann was rewarded for his efforts. In 1934 he became the first member of the Nazi party to receive the Nazi's Golden Medal of Honor (*Goldene Ehrenzeichen*), an honor bestowed only upon the original 100,000 members of the party (Lehmann joined the party in 1920; he also distinguished himself in both the Württemberg Freikorps and the Kapp Putsch). He was granted this award even before such Nazi notables as Gerhard Wagner, Walther Darré, Justice Minister Franz Gürtner, or Finance Minister Johannes Popitz. In 1935 the Nazi medical journal *Ziel und Weg* announced that Lehmann had been awarded the Adlerschild des Deutschen Reiches;[60] he was subsequently awarded honorary degrees at the universities of Tübingen and Munich.

Lehmann's takeover of the publication of the *Archiv für Rassen- und Gesellschaftsbiologie* in 1918 marked a fundamental shift in the political orientation of the German racial hygiene movement. The political Right began at this time to forge an alliance with the racial hygiene movement. Even though it is still possible after this time to distinguish between Right and Left or racist and nonracist forms of racial hygiene, by the end of World War I the forces on the Right held sway in the movement's leading journals, publishing houses, and professional societies.

In the course of the twenties, racial hygienists began to link themselves with the growing Nordic movement. In the late 1920s Ploetz visited Lehmann to see whether he might influence the rising Nazi Wilhelm Frick to establish a chair for social anthropology at Jena, and to have Hans F. K. Günther (known to his friends as "Rassen-Günther") occupy the position. Günther, who was to become one of Germany's most popular racial theorists, was appointed professor of anthropology at Jena in 1932 despite opposition by a majority of the university senate; Hitler attended Günther's inaugural lecture.[61] Ploetz himself, by the end of the twenties, had become a darling of the Nazi cause. In the first (1930) volume of the *National Socialist Monthly*, Ploetz was elevated into the ranks of the greatest heroes of the Nazi cause, among men such as Paul de Lagarde, General von Clausewitz, Horst Wessel, and Philipp Lenard. According to the long and laudatory review of his life and works, Ploetz had sought not only to preserve the health of the general population but also to maintain the higher stages of the "Nordic race."[62] The title of the review, published in the Nazis' leading theoretical journal, contained what would later become a slogan in much of Nazi literature: "National Socialism as the Political Expression of Our Biological Knowledge" (see Figure 6).

German racial hygienists found this an attractive idea. In fact, by 1930 links between the Nordic/Nazi and racial hygiene movements had become quite close. Fritz Lenz, coauthor of the most important textbook on genetics of Weimar Germany and editor of the *Archiv für Rassen- und Gesellschaftsbiologie,* could suggest in 1930 that there might not even have *been* a Nordic movement had it not been for Ploetz's racial hygiene.[63] In subsequent years the Nazi regime would credit Ploetz and his colleagues with having helped provide the "biological foundations" for the Nazi racial state. On January 9, 1936, Ploetz was appointed (honorary) professor of racial hygiene at Munich, in recognition of his services in the area of racial hygiene.[64] In the same year he was awarded the Goethe Medallion, Germany's highest honor for achievement in science and the arts. One year later, at age seventy-seven, Ploetz joined the Nazi party (no. 4,457,957).

By this time it had become difficult to distinguish the rhetoric of racial hygiene from that of official Nazi policy. Ploetz's critique of war, for example—one of the consistent early elements in his racial hygiene—now drew upon themes popular in Nazi ideology. In 1934, at the meeting of the International Federation of Eugenics Organizations in Zurich, Ploetz warned that another great war "would once again decimate the most virile males of the nations engaged," and that recovery from such a war would require many years.[65] He also argued, however, that the ill effects of war derived from the ways in which different elements of society were affected. Ploetz claimed that individuals of "Nordic stock" were especially hurt by wars—first of all, because such individuals are large and therefore tend to be put on the front lines; and second, because Nordics are "more willing to fight for their ideas." Jews, on the other hand, "tend to suffer least from war, partly due to their smaller physique and weaker constitution, and partly due to their lack of support for their fellow citizens and the state." As they enlist only half as often, and are killed only half as often, Jews suffer only a quarter as much as non-Jews from war.[66] Ploetz's views on this question were taken seriously: in 1936 he was nominated for the Nobel Peace Prize for his work in racial hygiene. Hitler himself apparently appreciated Ploetz's argument: in a speech before the German parliament on May 21, 1935, Hitler proclaimed that "Every war goes against the selection of the fittest," and concluded from this that National Socialism was "profoundly and philosophically committed to peace."[67]

I do not want to leave the impression that "racial hygiene" was a movement that wholly endorsed the rise of Nazism. As is true in the case of American eugenics, there were important figures within the German movement who rejected Nordic supremacy, and these people suffered to some extent under the Nazis. The Jesuit anthropologist Hermann Muckermann and the Weimar health minister Arthur Ostermann, for example, both opposed the Nordic movement and suffered for expressing their opinions.[68] After the rise of the Nazis, some medical philosophers wanted to distinguish between the homegrown, racially oriented *Rassenhygiene* and the more internationalist *Eugenik*. In 1933, for example, *Ziel und Weg* reviewed Karl Saller's book *Eugenische Erziehung* (Eugenic education) and criticized it for not paying sufficient attention to the Nordic question.[69] This was a common Nazi criticism of the eugenics movement. The publisher J. F. Lehmann, for example, once argued that after World War I, "Jewish-democratic and clerical circles" had tried to "neutralize" racial hygiene under the name of *eugenics,* and that this fault had been corrected only after the triumph of the Nazis.[70] Fritz Lenz, however, had tried to resolve this dispute as early as 1921, when he wrote:

> To those in Germany who find any mention of the word "race" unpleasant, and who wish to construct an opposition between racial hygiene and eugenics, it should be pointed out that the term "race" is important even in Galton's original [1883] definition of eugenics. Galton did not want to have the analysis of racial differences excluded from the science of eugenics.[71]

Differences between racist and nonracist versions of racial hygiene continued to appear from time to time in both the medical and popular press, even after the rise of the Nazis. In 1935, for example, Professor Hans Luxenburger of the Rüdin Institute in Munich delivered a lecture titled "Racial Hygiene and Genetic Issues of Our Times" at a rally organized by physicians in the town of Fürth. Luxenburger was attacked, however, for presenting an account of population policy, selection, degeneration, and other favorite themes of the racial hygiene movement without addressing "the Jewish question." The moderator of the evening's discussion—Dr. Friedrich Bartels, one of the leading figures in the Nazi Physician's League—protested

Luxenburger's speech, arguing that "a lecture on racial hygiene in which the word 'Jew' does not appear even once is a contradiction in terms."[72] The speaker after Luxenburger, the notorious anti-Semite Julius Streicher (editor of *Der Stürmer*), no doubt satisfied Bartels on this issue; yet the exchange does show that even after 1933, differences persisted in how the term *racial hygiene* was to be interpreted.

Weismann, Lamarck, and the Politics of Inheritance

Theobald Lang's celebration of Alfred Ploetz for the *National Socialist Monthly* is revealing for the light it sheds on the place of biology in Nazi ideology. The title of Lang's article is itself noteworthy: "National Socialism as the Political Expression of Our Biological Knowledge." Lang claimed that National Socialism was simply applied biology, and that a biological perspective was one of the defining features of the Nazi world view. This, Lang asserted, is what distinguishes National Socialism from Marxist socialism: Marxist socialism assumes the biological equality of humans and denies the importance of biological differences. National Socialism, in contrast, rests on the following three principles:

1. The genetics of particular individuals, races, and race mixtures are different.
2. We cannot consciously change the traits specified by genetics; nor does it appear likely that science in the foreseeable future will allow us to make such changes.
3. The current [liberal, Weimar] economic order and conception of civilization exert a negative selection on future generations, having as a consequence a general decimation of German peoples and thereby the entire world.

According to Lang, thousands of scientific articles from very different disciplines had confirmed each of these views (he cited August Weismann's work as especially important—see below). He claimed that National Socialism had founded itself upon these views, and that in this sense "National Socialist methodology is strictly scientific."[73]

One point raised by Lang is significant in Nazi ideology: he lists the "immutability of the human genetic material" as one of the fundamental principles of National Socialism. This was a common interpretation of the implications of genetics for political and social life at this time.[74] Weismann's doctrine of the immutability of the human genetic material was often used as a foil against calls for socialism or social reform. In the early decades of this century, questions of the mechanisms of human heredity, the plasticity of human character, and the origins and dynamics of human institutions were commonly confused with one another, and the science and mission of racial hygiene played a crucial role in perpetuating this confusion.

We know today that the question of the relative importance of nature and nurture in the development of human character and institutions can be addressed quite independently of particular questions of hereditary mechanisms. Whether acquired characters can be inherited, for example, says nothing about how or to what extent the environment may affect an organism in the course of its life. In the early part of the twentieth century, however, the question of the relative importance of nature and nurture often (and perhaps unfortunately) focused on the question of whether characteristics *acquired* by an organism in the course of its lifetime (calluses from sitting, longer limbs due to stretching, and the like) could be *inherited*. The "inheritance of acquired characteristics" was originally advanced by the French zoologist Jean-Baptiste Lamarck at the beginning of the nineteenth century in what is today regarded as one of the earliest attempts to provide a mechanism for the transmutation of species.[75] In the second half of the nineteenth century, and for several decades into the twentieth, many biologists accepted some form of Lamarckian inheritance.[76] The Lamarckian principle was conceived as consistent with, rather than in opposition to, the Darwinian principle of evolution by natural selection. Darwin, in fact, incorporated a kind of Lamarckian inheritance in his own theory of heredity—which he called pangenesis—according to which hereditary material was gathered from all parts of the body and collected into the germ cells (eggs, sperm), from where it could be passed on to subsequent generations. If germ cells for fingers came from the fingers, and germ cells for the eyes came from the eyes, then changes wrought by the environment on the fingers or the eyes might well be inherited in subsequent generations.

Throughout the nineteenth century most scientists had little or no sound theory for the mechanisms of hereditary transmission, and Lamarckian inheritance served as well as any other. The discoveries that were to change all this were announced by the Austrian monk Gregor Mendel, shortly after the publication of Darwin's *Origin of Species*. In 1866 Mendel published a paper in an obscure botanical journal presenting the results of experiments demonstrating the laws of assortment and segregation that today bear his name.[77] His paper, establishing the basic principles of modern genetics, went almost entirely unnoticed in European biological circles; it was not until 1900 that three biologists—Carl Correns in Tübingen, Hugo de Vries in Amsterdam, and Erich von Tschermak in Vienna—independently rediscovered the work. Shortly thereafter, biologists began to debate in earnest the question of whether hereditary transmission followed true to Mendelian or to Lamarckian principles.

The problem with Lamarckian inheritance was in one sense a mechanical one. It was difficult to imagine how something that affected the bodily parts of an organism could be transported to the germ cells of that organism. If a mouse lost its tail, how could this "information" (in modern terms) be transmitted to its offspring, as Lamarck and even Darwin believed? An even bigger problem, however, was empirical. In the 1880s the Freiburg zoologist August Weismann attempted to discover whether characters acquired in the course of an animal's lifetime could in fact be inherited. In what later became a widely publicized experiment, Weismann cut off the tails of a number of mice for several generations to see whether he could thereby breed a race of mice with shorter tails. The experiment failed, and Weismann's negative results subsequently became one of the most widely cited refutations of Lamarckian inheritance. (Critics of Weismann were nonetheless able to argue that such experiments did not disprove Lamarck's original hypothesis, because the kind of mutilations Weismann envisioned had nothing to do with the "needs" of an organism. In Lamarck's view, acquired characters were inherited only if they satisfied the needs of organisms; one would therefore not expect useless or mutilating traits to be inherited.)

Weismann proposed a model to explain his findings. In his view, organisms produce two kinds of cells: somatic and germ cells (*Somatoplasma* and *Keimplasma*). Somatic (or body) cells undergo development and yet play no role in heredity. Germ cells, in contrast, do not undergo development but are simply passed on to future generations as the genetic material. In such a model, it is easy to explain both the evolution of organisms and their stability in the face of environmental change. Evolution occurs through the random variation of germ cells, which then (in modern terms) code for a changed phenotype. At the same time, the stability of organisms is guaranteed by virtue of the fact that only the germ cells (and not the cells of the larger body) contain and transmit the genetic material. In Weismann's model the genetic material is largely impervious to environmental influences acting on the living organism.[78]

At the end of the nineteenth century Weismann's model of inheritance provided an attractive alternative to the Lamarckian model. When combined with Mendel's principles of the independent assortment of genetic traits, Lamarckian theories were dealt what ultimately proved to be a fatal blow. By 1913 William Bateson, the first to demonstrate the applicability of Mendel's laws to animals (Mendel had restricted his experiments to plants), could describe Lamarckian inheritance as "frankly inconceivable."[79]

The question of Lamarckian versus Mendelian (or "Weismannian") inheritance was not, however, a purely scientific one—at least if we conceive this in narrow terms. In the early years of the twentieth century, the question of Lamarckian versus Mendelian inheritance took on political overtones. At root was the question of the relative importance of hereditary (or race) and environment (or socialization) in the growth and expression of human character and institutions. Racial hygienists tended to reject the inheritance of acquired characteristics, along with any other theory stressing the importance of the environment in forming the human constitution. Racial hygienists appealed instead to the doctrine of Weismann, according to which the genetic material (germ plasm) was transmitted from generation to generation, uninfluenced by anything that happened to the rest of the organism (soma plasm) in the course of its life.[80]

For the racial hygienists, Weismann's radical separation of germ cells and body cells provided a central link in their argument that it was nature rather than nurture that provided the key to human character and institutions. The Society for Racial Hygiene underscored its debt to Weismann: the first issue of the *Archiv für Rassen- und Gesellschaftsbiologie* in 1904 was dedicated to Weismann (and Ernst Haeckel); Weismann (along with Haeckel) was named honorary chairman of the Society for Racial Hygiene when it was formed in 1905. A number of Weismann's students were among the earliest leaders of the society: Eugen Fischer, Fritz Lenz, and Wilhelm Schallmayer all studied under Weismann in Freiburg;[81] Heinrich Ernst Ziegler, editor of the ten-volume series *Natur und Staat,* was also a Weismann student. Weismann's principle of the separation of germ and somatic cells and his assertions that the germ cells remain unaltered (except for rare mutations) down through the generations were used by racial hygienists to argue that "mere social change" was impotent to alter the human condition.

Many of those who rejected Lamarckian inheritance did so as part of an effort to defend the goals of racial hygiene. Without appreciating this, it is difficult to understand the vehemence with which the Lamarckian doctrine was attacked (or defended).[82] Hermann Siemens, for example, in a 1918 article, "What is Racial Hygiene?" complained that "educators, philosophers, and socialists clutch maliciously and persistently onto the belief in the inheritance of acquired characters." He maintained that anyone who still believed in the Lamarckian doctrine could only be the product of "the crudest biological ignorance," combined with "superstition" and "a curious lack of clarity concerning the fundamental ideas of the science of genetics."[83] Obvious from his article, however, is that Siemens was less concerned to discuss evidence than to raise the political implications of the two theories. For Siemens, the inheritance of acquired characteristics implied a malleability of the human constitution that violated fundamental principles of race and inheritance. Racial hygiene, Siemens maintained, could not tolerate such plasticity in human character; he went so far as to argue that the science of racial hygiene "only had meaning" when one rejected, entirely, the idea that the environment might in any substantial way affect the human racial-genetic constitution.

Confusion is sometimes as important as clarity in the history of science. The question of the role of the environment in determining the structure of human character or institutions does not *necessarily* have anything to do with the question of whether biological inheritance is Lamarckian or Mendelian. (It may well have to do with whether there is such a thing as *cultural* inheritance, and whether that is "Lamarckian"—but that is an entirely different question.)[84] Yet the identification of racial hygiene with Mendelian genetics, and of human social plasticity with Lamarckian inheritance, are themes one commonly finds among biologists and racial hygienists in the 1920s and 1930s. In the first issue of the *Zeitschrift für Volksaufartung und Erbkunde* (1926), the Swedish racial hygienist H. Lundborg listed the inheritance of acquired characters as one of the three main "dogmas" racial hygiene had to overcome, alongside the dogmas of human equality and the omnipotence of education and the environment.[85]

Identification of Lamarckian inheritance with a belief in the plasticity of human behavior continued into the Nazi period. At a 1938 meeting of the German Genetics Society, the geneticist N. V.

Timofeev-Ressovsky argued that the genetic material could not be influenced by the environment; Timofeev drew from this the implication that one must reject both environmentalism, and the Lamarckian doctrine of the inheritance of acquired characteristics.[86] Others in the German medical community defended racial hygiene as a natural consequence of the triumph of Mendelian genetics over doctrines conceived to be exaggerating the power of the social or physical environment to shape the human species. It was in this sense that the Nazi's Office of Racial Policy was able to declare in 1938 that Mendel's discovery "made it possible to refute, once and for all, the liberal theory of the environment [*liberalistische Milieutheorie*]."[87] On similar grounds, Nazi medical philosophers were able to reject Marxism on the basis of evidence garnered by biologists—evidence supposedly establishing the primacy of race and biology over class and economy.[88]

In the German biomedical community, opinions on the question of Lamarckian versus Mendelian inheritance divided roughly along political lines. (I use *German* here in the sense of "German-speaking"—Paul Kammerer was an Austrian; debates in this period do not fall neatly within national boundaries.) On the one side, socialists such as Kammerer or members of the Association of Socialist Physicians defended Lamarck, arguing that the environment plays an important role in determining certain hereditary patterns.[89] On the other side, geneticists and eugenicists such as William Bateson, Erwin Baur, and Fritz Lenz defended Mendelian genetics (against Kammerer and the Lamarckians), based partly on their opposition to socialism.[90] The triumph of the Nazis in Germany, following upon the consolidation of Soviet rule in Russia, polarized this debate. In Nazi Germany, Lamarckian inheritance was commonly regarded as the folly of Marxists and liberals who naively assumed the "omnipotence of the environment";[91] Nazi racial hygienists rejected the inheritance of acquired characteristics as typical of the thought of "Jews and Free Masons."[92] In the Soviet Union, Mendelian inheritance was taken as part of the ideological apparatus used by bourgeois apologists to defend racial discrimination. The opposition of Nazi biologists to Lamarckian inheritance can be understood, at least in part, as a reaction against demands for social reform—especially those advocated by socialists and communists. Soviet support for Lamarckian inheritance can similarly be understood (especially after 1935) as partly a reaction against Nazi racial hygiene.

Historians have long recognized the importance of politics in the survival or resurrection of Lamarckian and neo-Lamarckian conceptions of heredity.[93] In the Soviet Union, for example, the doctrine of the inheritance of acquired characteristics was felt to allow for the rapid creation of a "new Soviet man," accumulating through his new experiences qualities that could be passed on to subsequent generations.[94] It was in this spirit that scientists such as Pavlov, and later Lysenko and the Michurinists, defended Lamarckian heredity against "Mendel-Morganism."

What has not been sufficiently appreciated is the extent to which the genetics of Mendel, Morgan, and Weismann was itself supported for political reasons. The origins of this point of view are easy to understand. Lamarck turns out to be wrong, and the principles articulated by Mendel, Morgan, and Weismann turn out to be more or less correct. And according to one conception of the relations of science and politics, it is easier to see politics behind the support for a false view than for what turns out to be a true view. There are two problems with this conception. First of all, it is not always clear, without the benefit of hindsight, what the most "reasonable" stance to take in such a controversy was, given the evidence available at the time. In the case of hereditary theory, it was not at all clear in 1918 whether or to what extent acquired characters might be inherited.

A second point that should be appreciated in this context is that political motivations can be as important in justifying correct views in science as they are in justifying false views. In the early twentieth century supporters of a strict Weismannian conception of the immutability of the germ plasm were attracted to the conservative implications of this idea. Those objecting, for example, to Paul Kammerer's experiments supposedly demonstrating the inheritance of acquired characteristics did so (in part) out of fears for the political implications conceived to flow from a doctrine that suggested a high degree of plasticity in the genetic or "racial" structure of life. This was what Siemens meant when he argued that racial hygiene stood or fell with the rejection of Lamarckian inheritance. Fritz Lenz made similar arguments (see Chapter 2). This helps us understand how Theobald Lang could consider biology and racial hygiene allies in the struggle of the Nazis against Marxism.

By 1930, when Lang celebrated the career of Alfred Ploetz for the *National Socialist Monthly,* Lamarckian inheritance was widely discredited in most of Western science. Revelations that certain parts of Kammerer's evidence had been doctored led many to believe that all of his results were unreliable. And yet for many on both sides of the debate, the political question remained a live one. Many in the young Soviet regime, for example, felt that Kammerer had been unfairly judged, even persecuted; a popular Soviet film at this time (*Salamandra*) dramatized the plight of Kammerer, driven to suicide by monks and right-wing racialist scientists.[95] German racial hygienists (Baur, Lenz), for their part, ridiculed any suggestion of Lamarckian inheritance, especially within Soviet science. Racial hygienists claimed that by upholding Lamarckian inheritance, Soviet ideologues had illegitimately imported politics into science in order to discredit racial hygiene. As early as 1931, Lenz protested that it had become *verboten* for Soviet professors to deny the inheritance of acquired characters; he also cited Schallmayer's 1911 warning that the day might come when the proletarian masses would proclaim a certain version of biological theory to be the "politically correct" one.[96]

Hereditary theory remained a point of political contention throughout the period of Nazi rule (and indeed, for some time after). In 1939 the Moscow Anthropological Museum sponsored an exhibit on "Race and Race Theory" attacking the Nazi ideal of Nordic supremacy as part of an "effort by the German ruling class to justify its domination over subjugated classes as 'natural'." Nazi physicians reporting on the exhibit claimed that by virtue of their support for the inheritance of acquired characteristics, Soviet biologists had abandoned the goal of "pure science"; Nazi physicians also suggested that the Soviets hoped, with the help of the Lamarckian doctrine, to "disprove the existence of racial boundaries" and thereby "facilitate the assimilation of Jews into the country."[97] By this time, however, Russia was not the only country issuing official proclamations on the nature of heredity. In 1937 the Nazi party published its official *Handbook for the Hitler Youth*, issued as required reading for the 7 million members of this organization. The *Handbook* presented a chapter titled "Race Formation: Heredity and Environment," including discussions of Mendel's laws of inheritance, Darwin's theory of the origin of species by natural selection, and the Lamarckian principle of the inheritance of acquired characteristics. It reviewed Weismann's experiments refuting the inheritance of acquired characteristics and then instructed the youth of Germany:

> What we need to learn from these experiments is the following: Environmental influences have never been known to bring about the forma-

tion of a new race. That is one more reason for our belief that a Jew remains a Jew, in Germany or in any other country. He can never change his race, even by centuries of residence among another people.[98]

According to the *Handbook,* experimental genetics had shown that "inheritance is in the long run always victorious over environmental influences," and that "political demands founded on a belief in the power of the environment are therefore false and weak."[99]

One could of course multiply such examples. The point I want to stress, however, is that biology was important for the Nazis: the Nazis appealed to biology to provide support for their idea that *nature,* rather than *nurture,* was the key to the development of human talents and institutions.

Pawns or Pioneers?

One often hears that National Socialists distorted science, that scientists perhaps cooperated more with the Nazi regime than they should have, but that by 1933, as one emigré said, it was too late—scientists had no alternative but to cooperate or flee. There is certainly some truth in this, but it misses the more important point that it was largely medical scientists who *invented* racial hygiene in the first place. Many of the leading institutes and courses on *Rassenhygiene* and *Rassenkunde* were established at German universities long before the Nazi rise to power. And by 1932 it is fair to say that racial hygiene had become a scientific orthodoxy in the German medical community. In the winter semester 1932–33, racial hygiene was taught in twenty-six separate courses of lectures in the medical faculties of most German universities; the major expansion in this department occurred *before* Hitler came to power (see Figure 7). Most of the leading journals of racial hygiene were established before the rise of National Socialism (see Table 1).

Racial hygiene received recognition from the German government prior to World War I. Some time around 1910, the Reich Health Office began to assemble a file on *Rassenhygiene,* including materials on population policy, birth control, anthropology, paleontology, and occasional papers on racial differences between Germans and Jews. In May 1920 the Prussian Interior Ministry established a Council for Racial Hygiene to discuss racial policy, including how to foster the growth of the German population and how to curb illegal abortions.[100]

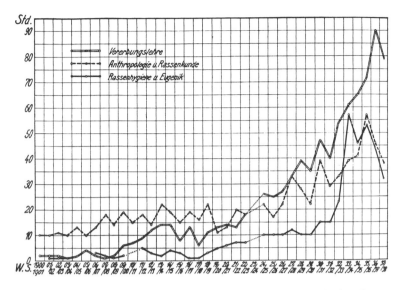

Figure 7. "Courses in Genetics (double line), Anthropology (broken line), and Racial Hygiene and Eugenics (solid line) Taught at German Universities since 1900." From *Der Biologe*, 9 (1938): 308.

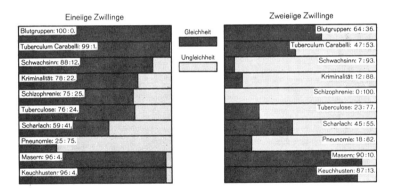

Figure 8. "The Relative Influence of Heredity and Environment for Various Diseases." Otmar von Verschuer and Karl Diehl compared identical and nonidentical twins to see to what degree identical twins share a higher concordance for a particular trait (identical twins, for example, are shown to be twice as likely to be "highly concordant" for tuberculosis as nonidentical twins). Verschuer and Diehl assumed that this provided a measure of the relative importance of heredity and environment for a given trait. The box on the left shows the degree of similarity (dark) and dissimilarity (light) in various traits for identical twins; the box on the right, for nonidentical twins. The chart purports to show that blood groups, tuberculosis, feeble-mindedness, criminality, and other human traits are highly heritable. From Verschuer and Diehl, *Zwillingstuberkulose* (Jena, 1933), p. 461.

Figure 9. "On the Cutting Edge of Racial Thinking." Racial hygienists at work in the archives of the Institute for Human Genetics and Racial Policy in Jena. The Jena Institute, directed by Rector Karl Astel, was one of Germany's thirty-odd institutes for racial science and racial care. From *Das Schwarze Korps*, July 1937, p. 3.

Table 1. Journals of racial hygiene and allied fields published prior to 1933

Journal	Period of publication
Archiv der Julius Klaus-Stiftung für Vererbungswissenschaft, Sozialanthropologie und Rassenhygiene	1925–
Archiv für Bevölkerungswissenschaft und Bevölkerungspolitik	1931–1943
Archiv für Rassen- und Gesellschaftsbiologie	1904–1944
Eugenik, Erblehre und Erbpflege	1930–1931
Das Kommende Geschlecht	1920–1934
Mitteilungen an die Mitglieder der Berliner Gesellschaft für Rassenhygiene	1917– ?
Monatsschrift für Kriminalbiologie und Strafrechtsreform	1904–1938
Politisch-anthropologische Revue	1902–1922
Verhandlungen der Deutschen Gesellschaft für Rassenforschung	1926–1944
Volk und Rasse	1926–1944
Zeitschrift für Psychische Hygiene	1928–1944
Zeitschrift für Rassenphysiologie	1928–1943
Zeitschrift für Volksaufartung und Erbkunde	1926–1930

One of the most important events in the institutionalization of racial hygiene in Weimar Germany was the establishment, in 1927, of the Kaiser Wilhelm Institute for Anthropology, Human Genetics, and Eugenics. In the summer of 1922 the Prussian Council for Racial Hygiene had recommended the establishment of a Reich Institute for Human Genetics and Population Science, staffed by three physicians and a statistician, whose mission would be to provide knowledge useful in the struggle against the "physical and mental degeneration of the German people." Research in the new institute was to include an anthropological survey of the German people; research into the effects of alcohol and venereal disease on the germ plasm; analysis of demographic trends and genealogies; and investigations into the heritability of feeble-mindedness, crime, nervous disorders, cancer, tuberculosis, and other human ailments.[101]

Support for the establishment of an institute devoted to anthropology, human genetics, and racial hygiene came from the highest levels of German health policy. Franz Bumm, president of the Reich Health Office, supported the project, as did the medical statistician Emil Rösle. Rösle argued that such an institute might help draft legislation to prevent the marriage of the mentally ill; statistical information gathered by such an institute might also be useful for insurance companies. He noted that other "cultured nations"—England, Sweden,

Norway, the United States, and Hungary—already had such institutes. Bumm similarly noted that the value of eugenics research had been convincingly demonstrated in the United States, where anthropological statistics had been gathered for 2 million men recruited for the American armed forces.[102]

Eugen Fischer was appointed director of the Kaiser Wilhelm Institute for Anthropology, Human Genetics, and Eugenics when the institute opened its doors in 1927. Fischer was a conservative and nationalist Catholic, who surrounded himself with like-minded colleagues (such as Hermann Muckermann and Otmar von Verschuer). His earliest scientific work cannot be considered particularly racist— his 1913 study of the "Rehobother Bastards" stressed the value of interbreeding for racial/genetic health. Even as late as January 1933, he was expressing views diametrically opposite to those of orthodox Nazi physicians. On January 29, 1933, one day before Hitler's *Machtergreifung,* Fischer delivered a speech to the Kaiser Wilhelm Gesellschaft maintaining that the racial mixing of Nordic with non-Nordic peoples of Europe—Alpine, Dinaric, Mediterranean—was not only not harmful but was in fact responsible for many of the spiritual achievements of present-day peoples. He even maintained that "where it has remained most pure, the Nordic race has brought forth no great cultural achievements."[103]

Shortly after the rise of the Nazis, however, on June 3, 1933, Fischer was replaced by the psychiatrist Ernst Rüdin as head of the Society for Racial Hygiene, as part of a broader effort by Nazi authorities to sever links with the more moderate wing of the Weimar eugenics movement.[104] Fischer was denounced by Karl Astel and Bruno K. Schultz of the Munich Society for Racial Hygiene; his name was struck from the list of editors of the *Archiv für Rassen- und Gesellschaftsbiologie.*[105]

Fischer continued, however, as director of the Kaiser Wilhelm Institute for Anthropology and indeed gained considerable power in July 1933, as he was named rector of the University of Berlin. In his inaugural address, and in a series of essays published shortly before, Fischer adopted attitudes more in tune with the times. He praised the Nazis as the first to realize that the culture of a people is not the product of its soil or its history alone but is instead "the product of the qualities of the *race* that has given rise to and carried on that culture." Fischer contrasted two fundamental philosophies of human health: "The Marxist socialist view concerns itself with the single individual; we [National Socialists], in contrast, concern ourselves with the family." According to Fischer, it was not particular sick individuals that are important in medicine but rather sick genetic *lines*. "Why," he asked, "do we have mandatory registration for contagious diseases such as measles, and diphtheria, but not for genetic diseases, such as schizophrenia, and mental illness? Why do we know a thousand crippling mutations of the fruit fly, *Drosophila,* and hardly any in man?"[106]

Fischer directed the research activities of his Institute for Anthropology, Human Genetics, and Eugenics into areas that fit well with Nazi biologistic goals. Records of the institute's activities for the period 1933–1936 reveal a wide range of projects designed to separate the effects of nature and nurture, genetics and environment. Scholars explored the heritability of a host of human traits and disabilities, including diabetes (Steiner), tuberculosis (Karl Diehl), manual dexterity (Schiff), patterns in the menstrual cycle (Petri), the structure of the internal and external ear (Thordar Quelprud), and certain brain diseases (Werner Wolfslast). Wolfgang Lehmann studied the heritability of rickets and muscular dystrophy; Bühler investigated racial patterns in blood types. H. W. Kranz analyzed 150 "criminal twins" as part of an effort to demonstrate the heritability of crime; K. Kühne examined X-rays of 10,000 individuals to determine the importance of heredity in the structure of the backbone. Wolfgang Abel traveled to Romania, where he investigated the effects of racial miscegenation among Gypsies; Johann Schäuble spent a year in Chile looking at Spanish-Indian racial miscegenation. Fritz Lenz explored the genetic origins of Down's syndrome; Peret explored the persistence of the "Cromagnon" racial type in certain populations. Work at the institute was serious and intense: by 1940 its fellows had published a total of 569 scholarly works on racial hygiene and allied fields.[107]

Scientists at the Fischer Institute were also involved in more practical activities during this period. Fischer, for example, served as a judge in Berlin's Appellate Genetic Health Court; Lenz and Fischer both helped evaluate the "genetic health" of individuals brought before such courts for sterilization (see also Chapter 4). Fischer and Abel provided Nazi officials (especially the Reichsstelle für Sippenforschung) with expert advice on racial purity (*Rassereinheit*); Fischer and Bühler provided expert testimony for civil courts in cases where paternity was in question. Fellows at the institute also taught courses for the National Socialist Teachers' Association (NS-Lehrerbund), National Socialist Physicians' League, and SS physicians' groups.[108]

On April 1, 1935, the Fischer Institute established a new division for genetic psychology (*Erbpsychologie*), headed by Dr. Kurt Gottschaldt from Bonn. The staff of this division cooperated with the Reich War Ministry in performing twin studies to determine who was fit for military service. In the summers of 1936 and 1937, Gottschaldt also established two special camps (*Erholungsheime*) on the North Sea exclusively for the study of twin children. The purpose of these camps was to discover whether Mendelian laws held true for human behavior. Fellows from the institute lived at the camp for weeks on end to study whether behavioral traits such as industry and perseverance were inherited or acquired.

The 1936 meeting of the board of directors of the Kaiser Wilhelm Institute for Anthropology listed the following "research activities" for the year 1935: the training of SS doctors; racial hygiene training; expert testimony for the Reich Ministry of the Interior on cases of dubious heritage; collecting and classifying skulls from Africa; studies in race crossing; and experimental genetic pathology. The magnitude of these efforts is difficult to capture in numbers; we do know, however, that by the end of 1934, according to institute records, the Kaiser Wilhelm Institute for Anthropology had trained 1,100 physicians in "genetic and racial care" (*Erb- und Rassenpflege*).[109] We also know that both the Rüdin and Fischer institutes were funded very well: in 1935 the Fischer Institute received 140,000 reichsmarks (RM) and the Rüdin Institute received 300,000 RM—more than the Kaiser Wilhelm Institutes for Physics and for Chemistry combined.[110]

One of the leading research efforts of Germany's racial hygiene institutes was twin studies (for example, studies of identical twins raised apart) designed to determine the relative importance of heredity and environment. Suggestions that the study of twins might be used for this purpose date back at least as far as Francis Galton's 1875 "History of Twins as a Criterion of the Relative Powers of Nature and Nurture."[111] In the Third Reich, twin studies were lavishly funded as part of an effort to prove that heredity was the key to many human talents and imperfections. Twin studies purportedly demonstrated the heritability of everything from epilepsy, criminality, memory, and hernias to tuberculosis, cancer, schizophrenia, and divorce.[112] In 1933 Otmar Freiherr von Verschuer published a book purporting to provide exact ratios of the relative influence of heredity and environment in a wide range of bodily traits; he derived his data from the study of several thousand identical and nonidentical twins (see Figure 8). Verschuer's studies were followed by hundreds of others. By 1936 Otto Reche's Institute for the Study of Race and Volk had examined 1,250 pairs of twins, recording forty-two separate physical or physiognomic traits for each pair.[113] Eugen Fischer called twin studies *the* single most important research tool in the field of racial hygiene; Verschuer called twin research the "sovereign method for genetic research in humans."[114] Racial hygienists were able to convince Nazi authorities that twin studies warranted substantial government support: in 1939 Interior Minister Wilhelm Frick ordered the registration of all twins, triplets, or quadruplets born in the Reich, for the express purpose of research to isolate the effects of nature and nurture in the formation of the human racial constitution.[115]

The Kaiser Wilhelm Gesellschaft was not the only body providing funds for research efforts in this area. The German Research Council (Deutsche Forschungsgemeinschaft—DFG) supported racial hygiene research through a special Division for Population Policy, Genetics, and Racial Care headed by Kurt Blome, the man responsible for Germany's postgraduate medical education. In 1934 the DFG provided Lothar Loeffler 7,000 RM to study the harmful effects of radiation on the human genetic material; in 1943 it provided thousands of reichsmarks to Loeffler's Institute for Racial Biology in Vienna to study the racial specificity of blood groups. The DFG supported Karl Valentin Müller's attempts to construct a "socio-anthropological profile" of (occupied) Bohemia and Moravia; funds were also supplied to SS officer and racial hygienist Falk Ruttke for work on a series of books constituting "a history of German law, grounded on the principles of racial science."[116] The DFG funded Otto Reche's work on criminal biology (5,000 RM) and Ludwig Schmidt-Kehl's work on racial biology. The council supported research at Berlin's Policlinic for Genetic and Racial Care on the genetics of asocial families and the family background of psychopaths; Karl Thums received support for his racial-biological examinations of German-Czech mixed marriages.[117] DFG support for racial hygiene was in some cases quite substantial. In 1938, for example, Otmar von Verschuer received 20,000 RM for work at his Institute for Racial Hygiene at the University of Frankfurt. Between 1937 and 1944 he received more than 160,000 RM for racial hygiene research, much of

44   Racial Hygiene

this coming after his appointment, in 1942, as successor to Eugen Fischer as head of the Kaiser Wilhelm Institute for Anthropology. Verschuer's DFG support continued long into the war years. In April 1944, for example, he received 10,000 RM to explore the genetics of tuberculosis; in May the Reichsforschungsrat awarded him 40,000 RM for research into comparative genetic pathology. At about the same time (1943–44) Verschuer received funds to help support the analysis of an extensive body of data (120,000 individual measurements) gathered from twins in Germany's concentration camps. This was also the period in which the SS physician Josef Mengele (Verschuer's former graduate student) served as Verschuer's assistant at the Kaiser Wilhelm Institute for Anthropology; Mengele helped supply the institute with some of the "scientific materials" he had acquired at Auschwitz. In his report to the DFG, Verschuer presented the following description of this project:

> My assistant, Dr. [Josef] Mengele (M.D., Ph.D.) has joined me in this branch of research. He is presently employed as Hauptsturmführer and camp physician in the concentration camp at Auschwitz. Anthropological investigations on the most diverse racial groups of this concentration camp are being carried out with permission of the SS Reichsführer [Himmler]; the blood samples are being sent to my laboratory for analysis.[118]

Verschuer noted that war conditions had made it difficult for his institute to procure "twin materials" for study; Mengele's position offered a unique opportunity in this regard, given the fact that the camp held such "diverse racial groupings." In the summer and autumn of 1944 Mengele had his Jewish slave assistant Dr. Miklos Nyiszli send other "scientific materials" to the institute, including the bodies of murdered Gypsies, internal organs of dead children, skeletons of two murdered Jews, and blood samples of twins infected by Mengele with typhus.[119]

The German Research Council supported most of the thirty-odd institutes for racial hygiene and anthropology established during or shortly before the Nazi period (see Figure 9; also Appendix B). Grant proposals were evaluated by a careful process of peer review: Rüdin wrote letters for Friedrich Stumpfl; Günther reviewed Ludwig F. Clauss's proposal for a project on "Race and Character." Günther wrote for Abel; Fischer, Mollison, Gütt, and Rüdin wrote for Eickstedt. Applicants for DFG grants were asked to indicate their racial identity and whether they had ever been a member of the Communist party or the SPD; applicants were also asked to respond to questions such as: "How long have you been a member of the Nazi party?" "When did you join the SA [Storm Troopers] or SS?" "Did your father fight in World War One?"[120]

German biomedical scientists thus participated in a broad program of racial research. The Nazis found biology and medicine a suitable language in which to articulate their goals; scientists found the Nazis willing to support many of their endeavors. Furthermore, racial hygiene was not "imposed on" the German medical community; physicians eagerly embraced the racial ideal and the racial state. This in fact was perceived by observers at the time. In 1933 Fritz Lenz noted:

> Whatever resistance the idea of racial hygiene may have encountered in previous times among German doctors, this resistance exists no longer. The German core [*Kern*] within the medical community has recognized the demands of German racial hygiene as its own; the medical profession has become the leading force in making these demands.

Lenz then cited the words of Gerhard Wagner, leader of the German medical profession:

> Knowledge of racial hygiene and genetics has become, by a purely scientific path, the knowledge of an extraordinary number of German doctors. It has influenced to a substantial degree the basic world view of the State, and indeed may even be said to embody the very foundations of the present state [*Staatsraison*].[121]

2 "Neutral Racism": The Case of Fritz Lenz

> It is the will of the Führer, that the demands of racial hygiene should be put into practice, without delay.
>
> —Fritz Lenz, 1933

The transformation of medical racial hygiene into Nazi racial science was not achieved without a struggle. Racial hygienists prior to 1933 were in fact divided over the question of Nordic supremacy. Some, such as the Jesuit anthropologist Hermann Muckermann or the Weimar health minister Wilhelm Ostermann, wanted nothing to do with the invidious racial judgments of the Nazis. Others, such as Ploetz, Lenz, and Rüdin, sympathized with the Nazis and hoped their racial ideals might be realized in the Nazi regime. Differences over this issue were regional, religious, and political. Members of the Berlin Society for Racial Hygiene (Schallmayer, Baur, Ostermann, Muckermann, Grotjahn) tended to be more reluctant than their Munich colleagues (Ploetz, Gruber, Lenz, Rüdin) to embrace the Nordic ideals of the rising tide of fascism.[1]

A Painful Oversight

By the mid-1920s, tensions within the Society for Racial Hygiene over the question of Nordic supremacy had grown sufficiently strong that the "liberal" (nonracist) wing of the society (led by Ostermann and Muckermann) seceded to form a new body, the German Association for Volkish Improvement and Genetics (Deutscher Bund für Volksaufartung und Erbkunde). The association maintained many of the traditional goals of racial hygiene, calling for sterilization of physical and mental inferiors and attacking venereal disease and narcotics as the "external enemies of inheritance."[2] But it also made clear its opposition to the Nordic movement. In the first issue of its journal, the association declared itself "free of all political and religious positions, and free from all particular racial tendencies [*sonderrassischen Bestrebungen*]."[3] Muckermann proclaimed that no conflict need arise between racial hygiene and religion (that is, Catholicism) as long as racial hygiene was applied to the human species as a whole, without differentiating between inferior and superior races.[4] These views were not uncommon among racial hygienists in the 1920s and 1930s. Leading figures in the Berlin branch of the Society for Racial Hygiene expressed concerns for the growing force of racism; on February 26, 1930, the Berlin Society for Racial Hygiene changed its name to the Berlin Society for Eugenics as part of an effort to dissociate itself from the Nordic supremacist and Nazi movements, which were increasingly looking to racial hygiene for support.

The division between the two factions of the society was short-lived. In 1931, after a series of compromises negotiated by Muckermann, the rift was healed and the society was reunited under the name Society for Racial Hygiene (Eugenics), with a renewed promise to unload the "ballast of racial ideology." The word *eugenics* was included in the title of the reconstituted society as a symbol of the supposedly "value-free" nature of the science, in contrast with the politicized polemics of the Nordic movement.[5]

By the end of the Weimar Republic, however, such pronouncements were not in tune with larger movements sweeping the country. Racial hygiene was no longer confined to the programmatics of a professional medical society; it was becoming a concept increasingly associated with National Socialism. As early as 1930, leading racial hygienists had begun to identify with this new political movement. In that year Fritz Lenz, editor since 1913 of the *Archiv für Rassen- und Gesellschaftsbiologie,* praised Hitler as "the first politician of truly great import who has taken racial hygiene as a serious element of state policy."[6] When Günther Just published *Eugenics and Worldview* in 1932, Lenz reviewed the book for one of Germany's most widely read medical weeklies and complained that it had failed to include "the Nazi point of view."[7] Lenz called this a painful oversight, given that eugenics had become a central part of the National Socialist world view. Other racial hygienists joined Lenz in praise of the Nazi revolution. In the spring of 1933, the editors of the *Archiv für Rassen- und Gesellschaftsbiologie* heralded "a new age of racial-biological revolution [*rassenbiologischer Umwälzung*]" and applauded Hitler for his promise to put race at the center of the policies of the new volkish state.[8]

The Grandfather of Racial Hygiene

The leaders of German racial hygiene in the 1920s included men such as Alfred Ploetz, Fritz Lenz, Ernst Rüdin, and Eugen Fischer. Among these, Lenz's work is perhaps most telling for the spirit of racial hygiene. Lenz was named Germany's first professor of racial hygiene at the University of Munich in 1923; it was Lenz who, with Eugen Fischer and Erwin Baur, coauthored the most important German textbook on genetics and racial hygiene of the interwar years. This was also the man who, in the early months of the war, would write to the head of the Office of Race and Settlement asking to participate in planning resettlement policy for the occupied East, providing detailed suggestions on how the region might be racially restructured.[9] And it was Lenz who, in 1972, on the occasion of his eighty-fifth birthday, would be honored in the first issue of the neo-Nazi *Neue Anthropologie* as the grandfather of racial hygiene in Germany.

Fritz Lenz was born in Pflugrade, Pomerania, in 1887, the son of a farmer.[10] Beginning in 1905 he studied medicine and philosophy, first at the University of Berlin and later at Freiburg, where he was intrigued by the neo-Kantian philosophy of Heinrich Rickert. From Rickert, Lenz gained an appreciation of the importance of the "value problem"—the problem of the nature and origins of good and evil. Lenz would later see racial hygiene as providing a solution to the value problem: race, he argued, is "the ultimate principle of value."[11] During medical school his favorite courses were those in the new science of genetics; he became convinced that human genetics might help unlock the secrets of a practical racial hygiene. In 1909 Lenz met Alfred Ploetz, the founding pioneer of racial hygiene, and the young medical student was moved to devote his life to the new science. Lenz was also strongly impressed at this time by Weismann's theory of the continuity and immutability of the germ plasm; for Lenz, as for many others at this time, Weismann's principle, when combined with Mendelian genetics, provided proof of the stability of the genetic substance in the face of environmental change. As early as 1914, Lenz rejected the Lamarckian doctrine of the inheritance of acquired characteristics.[12]

Lenz's rejection of Lamarckian inheritance was part of the broader rejection by racial hygienists of any substantial role for the environment in shaping human behavior and social institutions. For Lenz, "environmentalism" could be upheld only on ideological, not scientific, grounds. He repeatedly poked fun at Soviet attempts to "politicize" genetics by identifying the doctrine of the inheritance of acquired characteristics with socialist or proletarian science. Science, according to Lenz, was value free, and politics must not play a role in its development. Science, however, could and should inform the practice of politics. In 1930, in his celebration of Ploetz's seventieth birthday, Lenz wrote:

> Ploetz recognized as unsatisfactory from the very beginning the Marxist doctrine of historical materialism—a doctrine which, biologically speaking, derived from the principle of the omnipotence of the environment. The recognition that not all evil is determined by the environment, and that the roots of most evil lie instead in hereditary defects, became the decisive motivating force in racial hygiene.[13]

The search for hereditary defects had occupied Lenz since his years in medical school. Even before World War I, Lenz called for state-regulated marital counseling, obligatory registration of venereal disease, and prison terms up to two months (or fines up to 10,000 marks) for anyone who knowingly exposed another person to syphilis or gonorrhea. In 1912 he completed his doctoral work with a thesis on "The Diseased Genes of Males, and the Determination of Sex in Humans." In his thesis, Lenz gave expression to a principle that would guide much of his later work: "The only way to eliminate genetic illness is through the negative selection of the afflicted families."[14] This, combined with the belief that much of human suffering is the product of genetic illness, would become one of the major principles of racial hygiene over the next three decades.

After completing his studies, Lenz went to Munich, where he worked as assistant to Max von Gruber at the Institute for Hygiene. (Gruber, along with Ploetz and Rüdin, was one of the founders of the Munich Society for Racial Hygiene.) Over the next twenty years (from 1913 to 1933), Lenz edited the *Archiv für Rassen- und Gesellschaftsbiologie* and rapidly established himself as one of Germany's foremost racial hygienists. In 1923 he was appointed to the first German chair of racial hygiene at the University of Munich, a position that had evolved from Gruber's Institute for Hygiene. In

1933 Lenz was called to Berlin, where he was appointed professor (*Ordinarius*) for racial hygiene at Germany's most prestigious university. The appointment signaled a broader shift in German university policy: until 1933 this chair had been Germany's leading professorship for social hygiene, a position originally occupied by Alfred Grotjahn and subsequently by the socialist Benno Chajes. The replacement of Berlin's professorship for social hygiene by Lenz's new professorship for racial hygiene marked a sea-change in German academic policy that would last for more than a decade.

While in school at Freiburg, Lenz attended the lectures of the medically trained anthropologist Eugen Fischer. Fischer was impressed with the young geneticist, and in 1909 the two men collaborated to found a Freiburg branch of the Society for Racial Hygiene. The friendship that developed between the two men led to their cooperation, in 1921, with the geneticist Erwin Baur in publishing a massive two-volume work: *Grundriss der menschlichen Erblichkeitslehre und Rassenhygiene* (Outline of human genetics and racial hygiene), a monument of scholarship and careful argumentation. The book strongly influenced German biomedical thinking and provided scientific legitimacy for many of the views that came to be favored in the Nazi era (see Figure 10).

Let us explore, then, the elaborate vision of race and racial hygiene Lenz presents in the concluding chapter of the 1927 edition of his *Outline of Human Genetics and Racial Hygiene*.

Long Noses and Natural Lamarckians

Lenz introduces his chapter "The Inheritance of Particular Talents" with a series of questions: "Why is it that many persons are able, many others stupid, and the majority mediocre? Why are some people cheerful and others gloomy; some industrious and others slothful; some unselfish and others selfish?" Those "accustomed to thinking biologically," he answers, "have no difficulty understanding that characteristics of the mind, no less than those of the body, are rooted in the human hereditary equipment, and that environmental influences (including education in the narrower sense of the term) can do nothing more than help or hinder the flowering of hereditary potentialities."[15]

Clear, genetically based mental differences, Lenz continues, exist

Figure 10. Erwin Baur, Eugen Fischer, and Fritz Lenz (counterclockwise from top), authors of *Grundriss der Menschlichen Erblichkeitslehre und Rassenhygiene* (Munich, 1921–1940). They were leading figures in the 1920s and 1930s in the fields of genetics, racial hygiene, and anthropology. Lenz's picture is from "Lehrer der Heilkunde," published as a supplement to the *Münchener Medizinische Wochenschrift*, June 28, 1935; Baur's is from the *Galerie Hervorragender Ärzte und Naturforscher, Beilage zur Münchener Medizinische Wochenschrift*, no. 501 (1934); and Fischer's is from the *Festschrift* for Fischer in the 1934 *Zeitschrift für Morphologie und Anthropologie*.

Figure 11. "Adolf Hitler, Doctor of the German People." From *Die Volksgesundheitswacht,* Ostermond 1935, p. 3.

between the sexes, among the races, and among the individuals of any particular race. Consider the differences between men and women:

> Men are specially selected for the control of nature, for success in war and the chase and in the winning of women; whereas women are specially selected as breeders and rearers of children and as persons who are successful in attracting the male . . . Hence arise the essential differences between the sexes . . . Not only do these differences exist, but they are natural and normal.[16]

In intellectual ability, Lenz concedes, young girls do generally score as well as young boys; but one should not forget that girls mature more rapidly than boys, both mentally and physically. Women reach their peak earlier than men and, although female students may do well on university exams, their development is inevitably arrested shortly thereafter. That is why " 'great women,' endowed with 'greatness' in the sense of outstanding creative faculty are practically unknown." Women may occasionally equal men in powers of perception and in memory, but they invariably fall behind in powers of imagination and critical judgment.

Even greater than these differences in intellectual ability are differences in interest and in what Lenz calls "impulsive trends":

> A woman wishes, above all, to be regarded as beautiful and desirable, whereas a man wants to be regarded as a hero and as a person who gets things done. Man has more courage than woman in attack, whereas woman shows more valiancy in suffering. Since women are selected by nature mainly for the breeding of children and for the allurement of man, their interests are dependent upon those of man and of children, and are directed towards persons rather than towards things. Owing to the particular nature of her part in life, woman is endowed with more imaginative insight, more empathy, than men. She can more readily put herself in another's place, she lives more for others, her main motive being her love for her husband and her children.[17]

Lenz argued that differences between the sexes are greater even than differences among the races; so much so, in fact, that women and men should be considered "entirely different forms of organisms" living only in "symbiosis" with one another.[18]

Body size also reflects the character of an individual, according to Lenz. He is confident, for example, that if ten "musical" and ten "nonmusical" persons were placed in a room, he should be able to tell instantly which was which. A person with good hereditary equipment can be recognized from the size and shape of his forehead, chest, and nose. The size of the head gives some measure of intelligence; the size of the chest gives some idea of vigor. "Genius," writes Lenz, "is out of the question in persons the circumference of whose head is less than 56 cm."[19] And great men, he assures his readers, "tend to have long noses."

Lenz is most interested in differences among the races of mankind. Of all the races, the primitives of Australia "are certainly closest to our own apish ancestors." They make no weapons or tools of polished stone, and all attempts to teach them agriculture or to make them settle down have failed. Lenz leaves no doubts as to the cause of this failure:

> The chief cause of the inability of these primitive races to attain a higher degree of civilization would seem to be their lack of imagination . . . Those who hold a more favorable view of the possibilities of such primitive races should be reminded that these latter have had just as long a time as we have had to develop a higher civilization.[20]

The Negro, according to Lenz, is considerably advanced above the Australian aborigine. And yet, compared with European races, the Negro "certainly lacks foresight." This, he maintains, accounts for the propensity of Negroes both to commit crime and to fall into poverty. The Negro is "more strongly influenced than Europeans by the immediate impressions of the senses," and as a result he is "less inclined to work hard in the present in order to provide for well-being in a distant future." Lenz cites the opinion of Eugen Fischer:

> He [the Negro] is not particularly intelligent in the proper sense of the term, and above all he is devoid of the power of mental creation, is poor in imagination, so that he has not developed any original art and has no elaborate folk sagas or folk myths. He is, however, clever with his hands and is endowed with considerable technical adroitness, so that he can easily be trained in the manual crafts.[21]

American army intelligence tests from World War I provide Lenz with evidence of Negro inferiority. Negroes, he reports, scored consistently lower than whites, and those who did score well were usually of mixed blood. (Booker T. Washington, he notes, was the son of a white father and a black mother.) "Naturally," he concludes, "this extensive admixture of white blood has contributed to raise the intellectual level of the colored population." Furthermore, the difference between white and black intelligence seems to be lowest during childhood, because blacks (like women) suffer developmental retardation after puberty. The "widely reported cruelty" of the Negro is also the result of this developmental retardation. The Negro is essentially a child, and, as "we can often observe in our own children," the cruelty of the Negro derives from a lack of human sympathy. It is this childlike character, he asserts, that accounts for the supposed sexual prowess and promiscuity of the Negro: "the notorious lack of sexual control manifested by Negroes is not so much due to any exceptional impulse, as to a general childish lack of the power of self-restraint."[22]

The Mongol, for Lenz, greatly exceeds the Nordic man in mental development. And yet even so, "the Mongol's memory is stronger than his intellect"; his is more a capacity "for imitation than for invention." The Chinese excels in memorization and in apprehension, but falls behind in imagination, abstraction, and critical thought. "It is true," Lenz admits, that "the mariner's compass, the breeding of silkworms, and the spinning and weaving of silks, the making of porcelain, gunpowder, paper, and the printing press were all discovered in China." Nevertheless, Lenz counters, the Chinese have never developed mechanical techniques comparable to those of Europeans. And it even remains doubtful whether Mongols *were* in fact the true creators of Chinese civilization: "In modern China, there are millions of persons having a slender build, a narrow head, a narrow face, and a narrow prominent nose, whose general type, therefore, suggests a European origin."[23]

Lenz also describes "Alpine" and "Mediterranean" races of Europe, following closely the typology of Hans F. K. Günther. Perhaps his most extraordinary remarks, however, are those concerning the Jews, whom he classifies (along with Greeks and Armenians) as belonging to the "Near Eastern race." Much of what he says about Jews represents an attempt to explain, in biological terms, Jewish desires to assimilate to German culture.

According to Lenz, Jews can be recognized at once by their appearance, though the mental particulars of this race are even more distinctive than the physical. (He refers to the Jews as "a mental race.") Lenz imagines himself able "to recognize the literary work of a Jew (scientific writing included) by the way in which the thoughts are developed and by the method of expression," and then proceeds to list a wide range of examples for this thesis. Jews are especially interested in the sexual life (Freud, he says, is typical in this regard); in the medical sciences, Jews are conspicuous in fields of venereal disease, diseases of children, and diseases of the nervous system. Lenz claims that Jews are precocious and witty but lacking in genuinely creative talent; the Jew is more successful as an interpreter than as a producer of knowledge. His strength lies in the manipulation of numbers and in the use of formal logic (hence his "success at chess"); therefore genuinely creative thinkers, such as Einstein and Spinoza, cannot really be considered Jewish—these individuals must be considered more of the Oriental than of the Near Eastern type.[24]

Many Jews, Lenz reports, in the process of adapting to essentially alien surroundings, have tried to imitate the customs and appearances of their hosts in order to blend in and appear less conspicuous. He considers this a typical case of "animal mimicry," commonly observed "wherever a living creature gains advantages in the struggle for existence by acquiring a resemblance to some other organism." It is for this reason, he argues, that Jews are not just shrewd and alert, not just diligent and persevering, but possess as well an unusual sense of empathy—an ability to put themselves in the place of others and to induce others to accept their guidance.[25] The Near Easterner in general, and the Jew in particular, has been selected not for the control and exploitation of nature, but for the control and exploitation of other men. This in turn is reflected in the occupations Jews choose—they are most successful in businesses involving a capacity to influence people: the clothing trade, the theater, the press and publishing industries, the law, and so forth. The Jew knows what pleases and convinces people; the "hysterical Jew" has played a great part in revolutionary movements.[26] The Jew outdoes the Gentile in the arts of oratory and persuasion; the Jew is "a born actor." Industrial production and agriculture, in contrast, are foreign to the Jew. Lenz points out that Jews (in 1927) constitute only 3.6 percent of the Palestinian population engaged in agriculture. And thus, "owing to their deficient talent or inclination for the primary work of production, it would seem that a state consisting entirely of Jews would be impossible."[27] It would be wrong, he cautions, to suppose that Jews "are merely parasitic." The Jew contributes to production through the stimulation of needs and by mediating in their satisfaction. "Nevertheless," Lenz adds, perhaps with some sense of things to come, "it is true that whereas the Teutons could get along fairly well without the Jews, the Jews could not get along without the Teutons."²⁸

Most curious of all, perhaps, is Lenz's belief that the tendency toward "Lamarckism" is a genetically selected racial characteristic. The Jew, Lenz writes, has a peculiar fondness for Lamarckism, the doctrine of the inheritance of acquired characteristics. Hand in hand with this, "there usually goes a dislike of Darwinism, of the doctrine that the origin of species has been affected by the 'cruel' process of natural selection, not by way of the 'peaceful' inheritance of acquired characteristics." Lenz's explanation of the Jewish inclination toward Lamarckism is remarkable:

> The inclination of the Jews towards Lamarckism is obviously an expression of the wish that there should be no unbridgeable racial distinctions. For instance, it is extremely characteristic that Kammerer, who was himself both a Jew and a Lamarckian, should write that "the denial of the racial importance of acquired characteristics favors race hatred." I am personally acquainted with Jews of high mental attainments who feel themselves to belong to the German people and to German civilization, and to whom, therefore, it is a great tragedy of their lives that they should be looked upon as aliens. If acquired characters could be inherited, then, by living in a Teutonic environment and by adopting a Teutonic culture, the Jews could become transformed into genuine Teutons. This enables us to understand why the Lamarckian doctrine should make so strong an appeal to the Jews, whose fate it is to exist everywhere among the Gentiles as a sharply differentiated minority. But this, of course, can make no difference to the fact that the Lamarckian doctrine is an illusion . . . Jews do not transform themselves into Germans by writing books on Goethe.²⁹

A Nordic Racial Trait

As one might imagine, it is the Nordic race that for Lenz is the hero of history. The Nordic race created the Aryan Indo-Germanic languages and civilizations, from Hindustani and Persian to Hellenistic and even Roman. (Roman busts, according to Lenz, often "have a typically Brandenburg look.") Nordic blood was decisive in the discoveries and conquests of the Portuguese; Nordic blood produced the Protestant Reformation; the Dutch expertise in navigation; the empires of the British, the Russians, and the Spanish; and most of the world's great science and inventions.

Lenz is confident that in most respects the mental powers of Nordic man exceed those of other races. He cites Fischer's observations that the mentality of the Nordic includes industry, vigorous imagination, intelligence, foresight, organizing ability, artistic capacity, individualism, a willingness to obey orders, one-sidedness, an inclination toward meditation and flights of fancy, dislike for steady and quiet work, and devotion to plan or idea. To this Lenz adds the qualities of self-control, self-respect, respect for life and property, desire to know the unknown, a certain wander instinct, and fondness for the sea. According to Lenz, the Nordic mind strives above all else for clarity; Nordic idealism represents a "healthy realism," a sense of the actual and the essential. He also maintains that the deficiency of historical and geographical knowledge one finds among the British and the Americans is typically Nordic: the Nordic has less a sense of particular occurrences than of law and principle. This is turn he links with the Nordic's individualism and also his natural tendency toward Protestantism over Catholicism.[30] Selection has aided the Nordic—his cold northern climes have selected for intelligence and mastery of techniques. The same climate that among the Mongols selected for freedom from wants and capacity to endure has selected in the Nordic a love of order and of cleanliness; a love of sport, of danger, and of war; and a certain need for distance or detachment from other men and things (what Lenz calls Nietzsche's "pathos of distance"). Hence "objectivity is a Nordic racial trait."[31]

Such pronouncements may sound strange to the modern ear. Yet Lenz did in fact consider his science of race to be a neutral and objective science—indeed, he often warns against the dangers of "mixing values with science." For Lenz, human racial variation is simply a fact that science is called on to analyze; the purpose of constructing a racial typology is not to rank the various races in any moral sense:

> No race can be regarded as either "higher" or "lower" than another, because all such estimates of value imply the application of some standard of value other than that of race *per se*. We cannot say that the earth stands higher or lower than the planet Mars, or that the earth is at the same level as Mars, because the concepts "high," "low," and "level" are coined with reference to the earth itself.[32]

Lenz thus asserts that there is "no implication that we therefore regard our own race as having a 'higher' value in any objective sense." In similar fashion, he argues that one cannot speak of one sex as morally or intellectually higher than another: "Each sex has its own peculiar tasks to fulfill in the life of the race, and must be fitted for these tasks by the inheritance of particular bodily and mental characters."[33]

At several points Lenz takes pains to convince his reader that he is not an anti-Semite. He suggests that "contrary to the opinion of the 'anti-Semite,' " the Jews have played a constructive role in history: the Jew tears down, but generally with the aim of building up. The Jew is a good family man; he has a natural "business sense." Germans and Jews are more similar to one another than most have realized: "Next to the Teutonic, in fact," he asserts, "the Jewish spirit is the chief motive force of modern Western History." Lenz claims to have struck a prudent balance in his evaluation of "the Jewish question"— siding neither with "those writing in favor of the Jews" (Zollschau, Herty, Kahn), nor with those writing against them (Chamberlain, Fritsch, Ford).[34]

It should be recalled that Lenz, Baur, and Fischer's book remained the most prestigious genetics textbook of Germany for more than twenty years. Baur was professor of genetics at Berlin and director of the world-renowned Institute for Genetics in Potsdam; he was also editor of the *Zeitschrift für Induktive Abstammungs- und Vererbungslehre* and the *Bibliotheca Genetica*. Fischer was professor of anthropology at the University of Freiburg (and subsequently at Berlin) and editor of the *Zeitschrift für Morphologie und Anthropologie;* as head of the foremost anthropological institute in Germany, he was widely known as the "founder of human genetics" in Germany. Lenz himself was a prolific and highly regarded scholar in his time: between 1910 and 1943 he contributed 363 articles and reviews to the *Archiv für Rassen- und Gesellschaftsbiologie* and several hundred other articles and reviews to leading medical and social science journals in Germany and abroad.[35] His magnum opus, the Baur-Fischer-Lenz book on human heredity (from which I have quoted at length), was one of the most highly praised scientific texts of the times. Hans Stubbe called it the "standard work" in its field; Otmar von Verschuer called it "a masterpiece," the first great effort to unite "the previously separate sciences of genetics, Rassenkunde, and racial hygiene." Verschuer called Lenz's contribution "cautious and critical";

Lenz "lets the facts speak for themselves." Verschuer also noted that the work had played an important role in laying the scientific foundations for "the Nazi political and philosophical revolution."[36]

Reviews from outside Germany were also favorable. Soviet eugenicists praised the work: E. Kal'tsov, writing in the *Russkii evgenicheskii zhurnal*, gave it a positive review; the geneticist Filipchenko was so impressed with the book that he adopted some of its terminology in his own work.[37] The Dutch Nazi medical organization (the Medisch Front) displayed prominent advertisements for the book on the inside cover of its official journal, *Volksgezondheid*.[38] In Italy, Giulio Cogni linked Baur-Fischer-Lenz to both the Sterilization and the Nuremberg laws, calling it "the most comprehensive reference book that exists in this area." Cogni called the shift in world view associated with the book (and the German racial movement more broadly) "a Copernican scientific revolution," one that had "transformed morals, as well as science."[39] In the United States, the *Journal of Heredity* described the 1923 edition as "encyclopedic" and "worthy of the best traditions of German scholarship." Five years later, in 1928, this same journal hailed Baur-Fischer-Lenz as "the standard textbook of human genetics," not only in Germany but in the rest of the world as well.[40]

In 1931, when the first English translation of Baur-Fischer-Lenz appeared, the book was highly praised in both Britain and the United States. L. A. G. Strong, for example, writing in the *New Statesman and Nation*, called the work "a magnificent textbook" and "a masterpiece of objective research and cautious hypothesis." S. J. Holmes, in the *Journal of Heredity*, called it "a valuable source-book for many years to come," one that would stimulate "further observation and research."[41] Lenz received other favorable reviews in *The Spectator* and in journals such as *Sociological Education* and the *American Sociological Review*.[42] A reviewer for *Sociology and Social Research* called it the "standard monumental treatise on the general subject of human heredity." Prior to the translation of the book in 1931, the *Quarterly Review of Biology* had called the third German edition of the treatise "the best existing general book on human inheritance." "It is a pity," this reviewer had remarked, "that we have in English no such sound, comprehensive, and stimulating work as this on human heredity."[43]

Not all reviews were entirely favorable. Holmes, for example, cautioned that research in the field of racial differences still remained "full of pitfalls," and that works such as Baur-Fischer-Lenz should be considered suggestive, not conclusive. The American geneticist H. J. Muller in the journal *Birth Control* praised the genetics of the volume and yet mocked the views expressed by Lenz on the topic of racial differences.[44] In a review of the sixth (1936) edition, Frank H. Hankins in the *American Sociological Review* wrote that although the book was useful for its survey of contemporary research, it was also marred by its "failure to give any adequate discussion of the role of environment" and its "undue attachment to the ideologies of Gobineau, Chamberlain, and Günther." Hankins also maintained, however, that Lenz had presented what seemed to him "on the whole a dispassionate discussion of Jewish traits."[45]

A Principle of Value

Lenz first articulated his philosophy of race, science, and value in an article titled "The Renewal of Ethics," written for the first volume of *Deutschlands Erneuerung,* a protofascist journal founded by the publisher J. F. Lehmann in 1917.[46] (Lehmann's journal boasted itself as "the first monthly journal of a general political interest to give the question of race and racial hygiene its deserved and proper place.")[47]

Lenz's article, written at the height of World War I, posed the query, "What should be considered the absolute value of a people?" Lenz rejected utilitarianism on the grounds that the ideal of "greatest happiness for the greatest number" failed to consider whether individuals were sick or well, rich or poor, ethically valuable or ethically worthless. He also rejected science and technology as standards of value on the grounds that these present us only with means, not ends. Lenz argued that ethical questions were soluble "neither by the microscope nor the ballot box"; he recalled in this context Kant's dictum that we cannot "derive laws concerning that which *should be,* from that which *is.*"[48]

If neither science nor the greatest good for the greatest number, then what, Lenz asked, is the highest end? Kant considered the single individual to be the ultimate locus of value. And yet, Lenz asked, do we condemn the field commander who sacrifices thousands of soldiers to achieve a strategic goal? Certainly not. Man must locate himself within the larger organic unity—the unity from which he came and to which he may aspire to contribute. This is what Lenz called "the absolute value of race," a value that transcends the purely self-interested individual and on which all other values depend. It is this that justifies our men dying in battle: for "insofar as they died for the race, their death remains a service to life; indeed, they have found their fulfillment only in death."[49] Lenz ended his essay with an appeal to Plato's analogy of the metals, according to which some men are said to be made of gold, that they may rule; others are made of silver, and are destined to be the craftsmen and artisans; and still others are made of bronze, destined to be slaves. The most pressing task of the day, he concluded, is to ensure that "the fittest men come to the right position" in the months that lie ahead.

In the final years of the Weimar Republic, Lenz, like many others, believed that the triumph of National Socialism might well put "the fittest men in the right position." Certainly his own work seemed to fit the times. In 1933 his paper "The Renewal of Ethics" was republished with a title more in keeping with the times: "Race as a Principle of Value." In the preface, republished on the eve of the Nazi seizure of power, Lenz claimed that his article, first published in 1917, contained "all of the important features of National Socialist policy."[50] Baur-Fischer-Lenz also continued to enjoy success. Lenz probably derived satisfaction from learning that Hitler himself had read the book while in Landsberg prison, serving time for his role in the misfired Munich Beer-Hall Putsch of 1923.[51]

Lenz found National Socialism attractive, partly because he considered the alternatives inadequate. In 1931 he expressed his opposition to capitalism as overly "individualistic": he maintained that unrestricted laissez-faire could only lead to economic chaos and racial degeneration. Lenz had little confidence that the man on the street was capable of either recognizing or pursuing his own best interests. Socialism he considered to have certain ethical advantages over capitalism: Lenz appreciated the value of "socializing" child rearing by providing economic compensation for those who raise large and healthy families; but he also maintained that socialists were wrong when they assumed that social change alone could bring forth a "new man" and new society. Lenz had argued as early as 1917 that it was not the "socialism" in Social Democracy that bothered him, but the "democracy." (Lenz supported Alexander Tille's calls for "social aristocracy.") In 1931 Lenz claimed that the "tragedy" of modern socialism was that its lofty ideals could never be achieved with the racial quality of present-day man. Socialist ideals could be achieved only by *racial* means—through selection according to the principles of racial hygiene. Racial hygiene, Lenz argued, is the only path to true socialism.[52]

In 1930, three years before the triumph of National Socialism, Lenz lauded Hitler as the first politician "of truly great import, who has taken racial hygiene as a serious element of state policy."[53] And yet Lenz's attitude toward the Nazis was in certain respects ambivalent. In 1931 he expressed his disappointment with the "one-sided" character of the Nazis' anti-Semitism; he regarded it as unfortunate that men needed such "anti-feelings" to move them to action.[54] Lenz did not join the Nazi party until 1937 (no. 3,933,933), despite serving on government bodies such as the Committee on Population and Racial Policy, the body responsible for drawing up Germany's sterilization and castration legislation.[55] There is some evidence that he derived satisfaction from seeing his ideas reach practical fulfillment in the Nazi years; there is also evidence, however, that his notion of race differed in certain respects from that of many (other) Nazis. Lenz saw no fine line distinguishing the races; the variety of races presented a continuum flowing smoothly from one race to another. There were no "pure" races for Lenz; the peoples of Europe had been mixed for centuries through migration and wars. One could not even say that Germany was composed of several races, for Germany, like any other country, was composed of a mixture of various *genes,* not races. Lenz argued in 1934 that one must distinguish sharply between a race and a people (*Rasse und Volk*), and in doing so Lenz went against some of the more radical elements of Nazi racial doctrine.[56]

It is important to recall, however, that Nazi thought was not homogeneous, and that Nazi racial theory was not all of the knee-jerk "fanatical" variety of, say, a Julius Streicher. National Socialism was a mass movement, with different schools and competing factions. There were "refined," and "vulgar" versions of racialist doctrine. Fritz Lenz produced a body of literature that pretended to follow in the best traditions of German science. In 1936, as his book went into its fourth edition, he noted that race had become a central pillar in the philosophy of the new state. A new preface noted that certain passages had been dropped from the present edition; the authors explained that "it can now [1936] be assumed that the reader is familiar with the external racial characteristics of European and most important non-European races."[57] The fundamental ideals of racial hygiene had by this time become part of state policy; books like Lenz's had made it possible for Nazi-minded biologists and biology-minded Nazis to claim that "the National Socialist world view has conquered Germany, and a central part of this world view is biological science."[58] Lenz himself had done perhaps as much as anyone to create this view: in his 1931 magnum opus, Lenz had declared that National Socialism (unlike Marxist Socialism) could be considered applied biology.[59] When Rudolf Hess and other Nazi luminaries used such expressions after 1933, they were simply repeating slogans that leading German scientists—such as Lenz—had uttered several years before.

Two Functions of Neutrality

Lenz's appeal to science and to scientific objectivity is obviously something we cannot take at face value. Today we recognize that his racial hygiene and the racial science on which it was based were soaked with the values and prejudices of his time—values and prejudices that were probably invisible to many of those not on the receiving end of racial hygiene as it was put into practice. The guise of science helped to preserve this invisibility.

The appeal to scientific objectivity and neutrality served a dual social function. On the one hand, it allowed Lenz to don the guise of science in support of racial doctrine. In this sense science served to legitimize (or biologize) what in fact were common perceptions and prejudices of his time. This is a common feature of much of the racial science in the first decades of the twentieth century. In this as in other cases, the guise of scientific neutrality and objectivity served to mask the interests and values that motivated the research in the first place.

On the other hand, the ideal of objectivity also served as a *criterion* by which the races might be ranked and distinguished. Thus while Lenz considered Jews (and women) fundamentally "emotional" and thereby unable to distance themselves from human affairs, the Nordic race alone was capable of objective and impartial scientific inquiry. Science, in other words, was used by Lenz both to defend certain prejudices and then to construct a world view that prevented those who are the objects of that prejudice (women, blacks, Jews) from gaining access to the tools that might be used to refute such prejudices.

In the case of women and Jews, two groups important for Nazi racial science, the results of supposedly objective science were used both to describe their nature (they are irrational or emotional) and to make certain claims about their ability to do science (their irrationality makes them unable to practice good science). By casting such claims in the language of science, racial scientists such as Lenz were able to disguise the political character of their views. Whether or not this was a conscious effort (and in a sense, this does not really matter), the net effect was to insulate racial theory and practice from broader popular critique.

3 | Political Biology: Doctors in the Nazi Cause

> The National Socialist Physicians' League proved its political reliability to the Nazi cause long before the Nazi seizure of power, and with an enthusiasm [*Begeisterung*], and an energy, unlike that of any other professional group.
>
> —Dr. Hermann Berger, 1934

Biology and medicine both played an important part in Nazi ideology. Biology was commonly presented as providing the foundations for National Socialism;[1] Hitler was lauded as the great doctor of the German people (see Figure 11). Hitler himself called his revolution "the final step in the overcoming of historicism and the recognition of purely biological values." Medical imagery filled National Socialist literature; SS journals spoke of the need for selection to replace counterselection, borrowing their language directly from that of the racial hygienists (see Figure 12). Bavarian Cabinet Minister Hans Schemm declared in 1934 that National Socialism was nothing but "applied biology"; Rudolf Hess called the new movement applied racial science (*angewandte Rassenkunde*).[2] Several years before this, the National Socialist Physicians' League announced as one of its maxims "the primacy of national biology over national economy."[3]

In such a climate Hitler felt he could rely on the medical profession. In an early speech before the National Socialist Physicians' League, he argued that he could, if need be, do without lawyers, engineers, and builders, but that "you, you National Socialist doctors, I cannot do without you for a single day, not a single hour. If not for you, if you fail me, then all is lost. For what good are our struggles, if the health of our people is in danger?"[4] On April 5, 1933, Hitler asked that the German medical profession move with all its energy into the forefront in the race question; racial hygiene was to be the task of the German physician.[5]

Figure 12. "Selection" and "counterselection." From SS Leitheft 3, 5(1939): 18, 19.

Figure 13. Gerhard Wagner, Führer of the National Socialist Physicians' League and the German medical profession, 1933–1939. From *Deutsches Ärzteblatt*, 68 (1938), supplement to the August 17 issue, pp. 3, 4.

Figure 14. Physicians in the National Socialist Physicians' League meeting shortly after the Nazi seizure of power. Gerhard Wagner stands in the dark suit (front row, center). From *Deutsches Ärzteblatt*, 68(1938), supplement to the August 17 issue, p. 5.

Who Joined the Party and Why?

Medical science did not fail Hitler. Medical men were among the earliest adherents of National Socialism, and in the Reichstag elections leading to Hitler's seizure of power (*Machtergreifung*), nine physicians were elected members of parliament representing the Nazi party.[6] In 1929, at the Nuremberg Nazi Party Congress, a group of German physicians (forty-two men and two women) formed the National Socialist Physicians' League (*Nationalsozialistischer Deutscher Ärztebund*—NSDÄB) to coordinate Nazi medical policy and "to purify the German medical community of the influence of Jewish Bolshevism." The league listed among its primary goals the promotion of knowledge of racial hygiene, racial science (*Rassenkunde*), and eugenics; the league summarized its principal task as one of "providing the [Nazi] party and future state leadership with experts in all areas of public health and racial biology."[7] The first (1931) issue of *Ziel und Weg*, the official journal of the league, proclaimed the goals of the Nazi movement to be "the antithesis of the French Revolution"; the movement was to "overcome rationalism" and recognize "the German soul and German race." National Socialism embodied the performance principle (*Leistungsprinzip*) and the "old-fashioned Prussian fulfillment of duty." Nazi physicians attacked the bureaucratization (*Verbeamtung*) of medicine; league members were to be the Storm Troopers of the German medical profession.[8]

The Nazi Physicians' League was an immediate success. By the beginning of 1933 (that is, *before* the rise of Hitler to power), 2,786 doctors had joined the league. Doctors in fact joined the Nazi party earlier and in greater numbers than any other professional group.[9] The 2,800 doctors joining the league before Hitler's rise to power represented 6 percent of the entire medical profession (whereas only 2.3 percent of all engineers and less than half of 1 percent of all judges had joined).[10] In the spring and summer of 1933, physicians rushed to join the league. By October 1933, 11,000 physicians had joined,[11] and by 1934 the number waiting to join was so great that *Ziel und Weg* advised doctors to make no further applications until the present ones could be processed. Nazi physicians also organized regional branches of the league: on November 30, 1930, a number of "medical Brown Shirts" (*braune Männer des Aeskulap*) headed by Eugen Stähle founded a Gau Württemberg-Hohenzollern branch in Esslingen; other branches were established shortly thereafter in other parts of the Reich.[12] After 1933 the league also set up branches in other countries, including China and Argentina. Some countries, such as Finland and Holland, established independent Nazi medical associations. The Finnish National Socialist Physicians' League (*Duodecim*), for example, was headed by a Dr. Renpää, director of the Physiological Institute in Helsingfors; in Holland, Dutch Nazi physicians formed the Medisch Front headed by *Leider* G. A. Schalij. Exiled Russian physicians founded an Association of Aryan Russian Doctors (Verein der Arisch-Russischen Ärzte) in Prague.

In Germany itself, Michael Kater has estimated that as many as 45 percent of all doctors ultimately joined the Nazi party; according to Kater, 26 percent of all male doctors were in the SA (compared with 11 percent of all college teachers); more than 7 percent of all doctors were members of the SS (compared with less than half of 1 percent of the general public). In 1937 doctors were represented in the SS seven times more often than was the average for the employed male population.[13] Membership records for the Nazi Physicians' League indicate that nearly 40,000 physicians joined the league by 1942;[14] Georg Lilienthal has discovered archival evidence that by the beginning of 1943, some 46,000 physicians had joined.[15] If 90,000 physicians were active from 1931 to 1945, then roughly half of all physicians joined the Nazi party.

How does one account for the medical profession's support for the Nazis? How did this support manifest itself in particular policies? To what extent did Nazi racial ideology penetrate the German medical profession, and how did the profession help to construct this ideology? We shall return to these and related questions in subsequent chapters; here, however, let us briefly examine who joined the party in the case of Berlin and focus on some of the structural changes in the profession that followed the rise of the Nazis to power.

In 1937 the *Ärzteblatt für Berlin* published the results of a survey by Julius Hadrich presenting a comprehensive breakdown of the profile of the Nazi physician in Berlin in the early years of the Third Reich. In 1936 there were 6,319 physicians in Berlin. Of these, 23.3 percent were Jewish "by confession"; another 9 percent were of mixed (Jewish-German) race. In contrast, 61.5 percent of Berlin's insurance physicians (*Kassenärzte*) were "of German blood" (*Deutschblütige*—that is, non-Jewish). The survey also included statistics on physicians who joined the Nazi party. By 1936, 1,209 of Berlin's physicians had joined, representing 31 percent of those eligible (that is, non-Jewish physicians). Six hundred five physicians, or 15 percent of those eligible, were members of the SA; 212 Berlin physicians had joined the SS (5 percent); 114 physicians (3 percent) were members of the Hitler Youth.[16]

Hadrich's survey also presented the results of questions concerning the ages of the German physicians; this, coupled with information on the proportions joining the Nazi party, provides a profile of the ages at which Berlin physicians joined the party. In 1936 their age structure was as follows:

Age	No. of physicians	Percentage of all physicians
30 and under	808	13
31–40	1,712	27
41–50	1,572	25
51–60	942	15
Over 60	1,285	20
All physicians	6,319	100

Among those physicians who had joined the party, the age distribution was as follows:

Age	No. in Nazi party	Representation in Nazi party (percent)
30 and under	194	16
31–40	443	37
41–50	344	28
51–60	147	12
Over 60	81	7
All ages	1,209	100

It is also possible to compare different age groups to see which ones supported the Nazis most strongly. Only those physicians without Jewish ancestry were eligible to join the party; among these, what proportion did in fact join? In 1936, 61.5 percent of physicians belonging to Berlin's Reich Physicians' Chamber were "of German blood." Assuming that for each age group only 61.5 percent were eligible to join the party, one may calculate the following figures indicating the extent to which Berlin's non-Jewish physicians had joined by 1936:

Age	No. eligible	No. in Nazi party	Proportion of this age group in Nazi party (percent)
30 and under	497	194	39
31–40	1,063	443	42
41–50	967	344	36
51–60	579	147	25
Over 60	790	81	10
All physicians	3,896	1,209	31

We can see from this that the strongest support for National Socialism came from younger physicians, especially those forty and younger. In this age group, more than 40 percent of those eligible to join the party had done so by 1936. In contrast, only 10 percent of Berlin's non-Jewish physicians over age sixty had joined by this time. About half of all German physicians in 1936 were below age forty; among all Berlin physicians who had joined the party, the majority (53 percent) were forty or younger. Many Nazi medical leaders assumed positions of power within the profession at a relatively young age. Ernest Stuck became "Reich Dental Führer" at age thirty-nine; Friedrich Weber was named "Veterinary Führer" at age forty-one. Several leading figures in Nazi medicine assumed positions of power while in their thirties: Leonardo Conti was named health commissioner (*Staatskommissar für das Gesundheitswesen*) in the Prussian Ministry of the Interior in 1933 at age thirty-three; Karl Brandt became Reich health commissioner in 1942 at age thirty-eight. Walter Gross founded the Aufklärungsamt für Bevölkerungspolitik und Rassenpflege (in 1934 renamed the Office of Racial Policy) at age twenty-eight. Gerhard Wagner was relatively old compared with other medical leaders: he rose to the head of the Nazi Physicians' League in 1932 at age forty-four. (This is not out of line with what we know about the Nazi movement more generally: from the beginning it was a youth movement. By 1930 the National Socialist Student Association [NSDStB] was the most popular political organization on German university campuses, with 25,000–30,000 members.)

It is difficult to say how typical the case of Berlin is for the nation as a whole. There are no good statistics for party membership among physicians in Bavaria, for example, where the comparison with Berlin would be especially interesting. One thing we do know: the fact that so many Berlin physicians were Jewish (more than 50 percent in 1933) does not seem to have been the decisive factor in physicians' eagerness to join the party. In Pomerania (East Prussia), for example, where fewer than 8 percent of all physicians were Jewish, physicians joined the party in roughly the same proportions as in Berlin. By 1936, of 1,042 Pomeranian physicians eligible to join the party, 356 (34 percent) had joined. By this time, 28 percent had joined the SA, and 6 percent had joined the SS.[17]

Why did physicians join the Nazi party in such numbers? Professional opportunism certainly played a role: many reasoned that by driving out the Jews, jobs could be created for non-Jewish physicians—an important motive, given the overcrowding and financial stress suffered by the profession in the years before the rise of the Nazis (see Chapter 6). The traditionally conservative character of the medical profession was another factor. Prior to 1933, many German physicians identified with the Deutschnationale Volkspartei, a conservative and nationalistic party that eventually threw its support to Hitler. Most physicians shared a strong sense of national pride: in the spring of 1933, for example, the *Deutsches Ärzteblatt* noted that most German physicians had taken part in World War I and that 1,000 had died "on the field of honor."[18]

In the years preceding the triumph of the Nazis, physicians were faced with a series of economic shocks that moved many to realign their politics. Impoverishment after the war and economic collapse during the final years of the Weimar Republic polarized the profession politically. At the same time, physicians warned of a "crisis in medicine," a crisis variously construed as the bureaucratization, specialization, or scientization of medicine—problems blamed on the socialists, the Jews, or the numerous quacks that eternally plague the profession. Physicians expressed a desire to win back "the confidence of the people."

In the early 1930s many physicians imagined that National Socialism might solve the problems plaguing the profession. The Nazis would reverse the "degeneration" of German racial stock by making racial reform a centerpiece of social policy. The Nazis would restrict access to the profession and thereby put a halt, once and for all, to competition from natural healers and Jews. The Nazis would stand up to the Bolshevist threat and pull in the reins on Germany's powerful social insurance companies. The Nazis would restore the honor and dignity of the profession and recognize medicine as not a trade but a calling. Many physicians also anticipated new and enlarged powers and responsibilities under the Nazis. The physician would be entrusted with a special role, transcending that defined under previous governments. In December 1933, the *Deutsches Ärzteblatt*, Germany's leading medical journal, described the future of the profession under the Nazis in glowing terms: "Never before has the German medical community stood before such important tasks as that which the National Socialist ideal envisions for it."[19]

The *Gleichschaltung* of German Medicine

Shortly after the Nazis' rise to power, the medical profession was *gleichgeschaltet*—literally, coordinated or unified—into a single, hierarchical structure responsible to a vertical chain of command culminating in the National Socialist Physicians' League, which was in turn subordinated to the National Socialist party.

The authority of the National Socialist Physicians' League was consolidated within the very first months of Nazi rule. On March 21, 1933, Dr. Alfons Stauder, head of Germany's two major medical associations, met with key figures in the league (among them, Gerhard Wagner) to plan the reorganization of the German medical profession. On the same day, Stauder sent a telegram to Hitler, pledging the support of the profession to the new regime:

> To Reichskanzler Hitler. Berlin.
>
> The leading medical associations of Germany—the German Medical Association and the Hartmannbund—welcome with greatest joy the determination of the Reich government of national reconstruction to create a true Volk community of all estates, professions, and classes, and place themselves happily in the service of this great task of our fatherland, with the promise faithfully to fulfill our duty as servants of the people's health [*Volksgesundheit*].[20]

Two days later, Drs. Stauder, Schneider, and Reichert, representing the joint leadership of the German Medical Association (Deutsche

Ärztevereinsbund) and the Hartmannbund,[21] met again with Wagner in Nuremberg and issued the following announcement to all its members:

> In every part of the Reich, demands have been vigorously issued for a change in the executive leadership of the profession, insofar as members of this leadership are not in agreement with the political and philosophical [*weltanschauliche*] will of the overwhelming majority of the German people and the German medical profession.[22]

They suggested that these demands could best be achieved "without friction" and without endangering Germany's "carefully-constructed" medical organizations only if any and all dissent on the part of regional medical organizations was avoided. On behalf of Germany's two leading medical bodies, Stauder, Schneider, and Reichert issued a press release (also signed by Wagner) announcing that as of March 24, 1933, Gerhard Wagner, Führer of the Nazi Physicians' League, should be recognized as head of both the Hartmannbund and the German Medical Association. The announcement stated that such a measure was necessary "to counter divisions and new movements within the profession."[23]

The meetings of March 23–24 between representatives of the Nazi Physicians' League and Germany's medical associations were fateful ones for the profession. Stauder described the outcome of these meetings as the *Gleichschaltung* of the German medical profession.[24] The consolidation of this authority proceeded rapidly over the next month. On March 29 the German Pharmaceutical Association announced its own *Gleichschaltung*.[25] On April 2 the subordination of the Hartmannbund and the German Medical Association to the Nazi Physicians' League was formally approved by a majority of the members of the two professional bodies meeting in Leipzig. And on April 27 Gerhard Wagner officially took command of all local and regional branches of Germany's medical associations. Celebrating the victory of their movement within the profession, the journal of the National Socialist Physicians' League announced in banner headlines: "We take command!" (see Figures 13–15).

The process of *Gleichschaltung* continued through the summer and fall of 1933. On August 2, Germany's medical organizations were united into a single Association of German Health Insurance Physicians (Kassenärztliche Vereinigung Deutschlands—KVD) under Nazi leadership. The Nazis credited themselves with having established, for the first time, a unified and state-regulated structure for the German medical profession. Distinctive in this new structure was that henceforth the Führer of the KVD would also be Führer of the Nazi Physicians' League.[26] In this fashion, by the end of 1933 the German medical community had been unified into a single political entity, subordinated to the National Socialist Physicians' League and hierarchically organized in accordance with the Führer principle (*Führerprinzip*) and the principle of *Gleichschaltung*.

According to the Führer principle, responsibility for every aspect of German society was ultimately to rest with a single leader, or Führer, responsible only to his superiors. (In 1933 the Prussian Students' Association contrasted the Führer principle with the principle of "bureaucracy" overthrown by the Nazis.)[27] Führer were appointed for education and the arts, for law and medicine, for women's affairs, and for labor. There was a Reich Student Führer (*Reichsstudentenführer* Gustav Adolf Scheel), a Reich Youth Führer (*Reichsjugendführer* Artur Axmann) a Reich Sports Führer (*Reichssportführer* Hans von Tschammer und Osten), a Reich Teachers' Führer (*Reichsdozentenführer* Walter Schultze), and a Führer of German farmers (*Reichsbauernführer* Walther Darré). Gerhard Wagner was Führer of the German medical profession (*Reichsärzteführer*).

The Führer principle was applied not just to the medical profession as a whole, but also to the various specialties within the profession. On December 27, 1933, Interior Minister Frick ordered Friedrich Weber to consolidate Germany's veterinary organizations into a single *gleichgeschaltete* structure, with Dr. Weber assuming the position of Veterinary Führer of the Reich (*Reichstierärzteführer*).[28] Other leaders were appointed to head other parts of German medicine. Ernest Stuck was appointed Führer of Germany's dentists (*Reichszahnärzteführer*); Karl Schaeffer, Führer of Germany's dental technicians (*Reichsdentistenführer*); Albert Schmierer, Führer of Germany's pharmacists (*Reichsapothekenführer*); and Franz Ziegler, Führer of Germany's druggists (*Reichsdrogistenführer*). Ernst Kees was Führer of Germany's natural healers (*Reichsheilpraktikerführer*) and Emil Ketterer was Führer of the Deutsche Sportsärzte-Bund (*Reichsarzt der SA*).[29]

The July 3, 1934 Law for the Unification of Health Affairs (*Gesetz zur Vereinheitlichung des Gesundheitswesens*) further unified German medicine, subordinating the administration of public health af-

Figure 15. Ziel und Weg (Goal and path), official journal of the National Socialist Physicians' League. The headline in the spring 1933 issue reads: "We Take Command!"

Figure 16. Classes in the SA *Sanitätsschule* in Tübingen. From the Hoover Institution Archives, Foto-Willinger Collection.

Figure 17. Leaders of German universities meeting on November 11, 1933, in Leipzig to pledge allegiance to the new regime. From left to right, seated, are Schulrat Geyer, chief of staff of the NSLB, Saxony; Professor of Agricultural Chemistry Arthur Golf; Rector and Professor Dr. Schmidt; Professor Friedrich Karl Schumann; Professor of Church History Emanuel Hirsch; Arthur Göpfert; Rector and Professor of Philosophy Martin Heidegger; Professor of Art Wilhelm Pinder; Rector and Professor of Anthropology Eugen Fischer; and Professor of Medicine Ferdinand Sauerbruch. From *Illustrierte Zeitung*, November 23, 1933, p. 592.

fairs to the Nazi party's Office for Public Health (Hauptamt für Volksgesundheit der NSDAP). *Gauleiter* were appointed for each of Germany's 42 regional *Gau:* and within each *Gau,* regional leaders (*Kreisamtsleiter*) of the Office for Public Health were responsible for coordinating health affairs.[30] The *Gauleiter* for public health had at his disposal medical representatives from the SA, the SS, the Hitler Youth, German student bodies, the Deutsche Arbeitsfront, the NS Volkswohlfahrt, the German Red Cross, the NS Frauenschaft, and other Nazi formations. These lower-echelon leaders in German medicine, pharmacy, or dentistry (*Gaugesundheitsführer, Bezirksapothekenführer,* and so on) were responsible for bringing regional health affairs in line with national policies. In November 1933, Dr. Leonardo Conti (eventually to replace Wagner as Führer of the German medical profession) explained to those assembled at the Berlin Medical Society what the *Führerprinzip* would mean for the society: henceforth only the chairman of the Berlin Medical Society would be elected; this person would then appoint all other functionaries.[31]

Gerhard Wagner made it clear that the Führer principle also had a philosophical dimension: health care (*Gesundheitsfürsorge*) was to be replaced by health leadership (*Gesundheitsführung*); curative medicine (*Fürsorge*) was to be replaced by preventive medicine (*Vorsorge*); and individual hygiene was to be complemented by racial hygiene. Nazi doctors hailed a move "from the doctor of the individual, to the doctor of the nation." According to Nazi medical philosophers, the shift from health care to health leadership also implied a recognition of the importance of distinguishing between valuable forms of life and life "not worth living."[32] Traditional health care (in this view) had been designed to provide help only for those who could no longer help themselves; the new health leadership would minister to the strong, not just the weak.

The power concentrated in the hands of the National Socialist Physicians' League was enormous. By the end of 1933 the Führer of the league was clearly Germany's most powerful medical man. Wagner was not only Führer of the Nazi Physicians' League (his official title was *Reichsärzteführer*) but also head of the Reich Physicians' Chamber, the Hartmannbund, and the German Medical Association. He was also supreme authority for the Association of German Health Insurance Physicians, the Nazi party's Office for Public Health, the Office of Racial Policy, the Expert Committee for Public Health, and the Office for Genealogical Research (Amt für Sippenforschung). As we shall see, Wagner would play a major role in the construction of Nazi racial policy.[33]

The consolidation of the medical profession under Nazi rule implied dramatic and far-reaching changes in the structure of German medical practice. The new regime transformed the organization of the medical press, the nature of medical education, and the structure and priorities of medical research. It changed who could and who could not participate in German medical science and practice. It also reflected a broader shift in the philosophy of German medical practice.

The Medical Press

Prior to the Nazi seizure of power, German medical science was known throughout the world as one of the most vibrant and creative of all medical traditions. The German medical press was a vital part of this tradition. In 1933 more that 200 German journals reported on the technical and professional affairs of medicine.

At the beginning of 1933, there were two leading journals in Germany dealing with the nontechnical affairs of the profession. The *Ärztliches Vereinsblatt* had been published since 1872 as the official organ of the German Medical Association (Deutscher Ärztevereinsbund), the body primarily responsible for reporting on the organizational and ethical affairs of the medical community. A second journal, the *Ärztliche Mitteilungen,* published by the Hartmannbund, was devoted primarily to physicians' "historical struggle for freedom" against the medical insurance companies (*Krankenkassen*) and was intended to represent the economic interests of the profession. In the summer of 1933 Nazi medical leaders managed to have both journals merged into a single new one, the *Deutsches Ärzteblatt,* published as the official organ of the Reich Physicians' Chamber and the Association of German Health Insurance Physicians.[34]

The emergence of the *Deutsches Ärzteblatt,* following upon the *Gleichschaltung* of Germany's two leading medical societies, marks a turning point in the consolidation of Nazi control over the German medical press. During the next year, local medical journals reporting on the economic or social affairs of the profession were unified under a single chain of command; by the end of 1934 twelve such journals had been approved for publication throughout the Reich. On January

8, 1934, Wagner ordered all journals not of a "purely scientific character" to break relations with journals not explicitly approved by Nazi medical authorities.[35]

The *Gleichschaltung* of the medical press also marked the beginning of a campaign to eliminate Jews and all that might be identified as Jewish from German medical science. In the summer of 1933 the *Deutsches Ärzteblatt* announced that the German medical press would begin to "purge itself of non-German influences" in order to return the profession to "German-feeling" and "German-thinking." Part of this attempt was linguistic: new or foreign expressions were to be avoided wherever possible; medical journals published instructions on how to get along without a lot of "complicated" foreign terminology.[36] (On December 9, 1943, Propaganda Minister Joseph Goebbels ordered the word *catastrophe* eliminated from the German language. Goebbels advised that more "positive" words be found to express the situation after bombing attacks; he suggested that instead of *Katastropheneinsatz* [catastrophe aid], for example, people could use the expression *Soforthilfe* [first aid].)[37] More important, however, were changes to be made in personnel. Dr. Kurt Klare, newly appointed head of the Association of German Medical Press, announced in the fall of 1933 that "henceforth German medical journals must be edited and directed only by physicians of German origins; German doctors must be the only ones making decisions as editors and advisors for German medical journals."[38] In 1933 journals such as the *Deutsches Ärzteblatt* and the *Münchener Medizinische Wochenschrift* began to publish elaborate statistics on the numbers of Jewish physicians in various parts of Germany (see Figure 30 in Chapter 6). Medical journals also began to carry increasing numbers of articles on racial hygiene and racial policy. The *Medizinische Welt,* for example, carried a regular column called "Genetics and Racial Care" (*Erblehre und Rassenpflege*); beginning in the Weimar period, Rainer Fetscher published a regular "Racial Hygiene Review" (*Eugenische Rundschau,* continued after 1934 as the *Rassenhygienische Rundschau*) in the *Archiv für Soziale Hygiene und Demographie*. Many other journals followed suit.[39]

To further consolidate control over the German medical press, a Publishing House of the German Medical Profession (Verlag der Deutschen Ärzteschaft) was established to coordinate the publication of German medical journals. This new body, formed by expanding what had formerly been (until the summer of 1933) the publishing house of the *Ärztlichen Mitteilungen,* assumed publication of several of Germany's foremost professional journals. Under the leadership of Alfred Hoffmann, the publishing house was also greatly expanded. At the beginning of 1933 the publisher of the *Ärztlichen Mitteilungen* employed only 10 people; by 1939 the Publishing House of the German Medical Profession (renamed June 28, 1939, the *Reichsgesundheitsverlag*) employed 110 people.[40]

It is important to put this in perspective. The overwhelming majority of German technical medical journals (*Fachpresse*) continued publication with few or no references to larger political events. It would be difficult today for most people to tell whether a particular issue of the German journal of ophthalmology, or dental surgery, or internal medicine, was published in 1932, 1934, or 1936. The 150-odd technical journals of the profession generally survived the Nazi seizure of power unchanged; the majority showed little or no change in either editorial staff or policy (see Appendix A).

The case is otherwise, however, when we turn to nontechnical journals reporting regularly on the social or economic affairs of the profession (*Standespresse*). In early 1933 forty-seven German medical journals reported on nontechnical issues; by January 1934 these had been consolidated into little more than a dozen. Local journals, many now under the control of the Publishing House of the German Medical Profession, were required to affiliate with the Reich Physicians' Chamber. The purpose of this reorganization was at least in part ideological: the publishing house was formed to guarantee that publications of the German medical community remained within the bounds of the Nazi world view. And this strategy seems to have worked: after January 1933 it is difficult to find a single instance of criticism of Nazi racial policy in any of Germany's medical journals.

In terms of the sheer quantity of materials published by the medical community, German medical science did not substantially decline during the Nazi period—at least not until the onset of war in 1939. The number of books and articles published by the medical profession in the early years of the Reich is massive. In 1940 Alfred Hoffmann, director of the (newly renamed) Reich Health Publishing House, boasted that the amount of paper used by the publishing house in 1939 was 924 metric tons (92 boxcar loads)—enough paper to stretch 30,000 kilometers, or three-quarters of the way around the earth. He also noted that the financial situation of Germany's medical publishers was such that, for the first time, medical journals were able to pay their authors and editors for their services.[41]

The single most important class of journals that, generally speaking, did *not* survive the Nazi seizure of power were those publishing in the field of social hygiene (*Sozialhygiene*). These were journals concerned primarily with broader social or public health aspects of medicine, often from a socialist or communist point of view. The journal *Soziale Medizin,* for example, folded in the first year of Nazi rule, as did *Der Sozialistische Arzt,* the official journal of the Association of Socialist Physicians (see Chapter 9). In 1934 the *Fortschritte der Gesundheitsfürsorge* closed its doors, and by March 1935 most of Germany's oldest journals of social medicine had ceased publication, including the *Archiv für Sozialhygiene,* the *Zeitschrift für Gesundheitsverwaltung und Gesundheitsfürsorge,* the *Zeitschrift für Medizinalbeamte,* and the *Mitteilungen der Deutschen Gesellschaft zur Bekämpfung der Geschlechtskrankheiten.*[42] Certain journals of this sort did survive the Nazi takeover; these reoriented their focus from problems of a distinctively social, economic, or environmental nature to problems of race and racial health. The *Sozialhygienische Mitteilungen,* for example, began publishing articles on health and education among the Aryan peoples.[43] And in 1935 an ambitious new journal, *Der Öffentliche Gesundheitsdienst,* began publication (edited by Prussian Health Minister Arthur Gütt), taking over some of the functions of the earlier journals.

The Nazi medical community also published special journals designed either to popularize the new racial ideal or to keep Nazi physicians abreast of social and racial policy. *Ziel und Weg* was the primary journal responsible for articulating Nazi philosophy in the sphere of medicine. In 1931 it began publishing in editions of 3,000 copies; by 1934 this number had grown to 16,000; and by 1939 the journal was publishing 40,000 copies twice a month.[44] The Office of Racial Policy (Rassenpolitisches Amt) published the popular health magazine *Neues Volk* (New people), issued as the successor to the pre-Nazi journal *Das Hörrohr,* in editions that ran as high as 360,000 copies (in 1939); the office also published an in-house journal called the *Informationsdienst* (Information service) to keep its members informed on issues of racial policy. Circulation of the *Informationsdienst* was deliberately limited to 5,000 copies in order to be able to include confidential information; readers were asked not to repeat information published in the journal unless they withheld the source.[45] Published from 1934 to 1944, the *Informationsdienst* today serves as one of the most revealing sources of information on Nazi racial policy.

One of the largest of the popular medical magazines published under the Nazis was *Die Volksgesundheitswacht* (People's health watch), published from 1934 to 1944 in editions that ran to well over 100,000 copies. The journal was intended to be read in waiting rooms at hospitals and clinics, and like similar journals at this time, racial questions formed a leading theme. A sampling of the kinds of views put forth in the name of "people's health" can be seen from the *Gilbhart* 1934 issue of the journal. (*Gilbhart* was Old Norse for "October." As early as 1926 journals such as *Volk und Rasse* began using old "Nordic" names for the months of the year—*Julmond* substituted for January, *Eismond* for February, *Hornung* for March, and so forth.) In this issue Dr. Eugen Stähle of Stuttgart published an article titled "Blood and Race: New Research Results," advising the following:

> In describing the various races, we must not stop with the external shape of the body, nor even with mental characteristics in the classical manner of [Hans F. K.] Günther and Ludwig Ferdinand Clauss. We must go beyond this, to explore equally important differences in the inner organs of the body, differences that may reflect deeper, physiological differences among the races. Best known in this area is "racial smell." Europeans find the smell not only of Negroes, but of East Asians to be repulsive, even when they are clean; the Oriental himself will of course make similar claims.[46]

Stähle claimed that racial differences in musculature, nervous sensitivity, and longevity had been well documented; he asked his readers whether, among the various races of men (as among different species of animals), there might also be different kinds of blood. In support of this hypothesis, Stähle cited the discovery of blood diseases specific to certain races: diseases such as sickle-cell anemia in blacks and certain unspecified "accumulative diseases" (*Speicherungskrankheiten*) among Jews. (He called it an "irony of biology" that these accumulative diseases should afflict only Jews). Differences such as these, he claimed, prove beyond a shadow of a doubt that blood is "not merely symbolic, but has also a physical, material meaning," one that is rooted "in the very language and findings of science." Stähle referred in this context to the work of a Russian professor (E. O. Maniloff in Leningrad) who supposedly had been able to identify, by chemical means and with 90 percent accuracy, whether a certain sample of blood was "that of a Jew or a Russian." Stähle asked his readers to "think what it might mean, if we could identify non-Aryans in the test tube! Then neither deception, nor baptism, nor name change, nor citizenship, and not even nasal surgery could help [the Jew escape detection]. One cannot change one's blood."[47] One can only imagine how such claims must have sounded to people reading these magazines in the waiting rooms of their physicians. Stähle was not someone one could easily dismiss as a "quack": he was head of the medical profession for the state of Württemberg and claimed to be presenting what he described as "the latest results of scientific research."

Educational Reform

Educational reform was an important part of Nazi medical policy. In 1933 Propaganda Minister Joseph Goebbels asked that all German organizations be educated in "the eugenic way of thinking"; Bavarian Health Inspector Walther Schultze proclaimed that "no boy or girl must leave school without being made aware of the essence of blood unity."[48] At German universities support for racial hygiene also increased. In 1933 Fritz Lenz was the only full professor for racial hygiene in Germany, a position he had held for ten years. By 1936 professorships in racial hygiene had been established at Berlin, Bonn, Frankfurt, Giessen, Hamburg, Heidelberg, Jena, Königsberg, Munich, and Würzburg, and racial science was taught in the medical faculties of all other German universities (see Table 2). As early as 1922 the Society for Racial Hygiene had included within its charter a demand that racial hygiene be considered an obligatory field of study in the German medical curriculum. And throughout the 1920s the number of courses offered in this field continued to grow in German universities (see again Figure 7). In the spring of 1933 Walter Schultze asked Fritz Lenz to prepare his course on racial hygiene in the expectation that the field would soon be mandatory for all medical students; racial hygiene was to be incorporated into the state medical exams students had to pass in order to graduate and begin

80   Racial Hygiene

Table 2. Professorships of racial hygiene and allied fields at German universities, 1923–1944

University	Chair	Professor
Berlin	Rassenhygiene	Fritz Lenz (1933–1945)
	Anthropologie und Rassenbiologie	Wolfgang Abel (1943–1945)
Bonn	Rassenhygiene	Friedrich Panse (1937–1945)
Cologne	Erbbiologie und Rassenhygiene	Ferdinand Claussen (1939–1945)
Danzig	Erbbiologie und Rassenhygiene	Erich Grossmann (1942–1945)
Frankfurt	Erbbiologie und Rassenhygiene	Otmar von Verschuer (1935–1942)
		Heinrich W. Kranz (1942–1945)
Giessen	Erb- und Rassenforschung	Heinrich W. Kranz (1937–1942)
		Hermann Boehm (1942–1945)
Hamburg	Rassenhygiene	Wilhelm Weitz (1936–1945)
Heidelberg	Rassenhygiene	Ernst Rodenwaldt (1935–1945)
Jena	Menschliche Erblehre und Rassenpolitik	Karl Astel (1934–1945)
	Sozialanthropologie	Hans F. K. Günther (1932–)
	Rasse und Recht	Falk Ruttke (1941–1945)
Königsberg	Rassenbiologie	Lothar Loeffler (1935–1942)
Leipzig	Rassen- und Völkerkunde	Otto Reche (1927–1945)
Munich	Rassenhygiene	Fritz Lenz (1923–1933)
	Rassenbiologie und Rassenhygiene	Lothar Tirala (1933–1936)
	Rassenhygiene (honorary)	Alfred Ploetz (1936–1940)
Prague	Rassenbiologie, Rassenkunde	Bruno K. Schultz (1942–1945)
	Sozialanthropologie	Karl V. Müller (1942–1945)
Rostock	Erbbiologie und Rassenhygiene	Hans Grebe (1944–1945)
	Erb- und Rassenpflege (honorary)	Hermann Boehm (1937–1943)
Strassburg	Erbbiologie und Rassenhygiene	Wolfgang Lehmann (1943–1945)
Tübingen	Rassenkunde	Wilhelm Gieseler (1938–1945)
Vienna	Rassen- und Völkerkunde	Otto Reche (1924–1927)
	Rassenbiologie und Rassenhygiene	Lothar Loeffler (1942–1945)
Würzburg	Vererbungslehre und Rassenforschung	Ludwig Schmidt-Kehl (1937–1941)
		Günther Just (1942–1945)

Note: Most of these positions were established in medical faculties; some, however, were established in philosophical or legal faculties. Racial hygiene was often taught under the rubric of "anthropology" or "psychiatry"; I have not included these professorships here (for example, Eugen Fischer's chair for anthropology at Berlin, or Ernst Rüdin's chair at Munich). The people listed here represent only a few of the individuals who taught racial hygiene in German universities; most courses were offered not by full professors but by *Dozenten*. In 1941 *Der Biologe* (10[1941]:196) reported that thirty-two *Dozenten für Biologie und Rassenkunde* were active at twenty-three German colleges and universities and that the majority of these were young scholars between the ages of thirty and forty.

medical practice.[49] In 1936 many German universities established racial hygiene as an obligatory course of study and included questions in this field on medical exams.

Germany's state medical academies in Berlin and Munich also took up the cause of racial hygiene; this was especially important, as every one of Germany's medical students was required to attend courses at one of these two academies. In the fall of 1933 the State Medical Academy in Berlin offered its first course on genetics and racial hygiene. Some of Germany's premier racial hygienists, including Eugen Fischer, Otmar von Verschuer, Wolfgang Abel, Leonardo Conti, and Hans Reiter, presented lectures covering topics such as blood group research, anthropological measurement, twin research, and genetics. In the winter of 1935–36, the State Medical Academy at Munich offered courses on racial hygiene, criminal biology, racial law, war medicine, and organic medicine, along with more traditional courses in psychiatry, industrial hygiene, medical insurance, and maternal and child care. By 1937 Verschuer could claim that genetics and racial hygiene had become part of "the normal course of studies of medical students."[50]

Racial hygienists continued to call for the expansion of racial training in German medical schools. In 1937 Verschuer asked that medical studies include further coursework on racial hygiene, as well as new courses on genealogy, racial anthropology (*Rassenkunde*), and the study of constitutional body types (*Konstitutionslehre*). Medical students were also to be assigned practical exercises to learn basic "biogenetic methods"—including methods of genealogical and twin research, statistical genetics, and anthropometric techniques used in determining paternity. Praising the decision by the Ministry of Education to establish professorships for racial hygiene at all German universities, Verschuer urged university and medical authorities to take an even stronger role in promoting racial hygiene.[51]

Verschuer's advice did not fall on deaf ears. The April 1, 1939, curriculum regulations (*Studienordnung*) required that medical students in their ninth semester devote three hours of coursework per week to "human genetics as the foundation of racial hygiene"; in their tenth semester, students were required to devote two class hours per week to the study of racial hygiene.[52] Racial training was also incorporated into the courses physicians were required to attend to remain abreast of the latest developments in their fields (*Fortbildungskurse*);

physicians studied racial biology at the Fischer Institute in Berlin, or the Rüdin Institute in Munich, or one of the numerous university institutes for racial hygiene. Expansion of racial training in German medical schools continued even into the war years, despite curtailment of other aspects of the curriculum. When Hitler ordered the establishment of a German University at Posen in September 1939, racial research was seen as an integral task of the university. Posen was to be for the East what Strassburg was for the West; the university was intended to provide the "crystallization point for all Volkstums research in and for the German East."[53] As late as the fall of 1944, Reich Health Führer Conti asked that the number of required courses in racial hygiene be doubled.[54]

Apart from racial hygiene and racial science, the Nazis revived a number of alternative and organic forms of therapeutics. They emphasized medicine that would utilize natural methods and take into account "the whole man" (see Chapter 8). Nazi physicians stressed the importance of war medicine and sports medicine. One of Germany's medical leaders pointed out that, in accordance with the focus on child rearing in the new regime, pediatrics was to be raised for the first time to the level of traditional specialties such as internal medicine, surgery, and gynecology.[55]

In addition to the reorganization of the university medical curriculum around racial, military, or reproductive themes, the Nazi medical community also required that physicians participate in some form of postgraduate education. The 1935 Reich Physicians' Ordinance (*Reichsärzteordnung*) required that every five years all physicians under the age of sixty attend a three-week course on recent progress in medical science and techniques. By 1937, 300 training centers in sixty-eight localities had been set up for this purpose.[56] By 1936, 5,000 physicians a year were receiving specialized training in racial hygiene, marital counseling, sterilization techniques, and other fields on the frontiers of medical science. By 1939, 60 percent of all German doctors had gone through such training in educational centers throughout the Reich.[57] Justification for the training was simple. When Rudolf Ramm instructed medical students on the requirements of German medical education, he pointed out that in the new Germany, population policy and racial hygiene were areas "without the knowledge of which a physician cannot fulfill his new duties as marital counselor and guardian of the genetic constitution."[58]

The Doctors' Führer School at Alt-Rehse

One of the most renowned training centers was the SS Doctors' Führer School (SS Ärzteführerschule), established by the Nazi Physicians' League in the summer of 1935 in the tiny village of Alt-Rehse, near the Tollensee in Mecklenburg. Its purpose was to provide manual, mental, and moral training for promising young doctors, nurses, and midwives. Courses generally lasted about six weeks, during which time residents attended lectures on topics ranging from genetics and racial hygiene to nutrition and natural healing (one participant noted that it was first at Alt-Rehse that he learned the meaning of the word *organic*). Residents learned about the obligations they would face working in the medical divisions of the SA or the Hitler Youth and in fulfilling Hitler's four-year plan. Those who attended the school received credit for four weeks of the practical training required for the medical license; the intention was that eventually no physician in Germany would be able to establish a practice without having undergone training at Alt-Rehse.[59]

Training at Alt-Rehse was not intended to be exclusively intellectual. The school was intended to supplement rather than replace traditional medical education; Rudolf Ramm described it as a school for "building character" in the German doctor.[60] The central message, as one participant put it, was "crystal clear": the German doctor was to be trained as "a leader of his Volk."[61] Residents at the school followed a strict regimen of exercise and manual labor to bind themselves to the "blood and soil of their race and fatherland." They played ping-pong and soccer and practiced their skills in sailing; mornings from 6:00 to 6:20 were reserved for vigorous exercise. Photographs of residents at the school show physicians eating in common mess halls and running in military formation with shovels over their shoulders. Participants abandoned their civilian clothes for common camp uniforms; they sang the Horst Wessel song while hoisting the Nazi flag. On weekends they organized excursions to nearby Rostock or Warnemünde; after one such excursion a young physician claimed he could have written an essay on "The Genetic Basis for 'Attraction to Women' among Alt-Rehse Men."[62] Participants waxed poetic over their experiences at the school; medical journals in the mid-1930s are filled with praise for the virtues of the Alt-Rehse experience.

Genetics and racial science were a central focus of lectures at the school. The man most responsible for instilling the spirit of racial hygiene in German physicians was Dr. Hermann Boehm, honorary professor of racial care (*Rassenpflege*) at the University of Rostock and head of the Institute for Pathological Anatomy at Dresden's Rudolf Hess Hospital. In 1936 Gerhard Wagner appointed Boehm to instruct the German medical profession in the principles of National Socialist genetic and racial care and to incorporate these fields into the curriculum of the Doctors' Führer School.[63]

Boehm's conception of genetic and racial care was similar to that of many other racial hygienists of his day. He defended the study of racial hygiene on the grounds that medicine must concern itself not just with the health of comrades now alive but also with the health of the "German genetic streams" (*deutsche Erbströme*). Boehm complained that medical schools had been reluctant to venture into this "new and foreign territory" because of their reluctance to come to grips with preventive, rather than curative, medicine. This was not simply because genetics was a young science—the science of vitamins, Boehm pointed out, was younger still and yet had been taken up rapidly by the universities. The difference, according to Boehm, was that whereas vitamins had proved valuable for curing illness, genetics was valuable primarily for finding ways to prevent illness. Opposition to genetics in this sense had a political or philosophical basis: the short-sighted "individualism" of the Weimar Republic had blinded people to the value of this longer-term preventive science (genetics) and its practical application in racial hygiene. Racial hygiene, in Boehm's view, was not just a science but a *Weltanschauung*—a spiritual attitude grounded upon science. Science and politics were therefore not hostile or contrary forces; indeed, they required one another:

> National Socialism without a scientific knowledge of genetics is like a house without an important part of its foundation . . . Basic scientific knowledge is indispensable for anyone who wants to work in the area of genetic and racial care, and experimental genetics must provide the foundations for that care.[64]

In 1936–37, as part of the duties assigned to him by Reich Physicians' Führer Wagner, Boehm established an Institute for Genetics at Alt-Rehse in order to familiarize participants in the school with the principles of genetic and racial care. The institute was equipped to perform anthropological measurements and boasted facilities for identifying fingerprints and handprints, determining paternity, and so forth. The main room of the institute was equipped with facilities for fifteen to twenty people; separate laboratories were provided in the event that interested individuals wanted to delve into experimental genetics. The institute's library also allowed more contemplative study. Boehm noted that the goal of his institute was not just to teach but to produce scientific research. He qualified this, however, by noting that even in the case of "pure scientific work" the goal of science must be "to serve the people."

In designing and equipping his institute, Boehm was able to draw upon the help of some of Germany's top geneticists. Professor Hans Stubbe, for example, helped instruct the institute's staff in basic plant genetics and provided guidance in the selection of appropriate plant materials. Stubbe provided the institute (through his contacts with American geneticists) with samples of "every known mutant of corn" and helped Boehm construct "living chromosome maps" never before achieved in Germany. According to Boehm, Stubbe also helped to plan the design and construction of the institute "in a most loving manner." SS Führer Boehm expressed his appreciation for each of these contributions—he also thanked his teacher N. W. Timofeev-Ressovsky, director of the Institute for Genetics at the Kaiser Wilhelm Institute for Brain Research in Berlin, for providing the laboratories at the school with mutant forms of the fruit fly, *Drosophila*.[65] Many a budding young Nazi doctor first learned experimental genetics by crossing *Drosophila melanogaster* at the SS Doctors' Führer School in Alt-Rehse.

It is not yet clear what ultimately happened to the Doctors' Führer School. For a short time after the German invasion of Poland, its buildings were converted to wartime uses. In the spring of 1941 the school returned to its original goal of "imparting medical-biological knowledge based on the [Nazi] world view." In March and April of 1941, the school began instilling Nazi ideals in 1,200 ethnic German physicians "returned" to the Reich from regions now occupied by German armies. These included physicians from Alsace-Lorraine and Luxemburg, as well as thirty-three physicians from Holland invited to train at the school as personal guests of Reich Health Führer Leonardo Conti. A second series of courses was devoted to training physicians from Wolhynia, Bessarabia, and the Baltic countries.[66] In the same year, the official medical journal for the *Reichsgau* Wartheland (in occupied Poland) reflected on the achievements of the school, noting that the physician in the new Germany had become more than a curator of the ill; he was now a curator of genetic health and a health leader of the German people (*Erbpfleger und Gesundheitsführer*). The knowledge gained at Alt-Rehse was important, this journal argued, because "biology and genetics are the roots [*Erkenntniswurzeln*] from which the National Socialist world view has derived its knowledge, and from which it continues to derive new strength."[67]

The SS was not the only Nazi group to establish special medical training facilities. The SA (*Schutz Abteilung*, or Storm Troopers) also established its own school, the Reichssanitätsschule der SA, founded in 1933 by the SA-Gruppe Südwest in Tübingen. The school was designed to teach health officers (*SA-Sanitätsmänner und Unterführer*) "attitudes appropriate for the SA man in his capacity as propagandist for the enlightenment of the people on issues of race and inheritance." The school boasted that it did not want simply to teach first aid or how to become a good Samaritan, but rather how to acquire "the mental and physical fitness, the firmness in matters of world view, and the practical skills" required of the SA medical man. The school was equipped with laboratories, dental facilities, and operating rooms, along with a cafeteria and lecture halls designed to seat 150 men. Practical training was devoted primarily to developing skills required for field service, including treatment of wounds and injuries, physical therapy, and various sports. The school also had at its disposal the facilities of the nearby University of Tübingen, which allowed "a fruitful combination of theory and practice." The SA medical man was to be not only a commander of technical know-how, but also an advocate for National Socialism; he was to be a "spiritual leader" in questions of race and racial hygiene. The *Ärzteblatt für Berlin* summarized the atmosphere of the school as typical of that of the SA man himself: "simple, clean, and effective"[68] (see Figure 16).

A number of other schools were established by the Nazis to train medical personnel. In 1938 medical journals announced the founding of an SS Medical Academy in Berlin (later moved to Graz) to train physicians for duty in the Waffen-SS. Schools were also set up for the nursing profession. The Nazi Nurses' Association (NS-Schwestern) had a "mother house" in the Rudolf Hess Hospital in Dresden offering special training for Nazi nurses; beginning October 1, 1934, the Association offered intensive eight-week courses on the fundamentals of National Socialism.⁶⁹ On January 1, 1939, a school was established in Dortmund to train Nazi nurses; on February 20, SS Reich Physician Ernst Grawitz announced the establishment of Reich Führer Schools to train Red Cross personnel.⁷¹ And in 1943 plans were discussed to create a school for nurses caring for children in the Nazis' Aryan child-rearing program (*Lebensborn Schwesternschule*).⁷²

The Office of Racial Policy

One of the most important institutions in the Nazi state was the Office of Racial Policy (Rassenpolitisches Amt), established on May 1, 1934, "to coordinate and unify all schooling and propaganda in the areas of population and racial policy."⁷² Like the SA and SS, it had its own special training school for physicians. Medical students trained at the Reich School of the Office of Racial Policy in Neubabelsberg were supposed to work for the office after graduation from medical school; by 1937, twenty-eight of the "fittest" such students had begun to work there. The school also provided training for members of the SS; between July and December 1937, for example, the school trained 1,369 SS men.⁷³

The Office of Racial Policy, headed from its inception by Dr. Walter Gross, helped construct most of the principal racial programs of the Reich, such as the Sterilization Law, the secret sterilization of the *Rheinlandbastarde,* and the Nuremberg Laws (see Chapters 4 and 6). The office also conducted a broad campaign of "enlightenment" (*Aufklärungsarbeit*) to instill in the German public an appreciation of the need for racial policy. This enlightenment took various forms. The office offered special training in racial ways of thinking at the Reichsführerschule Bernau near Berlin, with lectures by racial hygienists such as Martin Stämmler, Walter Gross, and Lothar Loeffler. In 1937 the office sponsored a contest in cooperation with the National Socialist Teachers' Association and the Propaganda Ministry for high school teachers to develop methods of investigating the racial roots of local families. Reporting on the results of this contest, the *Ärzteblatt für Berlin* noted that one teacher, as part of his project for the contest, had managed to uncover a Jew among the ancestors of a certain family; the journal reported that the descendants of this Jew (baptized in 1685) had been entirely unaware of this aspect of their family background.⁷⁴

88 Racial Hygiene

Publications of the Office of Racial Policy included a wide range of what were known as "racial-political" analyses. The office issued reports on how to deal with "antisocial" elements of the population and published analyses of the "racial consequences" of marriage between cousins, or between uncles and nieces.[75] It also reported on attempts by biologists to clarify ambiguities in racial ancestry in order to determine who could and who could not meet the obligations of the new racial state. In one case, for example, an individual was denied the right to take over ownership of a farm when it was discovered that, in 1805, one of his ancestors on his father's side had been a "mulatto."[76] The office discussed the various standards of racial purity required by Germany's new racial bureaucracy; it clarified the distinction, for example, between the "small" and the "large" certificates of ancestry (*Abstammungsnachweis*). The small certificate, needed for government employment in accordance with the 1933 Civil Service Law, required proof that not more than one of an individual's four grandparents was fully Jewish. This was also the standard required for marriage with a "German" in accordance with the 1935 Blood Protection Law (see Chapter 6). Obtaining the large certificate was much more difficult, requiring a full record of one's ancestral lineage dating back to January 1, 1800, certifying that no "Jewish blood" whatsoever was present. According to the Office of Racial Policy, this was the standard for anyone wanting to join the NSDAP; it was also supposed to be the standard for applicants' wives. The Führer corps of the SS required an even stricter standard, documenting "purity" back to 1750.[77]

The Office of Racial Policy's confidential journal, the *Informationsdienst*, carried long articles on racial history and provided its readers with excerpts from the anti-Semitic works of figures such as Napoleon, Henry Ford, Paul de Lagarde, Hitler, Schopenhauer, and Fichte. The office reproduced anti-Semitic passages from Martin Luther, in which the Protestant reformer told his readers that the proper way to deal with Jews was

> to put their synagogues and schools to fire, and what will not burn, to cover with earth and rubble so that no-one will ever again see anything there but cinders . . . Second, one should tear down and destroy their houses, for they do also in there what they do in their schools and synagogues . . . And third, one should confiscate their prayer books and Talmud, in which idolatry and lies, slander and blasphemy is taught.[78]

Luther's anti-Semitism proved useful for the Nazis: after the war, Luther's words were read before the tribunal at Nuremberg as evidence that anti-Semitism was an old and honorable tradition in Germany, long before the Nazis.

The sheer scale on which the activities of the Office of Racial Policy were carried out is astonishing. In the three-month period from April to June 1938, it sponsored 1,106 public meetings attended by 173,870 individuals, as well as 5,172 school functions in which a total of 330,972 pupils participated. The office showed 350 films during this period—films designed to criticize what one medical journal called the "muddle-headed humanitarianism" (*Humanitätsduselei*) of those who squandered funds on the weak and inferior.[79]

The cumulative impact of the office's activities over the ten years of its existence must have been enormous. In 1938 the *Informationsdienst* reported that in the four years since its founding, the Office of Racial Policy had organized 64,000 public meetings and seminars, and that 4,000 Nazi party members had participated in thousands of eight-day conferences. The office had acquired 3,600 workers to help in its "work of enlightenment," and its affiliated journal, *Neues Volk*, had been printed in editions of as many as 300,000 copies.[80] It would have been difficult for anyone living in Germany at this time not to have been touched by the activities of the office.

The "Jewish Question" in German Medicine

Probably the most far-reaching consequence of the *Gleichschaltung* of German medicine was the expulsion of Jews from the profession. In his history of the early years of medicine in the Third Reich, Rudolf Ramm described this period as one in which "the dominant liberal-materialist spirit was replaced by the idealistic *Weltanschauung* of National Socialism." It was also at this time, Ramm states, that the liberal parliamentarian epoch was forced to bow before the Führer principle. From this time on, vital decisions of the profession would be made, not by the vote of the majority, but by the orders of professional leaders. Reflecting on the history of this period, Ramm put forth what today must seem a startling thesis:

> The overwhelming majority of the German medical community welcomed the assumption of leadership by the National Socialist Physicians' League. Their hope was that, in the National Socialist commu-

nity, the profession would once again come to be honored and respected. An important precondition for this was the exclusion [*Ausschaltung*] of inappropriate and politically unreliable elements, the reestablishment of discipline within the profession, and the reestablishment of high professional and ethical standards as the guiding principle of medical practice.[81]

Ramm's reference to "inappropriate and politically unreliable elements" in German medicine is clear—he is referring to Jews, social democrats, and communists. Many in the profession considered it "intolerable" that 13 percent of all German doctors were Jewish; in March and April of 1933, when medical leaders met to orchestrate the *Gleichschaltung* of the profession, the first resolution issued after the meetings was that Jews and other suspect colleagues must be removed from their posts throughout the Reich.[82] Nazi medical leaders declared themselves ready to eliminate all aspects of Jewish life and thought from medicine—from the universities and clinics, from the medical press, from German life as a whole. In his 1942 medical textbook, Ramm articulated the opinion of medical orthodoxy on this subject:

> One of the first measures of the National Socialist medical leadership [in 1933] was the cleansing of the profession from politically unreliable and racially foreign elements, to guarantee that the provision of medical care for the population would not be endangered. When one reflects upon the fact that in 1933, among 50,000 physicians active in Germany, 13 percent of these were Jewish, and that in Berlin, this was more than 60 percent; if we consider Austria, too, where the figures for Vienna were close to 67 percent, then one gets a sense of the enormous influence wielded by the Jew within medicine and upon health legislation until that time. Today, however, one can already see what a blessing it has been that the Jews were forcibly excluded from the vital [*lebenswichtigen*] professions and the offices of the state.[83]

Ramm blamed Jews for having introduced "advertising methods" and a "crass materialism" into the profession; he accused them of spreading "spiritually poisonous ideas" and of having destroyed the "genetic life" (*keimendes Leben*) of the German people. The Nazis, however, had put an end to this: Ramm, writing in 1942, commented on how fortunate it was that "today, there is no German-blooded man who is treated by a Jewish doctor"; indeed, as he noted, such practice had been illegal since 1938 (see also Chapter 6).

Action against the Jews was taken in the first months of the regime.

In March 1933, an official committee headed by Julius Streicher, along with Heinrich Himmler, Robert Ley, Hans Frank, and Gerhard Wagner, assembled to plan a coordinated strategy to deal with the opposition Nazi leaders expected to emerge against Nazi racial policies. On March 20 the committee issued orders that local party units were to organize boycotts of Jewish shops and businesses; on April 1 SA and SS troops blocked entrances to offices of Jewish doctors, lawyers, and businessmen. On April 4 the mayor of Munich announced that Jewish doctors working for the government could practice only on Jewish patients and would no longer be allowed to dissect non-Jewish cadavers. On April 22 the Baden Medical Association announced that all Jewish physicians would be dismissed from official posts and that Jews could henceforth practice only on other Jews.[84] Over the next several months Germany's other states followed suit.

The month of April 1933 marks the passage of the first important legal measure designed to exclude Jews from German life and society. On April 7 the German government passed the Law for the Restoration of the Civil Service (*Gesetz zur Wiederherstellung des Berufsbeamtentums*), a law that excluded anyone either of non-German heritage (Jews) or of questionable political sympathies (communists) from employment in the civil service (persons employed before August 1, 1914, were generally exempt from the law). A ruling of April 22 extended the law to Germany's medical insurance programs. This provision in particular made it difficult for many Jews to continue practicing medicine, given that the entire German labor force was soon to be included within the state medical insurance program. When Jewish doctors were no longer allowed to be part of this program, patients wanting to obtain treatment from Jewish physicians could no longer get reimbursed for their expenses.

In Germany civil service was a broader category than in many other countries. University professors were (then as now) employees of the state, and this meant that, according to the Civil Service Law, Jews could no longer teach at German universities. Members of the Communist party were also barred from government positions—although in fact this turned out to be of little consequence, since Communists had rarely been able to land government positions in the conservative atmosphere of Weimar or Wilhelmine Germany. In January 1933 few professors were Communists, even though the Communist party was one of the largest parties in the country.

The case was otherwise with respect to Jews. When the Nazis came to power, the majority of Berlin's physicians (for example) were either Jewish or from families of some Jewish ancestry. Nazi medical authorities used this fact time and again to argue that the profession was "saturated" by Jews (*verjüdete*). On March 24, 1933, the *Münchener Medizinische Wochenschrift* reported that 80–100 percent of the physicians of Berlin's city hospitals were either Jewish communists or social democrats; the journal reported that the contracts of these physicians would have to be terminated "at the next possible moment."[85]

Shortly after the subordination of the Hartmannbund and the German Medical Association to the Nazi Physicians' League in early April 1933, representatives of these organizations issued a directive asking that Jews and "those colleagues who do not feel an inner attachment to the new order" be removed from positions of leadership in the profession. The directive specified further that those in charge of the Association of German Health Insurance Physicians (Kassenärztliche Vereinigung) were to pressure insurance authorities to replace Jewish and Marxist physicians registered in these programs as soon as possible.[86] On April 1 Gerhard Wagner announced that he had asked the Ministry of the Interior to begin planning the exclusion of Jews from the insurance companies; he also called for the establishment of a new and unified medical order and for an increased role of the medical profession in the construction and administration of racial policy.[87]

On April 5 Hitler met with Wagner and representatives of the Hartmannbund and the German Medical Association to discuss the future of German medical policy. Hitler spoke of the need to suppress foreign influences in the cultural and intellectual life of Germany and promised that future German physicians would have much greater *Lebensraum* as a result of this suppression. After the meeting Wagner announced his appointment of new leaders of the Hartmannbund and the German Medical Association; he also declared that all future appointments to local and regional branches of these organizations would have to be approved by him.[88]

The exclusion of Jews and political unreliables from government employment meant that a substantial portion of Germany's university medical faculties was dismissed. At Berlin's famous Charité University Hospital alone, 138 members of the medical faculty were fired or forced to resign. At the Rudolf Virchow Hospital in Berlin, 26 out of 81 physicians were fired.[89]

The April 1933 Civil Service Law applied only to individuals employed in the German civil service. The majority of German physicians, however, were not employed by the government and thus were not affected by the law. Furthermore, many of those forced from government positions simply took up private practice. In order to solve this problem, the Nazi government passed a comprehensive Reich Physicians' Ordinance (*Reichsärzteordnung*) on December 13, 1935, subordinating the entire medical profession to the German government and allowing greater governmental discretion over who could and who could not obtain a medical license. German medical journals reported that the ordinance was intended to place the entire medical profession in the service of genetic-biological measures; the ordinance was also supposed to "maintain moral standards." One of its primary effects, however, was to bring medical practice within the rubric of the 1933 Civil Service Law. The ordinance allowed medical authorities to reject applicants for medical licenses if the applicant (or spouse) failed to meet the requirements specified by the Civil Service Law or if the percentage of "non-Aryan" physicians exceeded that of non-Aryans in the general population.[90] (In 1933, Jews constituted less than 1 percent of the German population, while approximately 13 percent of all physicians were Jewish.)

We shall return to the question of anti-Semitism in the German medical profession in Chapter 6. Let me simply note here, however, that one effect of the exclusion of Jews from the universities and other government posts was to free up a large number of positions in Germany's medical schools, institutes, and clinics. In the early years of the regime, many young, underemployed physicians were able to advance their careers by taking over positions left by Jews. This may well have been one of the reasons physicians were so willing to tolerate (and organize) the expulsion of Jews from the profession. It may also help to explain why so many physicians were willing and eager to support the new regime.

In light of the willingness of German physicians to embrace the Nazi cause, it is not surprising to find that the Nazi government considered doctors to be particularly reliable agents for their political agenda. Physicians were granted unprecedented power and prestige under the

Nazis. Two of the first five recipients of the German National Prize (*Deutschen Nationalpreises*) were physicians—Ferdinand Sauerbruch and August Bier.[91] Shortly after 1933, physicians were elevated to dominant positions in German universities. Two of the first rectors appointed by the Nazi regime were medical scholars: Eugen Fischer, appointed rector of the University of Berlin on May 3, 1933, and J. Reinmöller, appointed rector of the University of Erlangen shortly thereafter (see also Figure 17). Between 1933 and 1945 a higher proportion of Germany's top university offices was held by medical doctors than at any other time before or since. During the period of Nazi rule (1933–1945), the office of rector was occupied by medical doctors 30 percent of the time, in contrast with 19 percent for the period 1923–1932, and 18 percent for the period 1946–1967.[92] Medical faculties at German universities were also disproportionately represented in early statements of support for National Socialism. When the *Völkische Beobachter*, on March 4, 1933, published the names of 300 university professors pledging allegiance to the Nazi cause, professors in the medical faculties were represented in greater numbers than those of any other faculty. At the University of Berlin, a majority of those signing were from the medical faculty. At the University of Kiel, among a total of twenty-six *Dozenten* who signed the statement, twenty-two were from the medical faculty; among the four who signed from the philosophical faculty, all but one were professors of zoology.[93] It is not hard to understand why Leonardo Conti a decade later was proud to write that "doctors, among all the professions, were the earliest and most active participants in the National Socialist movement."[94]

Medical imagery and medical research were important in the Nazi view of the world. Biologistic research was conducted at the highest levels of the German scientific community; racial science penetrated leading research institutes and universities. But, as we shall see next, the biomedical community's interest in political biology was not confined to theoretical matters. The Sterilization Law enacted in 1933 demonstrates the massive levels of control exercised by the medical profession over the reproductive lives of German citizens.

4 | The Sterilization Law

> Whoever is not bodily and spiritually healthy and worthy, shall not have the right to pass on his suffering in the body of his children.
>
> —Adolf Hitler, *Mein Kampf*

On June 2, 1933, Reich Interior Minister Wilhelm Frick announced the formation of an Expert Committee on Questions of Population and Racial Policy (Sachverständigen-Beirat für Bevölkerungsfragen und Rassenpolitik) to plan the course of Nazi racial policy. The committee brought together the elite of Nazi racial theory: Alfred Ploetz, father of racial hygiene; Friedrich Burgdörfer, editor of *Politische Biologie* and a director in the Reich Statistics Office; Walther Darré, Reich Farmers' Führer and champion of "blood and earth"; Hans F. K. Günther, professor of social anthropology at Jena and Germany's leading racial anthropologist; Charlotte von Hadeln, second Führerin of the (short-lived) Deutsche Frauenfront; Ernst Rüdin, director of the Kaiser Wilhelm Institute for Genealogy in Munich; Bodo Spiethoff, professor of medicine in Jena and an expert in venereal diseases; Paul Schultze-Naumburg, member of the Reichstag and leader in the Nordic art movement; Gerhard Wagner, Führer of the Nazi Physicians' League; and Baldur von Schirach, head of the Hitler Youth. The chairman of the committee was Arthur Gütt, the man responsible for public health affairs in the Ministry of the Interior. Subsequent members included SS chief Heinrich Himmler; the industrialist Fritz Thyssen; and Fritz Lenz, Ploetz's protégé and editor of the *Archiv für Rassen- und Gesellschaftsbiologie*. The purpose of the group was to construct racial policy, replacing an earlier body formed in the Weimar Republic to address population questions.[1]

At the first meeting of the committee, Frick delivered a speech

96   Racial Hygiene

calling for a new German population policy, one that would reverse a host of threats to the health of the German people. The declining birthrate, he argued, would diminish both the quantity and the quality of the race. Germany was faced with an increasingly aged population, a population moving in the direction of the two-child family. Furthermore, Jews were immigrating in ever greater numbers from the East (4,000 to Berlin alone in 1930)—and as a result the number of mixed and "degenerate" offspring was also increasing. Frick also warned that the numbers of "genetically diseased" were growing in the population, owing to a lack of state-administered racial policy. He estimated the number of genetic defectives in Germany at 500,000, and noted that even this figure might be conservative, given that "some experts consider the true figure to be as high as 20 percent of the German population."[2]

Origins of the Law

Racial policy was not long in coming. On July 14, 1933, the same day Hitler outlawed the formation of political parties, the Nazi government passed the Law for the Prevention of Genetically Diseased Offspring (*Gesetz zur Verhütung erbkranken Nachwuchses*), or Sterilization Law, according to which an individual could be sterilized if, in the opinion of a genetic health court (*Erbgesundheitsgericht*), he or she suffered from any of several "genetic" illnesses, including feeble-mindedness, schizophrenia, manic-depressive insanity, genetic epilepsy, Huntington's chorea, genetic blindness or deafness, or severe alcoholism. The elaborate interpretive commentary on the law was written by three dominant figures in the racial hygiene movement: Ernst Rüdin, Arthur Gütt, and the lawyer Falk Ruttke (see Figure 18).

Racial hygienists (and much of the orthodox medical press) had long advocated sterilization as a means of improving the race. As early as 1892 the psychiatrist August Forel had tried to justify sterilization of the insane as a national sacrifice similar to that of the soldier in time of war.[3] Others took more practical steps: in 1897, for example, the Heidelberg gynecologist Edwin Kehrer sterilized at least one patient to guarantee that this person would no longer bring "inferior" descendants into the world.[4] Until 1933, however, sterilization was illegal in Germany, whether for eugenic purposes or for family planning. In 1903 the young psychiatrist Ernst Rüdin pro-

Gesetz zur Verhütung erbkranken Nachwuchses
vom 14. Juli 1933

mit Auszug aus dem Gesetz gegen gefährliche Gewohnheitsverbrecher und über Maßregeln der Sicherung und Besserung vom 24. Nov. 1933

Bearbeitet und erläutert von

Dr. med. Arthur Gütt
Ministerialdirektor
im Reichsministerium des Innern

Dr. med. Ernst Rüdin
o. ö. Professor für Psychiatrie an der Universität und Direktor
des Kaiser Wilhelm-Instituts für Genealogie und Demographie
der Deutschen Forschungsanstalt für Psychiatrie in München

Dr. jur. Falk Ruttke
Geschäftsführer des Reichsausschusses für Volksgesundheitsdienst
beim Reichsministerium des Innern

Mit Beiträgen:

Die Eingriffe zur Unfruchtbarmachung des Mannes
und zur Entmannung
von Geheimrat Prof. Dr. med. Erich Lexer, München

Die Eingriffe zur Unfruchtbarmachung der Frau
von Geheimrat Prof. Dr. med. Albert Döderlein, München

Mit 15 zum Teil farbigen Abbildungen

J. F. Lehmanns Verlag / München 1934

Figure 18. Title page of interpretative commentary on the "Law for the Prevention of Genetically Diseased Offspring," providing for the sterilization of genetic defectives. On March 6, 1934, Gerhard Wagner, Führer of the Nazi Physicians' League, required that all physicians purchase the book, published by Lehmann Verlag, at the special price of 3 reichsmarks.

Figure 19. "Only Genetically Healthy Offspring Ensure the Strength of the People." Inside caption reads: "We Do Not Stand Alone." The woman holds a baby and the man holds a shield inscribed with Germany's 1933 Law for the Protection of Genetically Diseased Offspring (Sterilization Law). The couple stands in front of a map of Germany, surrounded by flags of the nations that have enacted sterilization legislation. From *Neues Volk*, March 1, 1936, p. 37.

posed the sterilization of "incurable alcoholics" at the Ninth International Congress to Combat Alcoholism (in Bremen); his proposal was roundly defeated.[5] In 1914 bills were introduced (unsuccessfully) into German parliament to legalize voluntary sterilization. By the end of the Weimar period, journals such as the *Archiv für Gynäkologie* and the *Münchener Medizinische Wochenschrift* had joined the call for forced sterilization.

Germany was not alone in this movement. On September 3, 1928, the Swiss Canton of Waadt passed a law according to which the mentally ill and feeble-minded could be sterilized if public health authorities determined that such individuals were incurable and likely to produce degenerate offspring. The Swiss law was never of much consequence: by 1933 only twenty-one such sterilizations had been performed in this canton.[6] In 1929 Denmark became the second European country to legalize sterilization. Norway passed sterilization legislation in 1934, followed by similar laws in Sweden (1935), Finland (1935), Estonia (1936), and Iceland (1938).[7] Other states that passed sterilization laws were Vera Cruz (in Mexico), Cuba, Czechoslovakia, Yugoslavia, Lithuania, Latvia, Hungary, and Turkey. The Office of Racial Policy took great pride in the fact that Germany was not alone in its attempt to curb the reproduction of the unfit through sterilization (see Figure 19).

The American Connection

It was in the United States that theory was first turned into practice in this sphere. In 1907 Indiana passed the first laws allowing sterilization of the mentally ill and criminally insane; by the late 1920s twenty-eight American states and one Canadian province had followed suit, enacting legislation that resulted in the sterilization of some 15,000 individuals before 1930—many of them against their will and most while incarcerated in prisons or homes for the mentally ill.[8] By 1939 more than 30,000 people in twenty-nine American states had been sterilized on eugenic grounds; nearly half the operations (12,941) were carried out in California.[9]

During World War I, German racial hygienists expressed their concern that Germany's adversaries might surpass the fatherland in racial health. In 1917, when the Berlin branch of the Society for Racial Hygiene proposed strong measures to improve the quality of the race, American and English achievements in this field were held up as models worth emulating. Racial hygienists warned that serious consequences could follow if Germany's enemies were to advance in this field while Germany remained behind. Sterilization was not the only thing implied here: German racial hygienists also pointed to American emigration policies, according to which only "the fittest" were allowed in and inferiors sent back to the European motherland.[10]

After World War I, German racial hygienists continued to express their admiration of American achievements in this field. In 1924 Dr. Gustav Boeters, one of Germany's most persistent advocates of sterilization, defended the sterilization of "mental inferiors" with the following argument: "What we racial hygienists promote is by no means new or unheard of. In a cultured nation of the first order—the United States of America—that which we strive toward [that is, sterilization legislation] was introduced and tested long ago. It is all so clear and simple."[11] One year later Professor Otto Reche, chairman of the Vienna Society for Racial Care (Gesellschaft für Rassenpflege), expressed his fear that the Americans were becoming world leaders in racial hygiene and urged Germans to try to catch up. "Racial care," Reche asserted, "must become the *foundation* of all domestic policy, and at least a part of foreign policy."[12] In 1932, on the eve of Hitler's rise to power, the historian of science Reinhold Müller described the relation of America and Germany in this matter as follows:

> Racial hygiene in Germany remained until 1926 a purely academic and scientific movement. It was the Americans who busied themselves earnestly about the subject. Through massive investigations in the schools, they proved (with impeccable precision) Galton's thesis that qualities of the mind [*seelische Eigenschaften*] are as heritable as qualities of the body; they were also able to show that these mental qualities are inherited according to the very same laws as those of the body.[13]

As early as the late nineteenth century, German racial hygienists looked to America for leadership in racial hygiene. In the 1890s Alfred Ploetz had traveled to the United States to try to implement his racial ideals in the tiny utopian community of Icarus, in central Iowa. Although Ploetz's experiment failed, German medical authorities in subsequent years continued to refer to the United States for lessons on racial policy. At the turn of the century German health authorities studied legislation in North Dakota disallowing marriage of alcoholics, the insane, and individuals suffering from tuberculosis. Health authorities reported on laws passed in 1899 in Michigan according to which idiots, the insane, and individuals suffering from gonorrhea or syphilis were not allowed to marry and could be punished with fines up to $1,000 or prison terms up to five years for violating the statutes. In the early 1900s officials in the Reich Health Office (Reichsgesundheitsamt) took notice of these laws and included them as the first entry in what was to become a large file on racial hygiene.[14] German interest in American sterilization continued through the early 1930s. In the 1931 edition of his *Human Selection,* Fritz Lenz cited the American eugenicist Harry H. Laughlin's view that a proper sterilization effort in the United States would encompass 100,000 individuals in the first few years, rising to 400,000 a year by 1980. Laughlin had pointed out that with such a program, one could sterilize approximately 15 million individuals of inferior racial stock by 1980. Lenz noted that sterilization on such a scale would certainly contribute to the health of the race; he also claimed, however, that Laughlin's figures were modest and that one might well afford to sterilize an even larger fraction of the population.[15]

Sterilization was not the only area in which German racial hygienists learned from the Americans. In the Weimar period a number of American works on eugenics and racial theory were translated into German. In 1925 Madison Grant's *Passing of the Great Race* appeared in translation, as did Lothrop Stoddard's *Revolt against Civilization: The Menace of the Under Man.*[16] Two of the most widely cited American studies were Richard Dugdale's study of the Jukes and H. H. Goddard's study of the Kallikaks. According to Dugdale's celebrated study, Mr. Jukes, a colonial frontiersman, married into a defective family and produced a horde of degenerate offspring. Dugdale was able to trace 709 descendants and found that 181 were prostitutes, 106 were born illegitimately, 142 were beggars, 64 were housed at public expense, 184 had been prostitutes, and 70 had been convicted of criminal offenses (7 for murder). According to Dugdale, this single family cost the New York government more than $1,300,000 from 1730 to 1874. Equally famous was Goddard's story of the Kallikak family (one of the first works of American eugenics to appear in German translation in 1914). Martin Kallikak was the pseudonym given by the author to a New Jersey man who had married a "common tavern wench" of inferior racial stock. From this unhappy marriage came 480 offspring: 46 "normals"; 143 feebleminded; 33 immoral (mostly prostitutes); 8 bordello owners; 24 severe alcoholics; 3 epileptics; and "countless" other assorted degenerates. Kallikak also married a fine, upstanding, "healthy" woman, and from this second marriage came 496 descendants, all fit, healthy, and respectable citizens.[17] German racial hygienists commonly cited the Jukes and Kallikak studies as evidence of the primacy of heredity over environment.[18] They also sought and found their own examples of such families—the families Zero, Victoria, and Markus, for example—each of which told a story similar to those of the Jukes and the Kallikaks.[19] In each case the lesson was that heredity is more important than environment in the determination of moral and intellectual character, and that one single "genetic defective" can spoil an entire ancestral line.[20]

German racial scientists were also impressed with America's 1924 Immigration Restriction Laws and the antimiscegenation laws that existed in many states of the American South.[21] Bavarian Health Inspector Walter Schultze, for example, in a 1932 article, "The Nordic Ideal" written for the official journal of the Nazi Physicians' League, argued that racial hygienists must learn from the United States, where racial laws had recently been enacted to restrict the influx of Jews, Poles, and southern Europeans. Based on its experience in both the sterilization program and the immigration restriction laws, the United States was to be regarded as a nation where "racial policy and thinking have become much more popular than in other countries." (Schultze in subsequent years also praised South African legislation forbidding black-white intermarriage; he linked such laws with German efforts to restrict German-Jewish intermarriage.)[22] The importance of the United States as a model continued even after the rise of the Nazis to power. In the spring of 1933, with the beginning of the *Gleichschaltung* of the German medical profession, German medical journals declared that America had already solved its Jewish question by prudent emigration restrictions. The April 1933 issue of the *Deutsches Ärzteblatt* claimed that America (unlike Germany) had little need to defend itself against Jews, because its (1924) immigration restriction laws had already guaranteed that "unwanted racial elements" could no longer gain entry. The journal also noted that America had no intention of opening its doors to Jews fleeing Germany.[23] One could cite many other examples where German racial hygienists looked to the United States for inspiration; in this sense, German racial hygiene followed the American lead.

American eugenicists were in turn impressed with German achievements. Laughlin, Davenport, and other American eugenicists were envious of the thoroughness with which German racial measures were administered: when the Nazis opened the first Race Bureau for Eugenic Segregation in Dortmund, aimed explicitly at purifying the German race of its Semitic elements, one anonymous member of the Eugenics Record Office in Cold Spring Harbor remarked that Hitler "should be made honorary member of the Eugenics Record Office!"[24] (Laughlin also boasted that the German sterilization program had been inspired at least in part by his own "Model Sterilization Law.")[25] In 1936 Laughlin traveled to Heidelberg to receive an honorary doctorate; he returned to the United States with a copy of the propaganda film *Erbkrank* (The genetically diseased), which he showed to the staff of the Carnegie Institution at the Eugenics Record Office. Alice M. Hellmer of the office noted in a 1937 letter reproduced by the SS Office of Race and Settlement that Laughlin was so impressed by the film that he intended to make a similar one for American audiences.[26]

The Genetic Health Courts

Until 1933 sterilization was illegal in Germany, as in most other European countries. Proposals to allow some form of voluntary sterilization were rejected by Weimar legislators, despite periodic attempts by health authorities to have such laws passed.[27] Progress in this direction was finally made in the last years of the Weimar Republic. On July 2 and 3, 1932, the executive committee of the German Medical Association, along with the Prussian Health Council (Landesgesundheitsrat), met to discuss (among other things) the question of "eugenics in the service of the economy."[28] At a September meeting later that year, the council voted to approve limited medically supervised and voluntary sterilization, designed to stop the breeding of genetic defectives. In the fall of 1932, legislation was placed before the German parliament to allow voluntary sterilization.

The Sterilization Law passed by the Nazis in the summer of 1933 simply changed the language of the Weimar proposal to allow for compulsory sterilization on "eugenic indications." The new law allowed for the sterilization only of (supposedly) "homozygous" carriers of genetic disease; sterilization of "recessive" carriers was forbidden and remained punishable as a criminal offense. (This presupposed, of course, that the various indications for which one could be sterilized—feeble-mindedness, schizophrenia, alcoholism, and so on—were single-gene traits that followed the simple rules of Mendelian genetics; today we know that such a notion is virtually meaningless.) Germany's Sterilization Law was explicitly intended to be eugenic rather than punitive—that is, persons ordered sterilized were not to be considered perpetrators of a crime for which they were receiving punishment. Rudolf Ramm described sterilization as the sacrifice an individual makes as a result of the "personal tragedy" of having been born defective. By submitting to sterilization, such individuals "break their link in the chain of generation, as a sacrifice in the interests of the good of the Volk." Ramm did recognize that feeble-mindedness and other disorders covered by the law might be the product of environmental rather than hereditary influences; he nevertheless advised that it was better "to err on the side of caution" in such cases (that is, to go ahead with sterilization), as even slight impairment could conceal "more severe deficiencies."[29]

Although the German Sterilization Law was not intended to be punitive, some did believe that the sterilization of genetic defectives might help eliminate crime. The prison cleric (Strafanstaltspfarrer) Ebel, for example, maintained that both the Sterilization Law and the laws allowing castration for certain kinds of criminal acts (see Table 3) would have this effect. He argued that "when one reflects upon the fact that some proportion of the genetically ill are also morally defective and have broken the law, then one can easily understand how important sterilization may be in helping to reduce criminality."[30]

The new law was to be administered on a massive scale. Seventeen hundred genetic health courts (Erbgesundheitsgerichte) and appellate genetic health courts (Erbgesundheitsobergerichte) were originally envisioned to determine who should and who should not be sterilized. Racial hygienists reported to the international press that the costs of the program should run about 14 million RM (more than 5 million American dollars at this time); officials declared that this amount was negligible, however, compared with the costs of hereditary disease to the nation as a whole, estimated at 350 million to 1 billion RM annually.[31] Walter Gmelin, head of the Schwäbisch-Hall Health Office, predicted that the Sterilization Law would save Germany billions of marks in coming decades.[32]

In 1934, 181 genetic health courts and appellate genetic health courts were established throughout Germany to adjudicate the Sterilization Law.[33] The courts were usually attached to local civil courts and presided over by a lawyer and two doctors, one of whom was an

Table 3. German racial legislation, 1933–1945

Date	Legal measure
April 7, 1933	Gesetz zur Wiederherstellung des Berufsbeamtentums (Civil Service Law; required proof of Aryan ancestry and political reliability to hold government job)
July 14, 1933	Gesetz zur Verhütung erbkranken Nachwuchses (Sterilization Law)
September 29, 1933	Reichserbhofgesetz (farmers declared racial stock of nation; required that inheritors of family farms be "of German or related blood")
November 24, 1933	Gesetz gegen gefährliche Gewohnheitsverbrecher und über Massnahmen der Sicherung und Besserung (Law against Dangerous Career Criminals, or Castration Law; allowed the castration of sex offenders)
September 15, 1935	Gesetz zum Schutze des deutschen Blutes und der deutschen Ehre (Blood Protection Law; barred marriage or sexual relations between Jews and Germans)
October 18, 1935	Gesetz zum Schutze der Erbgesundheit des deutschen Volkes (*Ehegesundheitsgesetz,* or Marital Health Law; required certificate of health for marriage license)
November 15, 1935	Reichsbürgergesetz (Citizenship Law; distinguished "citizens" [Aryan Germans] from "inhabitants" [unmarried women, non-Aryans]; deprived Jews of civil rights)
September 1, 1941	Polizeiverordnung über die Kennzeichnung von Juden (all Jews required to wear Star of David)

Note: See Table 6 for legislation against Jews in 1938.

expert on genetic pathology (*Erbpathologie*). Especially after 1935, the courts also became involved in helping decide who was fit to marry whom, according to the 1935 Nuremberg Laws (see Chapter 6). The primary responsibility of the courts, however, was to adjudicate the Sterilization Law. According to its provisions, doctors were required to register every case of genetic illness known to them (except in women over the age of forty-five); article 9 of the law allowed fines of up to 150 RM for any doctor failing to register such a person. Individuals were usually first recommended for sterilization by their physician, who would present his analysis to the local genetic health court.[34]

German physicians recognized that the presentation of detailed medical records before a court without the permission of the patient altered the traditional privacy of the doctor-patient relationship; medical journals in the early years of the Third Reich frequently discussed how the rights of individuals to have their medical records kept confidential appeared to conflict with the broader obligation to maintain the genetic health of the German population. The question of privacy was ultimately resolved by requiring physicians to report cases of genetic illness in the same way they were required to report births and deaths or certain infectious or venereal diseases, and so forth. The proceedings of the courts were kept secret in order to preserve confidentiality. Physicians were also instructed, however, not to share information submitted to the courts with the patient whose reproductive future was in question. Such information was to be seen only by the physician bringing the charge and the officials of the genetic health court.[35] The courts were granted the power to subpoena medical records; hospitals and physicians were required to comply with these requests.

The proceedings of the genetic health courts were secret, and even today most of their records are protected under German laws guaranteeing that certain data will remain confidential (*Datenschutz*). Nevertheless, some sense of the philosophy and workings of the courts can be gleaned from legal and medical sources of the time, especially from the journal *Der Erbarzt* (The genetic doctor).

The Genetic Doctor

In 1934 *Der Erbarzt* was founded as a supplement to the *Deutsches Ärzteblatt* to provide a forum for discussion of methods, criteria, and grounds for sterilization. The journal carried a weekly column titled "Genetic Advice and Expertise" (*Erbärztliche Beratung und Begutachtung*), a kind of "Dear Abby" for physicians on how to determine genetic fitness, when to sterilize, how to counsel for a healthy marriage, and so forth; both doctors and laypersons wrote letters to the editor asking whether certain cases fell under the Sterilization Law.

The first issue of *Der Erbarzt* appeared on June 16, 1934. The editor, Dr. Otmar Freiherr von Verschuer, announced that his intention in publishing the journal was "to forge a link between the ministries of public health, the genetic health courts, and the German medical community." The goal was philosophical as well as practical:

the revolution of 1933, Verschuer insisted, recognized the poverty of individualism as a basis for medical practice; a patient was no longer to be treated as an individual, but only as "one part of a much larger whole or unity: his family, his race, his Volk."[36] Traditional health care was therefore to be complemented by genetic health care (*Erbgesundheitspflege*); population policy would have to attend "to the *quality* of its people, as well as its quantity." Verschuer claimed that the science of genetics had discovered the biological connection of Volk, family, and race; it had shown that "behind the life of every individual, there lives another life—the genetic current, which flows through the generations." The task of medicine was thus transformed: the traditional doctor of the individual would be replaced by the genetic doctor. The genetic doctor was not a new specialty but an entirely new kind of doctor: one who cared for the future of the race, one who put the good of the whole over the good of the part. "Every doctor," Verschuer proclaimed, "must be a genetic doctor" (*Jeder Arzt muss Erbarzt sein*).[37]

Authors for Verschuer's *Erbarzt* included some of Germany's most eminent biologists. The geneticist N. V. Timofeev-Ressovsky, for example, in a 1935 article argued that genetic pathologies accumulate in a population wherever civilization has interrupted the natural struggle for existence. Under such circumstances, pathological mutations multiply unchecked. It was important for racial hygiene not only to determine who was obviously genetically sick, but also to identify the heterozygous carriers who might show no symptoms. Timofeev maintained that this "would not only serve the purposes of racial hygiene, but would also help to facilitate the classification of certain genetic diseases."[38]

In his introduction to the first issue of the journal, Verschuer cited four legal measures that had begun to address the problems of racial hygiene: (1) the Civil Service Law of April 7, 1933, according to which all non-Aryans were dismissed from government posts; (2) the broad set of measures designed to allow the retraction of citizenship from elements of the population judged undesirable (especially recent immigrants); (3) the series of laws designed to prevent "further immigration of racial enemies"; and (4) the Sterilization Law. He also cited other measures designed to promote racial hygiene, such as loans for newly married couples (*Ehestandsdarlehen*); measures designed to relieve the tax burden for large families; incentives designed to keep German families on the farm (*Erbhofgesetz*); and the establishment of offices for family counseling (*Eheberatungsstellen*).³⁹ Verschuer drew attention to the wealth of new words that had been added to the German vocabulary as a result of racial hygiene: there were the *Erbkartei* (genetic files) and the *Erbklinik* (genetic clinics); people spoke of *Erbgesundheit* (genetic health), *Erbleiden* (genetic illness), and *Erbkrankheit* (genetic disease). There were the new sciences of *Erblehre* (genetics) and of *Erbrecht* (genetic law); there was the *Erbarzt* (genetic doctor) and the student of *Erbpathologie* (genetic pathology). There were the *Erbgesundheitsgerichte* (genetic health courts), the *Erbämter* (genetic officials), and the *Erbkammern* (genetic chambers); there were *Erbsünde* (genetic pollution) and the new *Erbhöfe* (hereditary farms). The term *Erblehre* (genetics) itself, Verschuer pointed out, was coined by Eugen Fischer in 1926 with the establishment of his Kaiser Wilhelm Institute for Anthropology, Human Genetics (*Erblehre*), and Eugenics.⁴⁰

The first genetic health court met on March 15, 1934, in Berlin. Over the next two months this court heard 348 cases and ordered 325 sterilizations. In 143 cases the application for sterilization was placed by the individual; in the remainder sterilization was requested by hospital directors, state or court physicians, or the legal guardian of the person to be sterilized.⁴¹ Most of those who received the so-called *Hitlerschnitt* (Hitler-cut) were between the ages of twenty and forty, but 5 percent were over fifty.

In the first year of the Sterilization Law (1934), genetic health courts received 84,525 applications for sterilization: 42,903 for men and 41,622 for women. During the same period 64,499 decisions were handed down by the courts: 56,244 in favor of sterilization and 3,692 against; 4,563 requests were either retracted or postponed. The courts decided in favor of sterilization in over 90 percent of the cases heard. The enthusiasm with which courts prosecuted "genetic inferiors" differed in different parts of the country. In the first year of the law, the Genetic Health Court of Dresden was the most vigorous in its prosecution, handling 4,152 cases. Berlin was next with 3,509, and the court at Hamm was third with 3,095. The fewest cases were recorded by Oldenburg with 473, Marienwerder with 285, and Braunschweig with only 212.⁴²

Individuals who had been ordered sterilized were guaranteed the right to appeal their decisions to appellate genetic health courts, and many did so. In 1934, for example, nearly 4,000 persons (about 7 percent of the total) appealed their decisions. Three hundred and seventy-seven were successful, but the great majority (3,559) failed. Individuals were guaranteed the right of appeal, whether the courts had ruled for or against sterilization. Thus in 1934, 287 people appealed court decisions refusing their applications for sterilization: 179 were successful; 108 were not.[43] As one might imagine, the overwhelming majority of those appealing decisions of the courts protested decisions to sterilize. (In one sample studied, there were 8,219 appeals protesting sterilization versus only 438 protests against decisions *not* to sterilize.) Throughout the Nazi period, only about 3 percent of appealed decisions were ever reversed.[44] Those who refused to submit to sterilization were generally sent to concentration camps.

The Office of Racial Policy reported in 1941 that many of those who had been sterilized bitterly condemned the state for having violated their personal freedom.[45] In the face of growing fears and anger, medical journals tried to spread the word that Germany's health offices (which often organized court proceedings) were cautious and conservative in their judgments on genetic illness; journals also tried to prove that the majority of those investigated were never ultimately sterilized. In the early war years, Germany's advisory centers for genetic and racial care (see Chapter 6) voiced concerns about the population's growing fear and distrust of medical authorities; Berlin's Policlinic for Genetic and Racial Care, for example, announced in 1941 that medical professionals must guard against the view that the advisory centers constituted a kind of genetic police (*Erbpolizei*).[46] The activities of the advisory centers and the courts were supposed to be viewed as "positive" rather than "eliminative" (*ausmerzende*).

Some evidence is available on the kinds of sterilizations performed in the early years of the law (see Table 4). Feeble-mindedness was generally the most common ground for sterilization; schizophrenia was next, followed by epilepsy and alcoholism. Although the proportions varied slightly from court to court, feeble-mindedness remained the primary target. In 1935 the chairman of the genetic health court in Kiel reported that the proportion of sterilizations for feeble-mindedness in his jurisdiction had risen to 75 percent. Feeble-mindedness, Dr. Bruman reported, had thus become "*the* question of eliminative racial care."[47]

The Sterilization Law was intended to be race neutral and was applied to men and women on a roughly equal basis. In 1935 the Reich Ministry of the Interior issued an ordinance that disallowed the

Table 4. Grounds given for sterilization in the adjudication of the 1933 Sterilization Law

Reason for sterilization	Study		
	K. H. Bauer[a]	Mikulicz-Radecki[b]	Verschuer[c]
Congenital feeble-mindedness	42.9%	66.8%	29.6%
Schizophrenia	25.4	22.6	34.4
Hereditary epilepsy	13.4	8.1	24.6
Severe alcoholism	5.0	0.5	6.8
Manic-depressive insanity	1.6	0.5	2.8
Hereditary deafness	1.4	1.5	0.6
Hereditary blindness	1.2	1.5	—
Huntington's chorea	0.2	1.5	0.3
Serious bodily malformation (hereditary)	0.2	1.5	0.9
Diagnosis not given	8.7	—	—
	100.0%	100.0%	100.0%

Source: Otmar Freiherr von Verschuer, *Erbpathologie: Ein Lehrbuch für Ärzte und Medizinstudierende* (1934), 2nd ed. (Dresden, 1937), p. 178.

a. Based on a sample of 6,052 men.
b. Based on a sample of 6,032 women.
c. Based on a sample of 325 men and women.

sterilization of girls under the age of fourteen; on June 26 and July 18, 1935, ordinances were passed extending the provisions of the law to "allow" (that is, require) abortions for women considered genetically unfit.[48]

New Techniques and Tests

Early estimates of the total number of people sterilized during the Nazi period ranged from 300,000 to 350,000; the true figure, as Gisela Bock has shown, is probably nearer 400,000.[49] In the ten regional districts (*Bezirken*) of Baden-Württemberg alone, some 11,400 individuals were sterilized, representing more than 1 percent of the entire population in that area.[50] Most of these were done in the first four years of the law (1934–1937), when the average number of sterilized in Germany as a whole exceeded 50,000 per year.

The sterilization of 400,000 people required an enormous effort from Germany's medical profession. Doctors competed to fulfill sterilization quotas;[51] sterilization research and engineering rapidly became one of the largest medical industries. Medical supply companies (such as Schering) made a substantial amount of money designing sterilization equipment. Medical students wrote at least 183 doctoral theses exploring the criteria, methods, and consequences of sterilization.[52]

The most common techniques of sterilization involved tubal ligation for women and vasectomy for men. The time and costs required for each was no small matter. The operation was relatively simple for men, requiring only local anesthesia and an operation lasting five to ten minutes. Yet for women, the operation (tying the fallopian tubes) typically required a hospital stay of eight to fifteen days and sometimes longer. Anticipating the importance of mass sterilization, physicians developed techniques that would allow more rapid sterilization on an outpatient basis. In the late 1920s the gynecologist Felix Mikulicz-Radecki perfected a method of "operationless" sterilization of women involving the scarification of fallopian tube tissue through injections of carbon dioxide. Though simpler than tying the tubes, this procedure was by no means risk free. In a 1935 study of 6,032 sterilizations using this technique, Mikulicz-Radecki found that thirty-three patients died of complications (most commonly, lung embolisms) arising from the operation. Scarification was not the only rapid technique developed. According to an ordinance passed on February 25, 1936, women over the age of thirty-eight or women for whom tubal ligation posed a risk could be sterilized by exposure to X-rays.[53] One study found that some 12 percent of all sterilizations were performed with X-rays—an operation that, as the Nazis were well aware, effectively amounted to castration of the patient. For all forms of sterilization, mortality rates averaged about half of 1 percent. If one considers that some 400,000 persons were sterilized, then approximately 2,000 must have died from the operations.[54]

Developments in sterilization technology continued throughout the Nazi period. In 1934 the firm G. Wolf of Berlin produced a model "hysteroscope" that could see in all directions and was thin enough (8 mm) not to require narcotics, yet large enough to allow the introduction of equipment into the uterus to remove tumors or to sever or scarify the fallopian tubes.[55] Especially after the onset of the war (and subsequent attempts to sterilize thousands of people in countries under German occupation), the Nazi government promoted further research into rapid sterilization techniques. In 1942 SS chief Heinrich Himmler granted gynecologists permission to develop methods of sterilization (using X-rays) that would not require a hospital stay and that could be used without the knowledge of the "patient." According to evidence presented after the war in the Nuremberg trials, victims in at least one instance were seated on chairs behind desks or counters and told to fill out questionnaires. X-rays from equipment installed under the chairs were then directed toward the genitals for two to three minutes, and sterility (as well as massive burns) followed immediately.[56] Developments in more traditional techniques also continued during the war. In June of 1943, the gynecologist Carl Clauberg announced to Himmler that by the end of the year, using techniques developed by Mikulicz-Radecki and with a staff of ten men, he should be able to sterilize as many as 1,000 women per day.[57]

Germany's massive sterilization program transformed the German medical profession. In Verschuer's words, every doctor had to become a genetic doctor. The new priorities were reflected in university research institutes and in academic training. By 1942 Germany's twelve leading university institutes for racial hygiene and racial care spent much of their time preparing expert testimony for the genetic health courts on cases of questionable parentage.[58] Every doctor in Germany was required to undergo training in genetic pathology and to become proficient in the analysis of racial traits.

Techniques developed in this science were ingenious indeed. The genetic doctor looked inside the mouth at the shape of the teeth, gums, and tongue. One doctor claimed to be able to determine racial ancestry by the "half-moon" at the base of the fingernails. (American physicians in the nineteenth century had suggested this as a way to determine the admixture of "Negro blood" in whites.)[59] In one signal example of Nordic thoroughness, a certain Dr. Thordar Quelprud, working at the Kaiser Wilhelm Institute for Anthropology, distinguished fourteen different physiognomic aspects of the external ear, claiming these could be used to determine racial ancestry. A colleague of Quelprud's, a research physician at Berlin's Poliklinik für Erb- und Rassenpflege, published an article in Germany's leading public health magazine arguing that he could discern various forms of racial degeneracy (criminality, feeble-mindedness, and so on) from the structure of the ear.[60] Doctors warned against confusing genetic with environmental factors, but behavioral characteristics were by no means excluded from the analysis of genetic pathology: Drs. Bauermeister and Küper advised looking at the position of the feet at rest and at the way of walking; Hans F. K. Günther, in his *Rassenkunde des jüdischen*

Volkes, published photographs of "typical Jewish posture" (*typische jüdische Haltung*).⁶¹

IQ tests developed by psychologists such as Wilhelm Stern (who coined the term *IQ*), F. von Rohden, and Walther Poppelreuter to measure "practical intelligence" were used to determine who should be sterilized.⁶² The psychologist Ferdinand Dubitscher suggested that the following tests be used in preparing evaluations for the genetic health courts:

> 1. *The suitcase test:* In a box 60 × 30 × 30 cm are twenty different objects of different shapes, such as books and bottles, which with careful packing exactly fill the box. Pack them all in such a way that the lid may be closed without force.
> 2. *The assignment test:* The subject is given [a] map and receives instructions to buy the following objects: half a hundredweight of potatoes, one-half pound of coffee, one-half pound of sausage, fifty pfennigs worth of fresh biscuits, and a pound of butter. He is further required to bring a pair of trousers to the tailor and a pair of shoes to the cobbler, as well as a ten-pound package to the post office. He is also required to pay a certain amount of tax at City Hall and to pick up a friend at the train station. The following rules are to be observed: The person leaves the house at 10:30. At 1:00 he should be back for lunch and have accomplished all his tasks. Now the tax office is open only from 8 to 10 A.M., fresh bread is available only after 11 A.M., and the friend arrives at the station at 12:30. The post office and all stores are open between 12 and 2. Between the apartment and the train station runs a streetcar—which takes one-quarter of an hour and may be used at will.⁶³

If the subject proved him- or herself fit to avoid sterilization by solving these "practical puzzles," there were further questions requiring more creative thought. The following problem was designed to measure ability to carry out orders:

> You are mayor of a city in time of war. Suddenly, from high command comes an order that all windows are to be removed. How should this be done, and what should be used in place of glass for the windows?⁶⁴

(This was before the development of plastics!). Other tests, some of which were widely reported in the international media, included questions such as: "What form of state do we have now?" "What are the German postal rates?" "Who were Bismarck and Luther, and who discovered America?" "Why are houses higher in the city than in the country?"⁶⁵ Physicians also tried to develop a more generalized "development quotient" (*Entwicklungsquotient*) test modeled on the IQ test that would provide a mathematical measure of mental retardation in children five, four, three, or even two years old.⁶⁶ These tests were developed explicitly for use in conjunction with German racial legislation.

The *Rheinlandbastarde*

The 1933 Sterilization Law made no provision for sterilization on racial grounds. (Jews, for example, were never specifically targeted by the law.) In 1937, however, on secret orders from Hitler, the 500 or so *Rheinlandbastarde*—offspring of black French occupation troops and native Germans—were sterilized in a joint Gestapo/genetic health court operation organized by Ernst Rüdin, Fritz Lenz, and Walter Gross, among others.⁶⁷

The mixed offspring were recognized as a "problem" as early as the 1920s, when Reichspresident Friedrich Ebert spoke of the black scourge (*schwarzen Schmach*) that had befallen the nation. Shortly after World War I, an Emergency Committee against the Black Scourge was formed in Munich, with the goal of "educating the public concerning the dangers facing the white race."⁶⁸ In 1927 Bavarian Health Minister Sperr wrote to the president of the Reich Health Office in Berlin to see if the children might be sterilized; the request was denied by the Reich Ministry of the Occupied Sectors.⁶⁹

On April 13, 1933, Hermann Göring ordered police authorities in Düsseldorf, Cologne, Koblenz, Aachen, and Wiesbaden to register all *Rheinlandbastarde* with state health offices. But it was not obvious what could be done with these individuals without encountering political repercussions. By 1934 Germany had already begun to suffer problems with several of its traditional "non-Aryan" trading partners. Quite apart from complaints from Jewish quarters, Germany had begun to receive complaints from allies in Ceylon, Japan, and India about the status of their compatriots under the new racial laws. Early in 1934 the Prussian minister of the interior met with the German foreign minister to discuss how to avoid the bad press Germany was getting in India, Japan, and Latin America. The interior minister recommended that special status be granted Japanese, Chinese, Indians, and all other non-Jewish foreigners who might otherwise suffer under the non-Aryan restriction laws. On January 10, 1934, the

German embassy in Tokyo recommended that Japanese be excluded from the restrictions of German racial law. German spokesmen were instructed to announce that the laws "did not imply that certain races were different in *value,* but merely in *kind.*"[70] The term *Aryan,* so it was explained, was intended to embrace all non-Jews. The Ministry of Foreign Affairs requested that Germany's racial legislation be changed to stipulate sanctions only against Jews—not, in other words, against Chinese, Japanese, or Indians living in Germany. Walter Gross, head of the Office of Racial Policy, relayed the message of Rudolf Hess that, although the fundamental racial philosophy of National Socialism could not be compromised, individual exceptions might nevertheless be made in particular cases of international import. By the time the Nuremberg Laws were written in the autumn of 1935, the more general term *non-Aryan* had been supplanted by the term *Jewish* explicitly for the purpose of satisfying foreign allies. By the middle of World War II, Germans were not even supposed to use the term *anti-Semitic,* for fear of offending Middle Eastern (especially Iraqi) "Semitic" allies.

On February 7, 1935, Division II of the Expert Committee for Population and Racial Policy met to discuss the use of X-rays in sterilization and to decide what to do about the *Rheinlandbastarde.* As a solution to the *Rheinlandbastarde* problem, the group decided that the children were to be sterilized illegally, bypassing the Sterilization Law, but only after obtaining the parents' permission. An anthropologically trained doctor would prepare briefs (*Gutachten*) on each of the children, documenting that the fathers were in fact occupation soldiers of African descent. Sterilization, to avoid complications, was to be "voluntary"; reliable party member doctors were to help "persuade" mothers that their children ought to be sterilized.[71]

In early 1937 a special commission was formed at Gestapo headquarters in Berlin; its task was to find and seize all *Rheinlandbastarde* and to deliver them to one of three commissions of anthropological experts (Eugen Fischer, Wolfgang Abel, Herbert Göllner), whose job would be to certify that the children were of African ancestry. The entire operation was to be carried out secretly and as rapidly as possible. The case of seventeen-year-old Mr. A. A., for which there is some documentation, might be taken as representative. According to information gathered by the Health Office of Germersheim, A. A., the son of a black French soldier from Madagascar and a German woman, was born on March 14, 1920, in Kandel. According to the physiognomic data in the report, A. A. showed typical "foreign-racial characteristics." The youth was ordered to appear before a commission in Ludwigshafen on January 10, 1937, but did not do so; police investigation determined that the youth was working on board a Dutch ship, transporting iron pyrite from Cologne to Kostheim by way of Ludwigshafen. Regierungsrat Thorn, head of the Duisberg base for the operation, ordered the youth seized, suggesting as a pretense that "the youth be accused of having been involved in activities against the state." On the night of June 28, Thorn received a call from the Gestapo reporting that the youth had been apprehended, and would appear the next morning in Cologne-Suelz. Because of the haste with which the operation was conducted, when the youth's case was evaluated, evidence of his half-breed status was simply taken from earlier information collected by the Germersheim Health Office and from earlier judgments of the anthropologist Göllner, based on a photograph he had seen of the youth. Under unclear circumstances (probably including some form of "persuasion" from the Gestapo), the mother and her new husband (she had meantime married a German) were convinced to give their permission to have A. A. sterilized. On June 30, one day later, the youth was sterilized by Professor Nieden, chief surgeon of the Prostestant Hospital in Cologne.[72] The other 500 *Rheinlandbastarde* were sterilized in similar circumstances.

The secret sterilization of the *Rheinlandbastarde* shows that German racial theorists were as concerned with German-African miscegenation as with German-Jewish miscegenation. This can also be seen in official Nazi racial policy: applicants for membership in the Nazi party were asked to certify that they had neither Jewish nor "colored blood" (*jüdische oder farbige Anschlag*) in their ancestry.[73] According to a theory popularized in Nazi circles, the Jew and the Negro were in fact related: the Jew was of an "impure race," consisting of a "hybrid" between the Negro and the Oriental.

The Slowdown

The sterilization program was brought largely to an end with the onset of World War II; only about 5 percent of all sterilizations were performed after 1939. Several reasons might be given for this slowdown. One possibility is simply that by 1939 not many people were left in Germany who fell within the criteria specified by the law and had not yet been sterilized. Another, more likely possibility is that the

German government had by this time decided to implement more dramatic methods. The year 1939 marks the beginning of the euthanasia program, in which individuals were not simply sterilized but killed (see Chapter 7).

A further reason for the slowdown appears to be that, beginning in the mid-1930s, conflicts arose within the Nazi leadership concerning the administration of the Sterilization Law. On May 19, 1937, Gerhard Wagner wrote to Hitler complaining that the Gütt-Rüdin-Ruttke commentary on the law allowed sterilization without adequate proof that the defects in question were in fact genetic. Wagner argued that in diagnosing feeble-mindedness or schizophrenia, the genetic health courts should rely less on physical exams or IQ tests and more on family history. He also wanted to shift the emphasis in the law away from defects in "the intellect," to deficiencies in the areas of "feelings and the will."[74] On January 24, 1938, Wagner wrote to Himmler outlining his objections to the sterilization of people without regard for "their total mode of living, and their total genetic heritage [*Erbgut*]"; he worried that if Germany's racial hygienists continued their "witch hunt" for inferiors (*Minderwertigkeitsschnüfflerei*), people would begin to lose confidence in the government's entire population policy.[75] He proposed that the Nazi party become more closely involved in the administration of the law.

Falk Ruttke, one of the authors of the commentary (and himself an SS officer), responded to Wagner's critique, noting that his commentary had distinguished clearly between feeble-mindedness (*Schwachsinn*) and stupidity (*Dummheit*) and had taken into account the fact that, whereas the latter affected only the intellect, the former affected the entire personality. Ruttke accused Wagner of thinking individualistically rather than in terms of "the species"; he also warned that if Wagner had his way, within a few generations the majority of German children would have to be operated on for harelip, congenital hip dislocation, or some other genetic defect.

In 1937–38 the internal debate over the Sterilization Law threatened to grow into a full-scale power struggle between Arthur Gütt in the Ministry of the Interior and Gerhard Wagner as Führer of the National Socialist Physicians' League. Wagner accused Gütt of having "falsified" the original intent of the law in his commentary; he called Gütt a "short-sighted genetic health fanatic" who had fallen victim to "medical overenthusiasm." At one point Gütt, the most powerful man in the Health Division of the Ministry of the Interior, wrote to Himmler for help, worried that he might have to resign over the affair; he asked that the matter be brought before an SS court of honor, on the grounds that both personal and professional reputations were at stake.[76]

The question was for a time resolved by the decision on May 18, 1938, to establish a committee composed of Wagner, Hans Pfundtner, and Hans-Heinrich Lammers to review the administration of the law; the recommendations that emerged from the committee reflected Wagner's concerns that the law be administered in closer consultation with the Nazi party.[77] On June 11, 1938, the Sterilization Law was modified to require that the genetic health courts be attended not just by physicians and lawyers but also by two laypersons who, "on the basis of their personal life experience, have an understanding of family life." Both participants were to be "of German or related blood"; section 2 of the revised law required that one of these lay members be a woman. In a secret internal memo justifying the law, Himmler stated that the new members of the courts should be concerned with "maternal affairs"; they were also supposed to be married, with children, and to have served in some leadership role in the Nazi party. According to the plans drawn up by Himmler's office for revising the Sterilization Law, local *Gauleiter* were to be notified before any application for sterilization could be submitted to the courts. The *Gauleiter* would then be able to present any objections he might have to court physicians responsible for recommending sterilization. Himmler's memo noted that decisions in the area of genetic care must not be considered purely medical matters; one also had to consider whether a decision contributed to the "productive value of the individual and his family for the Volk community." Decisions of the courts were to be reported to local *Gauleiter* in order to guarantee that the law was being administered in a manner "close to life and to the people" (*lebensnahe und volksnahe*).[78]

Himmler's decision to subordinate the administration of the Sterilization Law to party control may well have made physicians wary of recommending patients to be sterilized. Encumbered by the new restrictions and closely supervised by the party, doctors brought substantially fewer cases before the genetic health courts. Divisions within the party over how the law should be administered were compounded when it turned out that no one had consulted the Justice Ministry before rewriting the law. When the revisions were announced, Justice Minister Franz Gürtner became outraged that the decision to alter the law had been made without consulting him; on May 20, 1938, Security chief Reinhard Heydrich wrote to Himmler noting that, under such circumstances, the Reich Ministry of Justice was henceforth likely to ignore the genetic health courts entirely.[79]

In the summer of 1939, Gütt resigned from his post as head of health affairs in the Reich Ministry of the Interior after suffering injuries in a hunting accident on his East Prussian estate. He had been one of the strongest supporters of the sterilization program, and his resignation strengthened the hand of his critics. On September 1, 1939, German troops invaded Poland, and on the same day a government order went into effect asking that genetic health courts accept no further applications for sterilization unless there was an "exceptionally great danger" of the person in question producing offspring.[80] By this time, however, Nazi authorities were considering more ambitious programs to rid Germany of its defective genes (see Chapter 7).

The Sterilization Law was widely hailed as a signal example of the new government's determination to put a halt to German racial degeneration. The measures were dramatic, but not unprecedented. After the war, allied authorities were unable to classify the sterilizations as war crimes, because similar laws had only recently been upheld in the United States. West German authorities thus provided compensation for persons who had been sterilized only if they could prove they had been sterilized *outside* the provisions of the 1933 Sterilization Law—that is, if they could prove they were not genetically alcoholic, epileptic, feeble-minded, and so on.[81] Compulsory sterilization ended after the war in Germany, but it continued elsewhere.[82] The significance of the German law is that it set out to eliminate an entire generation of what were considered to be genetic defectives. In this sense, the sterilization program provided an early exercise for subsequent, more dramatic measures.

5 | The Control of Women

> National Socialism is the most *masculine* movement to have arisen in centuries.
> —Editorial in *Ziel und Weg*, 1933

Racial domination and the elimination of the weak and unproductive were not the only forms of oppression in the Nazi regime. One aspect of Nazi ideology that has come under increasing scrutiny in recent years is the masculine and machismo nature of that ideology.[1] The Nazi state was constructed and administered almost entirely by men; of the 2½ million members of the Nazi party in 1935, only about 5½ percent were women; women were explicitly barred from top positions in the Nazi ranks as early as January 1921.[2] Official Nazi policy was that politics is "man's business" (*Politik ist Männersache*). One Bavarian Nazi in 1930 declared: "We National Socialists take the position that politics is the business of men. The German woman is for us much too holy to be dirtied with the filth of parliament politics."[3]

Joseph Goebbels, in a novel called *Michael*, described a similar vision of the place of woman:

> The woman has the task of being pretty, and of bringing children into the world. That is not such a crude and old-fashioned idea as it sounds. The female bird cleans herself for her husband, and cares for the eggs. And in exchange, the male bird takes care of bringing home dinner. He also stands watch and fights away all enemies.[4]

The *Deutsches Ärzteblatt* expressed similar conceptions of the ideal Nordic woman:

Even after only a few months of the [Nazi] Revolution, one notices how the ideal of feminine beauty has markedly improved. Through the greatness of the Revolution—and the inner genetic power of National Socialism—the value of woman has changed, and today, one sees the ideal of the exceptionally Nordic woman thrust forward into the public arena.

A Most Masculine Movement

Despite such assertions, racial theorists before the Nazi revolution so concentrated on Nordic man that Nordic woman seems to have been somewhat difficult to imagine. In early 1926 a committee of German anthropologists and physicians sponsored by the publisher J. F. Lehmann announced a prize to find "the best Nordic head," male and female. Readers of Germany's most popular racial journals (*Volk und Rasse, Deutschlands Erneuerung,* and the like) were invited to send in photographs of individuals they considered to best represent the ideal Nordic man or woman; 500 RM were to be awarded for first place, 100 RM for second in each division. On October 1, 1926, when the contest closed, 793 male and 506 female photographs had been received. Eugen Fischer and Hans F. K. Günther served as judges for the contest. For the males, Fischer reported that there were "many excellent specimens"—so many, in fact, that the choice of the best was very difficult. But neither Fischer nor Günther felt that *any* of the female entries truly captured "the essence of the Nordic." Thus they decided that no first prize at all would be awarded to a woman; instead, three women were awarded second prizes (see Figure 20).[5]

The masculine character of the National Socialist revolution is obvious in the art and iconography of the time. The Nazis erected great statues of powerful Nordic man, statues that give forth an image of brute strength and ruthless determination.[6] This masculine imagery can also be seen on a smaller scale in medical and racial hygiene publications. Figure 21, for example, shows how the publisher Julius Friedrich Lehmann felt his company's cartouche should be changed to fit the times. Figure 22 shows two "silhouettes from medical life," printed in the journal responsible for German postgraduate education.

The masculine self-image of Nazi medical science was not something subtle or obscure in German medical publications. In a 1933 editorial in *Ziel und Weg,* the National Socialist Physicians' League proudly announced that National Socialism was "the most *masculine* [*männlichste*] movement" that had appeared in centuries.[7]

A Healthy Tendency toward Motherhood

One of the initial thrusts of Nazi population policy was to take women out of the workplace and return them to the home, where they were to have as many children as possible. This had long been one of the goals of the racial hygiene movement: in 1917 the Berlin Society for Racial Hygiene had described the role of women in society as not a "critical" (that is, intellectual) one, but rather one in which woman's "natural and healthy tendency toward motherhood" played the central role.[8] After 1933 this goal was also approved at the highest levels of the Nazi hierarchy. Rudolf Hess, for example, identified a country's possession of "a wealth of children" with "practical National Socialism."[9] To achieve this wealth, special loans amounting to about a year's salary (500–1,000 RM) were offered to married men whose wives would agree to give up jobs outside the home. For every child born, the principal owed on the loan was reduced by one-quarter. By February 1936 half a million loans valued at more than 300 million RM had been awarded, and by the end of 1940, 1,700,000 loans had been granted.[10] The government also began to push what it called the four-child family ideal, and on December 16, 1938, Hitler announced the establishment of the Honor Cross of German Motherhood (*Ehrenkreuz der deutschen Mutter*—modeled on the Iron Cross), awarded in bronze for four children, silver for six, and gold for eight (see Figure 23).[11] The first Honor Cross of German Motherhood was awarded on Mothers' Day 1939.

The number of these awards must have been sizable. In 1933, according to Nazi statistics, there were 14,317,000 married women in Germany; 25 percent of these women (3.6 million) had four or more children.[12] If similar ratios held for subsequent years (and in fact they increased), then the number of awards given for *kinderreiche* mothers (mothers with many children) must have been enormous. In 1939, for example, in the city of Lienz in East Tirol, a total of 13,727 women received the Honor Cross of German Motherhood. Gold medals were awarded to 745 women responsible for bringing a total of 7,372 children into the world.[13]

(Similar awards were not uncommon in other countries at this time: the Japanese government, for example, awarded 100,000 yen to families with more than ten children; 24,000 families were eligible for

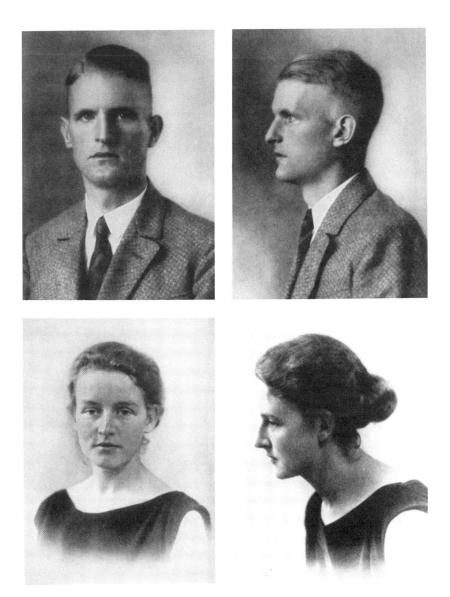

Figure 20. Prize-winning heads in the "best Nordic head contest." No first prize was awarded for the women's contest. From *Volk und Rasse*, 2(1927): 3–10.

J. F. Lehmanns Verlag / München 1930

J. F. Lehmanns Verlag / München 1936

Figure 21. Official cartouche of the Julius Friedrich Lehmann publishing house, before 1933 (above) and after 1933 (below). Lehmann was one of the largest medical publishers in the first half of the twentieth century as well as the single largest German publisher of works in the field of racial hygiene. The motto below the lion reads: "I Have Dared."

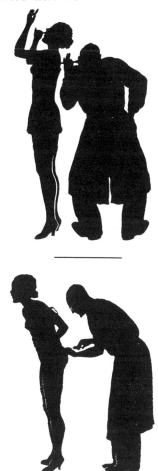

Figure 22. "Silhouettes from Medical Life." The lower caption reads: "Intra-gluteal Injection" and tells where copies of the artwork may be purchased. From *Zeitschrift für Ärztliche Fortbildung*, May 15, 1937, p. 303; October 1, 1937, p. 575.

Figure 23. The Honor Cross of German Motherhood, offered in bronze for four children, silver for six, and gold for eight. Hundreds of thousands of these awards were given to women during the Nazi period. From George Mosse, *Nazi Culture* (New York, 1968), p. iv.

these awards in 1940.[14] In 1926 the Toronto millionaire Charles Millar willed $700,000 to the Canadian woman who, by 1936, would have the most children. In 1930 the frontrunner was a certain Mrs. Brown who, at the age of forty, had already given birth to twenty-six children.)

Nazi efforts to increase the German birthrate involved a combination of propaganda, financial incentives, and special benefits. In 1937 the Health Office of Bremen established special "advising centers for the struggle against infertility." In 1938 all public officials (including professors) were required to marry or else resign; medical journals began to publish criticisms of unmarried or childless colleagues. After 1938 couples married for five years who had not yet raised a family incurred a penalty tax; grounds for divorce were broadened to include the inability of women to bear children. In 1940 the mayor of Berlin ordered all landlords owning more than four apartments to reserve at least one for families with more than three or four children. Even at the height of the war, research continued on ways to increase fertility. Professor Gauss of Tübingen, for example, explored ways that sauna treatments might cure infertility.[15] On July 16, 1942, Reich Health Führer Leonardo Conti ordered that "every means at the doctor's disposal should be used to help childless couples bear children"; for this purpose Conti ordered every German district (*Gau*) in the Reich to establish workshops (attached to local health offices) to help childless couples find ways of bearing children.[16] Even as late as 1944, Nazi medical authorities supported research to determine when in a woman's menstrual cycle it was optimal to conceive children.[17] There were also stronger measures taken, however, measures that discriminated according to race.

The Question of Abortion

As early as 1931 the Nazis introduced into parliament legislation requiring that "anyone who attempts to curb artificially the natural fertility of the German people" be punished by imprisonment for "racial treason" (*Rassenverrat*). (This statute also stipulated that anyone "contributing to the racial degeneration of the German people through intermarriage with members of the Jewish blood community" should be prosecuted in the same manner and to the same degree. This was section 5 of the *Gesetz zum Schutz der deutschen Nation.*) Soon after 1933 Nazi officials reaffirmed their opposition to any form of voluntary legalized abortion. Nazi laws allowed abortion only in cases in which the mother's life was at risk; Nazi physicians generally advised marriage as the solution to pregnancy out of wedlock.[18] (Nazi medical philosophy differed from that of socialist or communist physicians in this regard. For these latter groups, abortion was considered a fundamental right of all women—see Chapter 9). Abortion was in fact a common method of birth control in Eastern Europe in the early 1930s. In a survey of Czechoslovakian workers, Hugo Hecht of Prague reported in 1933 that three-fifths of all women of this class had had abortions—some as many as twenty-two times.[19] For the Nazis, however, abortion was "a crime against the body of the German people." In 1933 Gerhard Wagner complained that in post–World War I Germany, one fetus was aborted for every three or four babies born alive, representing some 300,000 to 500,000 pregnancies aborted every year.[20]

To reverse this trend, the Nazis enforced strict antiabortion laws inherited from the Weimar period, to which were now added stronger and broader penalties. In 1937 physicians convicted of performing abortions were commonly sentenced to ten years in prison and ten years' loss of civil rights.[21] By the beginning of the war in 1939, unauthorized abortion had been declared a treason against the "bodily fruit" of the German Volk, punishable in some cases by death. Not surprisingly, the effect of these strictures was to lower dramatically the number of applications for abortions. In the year prior to the Nazi seizure of power (1932), 43,912 German women applied for abortion on medical grounds; 34,698 of these applications were approved. In the five years between 1935 and 1940, however, there were only 14,333 applications for abortion in all of Greater Germany, and only 9,701 of these were approved.[22]

Nazi medical philosophers were not opposed to abortion under all circumstances. Bavarian Health Inspector Walter Schultze noted in 1933:

> The National Socialist state recognizes the fundamental legitimacy of section 218 [the pre-Nazi law outlawing abortion]. As a consequence of the pursuit of the selection demanded by racial hygiene, however, the state recognizes in addition to already existing exceptions [that is, where the life of the mother is in danger], the permissibility of abortion on eugenic grounds.[23]

Abortion, in other words, could be allowed if it was in the interests of racial hygiene. Schultze reflected broader Nazi opinion when he rejected "unconditionally" the legalization of abortion for family planning. In fact, sterilization and abortion for "healthy" German women remained illegal throughout the Nazi period; access to birth control in all forms was also severely curtailed.[24] At the same time, the Nazis did allow (and in some cases even required) abortions for women deemed racially inferior. The key measure was a June 26, 1935, emendation of the Sterilization Law, allowing abortions for women already slated to be sterilized.[25] The Nazis also made other exceptions. On November 10, 1938, a Lüneberg court declared abortion legal for Jews.[26] And in the spring and summer of 1943, Conti and Kaltenbrunner announced a series of measures designed to allow Polish and other women of Eastern extraction working in German factories to obtain abortions. Even in this case, however, a woman was not allowed to have an abortion if, according to her physician, the woman appeared to be "of German or related blood." If the woman made "a good racial impression," permission to have an abortion could be granted only by SS or police authority, and was generally denied. Eastern women who were granted permission to abort were commonly sent to university clinics and midwifery training schools, where medical students and midwives in training could learn to practice their trade on living models.[27]

A Solution to "the Woman Question"

The Nazi conception of women as reproductive rather than political beings was enshrined in legal doctrine. According to official Nazi policy, unmarried women were not even considered citizens of the state, but were relegated instead to a subordinate category (*Staatsangehöriger*), to which Jews were also assigned.[28] Women were granted job security in official positions only after the age of thirty-five, and beginning in 1936 women were barred from becoming lawyers, judges, and a host of other professions. The quota of female students was fixed at 10 percent. At the same time that women were denied basic civil rights, laws were passed (at the behest of Himmler) allowing "Aryan" women to bear children out of wedlock.[29] Women were also excluded from positions in which formerly they had exercised a certain amount of control. Before 1933, for example, women had occupied many of the leading positions in the German Red Cross. Under the Hitler regime, men took over most of these positions.[30]

The exclusion of women from academic and professional work was justified by German racial hygienists as a measure vital for the preservation of the race. Fritz Lenz, for example, as early as 1914 had complained: "By the time they have completed their studies, female academics, as a result of their advanced age, the loss of their beauty, and their neglect of training in home economics, are less appropriate for marriage than they once might have been. And for the overwhelming majority of girls who work outside the home, this is also the case."[31] He noted that in America the attendance of women at universities had removed the best women from the breeding population; he proposed that motherhood should be required of healthy women in the same way that military service was considered obligatory for men. Under such a system, women who by their twentieth birthday had not given birth to at least one legitimate child would be required to provide some other equivalent state or civil service, such as field work or employment by the government.[32] Lenz also opposed the rights of women to vote, to participate in sports, to attend university, and to have access to birth control or abortion.

Declining birthrates were consistently the most common theme in racial hygienists' discussion of "the woman question." What racial hygienists expected from women during this time must today be viewed as extraordinary. In 1913 Lenz reviewed an article Eugen Fischer had published in the German *Dictionary of the Sciences*. In his review Lenz rejected Fischer's judgment that a healthy woman ought to have "an average of eight or nine children" over the course of her life. He considered this figure much too low and presented instead his own opinion: "Now, it is a fact that a woman is capable of giving birth for a period of nearly thirty years. Even when we consider a woman giving birth only once every two years, this means a minimum of fifteen births per mother. Anything less than this must be considered the result of unnatural or pathological causes."[33]

Lenz's concerns were not uncommon at this time. Since the late nineteenth century, racial hygienists had warned that the German birthrate was declining; and by 1933 this had become a major concern of Nazi racial policy. In his speech of June 28, 1933, Interior Minister Wilhelm Frick declared that Germany was rapidly falling victim to the ideology of the two-child family and had already become "the most impoverished country in the world" in this regard[34] (see Figures 24–26). The birthrate had fallen from 36/1,000 in 1900 to less than 15/1,000 in 1932, particularly alarming in view of the fact that Moscow's rates had remained high throughout this period

Figure 24. "The Decline in Marital Fecundity." In 1890, one in three married women of child-bearing age (fifteen to forty-five) gave birth; by 1930, only one in eight gave birth in any given year. From *Volk und Rasse*, 8(1933): 174.

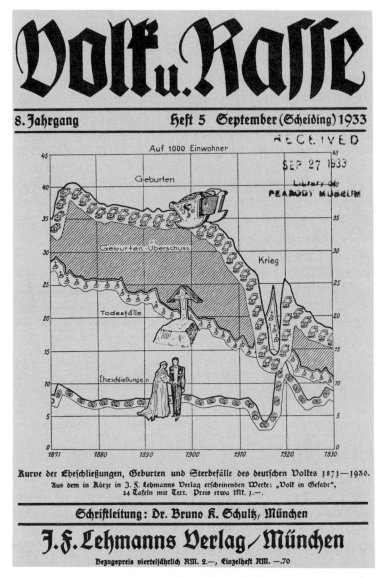

Figure 25. "Trends in Marriages, Births, and Deaths for the German People, 1871–1930." The graph shows the declining birthrate in Germany. The top line represents births; the middle, deaths; and the bottom, marriages. From the cover page of *Volk und Rasse*, 8(1933).

Figure 26. "Causes of the Decline in Births: Unemployment; Comfort; Miserliness and Greed; Poverty; Personal Prosperity; Love of Pleasure; Lack of Housing; Excess and Luxury; Fear and Timidity; Women Working outside the Home; Venereal Disease and Abortion." From Helmut, *Volk in Gefahr*, p. 51.

Figure 27. Title page of Paul Danzer, *Geburtenkrieg* (War of births), in the series *Politische Biologie*, edited by Heinz Müller. Note the Lehmann cartouche.

Figure 28. Birthrates for Germany (solid line) and Austria (broken line), 1927–1936. From Rudolf Schönhals, "Über die Auswirkung der nationalsozialistischen Bevölkerungspolitik in Marburg," *Archiv für Rassen und Gesellschaftsbiologie*, 33(1939): 44.

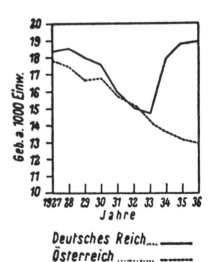

(see again Figure 4 in Chapter 1). Frick warned of the catastrophe that could ensue if such a trend continued; the racial hygiene journal *Politische Biologie* echoed Frick's fears and declared a "war of births" (*Geburtenkrieg*) to increase the population of Germany over that of its enemies (see Figure 27).

Competition with Germany's neighbors was only one of several reasons given for returning women to the home. Racial hygienists often provided economic arguments for the new policies: Otmar von Verschuer, for example, boasted in 1935 that the policy of returning women to the home was one of the principal ways the Nazis had managed to counter (male) unemployment in Germany.[35] Nazi population policy also provided an effective means of countering German feminism. In 1933, when Hitler assumed power, Germany had the largest feminist movement in the world, with over 600,000 registered members in a host of groups spanning the political spectrum. For the Nazis, however, feminism of any stripe represented a threat to the values of hearth and home. The women's movement was also commonly blamed for Germany's declining birthrates. In 1933, at a meeting of the German Society for Gynecology devoted to an examination of techniques required to implement the new Sterilization Law, Oswald Bumke, director of one of Germany's foremost psychiatric clinics, declared that "the greatest and most insane danger that threatens us is the birth strike [*Geburtenstreik*]; this threatens our entire people with extinction."[36] Martin Stämmler spoke of a "black plague" that went from door to door claiming its victims, even worse than a war or scourge in the damage it wreaked.[37] And as Hitler declared the woman's battlefield to be the home,[38] the German medical profession adopted appropriate measures: in 1933 Professor G. A. Wagner, director of the women's clinic of Berlin's Charité Hospital and editor of the *Archiv für Gynäkologie,* declared the nation's stock of ovaries a national resource and property of the German state. Wagner called for "mandatory care for these vital organs, vital not only for the individual, but for the health and future of the entire Volk."[39]

Three Million More Babies

Nazi population policy, directed toward what Wilhelm Frick called the solution to the woman question (*die Lösung der Frauenfrage*),[40] was remarkably successful in its own way—the birthrate jumped from 14.7/1,000 in 1933 to 18/1,000 in 1934 and continued to climb through the thirties. Mass marriages of SS and SA officials were held even before the *Machtergreifung* (Nazi seizure of power), and in 1933 marriages rose 23 percent over the previous year, representing what Friedrich Burgdörfer called an unprecedented achievement in world population history and a victory in the "war of births" (see Figure 28).[41] In 1938 German women gave birth to 1,347,000 children; Nazi medical statisticians took pride in pointing out that this was as many as England (with 737,000) and France (with 612,000) combined. By 1940 Germany's annual production of babies, now benefiting from newly acquired territories in the Greater German Reich (*Grossdeutschen Reich*), had jumped another 20 percent; in 1940 German women gave birth to 1,645,000 children.[42] Friedrich Burgdörfer calculated that as a direct result of National Socialist policies, the German people had produced 3 million more children than would have been born had pre-Nazi birthrates remained in effect.[43]

It is important to recognize the magnitude of the burden this placed on women. In the period 1933–1935, as the birthrate increased from 14.7/1,000 to 19/1,000, death rates due to childbirth increased by 15 percent, from 1.6 deaths/10,000 to 1.8/10,000. Despite the fact that maternal deaths per live birth dropped over this period (from 5.3/1,000 live births to 4.8/1,000 live births),[44] a total of 919 more women died in childbirth in 1935 than in 1933, as 290,000 more babies were born in Germany. The editorial staff of *Die Gesundheitsführung* cheerfully concluded from this that "every increase in live births by a thousand can be bought with the death of only three women."[45]

Ideology and Reality

Despite Nazi propaganda about returning women to the home, and despite real and dramatic increased familial burdens for women, female participation in the German labor force not only did not decrease, but actually increased throughout the Nazi era. Within a few years of the founding of the Third Reich, the proportion of women working outside the home was higher in Germany than anywhere else in the Western world. In 1938, 36 percent of German women were wage earners, compared with 26 percent in England, and 18 percent in the United States.[46] In 1937 one out of every four German employees was a woman; a total of 600,000 married women worked in factories. Child bearing does not seem to have been at the expense of women's employability. In fact, the probability of a German woman being employed was directly proportional to the number of children she had: in 1938, whereas 23 percent of women with only one child worked outside the home, 34 percent of women with five or more children did so.[47] In the Nazi period the proportion of women working outside the home grew even faster than that of men: the number of women in the German labor force increased by 16 percent from 1933 to 1938, whereas the number of men employed increased by only 6 percent.[48] The total number of women employed outside the home in 1938 was more than twice that in 1929, the most prosperous year of the Weimar Republic (13.4 million versus 6.2 million).

The forces behind these figures are not hard to understand. The ideology of keeping women in the home confronted a reality: the need to keep Germany's factories moving. As Hitler's military machine drew increasing numbers of men off the labor market, women took over jobs men had formerly held. Women thus served double duty. At the same time that women were financially coerced into having larger families, they were discouraged from competing for higher-paying professional jobs and forced to work in low-paying menial jobs.

As Nazi war plans drew women into the labor force, Nazi policymakers adapted employment policies to fit the refurbished ideology of motherhood. By modern standards, Nazi maternity-leave policy might even be considered progressive. From the sixth month of pregnancy until the third month after delivery, women were not allowed to do piecework or to work night shifts. From seven weeks before giving birth to a minimum of seven weeks after, women were not allowed to work at all. During this time working women received full pay. In the event that women were required to do other forms of labor while pregnant, they were not allowed to receive less pay for that work.[49]

After this period of grace, women returned to the factories. To reconcile the new ideal of motherhood with the need for female workers, the Nazi government established child-care centers at the workplace[50] and constructed visions of how work on the assembly line approximated life at home. Annemarie Tröger has recorded one such vision, expressed in a pamphlet issued by the Institute for Labor Research of the German Labor Front:

> The unskilled task ties a woman only loosely to her job and *above all only loosely to its purpose*. In her fantasy she enjoys visions of her children's happy faces while she is toiling for them . . . the fixed speed at the belts corresponds to the desires of women . . . they are spared

responsibility for initiative on a job which has no meaning for them. Therefore, they gladly forgo control over the pace of their work.[51]

Physicians published elaborate treatises on the mental and physical health of women who worked in factories.[52]

What about women's work as physicians? Despite Nazi prejudices against women filling professional positions, the number and proportion of women physicians actually increased throughout the Nazi period (see Table 5).[53] Editors of the women doctors' journal *Ärztin* pointed out in 1938, however, that even though there were more women physicians in Germany than ever before, this fact taken alone was misleading, because large numbers of women trained as physicians were not practicing medicine. Although the number of women graduating with medical degrees grew by nearly 20 percent between 1935 and 1938, many of these women had married, and married women were generally not allowed to practice as part of the companies responsible for administering German medical insurance (*Krankenkassen*). The number of female doctors *not* practicing medicine had grown from 278 in 1935 to 737 in 1937; taking this into account, the real increase in practicing female physicians over this period (1935–1937) was only about 6 percent—approximately

Table 5. Proportion of female physicians in Germany, 1876–1943

Year	Men and women	No. of women	% Women
1876	13,728	—	0%
1898	24,725	—	0
1909	30,558	82	0.3
1927	43,583	n.a.	n.a.
1931	47,275	2,801	6
1932	52,518	3,405	6
1934	51,673	3,602	7
1935	52,342	3,644	7
1937	55,259	4,339	8
1939	59,454	5,483	10
1943	73,960	9,426[a]	13

Source: Reichs-Gesundheitsblatt, no. 7 (1935); also *British Medical Journal*, December 4, 1937, p. 1107, and October 30, 1943, p. 554; and *Ärztin*, 15(1939): 128.

Note: These physicians include veterinarians and dentists. After 1932 the statistics include physicians from the Saarland and Danzig; data for 1939 are prewar figures for the "Altreich," including physicians in military duty.

a. Includes 1,200 women physicians brought into the Reich with the annexation of Austria (the Ostmark), Sudetenland, and eastern territories.

the same as for the profession as a whole.[54] The *British Medical Journal* reported along these same lines that, whereas in 1932, 74 percent of all of Germany's women doctors were practicing medicine, by 1937 this proportion had dropped to only 51 percent. Even in 1943, with nearly 10,000 female physicians in Germany, only about half (5,146) were salaried (that is, were admitted to practice as part of the national health insurance system); 2,210 had their own private practices, and 2,070 were not employed in any medical activity at all.[55] The *Deutsches Ärzteblatt* justified this situation by pointing out that many of these women were married and hence unable or unwilling to practice medicine.[56]

Women were represented disproportionately in certain specialties within the medical profession. In 1937, 30 percent of all pediatricians were women, whereas among other specialists fewer than 1 percent were women.[57] In 1938 only about 5 percent of Germany's 16,400 specialists (*Fachärzte*) were women, and in some fields women were not represented at all.[58] Women were also poorly represented on university faculties. In 1940 there were only forty-one women college teachers in Germany: twenty professors and twenty-one *Dozentinnen*.[59]

One reason the number of women physicians rose throughout the Nazi period was that women helped take up some of the slack when Jewish doctors were expelled from the profession. The July 1938 law excluding Jews from the practice of medicine reduced the number of male physicians practicing in Germany from 46,229 (as of January 1, 1938) to 44,089 (as of January 1, 1939). Yet the number of women practicing medicine actually rose slightly over this same period, from 3,503 to 3,636.[60] Growth in the number of women physicians continued even through the war years. When the Allied powers occupied Germany after the war, they found a surprising proportion of women physicians: Barbara von Renthe, vice president of the Board of Medical Affairs for the Soviet Zone, reported shortly after the end of the war that 35–40 percent of all doctors in Soviet-occupied sectors of Germany were women.[61] When army physicians returned to civilian duties, however, unemployment among physicians once again became a problem, and Allied forces responded in a way now familiar: Allied authorities in the Western sector maintained that "we cannot take the responsibility of permitting married women to practice when there are innumerable men who cannot make a living as resident doctors or as free practitioners."[62]

The growth in the numbers of practicing women doctors during the Nazi period can probably be attributed to a combination of the demand for physicians created by the expulsion of the Jews and the growing need for civilian physicians created by the militarization of German society. The number of Jewish physicians ultimately forced from their jobs (about 7,000) was about equal to the number of women who practiced medicine during the Nazi regime. The exclusion of such a large number of practitioners from the profession, even in times of relative unemployment, meant that the presence of women in the profession could be tolerated as the lesser of two evils. As we shall see in the concluding chapter, preparations for war eventually created a shortage of physicians—so much so that some Jewish physicians were rehired and women were encouraged once again to practice medicine. All of which shows that even the strongest of ideological structures may bend under the pressures of social, economic, or military expediency.

6 Anti-Semitism in the German Medical Community

> No one approves of the new Sterilization Laws more than I do, but I must repeat over and over again, that they constitute only a beginning.
>
> —Erwin Baur, director,
>   Kaiser Wilhelm Institut für Biologie, 1933

On November 2, 1933, Bavarian Health Inspector Walter Schultze announced in a speech before Munich's newly founded State Medical Academy that Germany's Sterilization Law would not be sufficient to stop the horde of psychopaths, feeble-minded, and other "inferior types" threatening the German race. Schultze declared that stronger measures could and would be taken, and that indeed "such measures have already to some degree been initiated in our present concentration camps."[1] Stronger measures were still to come.

The Nuremberg Laws

In the fall of 1935 Hitler signed into law a series of three measures—the so-called Nuremberg Laws—to further "cleanse" the German population from unwanted elements. The Reich Citizenship Law (*Reichsbürgergesetz*) of September 15, 1935, distinguished between citizens and residents (*Reichsbürger* and *Staatsangehöriger*). Citizens, the more exclusive category, included only those "of German or related blood who through their behavior make it evident that they are willing and able faithfully to serve the German people and nation." Jews in particular (but also single women!) were considered residents and were excluded from many privileges now accorded only to citizens.

Also on September 15, the Law for the Protection of German Blood and German Honor (*Gesetz zum Schutze des deutschen Blutes und der deutschen Ehre,* or Blood Protection Law) was announced, forbidding both marriage and sexual relations between non-Jews and Jews, and later extended to all "non-Aryans." A "full Jew" was defined as anyone with at least three grandparents who were Jews; individuals with lesser fractions of Jewish ancestry were considered "half-breeds" of either the first or second degree (*Mischlinge ersten oder zweiten Grades*). The Blood Protection Law specified very precisely which of these groups could marry which others (see Figure 29); for example, individuals with only one-quarter Jewish ancestry were considered Germans and allowed to marry other Germans—unless those other Germans were themselves one-quarter Jewish, in which case there was the danger that some of the offspring would be half Jewish (according to a peculiar kind of Mendelian logic), and so the marriage would be illegal. The Blood Protection Law further stipulated that Jews were forbidden to employ German servants under the age of forty-five in their households or to fly the national colors.

On October 18, 1935, the Nazi government passed a third and final measure in this series, the Law for the Protection of the Genetic Health of the German People (*Gesetz zum Schutze der Erbgesundheit des Deutschen Volkes,* or Marital Health Law), requiring couples to submit to medical examination before marriage to see if "racial damage" might be involved; the law forbade marriage between individuals suffering from venereal disease, feeble-mindedness, epilepsy, or any of the other "genetic infirmities" specified in the 1933 Sterilization Law. Those considered genetically ill (*Erbkranken*) were permitted to marry other genetically ill, but only after being sterilized to ensure that they would not leave any offspring.[2]

The Reich Citizenship Law was intended to deprive those "not of German blood" of all political rights; the Blood Protection Law, in contrast, was designed to separate Jews from non-Jews in the sphere of reproductive and familial relations. Sexual traffic between Germans and Jews was outlawed as "racial pollution" (*Rassenschande*); violations of the law could be punished by imprisonment in the years before the war and by death after the outbreak of war.[3]

"Sexual traffic" (*Geschlechtsverkehr*) was originally intended to refer only to sexual intercourse. It was not long, however, before the legal definition of this term was broadened to include almost any kind of sexual activity. In 1936, for example, a Hamburg physician was charged with racial pollution for attempting to kiss an eighteen-year-

Übersichtstafel, betreffend die Zulässigkeit der Eheschließungen zwischen Ariern und Nichtariern.

R.Bü.G. = Reichsbürgergesetz,
G.Sch.d.Bl. = Gesetz zum Schutze des deutschen Blutes und der deutschen Ehre.
AVO. = Ausführungsverordnung.

○	bedeutet: Staatsangehöriger deutschen oder artverwandten Blutes	◐ (horizontal)	von 2 jüdischen Großeltern abstammender jüdischer Mischling
◔	von 1 jüdischen Großelternteil abstammender jüdischer Mischling (§ 2 d. 1. VO. R. Bü. G.)	● (3/4)	von 3 oder 4 jüdischen Großeltern abstammender Jude (§ 5 d. 1. VO. R. Bü. G.)

Lfd. Nr.	Beabsichtigte Ehepartner	Zulässigkeit der Ehe	Lfd. Nr.	Beabsichtigte Ehepartner	Zulässigkeit der Ehe
	Gruppe I:			**Gruppe III:**	
1	○+○	zulässig	9	◐+○	wie bei Nr. 3
2	○+◔	zulässig	10	◐+◔	wie bei Nr. 7
3	○+◐	a) zulässig mit besonderer Genehmigung; § 3 AVO. G.Sch.d.Bl.	11	◐+◐	zulässig (in AVO. G.Sch.d.Bl. nicht erörtert)
		b) verboten in den Sonderfällen a bis d; § 5 (2) d. 1.VO. R.Bü.G.	12	◐+●	zulässig, aber der jüdische Mischling wird Jude n. § 5 (2) b d. 1.VO. R.Bü.G.
4	○+●	verboten § 1 G.Sch.d.Bl.			
	Gruppe II:			**Gruppe IV:**	
5	◔+○	wie bei Nr. 2	13	●+○	wie bei Nr. 4
6	◔+◔	soll nicht geschlossen werden; § 4 AVO. G.Sch.d.Bl.	14	●+◔	wie bei Nr. 8
7	◔+◐	a) zulässig mit besonderer Genehmigung, § 3 AVO. G.Sch.d.Bl.	15	●+◐	wie bei Nr. 12
		b) verboten in den Sonderfällen a bis d; § 5 (2) d. 1.VO. R.Bü.G.	16	●+●	zulässig
8	◔+●	verboten § 2 AVO. G.Sch.d.Bl.			

Figure 29. "Overview of the Admissibility of Marriage between Aryans and non-Aryans." This chart depicts who might marry whom, according to Germany's racial legislation. The white circles represent "pure Germans"; the circles with black indicate the proportion of "Jewish blood." "Allowable" (*zulässig*), for example, was a marriage between a full Aryan and a one-quarter Jew (case 2). "Not allowed" (*verboten*) was a marriage between a one-quarter Jew and a three-quarters Jew (case 8). The chart was constructed by Dr. Spranger of the Reich Health Office. From *Zeitschrift für Ärztliche Fortbildung*, 33(1936): 115.

Figure 30. "The Trend in Racial Pollution." The graph shows the growing danger of German-Jewish miscegenation. The side caption cites Goethe's words: "The important thing is that the race remains pure: in this way, we become a people! And only in this way will we be able to preserve and enhance the German character." From *Volk und Rasse,* 12(1937): 390.

old "Aryan" patient; the physician was convicted and sentenced to 2½ years for his crime. (The editors of the exiled socialist physicians' *Internationales Ärztliches Bulletin* responded curiously to this conviction, arguing that "every expert knows that young women often do not have the ability to distinguish true experience from fantasy.")[4] Penalties even for such minor infractions stiffened after 1939. On March 13, 1942, for example, a Nuremberg court convicted a Jewish man for having violated the law and sentenced him to death, despite the fact that the only evidence presented was that he had kissed and embraced a woman "of German blood."

"Justice" according to the Nuremberg Laws was meted out differently to women and to men. Men accused of violating the Blood Protection Law were accused either of "an attack on German blood" (if they were Jewish) or of "treason against their own blood" (if they were "German"). But according to section 2 of the law, women (whether Jewish or not) could not be punished for violations of the law because, it was argued, women are "passive" in the sphere of sexual relations.[5]

These were the legal provisions. In practice, the situation could be quite different. After serving their time, individuals convicted of violating the Blood Protection Law (usually men) had their case brought before the local Gestapo for review to determine whether further "protective custody" was required. For Jews, this almost invariably meant transfer to a concentration camp. Non-Jews were also often detained on the grounds that they presented a "health risk" to the broader German population.[6] On June 12, 1937, SD chief Reinhard Heydrich ordered that Jewish women convicted of violating the Blood Protection Law be taken into custody if they posed a "health risk" to the German public; non-Jewish women were to be taken into custody only if they had Jewish relatives or children.

When the Nuremberg Laws were announced in the fall of 1935, German medical journals applauded the measures. Several journals published charts indicating whether individuals with a certain fraction of "Jewish blood" were fit to marry individuals of a given fraction (see again Figure 29).[7] The *Deutsches Ärzteblatt* saluted the Blood Protection Law as a measure "of historic importance," arguing that the law would help protect the German "body" against further encroachment of "foreign racial elements" and help to "cleanse the body of our Volk." The journal greeted the Marital Health Law passed shortly thereafter as "completing" the earlier Blood Protection

Law; the Marital Health Law would "help secure the health and strength of the people for centuries to come."[8]

The fact that medical journals praised the Nuremberg Laws is not surprising, given the context of the times. What is perhaps more surprising is that several journals were active in calling for such laws early in the Nazi regime. In the summer of 1933, for example, the *Deutsches Ärzteblatt* warned against the marriage of Jews and non-Jews and called for a ban on all interracial marriage.[9] Germany's popular racial hygiene journals also joined in this call (see Figure 30).

Demands for an end to German-Jewish intermarriage were commonly defended as part of a broader program of genetic and racial care. On August 25, 1933, for example, Walter Gmelin, head of the Health Office of Schwäbisch-Hall, published an article in the *Ärztliche Rundschau* asking physicians to help construct racial legislation. In harmony with racial hygiene orthodoxy, he noted that such legislation encompassed both negative and positive measures. Negative measures included the Sterilization Law, marital sanctions, certain forms of birth control or abortion, and increased powers to confine individuals to psychiatric institutions. The more important positive measures included support for "valuable genetic lines" and incentives for families of good stock to have many children. Gmelin also mentioned a further aspect of "positive racial policy": legislation designed to separate Aryan from non-Aryan families.[10]

Gmelin argued that the effective separation of Aryan from non-Aryan families required the establishment of exact anthropological criteria for racial affiliation. This would be important not only for carrying out the provisions of the Civil Service Law but also for impending legislation that would determine German citizenship on racial grounds. Section 4 of the Nazi party program had required that "Volk comrades" be "of German blood, independent of religion"; Gmelin pointed out that this would also soon become one of the legal foundations of the Nazi state, and that as a consequence physicians trained in genetics would come to exercise a new and important role in society. Geneticists, Gmelin claimed, would determine who was a Jew and who was not. This would not be an easy task because racial lines no longer followed confessional lines. Given the large numbers of Jews who had converted to Protestantism or Catholicism, Gmelin argued, religion alone was no longer a reliable measure of one's race; only the use of physicians trained in genetics would ensure that racial policy was grounded in "a sound scientific basis."[11]

Gmelin therefore suggested that the German government launch a massive effort to construct a comprehensive genetic registry (*erbbiologische Registrierung*) of the German population in order to determine the scale of the problems German health authorities would have to face.[12] Gmelin was not the only one calling for the construction of genetic registries at this time. As early as 1930 Kurt Thomalla had proposed that all Germans carry a health pass (*Gesundheitspass*), which would include vital information on one's genetic and racial health. Shortly thereafter, Walther Darré recommended the establishment of racial offices (*Rassenämter*) headed by physicians trained in genetics, whose duties would be to construct comprehensive files on genetic defectives.[13] On February 17 and 18, 1935, the Nazi party newspaper *Völkischer Beobachter* announced the introduction of ancestral health books (*Gesundheitsstammbücher*) to be carried by everyone in the Reich; the paper claimed that the purpose of these books was not to track down defectives but to facilitate "planning the health of the population." And on May 21, 1935, Wilhelm Frick ordered every health office in the Reich to establish special advisory centers for genetic and racial care (*Beratungsstelle für Erb- und Rassenpflege*), whose purpose would be not only to certify couples as "fit to marry" but also to construct a comprehensive "genetic-biological map" covering every region of the country and several regions outside the country as well.[14]

The participation of physicians in the administration of the Nuremberg Laws was intended to guarantee that concerns such as those raised by Gmelin were carefully considered. Early in 1936 the Reich Ministry of the Interior announced the creation of a Committee for the Protection of German Blood (*Reichsausschuss zum Schutze des Deutschen Blutes*), whose duties would be to receive all applications for marriage between Jews and non-Jews. Members of the committee included Secretary of State Wilhelm Stuckart; SA Sanitätsgruppenführer Hermann Brauneck, head of the Bremen Health Office; Arthur Gütt, head of health affairs for the Ministry of the Interior; Gerhard Wagner, head of the National Socialist Physicians' League; Walter Gross, head of the Office of Racial Policy; Oswald Pohl, chief administrative officer in the Reich Security Office; and Erich Volkmar of the Reich Ministry of Justice. Among the seven members responsible for supervising the adjudication of the Blood Protection Law, five were medical doctors.[15]

Given the (self-) censorship of the German medical press, it is perhaps not surprising that there is no record of opposition to the Nuremberg Laws in any German medical journal of the time. It should be clear, however, that this was not because physicians were not involved in the laws. Physicians were commonly hailed as pioneers in both the construction and the administration of the laws. When Gerhard Wagner died in the spring of 1939, Fritz Bartels noted that Wagner's name would "forever" be remembered in association with the Nuremberg Laws regulating genetic disease and racial miscegenation.[16]

Marital Counseling: The Medical Rx for Racial Miscegenation

Legal sanctions against racial miscegenation were not new to Germany in the 1930s. In 1908 the German Reichstag had passed legislation outlawing intermarriage between German citizens and the indigenous populations of German Southwest Africa; the law declared null and void all previous marriages of this kind. Physicians in the nineteenth century had commonly argued that racial intermarriage produced either infertility (what in America was known as "mulism") or some other form of racial degeneration. Such views continued long into the twentieth century. Until sometime in the 1930s or 1940s, most geneticists in Europe and America assumed that the crossing of widely divergent races (such as black and white) would produce degenerate offspring.[17] Eugen Fischer's study of the effects of racial crossing between native Hottentots and white settlers in Southwest Africa (the so-called Rehobother Bastards) was an attempt not only to demonstrate Mendelian inheritance in humans but also to discover any negative medical consequences of racial intermarriage. Fischer himself had tried to remain neutral on this question; most of his colleagues, however, did not. Fritz Lenz, for example, in his 1931 *Menschliche Auslese,* argued that racial miscegenation was indeed harmful, given that only a defective individual would ever entertain marriage with someone from another distant race. He claimed that white men who entered into unions with "native" women were generally inferior to men who remained with their own kind; the same could be said for women who entered into such a liaison. Lenz cited the nineteenth-century naturalist Louis Agassiz in support of the concept of hybrid inferiority; he also hoped that with the growth of "Nordic" and of "Zionist" consciousness, German-Jewish miscegenation could be held in check.[18] During World War II, German soldiers were not allowed to marry women who had previously been married to Jews; the reason given for this restriction was that such women had shown themselves to lack an appropriate "racial instinct."[19]

The danger of racial miscegenation was a common theme of early Nazi medical writings. In 1932 the historian of science Reinhold Müller published an article in *Ziel und Weg* claiming that the degeneration of the Nordic race had begun on August 2, 338 B.C., when Phillip of Macedon defeated Athens and Thebes in the battle of Choronea. According to Müller, this battle marked the beginning of an era of Alexandrian and Hellenistic internationalism, along with the first great emancipation of the Jews, and the eventual downfall of Rome due to racial mixing. Müller asserted that the "Verniggerung" and "Verjudung" of the Nordic race had gone so far in some countries (for example, France) that rehabilitation would be almost impossible.[20]

One of the major thrusts of Nazi policy was to reverse the trend toward racial intermarriage. In 1931 the SS required that members of the elite corps desiring to marry had to follow strict rules preventing marriage "outside the race." On December 31, 1931, Himmler established a special Racial Office of the SS (Rasseamt der SS), responsible for guaranteeing that all SS marriages—and later, all sexual relations on the part of SS men—were in accord with Nazi racial principles. (According to SS regulations, only SS physicians could approve SS engagements or marriages.) The duties of this office were substantial: in the early years of the Nazi regime, the office (headed by Walther Darré and then by SS Brigadeführer Reischle) approved an average of 1,100–1,700 engagements each month.[21] The principles developed for SS marital exams, praised by Germany's leading racial hygienists,[22] were also later used as a model for broader civilian racial legislation. In the course of the 1930s, as the Racial Office became involved in certifying civilian marriages, its activities increased substantially. In the single month of May 1937, the genealogical bureau of the office (the Sippenamt) examined 20,000 applications for engagement.[23]

The administration of the Nuremberg Laws was made easier by the fact that there was already an institutional apparatus in Germany for "marital counseling." Shortly after World War I, the German government took steps to involve the state in counseling. On January 11, 1920, the Weimar government passed a law authorizing the publication and distribution throughout the Reich of a "Pamphlet for Couples Engaged to be Married." The pamphlet urged anyone considering marriage to seek expert medical advice and to be wary of the dangers of venereal disease, tuberculosis, mental illness, and other ills that might ruin a healthy marriage. The government authorized the establishment of counseling centers to help people decide on "a quality marriage"; and in 1926 the counseling program was expanded to allow for counseling based on the principles of racial hygiene.[24] German physicians generally welcomed this move.

By the end of the Weimar period, Berlin could boast more than a dozen marital counseling centers, and Berlin was not unusual in this regard. In 1932, of the ninety-eight German cities with more than 50,000 inhabitants, forty-nine had marital counseling centers (*Eheberatungsstelle*); in 1930 the state of Prussia alone had 200 such centers.[25] Rainer Fetscher pointed out at the beginning of 1933, however, that most of these centers did little more than pencil pushing. In 1931, for example, the three largest centers in Germany received a total of only 1,822 visits for marital, premarital, and sexual counseling. The most active of these was Fetscher's own center in Dresden with 1,066 visitors; Berlin's center received only 270 visitors; and only seven centers in the entire country counseled more than 100 people that year.[26]

The Nuremberg Laws enacted in the fall of 1935 modified and expanded activities previously covered by marital counseling centers. The new laws made obligatory what had earlier been voluntary and greatly increased the scope of such counseling. Counseling was now to become an integral part of German public health; counseling bodies were attached to the Reich Health Office, the official government body responsible (since 1871) for health affairs of the German populace. Preparations for an expanded role of marital counseling began several months before the passage of the Nuremberg Laws. The July 3, 1934, Law for the Unification of German Health Affairs required that Reich health offices investigate not only general health but also genetic health and genealogy. With the passage of the Nuremberg Laws in the fall of 1935, the advisory centers for genetic and racial care attached to local health offices took over primary responsibility for administering the laws.

Medical journals described the activities of these advisory centers. Physicians employed there were responsible for issuing certificates testifying that one was "fit to marry" (*Ehetauglichkeitszeugnisse*);

these certificates were required in order to obtain a marriage license. For the marital health certificate, one had to submit to a medical examination, which generally lasted about three-quarters of an hour (longer, one journal reported, if the individual had passed only the third or fourth grade). The physician would typically take blood samples and lung X-rays and perform other clinical or neurological tests. In ambiguous cases, experts from one of Germany's thirty-odd institutes for racial hygiene might be consulted (see Appendix B). Examinations usually cost the patient about five RM; the certificate issued was valid for only six months after examination.[27]

Individuals who failed the genetic health exams and were refused the marital health certificate could appeal this decision to their local genetic health court. Physicians at Berlin's Policlinic for Genetic and Racial Care, however, reported that only about 5 percent of those examined were ever turned down. Physicians at the clinic stressed the importance of early counseling—preferably before engagement—in order to minimize trauma for all parties involved. They also cautioned that marital counseling centers must not get the reputation of being a kind of genetic police (*Erbpolizei*).[28]

Anyone found violating an advisory center's decision against marriage could be sentenced to prison. In one case, a woman who had been sterilized for feeble-mindedness in 1935 married a "healthy German" at the beginning of World War II. The two were discovered and were convicted of violating the Marital Health Law; the man was sentenced to four months of prison, and the woman to two months.[29]

The duties associated with the measurement of marital fitness expanded the responsibilities of the German physician nearly as much as did the Sterilization Law. One Berlin counseling center examined 10,000 individuals over a period of three years (1934–1937). By 1937 this particular center had constructed more than 400 genetic files (*Erbkartei*) and 13,000 regional files on individuals in the area. Arthur Gütt claimed that from the work of these centers would eventually come "a genetic registry of the entire German people," making possible for the first time universal marital counseling.[30]

In order to keep up with these new duties, the Reich health offices were greatly expanded. By the beginning of 1937, 742 health offices had been established throughout the Reich, to which were appointed 2,000 full-time physicians, 4,000 part-time physicians, 3,700 nurses, 800 technical assistants, 800 health inspectors, and 2,000 clerical personnel.[31] The office continued to grow over the course of the next several years. In 1937 the Central Reich Health Office in Berlin was enlarged; the new office contained special divisions for marital counseling, for sterilization, for genetic registration, and for questions of Jewish miscegenation. These were all included under the rubric of "genetic and racial care."[32]

Some sense of what genetic and racial care comprised can be seen from the following description of one of the special institutes established by the Reich Health Office. In December 1937 Dr. Franz Orsós, president of Hungary's National Association of Physicians (Mone), reported in German medical journals on his recent tour of the Reich Health Office in Berlin. Orsós was impressed with the activities of the Institute for Racial Protection, Criminal Psychology, and Criminal Biology, established as part of the expanded Reich Health Office. Research at the institute included the study of the physical and mental condition of German workers, criminal biology, the question of "half-breeds" (*Mischlingsforschung*), and experimental genetics.[33] Investigative medical personnel at the institute had also been granted broad police powers to ensure that individuals responsible for spreading venereal diseases could be identified and treated.

Orsós was especially intrigued by the institute's research into the question of Gypsy-German miscegenation. The Hungarian medical leader reported that German research had uncovered the fact that "pure" Gypsies were relatively "harmless and upstanding," and that problems really only arose when Gypsies bred with Germans. Orsós was also impressed with the efforts that had been put into the demonstration of such claims. In 1937 health officers at the institute could show him "a table several meters in length on which in tiny, millimeter-size letters and numbers the genealogical tree of all Gypsies living in Germany for the last ten generations had been charted." Orsós reported that "no one—least of all the Gypsies themselves—had ever imagined there might be created such an institute, or that such an institute might be able to undertake such a careful and comprehensive analysis of the origins and descent of a Gypsy stock [*Zigeunerstamm*]." Officials at the institute told Orsós that information gathered there would be used to help research the "future development of all peoples, especially the German."[34]

The intent of the Marital Health Law was that ultimately everyone should have a certificate prior to marriage. Practically speaking, however, this was impossible. The Reich Health Office recognized the need for a transition period during which only those suspected of "genetic infirmity" or other health violation would be expected to produce such a certificate. Even so, German health authorities were never able to comply fully with section 2 of the Marital Health Law, requiring that *all* individuals wanting to marry must undergo a marital health exam. In February 1938 Arthur Gütt admitted in a letter to Himmler that the resources of the Reich Health Office were simply not sufficient to guarantee that every individual could obtain a medical certificate before marriage. Permission to marry was often granted after only a cursory examination; health officials ordered comprehensive examinations only when it appeared to the examiner that an individual's "fitness" was in question. This, Gütt argued, helped prevent the overwhelming bulk of defective marriages (*gröbste Unheil*), without bringing to a halt the entire process of marriage.[35]

The laws nevertheless had their effect. The Nuremberg and Sterilization laws were probably responsible more than anything else for the expansion of German medical services in the early years of the Nazi regime. Despite the exclusion of the Jews, the total number of medical personnel actually rose throughout the Nazi period, from 287,000 in 1935 to 300,000 in 1939.[36] After a slight decline in 1933, the number of physicians in Germany grew from 52,342 in 1935 to more than 70,000 in the war years (see Chapter 5). Medicine prospered under the Nazis, as Germans under Nazi guidance became increasingly obsessed with marital, racial, and physical fitness.

(It was in the Nazi period that German physicians apparently first instituted the regular "checkup." Beginning in the early years of the regime, everyone in Germany was required to undergo a medical exam at age six [before entering school]; ten [for entry into the Deutsches Jungvolk or the Bund Jung Mädel]; fourteen [for graduation from elementary school and admission into the Hitler Youth]; and eighteen [for entry into the army or Reich Work Service]. At each of these stages, one received a medical certificate.)[37]

Perhaps what is most disturbing is that the Nuremberg Laws were generally considered *public health measures*. The Blood Protection Law was viewed not simply as an anti-Semitic law but as a health law, and was listed among the official measures of German health legislation, in the *Sammlung Deutscher Gesundheitsgesetze*.[38] German medical journals commonly described racial miscegenation as a "public health hazard"; scholars analyzing the racial makeup of a particular community claimed to be producing a "racial diagnosis" (*Rassen-

diagnose).³⁹ Germany's leading health officials saw the prevention of human genetic disease, along with the prevention of racial miscegenation, as part of a single program of responsible public health policy.⁴⁰

The Origins of Anti-Semitism in the Medical Profession

Jews joined the European medical profession in large numbers beginning in the Middle Ages, partly because medicine was one of the few professions open to Jews. Prior to the nineteenth century, Jews could not own land, hold public office, or participate in other social or community affairs.⁴¹ Jews were first admitted to a German medical school at Frankfurt an der Oder in 1678; in 1721 the first Jew graduated from a German university.⁴² In the nineteenth century Jews began to enter the medical profession in larger numbers, especially after the opening up of the universities in the 1830s and 1840s. By the end of the century they constituted about 16 percent of the German medical profession, despite being (according to the census of 1871) only about 1 percent of the German population. In Berlin at this time, approximately one-third of all physicians were Jewish.

The turning point in the marriage of medical racial hygiene and Nordic supremacy was World War I. Prior to this time, the racial hygiene movement was less anti-Semitic than nationalist or meritocratic. Jews were not barred from the movement, and there were in fact a few members with Jewish ancestry.⁴³ Alfred Ploetz ranked the Jews among the "cultured races" of the world (by virtue of their "Aryan ancestry"); Lenz and other leaders in the early movement did not consider themselves anti-Semitic. Even the Nordic supremacist *Politisch-anthropologische Revue* reported periodically (and without comment) news from Jewish publications such as *Ben Israel* and the *Jüdisches Volksblatt*.

This is not to say that anti-Semitism was not an important part of German society before this time. By World War I anti-Semitism had already become a political force in Germany. Support for the Anti-Semitic People's party (Antisemitische Volkspartei) grew from 12,000 votes in 1887 to 264,000 in 1893 and 350,000 on the eve of World War I. In the 1907 national elections, the Anti-Semitic party (and affiliated bodies) won twenty-one seats in the German Reichstag. The volkish and Nordic movements that coalesced around Hitler's National Socialist Workers' party in 1919 and 1920 were able to draw upon nationalist movements (such as the Anti-Semitic party and the Pan-German League) organized prior to the war.

The effect of the war was to exacerbate the chauvinism of the prewar period; this was as true for physicians as for anyone else. Thousands of German physicians returned from World War I only to face a destroyed economy and massive unemployment. Hundreds of immigrant Jewish physicians, fleeing Tsarist pogroms (or the pressures of revolutionary Russia), arrived in Germany looking for work; competition from these physicians helped fuel anti-Semitism within the profession. Jews became a convenient scapegoat for the troubles of the twenties: Jews were blamed for having lost the war or for sowing the seed of revolution; Jews were accused of stealing German jobs or of trading intuitive, "people-oriented science" for theoretical abstractions. Jews were attacked as individualists or socialists, materialists or formalists; Jews were singled out as the cause of both capitalist chaos and Bolshevist tyranny. Jews were accused of organizing mysterious financial forces to control the world economy.[44]

The growth of chauvinism or racism can never be entirely explained by reference to larger social and economic processes; these processes can, however, be important for understanding how such views become attractive to large masses of people or to leaders people are willing to follow. Views judged extreme in one context can become mainstream in another; attitudes become plastic or polarized in times of political or economic crisis. The growth of anti-Semitism in the German medical profession must be understood with reference to a series of transformations in the social and economic status of physicians in the early decades of the twentieth century.

The years before the rise of the Nazis saw the bureaucratization, socialization, and scientization of German medicine. One of the most important new institutions that arose in the last decades of the nineteenth century were the so-called *Krankenkassen*—state-supported companies established under Bismarck (in the 1880s) to provide medical insurance for the German population. In 1883 the German government approved the first comprehensive medical insurance program in history. In 1884 this was extended to cover accident insurance, and in 1889 to social security for the elderly (*Rentenversicherung*). The establishment of socialized medicine was in one sense a victory for the Social Democrats, long-time advocates of such reforms. It was also a successful attempt on the part of moderate social forces to steal the socialists' thunder. In the Bismarckian era emerged a host of sweeping social reforms—conceded by German government and industry only because, without such reforms, revolutionary Social Democracy would probably have made even more rapid inroads into the German population.[45]

The establishment of medical insurance companies in the late nineteenth century followed closely upon the establishment of scientific laboratories in industry and universities. Medical insurance companies moved to create large, laboratory-based clinics within which member physicians of a particular company would locate their offices. In the earliest years of socialized medicine, private practice differed from insurance-supported practice only in the manner of funding. In the last decade of the nineteenth century, however, clinics began to take on more bureaucratic features—including waiting rooms, scheduled appointments, and centralized services. Medicine (as the Nazis would later complain) was becoming a "business."

In the decades before the rise of National Socialism, the proportion of Germans covered by socialized medical insurance grew dramatically: from 1883 to 1928 the proportion rose from only 9 percent to 33 percent, and the power of the insurance companies grew correspondingly. Companies began to regulate the workload of doctors in order to distribute services more evenly or more profitably. They implemented quality and cost controls. They regulated the access of patients to doctors, and patients began to lose the right to choose their own doctors. Insurance companies, in other words, came to exercise increasing control over the organization of medical practice. In 1894 they were granted the right to exclude physicians who persisted in maintaining a private practice.

Many physicians resented the increasing power of the insurance companies. Doctors in private practice saw the "socialization" of medicine as a threat to their ability to attract patients, particularly when a growing proportion of the population belonged to programs that reimbursed only those costs incurred from approved company-member physicians.

In 1900 a group of doctors, inspired by the Leipzig physician Hermann Hartmann, organized to form an association (later called the Hartmannbund) to strengthen the bargaining power of physicians vis-à-vis the insurance companies. By 1911 more than 95 percent of Germany's physicians had joined the Hartmannbund.[46] A key issue was whether patients would have the right to choose their own physicians. Dissatisfaction within the profession over this and other issues was such that in 1913 doctors went on strike for nearly a year to achieve their demands.

The result of the physicians' strike was that for ten years physicians gained the right to have patients choose their doctor. In 1923, however, the medical insurance companies, with the assistance of the Social Democrats, managed to have this right abolished. Insurance companies argued that social medicine required the "rationalization" of decisions concerning the allocation of medical resources, and that without such rationalization, socialized medicine (that is, the insurance companies) might not survive the economic distress of the postwar period.

With the rise of the Social Democrats to power after World War I, many physicians blamed the insurance companies for the economic difficulties of the profession. The peculiar situation of physicians fostered what seems today like a curious set of ideological allegiances. The insurance companies had been fostered in the name of socialism—socialized medicine—as part of a broader series of reforms advocated by the (Marxist) Social Democrats, designed to guarantee a minimum standard of health for the German population. And yet, to many physicians, the insurance companies were large, impersonal bureaucratic structures exercising a powerful influence over how, when, and for whom a physician might practice medicine. The companies were equated not just with socialism but also with liberalism and capitalism. The companies were, after all, profit-making institutions: relations between doctor and patient were seen essentially in economic terms. Physicians who resented the power of the companies were able to attack them as both socialist and capitalist; physicians accused the Social Democrats of having delivered German medicine into the hands of the capitalist, socialist, and (as we shall see) Jewish health care monopoly.

The growth of anti-Semitism in the German medical profession was tied to this broader climate of dissatisfaction with the economic organization of the profession. There are several elements to this. First, Jews were a conspicuous and growing minority within the medical community. In the wake of World War I, 75,000 Jews immigrated into Germany from the East, increasing Germany's Jewish population by nearly 20 percent.[47] In the liberal climate of the Weimar period,

Jews managed to obtain positions in German universities and in German government. They were also active in socialist politics: most of the leading figures in the Association of Socialist Physicians, for example, were Jewish (see Chapter 9). Jews played an active role in the administration of Germany's social insurance companies—companies the Nazis would later identify with "Jewish-Bolshevist capitalism."

Jews had long served as an easy scapegoat in troubled times, and in the economically depressed postwar years anti-Semitism began to take on stronger forms. Many doctors saw Jews as taking jobs that "Germans" might have assumed; high unemployment among physicians accentuated these sentiments. Among doctors, competition for practice within the insurance companies had already begun in the late nineteenth century and sharpened with the rapid growth in the number of doctors graduating from German medical schools. In the period 1887–1898, for example, the number of doctors in Germany grew by more than 52 percent, although the German population grew by only 14 percent. Competition for positions in the insurance companies was intensified by the fact that, in the early months after World War I, 5,000 physicians returned from war duty looking for work, only to face an overburdened job market and a devastated economy.

The difficult times of the twenties helps to explain why, in 1933, so many young physicians voted National Socialist. Most Nazi doctors received their education in the period 1920–1930, a time of growing nationalism and massive unemployment. Anti-Semitism became a common feature of medical ideology. In July 1920, the German Medical Association debated the "Jewish question" and resolved that issues of race or politics should not be introduced into medical schools and that Jewish students should not be refused posts at hospitals. In the mid-twenties, however, medical students in Graz refused to allow Jews in their medical organizations; and in Königsberg, Jews and foreign students were in one instance actually thrown from university classrooms (the faculty, however, refused to accept student demands that they be expelled). In 1923 Ludwig Plate, one of the earliest members of the Society for Racial Hygiene and successor to Ernst Haeckel's chair of zoology at Jena, advised Jewish students against taking his course, on the grounds that they would probably find what he had to say objectionable.[48]

The Exclusion of Jews from German Medicine

Nazi propagandists exploited the intimacy of the traditional doctor-patient relationship to argue that Jewish physicians posed a special danger to the German people. In the summer of 1933, one of the rallying cries of the new journal *German Public Health from Blood and Earth* was to "put an end to the pernicious influence of Jews in medicine." The journal carried a biweekly cartoon caricaturing the "Life and Deeds of Mr. Isidor Färben," a physician with exaggerated Jewish features invented to attack "Jewish medicine." Kurt Holz, editor of *Der Stürmer,* argued in the new journal that, bad as it was that Jewish lawyers, journalists, and politicians had for decades "injected their poisons" into the German people, "a thousand times worse" was the fact that Jews had come to dominate German medicine. Holz claimed that nearly all the great figures of German medicine—Neisser, Wassermann, Ehrlich, Virchow, Koch, von Behring—were either Jews or "under the control of Jews" (Koch and Behring had Jewish wives; they were therefore to be counted among the Jews).[49]

Rhetoric on the dominance of Jews in the profession was not confined to popular journals. Many of Germany's medical journals published statistics on the numbers of Jews in German medicine (see Figure 31). According to the *Deutsches Ärzteblatt,* 60 percent of Berlin's doctors were Jewish when the Nazi government took power.[50] By July 31, 1934, this proportion had only decreased to 46 percent, and it remained as high as 44 percent even in 1935, a fact that Nazi propaganda organs were to exploit into the late 1930s (see Figure 32).[51]

Nazi medical philosophers justified the exclusion of Jews from the profession as a means of rectifying what was presented as Jewish hegemony in the field of medicine. For example, after reviewing racial statistics for the *Ärzteblatt für Berlin,* Hans Löllke, head of Berlin's Medical Chamber, proclaimed that the preponderance of Jews in the medical profession "must of course be considered an intolerable situation, seen from the long-run point of view."[52]

With the rise of the Nazis, universities and medical organizations took immediate and drastic action to solve this problem. In April 1933 the University of Leipzig announced that, in order to redress the imbalance in the numbers of Jewish students relative to their proportions in the German population, no Jews would be admitted to the university over the next ten semesters. The April 25, 1933, Law against Overcrowding at German Schools and Colleges required that the proportion of non-Aryan students never exceed that of the general population. At the University of Berlin, non-Aryan students were allowed to continue attending lectures, but only after receiving special identification papers—colored yellow, in contrast with the usual gray now held only by Aryan students.[53]

The most important measure excluding Jews from German medicine was the April 7, 1933, Civil Service Law, which forbade anyone of either Jewish descent or communist sympathies from holding a position in government service. The Civil Service Law excluded Jews and socialists from teaching at universities or working at government research or public health facilities. During 1933 and 1934, hundreds of Jewish and/or socialist physicians were dismissed in accordance with the law. By January 1934 the *Internationales Ärztliches Bulletin* (the most important publication of the medical resistance in exile) could list the names of 115 professors of medicine and medical researchers fired or arrested by the Nazi regime. Over the next few years this list would grow substantially.[54] When Arthur Kronfeld was dismissed from his position as professor of psychiatry and neurology at the University of Berlin in the early weeks of 1935, the *Bulletin* reported that there was no longer a single non-Aryan professor teaching in Berlin.[55]

Physicians were also forced from positions of a semiprivate nature, based on a broad reading of the 1933 Civil Service Law. Jews were expelled from the institutes of the Kaiser Wilhelm Gesellschaft, for example, on the grounds that the Gesellschaft received most of its funds from the government.[56] Jews were forced from the Medical Chambers and from service in the state-supported social insurance system. On May 17, 1934, Dr. Oskar Karstedt in the Ministry of Labor announced that non-Aryan physicians and physicians with non-Aryan spouses would no longer be allowed to practice medicine as part of the social insurance program. By this time, however, the purging of German insurance companies was well under way: in 1933 alone, 2,800 physicians were driven from the *Krankenkassen*.[57] This was a severe blow to the livelihood of "non-Aryan" (Jewish) or "communist" (left-leaning) physicians, for by then most medical services in the Reich were administered through these companies.[58]

The April 1933 Civil Service Law transformed the lives of many

Nichtarische Kassenärzte in v. H. der Gesamt-
zahl der Kassenärzte
(Stand Ende März 1933)

Arztregisterbezirke (Oberversicherungs-ämter)	Kassenärzte insgesamt	davon nichtarisch	in v. H.
Königsberg i. Pr.	724	99	13,7
Potsdam	1 177	123	10,5
Berlin	3 605	1 879	52,1
Stettin	730	73	10,0
Breslau	1 527	339	22,2
Oppeln	459	101	22,0
Merseburg	1 687	112	6,6
Schleswig	626	8	1,3
Hannover	1 243	79	6,4
Osnabrück	291	4	1,4
Dortmund	1 114	55	4,9
Münster	578	19	3,3
Minden	389	15	3,9
Wiesbaden	1 023	300	29,3
Kassel	510	41	8,0
Aachen	312	23	7,4
Düsseldorf	2 010	157	7,8
Köln	832	121	14,5
Koblenz	366	19	5,2
Trier	173	6	3,5
München	1 343	146	10,9
Augsburg	429	14	3,3
Landshut	481	10	2,1
Nürnberg	800	125	14,3
Würzburg	343	27	7,9
Speyer	420	47	11,2
Dresden	1 000	47	4,7
Leipzig	705	79	11,2
Chemnitz	851	41	4,8
Stuttgart	1 270	97	7,6
Karlsruhe	1 317	181	13,7
Gotha	778	34	4,4
Darmstadt	774	88	11,4
Hamburg	873	265	30,3
Schwerin	384	21	5,5
Oldenburg	210	3	1,4
Braunschweig	274	23	8,4
Bremen	251	10	4,0
Detmold	84	6	7,1
Lübeck	99	3	3,0
zusammen	32 152	4 840	15,5
dazu die Verzogenen		468	
		5 308	
Dagegen Stand vom Frühjahr 1934	rd. 52 000	3 641	11,4

Figure 31. "Non-Aryan Doctors as a Proportion of Total Doctors, at the End of March 1933." From Julius Hadrich, "Die nichtarischen Ärzte in Deutschland," *Deutsches Ärzteblatt,* 64(1934): 1245.

Figure 32. "After Four Years, Still No Loss Can Be Determined." This SS cartoon complains that after four years of National Socialism, there appeared to be no reduction in the number of Jewish doctors in Berlin. From *Das Schwarze Korps*, October 14, 1937, p. 1.

German doctors. One official count of October 1933 listed the majority of Berlin's physicians as non-Aryan. According to this count, out of a total of 3,481 Berlin physicians practicing medicine within the state-supported insurance programs, only 1,404 were "of German origin." Nearly 2,000 (1,888) were "of foreign origin"; and the remaining 189 were of "ambiguous" origins. Home to more than half of Germany's Jewish physicians, Berlin was to bear the brunt of anti-Semitic legislation. By 1934, 1,144 physicians had been forced from Berlin's social insurance programs. The Reich Ministry of Labor calculated about this time that 827 physicians, 174 dentists, and 52 dental technicians had been dismissed. Most (but not all) of these dismissals were for racial reasons; about 10 percent of those dismissed were listed as communists, not as non-Aryans.[59]

Especially after 1933, it was not always so easy to say just what was meant by *Jewish. Jewish* was used primarily as a racial rather than a religious term; Nazi documents commonly distinguished between the "mosaic religion" and the "Jewish race." After passage of the 1935 Nuremberg Laws, the Nazis generally avoided the term *non-Aryan* and used instead the more specific term *Jewish,* contrasting this with *German-blooded.* Nazi laws distinguished *full Jews, half-Jews,* and *quarter-Jews,* according to whether one had four, two, or only one Jewish grandparent;[60] individuals were also sometimes considered Jewish, however, if they had a Jewish wife or husband—or (according to Ternon and Helman) for no other reason than that they could not prove the contrary.[61]

In certain cases, contact with a person (especially blood or sexual contact) was sufficient to acquire the stigma of being Jewish. The court rulings on some of these cases were curious indeed. In the winter of 1935, for example, the *Strassburger Neueste Nachrichten* reported that an SA man from southern Germany had been hit by a car near a Jewish hospital and was taken to the hospital, where he was given a transfusion (of "Jewish blood"). After the man recovered, he was brought before an SA disciplinary court to determine whether he had lost the racial purity required of all members of the SA (the Brownshirts). The court ruled that, strictly speaking, the man should be excluded from the SA. The court also noted, however, that the donor at the Jewish hospital (who was Jewish) had fought at the front during World War I; the court was therefore able to rule in accordance with the Civil Service Law that the man should be allowed to remain in the SA.[62]

Ambiguities in racial definitions persisted, especially when it came to other European nationalities. Were the Turks, for example, to be considered German-blooded? In their 1936 *Commentary* on Germany's racial legislation, Wilhelm Stuckart and Hans Globke argued that any people permanently settled in Europe and whose non-European descendants had maintained their lines "pure" could be considered "of German blood." Turks or people of Turkish descent were thus included as "Germans."[63] But what about Persians or Egyptians?

Beginning in the mid-1930s, anthropologists and human geneticists tried to develop techniques that would reveal who was a Jew and who was not. Germany's foremost public health journal published detailed reports on how to determine racial affiliation.[64] The anthropologist Hans F. K. Günther published pictures of "typical Jewish posture"; one physician advised investigating the shape of the forehead, brow, eyelids, and various passages and contours in the nose, eyes, and ears to determine paternity and/or racial ancestry.[65] Hitler is reported to have thought one could identify a Jew by whether the earlobes were attached to or separate from the neck; he once asked his photographer Heinrich Hoffmann to take pictures of Stalin's ears to see whether he was Jewish. Hitler is reported to have considered this "very important to know."[66]

Blood groups provided a hope for many that the various races could be accurately distinguished. Otto Reche, professor of racial science at the University of Leipzig, was one of the pioneering researchers in this field. Reche (along with Paul Steffan) was founder of the German Society for Blood Group Research (in 1926) and also (again with Steffan, in 1928) of the *Zeitschrift für Rassenphysiologie*. He was one of the leading figures in German anthropology and racial theory in the Weimar and Nazi periods.[67]

Reche claimed to have founded the Society for Blood Group Research as part of an effort to find a precise physiological measure of differences among the various races.[68] (He was by no means the first to suggest an uneven distribution of blood types across "races": Karl Landsteiner had suggested this earlier in the century, and subsequent research in the Nazi period cited Landsteiner's work.)[69] According to Reche (based on his studies of the rural inhabitants of northwest Germany), the long-headed European races were originally characterized by blood type A. Another, less well defined race with origins somewhere in Asia was characterized by blood type B, whereas the pure-blooded inhabitants of pre-Columbian America had neither type A nor B but were exclusively of type O. Reche concluded that a strong correlation had once existed between race and blood type, and that subsequently, through racial intermarriage, the races had become intermingled.

Reche felt that blood group research had important policy implications for the Nazi state. He described in vivid terms the negative consequences of allowing enemy (*feindliche*) blood groups (A and B, for example) to mingle with one another. If a person of blood type A, for example, were to receive blood from an individual of type B, this could result in the destruction of the circulatory system and possibly even in the death of the recipient. He noted that the ability to distinguish blood types was important in police work and in the determination of paternity: "In some cases, it can be ascertained whether or not an illegitimate child is the offspring of a Jewish father, because the Asiatic B blood type is more common among Jews than among Europeans."[70] Reche conceded that such tests were never conclusive, given that no single blood type was typical among Jews; most Nazi physicians admitted this was the case.

Reche and others, however, believed that even though there was no necessary correlation between race and blood type, the methods developed in the new science were important for Germany's new racial legislation. In 1939 Peter Dahr, for example, cited a case in which a (non-Jewish) woman married to a Jew had three children and wanted to claim that one of them stemmed from an extramarital relationship with a "German" and should therefore not be considered Jewish. Dahr showed how blood types could be used to determine paternity and resolve the racial status of the child. The mother was type OO, the father AB. Because the child in question was type OO, it could not have been fathered by the woman's husband. The child could therefore be considered German under Nazi law.[71]

The study of the racial specificity of blood types was supported by Germany's leading scientific bodies. The Kaiser Wilhelm Gesellschaft and the German Research Council both supported research in this area, and many of Germany's medical and anthropological journals published articles on this topic.[72]

The exclusion of Jews from German medical practice was achieved through a combination of propaganda, harassment, and legislation. Legal exclusions followed soon after the consolidation of Nazi rule in 1933. As of May 17, 1934, non-Aryan physicians and physicians with non-Aryan wives were no longer allowed to begin practice as part of Germany's state-supported health insurance scheme. On August 12, 1934, the Nazi government required that all pharmacists submit proof of Aryan ancestry. After December 8, 1934, proof of Aryan descent was required for admission to pharmaceutical exams, and on October 28, 1935, all students (*Kandidaten*) of pharmacy were required to show proof of Aryan ancestry. On April 15, 1937, the Reich minister for science and education announced that Jews would no longer be allowed to take exams for the doctorate; Jews who had already fulfilled all requirements for the degree—even those with completed dissertations—were allowed to graduate only if they had scheduled their exams to take place within three months of the date of announcement. After June 9, 1938, Jews were not allowed to audit classes at German universities. In 1938 all books by Jews were required to be published in "Antiquascript," to identify them easily as written by Jews; all books by Jews had to be submitted for censorship before publication.

The Nazi message was not subtle or obscure; many Jews recognized early on that the Nazis could be taken at their word. The exodus of Jews from Germany began shortly after the rise of the Nazis to power. From January 1933 to the end of 1939, 319,900 of Germany's 500,000 Jews fled the Reich.[73] Jewish physicians began to flee Germany in large numbers in the spring and summer of 1933; by September more than 200 Jewish physicians had fled to England alone. The pace of emigration continued throughout the 1930s. In 1933, 578 Jewish physicians fled the Reich and 1,667 Jews were forced from the insurance companies. By May 1935 the number of Jewish physicians who had fled increased to 1,307, representing more than 20 percent of all Jewish physicians in the Reich.[74]

We have some idea of where physicians went after leaving Germany. One survey of those who left in 1933 and 1934, for example, found that 45 percent remained in Europe; 33 percent went to Palestine; 13 percent to America; 5 percent to Asia; and 3 percent to Africa. Among those emigrés who stayed in Europe (as of 1935), 8 percent went to France, 8 percent to England, 6 percent to Switzerland, and 2 percent to Czechoslovakia.[75] After the annexation of Austria in the spring of 1938, the Turkish government agreed to accept 200 Austrian physicians into the country.[76]

Many Jewish doctors remained in Germany, however, even after they were forbidden to practice medicine (except for providing treatment for other Jews) in 1938. In 1935 the *Deutsches Ärzteblatt* reported that Jews had actually begun to return to Germany, after recovering from an initial "scare."[77] According to a survey of April 10, 1937, there were 4,121 Jewish physicians in Germany.[78] Seven percent of all physicians in Germany at this time were Jewish (down from 13 percent in 1933); Nazi medical statisticians reported that in Berlin the percentage of Jewish physicians had fallen from over 60 percent to 23 percent. Professional medical journals continued, however, to attack the presence of Jews within the profession, especially in the Berlin "bastion." At the end of 1937 the *Ärzteblatt für Berlin* reported: "No other city in the Reich still suffers so much from its medical profession being overrun by Jews [*Überjudung*] than Berlin. Even today—nearly five years after the Nazi seizure of power—more than a third of Berlin's physicians associated with the insurance companies [*Kassenärzte*] are Jewish."[79] One reason for this situation was that between 1935 and 1938, many Jewish physicians from some of the more isolated parts of Germany had fled to Berlin in the hope that in Germany's cosmopolitan capital they would find at least a modicum of tolerance.

The exclusion of Jews from German medical practice accelerated in the early months of 1938. At the beginning of this year, Jewish physicians were barred from service in welfare institutions, in the postal service and police, and in a host of other institutions. Jewish physicians were barred from working with public utilities (such as the Allgemeine Elektrizitätsgesellschaft), public transport (such as the Berliner Verkehrsgesellschaft), and a number of private firms (such as the Siemens-Werke).

The final and most comprehensive law excluding Jews from the practice of medicine was the July 25, 1938, Fourth Ordinance of the Citizenship Law, requiring that as of September 30, 1938, medical licenses be revoked from all Jews; henceforth Jews would be allowed to provide medical treatment only for other Jews, and even this required special permission. Any Jew providing medical service would be considered not a physician (*Arzt*), but an attendant (*Krankenbehandler*). In Berlin 300 "attendants" were permitted to continue practicing at Jewish hospitals; another 150 were allowed to practice in other parts of the Old Reich.[80] (The fact that some Jewish physicians were allowed to continue in a limited practice may have been the result of fears that the loss of *all* Jewish services would overburden non-Jewish physicians. On February 7, 1938, Arthur Gütt wrote a letter to Himmler arguing that although he supported the exclusion of the Jews from German medicine, the exclusion of all Jews from the profession would create a shortage of physicians in certain areas, straining already overburdened physicians in the party's Office for Public Health.)[81] Under this same legislation, landlords housing Jewish medical offices were required to evict their tenants by September 30 unless they could prove that it would be difficult to find new tenants.[82] Jewish physicians were also deprived of all retirement privileges and pensions. The 1938 ordinance excluding Jews from German medicine was immediately incorporated into German medical textbooks and regulations. Rudolf Ramm, in his 1942 textbook on the professional, ethical, and legal responsibilities of the physician (commissioned as required reading for all of Germany's medical students), stated as a simple matter of fact that "it is explicitly forbidden for Jews to provide medical treatment to individuals of German blood."[83]

The measures noted above are, of course, only some of the hundreds of legal measures implemented to remove Jews from public life in Germany (see Table 6). Between April 7, 1933, when Jews were forced from all public posts, and September 1, 1941, when Jews were required to wear the Star of David, more than 250 laws, decrees, and ordinances were issued to exclude them from public life.[84]

In medicine as in other spheres of life, these measures were successful. In 1942 Rudolf Ramm, the man responsible for supervising the quality of German medical education, presented statistics showing that, whereas in 1933, 13 percent of German doctors had been Jewish, by the beginning of the 1940s this "problem" had been "solved" by National Socialist policies. Ramm proudly reported that "today, no man of German blood is treated by a Jewish doctor."[85] Nazi physicians hailed the 1938 law excluding Jews from German medicine as an event of historical import: Dr. H. H. Meier, in an article titled "The End of Jewish Medicine," celebrated the year 1938 as "one of the most important years in all of German history."[86]

Curiously, by the early 1940s it may have become obvious to some within the party hierarchy that the suppression of the Jews had been, if nothing else, a tactical error for the health of German science. Shortly after the outbreak of war, and especially after the large numbers of casualties on the Russian front, German armies suffered a shortage of medical personnel; the German government in 1941 thus ordered the mobilization of a number of Jewish doctors and nurses to

Table 6. Legal measures enacted against Jews in 1938

Date	Legal measure
January 1	Jewish physicians no longer able to practice in Ersatzkassen.
January 5	Law makes it illegal to change one's first or last name; Jews specifically barred from taking "German names."
March 28	All Jewish organizations required to register with government authorities.
April 17	Ordinance designates 316 names as officially "Jewish" (185 for men and 131 for women); Jews with other names required to add "Israel" or "Sarah" to their names.
April 22	Field Marshal Göring issues proclamation making it a crime to conceal the "Jewish character" of a shop or business.
April 26	Jews and their spouses required to register all their property with the authorities.
July 1	Parents of "Aryan" descent prohibited from giving a child a name "of Jewish origin, which has a Jewish sound, or which for the German people will be considered 'typically Jewish'—such as 'Joshua'."
July 6	Jews banned from a host of occupations, including work in real estate, mortuaries, and loan negotiations.
July 23	Jews required to apply for special papers identifying them as Jewish, to carry these papers with them at all times, and to show them at all official places without being asked.
July 25	All Jewish physicians have their licenses withdrawn.
July 27	All streets named after Jews required to be changed.
October 6	All Jewish physicians removed from the official registry of licensed physicians and allowed to practice medicine only on other Jews and only after obtaining special permission from the Kassenärztliche Vereinigung.
November 12	Goebbels orders that Jews be prohibited from attending German theater, concerts, lectures, cabarets, circuses, variety shows, dances, or cultural exhibitions; that Germany's Jewish community pay compensation for the murder of the German ambassador to France; and that damages from the events of "Kristallnacht" be paid for by Jewish residents of damaged areas. Jews forbidden (effective January 1, 1939) to operate mail-order businesses or independent handicrafts, to offer services at public markets, to take orders for goods, or to hold leadership positions in German factories.
November 15	Jews barred from attending German schools.
November 28	Security (SD) chief Reinhard Heydrich authorized to restrict the movement of Jews within certain areas and to confine Jews to their houses.

Source: Reports on German racial legislation in *Informationsdienst, Rassenpolitisches Amt der NSDAP* (1938–1939).

assist in care for the wounded. Similar mobilization orders were issued in Hungary, Slovakia, and Romania.[87] (Jewish physicians rehabilitated under these orders were not permitted to employ Aryan nurses; Jewish nurses were not allowed to work for non-Jewish doctors.) In 1942 General Dr. Wolff blamed the failure of medical preparations at the eastern front on Conti's obsession with ideological purity; Wolff asked that Jewish physicians be rehabilitated for service in sanitation and health fields, a request that was only partially accepted. Hermann Göring at about this time asked that restrictions on scientists with Jewish wives be relaxed to allow them to remain productive. And in the fall of 1941, the Romanian Red Cross, now under Nazi rule, announced it would accept donations of "Jewish blood" for transfusions, owing to a shortage of "Aryan blood."[88] It remains unclear today how far any of these measures were put into practice. Yet they do show that, as elsewhere, the exigencies of war forced cracks into some of the toughest parts of the Nazi ideological fortress.

Economic Stress and the Search for a Scapegoat

Anti-Semitism is not an attitude that exists in isolation. Like other forms of chauvinism or racism, anti-Semitism in recent history has generally been attached to other kinds of fears—fears of unemployment or impoverishment, of communism, or of mysterious and powerful forces conspiring to shape the course of history. In the early decades of the twentieth century these were not new fears, but they became accentuated with the impoverishment suffered by many in the early years after World War I and in the final years of the Weimar Republic.

In May 1926 the Hartmannbund published figures claiming that among 28,784 doctors working in the insurance companies, 42 percent earned less than 2,000 RM per year. Twenty-eight percent earned 2,000–6,000 RM, and fewer than 10 percent earned more than 12,000 RM per year. In 1926 prices, this meant that nearly half of all doctors were earning a salary only slightly above that of an average industrial worker.[89] The depression made this situation worse. In 1928 Germany's gross national product was 75,400 million RM; by 1932 this amount had fallen by over 40 percent to 45,175 million RM.[90] The economic collapse of 1929–1932 affected physicians as much as it did many other workers. In 1932 only 10 percent of all doctors earned more than 15,000 RM a year. Even in 1929, before the Great Depression, 48 percent of all German doctors earned less than what one observer called the minimum necessary to survive (*Existenzminimum*). By 1932, according to Julius Hadrich, writing in the *Ärztliche Mitteilungen,* this proportion had jumped to 72 percent.[91] Writers of the time report that 10 percent of all German doctors were "starving" in the deepest years of the depression.[92]

One must, of course, take such reports with a grain of salt. The historian Walter Wuttke-Groneberg has pointed out that contemporary reports of the impoverishment of the German physician may have been exaggerated. German medical bodies admitted their reluctance to publicize statistics on physicians' income; cries about the "proletarization" of the German doctor must be evaluated in this light. Even Wuttke-Groneberg concedes, however, that the income of physicians fell substantially in the years prior to the rise of the Nazis. He reports research showing that physicians' taxable income (after deduction of expenses) fell from an average of 13,200 RM in 1927 to 9,600 RM in 1932.[93] By any account, physicians suffered substantial financial losses in the years prior to the Nazi rise to power.

Medical insurance companies also felt the crunch. In 1930, 20.3 million persons were covered by Germany's socialized medical insurance companies (*Krankenkassen*). By September of 1932, however, this number had fallen to 16.6 million. In 1931 the average annual payment of members for medical insurance was 74.35 RM; in 1932 this fell to 70.68 RM. Whereas income to the insurance companies in 1929 was about 400 million RM, by July 1932 a survey of the Hartmannbund showed this to have dropped by nearly 30 percent. The decline from 1931 to 1932 alone cost Germany's medical insurance companies 771 million RM.[94] The *Münchener Medizinische Wochenschrift* wrote at the beginning of 1933: "Six thousand physicians are looking for work and bread in Berlin, and see their margin of subsistence grow narrower and narrower as a consequence of the growing impoverishment of the population. In the free play of forces, the competitive struggle takes on ever sharper forms; the struggle of each against all appears almost unavoidable."[95]

Despite increasing unemployment among doctors, the number of doctors practicing within Germany's state-supported insurance program increased substantially in the years of the depression—from 28,700 in 1929 to 32,000 in 1932. Enrollments in medical school also increased dramatically over this period: in 1932 nearly 22,000 students studied medicine at German universities—5,000 of these in their first year. University studies were (then as now) one way to escape unemployment; in the deepest years of the depression, students flocked to the universities in record numbers (see Table 7). In 1911 there had been only 19,000 graduating high school seniors (*Abiturienten*); by 1932 this number had increased to 45,000. Whereas unemployment among academics before World War I had been essentially zero, by 1932 there were 30,000–40,000 unemployed academics in Germany. In 1932 alone, 30,000 academics graduated with doctorate or professional degree in hand, with openings for only 10,000.[96] Some expressed a fear that unemployment among academically trained professionals might reach 200,000 by 1935.[97] In January 1933, Germany's most important medical journal warned that if the present situation were to continue, the medical profession would soon face "a catastrophe."[98]

Medical journals in this period reported nearly every week on the overcrowding in medical schools and on the effect this would have on medical services and teaching. One medical student rendered the following account of the situation on medical campuses in 1932:

> Even the most casual observer, seeing the enormous number of students filling the medical institutes and clinics, cannot help but notice the severe overcrowding. Between classes, the medical areas of nearly every university are flooded by a powerful, frenzied, and unceasing flow of humanity, rushing from one clinic to the next. Everyone tries to outdo his fellow student in speed, just in order to secure a seat in the lecture hall. Those engaged in sports, of course, have a natural advantage; but even these often find they cannot gain a seat, as others will have already been waiting for an hour at the lecture hall. The following anecdote, circulating among medical campuses, may best illustrate the surest

Table 7. Students enrolled at German universities

Year	Total	Women	Students per 100,000 inhabitants
1911	63,000	2,300	100
1914	69,500	3,800	106
1925	81,500	6,900	127
1931	131,000	21,000	200
1932	150,000	n.a.	n.a.

Source: Carl Bauer, "Massnahmen gegen die Überfüllung der Hochschulen," *Ärztliche Mitteilungen,* 33 (1932): 802.

method of finding a seat. One night, so the story goes, the police discovered at about two o'clock in the morning a group of young men lingering around the anatomy building, and ordered them to disperse. As it turned out, however, these were actually students standing in line, trying to ensure themselves a good seat in the lecture hall for the following morning.[99]

In 1932, universities were producing trained medical graduates at two to three times the rate they could be absorbed under existing market conditions. Stopgap measures were imposed, including career advising, an obligatory work-year for doctors, limits on the admission of students into medical school, and increases in the number and difficulty of qualifying exams.[100] At the beginning of 1933, the *Deutsches Ärzteblatt* reported that even if these and similar measures were undertaken, the growth in the number of physicians in two or three years would still be far in excess of what was needed; such a situation would threaten both the economic livelihood and the moral integrity of the profession. The journal cited George Bernard Shaw's words to the effect that "the greatest danger a people may face in times of need is the impoverishment of its physicians."[101]

In such a climate, doctors were desperate to find a solution to the overcrowding in the profession. The Hartmannbund encouraged medical students to study abroad, in the hope that some would not return to Germany. Medical journals urged physicians to prescribe more drugs, to provide pharmacists with an income. Some proposed more drastic measures, based on their conviction that it was women or Jews who were responsible for overcrowding at the university and for "stealing German jobs." Fritz Lenz, for example, noted in 1933 that the number of unemployed in Germany was "not coincidentally" exactly equal to the number of working women (6 million).[102] Women and Jews were frequently blamed for saturating the academic labor market. In the late 1920s and early 1930s, doctors writing in professional medical journals advised that the admission of women to universities be reduced, on the grounds that in recent years, female enrollment had increased at a faster rate than that of men.[103] Others demanded the exclusion of Jews and "other foreigners" from medical studies. Each of these measures would be undertaken, but not before the Nazi rise to power.

Appreciating this, one can see one of the reasons why National Socialism appealed to the German medical man. The social Darwinian rhetoric of the struggle for existence struck a familiar chord for physicians struggling with overcrowding and economic insecurity. National Socialism promised to restore the lost status of the doctor, to overcome the "impotence and apathy" of Weimar liberalism. In June 1932 the Verband Deutscher Medizinerschaften petitioned the Weimar government to put a lid on medical enrollments at German universities, but the government refused, fearful that the measure would only further inflate already bulging unemployment rolls.[104]

Aid for the German medical man was brought shortly after the rise of Hitler to power. To ensure a minimal level of economic prosperity, the government passed measures guaranteeing all physicians belonging to the Association of German Health Insurance Physicians (Kassenärztliche Vereinigung Deutschlands) an annual salary of 1,000 RM.[105] To relieve the overcrowding at medical schools, the government established quotas on the numbers of students that could be admitted in any given semester. To these were also added racial quotas: the April 25, 1933, Law against Overcrowding at German Schools and Colleges required that the proportion of non-Aryan students at German schools and colleges never exceed that of the general population. The government also instituted new and stiffer requirements for admission to German universities: a measure passed early in the regime required that high school diplomas indicate whether students possessed "the spiritual and human qualities necessary for higher education." Students who did not possess these qualities and yet chose to pursue higher education could be excluded from financial aid and be asked to take extra exams in their first semester of studies. Admission to studies and to qualifying exams for the medical degree was also made contingent upon a student's "natural and moral trustworthiness."[106] Editors of the *Münchener Medizinische Wochenschrift* saluted these and other measures as proof that the new regime was serious about coming to grips with the "unbearable" overcrowding of the academic professions.[107]

The various state governments took additional measures. In April 1933 the Prussian Ministry of the Interior announced that foreigners could no longer expect to be licensed as German physicians, dentists, or pharmacists.[108] In the same month, Bavarian Interior Minister Adolf Wagner announced that Germany's need for physicians had now been covered for the next nine years; he also warned that further admission to medical studies would only endanger the profession. Wagner ordered that the number of medical students at the universities of Munich, Würzburg, and Erlangen be limited to 345, 120, and 98, respectively; he also announced that members of the Jewish race were "henceforth totally excluded from admissions to medical study."[109]

Nazi efforts to relieve the overpopulation of medical schools and universities were successful. Between the winter semesters 1933–34 and 1935–36, the number of students taking medical exams dropped from 4,970 to 2,769.[110] Women were discouraged from studying medicine, and the proportions of women with medical degrees *not* practicing medicine rose from about 25 percent in 1932 to nearly 50 percent in 1937.

The exclusion of the Jews was by far the most important element in the program to reduce the overcrowding of the profession. Even before 1933, Nazi medical philosophers had proposed the exclusion of the Jews as one of the ways to achieve full employment for "German-blooded" physicians: at the 1931 meeting of the Hartmannbund, Hans Deuschl, cofounder of the National Socialist Physicians' League, defended this point of view with the argument that "every German-blooded doctor must first have a job, before we can think of guaranteeing others work and bread."[111] After 1933 Germany's medical journals supported this view quite openly. In April 1933 the *Deutsches Ärzteblatt* linked the suppression of "foreign racial elements" with the winning of *Lebensraum* and employment for young German physicians.[112] Medical journals beginning in 1933 are filled with advertisements announcing "Aryan doctor wanted to fill position recently vacated by Jew." Young "Aryan" physicians seeking to establish a practice frequently included their political or racial qualifications in these ads (see Figure 33).

Anti-Semitism in the Nazi era did not go unrewarded. Non-Jewish physicians profited from the thousands of positions opened up when Jews lost their jobs. With an important part of their competition forced from the profession, physicians' salaries began to grow. In 1933 the average taxable income for a physician was 9,280 RM; by 1938 this had grown to 14,940 RM. In 1928 lawyers' income exceeded that of physicians 18,428 RM to 12,616 RM. By the end of 1933, however, doctors had pulled even with lawyers; and by 1935 physicians earned an annual salary nearly 2,000 RM greater than that of lawyers.[113] In purely financial terms, the majority of German physicians prospered under National Socialism. Nazi policies provided a bonanza for those willing and able to move with the regime.

The general point to be made in this context is that under financial pressures, solutions to problems that seem extreme or inhumane in one context may become banal to large numbers of people in another.

162   Racial Hygiene

Prior to the 1930s, anti-Semitism was not a central feature of German medical writings. But in the final years of the Weimar Republic this changed. Nazi physicians were able to link a supposed "Jewish menace" with the joint specters of communism, impoverishment, and a host of other fears facing the profession (proletarization, bureaucratization, and so on). In this fashion it was not difficult for a vocal minority to enlist a substantial portion of physicians in the service of the Nazi cause.

"Jewish Medicine"

The tasks posed to the German medical man by the Nazi movement were intellectual as well as practical. In attempting to understand the role of anti-Semitism in the medical profession, it is important to recognize the philosophical critique Nazi physicians raised against what they saw as "Jewish science." Jews were blamed for a broad range of problems faced by modern science and medicine. Medical anti-Semitism represented in this sense not just a desire to gain the jobs of Jews but also a vehicle for launching a more general attack on science and its place in society.

The 1920s and 1930s constituted a period when authors of various political persuasions began to write about the importance of politics, religion, and national character in the structure of scientific knowledge. Max Scheler coined the expression "sociology of knowledge" (*Wissenssoziologie*) in his 1926 *Die Wissensformen und die Gesellschaft;* many of the other classics in this field—works by Lukács, Hessen, Bauer, Borkenau, Fleck, or Zilsel—date from this period.[114]

Physicians in the Nazi period were similarly intrigued by the notion that Jews and Germans might have different forms of knowing. The most common view was that Jewish science was somehow "foreign" to the needs or values of the Nordic, German man. The Swiss psychoanalyst Carl Jung, appointed head of Germany's International Society for Psychotherapy after the expulsion of Ernst Kretschmer in 1933, considered the question of religion in science a legitimate one; Jung found it difficult to understand why Jews should be so hostile to the idea of a distinctive "Jewish psychology":

> Can one not say that there is also a Jewish psychology which bears the marks of Jewish blood and history? Can one not ask what are the particular differences between an essentially Jewish, and an essentially

Figure 33. Advertisements for "Aryan doctors" in Munich's foremost medical journal. In the center of the page in bold letters the J. F. Lehmann publishing house advertises recent books in the field of racial science and racial hygiene. Immediately above, a technical assistant advertises that she is "Aryan" (*arisch*). Another advertisement requests that applicants for a position in Munich be Nazi party members (*Pg.*). From *Münchener Medizinische Wochenschrift*, 80(1933): 10.

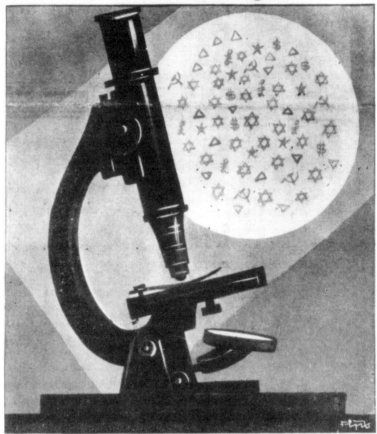

Figure 34. "Infectious Germs." Under the microscope are symbols for Jews, communists, and homosexuals (triangles), alongside the British pound and the American dollar. The poem at the bottom reads: "With his poison, the Jew destroys / The sluggish blood of weaker peoples; / So that a diagnosis arises, / Of swift degeneration. / With us, however, the case is different: / The blood is pure; we are healthy!" / From *Der Stürmer*, April 15, 1943, p. 1.

Christian conception? Can it really be the case that I am the only one among the psychologists who possesses a distinctive and subjectively prejudiced organ of knowledge [*Erkenntnisorgan*]? Why does the Jew appear deeply hurt when one supposes that he is a Jew? Surely the Jew does not want us to suppose that he, as a knowing being [*Erkennender*], is a "nothing," without content, or that his brain only today has emerged from the sea of historylessness? I simply cannot understand why it should be a crime to speak of "Jewish" psychology.[115]

Jung was not alone in his attempt to discover the peculiarities of "Jewish psychology"; this was a widespread trend in European psychology and anthropology. But many Nazis (unlike Jung, who never joined the Nazi party) went beyond this to argue that Jewish science was not just different but was also one-sided, misguided, or in various respects dangerous or defective. Hermann Berger, for example, claimed that the majority of German physicians had rejected Freudian psychoanalysis even before 1933 because they found it "disgusting."[116] Others argued that the distinctive character of Jewish science derived from certain basic "defects" in Jewish faculties of perception. Thus in 1936, Dr. Heinrich Chantraine published an article in the official journal of the Nazi Physicians' League claiming that Jews have problems with spatial and depth perception; this was why "the Jews never developed X-ray stereoscopy, even though they dominate the science of radiology."[117] Chantraine discussed a number of other "defects" of the Jewish spirit: Jews are "rationalists" and therefore suspicious of sensory experience; they excel in working with ideas (*Begriffsarbeit*) but lack a broader perspective (*Anschaulichkeit*). The Jewish mentality is Oriental and therefore merely "practical" or "technical"; Jews are obsessed with profitability and usefulness. For the Nordic man, in contrast, science springs from a grasp of things in themselves, from a "natural bond to nature." Genuine science, Chantraine maintained, "is not a form of calculation, or a form of logical acrobatics," and that is why "there never has been genuine science outside of that produced by the Nordic race. Only through Nordic science has man learned to direct nature according to our wishes. Outside of Nordic science, there is only practical experience."[118] (Professor Alexander von Senger of Munich constructed an equally creative argument for the case of art: Jewish art was always "two-dimensional"; only "Nordic man" could see and build in three dimensions. Senger published examples of artwork produced by Jewish and German children in *Ziel und Weg* to illustrate his point.)[119]

One of the most common charges raised against "Jewish science" (or medicine) was that Jews were responsible for bringing an impersonal, businesslike mentality into medicine. Jews were accused of transforming the hospital into a business and the clinic into a factory. "Factory medicine" (*jüdische Fabrikmedizin*) was a slogan used by the Nazis to denigrate the large, impersonal clinics established by Germany's medical insurance companies. The entrée of Jews into academic science in the nineteenth century coincided with the growth of laboratory-based clinical methods, and it was not hard for the Nazis to portray this as cause and effect. Nazi medical philosophers blamed Jews for many of the ills associated with modern, scientific medicine. Jews were blamed for having tried to suppress natural "organic" methods in favor of modern laboratory-based medicine. They were accused of promoting hospital births (versus birthing by midwives) and Caesarean sections (versus natural childbirth).[120] They were accused of encouraging abortions and providing indiscriminate birth control. In short, Jews were accused of having imported a philosophy of medicine that was foreign to native German traditions.

Perhaps the single most comprehensive discussion of Nazi medical philosophy was presented by Karl Kötschau in a series of articles published between 1933 and 1935 titled "The National Socialist Revolution in Medicine."[121] Kötschau was the leading spokesman for "organic" medicine in Germany; he was appointed professor of organic medicine at the University of Jena in 1934, and subsequently organized a synthesis of academic and organic medicine on a scale never before achieved in Germany (see Chapter 8). Kötschau argued that medicine had suffered in recent years from the encroachment of a materialistic, mechanical spirit, which turned the clinic into a laboratory and medicine into a business. In the last 100 years or so, he wrote, science has turned from "systems" to "analysis," from the recognition of human subjectivity to a belief in "objectivity" and in a "science free of suppositions." Kötschau criticized those who claimed that medicine is just a branch of biology or that there can be no "national medicine," no more than there can be a "national biology." This, he complained, "has become the ideology of our age: that there is only one science, and that this is exact, natural science—all else is nonscience, a regression into pre-science or romanticism. There is no vision of an 'alternative science'."[122]

Kötschau argued that it was the task of National Socialism to challenge this narrowly mechanistic vision of the sciences. He asserted that central in the Nazi conception of science was a new appreciation of the importance of world view—*Weltanschauung*—in the structuring of knowledge. Kötschau conceded that there were still those who claimed that science has nothing to do with such matters, those who say, "I am a doctor, a scientist; *Weltanschauung* does not concern me." But those who think this way have not yet sensed the spirit of the times; for "the National Socialist confronts all questions and problems from the point of view of a particular *Weltanschauung*, even those in the sphere of science."[123] This, Kötschau argued, cannot help but be the case, for knowledge is invariably dependent upon a particular context. Those who deny this are simply bad philosophers, unconscious of their allegiances, for science is not and cannot be "value free": value neutrality is itself a dogma, the dogma (Kötschau claimed) of the "Jewish-international conception of the world."

This idea of the Jews as responsible for the rise of impersonal and neutral science is a recurrent theme in Nazi ideology (see also Chapter 10). National Socialists criticized the apathy, the equanimity (*Gleichgültigkeit*) of the Weimar Republican Jewish spirit, according to which science was supposed to be apolitical, or value free. Nazi medical philosophers cited the words of the Nazi classic *Rembrandt als Erzieher* that the ultimate goal of genuine science was not "to prove facts," but rather "to render value judgments."[124] In a 1935 commentary on the International Medical Congress held in Montreux, Switzerland, on September 9–14, Gerhard Wagner ridiculed as "purely Jewish" (*echt jüdisch*) the following resolution of the congress: "Science is simply a matter of truth, and thus can never be national. It can only be international, bound to a common humanity; science can therefore only be apolitical."[125] Wagner declared that it was obvious that no German could take part in a meeting where such views were expressed.

Pragmatism, materialism, and even value neutrality were not the only supposed characteristics of Jewish science. In a 1935 article titled "The Solution of the Jewish Problem," Professor of Medicine Alfred Böttcher argued that the "Jewish internationalist materialist spirit" had exercised a destructive influence upon the sciences, primarily by virtue of its divisive, "analytic" character. Böttcher claimed:

> The thought of the Jew is distinguished by a certain analytic or destructive character which, like his blood, derives from its chaotic or impure

origins. The Jew always has the tendency to split and divide everything into its atoms, thereby making everything complicated and incomprehensible, so that the healthy man can no longer find his way in the desert of contradictory theories . . .

The healthy non-Jew, in contrast, thinks simply, organically, creatively. He unifies, builds up! He thinks in terms of wholes. Briefly put, the blood-law of the Jew demands: chaos, world revolution, and death! And the blood law of the creative-heroic man demands: an organic world view, world peace, and life![126]

Hence in science, also, Jews became a convenient scapegoat for many of the problems facing German physicians in the early decades of the twentieth century. Jewish science was either "too practical" or "too theoretical"; Jewish medicine was tainted by "individualist-capitalism" or "Bolshevist-communism." Jewish medicine was either too analytical or too contemplative; too involved or too detached. Jewish medicine was "international" and "value free," or idiosyncratic and one-sided. Some blamed Jews for "suppressing natural medicine"; others accused them of being quacks.[127] Jewish medicine, in short, became a metaphor for all that was wrong in modern medical science and practice. By locating all the problems of medicine in the person of the Jew, the Nazis were able to propose a single, sweeping solution to the problems confronting German science and society.

International Anti-Semitism

Germany was not alone in its persecution of Jewish physicians. By the end of the 1930s, Nazi medical publications could note that countries as diverse as Bulgaria, France, Italy, Norway, Poland, and Romania had passed laws restricting the proportion of Jews allowed to practice medicine in those countries. On June 30, 1939, Slovakia restricted the proportion of Jewish doctors to 4 percent.[128] In other countries, limits were placed on either the number of immigrants accepted or their eligibility to work once they had arrived. Many of these measures were passed before the military expansion of the Nazis. Holland, for example, commonly denied working permits to Jews fleeing Germany in the late 1930s; Bulgaria closed its borders to Jews in 1939. In Belgium, in 1939, as the influx of Jewish refugees reached 1,250 per month, the Flemish Nazi leader Braun announced a Nazi-supported campaign to exclude the "white Negro" (*weisse Neger*) from further immigration.[129] At the German University of Prague and at the technical colleges in Prague and Brno, many Jewish professors and *Privatdozenten* were relieved of their posts in the months prior to the German invasion in March 1939. In January and February, Czechoslovakian physicians and lawyers petitioned the government to pass a "Law for the Protection of Czechoslovakian Physicians and Lawyers from Jewish Domination," setting limits on the numbers of Jews allowed to practice medicine and law.[130]

Germany's eastern neighbors were among the countries most ardent in their anti-Semitism prior to Germany's military expansion in 1938 and 1939. In the spring of 1937, the (German) Polish Medical Association voted 120 to 104 to exclude Jewish members from that organization.[131] In 1938 the Hungarian Medical Chamber ruled that the number of Jewish physicians in the chamber could not exceed 20 percent.[132] According to a Hungarian law of December 22, 1938, Jews were forbidden to work in state or local government; Jewish representation in law, engineering, theater, and the press was restricted to a maximum of 6 percent.[133] Even before the implementation of these measures, German medical journals hailed Hungarian medicine as a signal example of racial responsibility: in 1937 the *Deutsches Ärzteblatt* reported that Hungarian physicians "are rightly proud of the fact that they were the first among the world's medical professionals to solve the problem of the racial future of the profession." The journal noted that the number of Jewish students in Hungarian medical schools had been fixed at 5 percent for many years, and that the Hungarian Medical Association had taken the lead in establishing and protecting these quotas.[134]

In 1940 and 1941, after Germany's military expansion, anti-Semitic policies were enacted in most of the countries now in the German sphere of influence. In April 1940 Czechoslovakian physicians resolved at their national meeting that Jewish doctors should be barred entirely from the practice of medicine; the Bohemian provisional government at this time ordered all Jewish employees in government service to be fired, a measure directed primarily against Jewish physicians.[135] In September 1941, German medical journals reported that in Bulgaria, only twenty-one Jewish physicians were allowed to practice medicine; limits were also established at this time on the number of Bulgarian Jews allowed to practice as veterinarians (two), dentists (seven), lawyers (twenty), and other professionals.[136] In 1942 the Hungarian government passed its equivalent of the Nuremberg Laws, preventing marriage or sexual relations between

Jews and non-Jews; the Hungarian parliament also proposed legislation at this time to limit the proportion of Jewish physicians to 6 percent. In 1943 the Romanian government required that physicians be of either "Aryan or Turkish origins"; Jewish physicians who had been in Romania since 1919 were allowed to join a special, segregated division of the Romanian Medical Association.[137]

In England limits were set on the number of refugee physicians allowed to practice medicine soon after the first refugees arrived in 1933. At the end of 1933, Lord Dawson, personal physician of the British monarch, declared, "We cannot remain indifferent in the face of this invasion of students of another nation into our medical schools." Dawson complained that there was already an excess of physicians in England and that the admission of more would compromise the standard of living of English physicians.[138] Policies on this matter sharpened in the late 1930s: on July 14, 1938, in response to a parliamentary inquiry, Home Secretary Samuel Hoare stated flatly that "a policy of unrestricted admission to this country for qualified doctors or dentists would be out of the question." Some British physicians objected even to the limited numbers granted permission to practice. On July 2, 1938, for example, a Mr. Higgs cautioned in parliament that medical practitioners were "very concerned at the intention of the Home Office to admit further alien doctors into this country." On the same day, a Mr. Kirby asserted that with respect to (German Jewish) refugee physicians, "the medical profession strongly resents their entry and consequent competition with them on a lower standard of training than is required here." Partly as a result of such sentiments, by 1938 only 185 refugee doctors and 93 dentists had been granted permission to practice in Britain.[139] After 1938, refugee physicians were able to practice medicine only if approved by a committee representing the Royal College of Physicians, the British Medical Association, the Royal Society of London, and the University of London.[140]

The case of Austria is revealing. As one might expect, Austrian racial policy followed closely that of Germany after the *Anschluss* in the spring of 1938. What is perhaps more surprising is the extent to which Jews were excluded from the medical profession several years before German armies marched into Vienna. In fact, it is possible to argue that Austrian medical and racial policy followed many of the directions taken by Germany, long before the "return" of Austria to the Reich. In early 1935 the Austrian *Mitteilungsblatt der Vereini-*

gung jüdischer Ärzte reported that for the past twenty-two months, young Jewish physicians were no longer being admitted to Austria's government medical insurance programs (*Fondspitäler*) and city hospitals. The problem had reached "catastrophic" dimensions—especially for younger physicians, many of whom had taken their own lives out of despair. The journal also reported that in the previous twenty-two months (that is, since the rise of Hitler), the number of Jewish physicians (*Hilfsärzte*) employed in Austrian hospitals had fallen by more than half. Jews were being forced entirely from many Viennese hospitals: by July 30, 1935, the last Jewish resident physician (*Sekundararzt*) was supposed to leave Vienna's General Hospital, and the case was similar with many other hospitals in the country. In several of Vienna's large medical insurance companies, Jewish *Aspiranten* were no longer able to obtain gynecological training (see also Chapter 9).[141]

The situation in Prague was similar in certain respects to that in Vienna. By the spring of 1935, many of the physicians of German extraction in Prague had declared their support for National Socialism. The *Internationales Ärztliches Bulletin* reported at this time that many of the German academic youth in Czechoslovakia supported the Nazis; indeed, all organized German student bodies in Czechoslovakia were now under Nazi control. The journal also stated that support for the Nazis was especially strong in the medical faculties.[142]

In the case of Czechoslovakia, it is important to distinguish differences in this regard between the government and the universities. The German University of Prague (the oldest German university) was an early center of Nazi sympathies; the Czech government was not. In the early 1930s, whereas Romania, Poland, and Hungary all had quotas on the number of Jews who might study medicine, Czechoslovakia did not.[143] In fact, the Czech government was generally critical of Nazi racial policies, and of the far-right sentiments of the German medical faculties. Today it seems hard to believe that a liberal government (relatively speaking) could ban a prestigious medical journal for its political content, but in the mid-1930s that is precisely what happened: the Czech government regarded J. F. Lehmann's *Münchener Medizinische Wochenschrift* as so infused with Nazi ideology that it banned the journal as a subversive political publication.

One of the early centers of support for German fascism in Czechoslovakia was the medical faculty at the German University of Prague, where professors Anton Ghon, Karl Schloffer, and Wilhelm Nonnenbruch organized the student body in support of Nazi racial and political goals. In the late 1920s, students at Prague had organized a boycott after a Jew (Steinherz) was named rector of the university; the boycott was organized by the faculty and students at the Institute for Pathological Anatomy, headed by Professor Ghon. In the early 1930s, Nazi-oriented student clubs such as the Barden were strong at Prague, especially in the traditionally conservative medical fields of surgery, internal medicine, and gynecology. Professors in these fields wore the blue pins of the right-wing Barden on their laboratory coats and helped maintain control of the student body and exclude Jews. The political role of the medical professoriate at Prague was widely recognized at the time: when the journal *Prítomnost* reviewed the penetration of Nazi ideology into Czechoslovakian universities in the period 1933–1935, it stated bluntly that "the center of the German national movement is at the medical faculty in Prague."[144]

Support provided to the Nazis by members of the German medical faculty at Prague was not merely symbolic. After 1933, German physicians at the University of Prague falsified records of persons fleeing German concentration camps, destroying evidence that they had been subjected to torture. Jewish faculty in the mid-1930s were harassed to a point that many found difficult to endure; on March 21, 1935, for example, the Jewish physician Josef Gach committed suicide after being ostracized by anti-Semitic colleagues at the surgical clinic of Professor Schloffer. In the note he left behind, Gach wrote that "Schloffer and Wenzel have driven me to death."[145] The Gach affair created a minor sensation in the Czechoslovakian press. Although criminal charges against the German physicians under Schloffer and Wenzel were eventually dismissed, the spirit in which the entire inquiry was conducted made it clear that larger issues were at stake. The official journal of the German Medical Association in Czechoslovakia denied any wrongdoing by German physicians and printed a statement claiming that Dr. Gach had suffered from "certain genetic disorders," compounded by "a long-standing brain disease" that had led to his unusual behavior.[146] German socialist physicians exiled in Prague ridiculed the suggestion that Gach's suicide could be traced to genetic or psychiatric infirmities and not to the wave of political anti-Semitism sweeping across eastern Europe.

Italy, as Germany's closest ally, was encouraged to follow Germany's lead in excluding Jews from public life. A debate that emerged between Germany's racial scientists and the Catholic church over the question of racial policy reveals something about both the extent of anti-Semitism and the broader philosophy of Nazi science.[147] On July 14, 1938, the *Giornale d'Italia* published a "Racial Manifesto" authored by leading representatives of the Italian racial movement, including Guido Landra and Marcello Ricci. Shortly after this, on August 1, 1938, the journal *La Difesa della Razza* first appeared in Rome, edited by Landra, Ricci, Lidio Cipriani, Leone Franzi, and Lia Businco, the same scholars who had coauthored the "Racial Manifesto."[148] The Catholic church immediately issued a criticism of the manifesto, arguing that it threatened to replace church by state authority in the sphere of marriage, and that it represented an attempt on the part of the Italian government to imitate certain features of German policy.

Nazi medical officials countered papal criticism of racial science and policy by attempting to cast the criticism as only the latest round in the age-old conflict between science and religion. Medical Führer Gerhard Wagner defended German racial science, arguing that the church could not continue forever to exercise authority over areas that had been revolutionized by the progress of science. Wagner pointed to the "unscientific" calculation issued by Pope Gregory XIII dating the creation of the earth at 5199 B.C.; he maintained that such views must bow before the findings of modern paleontology. Wagner suggested a parallel between the criticism of German racial science abroad and the persecution of Copernicus and Bruno at the hands of the Inquisition; he argued that, despite criticism by the church, the future of Nazi racial science was still a hopeful one, for "science never allows itself for long to be forced into the rigid confines of dogmatic beliefs." Wagner proclaimed:

> Science has always triumphed in the end, and thus, in like fashion, the Racial Idea of our own time will one day spread throughout the earth, despite all the dogmatic attacks against it . . . From the racial teachings of the National Socialist movement will come a revolution in the conception of the history of the human past and the human future, just as the discovery of the revolution of the earth about the sun led to a revolutionary reorientation in our general picture of the universe.[149]

On August 12, 1938, the *Osservatore Romano* published a qualification (the Germans considered it a retraction) of the Vatican's earlier criticism of the Italian "Racial Manifesto"; the journal made the point that when the pope spoke of racial science (*Rassenlehre*), he intended to distinguish Italy and Germany in this regard; furthermore, he "had not intended to do the Jews a service, but rather had simply affirmed that all men are brothers."[150] Mussolini at this time was concerned about suggestions by church authorities that his government was being pressured to go along with German racial policies; to counter these insinuations, Il Duce announced in a speech of July 31, 1938, before the avant-garde Fascist youth, that even though Italy was indeed "marching forward unerringly in the racial question," it was "absurd" to say that Italian Fascism had "imitated anyone or anything." When the German Office of Racial Policy reported Mussolini's remarks, it noted that the hue and cry raised over this issue by the Italian press and papacy was unfounded, given that "all countries—even England, the United States, and France—have racial laws in more or less overt forms."[151]

On September 1, 1938, the Italian government announced a program to deport all Jews residing in Italy and its occupied territories who had arrived after January 1, 1919. (The *Informationsdienst* in 1938 reported that 44,000 Jews resided in Italy in the mid-1930s.) On October 6, 1938, the Italian government announced a series of legal measures equivalent in effect to the German Nuremberg Laws; the laws excluded Jews from the Fascist party and forbade Jews from marrying non-Jews.[152] A 1939 extension of the laws barred Jewish doctors, pharmacists, and lawyers from practicing in Italy (except for providing services to other Jews); further extensions on March 1, 1940, excluded Jews from positions in journalism, law, pharmacy, engineering, architecture, and other professional employment.[153]

The reaction of the Catholic church to these new racial measures was ambivalent. The position of the church, as expressed in the 1931 *Encyclical on Marriage,* was that marriage between Catholics and non-Catholics should be disallowed, not on the basis of race, but on the basis of religion. Nazi racial theorists took advantage of this statement to argue that it was not the *effects* of Germany's racial legislation that bothered the church, but rather the fact that the Nazi regime had usurped a realm of control formerly belonging solely to the church.[154]

Medical anti-Semitism was not restricted to European countries. In 1939 Mexico's parliament debated motions to bar all further immigration of Jews; Bolivia passed a similar resolution in 1942. And in Palestine, Jewish doctors fleeing Nazi persecution arrived on the shores of "the promised land" only to be met with demands of the Arabic Doctors' Association that Jewish physicians not be granted license to practice.[155]

In the United States, immigration of Jews (along with other "undesirable" groups) had already been drastically curtailed by the 1924 Immigration Restriction Acts. In the period 1900–1924, immigrants were accepted into the United States at a rate of about 435,000 per year. In the period 1925–1939, however, after quotas were imposed, this figure dropped to 24,430 per year, a tiny fraction (5 percent) of the former rate.[156] (In 1934 Harry H. Laughlin of the Eugenics Department of the Carnegie Institution proposed stronger immigration restrictions against Jews fleeing Nazi Germany. Today we know that thousands of Jews seeking asylum in the United States were turned back from Ellis Island in the 1930s after quotas had been filled; some of these were later killed in concentration camps in the countries from which they had tried to flee.)

German racial hygienists looked to the United States as an example of a country effectively dealing not only with the problem of the genetically unfit but also with immigration policy. In August 1932, at a course organized by the Nazi Physicians' League to allow physicians to brush up on their racial hygiene, organizer Heinz Kürten called attention to the trail blazed by America in the field of racial hygiene. America, according to Kürten, had been invaded by a flood of immigrants—10 million in the first decade of the twentieth century—largely of the "dirtier southern European stocks." Kürten argued that these immigrants threatened to spoil the achievements of the whites, "who had originally discovered and conquered the land." But thanks to the "educational activities" (*Aufklärungsarbeit*) of men such as Lothrop Stoddard, Madison Grant, and Harry Laughlin, the tide might be turned, especially if immigration restriction rules could be enforced. Kürten was not alone in this view. In 1933 Physicians' Führer Gerhard Wagner praised America for her stringent racial policy and implored his own countrymen to follow her example. Wagner praised American restrictions on alien movements and behavior—restrictions that, according to Wagner, had allowed the U.S. government to send some 30,000 violators of immigration rules back to their country of origin over the two-year period 1929–1930.[157]

In the mid-1930s, Nazi medical journals were able to report that anti-Semitism was a common feature of American university and medical life; journals noted that many of America's leading universities boasted quotas on Jewish student enrollments. The *Deutsches Ärzteblatt,* for example, noted in 1937 that of 1,319 American colleges and universities, 477 had no Jews whatsoever; the journal concluded that in many areas Americans had recognized "the danger of the swamping of the intellectual professions by aliens."[158] In 1939 the journal reported that American newspapers and journals were complaining about the "flooding" of New York City by immigrant Jewish physicians.[159] German academic journals also made much of the fact that American black-white miscegenation laws were generally much stricter than Germany's own Nuremberg Laws; German medical journals took notice when the American Medical Association rejected the request of 5,000 black physicians to join the prestigious American body.[160] In 1939 Germany's leading racial hygiene journal reported the refusal of the University of Missouri to admit blacks; one year later the journal reported legislation introduced by Mississippi Senator Bilbo to send 2.5 million American Negroes back to Africa.[161]

American eugenics publications in turn hailed German racial legislation as the most advanced in the world. In 1934, editors of the American journal *Eugenical News* reported:

> The city of Berlin quite logically is trying to reduce the number of its Jewish physicians, which is not in keeping with the racial composition of the general population. According to the last census Berlin had a population of 4,236,400, of which 155,000, or 3.6 percent, were of Jewish religion. Assuming that that part of the population which is Jewish by racial descent is twice as large, we must still admit that 47 percent Jews among the medical men of Berlin is hardly justified.[162]

In 1943 Rudolf Ramm, the man in charge of supervising German medical education, summarized ten years of German racial legislation. He noted that in 1933 there had been three distinct dangers facing the German people: racial miscegenation; a declining birthrate; and the growth of inferior elements in the German population. The origins of these dangers could be traced, in Ramm's view, to a disregard for natural laws, a disregard fostered by both church dogma and the spread of "the materialistic ideologies of liberalism and Marxism." Ramm blamed the political parties of the Weimar period (the so-called *Systemzeit*) for having failed to utilize modern biological knowledge to combat these dangers; it was not until the triumph of National Socialism that Germany had seen a "fundamental transformation in the conception and application of biological research." Ramm listed five key measures in the achievement of this transformation: the Civil Service Law, the Blood Protection Law, the Sterilization Law, the Castration Law, and the Marital Health Law. These, he wrote, had become the "milestones" along the path of restoring racial purity. The Civil Service Law was designed to exclude "the Jew and Jewish half-breed from state and other public positions"; the Blood Protection Law put a halt "once and for all" to miscegenation between men of German blood and "the inferior Jewish race." The three other measures served to improve the genetic health of the population by a process of selection and elimination (*Ausmerze und Auslese*). The Sterilization Law and the Castration Law prevented "the genetically ill and morally inferior from transferring their genes to future generations"; the Marital Health Law served to prevent the "marriage [*Koppelung*] of diseased, inferior, or dangerous genetic material with superior material." Each of these laws was supposed to have been based on the latest results of genetics.[163]

These are claims that were published in a book intended to be required reading for all German medical students: this was Germany's leading textbook on "legal and ethical aspects of the profession." Ramm (writing in 1942) was proud of the fact that Germany's efforts to suppress the Jews had found widespread imitation in many other European states. He thus issued a prophesy, directed to all medical students in the Reich, that "the radical solution of the Jewish question becomes in this sense a European problem. The faster and more thoroughly it is solved, the more rapid (and better) will be the reformation [*Gestaltung*] of the European continent upon a racial basis, and the happier will be its future."[164]

The persecution of the Jews under the Nazis derived support from a complex of philosophical doctrines embodied in legal and medical practice. Germany carried to an extreme policies that were present in milder forms in other countries. Justifications for this persecution were based on certain conceptions of science and of race—conceptions that, when combined with a unique set of social and economic events at the end of the Weimar Republic, made National Socialism attractive to a substantial portion of the German medical community. But there is a further aspect of medical anti-Semitism, one that must be explored if we are to understand the role of medicine under the Nazis. As we shall see next, Nazi medical philosophers did not simply say that Jews were stealing German jobs or bringing a "materialist" or "apathetic" spirit into the medical profession. In the Nazi medical view, the Jew, to be destroyed, had to be rendered "sick"—what one doctor called "a diseased bacillus, eating its way into the body of the German people"[165] (see Figure 34). The Jews, along with other social, sexual, and political "undesirables," would be rendered "life not worth living"; this would also become a medical task.

7 The Destruction of "Lives Not Worth Living"

> The needle belongs in the hand of the doctor.
> —Viktor Brack, head of the
> German euthanasia program, 1939

In early October of 1939, designated by the government as the year of "the duty to be healthy," Hitler authored a secret memo certifying that "Reichsleiter Bouhler and Dr. Brandt are hereby commissioned to allow certain specified doctors to grant a mercy death [*Gnadentod*] to patients judged incurably sick, by critical medical examination."[1] By August 24, 1941, when the first phase of this "adult operation" was brought to an end, over 70,000 patients from more than a hundred German hospitals had been killed, in an operation that provided the stage rehearsal for the subsequent destruction of Jews, homosexuals, communists, Gypsies, Slavs, and prisoners of war.[2]

Historical Background

The idea of the destruction of "lives not worth living" had been discussed in legal and medical literature long before the Nazi rise to power. In the late nineteenth century, scholars writing for the British *Westminster Review* had debated the merits of destroying the insane in order to relieve society of "this terrible burden." In 1912, at a meeting of the Hungarian Psychiatric Association, a Dr. Namenyi recommended that "useless idiots" be killed according to the principle of euthanasia.[3]

Euthanasia has, of course, meant different things to different people. The word originally simply meant "an easy or gentle death"; the English use of the word in this sense dates back at least to the seventeenth century. Nineteenth-century advocates of euthanasia defended the right to choose the time and manner of one's death or to end one's life with a minimum of pain and suffering. In the twentieth century, however, euthanasia has also been recommended as a means of cutting costs or ridding society of "useless eaters."

It is one thing to guarantee someone the right to die without suffering or without the use of heroic or extraordinary measures. It is another thing to require that certain individuals or groups be forcibly destroyed as lives useless to the community—lives not worth living. The logic in each case is different: in the first, the goal is to provide individual happiness in the final moments of life; in the second, the goal is an economic one—to relieve society of the financial burden of caring for lives considered useless to the community. It was the achievement of the Nazis to confuse these two very different senses of euthanasia: voluntary and compulsory, the one based on relieving suffering, the other based on minimizing medical costs. The confusion, however, was not entirely an invention of the Nazis.

In 1920 Alfred Hoche, a professor of medicine, and Rudolf Binding, a professor of law, published their book *Release and Destruction of Lives Not Worth Living,* in which they argued that the principle of "allowable killing" should be extended to the incurably sick (they also defended the right to suicide). The right to live, they asserted, must be earned and justified, not dogmatically assumed. Those who are not capable of human feeling—those "ballast lives" and "empty human husks" that fill our psychiatric institutions—can have no sense of the value of life. Theirs is not a life worth living; hence their destruction is not only tolerable but humane.[4]

The idea of systematically killing mental patients gained broader currency after the deprivation suffered in World War I. Racial hygienists (such as Gustav Boeters) claimed that the costs of "maintaining defectives" had become prohibitive during the war; this argument was made more acceptable by the fact that even some doctors in this period were going hungry. Food and medical supplies were rationed after the British blockade of German ports, and "defectives" were low on the list to obtain supplies. As a result, nearly half of all patients in German psychiatric hospitals perished from starvation or disease.[5] It was in this context that Hoche and Binding proposed the killing of the mentally ill.

Hoche and Binding's call for "a release from this national burden" prompted a nationwide debate on when—if ever—a physician was justified in taking life. Ewald Meltzer criticized Hoche and Binding's proposal, linking it with the morality of the "breeding state"; the Weimar Reich Health Office included a review of Meltzer's book in its files on racial hygiene. Heinrich Hoffmann and Max Nassauer both advocated "dying help" (*Sterbehilfe*) for the incurably sick; I. Malbin defended the destruction of "lives not worth living" as a natural practice common to peoples throughout history.[6] In 1922 Ernst Mann published a novel portraying the destruction of the poor as a means of eliminating poverty.[7] In 1925 E. Kirchner linked Hoche and Binding's proposal with Nietzsche's view that "the sick person is a parasite of society"; he also noted that the Liegnitz town council in the early 1920s had recommended the formation of a commission to determine whether money might be saved by eliminating the insane. Two years later, Kirchner applauded Hoche and Binding for their "creative solution" to problems posed by Plato, Thomas More, and Nietzsche.[8]

Calls for euthanasia (in the various senses of the term) were not restricted to Germany. In 1932 Kilock Millard, president of Britain's Society of Medical Officers, proposed legislation regulating voluntary euthanasia. In 1935 a number of British physicians formed the Voluntary Euthanasia Legalization Society, headed by Lord Moynihan, president of the Royal College of Surgeons. In 1936 the Euthanasia Society submitted a bill before the House of Lords to allow voluntary euthanasia, and over the next five years (1936–1941) the *British Medical Journal* carried on a lively debate over this question. A not uncommon view in this debate was that euthanasia should be considered an option for the (otherwise healthy) mentally retarded.[9]

The facile language used in such debates often sounds strange to the modern ear. Consider the following extraordinary assertion by the philosopher Bertrand Russell, taken from his 1927 *Marriage and Morals:* "It seems on the whole fair to regard negroes as on the average inferior to white men, although for work in the tropics they are indispensable, so that their extermination (apart from questions of humanity) would be highly undesirable."[10] Though Russell's remarks are not made in the context of the euthanasia debate, they do reveal how broadly nets were cast over questions of who will live and who will die.

American discussion of the "euthanasia question" peaked (predictably) in the period 1936–1941. As in Britain, most advocates claimed that people should have the right to choose when or how they want to die. Euthanasia was primarily intended to help guarantee the rights of individuals to what we today would call death with dignity. Many American advocates also argued that euthanasia might be a good way to save on medical costs.[11] Dr. W. A. Gould, for example, in the *Journal of the American Institute of Homeopathy*, defended euthanasia as one way of resolving economic difficulties; he asked his readers to recall in this context the "elimination of the unfit" in ancient Sparta.[12] Some offered more radical suggestions: in 1935 the French-American Nobel Prize winner Alexis Carrel (inventor of the iron lung) suggested in his book *Man the Unknown* that the criminal and the insane should be "humanely and economically disposed of in small euthanasia institutions supplied with proper gases."[13] W. G. Lennox, in a 1938 speech to Harvard's Phi Beta Kappa chapter, claimed that saving lives "adds a load to the back of society"; he wanted physicians to recognize "the privilege of death for the congenitally mindless and for the incurable sick who wish to die; the boon of not being born for the unfit." Lennox was also astute enough to perceive that "the principle of limiting certain races through limitation of off-spring might be applied internationally as well as intranationally. Germany, in time, might have solved her Jewish problem this way."[14]

American support for the concept of euthanasia dwindled in the early 1940s, after rumors of German exterminations began to filter into the American news media. The issue was not entirely dead, however. In 1942, as Hitler's psychiatrists were sending the last of their patients into the gas chambers. Dr. Foster Kennedy, professor of neurology at Cornell Medical College, published an article in the official journal of the American Psychiatric Association calling for the killing of retarded children aged five and older—children whom the author called "those hopeless ones who should never have been born—Nature's mistakes."[15] Kennedy cited Justice Holmes's remarks (made originally in support of sterilization, not of euthanasia) that "three generations of imbeciles are enough," and he was apparently not alone in this opinion: a 1937 Gallup Poll showed that 45 percent of the American population favored euthanasia for defective infants. After the war, physicians accused of having organized the euthanasia operations were able to point to America to argue that the idea of destroying inferiors found supporters outside Germany.[16]

Wonderful Parks and Gardens

According to the postwar testimony of Hitler's personal physician Karl Brandt, Hitler decided even before 1933 that he would one day try to eliminate the mentally ill. In fact, shortly after the rise of the Nazis, several NSDAP *Gauleiter* were authorized to perform secret euthanasia operations in certain insane asylums.[17] It was not until 1935, however, at the Nazi Party Congress in Nuremberg (the *Parteitag der Freiheit*), that concrete plans for the destruction of all of Germany's "lives not worth living" were discussed. The logic for the destruction was presented by Gerhard Wagner, Führer of the National Socialist Physicians' League, in a speech before the congress (see Figure 35).

In his speech Wagner assailed liberalism and Marxism for having denied "the inherently different value" of the lives of different individuals. According to Wagner, the doctrine of equality (*Gleichheitslehre*) was even worse in its effects ("biologically speaking") than the Russian revolution, insofar as it led one "to value the sick, the dying, and the unfit on a par with the healthy and the strong." Wagner appealed to Fritz Lenz to argue that the average family size of "inferiors" was nearly twice that of healthy families; as a result, the number of mentally ill had grown by 450 percent in the last seventy years, while the population as a whole had increased by only 50 percent. Inferiors thus lived on at the expense of the healthy: "more than one billion reichsmarks is spent on the genetically disabled; contrast this with the 766 million spent on the police, or the 713 million spent on local administration, and one sees what a burden and unexcelled injustice this places on the normal, healthy members of the population." Wagner noted that steps were being taken to reverse this trend, and that, indeed, while much of the world still clung to what he called the insane idea of equality (*Wahn der Gleichheit*), Germany as a nation had begun to recognize, once again, "the natural and God-given inequality of men."[18]

Not included in published records of the time, however, was Wagner's solution to the problem. According to Brandt's postwar testimony, Hitler told Wagner at this time that if a war should break out, then he (Hitler) would authorize a nationwide program of euthanasia; Brandt also recalled that "the Führer was of the opinion that such a program could be put into effect more smoothly and rapidly in time of war, and that in the general upheaval of war, the open resistance anticipated from the church would not play the part that it might in other circumstances."[19]

The association of euthanasia and war was not fortuitous. If the healthy could sacrifice their lives in time of war, then why should the sick not do the same? This was Hoche and Binding's argument, and it became a fashionable one among the Nazis. One American writer recognized this thinking as early as 1941, when he pointed out that the handicapped and mentally ill "were not killed for mercy. They were killed because they could no longer manufacture guns in return for the food they consumed; because beds in the German hospitals were needed for wounded soldiers; because their death was the ultimate logic of the national socialist doctrine of promoting racial superiority and the survival of the physically fit."[20] The Nazis made this link explicit. On August 10, 1939, when Nazi leaders met to plan the euthanasia operation, Philipp Bouhler, head of the Party Chancellery, declared that the purpose of the operation was not only to continue the "struggle against genetic disease" but also to free up hospital beds and personnel for the coming war.[21] The underlying philosophy was simple: patients were to be either cured or killed. Accordingly, Leonardo Conti, Wagner's successor as Reich Health Führer, allowed individuals capable of productive work to be excluded from the operation.

The concept of sacrificing the less than physically fit reverberated through other areas of Nazi legal and medical policy. In March 1937 the *Frankfurter Zeitung* reported on the case of a farmer who had shot to death his sleeping son because the child was "mentally ill in a manner that threatened society" (*gemeinschaft-gefährlich geisteskrank*). The father was charged with murder and brought to court, where he defended his action on the grounds that the son had become (among other things) a financial burden to the family. The prosecutor asked for the death penalty. Karl Astel, president of the Thuringen Health Office, came to the father's defense and influenced the court to grant a reduced sentence of three years in prison. The mental condition of the murdered son played an important role in the decision.[22]

The destruction of life not worth living was also glorified in Nazi literature and art. In 1936 the ophthalmologist Helmut Unger published his widely read novel *Sendung und Gewissen* (Mission and conscience), which told the story of a young woman who, suffering from multiple sclerosis, decides that her life is no longer worth living and asks to be relieved of her misery. Her husband, a doctor, recog-

Figure 35. Gerhard Wagner and Adolf Hitler at the Nazi Party Congress in Nuremberg in 1935, at which Hitler discussed with Wagner the "euthanasia" of the mentally ill. From *Deutsches Ärzteblatt*, 65(1935): 913.

Figure 36. "The Prussian Government Provides Annually the Following Funds for: a Normal Schoolchild (125 RM); a Slow Learner (573 RM); the Educable Mentally Ill (950 RM); and Blind or Deaf-Born Schoolchildren (1,500 RM)." This illustration depicts the burden of maintaining the socially unfit. From *Volk und Rasse*, 8(1933): 156.

Figure 37. "You Are Sharing the Load! A Genetically Ill Individual Costs Approximately 50,000 Reichsmarks by the Age of Sixty." This poster, from an exhibit on racial hygiene produced by the Reichsnährstand, illustrates the burden of the mentally ill on the healthy German population. From Walter Gross, "Drei Jahre rassenpolitische Aufklärungsarbeit," *Volk und Rasse*, 10(1935): 335.

nizes her plight and agrees to give her poison. In a grand act of humanity, the husband gives his wife a fatal injection of morphine, while a friend of his (also a doctor) accompanies the act with soothing and romantic music at the piano. The doctor, Terstegen, is accused of murder and brought to trial, where he refuses to let his colleagues invent an alibi for him, because he is convinced he has done no wrong. "Would you," asks Terstegen, "if you were a cripple, want to vegetate forever?" He is finally acquitted on grounds that his act constituted an act of mercy; in a critical scene, the words of the Renaissance physician Paracelsus are recalled: "medicine is love."[23]

Unger's novel was important in helping to prepare the ground for the euthanasia program. In the fall of 1935, Gerhard Wagner ordered the book made into a movie designed to dramatize the plight of the incurably ill. The film (*Ich klage an!*) was released in Berlin in the early war years, where it was a great success.[24]

Humanistic propaganda notwithstanding, the argument for the destruction of life not worth living was at root an economic one. In 1934, for example, the journal *Deutsche Freiheit* in Saarbrücken published a small pamphlet by Dr. Heilig, a representative of the Nazi Physician's League for Altena and Lüdenscheid. In his pamphlet, Heilig argued:

> It must be made clear to anyone suffering from an incurable disease that the useless dissipation of costly medications drawn from the public store cannot be justified. Parents who have seen the difficult life of a crippled or feeble-minded child must be convinced that, though they may have a moral obligation to care for the unfortunate creature, the broader public should not be obligated ... to assume the enormous costs that long-term institutionalization might entail.[25]

Heilig also stated that it made no sense for persons "on the threshold of old age" to receive services such as orthopedic therapy or dental bridgework; such services were to be reserved for healthier elements of the population.

Heilig's comments are typical within the Nazi medical profession. Popular medical and racial hygiene journals carried charts depicting the costs of maintaining the sick at the expense of the healthy (see Figures 36 and 37); schoolbooks asked students to calculate the costs of maintaining the frail and invalid. Adolf Dorner's 1935–36 high school mathematics textbook, for example, included the following problems:

Problem 94
In one region of the German Reich there are 4,400 mentally ill in state institutions, 4,500 receiving state support, 1,600 in local hospitals, 200 in homes for the epileptic, and 1,500 in welfare homes. The state pays a minimum of 10 million RM/year for these institutions.
  I. What is the average cost to the state per inhabitant per year?
  II. Using the result calculated from I, how much does it cost the state if:
     A. 868 patients stay longer than 10 years?
     B. 260 patients stay longer than 20 years?
     C. 112 patients stay longer than 25 years?

Problem 95
The construction of an insane asylum requires 6 million RM. How many housing units @ 15,000 RM could be built for the amount spent on insane asylums?[26]

Such problems did not remain in the realm of theory. After the war, documents presenting detailed calculations of the "savings" achieved through the euthanasia operation were found in a safe in the castle at Hartheim (one of six euthanasia institutions equipped with gas chambers). Euthanasia officials calculated that the "disinfection" (murder) of 70,273 individuals in the course of the operation had resulted in savings of the following food items (in kilograms):

Bread	4,781,339.72 kg
Marmalade	239,067.02 kg
Margarine	174,719.23 kg
Schmalz	5,311.40 kg
Coffee substitute	79,671.38 kg
Sugar	185,952.86 kg
Flour	156,952.86 kg
Meats and sausage	653,516.96 kg
Potatoes	19,754,325.27 kg
Butter	50,458.49 kg[27]

Altogether, the euthanasia operation had saved the German economy an average of 245,955.50 RM per day (88,543,980.00 RM per year); if one assumed an average institutional life expectancy of ten years, the Reich had been saved expenses in excess of 880 million RM. Officials also noted that by the end of 1941, 93,521 hospital beds had been freed up by the operation.[28]

Even before the euthanasia operation, other aspects of Nazi social policy reflect this same philosophy. In 1933, the first year of Nazi government, expenditures for the handicapped and invalid were drastically cut. In 1933 German medical insurance companies paid 41.5 million RM for invalids—10 million less than in 1932, in the depths of the recession.²⁹ Many homes for the elderly or infirm closed in the early years of the Nazi regime; the total number of nurses caring for the ill dropped from 111,700 in 1933 to 88,900 in 1934. According to the Statistische Reichsamt, the number of hospitals and other medical care institutions fell from 3,987 in 1931 to 3,219 in 1935; the number of beds per 1,000 population fell in the same period from 5.7 to 4.5.³⁰

These policies were supported by Germany's most prominent racial hygienists. Otmar von Verschuer, for example, attacked Germany's entire system of socialized medicine on the grounds that it interfered with the natural tendency for individuals to sort themselves out according to "inner genetic potential." Verschuer argued that socialized medicine could seriously impair the racial hygiene of a people, and that the German state had been far too eager to support "the weak, the laggard, and the inferior."³¹ Fritz Bartels, Gerhard Wagner's right-hand man in the Nazi Physicians' League, phrased this in even stronger terms. He accused Marxists in the "14-year humiliation" (*14 Jahre Schmach*—Nazi language for the Weimar Republic) of having built "palaces for the mentally ill," "wonderful parks and gardens" for those inferior beings that inhabit Germany's mental institutions. Bartels noted that this would soon have to stop. This, after all, was the lesson of history: "From time immemorial, the nation has always eliminated the weak to make way for the healthy. A hard, but healthy and effective law to which we must once again give credence. The primary task of the physician is to discover for whom health care at government expense will be worth the cost."³² For the Nazi medical philosopher, support for the mentally ill was simply not worth the cost. In the course of the thirties, funds allotted to care for the mentally ill gradually fell, reaching 40, 39, or even 38 pfennig per person per day.³³ It was not such a large step from here to remove all care entirely.

The Child-Murder Operation

The program to destroy lives not worth living began in a relatively innocuous fashion. In the fall of 1938, a father by the name of Knauer wrote to Hitler asking that his child, born blind, retarded, and without an arm and a leg, be granted a "mercy death," or euthanasia. Hitler instructed his personal physician Karl Brandt to determine in consultation with the child's physicians whether or not the facts were as stated in the father's letter. Brandt was instructed that if the report proved to be accurate, then he was empowered to allow the physicians to grant the child euthanasia. Werner Catel, the physician in charge of the child, agreed to allow the child to die a "merciful death."

The case of Knauer provided a model on which other euthanasia actions would be carried out. In May 1939, only a few months later, Brandt notified Hans Hefelmann that Hitler had asked him (Brandt) to appoint an advisory committee to prepare for the killing of deformed and retarded children. Hitler's Chancellery was to be directly responsible for the operation; but to maintain secrecy, the project was organized under the cover name Committee for the Scientific Treatment of Severe, Genetically Determined Illness (Reichsausschuss zur wissenschaftlichen Erfassung von erb- und anlagebedingter schwerer Leiden). Members of the committee included Karl Brandt, Helmut Unger, the pediatrician Ernst Wentzler, the psychiatrist Hans Heinze, and the pediatrician Werner Catel. The entire process of euthanasia was to be conducted under the strictest secrecy (*Geheime Reichssache*); Hefelmann, in testimony after the war, noted that only those physicians from whom a "positive attitude" could be expected were asked to participate in the operation.[34]

On August 18, 1939, just fourteen days before the invasion of Poland, the Committee for the Scientific Treatment of Severe, Genetically Determined Illnesses produced a secret report, delivered to all state governments, asking that midwives or doctors delivering any child born with congenital deformities such as "idiocy or Mongolism (especially if associated with blindness or deafness); microcephaly or hydrocephaly of a severe or progressive nature; deformities of any kind, especially missing limbs, malformation of the head, or spina bifida; or crippling deformities such as spastics [*Littleschen Erkrankung*]" register that child with local health authorities. The ostensible reason given for this registration was "to clarify certain scientific questions in areas of congenital deformity and mental retardation."[35] The order also required that doctors with any child in their care up to the age of three and suffering from any of these infirmities report this child to local health offices; doctors throughout the Reich were sent elaborate questionnaires for this purpose. Registration orders were published in many medical journals; the ailments listed in the orders were simply added to the list of other things requiring medical notification—such as venereal disease, births and deaths, childbed fever, certain contagious diseases, and genetic illnesses falling under the Sterilization Law.[36] Midwives were paid 2 RM for every registration.

Questionnaires returned by physicians or midwives were assembled in Berlin at the desk of Hans Hefelmann, business director of the operation. Hefelmann sent the questionnaires to Professors Catel, Heinze, and Wentzler to be sorted for "selection" (extermination). Children slated to die were marked with a plus sign; children allowed to live were marked with a minus sign. Decisions were made entirely on the basis of these questionnaires; those doing the selection never examined the children in person or consulted the families or guardians. Children marked with a plus sign were ordered into one of twenty-eight institutions rapidly equipped with extermination facilities, including some of Germany's oldest and most highly respected hospitals (Eglfing-Haar; Brandenburg-Görden; Hamburg Rothenburg and Uchtspringe; Meseritz-Obrawalde, among others). Parents were told that the transport was necessary to improve treatment for their child.[37]

Methods of killing included injections of morphine, tablets, and gassing with cyanide or chemical warfare agents. Children at Idstein, Kantenhof, Görden, and Eichberg were not gassed but were killed by injection; poisons were commonly administered slowly, over several days or even weeks, so that the cause of death could be disguised as pneumonia, bronchitis, or some other complication induced by the injections. Hermann Pfannmüller of the hospital at Eglfing-Haar slowly starved the children entrusted to his care until they died of "natural causes." This method, he boasted, was least likely to incur criticism from the foreign press or from "the gentlemen in Switzerland" (the Red Cross).[38] Others simply left their institutions without heat, and patients died of exposure. Nazi medical men could thus argue that their actions were not technically murder, for they were simply withholding care and "letting nature take its course."[39] Parents were informed with a standardized letter, used at all institutions, that their daughter or son had died suddenly and unexpectedly of brain edema, appendicitis, or other fabricated cause; parents were also informed that, owing to the danger of an epidemic, the body had to be cremated immediately.

This first part of the children's euthanasia was originally restricted to children up to three years old. In December 1940, however, Hefelmann, in conference with hospital doctors administering the program, agreed that the three-year-old boundary might "occasionally be overstepped."[40] On July 12, 1941, Reichsstatthalter Mehlhorn ordered all doctors, nurses, and medical personnel to register not just infants but all minors known to have crippling handicaps; teachers who noticed such handicaps among their pupils were required to register those children with health authorities. Anyone failing to register such individuals could be fined up to 150 RM or face imprisonment up to four weeks.[41] By the autumn of 1941, the children's euthanasia program had been expanded to include children up to eight, twelve, and even sixteen and seventeen years old, partly to make up for the slowdown of the adult program[42] (discussed later in this chapter).

Jewish children were originally excluded from this operation, on the grounds that they did not deserve the "merciful act" (*Wohltat*) of euthanasia. In 1943, however, the program was broadened to include healthy children of unwanted races: in May 1943 the psychiatric hospital at Hadamar began exterminating Jewish children. Altogether, more than 5,000 children were killed in this first phase of the German euthanasia program.[43]

Adult Euthanasia

The child murders were only one part of a much larger program designed to rid Germany of its weak, handicapped, and "inferior." Here again, the program was planned and administered by medical professionals.

On July 18, 1939, Hans Hefelmann reported to Viktor Brack that Hitler had authorized Leonardo Conti to begin a process of adult euthanasia (*Erwachseneneuthanasie*). The message had been given to Hefelmann, in utmost secrecy, by the ophthalmologist Helmut Unger; Unger, in turn, had been informed of the authorization earlier in the year by Reich Physicians' Führer Gerhard Wagner. By the summer of 1939, Conti (Wagner's successor), Philipp Bouhler (Party Chancellery leader), and Herbert Linden (coauthor of the Blood Protection Law) had worked out a plan for the extermination of all of Germany's mental patients. Three ostensibly scientific/medical organizations were created to administer the destruction of mental patients and handicapped children. The Working Committee for Hospital Care provided letterhead for operations correspondence; the Charitable Foundation for Institutional Care was responsible for arranging financial details; and the Nonprofit Patient Transport Corporation was responsible for transporting patients to extermination institutions.[44] Each organization was subordinated to the Committee for the Scientific Treatment of Severe, Genetically Determined Illness, the body established in the summer of 1939 to administer all euthanasia operations. The operation was given the code name T-4, derived from the address of the Nonprofit Patient Transport Corporation, located at Tiergartenstrasse 4 in Berlin.

In October 1939 the first euthanasia applications were sent to psychiatric institutions, where they were evaluated by forty-eight medical doctors—including most notably Werner Heyde, Friedrich Mauz, Paul Nitsche, Friedrich Panse, Kurt Pohlisch, Carl Schneider, and W. Villinger. For their services, the physicians received five pfennig per survey if they evaluated more than 3,500 applications per month, and ten pfennig if they evaluated fewer than 500 per month. From a total of 283,000 applications evaluated, roughly 75,000 patients were marked to die.[45]

The first executions of adult mental patients were carried out during the military campaign against Poland. On January 9, 1940, Dr. Hildebrandt, the future head of the Office of Race and Settlement, reported to Himmler the "elimination [*Beseitigung*] of approximately 4,400 incurable mentally ill from Polish insane asylums," and further, "the elimination of approximately 200 incurable mentally ill from the asylum at Konradstein." Most of these were simply shot, as part of the cleanup work of *Einsatzgruppen* deployed by the Security Service (SD) close behind advancing German armies. Patients were also killed in certain parts of Germany near the front—especially in Pomerania (near Danzig)—and in West Prussia.[46] At about the same time, physicians began to develop techniques that could be used to destroy the entirety of Germany's mental patient population. In early January 1940, Brack, Brandt, Conti, and Bouhler met in the psychiatric hospital at Brandenburg, near Berlin, to conduct the first large-scale test of adult euthanasia. August Becker, a chemist employed by the Reich Criminal Police Office, described this first "experiment" as follows:

> I was ordered by Brack to participate in the first euthanasia trial run in the Hospital at Brandenburg, near Berlin. It was in the first part of January 1940 that I traveled to the hospital. Special apparatus had been constructed for this purpose at the hospital. A room, similar to a shower

with tile floors, had been set up, approximately three by five meters and three meters high. There were benches around the edge of the room, and on the floor, about ten centimeters above the ground, there was a water pipe approximately one centimeter in diameter. In this tube there were small holes, from which the carbon monoxide gas flowed. The gas containers were outside the room and were already attached to one end of the pipe . . . In the hospital there were already two crematoria ovens ready to go, for burning the bodies. At the entrance to the room, constructed similar to that of an air-raid shelter, there was a square peep hole through which the behavior of the subjects [*Delinquenten*] could be observed. The first gassing was administered personally by Dr. Widmann. He operated the controls and regulated the flow of gas. He also instructed the hospital physicians Dr. Eberl and Dr. Baumhardt, who later took over the exterminations in Grafeneck and Hadamar . . . At this first gassing, approximately 18–20 people were led into the "showers" by the nursing staff. These people were required to undress in another room until they were completely naked. The doors were closed behind them. They entered the room quietly and showed no signs of anxiety. Dr. Widmann operated the gassing apparatus; I could observe through the peep hole that, after a minute, the people either fell down or lay on the benches. There was no great disturbance or commotion. After another five minutes, the room was cleared of gas. SS men specially designated for this purpose placed the dead on stretchers and brought them to the ovens . . . At the end of the experiment Viktor Brack, who was of course also present (and whom I'd previously forgotten), addressed those in attendance. He appeared satisfied by the results of the experiment, and repeated once again that this operation should be carried out only by physicians, according to the motto: "The needle belongs in the hand of the doctor." Karl Brandt spoke after Brack, and stressed again that gassings should only be done by physicians. That is how things began in Brandenburg.[47]

The carbon monoxide used in this and subsequent operations (or "disinfections," as they were commonly known) was recommended for use by toxicologists at the Reich Criminal Police Office's Institute for Criminal Technology.[48] After taking the gold out of the teeth, the bodies were sent to be burned in newly installed crematoria.

The Brandenburg experiment served as a model for subsequent executions. Hospitals at Grafeneck, Bernburg, Sonnenstein, Hadamar, Brandenburg, and the castle at Hartheim near Linz were all specially outfitted with gas chambers disguised as showers and crematoria to burn the bodies.[49] Young, inexperienced doctors were chosen to run the facilities.

The original intent of those who planned the euthanasia operation was to scale it according to the formula 1,000:10:5:1—that is, for every 1,000 Germans, 10 needed some form of psychiatric care; 5 of these required continuous care; and among these, 1 should be destroyed.[50] Given a German population of 65–70 million, this meant that 65,000–70,000 individuals should have been included within the operation. And in fact the program kept closely to this schedule. By the end of August 1941, when the gassing phase of the operation was stopped, 70,273 individuals had been killed. The committee responsible for overseeing the operation kept meticulous records, and today we have an accurate account of how many were killed, and where.[51]

Killing stations	Period of operation	Numbers killed
Grafeneck	Jan.–Dec. 1940	9,839
Brandenburg	Feb.–Sept. 1940	9,772
Bernburg	Jan.–Sept. 1941	8,601
Hadamar	Jan.–Aug. 1941	10,072
Hartheim	May 1940–1941	18,269
Sonnenstein	June 1940–Aug. 1941	13,720

It is important to recognize the banality of the operation. In 1941 the psychiatric institution at Hadamar celebrated the cremation of its ten-thousandth patient in a special ceremony, where everyone in attendance—secretaries, nurses, and psychiatrists—received a bottle of beer for the occasion.[52]

Operations on such a scale are not easy to keep quiet. Rumors had begun to spread in 1940 that children were being killed. Some people began to notice identical form-letter death announcements appearing in newspapers; others complained when they were notified that their child had died of "appendicitis," even though the child's appendix had been removed years before. Suspicions also began to grow (especially around the hospital at Hadamar) that homes for the elderly were going to be emptied; some elderly began to refuse commitment to rest or retirement homes. In the spring of 1940, after a number of parents complained that their children had been killed, state prosecutors filed charges of murder against the directors of two institutions. Charges were quickly dropped, however, when the courts were informed that Hitler himself had guaranteed the immunity of all persons involved. Subsequently procedures were developed to prevent such difficulties. Martin Bormann ordered that letters notifying parents of their child's death be varied in both form and content. Himmler suggested showing films on heredity and mental disease in order to quell the "ugly public opinion" that had grown in the mountainous area surrounding the extermination hospital at Grafeneck;[53] such films had been used since early in the regime as part of an effort to harden public attitudes against "weaker" elements in the population.[54] The regime also took more forceful steps. Parents who resisted turning over their children to the hospitals were declared incompetent and deprived of custody. In other cases, reluctant parents were sent to forced labor camps, and their children were placed in the custody of the state. By the summer of 1941, protests (especially from the Catholic church) had become sufficiently frequent to cause a certain amount of concern among those administering the operation; on August 24, 1941, Hitler ordered Brandt to stop gassing patients in psychiatric institutions. By this time, however, the original goal of eliminating 65,000–70,000 patients had already been achieved.

The killings continued, however, throughout the war and even for some time after. After the fall of 1941, the character of the euthanasia operation changed dramatically. Until August 1941, the program had been centrally administered through Hitler's Party Chancellery. Beginning in 1942, responsibility for administering euthanasia was shifted away from the Chancellery and back to individual hospitals. The methods of killing also changed. Whereas earlier killings had been primarily by means of gas chambers, killings after the fall of 1941 were achieved through a combination of injections, poisonings, and starvation. Euthanasia took on less the character of a single, Reichwide "operation" and more the character of normal hospital routine.[55]

This routine character of euthanasia operations continued in at least one instance for some time after the end of the war. Peter Breggin, in his article "The Killing of Mental Patients," has described his interview with Robert Abrams, a twenty-four-year-old soldier, reporter, and public relations officer at the time of the American occupation. According to Abrams:

> It was a full three months after the start of the occupation when a German doctor told a story that no one could at first believe. The doctor had returned home from the war to discover that the state hospital near his village was exterminating its mental patients, and that this was going on unabated within a few hundred yards of an American M.P. unit. The chief psychiatrist of the hospital had actually been arrested as a Nazi, but the remaining doctors, nurses, and attendants in the hospital had continued on quietly with their murder of the inmate population.

Breggin continues:

> On July 2, 1945, Abrams and a carload of soldiers entered the town, Kaufbeuren, and saw the institutional buildings in the distance . . . The third doctor in command was now the chief and he told Abrams that the last child patient had been killed on May 29th, 33 days before the occupation of the nearby village. The last adult had died twelve hours before Abrams' arrival, and only the drawn guns of the Americans had put an end to the "destruction of useless eaters."[56]

Doctors were never *ordered* to murder psychiatric patients and handicapped children. They were *empowered* to do so, and fulfilled their task without protest, often on their own initiative. Hitler's original memo of October 1939 was not an order (*Befehl*), but an empowerment (*Vollmacht*), granting physicians permission to act. In the abortive euthanasia trial at Limburg in 1964, Hefelmann testified that "no doctor was ever ordered to participate in the euthanasia program; they came of their own volition." Himmler himself noted that the operations undertaken in psychiatric hospitals were administered solely by medical personnel.[57]

Two further dimensions to this situation have emerged from recent research. First, most of those physicians who did object complained primarily that the operation was not, strictly speaking, *legal*. In the early years of the program, some of those administering the operation (Brack and Lammers, for example) were sufficiently concerned about this complaint that they drew up plans for a euthanasia law with the help of several of Germany's racial hygienists (such as Fritz Lenz). One version of the law, drafted in 1940, included the following provisions:

> 1. Anyone suffering from an incurable illness that leads to strong debilitation of either oneself or others can, upon explicit request of the patient and with permission of a specially appointed physician, receive dying help [*Sterbehilfe*] from a physician.
> 2. A patient who, as a consequence of incurable mental illness requiring lifelong care, can, through medical intervention and without his knowledge, have his life terminated.[58]

Proposals for establishing a euthanasia law were widely discussed, and yet the law was never passed. The decision was made instead to keep the question of euthanasia a "private matter"—between doctors and their patients. The killings were performed contrary to German law, though authorized by government officials; Hitler assured those responsible for administering the program that he would bear full responsibility for all that was done.[59]

The West German historian Götz Aly has shown that in many cases, parents of handicapped or retarded offspring were eager to rid themselves of the stigma of having "defective children." Many parents wrote to hospitals to ask if their child could be relieved of his or her misery and be granted euthanasia. The euthanasia operation was not an entirely unpopular program; in fact, it appears to have received a broad level of public support throughout the country.[60] Nazi authorities anticipated this before the onset of the program. In 1920 Ewald Meltzer had surveyed the parents of 162 handicapped children, asking whether they would be willing to have their child put to death, and if so, under what circumstances. A surprisingly large number of the respondents advocated some sort of euthanasia for their children: 119 (73 percent) said yes, with various degrees of qualification; only 4 rejected the suggestion under any circumstance. Meltzer's survey was cited by Nazi authorities exploring how to administer the child-euthanasia program: when Hitler's personal physician Theo Morell helped draw up plans for the operation in the summer of 1939 he referred to Meltzer's survey, noting that many of those who said yes had also expressed the hope that they would never be told the true cause of their child's death. Nazi physicians used this to justify disguising the true nature of the operation from the parents or guardians of the victims.

Similarly, the elimination of the adult mentally ill was not an entirely unpopular program. By the end of the thirties, propaganda bodies had whipped up such fear and hatred for the mentally ill—one Bielefeld physician compared the genetic defective to a "grenade" waiting to explode[61]—that the elimination of these people seemed a logical or even humane measure. Support for the euthanasia of the mentally ill was apparently one reason that steps were taken, in the spring and summer of 1939, to coordinate a single, nationwide euthanasia program: as Aly has shown, Nazi authorities formulated standardized procedures for killing mental patients partly out of fear that, in war conditions, individual *Gauleiter* might begin destroying patients on their own.[62]

The Medicalization of Anti-Semitism

Historians exploring the origins of the Nazi destruction of lives not worth living have only in recent years begun to stress the links between the destruction of the handicapped and mentally ill, on the one hand, and the Jews, on the other. And yet the two programs were linked in both theory and practice. One of the key ideological elements was the "medicalization of anti-Semitism"—the view developed by Nazi physicians that the Jews were "a diseased race," and that the Jewish question might be solved by "medical means."[63]

According to Walter Gross, head of the Office of Racial Policy, it was first with the Nuremberg Laws of 1935 (and especially the Blood Protection Law) that the explicit link was made between the genetically healthy (*Erbgesunden*) and the German blooded (*Deutschblütigen*). The 1933 Civil Service Law (which excluded non-Aryans from government employment) was primarily a "socioeconomic," not a "medical or biological," measure; according to Gross, it was not until the Nuremberg Laws banned marriage and sexual relations between Jews and non-Jews that German racial legislation was put on a "biological basis." All subsequent legislation in the sphere of race and population policy, Gross claimed, was based on this distinction between "healthy" and "diseased" races.[64]

The Nazi conception of healthy and diseased races was at one level expressed in metaphors of the Jew as "parasite" or "cancer" in the body of the German Volk. One physician phrased this in the following terms: "There is a resemblance between Jews and tubercle bacilli: nearly everyone harbors tubercle bacilli, and nearly every people of the earth harbors the Jews; furthermore, an infection can only be cured with difficulty."[65] Peltret also contrasted the "biological" character of National Socialism with the "pathological" character of communism and the "artificial" (*künstlich*) character of imperialistic fascism.

Nazi physicians also claimed, however, that Jews actually suffered from a higher incidence of certain metabolic and mental diseases. In his speech before the 1935 Nazi Party Congress at Nuremberg (the same meeting at which Hitler proposed the murder of the mentally ill), Gerhard Wagner argued that for every 10,000 inhabitants in the Reich, there were 36.9 mentally infirm among the Germans and 48.7 among the Jews. Wagner cited the "interesting figures" of the "Jewish doctor Ullmann," documenting the fact that between the years 1871 and 1900 the relative proportions of Jews and Germans in psychiatric institutions rose from 29:22 to 163:63. Interesting as well, Wagner noted, was the fact that Jews showed a higher rate of sexual deficiency, expressed, for example, in the blurring of secondary sexual characteristics. This, he affirmed (citing the "Jewish doctor Piltz"), explained not only the higher incidence of homosexuality among the Jews but also the prominence of female Jews in "masculine pursuits" such as revolutionary political activism. Wagner concluded that Jews were "a diseased race"; Judaism was "disease incarnate."[66]

Wagner was not of course the first to make such claims. Nazi medical theorists were able to draw upon a broad body of literature documenting differential racial susceptibilities to disease. In 1902, for example, Alexander Pilcz had reported in one of Austria's leading medical journals that Jews suffered disproportionately from acute psychosis and insanity and were especially susceptible to psychoses of a "hereditary-degenerative nature."[67] A Dr. Rajanski noted that the 1871 German census showed that Jews were nearly twice as likely to suffer from mental illness as Christians; and in Vienna, a Dr. M. Engländer presented statistics to demonstrate the higher incidence of idiocy, myopia, glaucoma, diabetes, and tuberculosis among Jews than among non-Jews, attributing these higher rates to poor nutrition and inbreeding.[68] Much of this research was published in Jewish journals: Dr. L. Silvagni, for example, in the 1902 *Jüdisches Volksblatt*, reported a higher incidence of nervous disorders, gallstones, bladder and kidney stones, neuralgia, chronic rheumatism, and brain malfunction among Jews (but also reported a lower susceptibility of Jews to lung infections, typhus, various fevers, syphilis, and alcoholism).[69] Gerhard Wagner cited these and other articles as evidence for his claim that Jews suffered from many diseases that non-Jews did not have, and concluded that the interbreeding of Jews and non-Jews therefore posed grave risks to German public health. Wagner argued that if Germans continued to allow the mixing of "Jewish and non-Jewish blood," this would result in the spread of the diseased genes (*krankhafte Erbanlagen*) of the "already bastardized Jewish race" into the "relatively pure European stocks."[70]

The study of the racial specificity of disease was to become one of the chief priorities of biomedical science under the Nazis. Otmar Freiherr von Verschuer, director of the Frankfurt Institute for Racial Hygiene, was one of the leaders in this effort. In his 1937 book on genetic pathology, Verschuer identified more than fifty different ailments suspected of being genetic in origin. He also classified diseases according to how common they were among particular racial groupings. Measles, Verschuer argued, was rare among Mongols and Negroes; myopia and difficulties associated with giving birth were more common among civilized than among primitive peoples of the world.

He produced evidence to show that Jews suffered more from diabetes, flat feet, staggers (*Torsionsdystonie*), hemophilia, xeroderma pigmentosum, deafness, and nervous disorders than non-Jews; both Jews and "coloreds" (*Farbige*), Verschuer wrote, suffered higher rates of muscular tumors. Interestingly, tuberculosis was the only disease Verschuer listed as *less* prevalent among Jews than among non-Jews. To explain this, Verschuer adduced an adaptive story. Jews, Verschuer claimed, have for centuries lived in the cities. Their long-standing urban life has led them to develop resistance against diseases commonly found in cities (such as tuberculosis) and to become susceptible to ailments such as flat feet.[71]

Nazi physicians sometimes speculated that Jewish racial degeneracy might be explained in terms of the supposedly hybrid character of the Jewish race. In 1935, for example, Dr. Edgar Schulz of the Office of Racial Policy published an article demonstrating higher rates of insanity (manic depression and dementia praecox), feeble-mindedness, hysteria, and suicide among Jews than among non-Jews.[72] Schulz claimed that these and other disorders arose from the fact that Jews were not, strictly speaking, a single race but rather were an amalgam of Negro and Oriental blood. As a result of this "impure" racial constitution, Jews suffered "tensions and contradictions" that became manifest as disease. This phenomenon was supposedly observed not just among Jews but among any population that experienced racial mixing.[73] The anthropologist Wolfgang Abel in 1937 thus described the *Rheinlandbastarde* as suffering from a host of racial maladies—including tuberculosis, rickets, bad teeth and gums, gout, flat feet, bronchial problems, and nervous disorders such as nail biting, eye twitching, speech defects, and crying in the night.[74] Eugen Fischer's early studies of the "Rehobother bastards" were supposed to have proved that children of interracial marriages scored lower on standardized tests than their classmates.[75]

Racial scientists were remarkably creative in their attempts to explain the odious effects of racial miscegenation. Wilhelm Hildebrandt, for example, in his 1935 *Racial Mixing and Disease*, argued that the maladies produced by racial miscegenation were a product of the fact that different races have different life spans and that bodily organs therefore mature and degenerate at different rates. If a long-lived person were to mate with a short-lived person, then the various organs might mature and die at different rates, disturbing the "equilibrium" found in relatively pure races.[76]

Interestingly, differential racial susceptibility to disease was one topic Jews were permitted to write about, even at the height of the Nazi regime. In 1937 Drs. Franz Goldmann and Georg Wolff presented statistics demonstrating lower rates of infant mortality and tuberculosis among Jews than among non-Jews. These authors, writing for Germany's officially sanctioned Jewish body (the Reichsvertretung der Juden in Deutschland), also pointed out that Jews suffered higher rates of mortality from diabetes, diseases of the circulatory system (especially arteriosclerosis), and suicide. From 1924 to 1926, suicide rates among Jewish men were 20 percent higher than for non-Jewish men (the difference between Jewish and non-Jewish women was even higher—30 percent); by 1932–1934, the Jewish suicide rate was 50 percent higher than the non-Jewish rate.[77]

There is evidence that some Nazis did recognize that differences in susceptibility to disease might be due to social rather than racial causes. In 1940, for example, Martin Stämmler and Edeltraut Bieneck analyzed demographic shifts among Jewish and non-Jewish inhabitants of Breslau in the period 1928–1937. Stämmler and Bieneck noted that Jewish birthrates had declined considerably over this period, and that consequently the proportion of elderly was higher among Jews than among non-Jews. This fact, the authors said, helped account for the higher rates of mortality Jews suffered from disorders such as cancer, diabetes, and circulatory failure; it also helped explain the lower death rates from tuberculosis and infectious diseases, ailments that commonly strike the young.[78] They also noted that Jewish mortality rates had risen dramatically over this period: from 14.2/1,000 in 1928 to 21.2/1,000 in 1937. As the *British Medical Journal* pointed out, however, nowhere in their analysis did Stämmler and Bieneck discuss the role of state violence or the barbarities of the concentration camps in producing these statistics.[79]

The interpretation of the Jewish problem as a medical problem was to prove useful in Nazi attempts to find a "final solution to the Jewish question in Europe." In the early months after the invasion of Poland in 1939, Nazi officials turned to medicine to justify the concentration and extermination of the Jews. Just how this was done illustrates something not only about the role of medical ideology in the persecution of Germany's minorities, but also about how the concept of the Jew as "disease incarnate" began to take on the character of a self-fulfilling prophecy.

Genocide in the Guise of Quarantine

On September 1, 1939, Hitler's armies invaded Poland on the pretext of retaliation for an attack on a German border station by Polish troops—an attack we now know to have been staged by SS guards disguised as Polish officers. Shortly after the occupation of Poland, SS officers were ordered to confine all of Poland's Jews into certain ghettos, including first and foremost, the traditional Jewish ghetto of Warsaw.

In territories occupied by the German army, Nazi medical authorities used the danger of disease as a pretext to justify a series of repressive measures against the Jewish population. In Warsaw, when the Nazis established a separate section for Germans on the city's streetcars, the Nazi-controlled *Krakauer Zeitung* explained: "The separation of the Germans from the Poles—and particularly from the Jews—is not merely a question of principle; it is also, at least as far as Warsaw is concerned, a hygienic necessity."[80] When the Nazis banned Jews from unauthorized railway travel in occupied Poland, Nazi newspapers printed headlines announcing: "Germ-carriers Banned from Railways."[81] Hygiene was commonly listed as the reason for excluding Jews from a wide range of activities in the *Generalgouvernement*.[82]

One of the most brutal forms of persecution for which hygiene was used as a pretext was the confinement of Jews to the ghettos. In February 1940 more than 160,000 Jews from the areas surrounding the industrial town of Lodz (renamed Litzmannstadt after German occupation) were rounded up and forced into one small part of the town. The original intention was to remove all Poles and Jews, thereby leaving the town entirely "German." When this proved impractical, Nazi authorities decided to confine the Jews to the northern part of town and to regulate all trade or interchange between the Jewish and non-Jewish sectors. On April 30 the Jewish quarter was sealed off and surrounded by a wall, similar to the one being erected around the Jewish ghetto in Warsaw. German newspapers reported that the ghetto in Lodz was the "most perfect" of all the settlements established by the Germans in occupied Poland; one author called it the "purest temporary solution to the Jewish question anywhere in Europe."[83] Similar ghettos were subsequently established on a smaller scale in Cracow, Lublin, Radom, and other parts of occupied Poland.

In each of these cases, hygiene was proferred as one of the principal grounds for concentration. The establishment of the Jewish ghetto at Lodz, for example, was justified as a measure necessary to protect against the dangers of epidemic disease.[84] And soon after concentration, of course, Jews in these ghettos did begin to suffer from higher rates of infectious disease. These outbreaks of disease allowed Nazi medical philosophers to justify the continued concentration of the Jews in terms of a medical quarantine. Medical police powers were often invoked for such actions: on December 1, 1938, the German government had granted health authorities broad powers to confine anyone suspected of being a carrier of infectious disease. This allowed officials to confine individuals to a certain area or to transport them to hospitals or other "appropriate" areas.[85] The measure was most commonly used for tuberculosis victims, but it was also used for racial deportations.

It was in the Warsaw ghetto, however, that the Nazis were able to realize to the fullest their prophecies of "Jewish disease." Shortly after the invasion of Poland, German radio stations carried a report of an associate of Goebbels who had recently returned from a visit to Warsaw and Lodz. The author of this report described the Jews of the ghettos as "ulcers which must be cut away from the body of the European nations"; he claimed that if the Jews of the ghettos were not completely isolated, the "whole of Europe would be poisoned."[86]

Before the war, the population of Warsaw was approximately 1.2 million including 440,000 Jews, two-thirds of whom lived in the ghetto in the northwest part of town.[87] When Nazi occupation forces began forcibly concentrating Poland's rural Jews into the ghetto, the effect was to create a breeding ground for disease. The crowded living conditions were exacerbated by shortages of food and clean water. In 1940 and 1941, as the number of Jews arriving in the ghetto grew from 500 per day to over 1,000 per day, diseases began to break out, soon reaching epidemic proportions. The world medical press was not unaware of these conditions. The July 6, 1940, issue of the *British Medical Journal* reported: "Typhoid fever is still raging in Warsaw, where there are from 200 to 300 cases every day. Fully 90 percent of the victims are Jews. The German authorities have increased the number of disinfecting stations from 212 to 400, but have made no attempt to eradicate the source of the disease by clearing out the worst part of the ghetto, where tens of thousands of Jews are confined under pestilential conditions."[88]

The situation was to become much worse. Before the war, mortality in the ghetto due to all causes had been about 400 deaths per month. By January 1941, nearly 900 people were dying every month, and death rates were increasing week by week. By March the number of deaths had grown to 1,608 per month, and in the single month of June 1941, 4,100 people died from infection and disease, compounded by starvation, physical abuse, and lack of adequate medical supplies.[89] According to Wilhelm Hagen, the German commissioner of the ghetto (a Dr. Auersbach) sabotaged efforts on the part of well-meaning German doctors to alleviate the situation by his order to block shipment of food and medical supplies to the city. By the end of 1941 official rations had been reduced to bread worth about 2,000 calories per person per day, and many were receiving even less than this. Hunger and epidemic disease reinforced each other as mortality rates from tuberculosis alone rose from 14/100,000 in 1938 to more than 400/100,000 in the first quarter of 1941. The case was even more dramatic with typhus. In the single month of October 1941, health authorities responsible for the Warsaw ghetto recorded 300 deaths from typhus—nearly as many as from all causes combined before the German occupation.[90]

Epidemics that raged inside the Warsaw ghetto in 1941 and 1942 provided Nazi occupation forces with a medical rationale for the isolation and extermination of the Jewish population. On October 29, 1940, the *Hamburger Fremdenblatt* noted that 98 percent of all cases of typhoid and spotted fever in Warsaw were to be found in the ghetto. In the spring of 1940 non-Jewish doctors were barred from treating Jewish patients; on March 12 the *Krakauer Zeitung* explained this ban as follows: "This decree is based on the fact that infectious diseases, particularly spotted fever and typhoid, are widespread especially among the Jewish population. When Jews suffering from those diseases are treated by non-Jewish doctors—doctors who are at the same time treating the sick of other races—there is a danger of their transmitting diseases from the Jews to the non-Jewish population."[91]

In the first months of the German occupation of Poland, traffic between Jews and non-Jews in and outside the Warsaw ghetto was not restricted; Germans and non-Jewish Poles were allowed to enter the ghetto. After 1940, however, contact with Jews was declared a "threat to public health"; Jews trying to escape from the ghetto were shot on the grounds they were violating the quarantine imposed by the Nazis. Years later, long after the war, when the Nazi chief of police for Warsaw was brought before a West German court to be tried for ordering the shooting of Jews trying to leave the ghetto, defense attorneys argued that this action had been a "necessary precaution" to preserve the quarantine.[92]

Criminal Biology

Criminal biology was to forge a further link in the medical solution to the Jewish question. According to the psychiatrist Robert Ritter, the "urgent task" of criminal biology was "to discover whether or not certain signs can be found among men which would allow the early detection of criminal behavior, signs which would allow the recognition of criminal tendencies *before* the actual onset of the criminal career."[93] Such efforts were not, of course, the invention of the Nazis. Criminal biologists had tried, at least since Cesare Lombroso's *L'uomo delinquente* in the late nineteenth century, to construct a medical-forensic system linking moral, criminal, and racial degeneracy. Crime, in this view, was a disease; criminality was linked with certain physical manifestations such as facial shape or body hair. (Lombroso's work was rarely cited by Nazi criminal biologists, probably because of his Jewish ancestry.)

In the twentieth century, spurred by advances in genetics and hopes for eugenics, criminal biology became an important research priority in the German scientific community. Concerns on the part of criminal biologists were close in many ways to those of the racial hygienists. Criminal biologists argued that crime is both genetically determined and racially specific; they worried that criminals were reproducing at a faster rate than noncriminal elements of the population (see again Figure 1). In the Nazi period, government statistics offices attempted to determine what proportion of murderers (for example) were genetically defective: in 1938 government statisticians provided data to show that, whereas in 1928–1930 only 14.5 percent of all murderers were genetic defectives (*erblich belastet*), by 1931–1933 this proportion had supposedly grown to 20.1 percent.[94] Twin studies here again provided the vital empirical link between theory and policy: racial theorists argued time and again that studies of identical and nonidentical twins proved that crime was the product of hereditary disposition and not just social environment.[95] Racial hygienists in the Nazi period drew important political implications from such studies: at the fourth Congress of Criminal Biology at Hamburg in June 1934, Rainer Fetscher predicted that a thorough implementation of the Sterilization Law would lower criminality as a whole by 6 percent and "moral" (sexual) crimes by 30 percent.[96] Fetscher himself had begun in 1927 to construct a comprehensive "criminal biology map of the Free State of Saxony" (*Kriminalbiologische Kartei des Freistaats Sachsen*),[97] which he later used to identify individuals for sterilization.

Interest in criminal biology accelerated with the rise of the Nazis. By 1935, legal and medical journals were regularly reporting that crime and other "antisocial behavior" were genetically determined racial characteristics. J. F. Lehmann's *Monthly Journal of Criminal Biology and Penal Reform* had, since 1904, pioneered the study of the "genetics" of crime; after World War I, many other journals followed suit.[98] By the mid-1930s most German universities offered instruction in this area—often in conjunction with courses on racial hygiene.[99] The German government supported research in this area in several ways. In October 1936 Justice Minister Franz Gürtner ordered the establishment of fifty examination stations throughout Germany to explore the genetics and racial specificity of crime. The main targets of these stations (modeled on similar institutions existing since 1923 in Bavaria) were individuals under the age of twenty-five serving long-term prison sentences; everyone serving a three-month sentence or longer was required to be examined. In addition, larger criminal biology research stations (*Kriminalbiologische Sammelstelle*) were established at Munich, Freiburg-Breslau, Cologne, Münster, Berlin, Königsberg, Leipzig, Halle, and Hamburg to evaluate the effects of various measures on the incidence of crime—especially the 1935 Castration Law.[100] In 1939 the *Deutsches Ärzteblatt* reported Himmler's orders that henceforth, examination of the genetics and genealogy of criminal suspects was to become a routine part of criminal investigations.[101]

Criminal biologists also addressed the Jewish question. The conceptual link here, as one might imagine, was the theory that Jews were racially disposed to certain forms of crime, just as they were racially disposed to certain kinds of disease. One should recall that "disease" for the Nazis was often broadly construed to cover not just physical disorders but also behavioral and cultural maladies. Johannes Schottky, for example, in his 1937 book *Race and Disease,* argued that Jews were racially disposed to suffer disproportionately not just from flat feet or gout but also from mental disorders such as feeble-mindedness, hysteria, various sexual disorders, and pathological drives for recognition and power.[102] It was not a large step from here to argue that Jews were racially disposed to commit certain forms of crime. Indeed, Fritz Lenz had put forth this thesis in his textbook on human genetics, written with Erwin Baur and Eugen Fischer. One of the distinctive racial qualities Lenz attributed to the Nordic man was a certain sense of "foresight," a quality that, according to Lenz, led the German (unlike the Jew) to respect the life and property of others. Lenz presented statistics to buttress this point. For the decade 1892–1901, he listed as follows the relative incidence of crime (per 100,000 population) among German Catholics, Protestants, and Jews.[103]

Crime	Catholics	Protestants	Jews
Offenses in general	1,361	1,112	1,030
Minor assaults	67	54	44
Grievous bodily harm	314	186	75
Fraud	68	58	113

From such statistics, one might think it difficult to argue that the Nordic was less prone to crime. Lenz, however, asserted that these data disguised what was really going on. If one compared Jews, not with the non-Jewish population as a whole, but with those parts of the non-Jewish population of similar economic status, then one would find (Lenz claimed) that violent crimes were "no less common among Jews than non-Jews." Lenz was willing to take other parts of his statistics at face value, however: "Fraud and the use of insulting language really are commoner among Jews"—as is "the circulation of obscene books and pictures" and "the white slave trade."[104]

Nazi medical authorities followed this lead. Gerhard Wagner, in the same speech in which he attacked the "exorbitant costs" of supporting the mentally ill, declared that the incidence of criminality was higher among Jews than among non-Jews, as was the incidence of bankruptcy (fourteen to thirty times higher for Jews), distribution of pornography ("exceptionally Jewish"), prostitution, drug smuggling, purse snatching, and general theft.[105] Wagner and other Nazi medical leaders were able to cite the work of Lenz and others in the racial hygiene community in support of this thesis.

Science thus conspired in the solution to the Jewish question: Jews were racially disposed to commit crime, as they were racially disposed to suffer from a host of other diseases. By the late 1930s, German medical science had constructed an elaborate world view equating mental infirmity, moral depravity, criminality, and racial impurity. This complex of identifications was then used to justify the destruction of the Jews on medical, moral, criminological, and anthropological grounds. To be Jewish was to be both sick and criminal; Nazi medical science and policy united to help "solve" this problem.

The Final Solution

The German census of May 17, 1939, revealed that there were 330,892 Jews in Germany (now including Austria); there were in addition 72,738 "half-breeds" (*Mischlinge erster Grad*), and 42,811 quarter-Jews (*Mischlinge zweiter Grad*). In six years of Nazi rule, the number of Jews in Germany had fallen by 390,000.[106] For those remaining, a variety of "solutions" were proposed, and medical doctors were among those leading the search for solutions.[107]

Publicly, Germany's medical journals made it clear that Jews were to have no place in the New German Order. Dr. W. Bormann, for example, writing in the *Ärzteblatt für den Reichsgau Wartheland*, declared that the "retrieved" German territories of the occupied East were to be settled "exclusively with German men."[108] On November 23, 1939, when laws were passed requiring Jews in occupied Poland to wear the yellow star, Germany's foremost medical journal justified this as necessary "to create an externally visible separation between the Jewish and Aryan population." The journal argued further that in order to establish a "geographical" separation between the races, there were two possible solutions: the creation of a separate Jewish state and confinement to a ghetto. The latter solution was preferable, because "it could be implemented more rapidly and with greater effect."[109] The *Deutsches Ärzteblatt* reported with satisfaction that, as a result of Nazi policies, areas of mixed Polish-Jewish population had already begun to disappear, and Jewish businesses were gone. Furthermore,

> for the first time in centuries, the Jew has been forced to change his lifestyle; for the first time, he is required to work. For this purpose, Jews have been organized into forced labor brigades. At the head of each of these brigades there is a Jew who supervises his racial comrades and is

responsible to German authorities for ensuring that the work assigned to his brigade is carried out in an orderly manner. This procedure has proven to work exceptionally well in the *Generalgouvernement*.[110]

The journal claimed that this arrangement was intended to last for two years, after which a specially appointed committee of Jews was to organize accommodations and work for Polish Jews—work primarily "of a handicraft nature."[111]

Privately, Nazi intellectuals advocated more radical measures. Hans Hefelmann suggested deporting all Jews to Madagascar; Otto Reche recommended that this option be included as one condition of a general peace treaty with England and France.[112] Others proposed the establishment of a huge Jewish reservation near Lublin for permanent settlement, an option that would allow German scholars to pursue "Jewish studies." The official medical journal for the Reichsgau Wartheland defended proposals to establish Jewish studies at the new German University at Posen, on the grounds that scholars at the university would be uniquely placed to study Jews "in their more or less 'natural condition' [*Naturzustand*]."[113] Still others advocated measures utilizing the tools of racial hygiene. Philipp Bouhler favored sterilizing all Jews by X-rays; Viktor Brack recommended sterilization of the 2–3 million Jews capable of work, sparing (only) these from extermination. In postwar testimony at Nuremberg, Brack recounted the alternatives pondered by Nazi authorities:

> In 1941, it was an "open secret" in higher party circles that those in power intended to exterminate [*ausrotten*] the entire Jewish population in Germany and occupied territories. I and my co-workers, especially Drs. Hefelmann and Blankenburg, were of the opinion that this was unworthy of party leaders and humanity more generally. We therefore decided to find another solution to the Jewish problem, less radical than the complete extermination of the entire race. We developed the idea of deporting Jews to a distant land, and I recall that Dr. Hefelmann suggested for this purpose the island of Madagascar. We drew up a plan along these lines and presented it to Bouhler. This was apparently not acceptable, however, and so we came up with the idea that sterilization might provide the solution to the Jewish question. Given that sterilization is a rather complicated business, we hit upon the idea of sterilization by X-rays. In 1941 I suggested to Bouhler the sterilization of Jews by X-rays; this idea was also rejected, however. Bouhler said that sterilization by X-rays was not an option, because Hitler was against it. I worked on this program further and finally came up with a new plan.[114]

Brack's new plan was simply another version of the plan to induce sterilization by X-rays. Jews were to be radiated with sufficient quantities of X-rays (500–600 roentgen for men; 300–350 roentgen for women) to destroy the reproductive capabilities of the testicles or ovaries. This, Brack suggested, might be best achieved by having individuals stand in front of a counter where they would be asked to fill out a form; an official standing behind the counter would operate the apparatus, administering to the genitals a dose of radiation for the time it took to fill out the form (two to three minutes), thereby castrating the individual. With twenty such setups, Brack figured that one could sterilize perhaps 3,000–4,000 people per day.[115]

Sterilization was ultimately rejected as a solution to the Jewish question. The decision to destroy Europe's Jews by gassing them in concentration camps emerged from the fact that the technical apparatus already existed for the destruction of the mentally ill. In the earliest phases, both the children's and the adult euthanasia operations were to be administered only to non-Jews: Jews were explicitly declared not to deserve euthanasia.[116] But the operations were eventually extended to Jews, and in mass fashion. On August 30, 1940, the Bavarian minister of the interior ordered all Jewish patients in psychiatric hospitals to be transported to the hospital at Eglfing-Haar, near Munich; a memo of December 12 that year justified this move on the grounds that the mixing of German and Jewish patients posed "an intolerable burden on both nursing personnel and the relatives of patients of German blood." In fact, Jewish psychiatric patients from the hospital at Berlin-Buch had begun to be rounded up and sent to gas chambers at Brandenburg since earlier that summer (June 1940).[117] In early September 1940, 160 Jewish patients at Eglfing-Haar were filmed as part of the propaganda film *Scum of Humanity* (*Abschaum der Menschheit*). On September 20 these patients were sent to Brandenburg, where they were gassed on September 22.

In early 1941 the Reich Ministry of the Interior ordered that all Jews in German hospitals be killed—not because they met the criteria required for euthanasia, but because they were Jews.[118] The Jews were not the first group to be singled out for extraordinary euthanasia. Criminals in Germany's hospitals had already been disposed of by this time; and in the course of 1941 a number of other groups would fall within the shadow of the program. On March 8, 1941, Werner Blankenburg wrote to local *Gauleiter* asking that all "asocials" and "antisocials" in Germany's workhouses be registered with euthanasia officials. In April Germany's concentration camps began a new program designed to destroy inmates no longer capable or willing to work. This project, within which Jews were also to be included, was code-named "14 f 13."

Operation 14 f 13 represents the transition from the systematic destruction of the handicapped and the mentally ill to the systematic destruction of the ethnically and culturally marginal. In 1941 Buchenwald Commandant Koch announced to SS officers in his camp that he had received secret orders from Himmler that all feeble-minded and crippled inmates of Germany's concentration camps were to be killed. Koch also announced at this time that all Jewish prisoners were to be included in operation 14 f 13. In December 1941, SS Lieutenant Colonel Liebehenschel notified the concentration camps at Sachsenbuch, Gross-Rosen, Neuengamme, Mauthausen, Auschwitz, Flossenbürg, Niedernhagen, Sachsenhausen, and Dachau that a medical commission would soon arrive to select prisoners for "special treatment." Camp officials were instructed to prepare the necessary paperwork; forms were to be filled out indicating the "diagnosis" of the inmates, including information on race and whether the individuals were suffering from "incurable physical ailments." SS Lieutenant Colonel Friedrich Mennecke, head of the Eichberg State Medical Hospital, arrived in Gross-Rosen in mid-January 1942 to begin selecting prisoners for destruction. By this time, "selection" had moved some distance from what we today would consider criteria for health. Psychopaths, criminals, asocials, antisocials, and individuals foreign to the community (*Gemeinschaftsfremde*) were now all included; people were being taken from tuberculosis hospitals and from workhouses, along guidelines established by the euthanasia experts Nitsche, Heyde, and Brack. (The elderly infirm were generally excluded from the euthanasia operation, out of fear for the reaction this would arouse among the general population. In August 1941 Nitsche wrote to Linden complaining that there were many people in Protestant and Catholic hospitals for the elderly who should fall within the euthanasia operation; the euthanasia enthusiasts, however, were rarely able to ever touch this "material.")[119]

According to Mennecke's testimony after the war, the selection of Jews alongside the mentally ill began first either in Buchenwald or in Dachau.[120] Throughout the remaining years of the war, cooperation continued between concentration camps and psychiatric hospitals ad-

"Lives Not Worth Living" 209

ministering euthanasia. From July 1944 through the spring of 1945, for example, 400 Russians and Poles were gassed in the psychiatric hospital at Hadamar—now with years of experience in execution by gas chamber.[121]

It is important to realize today that for Nazi physicians no sharp line divided the destruction of the racially inferior and the mentally or physically defective. The physicians responsible for administering the euthanasia operation in German hospitals (T-4) were also responsible for formulating criteria and administering the first phases of the destruction of the Jews and handicapped in Germany's concentration camps (14 f 13). When cross-examined after the war at the Nuremberg trials, physicians pointed out that they did not always distinguish whether certain exterminations were for racial, political, or medical reasons. The testimony of Dr. Mennecke, questioned by the defense attorney for Karl Brandt, made this clear:

Attorney: When was the decision made to exterminate individuals based on racial and political considerations? Had this already been decided by the time you first visited a concentration camp?

Mennecke: No.

Attorney: When was it then?

Mennecke: As far as I can remember it first began in Buchenwald or Dachau.

Attorney: How was it done prior to this? What was your task in the concentration camps?

Mennecke: The examination of certain prisoners with respect to the question of psychosis or psychopathology.

Attorney: So it was first a question of mental illness?

Mennecke: A medical question.

Attorney: And later it became a political and racial question?

Mennecke: Yes. That is, alongside the political and racial question I also had to make purely medical judgments.

Attorney: So, you had two kinds of cases: the mentally ill, which had to be evaluated according to medical criteria, and those which had to be evaluated according to political and racial criteria?

Mennecke: One simply cannot distinguish the two, Herr Attorney. The two cases were simply not divided and clearly separated from one another.[122]

American army officials discovered shortly after the war that concrete plans for the final solution (*Endlösung*) of the Jewish problem in

Europe were made at a luncheon organized by SD chief Reinhard Heydrich at Wannsee castle (near Berlin) on January 20, 1942. At this meeting thirteen high-ranking Nazi and Reich government officials were shown photostatic copies of a letter from Hermann Göring charging Heydrich with the task of finding a "final solution to the Jewish question." Records from the meeting were discovered in the files of the physician Philip Hoffmann, head of the SS Race and Settlement Office.[123]

We also know that Germany's political elite discussed these issues openly well before final plans were made. On January 20, 1939, for example, Hitler announced in his infamous speech before the Reichstag: "Today, I will once again be a prophet: if international financial Jewry inside Germany and abroad should manage to force the peoples of the world once more into a world war, then the result will be not the 'Bolshevization' of the earth, and thereby the victory of Judaism, but rather the destruction of the Jewish race in Europe."[124] Hitler repeated this promise several times in subsequent years;[125] his underlings made similar claims. On March 23, 1941, for example, Himmler presented a report to Hitler announcing that "the very idea of Jews I hope . . . to see fully extinguished" (*Der Begriffe Juden hoffe ich . . . völlig auslöschen zu sehen*). Four months later, on July 31, 1941, Hermann Göring entrusted Heydrich with "the solution of the entire Jewish question in the German sphere of influence in Europe." And on November 16, Alfred Rosenberg announced at a press conference the intention of the government to find a final solution to the Jewish question.[126]

Earlier than this, it is possible to find numerous references from German doctors to the need for a solution to Germany's Jewish problem. In 1939, for example, Edith Lölhöffel, editor of the women doctors' journal, praised Hitler for the reunification of Austria and Germany, and for his "elimination [*Ausschaltung*] of all foreign races from Germany."[127] Reich Health Führer Leonardo Conti, in a speech before a meeting of government physicians on December 14–15, 1938 in Berlin, announced it was the intention of the government to find a final solution (*endgültige Lösung*) to the Jewish problem in Europe.[128] In 1938 Walter Gross announced that the work of the Office of Racial Policy would not be finished until "the disappearance of the last Jew from our Reich."[129]

Discussion of the Jewish question was a common feature in several of Germany's medical journals in the Nazi period. Popular medical

"Lives Not Worth Living" 211

journals discussed the history of the Jews, in some cases complete with pictures portraying the exodus of the Jews from Egypt, the problems of Zionism, and so forth.[130] In the early war years the *Deutsches Ärzteblatt* carried a regular column on "Solving the Jewish Question," which reviewed current attempts at solutions not just in Germany, but in Romania, China, Japan, Italy, and other countries.[131] The journal worried that Britain was building "an army of 100,000 Jews in Palestine," an army that "could and would be used against the Germans." It reprinted Hitler's words (in boldface) that another war in Europe would mean not the "Bolshevization" of the earth, but the destruction of the Jewish race in Europe.[132]

Racial hygienists also carried forth this banner. Otmar von Verschuer described in his textbook the need for a "complete solution of the Jewish question" (*Gesamtlösung des Judenproblems*).[133] On March 27–28, 1941, at opening ceremonies for the Institute for Research on the Jewish Question (Institut zur Erforschung der Judenfrage) in Frankfurt, Eugen Fischer and Hans F. K. Günther were guests of honor at a meeting where possible solutions to the Jewish question were discussed.[134] At this meeting Walter Gross reviewed the shortcomings of previous efforts in this regard (emancipation, persecution, partial annihilation, and so forth) and claimed that a final solution could come only with the complete "removal of Jews from Europe."[135] Racial hygienists appreciated Nazi efforts to solve the Jewish question. In 1944, not long after he accepted Josef Mengele as his scientific assistant, Verschuer proudly claimed that the dangers posed by Jews and Gypsies to the German people had been "eliminated through the racial-political measures of recent years." He also noted in this context that the purification of Germany from "foreign racial elements" required a larger effort extending across the entirety of Europe.[136]

In November 1942 the *Informationsdienst des Hauptamtes für Volksgesundheit der NSDAP,* a journal published by the Reich Health Publishing House, noted that in the "Confidential Information of the Party Chancellery" there had appeared a paper (no. 881) titled "Preparatory Measures for the Final Solution of the European Jewish Question."[137] Copies of this journal were circulated within the medical faculties of certain universities (for example, Giessen); one can only wonder what crossed the minds of these professors upon seeing the title of this paper.[138]

The continuities linking the various phases of the Nazi's program to destroy lives not worth living were both practical and ideological. In the fall of 1941, with the completion of the first major phase of the euthanasia operation, gas chambers at psychiatric institutions in southern and eastern Germany were dismantled and shipped east, where they were reinstalled at Belzec, Majdanek, Auschwitz, Treblinka, and Sobibor. The same doctors and technicians and nurses often followed the equipment.[139] Germany's psychiatric hospitals forged the most important practical link between the destruction of the mentally ill and handicapped and the murder of Germany's ethnic and social minorities.

Sexual and Racial Pathologies

It was not just the Jews or the mentally or physically handicapped, but other groups as well that were stigmatized as "sick" and "degenerate" by German racial scientists. Jews, Gypsies, communists, homosexuals, the feeble-minded, the tubercular, and a wide class of "antisocials" (alcoholics, prostitutes, drug addicts, the homeless, and other groups) were all marked for destruction.

Consider the case of homosexuals. By the 1930s Nazi medical leaders could draw upon a sizable literature documenting the supposedly pathological character of (male) homosexuality. In the first (1904) volume of the *Archiv für Rassen- und Gesellschaftsbiologie,* Ernst Rüdin argued that homosexuality was a genetically determined "diseased form of degeneracy."[140] In 1924 Dobrovsky published an article claiming that gay men showed abnormal gum and tooth development; an article by Arthur Weil in the same year purported to discover distinctive bodily deformities in homosexual men.[141] Nazi racial hygienists built upon views common in pre-Nazi research. In the summer of 1934, Professor Lothar Tirala of Munich argued that homosexuality was a "moral pathology" and advised that Germans use "all possible means to suppress such sick perversions in the body of our people."[142]

By the mid-1930s physicians in Germany were united in arguing that homosexuals posed a threat to public health. Physicians writing in Germany's leading public health journal, *Der Öffentliche Gesundheitsdienst,* regularly described homosexuality as a "pathology" and homosexuals as "psychopaths."[143] The magnitude of the threat was not something to be taken lightly: in 1938 the Office of Racial Policy reported that Germany was faced with an "epidemic of some 2 million homosexuals, representing 10 percent of the entire adult male population."[144]

The most common theory of homosexuality advanced under the Nazis was that homosexuality was an inborn, biologically determined disorder. In 1939, for example, a physician by the name of Deussen published an article titled "Sexual Pathology" supporting this view in the journal *Progress in Genetic Pathology*.[145] Deussen cited Theobald Lang's work purportedly showing that the sisters of male homosexuals tend to exhibit particularly "masculine" characteristics; this led both Deussen and Lang to accept Richard Goldschmidt's theory of the male homosexual as a "genetic female."[146] Interestingly, belief in a genetic basis of homosexuality was not confined to the political Right. In 1937 the socialist physicians' *Bulletin* in exile published an article claiming that homosexuality was "inborn, and hence not subject to the free will of the individuals who come into the world with this inversion."[147] The journal advocated abolishing section 175 of the Prussian criminal code criminalizing homosexuality.

In light of such arguments, some Nazi physicians disputed the claim that homosexuality was a genetic disorder. In June 1938, for example, a physician writing for the Office of Racial Policy characterized homosexuals as "weak, unreliable, and deceitful"; they were typically "servile and yet power hungry, . . . incapable, in the long run, of functioning in a positive manner in society as a whole." This author argued that homosexuality was *not,* however, a genetic disease: the view that homosexuality was inherited simply played into the hands of those who wanted to assert that homosexuality was not a matter of choice. This was the argument "upon which the entire ideology of homosexuality is based"—namely, that these people "cannot do otherwise." The author estimated that although perhaps only 2 percent of all homosexuals were actually "genetically sick," these people exerted an enormous influence in society: "40,000 abnormals—whom one might well expel from the community—are in a position to poison 2 million citizens." Homosexuals, in this author's view, were like the Jews: they build a "state within a state, they are state criminals. They are not 'poor, sick' people to be treated, but enemies of the state to be eliminated!"[148]

Homosexuality was illegal in the Weimar Republic; the Nazis, however, imposed a series of new and far more repressive measures against this group. On the night of June 30, 1934, most of the (largely homosexual) leaders of the SA (including, most notably, Ernst Röhm) were assassinated, in what subsequently became known as the Röhm putsch or "night of long knives." The Röhm putsch marked only the first phase of the Nazi persecution of homosexuals. Beginning soon after the *Machtergreifung*, Nazi officials had begun to construct an inventory of all representatives of the so-called third sex; these lists were subsequently used to "cleanse" the German population of these people. In the mid-1930s, thousands of individuals identified as homosexuals were arrested and sent to concentration camps, where they were detained so as not to "infect" the broader population. Thousands of camp inmates wearing the pink triangle were ultimately sent to the gas chambers, as part of the attempt to rid Germany of this "pathology."[149]

Other groups were singled out for destruction, and here again the cooperation of medical personnel on both ideological and practical levels was crucial. Beginning early in the Nazi regime, the Reich Health Office began constructing elaborate genealogical tables of all Gypsies in Germany.[150] In 1938 public health authorities were asked to register with the police all Gypsies and Gypsy "half-breeds," based on information gathered from genealogical tables or genetic registries.[151] This information was then used by police authorities to round up Gypsies for deportation. An article in the *Deutsches Ärzteblatt* described some of the tasks faced by the physician in sorting out the Gypsy question:

> Experience gathered thus far in the struggle against the Gypsy plague [*Plage*] reveals that half-breeds are responsible for the largest fraction of criminal offenses among the Gypsies. It has also been shown that attempts to make the Gypsies settle down have failed, especially among the purest strains of this race; this is because of their strong wander instinct. It has thus become necessary to separate pure and half-breed Gypsies, for the purpose of coming to a final solution of the Gypsy problem [*endgültigen Lösung der Zigeunerfrage*]. Toward this end, the SS Reichsführer and chief of German police [Heinrich Himmler] has issued elaborate instructions. In order to achieve this goal, it will be necessary to determine the racial affiliation of all Gypsies living in the Reich, also that of all people living like Gypsies.[152]

This article specified that all Gypsies were to be registered with the Reich Criminal Police Bureau, in a special division created for this purpose (the Reichszentrale zur Bekämpfung des Zigeunerwesens).

Gypsies, like Jews and homosexuals, were often described by Nazi medical authorities as a "health risk" to the German people. Otmar von Verschuer claimed that 90 percent of Germany's 30,000 Gypsies were "half-breeds," and that most Gypsies were "asocial and genetically inferior."[153] In 1944 medical authorities in Bulgaria "ascertained" that Gypsies, by virtue of their migrant lifestyle, were responsible for spreading infectious diseases; Bulgarian authorities ordered all Gypsies to give up their wandering lifestyle and settle in a single location.[154] Medical involvement in the destruction of the Gypsies was also more direct. In the winter of 1941–42, Dr. Robert Ritter, a prominent German criminal biologist, participated in a conference at which the drowning of Germany's 30,000 Gypsies by bombardment of their ships in the Mediterranean was proposed.[155] Ritter ultimately became one of the chief organizers of the genocide of this group. Beginning in the mid-1930s, he received funds from the German Research Council (DFG) to research the Gypsy question at his Racial Hygiene and Population Biology Research Division within the Berlin Health Office. On January 20, 1940, Ritter reported to the DFG that the Gypsy question could be solved only "if the majority of asocial and useless Gypsies can be rounded up and put to work in special camps, where they can be prevented from any further reproduction." He helped prepare evaluations (*Gutachten*) used for identifying Gypsies to be destroyed; on January 31, 1944, Ritter reported that he had recently completed evaluation of 23,822 Gypsy "cases."[156]

The campaign against tuberculosis took on a similar—if more controversial—character under the Nazis. Even before their rise to power in January 1933, the Nazis claimed that the eradication of tuberculosis was one of their highest goals. Opinions were divided, however, on what the appropriate attitude toward the disease should be. Some complained about the exorbitant costs associated with treating the disease. F. Koester, for example, writing in Germany's leading tuberculosis journal, stated in 1938 that care for Germany's 400,000 tubercular cost the government 4 or 5 billion RM annually. Others expressed doubts whether it was a good idea even to try to eradicate tuberculosis, given that this would eliminate an important means of "natural selection."[157] Tuberculosis had been recognized as an infectious disease since Koch's discovery of the tubercle bacillus at the end of the nineteenth century, yet many also recognized that infection with the bacillus was not a sufficient condition for someone coming down with the disease. People knew that one had to be in a weakened physical state to contract the disease—but opinions differed on the nature or origins of this state. Many argued that the "white plague" was largely the product of nutrition, living space, or working conditions; others argued that although environmental factors were important, one's physical or racial constitution was the crucial variable. Followers of Kretschmer's *Konstitutionslehre,* for example, argued that those with the leptosome body type were especially susceptible to the disease, and concluded that such individuals should be advised not to go into nursing or medicine (where they were more likely to be infected). Fritz Lenz argued that members of the Nordic race (or light-skinned individuals more generally) were particularly resistant to the disease; Hans Luxenburger postulated a correlation between schizophrenia and TB.[158]

Even prior to 1933, the widespread conception of tuberculosis as a genetically inherited disease[159] prompted many to call for the isolation of those with the disease from the "genetic stream" of the population. Alfred Grotjahn, as early as 1915, advocated celibacy for the afflicted; others proposed that the actively tubercular not be allowed to obtain a marriage license. Still others argued that tuberculosis should constitute grounds for eugenic sterilization—a proposal that F. Redeker criticized as early as 1931 as "only the most recent demand in the fool's paradise [*Wolkenkuckucksheim*] of eugenics."[160] After 1933, health officials stepped up their struggle against the disease. Despite continued calls for sterilization or marriage bans (and even some calls to promote the breeding of the "muscular" over the "leptosomal" body type in the German population),[161] tuberculosis was never included within the sterilization or marital health laws. TB did, however, become the most common ground for abortion in Nazi Germany, and health officials initiated a massive campaign for early detection of the disease, along with obligatory chest X-rays for everyone in the SS, the army, the SA, and workers in the armament industry.[162] On December 1, 1938, the Order for the Struggle against Contagious Diseases required that all cases of tuberculosis be registered with state health authorities; the order also allowed the forcible confinement of individuals with the disease.

During World War II, the struggle against tuberculosis took on a more urgent nature, especially in occupied territories. On May 1, 1942, the *Gauleiter* for the Wartheland region in occupied Poland wrote a letter to Himmler suggesting that Poland's 35,000 incurable and infectious tubercular be exterminated, and that preparations for this operation be made as soon as the region's remaining 100,000 Jews were destroyed. Reinhard Heydrich approved the operation in a letter of June 9, 1942, on the condition that health authorities could determine which cases of the disease were incurable. Kurt Blome, head of Germany's medical postgraduate education program and now deputy chief of the Nazi party's Office for Public Health, was asked to explore the alternatives open to German authorities to deal with the matter. Blome distinguished three possible options: "special treatment" (*Sonderbehandlung*—Nazi language for extermination); isolation of the severely infected; or creation of a special reserve for all tubercular. Blome estimated that the first of these options—the one favored by Heydrich and Himmler—would take six months to complete. He also cautioned, however, that the operation would have to be kept secret; if the operation were to become public, Germany's enemies would be able to mobilize the "doctors of the world" against Germany, and opposition would be even greater than to the euthanasia operation. Blome therefore recommended the creation of a reservation, comparable to a leper colony.[163] It remains unclear today how far plans for such a colony were ever put into effect.

The Medical Experiments

No account of the Nazi destruction of life not worth living would be complete without at least a brief examination of the role of physicians in the notorious medical experiments of the 1940s. Evidence that physicians participated in experiments in the concentration camps was presented in the "doctors' trial" in Nuremberg in the spring and summer of 1947. At the trial, physicians from the concentration camps in Dachau, Auschwitz, Buchenwald, and Sachsenhausen were accused of having forced prisoners to drink seawater, to suffer extremes of cold or low pressure, or to undergo bone or limb transplants that often ended in death or crippling mutilation. The experiments were undertaken not out of sadism, but to gain knowledge about certain conditions faced by German military men. Prisoners were immersed in ice water to discover how long German pilots, downed by enemy fire, could survive in the icy waters of the North Sea; they were forced to drink seawater to determine how long a man stranded at sea might survive without fresh water; they were subjected to mutilating limb transplants to improve techniques that might prove valuable in genuine medical emergencies; and they were wounded or injected with infectious bacteria to determine the effectiveness of new antibacterial drugs.

The medical experiments were begun in conjunction with a series of new priorities established by the Nazi regime in the war years. Plans for the occupied East (the so-called *Generalplan Ost*) involved a dual strategy of "negative demography" and "racial resettlement." According to these plans, 8 million Germans would resettle the occupied territories over thirty years; this program would be combined with sterilization and other more drastic means of removing local non-German populations. Several of the experiments undertaken in Germany's concentration camps were designed to devise techniques for controlling fertility in the newly conquered eastern territories. Carl Clauberg, for example, experimented with ways to induce sterility; Horst Schumann explored new techniques for castrating men.[164] Hundreds of people were mutilated or killed in the course of these experiments, which lasted from 1942 through the end of the war.

A further priority that emerged during the war was to find new means of combating infectious diseases faced by troops moving into Africa or southern and eastern Europe. Spotted fever, for example, became a problem during the invasion of the Soviet Union; in response, Professor Gerhard Rose ordered tests of new vaccines against the disease in the concentration camp at Buchenwald. Rose's experiments (which proved fatal for many of the subjects involved) were planned in consultation with Germany's chief medical authorities— Leonardo Conti, Hans Reiter, and Ernst Grawitz—in the hope that such experiments might help to solve problems facing German armies.[165] Other, less fatal, methods were also tested: at the SS hospital in Dachau, Ernst Grawitz tested homeopathic preparations to see if they were effective in combating infection (he found they were not).[166]

One of the supervisors of medical experiments at Dachau was Hans Deuschl, a personal friend of SS chief Himmler and head of the Doctors' Führer School at Alt-Rehse. In 1940 or 1941, Deuschl left Alt-Rehse to take up war duties on the eastern front, where he was appointed chief of health affairs in Estonia. As an SS man and longstanding leader in the Nazi Physicians' League, Deuschl reported directly to Himmler. In a letter of January 24, 1942, he wrote to Himmler asking for permission to deal "radically" with an epidemic of spotted fever that had broken out among a group of Russian prisoners of war in Estonia, near Fellin. Deuschl noted in his letter that 1,400 Russian prisoners of war had fallen ill, and only about 25 percent were capable of work. In view of this situation, he advised that "radical measures" be taken: half the Russian prisoners were to be shot, so that the remaining half could be given twice the previous rations. Deuschl commented that this would also reduce the danger of epidemic disease in the camp—an important benefit, given that the summer months would bring a renewed risk of dysentery and typhoid. Deuschl made the premise upon which his decision was based quite clear: "I would rather see the death of 500 Bolshevist beasts (who will probably eventually die anyway—of hunger, cold, or disease), than see one German soldier—or even one Estonian soldier—perish from epidemic disease." Himmler wrote back, granting Deuschl permission to implement his "radical measures."[167]

In the summer of 1943, Himmler asked Deuschl if he would be willing to supervise a series of medical experiments at Dachau; Deuschl accepted the offer. Dachau was the first concentration camp to engage in human experimentation. In 1939 Sigmund Rascher had begun a series of experiments on blood-clotting factors; in subsequent years he helped to organize the infamous low-pressure and cooling experiments, sponsored in conjunction with air force medical bodies. In these experiments, prisoners (primarily Russian prisoners of war) were submerged in ice water or subjected to low pressure for hours at a time, often until death.[168] The purpose was to discover how long pilots forced to bail out over water or at high altitudes could survive in conditions of extreme cold or low pressure. As of July 1943 there were (according to one observer) "three to five" separate sets of experiments running at Dachau.

Deuschl was chosen by Himmler to supervise the experiments, partly because he had been a long-time personal friend. Himmler doted on Deuschl, sending him flowers, china, cognac, fresh fruit, and chocolates during the war, when these were difficult to obtain without special connections. In 1943 Deuschl was able to acquire a house in Starnberg, a small town in the foothills of the Bavarian Alps (the house had recently belonged to a Jewish family). Deuschl's rewards were political as well as pecuniary: in January 1944 he was named mayor of the town.

Personal reward was only one of several reasons physicians became involved in the experiments. At the Nuremberg trials, physicians justified their participation in the experiments on a variety of grounds. Karl Gebhardt carried out a series of experiments with sulfonamide, in his words, to clear himself of suspicion in the death of SS General Reinhard Heydrich.[169] Others argued that prisoners were being sacrificed to help save the lives of other, more "valuable" individuals. If concentration camp prisoners were condemned to die anyhow, what harm could there be in using them in this way? Furthermore, those who survived the first run of "terminal" experiments were supposed to be granted a stay of execution. (Physicians at the camps admitted, however, that this did not apply to Poles and Russians; nor is there evidence that Jews or Gypsies were ever granted such a reprieve.) Physicians compared their work with medical experimentation in other countries, at other times. Defense attorneys after the war were able to cite instances in the United States in which experiments had been performed on unwilling or unknowing human subjects.[170]

Perhaps the most common argument was that such experiments were done on orders "from the professors in Berlin." This of course was a convenient excuse. Physicians claimed that if they had disobeyed orders, then they themselves might have become victims. There is, however, little evidence that physicians ever refused to participate in Nazi programs; those few who did (in the euthanasia operation, for example), do not seem to have suffered for their refusal. As noted earlier, physicians were never ordered to participate in the experiments; those who participated did so because they were given the opportunity and volunteered.

It is curious that, immediately after the war, people were eager to argue that Nazi medical experiments "were not even good science." The American prosecutor at Nuremberg, for example, felt compelled to point out that Nazi medical experiments were "insufficient and unscientific," "a ghastly failure, as well as a hideous crime."[171] One is almost left with the impression that if such experiments had been "good science," this would somehow make a difference in our attitudes toward them. And yet the cruelty of an experiment is not lessened by its scientific value. Furthermore, Nazi experiments were not entirely "insufficient and unscientific," in the restricted sense of these terms. The experiments were undertaken by trained professionals; the results were presented at prestigious conferences and scientific academies. Karl Gebhardt and Fritz Fischer, for example, ordered a series of experiments whereby women were infected with gas bacilli, staphylococcus, or malignant edema to determine the effectiveness of new drugs produced by the German pharmaceutical industry. Gebhardt and Fischer presented the results of these experiments at a May 24–26, 1943, meeting at the Military Medical Academy in

"Lives Not Worth Living" 221

Berlin; prominent German physicians (such as Ferdinand Sauerbruch) participated in discussions of the experiments, which had been performed at the concentration camp at Ravensbrück.[172] Results of these and other camp experiments were published in scientific books and articles.[173] German industry also profited from the experiments: the firm Behring-Werke, for example, used concentration camp prisoners to test new vaccines against spotted fever; Bayer Pharmaceutical Company purchased female experimental subjects from Auschwitz (for 700 RM each) in order to perform experiments on this "captive population."[174]

Part of our revulsion for Nazi medical experiments stems from the fact that they violated a relationship of supposedly unique confidence and trust. In the Nazi period, the doctor-patient relationship was exploited to achieve goals that would have been difficult to attain by other means. At Buchenwald, for example, 8,000 Russian prisoners of war were executed in the course of supposed medical exams; unsuspecting prisoners were taken to an examination room, where they were told to stand in front of a device apparently designed to measure their height. Prisoners were then shot in the head from a secret cavity built into the device. (This device can still be seen as part of the exhibit the East German government has established among the ruins of the former concentration camp.) The traditional doctor-patient relationship was exploited in other ways as well. SS troops suspected of disloyalty were executed under the guise of medical treatment—through intravenous injection of phenol or gasoline.[175] Phenol and gasoline left odors on the body, however, which caused problems with high-ranking Nazis whose bodies had to go on public display at state funerals. Nazi physicians thus developed methods of execution that would simulate "natural causes" of death. For example, Professor Heissmeyer, one of Karl Gebhardt's associates at the SS hospital in Hohlenlychen, developed a technique to induce acute and fatal miliary tuberculosis by intravenous injections of live tubercle bacilli. Sigmund Rascher at Dachau developed cyanide capsules that could be used either for executions or for suicides.

It is possible of course, in hindsight, to separate analytically the sterilization program (eugenics), the destruction of the mentally ill (euthanasia), and the destruction of Germany's racial minorities (the final solution). The fact is, however, that each of these programs was seen as a step in a common program of racial purification. Medical journals used the expression "life not worth living" to refer to those sterilized under the 1933 Sterilization Law,[176] to those killed in psychiatric hospitals, and to those killed in concentration camps.

If we want to understand the logic of the Nazi racial program, then it is not possible to draw a sharp line between what happened before and after 1939. Nor is it possible to maintain that Germany's biomedical community restricted its participation only to the earliest or more "theoretical" phases of this process. Physicians played an active role in both the theory and the practice of each phase of the Nazi program of racial hygiene and racial destruction.

In this light, we can appreciate the conclusion reached by Max Weinreich in his *Hitler's Professors:*

> It will not do to speak in this connection of the "Nazi gangsters." This murder of a whole people was not perpetrated solely by a comparative small gang of the Elite Guard or by the Gestapo, whom we have come to consider as criminals . . . the whole ruling class of Germany was committed to the execution of this crime. But the actual murderers and those who sent them out and applauded them had accomplices. German scholarship provided the ideas and techniques which led to and justified this unparalleled slaughter.
>
> [Those involved] were to a large extent people of long and high standing, university professors and academy members, some of them world famous, authors with familiar names.[177]

8 | The "Organic Vision" of Nazi Racial Science

> Today, the German people may well be considered first in the world in terms of the organic views of its leaders.
>
> —Hans Reiter, president of the Reich Health Office, 1937

In 1933, in the first of a series of articles for *Ziel und Weg* called "The National Socialist Revolution in Medicine," Dr. Karl Kötschau, one of Germany's leading advocates of "natural healing," argued that only the first and formal stages of the National Socialist revolution had been achieved. The most difficult tasks—the penetration of the National Socialist world view into science and culture—remained for the future. Central in the coming revolution would be the Nazis' "organic" vision of science and medicine.

More Goethe, Less Newton

Kötschau's demands were sweeping: the thrust of the Nazi revolution must be to replace the mechanistic thinking of recent medicine by a new and more organic (*biologische*), holistic view of the world. It was not enough, Kötschau declared, for surgery to make technical advances; indeed, the primacy of technical or mechanistic thinking had stifled the search for alternative methods and made difficult the preservation of valuable traditional therapies. Natural methods of healing (*Naturheilkunde*) had as a result been replaced by exclusively physicochemical models and techniques; time-tested methods such as homeopathy had been supplanted by modern pharmacology and mass-produced chemical products. Kötschau complained that two, separate sciences had developed: one for the laboratory and one for the bedside. Science had become "separate from the people."

Kötschau called for a new philosophy of medicine, a philosophy that would reorient medicine toward "more Goethe, and less Newton."[1]

The Nazi vision of a more natural or organic way of life reflected, in part, Nazi desires to return German society "to the earth," to a premodern or rural way of life, free of the troubles and complexities of modern civilization. The Nazis were troubled by the social dislocation and deprivation that followed World War I, and expressed their concerns for the (real or imagined) problems of capitalist, urban industrial life. The Nazi vision of "more Goethe, and less Newton" was linked with a vision of society supposedly more in tune with nature. Alfred Rosenberg, for example, attacked the "unbiological" position of "hollow internationalism" (a veiled reference to Jews and communists) and demanded instead the creation of "a mode of thought that corresponds to organic, natural laws." The greatest task of National Socialism, according to Rosenberg, was "to construct a common destiny that accords with the natural laws of life and the eternal demands of the German racial soul."[2] Ferdinand Sauerbruch criticized the totalitarianism (*Totalanspruch*) of the "mechanical way of looking at the world," and stressed instead the need to return to the primacy of "the personal character of the physician" over mere medical technique.[3]

It is important to recognize, however, that this "organic" vision of National Socialist ideology was not just a form of social apologetics; it also informed the practice of science.[4] The Nazis provided support for areas that today would be considered alternative, organic, holistic, or otherwise heterodox—areas such as ecology, toxicology, and environmental science. These sciences were linked with broader social movements that were trying to reorient German science and medicine toward more natural or "volkish" ways of thought and living.

The Origins of Organic Medicine

These concerns were not new in German society of the 1930s. Organic or heterodox medicine arose as obverse and reverse of the process of professionalization during the nineteenth century. In a sense, much of medicine was "organic" prior to the growth of clinical medicine and chemical methods. In the nineteenth century, however, this changed. The key intellectual transformations in this process were the suggestion by Rudolf Virchow of the cellular basis of disease

(1858); the discovery by Robert Koch that bacteria are the cause of anthrax (1876); and the development by Ehrlich and others of modern chemotherapy (the discovery of the antibiotic effects of salvarsan). The key social transformations included the proliferation of laboratory techniques, the growth of the clinic (and in Germany, the insurance companies associated with these clinics), and the standardization of medical treatment through the exclusion of "irregular" practices.

By the middle of the nineteenth century, a dual medical system had developed in Europe. On the one hand, there was a growing body of urban-based professional physicians that relied increasingly on laboratory and chemical methods. They were trained at the university, were licensed by the state, and practiced "regular medicine" according to standards of performance set by government bodies. On the other hand, there was a larger body of primarily rural-based folk healers, who provided traditional remedies independent of (and often in opposition to) the new methods of laboratory science. These practitioners were generally unlicensed and unregulated; they lacked academic training and practiced according to traditional methods passed down from generation to generation.

The nineteenth century saw the replacement of many folk traditions by "regular medicine," as well as attempts by folk practitioners to organize alternative forms of practice. In 1829, for example, followers of the physician Samuel Hahnemann (1755–1843) founded what was eventually to become Germany's principal homeopathic organization (the Deutsche Zentralverein homöopathischer Ärzte). Other movements stressed very different methods. Healers trained in the tradition of Sebastian Kneipp advocated a healthy diet, medicinal herbs, and exercise. By the end of the century there were eighty-five local Kneipp physicians' associations in Germany, with a total membership of 14,000.[5] Perhaps the most popular organized form of alternative therapy was that offered by the followers of Vinzenz Priessnitz (1799–1851). Priessnitz physicians used cold water to transform chronic into acute illness, provoking a crisis and (hopefully) a cure. In 1832 Eucharius Ortel founded an association based on Priessnitz' methods; subsequent followers established what became known as the Priessnitzbund, emphasizing the importance of light, air, sunshine, and water in maintaining human health and treating disease. Membership in the Priessnitzbund grew from 19,000 in 1889 to

148,000 in 1913. The Priessnitzbund, loosely affiliated with the Social Democratic party, published the journal *Naturarzt* in editions as large as 160,000 on the eve of World War I.[6]

The popularity of such movements in the early twentieth century should be understood not merely as a romantic yearning for preindustrial society but also as evidence of a perception (even among physicians) that something was wrong with the way medicine was heading. Physicians in the 1920s and early 1930s commonly spoke of a "crisis" of modern medicine.[7] Physicians criticized the shift of medical attention from individual patients to particular organs, as well as the extreme specialization accompanying the rise of science-based medicine. Some warned that the crisis of medicine was also a crisis in human health: people began to notice that cancer and heart disease rates were on the rise, and that the same was true for many other ailments (venereal disease, diphtheria, suicide).

Professional concerns about a crisis in modern medicine, combined with popular distrust of medical orthodoxy, allowed alternative healers to withstand repeated attempts to standardize or "scientize" medical practice in the early decades of the twentieth century. In 1933, just prior to the Nazi rise to power, German natural medicine was highly organized and diversified. Local healing associations were organized into several large umbrella bodies (*Grossverbände*); one of these—the Biochemische Verband—boasted 400 local and 19 state associations (*Landesverbände*). Local associations published their own newsletters and journals: in early 1933 the *Deutsches Ärzteblatt* reported that 70 periodicals had taken it upon themselves "to struggle against scientific medicine." Naturopathic physicians, by their own count, claimed to have as many as 150 journals.[8]

Natural medicine was not, in other words, something invented by the Nazis. New in the Nazi period was the government's apparent willingness to revive and regulate certain of these traditions and to place them on a par with other forms of medical practice. Also new was the attempt to link natural medicine with the ideals of social Darwinism, racial hygiene, and Nordic supremacy.

The New German Science of Healing

Nazi encouragement for new and more organic forms of medicine must be seen as part of a broader movement to restore more natural ways of living to the German people. Women were supposed to avoid make-up so they would not destroy their "natural beauty." The Nazis emphasized the importance of protecting animal life and conserving natural resources;[9] in the early years of the regime, veterinary journals reported on Nazi legislation designed to protect rare or valuable varieties of plants and animals. Nazi philosophers also commonly expressed concerns about cruelty toward animals. In early 1933, Nazi representatives in the Prussian parliament called for legislation barring vivisection.[10] And on August 17, 1933, Hermann Göring, chairman of the Prussian Ministerial Cabinet, issued orders that henceforth "vivisection of animals of whatever species is prohibited in all parts of Prussian territory," and that "persons who engage in vivisection of animals of any kind will be deported to a concentration camp."[11]

Nazi physicians linked their concerns for the protection of nature and nature's creatures with the supposed need for a retreat from the impersonal, "capitalist," "socialist," or "Jewish" forms of medicine that had dominated the earlier liberal age. Jews were blamed for having suppressed German folk traditions in favor of "internationalist" medicine (see Figure 38). Nazi physicians promised to redress these grievances. Early in the regime, the National Socialist Physicians' League announced the return of the house call and the family physician, and related both of these to the new emphasis on the family.[12] The Nazis also allowed the reemergence of traditional forms of healing previously declared illegal: on October 20, 1933, for example, the Ministry of the Interior announced it would allow faith healers to practice once again.

Nazi support for alternative forms of medicine was not out of touch with popular sentiments at this time. In 1933 the *Deutsches Ärzteblatt* reported the estimate of Nazi medical hero Erwin Liek that more than half of all illnesses in Germany were treated by nonlicensed medical personnel. The *Deutsche Invalidenversicherung* pointed out that probably 50,000 people in Germany offered medical treatment without a license—more, in other words, than the total number of physicians.[13] In 1936 the *British Medical Journal* reported that more than half the German population followed some form of "nature medicine."[14]

The scale of this popular support is impressive even today. In the single month of November 1934, for example, more than 270,000 people paid out of their own pockets for treatment by natural healers (*Heilpraktiker*) rather than going to regular physicians, whose fees were paid by the government.[15] German medical journals pointed out that in the years prior to the Nazi seizure of power, the numbers of those registered by the state to provide treatment without a medical license grew even more rapidly than the numbers of physicians. In 1876 there were only 670 registered *Kurpfuscher* ("quacks,"[16] or those providing treatment without a medical license) in Germany; by 1930 there were 12,942. In Prussia at the end of 1930, there was one registered healer for every four physicians; in Bavaria, there was one for every five; and in Saxony, one for every two. These figures do not even include the larger body of unregistered free practitioners who managed to avoid government accounting altogether.

The natural health movement enjoyed support from the highest ranks of Nazi leadership. Hitler was a vegetarian and did not smoke or drink. Rudolf Hess, Hitler's second in command, attended congresses of homeopathic medicine and supported the development of homeopathic science. SS chief Himmler was an ardent fan of organic health; during World War II he organized special homeopathic field hospitals for use on the Russian front and sponsored experiments in concentration camps on lead poisoning. Julius Streicher, the rabid anti-Semite and early Hitler supporter, was head of one of Germany's largest organic health movements: the People's Health Movement (Volksgesundheitsbewegung), said to have a broad following of some 6 million persons (see Figure 39). In 1933 Streicher imagined himself eventually assuming a position as Reich health minister after the consolidation of the natural health movement in the new regime.[17]

Nazi support for alternative forms of medical care was institutionalized before the rise of the Nazis to power (not, however, before the organization of regular physicians into the National Socialist Physicians' League). In the fall of 1930 a number of German natural healers met in Hanover to form the Association of National Socialist Healers of Germany, a short-lived body that declared itself ready and willing to coordinate Nazi efforts in the field of natural medicine. The new organization called for the rights of natural healers to practice free from government restrictions.[18]

It is not yet clear what became of the Association of National Socialist Healers. By 1933 the body had disappeared, and none of its leaders seem to have played a major role in the *Gleichschaltung* of Germany's top natural health bodies. Initiative for the reorganization of Germany's natural health associations appears to have come from other sources. In the spring of 1933 the Ministry of the Interior

Figure 38. Article titled "Stop the Thief: The Role of Jews in Medicine," in a popular anti-Semitic journal supporting the organic health movement. The cartoon shows "Jewish-influenced medicine" suppressing "natural healing methods"; the caption asks: "How Much Longer Will the Jewish Spirit Be Allowed to Muzzle German Reforms?" From *Deutsche Volksgesundheit*, November 1933, p. 1.

Figure 39. Julius Streicher and Gerhard Wagner at the 1936 meeting celebrating the founding of a New German Science of Healing. Streicher was head of the People's Health Movement, an organization with a membership said to number in the millions. From *Volksgesundheitswacht*, Brachet 1935, p. 5.

announced the formation of a Healers' League of Germany (Heilpraktikerbund Deutschlands), with 500 members representing practitioners of homeopathy, *Biochemie* (a variant of homeopathy), and other folk medical arts, including treatments with mudpacks, herbal remedies, and various kinds of magnetic and radiation therapies (*Magnetopathie und Bestrahlungsarten*). Other bodies were agglomerated in similar fashion. In late November 1933, 300 physicians and natural healers met in the Rudolf Hess Hospital in Dresden for the first meeting of what would soon become known as the Association of Nature-Physicians (Reichsverband der Naturärzte), headed by Oskar Väth of Munich. This body was subsequently subordinated to the Healers' League of Germany, headed by Ernst Kees of Munich.

As one might imagine, the reorganization of natural healing under the Nazis was accompanied by the exclusion of Jews from organized healing bodies. Jews had long been active in the natural healing community. The socialist and Reichstag member Julius Moses, for example, was a major supporter of folk medicine; he once argued that if healers lost the freedom to practice (*Kurierfreiheit*), the result would be "the monopolization of medical care by orthodox medicine."[19] Nazi natural healers, like orthodox physicians, argued that Jews exercised a disproportionate influence in the community; one healer claimed that more than half the members of the Berlin branch of the Association of Nature-Physicians were Jewish.[20] Exclusion of the Jews became an early priority of the Nazi-led healers' movement, and by 1936, at the one hundredth anniversary of the founding of the German Folk Health Movement (*Volksheilbewegung*), Reich Healers' Führer Ernst Kees could announce that the "cleansing" of Jewish elements from the natural healing community had been essentially completed; the healing community (except for a few "isolated cases") was now essentially "free of Jews" (*judenfrei*). He also boasted that natural healers were more "advanced" than orthodox physicians in this regard, as roughly 10 percent of all regular physicians were still Jewish.[21]

The Nazi Physicians' League played a key role in organizing strong and early support for natural healing. On November 26, 1933, Gerhard Wagner delivered a speech at the annual convention of natural healers (*Tagung der Heilpraktikern*) in Munich, contrasting natural medicine with academic medicine. Academic medicine, he charged, used complicated methods to diagnose problems in particular parts of the body, while ignoring the person as a whole. He blamed orthodox physicians for having ignored what is true and valuable in alternative therapies; alternative methods, he pointed out, had been adopted by "nonprofessionals" only because orthodox physicians had stubbornly ignored these methods. Wagner also remarked on a political dimension in the problem. The liberal era of "laissez faire, laissez aller" had assumed that government regulation of natural healing was unnecessary or ill-advised. Under National Socialism, however, such freedom could not be tolerated: either all natural methods were to be banned, or their practice would have to be regulated so that "anyone who wants treatment by a natural healer can rest assured that the healer has been adequately trained in the art of his trade." The German Physicians' Führer called for an end to the unregulated practice of medicine and declared that the only legitimate body representing natural healers was the Healers' League of Germany. Other bodies, Wagner said, "will have to disappear."[22]

Others in the Nazi medical hierarchy expressed similar views. Walter Gross contrasted "popular healing" with "dogmatic school medicine." Kurt Blome pointed out that tensions between scientific and natural medicine had existed for centuries, but that in recent years overspecialization risked losing the forest for the trees. Louis Grote celebrated what he called the coming of an entirely new era of medicine—one that would challenge Galileo's demand "to measure what is measurable, and to make measurable, what is not."[23]

The high point of support for natural medicine in Nazi Germany (at least in terms of fanfare and propaganda) was a meeting of the Association of Nature-Physicians in Nuremberg on May 25–26, 1935. Some 1,200 physicians and healers representing various parts of the movement were in attendance; the meeting was cosponsored by Julius Streicher, one of the popular leaders of Germany's natural health movement.

Speeches delivered at the Nuremberg meeting promised a broad reorientation of German medicine. Gerhard Wagner addressed the meeting, promising that concrete steps would be taken to bridge the gap between academic medicine and organic healing; Wagner announced that organic care stations (*biologische Pflegestätten*) were being planned for Munich and Dresden. The highlight of the meeting, however, was Wagner's announcement of the formation of a Committee for a New German Science of Healing (Reichsarbeitsgemeinschaft für eine Neue Deutsche Heilkunde), headed by Karl

Kötschau of Jena and assisted by Oskar Väth from the Association of Nature-Physicians.[24]

Alfred Brauchle, "organic physician" at the Rudolf Hess Hospital in Dresden, outlined for the meeting some of the philosophical principles behind the New German Science of Healing. Brauchle argued that prevention must be united with cure, and that patients must take it upon themselves to learn what makes one healthy or ill. Ultimately the body heals itself; medicine can do nothing but help facilitate this process. The proper task of medicine is to remove obstacles blocking the body's own natural defense mechanisms; more than this may be excessive or dangerous. Brauchle denounced the radical separation of diagnosis and treatment and stressed instead the value of cleanliness, a natural diet, periodic fasting, and the consumption of raw fruits and vegetables.[25]

Karl Kötschau, Führer of the new committee, stressed that organic medicine was intended to complement—not replace—traditional medicine, and that the goal was "more science," not less: "It is not our intention to ignore the results of the exact sciences. The organic physician must have the opportunity, however, to prove his art through his own institutions. The goal of organic medicine is not fantastic speculation, but rather more science . . . Organic medicine is ready to show that it can produce considerable results in the struggle against infectious epidemics."[26] Kötschau pointed out that the organic physician opposed the "alienation from nature" accompanying the sterilization, preservation, and pasteurization of foods; as a result of such processes, one could already observe an "unusual diminishment of capacity" among Germany's school children.

Organic medicine was also to fit within the broader racial goals of the new state. According to Kötschau, organic medicine was to ensure that Germany's "existing genetic material" would be allowed to develop "to its fullest potential"; this would guarantee Germany "a strong and capable race." He recommended that organic medicine be incorporated into the medical school curriculum as a primary field for examinations.[27]

The Committee for a New German Science of Healing was to embrace most of Germany's alternative medical community: all naturopathic and Kneipp physicians, all homeopathic and anthroposophical doctors, and all balneologists and physicians in the German psychotherapy movement.[28] The committee was to sponsor meetings to unite academic and natural medicine and was to oversee the establishment of professorships in the New German Science of Healing (*Neue Deutsche Heilkunde*) at German universities. The committee, subordinated to the Reich Physicians' Führer, was supposed to be eventually incorporated into the Reich Medical Chamber.

On April 20, 1936, on the occasion of Hitler's forty-seventh birthday, 2,000 physicians, Nazis, and natural healers met in Wiesbaden for the first (and last) Congress of the New German Science of Healing. The congress, sponsored jointly by the prestigious Society for Internal Medicine and the newly formed Committee for a New German Science of Healing, was widely hailed as the first time that academic physicians had met with organic healers as part of an effort to combine forces. The intent of the congress, in the words of one participant, was "to bridge the gap that separates academic medicine from the feelings and desires of the people."[29] Claims made for this effort were not modest. Professor Alfred Schwenkenbecher of Marburg, in his opening speech before the congress, hailed an era of new thinking in medicine, characterized by "a retreat from purely scientific attitudes." German medicine had come to a crisis, or turning point, from which would come a new kind of medicine, one "closer to the people" and dealing with "the wholeness of the human personality." Gerhard Wagner also addressed the meeting, repeating again the themes he had stressed the year before at Nuremberg. He declared that physicians must become both "allopaths" and "homeopaths," and that in the future there must be no difference between school medicine and organic medicine.[30] (At the opening of the twelfth International Congress of Homeopathic Physicians in Berlin in 1937, Wagner announced that "if something is good for the Volk, it doesn't matter where it comes from—whether that be the university professor, or the herbalist [*Kräuterweiblein*].")[31] Karl Kötschau also repeated some of the claims he had made the previous year. He contrasted the duties of preventive and curative medicine (*Vorsorge und Fürsorge*): the purpose of preventive care was to strengthen the organism so that it can fight illness on its own; the purpose of curative care, in contrast, was to treat deviations from the organism's normal condition, intervening at a point where natural methods are no longer appropriate. Kötschau argued that the goal of the New German Science of Healing was not to eliminate curative medicine but to render it unnecessary.[32] The Wiesbaden congress concluded by issuing a resolution that German medical science had won its worldwide reputation by virtue of its love of truth and its exacting research standards; the congress resolved to test the methods of natural healing using these same strict and unbiased standards.[33]

In the years following the 1935 and 1936 Nuremberg and Wiesbaden meetings, natural healing enjoyed unprecedented status in Germany. The government established homeopathic hospitals and funded popular lectures and exhibits on organic medicine. Several journals of the movement expanded publication.[34] Natural medicine was for the first time in many years taught in German universities; plans were made to establish a number of professorships in this area.[35] Orthodox medical journals reported on the value of natural healing for internal medicine, pharmacy, and surgery; in 1936 Berlin's Academy for Postgraduate Medical Education offered courses on homeopathy.[36]

The Nazi period also sees the establishment of several hospitals devoted to one or another variant of heterodox medicine. In 1934 construction was completed at the Rudolf Hess Hospital in Dresden, acclaimed as "a school of Hippocratic thought and ideals." Separate natural healing and medical clinics were provided in the hospital, each with 250 beds. The hospital was designed to treat pneumonia, rheumatism, bronchial asthma, stomach and intestinal tumors, circulatory problems, and cirrhosis of the liver by homeopathy and other "natural" techniques.[37] In 1940 construction was completed of the huge Robert Bosch Homeopathic Hospital at Bad Lannstatt (near Stuttgart); the hospital was hailed as the first exclusively homeopathic hospital in the world, with 300 beds and modern conveniences including telephones and radios in every room. Natural healers were impressed with these gains. Rudolf Tischner noted in 1937 that "in the Third Reich, organic medicine has found a respect that it never, not in its wildest dreams, imagined it might achieve."[38]

The New German Science of Healing was to draw from both old and new traditions of medicine. It was to be rooted in the "blood and earth" of German history and to present a challenge to certain strains of modern scientific medicine. This can be seen, for example, in the fascination of Nazi medical writings with the sixteenth-century physician and philosopher Paracelsus von Hohenheim. Paracelsus appeared in Nazi books and magazines as the personification of German medical science. Paracelsean medicine was said to embody the natural, earthbound, experimental character of German medicine—medicine that was "close to the people" and not based on "a lot of complicated theories." It embraced "the whole man," not just particular organs or ailments. The historian Paul Diepgen hailed Paracelsus as the "most German" of all of Germany's medical men in the period of the Reformation.[39] Paracelsean medicine was supposed to provide a model for the New German Science of Healing.

Enthusiasm for the teachings of Paracelsus spilled over into popular cultural events. In 1935 Julius Streicher founded a Paracelsus Institute in Nuremberg. On August 7–8, 1937, at a meeting of the German Folk Health Movement in Düsseldorf, the playwright Martha Sills-Fuchs opened an exhibit on the life and times of Paracelsus; opening ceremonies were attended by Gerhard Wagner and Georg Wegener. Sills-Fuchs also staged a performance of a play she had written on the physician-philosopher; the play, performed at Düsseldorf's Operettenhaus, was so popular that it was held over for an extra evening.[40] In the fall of 1941, Nazi medical authorities met in Salzburg to celebrate the life and work of Paracelsus on the four hundredth anniversary of his death. Frick called the German physician a "scientific revolutionary"; Conti proclaimed that, although Paracelsus could not exactly be called a National Socialist, he nevertheless should be considered a philosophical ally of the movement.[41]

Nazi efforts to organize and reorganize German natural healers continued into the war years. On May 24, 1939, Conti announced the dissolution of the Association of Nature-Physicians and the Kneipp Physicians' League as part of a campaign against the sectarianism (*Sektiererei*) of the various alternative medical groups.[42] In 1941 the Committee of Associations for Natural Methods of Living and Healing[43] was reorganized into the German People's Health Association (Deutsche Volksgesundheitsbund, or DVB); this new body included the Deutsche Gesellschaft für Lebensreform, the Priessnitzbund, the Kneipp-Vereinigung, the Reichsbund für Homöopathie und Lebenspflege, and the Biochemische Bund Deutschlands.[44] These groups continued to be active in the final years of the Third Reich. The DVB sponsored training in paramedical skills such as homeopathy, first aid for war-wounded, care for teeth and skin, gymnastics, and the use of medicinal teas. In 1942 alone, the DVB trained 7,000 people in centers established throughout the Reich: in 1943 leaders of the Bund announced that the DVB had become the "shock troops" of Nazi health leadership on the home front.[45]

A number of historians have recently argued that much of the Nazis' attempt to reorient medicine toward more organic forms was a failure.[46] The celebrated Committee for a New German Science of

Healing was supposed to unify all branches of German natural medicine; in fact the organization never transcended the level of propaganda. Natural medicine met with resistance, not only from orthodox physicians but also from natural healers who resented efforts to unify all variants of natural medicine under a single chain of command. At the end of 1936, Gerhard Wagner ordered the Reich Committee for a New German Science of Healing dissolved, amid criticism from various quarters.[47] For the remaining years of the Reich, the Nazis never managed to control the diverse and splintered factions of the healing community as cleanly and as easily as they controlled the orthodox medical community.

This is not to say, however, that attempts to reorient medicine toward more organic forms were without effect. Whatever success or failure the Nazis had in bringing about particular institutional reforms, one cannot deny that support for organic health and healing did transform certain aspects of German society. One example of this success can be seen in what was widely debated as the "whole-grain bread question" (*Vollkornbrotfrage*).

The Whole-Grain Bread Operation

In 1935 Reich Physicians' Führer Gerhard Wagner launched an attack on the recent shift from natural whole-grain bread to highly refined white bread. He denounced the modern world's white bread as "a chemical product" and advocated a return to healthy whole-grain bread. (German *Vollkornbrot* is actually quite a different substance from American whole-grain bread. The former includes the entire kernel of wheat, rye, or other grain, and is much heavier than what usually passes for whole-grain bread in the United States.) In a speech before the 1938 Nuremberg Nazi Party Congress, Wagner linked the "bread question" to a broader need to return to a diet of less meat and fats, more fruits and vegetables, and more whole-grain bread.[48] Many of Germany's leading medical journals seconded Wagner's appeal. Professor Arthur Scheunert warned that the shift from whole-grain to white bread had resulted in the loss of both fiber and vitamins, and that this probably meant the loss of the primary health value of the bread.[49] Karl Kötschau called whole-grain bread the German people's future bread of peace (*zukünftige Friedensbrot des deutschen Volkes*).[50] Franz Wirz, a member of the NSDAP's Committee on Nutrition, expressed similar views: "We don't want to have whole-grain bread as the only bread [*Einheitsbrot*]; no-one is suggesting that. We don't want to force anyone to eat whole-grain bread. But we do want to enlighten, to teach, and to convince."[51] The *Ärzteblatt für Berlin*, commenting on Wirz's remarks, noted that one could shortly expect state regulations governing how finely grain for bread could be ground.

In 1935 Wagner ordered that German bakeries reorient production from white bread to whole-grain bread. To carry out Wagner's orders, a Reich Whole-Grain Bread Committee was formed, with ninety-six members representing the German government, the Nazi party, and interested parties in science, industry, and regulatory bodies governing German bakeries.[52] The purpose of the committee was to find "a solution to the bread question" (*Lösung der Brotfrage*), and to do this by implementing an operation designed to make whole-grain bread the primary "people's bread" (*Volksbrot*). In cooperation with this program, Goebbels' propaganda office designed and printed a poster showing a mother serving her children whole-grain bread.

During the war years Nazi medical authorities raised the whole-grain bread campaign (*Kampf ums Brot*) into a leading issue of public health for the German nation. On March 8, 1940, the Nazi Physicians' League sponsored a conference in cooperation with the Whole-Grain Bread Committee to advertise the nutritional and medicinal value of bread. Speakers at the conference presented evidence of research showing that whole-grain bread was good for diabetes, gout, cirrhosis of the liver, constipation, kidney stones, nephritis, and various allergic disorders. Whole-grain bread was said to help maintain a healthy bite and to protect one against falling asleep.[53]

During the early months of the war, the Whole-Grain Bread Committee was granted extensive powers to reorient German consumption and production patterns.[54] The committee also established special institutes to supervise the quality of bread; three such institutes, attached to medical facilities in Munich, Dessau, and Cologne, monitored the production of German bread, testing not just smell and taste but also mineral, fiber, and water content, and firmness of the crust. At the same time, German health authorities continued a widespread public relations effort to get Germans to eat a better bread. In the spring of 1940, the Reich Work Service of the Sudetenland ordered that workers be served only whole-grain bread.[55] On March 21, 1941, at 6:30 P.M., Reich Health Führer Leonardo Conti addressed the German nation in a radio broadcast, asking people to turn from white bread to whole-grain bread for the good of their health and the strength of the nation.[56]

The whole-grain bread operation (*Reichsvollkornbrotaktion*), as this program was known, was a tremendous success. In 1939 only 2,420 German bakeries (or 1 percent of all bakers) produced whole-grain bread. By 1943, however, this number had risen to 27,454 bakeries, representing nearly a quarter (23 percent) of all bakeries in Germany.[57] This success was not entirely due to good propaganda. Whole-grain bread is easier to make than highly refined white bread, and the shift to the coarser whole-grain bread could be justified not only as a healthy measure but also as an austerity measure necessary in time of war.

Alcohol, Tobacco, and Other "Genetic Poisons"

One reason for the appeal of natural medicine was its link with the broader goals of racial hygiene. For leaders in the Nazi organic health movement, these two movements were connected in both theory and practice. Karl Kötschau, for example, claimed that "the heroic man of National Socialism and the organic, fully developed [*vollwertige*] racial man—these are one and the same."[58] The New German Science of Healing was supposed to harken back to traditional "Aryan medicine" of an ancient and bygone era; the return to natural medicine was to restore the natural and original practices of Germany's racial ancestors.

Nazi concern for racial health was also associated with efforts to improve the quality of the environment. The Nazi government provided extensive funds for research into the effects of environmental toxins on the human genetic material. Scientists documented the hazardous effects of radiation and established elaborate classifications for the kinds of diseases one might expect from exposure to irritants such as asbestos or to heavy metals such as lead, cadmium, and mercury.[59] German medical journals in the 1930s and 1940s warned against the ill effects of artificial colorings and preservatives in food and drinks, and stressed a return to organic or "natural" ingredients in pharmaceuticals, cosmetics, fertilizers, and foods. Advertisements in popular magazines boasted that their products were free of genetic poisons (*erbgiftfreie*) or that they helped strengthen the genetic material (*erbmassstärkende*).[60] Government officials took the matter of genetic poisons seriously: Hitler's personal physician Theodor Morell declared the pesticide DDT both useless and dangerous, and prevented its distribution until 1943 on the grounds that it posed a threat to health.[61]

Racial hygienists had warned against the dangers of various genetic poisons since before World War I. In the 1920s and 1930s, Bluhm, Ploetz, Rüdin, Lenz, and others spent a great deal of their time trying to prove the damaging effects of alcohol on the germ plasm.[62] As early as 1923, Lenz had warned that pharmaceuticals such as quinine, mercury, iodine, and arsenic, and commercial substances such as lead, phosphorus, benzene, or aniline dyes might harm the germ plasm; he linked his critique of the excessive or careless use of such substances to a more general critique of life in the big city.[63] Lenz once suggested that "mongolism" (Down's syndrome) might be the product of genetic defects causes by harmful substances in the environment, especially chemicals used to prevent contraception or induce abortion;[64] he also argued that X-rays could damage the genetic material, not just at the levels used for sterilization but in much smaller doses as well. Lenz incurred criticism from some colleagues (such as Albert Döderlein) when he asked for greater precautions in using radiation for medical purposes.[65]

In the Nazi period, medical authorities incorporated these concerns into state policy. Hans Reiter, president of the Reich Health Office in Berlin, declared in 1937 that three fundamental tasks formed the centerpiece of Nazi "health leadership":

> First, to guarantee that valuable genetic material can be transmitted unaltered—that is, undamaged by environmental influences.
>
> Second, to ensure that inferior genetic material will be excluded from further transmission.
>
> Third, to guarantee that mediocre (*mittelmässige*) genetic material can be improved in whatever way possible, and harmed as little as possible.[66]

Reiter declared that protection of German genes against environmental poisons must be a vital part in any such efforts; he also noted that the two greatest sources of environmental poisons were those that issue from the workplace and those in the food we consume.

Analysis of the effects of environmental toxins on human health was one of the chief priorities of Nazi medical research. Government medical publications tried to discover the extent to which rising cancer rates could be blamed on exposure to radiation, consumption of meat and chemical preservatives, or simply the fact that people were living longer.[67] Max Brandt of Posen wanted to found a new science of "geopathology" that would study the effects of different environments on the diseases of peoples throughout the world. Nazi doctors also stressed the importance of cancer prevention rather than cancer cure: Erwin Liek, editor of the Hippokrates Verlag and one of the early idols of Nazi medicine, predicted in the 1920s that cancer would be found to be closely connected to diet.[68]

In accordance with this concern for the health of the "German germ plasm," the Nazi government sponsored research into the health effects of alcohol and tobacco. In 1938, in a speech before the Reichsparteitag, Gerhard Wagner complained that since 1933, consumption of brandy had increased from 397,000 hectoliters to 761,000 hectoliters, and that cigarette smoking—Germany's "deadliest consumer poison"—had grown from 31.3 billion cigarettes per year to 41.2 billion per year (see Figure 40). Wagner worried that this could damage not just present but also future generations; he cited evidence showing that nicotine passed into mothers' milk and into the developing fetus, and that exposure to nicotine could result in sterility or miscarriage.[69] He did not want to ban the use of tobacco or alcohol altogether, but warned that people should not be misled by the "boundless propaganda issued by nearly every German magazine" encouraging people to smoke.

In July 1939 Reich Health Führer Leonardo Conti founded a Bureau against the Dangers of Alcohol and Tobacco (Reichsstelle gegen die Alkohol- und Tabakgefahren), under his personal leadership. The Reich Health Office at about the same time ordered an investigation of the effects of nicotine on human chromosomes and offered substantial prize money for the best research in this area.[70] Medical journals reported on the absorption of nicotine into mothers' milk and campaigned for women to stop smoking while pregnant; in 1943 one of Germany's leading gynecological journals reported that women who smoked three or more cigarettes a day were nearly ten times as likely to be childless as women who did not smoke.[71] After the outbreak of war in 1939, cigarettes were rationed, and tobacco sales fell so drastically that many shops had to close. Health authorities used this as a way to stop certain groups from smoking altogether. Groups that, according to medical officials, "do not or should not smoke"—including legal minors, women under twenty-five, women over fifty-five, and people in hospitals, rest homes, or homes for the physically handicapped—were denied rationing coupons. In the spring of 1944, smoking on city trains (*Strassenbahnen*) and buses was banned.[72]

Alcohol was another area in which the Nazi government took steps to protect the health of the race. In 1937 the SS ordered stronger restrictions on the sale of alcohol to minors.[73] During the war, the sale of beer and wine was restricted and the sale of high-proof alcohol was prohibited altogether. The Nazi government also enacted legislation allowing stiff penalties for anyone caught drunk while driving; early in the regime, laws were passed requiring motorists suspected of intoxication to submit to medical exams to determine blood alcohol content.[74]

In 1942 the German state of Saxony established at the University of Jena the first Institute for the Struggle against Tobacco (Institut für die Bekämpfung des Tabakwesens), to which Hitler gave 100,000 RM of his own personal funds. Hitler, as already noted, was a vegetarian and did not smoke or drink; nor would he allow anyone to smoke in his presence. (The American *Scientific Temperance Journal* in 1933 praised the German leader for his disapproval of alcohol.)[75] SS chief Heinrich Himmler shared Hitler's opposition to the consumption of alcohol. As part of the effort to discourage drinking, the SS supported the production of fruit juices and mineral waters; by the end of the war, the SS controlled the production of 75 percent of Germany's mineral water.[76]

Nazi health officials defended the attack on alcohol and tobacco on the grounds that, under National Socialism, one could no longer accept the liberal ideal of absolutely separate spheres of public and private life. Hans Reiter, in a 1941 lecture titled "Current Scientific Research on the Tobacco Threat," pointed out that personal health was now an integral part of the German national interest. According to Nazi philosophy, "the good of the whole comes before the good of the individual" (*Gemeinnutz geht vor Eigennutz*); hence the responsible Nazi doctor could no longer tolerate substances that damaged the society as a whole, even if certain individuals found them pleasurable.[77]

Medical leaders in the Nazi government commonly spoke of the need to reorient medicine from an emphasis on curing ailments to an emphasis on preventing them. The racial hygiene program was itself conceived along these lines: racial hygiene was intended to provide

Wir rauchen je Jahr fast 45 Milliarden Zigaretten!

Ist Rauchen gesundheitsschädlich?

Was geben wir für das Rauchen aus? | Wie wirkt der Tabakgenuß? | Dürfen Frauen rauchen?
„Nicht weniger, aber nikotinarm" rauchen?

Der Verbrauch an Genußmittel-Giften, Kaffee, Tee, Alkohol, Nikotin, ist in den letzten Jahrzehnten, insbesondere aber auch in den letzten Jahren unaufhaltsam und erschreckend angestiegen. Noch vor 6 Jahren, im Jahre 1933, sind in Deutschland 10 Milliarden Zigaretten weniger geraucht worden, als jetzt. Aber schon damals betrug der Jahresverbrauch bereits 31 Milliarden und 348 Millionen Zigaretten (1933), um von da ab, Jahr für Jahr um durchschnittlich 2 Milliarden Stück zuzunehmen. 1938 wurden in Deutschland schließlich 41 Milliarden und 285 Millionen Zigaretten verraucht, zu denen noch 3 bis 4 Milliarden selbstgedrehter Zigaretten, etwa 10 Milliarden Zigarren und große Mengen an Pfeifen-, Kau- und Schnupftabak hinzutreten. — Die Frage:

Können wir uns das leisten?

ist also im wirklichen Sinne des Wortes brennend geworden. Unsere Tabakeinfuhr aus dem Auslande betrug 1931 1,4 Millionen Zentner, sie betrug 1935 bereits 1,75 Millionen. Das Gewicht dieser ungeheuren Mengen gleicht etwa dem Gewicht von 1 Millionen erwachsener Menschen.

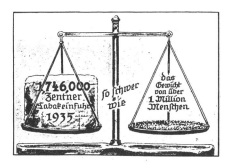

1936 betrugen die finanziellen Lasten, die wir uns für Rauchwaren aufbürden:
für fast 9 Milliarden Zigarren . . . . 760 Millionen RM.
für 38,5 Milliarden Zigaretten . . . . 1300 „ „
für Rauch-, Kau- und Schnupftabak . . 280 „ „
Jahreslast für Tabak zusammen: . . . 2340 Millionen RM.

Das war 1936! Zur Zeit paffen wir je Jahr über 2,5 Milliarden Reichsmark in die Luft! Um uns von dieser ungeheuren Summe einen Begriff zu machen, sei darauf hingewiesen, daß eine einzige Tabak-Jahreslast ausreichen würde, um unser Volk auf einen Schlag mit 2,5 Millionen Stück Auto-Volkswagen zu versehen!
Es gibt nützlichere, gesündere und wertvollere Ausgaben, nicht

Figure 40. "Is Smoking Hazardous to Your Health?"—an article in a popular health journal. The illustration on the left shows that the amount of tobacco consumed by the German population in one year (1935) is equal to the weight of 1 million people. The illustration on the right points out that in one year "our people spend 2.5 billion reichsmarks on tobacco products; for the same amount of money, we could buy 2.5 million Volkswagens!" From *Gesundes Volk*, April 1939, p. 59.

Figure 41. Nazi midwives meeting in Berlin to celebrate the thirtieth anniversary of Frau Nanna Conti's practice of midwifery. Conti (seated, holding the bouquet) was head of the Reichsfachschaft deutscher Hebammen and mother of Reich Health Führer Leonardo Conti. From the 1941 *Zeitschrift der Reichsfachschaft deutscher Hebammen.*

The "Organic Vision" 241

long-term preventive care for the human genetic material. Gerhard Wagner, speaking at the Third International Congress for Postgraduate Medical Education, stressed: "It is not enough for the National Socialist health policymaker to eradicate already existing diseases; he must avoid and prevent them. The healthiest people is not that which possesses the best, or the greatest number of hospitals, but rather that which needs the fewest."[78] The Nazi attack on alcohol and tobacco coincided with this new emphasis on prevention.

Concern for the effects of genetic poisons was often conceived within a hereditarian framework. Fritz Lenz, for example, argued not only that alcohol could damage the germ plasm, but also that the tendency to drink was itself the product of genetic infirmity.[79] Otmar von Verschuer made a similar argument for dust-induced lung diseases. In the late 1930s he tried to prove that susceptibility to diseases caused by dust was a genetically inherited trait. Verschuer examined 20,000 individuals from the Ruhr Valley suffering from dust-related diseases and concluded that certain groups had a constitutional predisposition to suffer from these diseases.[80] Racial hygienists worried about the effects of carcinogens in the environment, yet they also pursued research attempting to demonstrate a hereditary basis for cancer.[81] Efforts such as these show that Nazi racial hygienists often combined their fear of genetic poisons with an assumption that one's genetic constitution can play an important role in whether one will succumb to such poisons.

Nazi Support for Midwifery

The Nazi emphasis on a return to natural and in some cases traditional medical procedures can also be seen in the support for a return to midwifery. In the nineteenth and early twentieth centuries, the practice of midwifery was nearly destroyed by the professionalization of medicine and the replacement of midwifery by gynecology. Whereas in 1909 there were nearly 38,000 midwives in Germany, by the end of the Weimar period there were just over 20,000.

Early in the Nazi regime, health authorities consolidated Germany's professional midwifery organizations into a singly body[82] and launched a program to support birthing by midwives. In 1933, 29 percent of all German babies were delivered by midwives; by 1935 this had increased to 39 percent. By 1937 *Ärztin*, the women doctors' journal, could report that three-quarters of all German births were attended by midwives, and only about one-quarter took place in hospitals.[83] In 1939 a law was passed (the *Hebammengesetz*) requiring that *all* German babies be delivered by German midwives.

German midwifery, like all other medical organizations, was *gleichgeschaltet* in the early years of the Nazi regime. Midwives were required to join the Reichsfachschaft Deutscher Hebammen (the official midwife's organization), and by 1938 there were 25,000 registered members of this organization. By 1943 this number had grown to more than 27,000.[84] The attempt of the Nazis to shift the burden of birth assistance from doctors to midwives was successful. Whereas in 1933 midwives delivered (on average) twenty-nine babies per year, by 1935 this had grown to thirty-nine, and in 1941 the average German midwife assisted in the birthing of nearly fifty babies.[85] After the war began, the proportion of babies born to midwives increased: in 1943 Nanna Conti could report that about 73 percent of all births were attended by independent midwives (practicing outside hospitals), and another 25 percent were delivered by midwives employed in hospitals. She proudly concluded that "every German child is lovingly received into the world by the hands of knowledgeable German midwives."[86]

The rebirth of midwifery in Nazi Germany was aided in part by the fact that the mother of Reich Health Führer Leonardo Conti, Nanna Conti, was chief of Germany's midwives (Leiterin der Reichsfachschaft Deutscher Hebammen—see Figure 41). Conti was a follower of Theodor Fritsch and an early supporter of National Socialism. She argued that, as a consequence of the renewed emphasis on motherhood, German physicians had become especially interested in developing ways to ensure safe childbirth. She was also able to point to evidence that birthing by midwifery was safer than hospital births. Conti published statistics demonstrating that among industrialized countries, maternal mortality was highest in those countries for which hospital births had become the exclusive method of birthing: America (except for four states where midwifery was still practiced), Canada, and New Zealand. In 1934, when the Prussian Ministry of the Interior ordered that midwives should accompany all births, this was justified on the grounds that it would lower infant and maternal mortality.[87] In 1936 German midwives delivered nearly three-quarters of a million babies, with an infant mortality rate of only 3.4 percent.[88]

The January 1, 1939, Reich Midwifery Law (*Reichshebam-*

mengesetz) specified new standards for the training and practice of German midwives.[89] The law stated that in order to obtain a license, midwives were required to undergo eighteen months of intensive training, including 900 hours of instruction, extensive clinical experience, and assistance in a minimum of fifty actual births. In 1944 Nanna Conti calculated that since 1939, German midwives had attended 7,000 technical lectures and lectures on questions of world view.[90] Women between the ages of eighteen and thirty-five were eligible for training as midwives; these women were often from rural or working-class backgrounds. Midwifery was a popular profession in the Nazi period: applications generally exceeded positions at the schools by a factor of about four to one. Conti noted that the state of Saxony guaranteed its midwives an annual income of 1,400 RM.

Nazi physicians justified midwifery as healthier and more natural than hospital births. Nazi medical philosophers reminded their colleagues that birth was a natural process, and that medical intervention—whether by drugs to induce labor or by Caesarean section—should be considered only when absolutely necessary. Similar philosophies were extended to early child care. Women were encouraged to breast-feed their children, on the grounds that this provided healthier nutrition than artificial formulas. Women were given a daily allowance (*Stillgeld*) of fifty pfennig for every day they nursed their children up to twenty-six weeks. To aid those infants who for one reason or another did not have access to mothers' milk, the Nazi government encouraged women to donate their milk. In 1941 German women donated 92,500 liters of milk to this program; in 1943, 11,000 women contributed nearly 130,000 liters.[91]

The Nazi Retreat from Natural Medicine

The Nazis' support for alternative or organic forms of medicine led them into certain contradictions with broader movements in German society. On the one hand, the Nazis wanted to return to what they saw as the original, natural state of human life and society. On the other hand, Nazi medical authorities also wanted to breed a better human, and this induced them to entertain radical measures to alter and "improve" the course of human biological history.

This tension in Nazi medical ideology between the ideals of the organic life and the imperatives of human racial improvement led to a curious set of ideological allegiances. Walter Gross, for example, was head of the Office of Racial Policy and responsible for a massive propaganda program advocating the elimination of Jews and "the unfit" from German life. Yet Gross (like many other Nazi physicians) was also critical of all that was "unnatural" in modern life. Gross thus criticized American scientists for experimenting with ways of "breeding children by artificial insemination"; he warned that techniques of clinical fertilization might one day be used by women "who have an ineradicable hostility toward men" to circumvent the need for fathers altogether. Gross claimed that it was difficult for him to imagine how anyone could undertake such "tasteless" and "unnatural" experiments in the name of progress. He accused American scientists of having become alienated from nature (*naturentfremdet*), and attributed this to the hegemony of "Jewish-mechanistic thought."[92]

The enthusiasm of Nazi physicians for natural medicine was ultimately compromised by their allegiance to techniques and traditions that only the orthodox profession could provide. The bodies of knowledge associated with racial hygiene (genetics, anthropology, and the like) were generally the province of orthodox, not heterodox, medicine; the techniques required for sterilization, castration, and so on, were not something that organic medical traditions could offer.

More important, physicians wanting to forge an alliance between organic and regular medicine ran into resistance from orthodox physicians who resented this move. Important parts of the medical profession had opposed the natural healing movement for quite some time, and many physicians hoped that the Nazis would pull in the reins on "irregular" medicine. Many German physicians supported the Nazis on precisely these grounds—they were convinced that support for National Socialism would help bring natural healing under government control and put an end to the unregulated practice of (natural) medicine.

In the early months of the Nazi period, the *Deutsches Ärzteblatt* launched an extended attack on medical "quackery" (*Kurpfuscherei*). Editors of the journal pointed to the irony in the fact that, whereas "healers" were free to provide treatment to fellow humans without a license, one had to have a license to treat pigs or horses.[93] The freedom to practice medicine without a license (in this view) was the product of an earlier and one-sided liberal age in which free trade ruled in the sale of drugs and medical services. The journal admitted that physicians had perhaps been too eager to turn to surgery or synthetic drugs, but also warned that one must not forget the powerful results achieved in the age of scientific medicine. The journal demanded an immediate halt to the practice of medicine by unlicensed healers, and warned that it would be "irresponsible" if the great ideas of eugenics and racial hygiene were to be turned over to quacks instead of responsible medical authorities.[94]

The professionals' attack on unprofessional healers sometimes took sharper forms. On April 30, 1933, physicians in the Württemberg Medical Association accused half of Germany's natural healers (*Heilpraktikern*) of being criminals. When Rudolf Hess and Gerhard Wagner declared their support for a "cross-fertilization" of natural healing and academic medicine in the fall of 1933, this was met with such criticism from within orthodox medical circles that both men were forced to qualify their remarks, adding a disclaimer to the effect that one must distinguish sharply between genuine healers and quacks.[95] Popular health magazines throughout the Nazi period instructed readers on how to guard themselves against charlatans in the field of medicine.[96]

As support for natural healing grew in the early years of the Third Reich, so did orthodox criticism. In fact, natural medicine is one of the few areas in which it is possible to find criticism of Nazi policies in German medical journals. Nazi support for natural healing encountered opposition from the insurance companies, the medical administrative bureaucracy, and the pharmaceutical industry. In 1936 the world-renowned surgeon Ferdinand Sauerbruch warned that the abandonment of scientific thinking would only exacerbate the "crisis of confidence" in medicine and bring about a revival of "chaos and mysticism."[97]

In 1937 Hermann Berger attacked the New German Science of Healing in an article in the *Münchener Medizinische Wochenschrift*. He told the story of a homeopathic physician in Frankfurt who treated two children for throat infection. Two days after treating the children, the physician realized the children were suffering from diphtheria; in spite of this, the physician kept the children at home, without isolating them or notifying the authorities. After one week the mother had contracted the disease. Only after a regular physician had been called was the family taken to a hospital. By this time, however, it was too late: all three patients eventually died from the disease. The homeopathic physician was brought to court and accused of negligence in the death of the children. He was absolved of criminal charges, however, and was simply fined 3,000 RM by a disciplinary court of the Reich Medical Chamber for having failed to impose a quarantine or to register the cases with health authorities. Commenting on this case, Berger noted that although the dangers posed to German health by the new medicine were not yet great, they might well increase "year by year, as these dangerous doctrines spread and penetrate German medical education."[98]

Natural healing journals recognized that the government was not willing to support all the demands put forth in the name of natural medicine. In 1934, for example, Albert Wolff, editor of the prestigious homeopathic journal *Fortschritte der Medizin,* published an article criticizing government support for mandatory vaccination. In January 1935, after Nazi medical authorities initiated proceedings against Wolff for having published the article, Wolff complained that the regime would soon be taking "even stronger measures against many other journals" for opposing government policies.[99] Shortly after this, Wolff's journal published an order by Wagner forbidding any further "criticism or agitation" by German medical journals on the question of vaccination.[100] Wagner declared that "reactionary" criticisms of government policy would not be tolerated, and that laws requiring vaccination must be followed.[101]

Foreign observers followed with interest the growing tensions between orthodox physicians and natural healers. As early as 1934, the socialist Theodor Gruschka could note in reference to these tensions that it was no longer the Jews but the natural healers that were giving the German medical profession competition.[102] One year later Wagner cautioned against "eccentricity" on the part of organic physicians, and medical journals began to report on growing divisions between Wagner and Julius Streicher's movement,[103] culminating in Streicher's *Deutsche Volksgesundheit aus Blut und Boden* being forced to cease publication, largely as a result of its continued hostility to government vaccination policies. In August 1937, in a move that was to cause considerable consternation within the natural healing community, Wagner declared that German healing (*Heilkunde*) must be based on "knowledge gained in higher education"; Wagner also stated that *natural* medicine was to be incorporated into *orthodox* medicine, and not vice versa. He rejected suggestions that a new generation of healers should be educated in special schools designed for that purpose.[104]

In fact, the numbers of those licensed to practice natural healing did not substantially increase during the Nazi period. In 1927, for example, there were 11,761 registered natural healers in Germany. Ten years later there were only 12,417. Whereas the number of regular doctors grew by more than 26 percent over this period, the number of natural healers recognized by the government grew by only about 5 percent.[105] After 1937 the Nazi government posted increasingly strict rules on the practice of natural medicine. The Natural Healer's Law (*Heilpraktikergesetz*) of February 17, 1939, established natural healers as a licensed and registered profession; all healers were required to belong to the Association of German Healers (Deutsche Heilpraktikerschaft, e.V.), a body subordinated to the Reich Physicians' Chamber. (Membership in the association required, of course, that members and their spouses be "of German or related blood.")

In 1942 Rudolf Ramm estimated that under the new law, the number of individuals licensed to practice natural healing would not exceed 3,000–3,500. By this time, however, the German medical community had already acted to guarantee that these healers would ultimately disappear from Germany. The 1939 law regulating natural medicine dissolved all natural healers' schools and forbade the establishment of new ones. Practitioners of the art were no longer allowed to train new apprentices. Ramm flatly stated that the law was designed to place the entire field of health care "in the hands of state-licensed physicians." The only exception would be a limited number of "physicians of natural healing" (*Ärzte für Naturheilkunde*), a position that required three years of apprenticeship with a practicing healer and six months of clinical experience in a hospital. Ramm pointed out that the Natural Healer's Law was intended to encourage those interested in natural healing to pursue a normal course of university medical studies.[106]

Criticism of natural healing continued into the years of World War II. In July of 1942, Leonardo Conti attacked Schüssler's *Biochemie* as one-sided and sectarian; he maintained that there was hardly a single member of the Biochemischer Bund innocent of charges of corruption, deceit, or "Marxist-Jewish tendencies."[107] Practical steps were also taken to rid Germany of more extreme forms of quackery. On October 26, 1942, DAF leader Robert Ley established an Office for the Occult (Hauptstelle Okkultismus), whose primary purpose, according to its chief, Dr. Bernhard Hörmann, was to combat the "flight into the occult" that "invariably accompanies the outbreak of war." Hörmann noted that in time of war, people want to communicate with a fallen son or try to determine (through astrology, for

248 Racial Hygiene

example) whether a betrothed soldier will return from the front. He claimed that the task of the office was to combat these occultist tendencies by appealing to "positive observation and experience." The activities of the office included attempts to discredit a broad range of practices, such as fortune telling, mind and palm reading, numerology, astrology, communication with the dead, and faith healing.[108]

It would be a mistake, then, to argue (as some early emigrés did)[109] that the Nazis tolerated all forms of natural, mystical, or folk-occult forms of medicine. Nazi medical philosophers argued that the unrestricted provision of medical treatment contradicted the fundamental principles of National Socialism. The Nazis equated absolute freedom to practice medicine with the chaos of an earlier, liberal era in medicine, when one was free to provide or enjoy any and all kinds of marginal or exotic medical treatment. The Nazis attacked as a liberal perversion the view that one should have "the right to dispose of one's own body" (*Recht auf den eigenen Körper*) in whatever way one saw fit. This liberal principle was to be replaced by the Nazi principle of the "obligation to be healthy" (*Pflicht zur Gesundheit*). Rudolf Ramm maintained that those who had once warned of a crisis in medicine had often done so out of self-interest, in order to open the door to all kinds of "quacks and charlatans, astrology and magic."[110] National Socialist medicine, Ramm maintained, would not tolerate such things. The Nazis, unlike those in the previous liberal era, would no longer stand for "quackery" in the sphere of medicine.

Natural Medicine and Preparations for War

Nazi fascination with preventive medicine, natural healing, natural foods, and so forth, may appear odd to someone not familiar with Nazi philosophy. But such movements served a variety of not so obvious functions. On an ideological level, the "organic" metaphor served to stress the unified character of the Nazi state and society; the metaphor of organic harmony could be used to stifle dissent as "inorganic," "inharmonious," or destructive of the volkish body, nation, or state.[111] The ideal of a movement bound "to the earth" also served to link present events to past glories and provided hope for an escape from the crises facing Germany in the 1920s and early 1930s. On a more direct or practical level, the emphasis on organic methods also served military interests. While research into herbal cures was most commonly justified as simply an addition to the store of pharmaceutical knowledge, it was also encouraged by public health officials as part of a conscious program to help prepare the German populace to cope with shortages in the event of war.[112]

In 1935 the Nazi party's Office for Public Health founded a Reich Committee for Research and Collection of Medicinal Plants based in Weimar. The committee encouraged people all over Germany to collect and photograph plants useful for medicinal purposes; archives were established at the medical clinic in Heidelberg to process and classify these materials.[113] The committee also launched an ambitious effort to supplement the German diet with natural herbs and teas. Thus in 1941 the committee supplied the German people with 1.9 million kilograms of dried pharmaceutical plants, 230,000 kilograms of fresh plants, and 1 million kilograms of horse chestnuts (used to supplement animal feeds) gathered from areas around Westphalia, Württemberg, Hanover, Baden, Vienna, the Sudetenland, and Bohemia and Moravia. In April 1941 Franz Wirz reported that in the past year, a German-Bulgarian Rosehip-Gathering Operation (*Hagebutten-Sammelaktion*) had produced 1.2 million kilograms (240 boxcar loads) of the flower; Wirz expected this to increase fivefold in the current year.[114] The flowers gathered in this operation were blended into cakes, chocolates, marmalades, and ciders, in addition to being used as teas. Rosehips were recognized by German health authorities as an important source of vitamin C; in fact, the Rosehip Operation was initiated as a means of ensuring the German population an adequate supply of vitamins during the war.[115] The project was a success: in 1942 the Office for Public Health of the NSDAP reported that in the midst of the war years, the committee was able to supply both the army and civilian populations with all the medicinal herbs they needed. Orthodox medical and pharmaceutical organizations supported the work of the committee; the project was headed by Reich Pharmaceutical Führer Albert Schmierer, and German medical journals hailed the project with bold headlines proclaiming: "German Physicians Use Native Medicinal Plants!"

The Reich Committee for Medicinal Plants was not the only group promoting this kind of activity. In the war years, Hitler's Party Chancellery issued secret orders requiring the gathering of berries, mushrooms, herbal teas, and wild fruits and vegetables.[116] Popular medical journals encouraged readers to learn all they could about local herbs and plants and to develop a taste for herbal teas that might substitute for import varieties.[117] The SS was also interested in natural herbs and pharmaceuticals. The elite paramilitary corps financed experimental gardens in and around Munich to test the effectiveness of various plants for medicinal purposes. At the concentration camp at Dachau, the SS organized farms for cultivating herbal medicines; the project was organized on such a scale that contemporary accounts dubbed it "the largest research institute for natural herbs and medicines in Europe."[118]

Such preparations were defended as valuable not only for improving the general store of German medicine, but also for ensuring supplies should Germany lose its access to foreign markets. Wartime self-sufficiency and war preparedness were in fact among the major arguments given for supporting natural medicine in the thirties and early forties. DAF chief Robert Ley linked the crackdown on intoxicants (*Genussgifte*) to the need to prepare the German populace for war; as early as 1935, Georg Wegener instructed his fellow natural healers on how to create "a people ready and willing to fight [*wehrtüchtigen, wehrwilligen*]."[119] Reich Health Führer Leonardo Conti described the task of health leadership as "work for an organic victory"; and when the Nazi party's Office for Public Health celebrated its sixth anniversary in 1940, medical journals emphasized the importance of "health as a weapon in war."[120]

Ultimately, Nazi support for natural healing was subordinated to the quest for medicines that would help fight and win the war. Those parts of medicine seen as vital for this effort were preserved; others were allowed to wither. The Nazis, in other words, supported "organic" medicine when it suited their purposes. Some supported the new medicine; others opposed it. One should not, however, imagine that the Nazis were more fond of organic than of orthodox medicine, or that National Socialism appealed more to natural healers than to orthodox practitioners. There is simply no evidence this was the case. The Nazis appealed to regular as well as to irregular medicine, and both responded with their services.

9 | Medical Resistance: The Association of Socialist Physicians

> Fascism is the end of European culture. With terror, tyranny came to power, and with terror, it holds onto its power. The sciences have been subordinated to authoritarian rule. Biology has been falsified, in order to eternalize the privileges of the propertied classes.
>
> —Manifesto of the Second International Congress of Socialist Physicians in Brno, Czechoslovakia, 1934

There are two kinds of lessons to be learned from the experience of medicine under the Nazis. First, scientists or physicians were not impervious to the political movements of the times. No less than anyone else, they participated fully and actively in the Nazi movement; in fact, physicians were leaders in the Nazi vanguard. Second, not all Germans were Nazis. Many Germans resisted the onslaught of Nazism, and physicians were important within this resistance. To gain an accurate and fuller picture of these times, we must recall some of the voices of opposition in German medical science. The efforts of the most organized form of medical opposition, the Association of Socialist Physicians, provide us with a hint of how medicine in Germany might have evolved had history taken a different path.

Forms of Resistance

The rise of National Socialism disturbed many in the German medical community, even many of the "Aryan," noncommunist physicians not subject to racial or political persecution. On July 26, 1932, physicians of various political persuasions demonstrated against fascism.[1] Even after 1933 it is possible to name instances in which medical faculty opposed the dismissal of Jewish colleagues. In Halle, Professor

Emil Abderhalden tried (unsuccessfully) to obtain a two-year delay in the dismissal of Dr. Ernst Wertheimer. In the Medical Academy of Düsseldorf, Professors Edens and Huebschmann defended Jewish members of the academy with such fervor that the Nazi gynecologist Friedrich Siegert wrote to Goebbels (in April 1933) that the academy was guilty of "a systematic protection of its Jewish professors."[2] In 1935, after Albert Ekstein was forced from the Düsseldorf Pediatrics Clinic, nurses at the clinic took up a collection to buy him a medal; they were fined 10 RM each for this action.[3]

The most systematic and sustained resistance against the Nazis was provided by communist groups. Georg Groscurth, for example, was professor of internal medicine at the University of Berlin (after 1939) and a member (1933–34) of an illegal Marxist circle headed by Hans Seigewasser; Groscurth helped provide Jews with forged passports and certificates of Aryan identity. He treated Rudolf Hess and other high-ranking Nazi functionaries, and was thereby able to gain access to information and pass this on to resistance groups. Groscurth also established contacts with resistance groups inside the concentration camp at Oranienburg; he worked with the Russian camp physician Galina Romanova to supply resistance leaders inside the camps with medicines and materials to build radios. Groscurth attracted other physicians (such as Heinz Schlag and the dental technician Paul Rentsch) to the anti-Nazi movement, but in September 1943 he was arrested by the Gestapo (along with Schlag, Rentsch, Romanova, and others), brought before a German court, and charged with treason. After his conviction, Groscurth refused to cooperate with the Nazis in order to obtain a pardon and was executed on August 15, 1944.[4]

The broad persecution implemented by the Nazis fostered a curious set of allegiances. Rainer Fetscher, for example, supported the communist resistance despite the fact that he was, by his own admission, a "bourgeois democrat." By virtue of his close connections with police and prison officials, he was able to provide resistance leaders with information concerning Nazi plans to blow up electrical, water, gas, transport, and hospital facilities before the advancing Red army. In 1944 Fetscher helped draw up secret plans for the postwar reform of German health policy. Unfortunately Fetscher himself never lived to see those plans: on May 8, 1945, only days before the defeat of the German army, he was murdered by the SS.[5]

Published forms of resistance (*criticism* or *dissatisfaction* are perhaps better terms) were most often religious in origins. Emil Abderhalden's journal *Ethik,* for example, presented occasional criticisms of the slide toward euthanasia in the mid-1930s, largely from a Christian point of view. Georg Bonne, a seventy-five-year-old physician writing in this journal, complained in 1935: "Today, people express support for not just the sterilization of inferiors, but also for the 'elimination of inferiors' with the help of 'euthanasia'—an easy and comfortable death (or murder?), based on 'human' or 'fiscal'(!) grounds."[6] Bonne did not deny that "growing hordes" of alcoholics and mental defectives were corrupting the German race; he simply advised that the sterilization and euthanasia advocated by racial hygienists were not the best ways to combat these evils. Instead, people should "follow the example of the Führer" and avoid all drink and tobacco. One could thereby combine Nazi and Christian values. Bonne noted that the Nazi state was based on what he called "practical Christianity," and that the only alternative was "Moscow, Bolshevism, and chaos."[7]

Other protests were expressed in terms of what was lost to the German nation. The physicist Max Planck, for example, as president of the Kaiser Wilhelm Gesellschaft, met with Hitler in May 1933 and raised the issue of Jews losing their jobs. The expulsion of Jews from physics, Planck argued, was hurting German science. He pointed out that "there are all kinds of Jews, some worthless to humanity, and some very valuable," and that some discrimination ought to be used in such matters.[8] In a similar vein editors of the *Danziger Äzteblatt* protested: "The German medical profession cannot remain silent when a great doctor is branded a Jew . . . Even if Germany finds itself in a state of siege from world Jewry, we cannot deny the individual contributions of an Ehrlich or a Wassermann."[9] Even within the racial hygiene community, some refused to go along with Nazi notions of race. Karl Saller, for example, Professor of Racial Science at Göttingen, was dismissed in 1935 because he described Alfred Rosenberg's notion of geographical races as nonsense. Saller advocated instead a theory of "social races," which held that races were supposed to arise anew continually through environmental influences.[10]

Some physicians, basically sympathetic to Nazi policies, cautioned against an excessive zeal on the part of those administering the policies. Professor August Mayer of Tübingen wrote in the 1934 *Zentralblatt für Gynäkologie* that the participation of physicians in the genetic health courts was eroding public trust in doctors; if this were to continue, "patients will turn from doctors to quacks, which is certainly not in the interests of public health." Mayer suggested that patients (and not physicians) should be the ones to apply for sterilization, and that doctors "should not be overeager to sterilize; we should not ask 'who *can* I sterilize?' but rather 'who *must* I sterilize?' "[11]

There are even cases in which the Nazi government felt compelled to restrain overzealous physicians eager to sterilize their patients. In 1934 the interior minister for the state of Baden ordered physicians to be more careful in their selection of patients for sterilization. "It simply makes no sense," he pointed out, "to burden the genetic health courts with applications to sterilize sixty-year-old alcoholics, or ten-year-old feeble-minded children, or vegetating idiots, or catatonic women over the age of forty-five—especially when there are others still of breeding age in need of sterilization." The minister also argued that sterilization of individuals with six fingers, harelip, congenital hip dislocation, or other minor defects should be left to a time when carriers of more "dangerous" genetic deformities had been sterilized.[12]

One might imagine that the euthanasia operation generated the greatest opposition. Here as elsewhere, however, resistance was feeble. Indeed, Ernst Klee argues that one cannot speak of genuine resistance on the part of German physicians in this operation: protests came from legal circles and the churches, but not from medicine.[13] There are, of course, isolated exceptions. In July and August of 1940, for example, Karsten Jaspersen of Bethel attempted to organize German professors of psychiatry to protest against the operation and managed to gain the support of one or two other physicians. Gottfried Ewald, one of those asked to help evaluate patients for destruction, refused to participate, as did several others. Most of those who complained about the operation, however, complained not because they opposed the operation in principle, but because it had not (yet) been sanctioned by German law.[14]

But which of these various actions can really be called *resistance*? Was it resistance simply to express dissatisfaction with some part of Nazi policies? Was it resistance when certain SS physicians sought to keep the number of deaths in concentration camps "to a minimum"? Was it resistance when a physician in Berlin charged large sums of money to the frozen bank accounts of Jews in order to return that money to the victims? Was it resistance, as some have suggested, to have done nothing more than continue one's scientific work in silent protest, joining what some have called the great inner emigration?[15]

It is important to distinguish resistance from dissatisfaction with one or another aspect of Nazi policies. The group I will focus on here is one that, with limited resources, struggled against fascist trends within German medicine both before and after 1933. Although its members (many of whom were Jewish) were ultimately imprisoned or forced into exile, the Association of Socialist Physicians distinguished itself by providing an alternative vision of how medicine might be organized, one that contrasts sharply with that presented by Nazi physicians.

Early Socialist Medicine

Political tensions were not new in 1933 to the German medical profession. Throughout much of the nineteenth century, German physicians played an active political role in German society. During the revolution of 1848, for example, Rudolf Virchow and R. Leubuscher founded the journal *Die Medicinische Reform* in order to champion the cause of German unity, socialism, and medical reform.[16] Virchow suggested that the causes of health or disease were to be found not in climate or "miasmas" but in the social conditions of the home and workplace. His efforts provided a model for the role many physicians would play in the establishment of socialized medicine and other medical reforms in the latter half of the nineteenth century.

Radical medicine did not die with Virchow's journal. Beginning especially in the 1880s, physicians excited by the prospect of socialism in Germany applied the principles of this movement to medicine. Important in this regard was the rise to power of the (Marxist) Social Democratic party. Between 1890 and 1910, support for the Social Democratic party grew from 100,000 votes to more than 4 million. In the elections of 1912, the Social Democrats won more than half the popular vote, and on the eve of World War I, the SPD was clearly the largest political party in the country.

Physicians played an active role in shaping the policies of the early Social Democratic party. A certain tension also developed, however, between the SPD and the medical community in this period. Most physicians were quite conservative and opposed SPD efforts to establish and extend state-supported medical insurance. The SPD, in turn, although it supported social medicine, was skeptical of physicians' efforts to organize outside the party framework. SPD policy had been to deny physicians the right to form coalitions, on the grounds that this would create divisions serving special interests. Socialist doctors who wanted to join or were already members of the Hartmannbund (for example) were threatened with expulsion from the party; *Vorwärts,* the official newspaper of the SPD, warned readers of the "excessive demands" being made by physicians.[17]

Tensions between physicians and the Social Democratic party were ideological as well as political. The party tended to view the struggles of physicians in this period (for example, to establish the patient's right to choose a physician) as the product of "bourgeois-reactionary sentiments." SPD leaders were generally skeptical of the political values of doctors and, to an increasing degree, of scientists. Karl Kautsky, in his 1906 *Ethics and the Materialist Conception of History,* argued that although science throughout most of history had been a progressive force, in recent years, science (at least in its "undialectical form"—the form of Büchner and Haeckel) had made its peace with the bourgeoisie and had now become a largely conservative institution.[18]

In 1913, shortly before World War I, a group of Germany's politically conscious physicians formed a Social Democratic Doctors' Association (Sozialdemokratischen Ärzteverein) under the leadership of Ignaz Zadek to champion the cause of socialist medicine (see Figure 42). Their intention was to support the SPD in matters of health policy; members of the association were all in the Social Democratic party.[19] In the early years after the war, however, as political differences began to split the SPD, divisions also began to appear within the socialist physicians' community. In 1924 the left-leaning majority of the Social Democratic Doctors' Association followed Ignaz Zadek (brother-in-law of Eduard Bernstein) and Ernst Simmel in breaking with the Social Democrats to form an independent body: the Association of Socialist Physicians (Verein Sozialistischer Ärzte—VSÄ). The new association was intended from the beginning to be nonsectarian, bringing together socialist physicians from the SPD, the Independent Social Democratic party (USPD), and communist factions of the larger socialist movement. The association was to provide a "united front" of progressive-minded physicians, independent of particular issues dividing the movement. (Stephan Leibfried and Florian Tennstedt note that the association was one of the very few professional associations in this period with both SPD and Communist party membership.)[20] It was also clear, however, that many in the new

Figure 42. Ignaz Zadek (1858–1931), founder of the Association of Socialist Physicians. From *Der Sozialistische Arzt*, August/September 1931, p. 213.

Figure 43. Otmar Freiherr von Verschuer, former director of the Kaiser Wilhelm Institute for Anthropology, Human Genetics, and Eugenics. After the war many of Verschuer's students went on to become leading figures in the postwar German science of human genetics. From *Homo*, 7(1956): 66.

association were critical of the increasingly conservative and nationalist stance taken by the SPD. Many objected to the party's support for German militarism in World War I; many were also critical of the party's unswerving support for the *Krankenkassen,* the large (and growing) state-supported medical insurance companies established under Bismarck. Radicals within the party complained that the party leadership had tied itself too closely to these companies;[21] the socialist physicians generally wanted more decisive support for socialized medical practice.

The severe economic conditions of the years after World War I were important in politicizing the German medical profession. The hunger and poverty that followed the war produced a crisis in German health and health care; the incidence of diseases such as tuberculosis grew dramatically.[22] In 1918 rations fell from seven pounds of potatoes per week to three and then one pound. The armistice finally declared in 1918 was followed by the November 1918 revolution and a bloody civil war until early 1920. In 1922 and 1923 Germany suffered the highest rate of inflation in history—in little over a year, the value of the German currency fell from several reichsmarks per dollar to a point where billions of reichsmarks were almost worthless.

These events left their mark on the medical profession. During the civil war Germany's major political parties maintained their own underground armies, to which doctors and nurses were often attached. Many of Germany's subsequent Nazi medical leaders (for example, Schmierer, Wagner, Weber, and Verschuer) joined the anticommunist paramilitary *Freikorps* in this period; socialist and communist physicians also organized their own medical bodies. In 1921, for example, communist physicians established a Proletarian Health Service (Proletarischer Gesundheitsdienst) to provide, among other things, first aid for workers injured in industrial accidents.[23]

Economic difficulties transformed other aspects of medical life. Käte Frankenthal, one of the leading socialist physicians in the Weimar Republic (and a member of the Prussian parliament), described the emergence in the early 1920s of a barter economy in which physicians' services were traded directly for goods or services. Hostilities sharpened between doctors and the insurance companies, especially when suspicions arose that the companies were delaying paying physicians in order to profit from the rapidly declining value of the currency. In 1922 Berlin physicians organized a strike against the insurance companies. Physicians continued to treat patients but demanded direct payment, circumventing the insurance system. The strike (and there were several others in this period) divided the medical community. Although most physicians supported the strike, socialist physicians generally opposed it on the grounds that it was forcing the poor to pay out of their own pockets for medical services.[24] The Social Democratic Doctors' Association and the Proletarian Health Service both established emergency medical stations for the duration of the strike.

Some of the first physicians to break with the Social Democrats were those associated with the short-lived Bavarian Soviet Republic. In the revolutionary climate immediately after the war, Mieczyslaw Epstein and Friedrich Bauer founded the Munich Association of Socialist Physicians; in 1922 the association held its first nationwide Socialist Physicians' Congress. By this time the Social Democratic movement in Germany had split into three groups: the orthodox and increasingly conservative Social Democratic party (SPD); the Spartacus movement, formed in 1914 by Rosa Luxemburg and Karl Liebknecht in opposition to the SPD's support for the war (reorganized in late 1918 as the Communist party of Germany—KPD); and the Independent Social Democratic party (USPD), formed in 1917 in opposition to both the SPD's war policy and the revolutionary demands of the Communists. Although the Association of Socialist Physicians tried to maintain a broadly united front, it was often accused by both SPD and conservative bodies of being a predominantly communist organization, a charge the association denied. In 1928, leaders of the association pointed out that fewer than one-eighth of its members were Communists and that its board of directors was composed of eleven Social Democrats and only four Communists.[25]

Bourgeois Medicine, Proletarian Medicine

The political attitudes of German physicians in the early decades of the twentieth century depended in part on their field of specialty. Physicians in older specialties, such as surgery, internal medicine, and gynecology, tended to be more conservative. Physicians in some of the newer specialties—social, industrial, or public hygiene, for example—or those treating diseases most obviously caused by economic or environmental conditions (*Armenärzte*, for example) tended more toward the left wing of the political spectrum. Ignaz

Zadek, founder of the Association of Socialist Physicians, specialized in social hygiene; many socialist physicians shared his interests.

Beginning in 1925, the association published a journal, the *Mitteilungsblatt,* soon renamed *Der Sozialistische Arzt* (The socialist physician). The journal addressed social, political, and economic questions of the day, especially those touching on health and medical policy. Centered in Berlin, the journal allowed socialist physicians to keep abreast of developments in the movement.

The association was active in a broad range of political causes. It supported the Emergency Association for Wives and Children of Political Prisoners, a group established to support families of socialists and communists interned by the Weimar government. Physicians joined other intellectuals and activists in this effort, figures such as Käte Kollwitz, Helene Stöcker, Albert Einstein, and Eduard Fuchs. The association was active in advising socialist parties in the Reichstag on matters of health policy; it also fought for the establishment of ambulatory clinics (*Ambulatorien*) and other forms of health care serving the working poor. Many writers for the association's journal were Jewish, and the journal reported frequently on health care in Palestine.

According to the philosophy of the association, "every doctor who wishes to practice his art effectively must be a socialist."[26] Ernst Simmel, chairman of the association and one of its founders, argued in 1925 that genuine medicine was a much larger project than that generally conceived by "the bourgeois doctor." In the Marxian view of the world, Simmel explained, capitalism is the greatest malady afflicting industrial society: capitalism concentrates the means of production in the hands of a few; capitalism forces wage earners "to squander and waste the only thing they possess—their labor power and their health." Failing to remedy this larger social and economic illness, the traditional role of the physician as "adviser" to his patient falls short of what is needed:

> What good is all the hullabaloo about "medical advice," in word or in film, concerning how one should raise one's children, or what foods one should eat, or how one should work and sleep in a healthy fashion? What good is it to know that one should wash one's hands, or that spitting may injure the health of our neighbors—what good is it to know these things, if the natural means of maintaining health—adequate food, sunlight, fresh air, sleep, and especially, peace and quiet—are luxury items only for the propertied classes?[27]

Simmel conceded that there were bacteria against which one should protect oneself, but he also protested that "people do not die from deadly bacteria alone, but rather from the fact that anyone exhausted from brutal exploitation by industry becomes easy prey for whatever germs they happen to encounter."[28]

The *Sozialistische Arzt* asked that doctors take into account not just the *symptoms* of disease but also the longer-term *social causes* of disease. The May 1931 issue distinguished two fundamentally different kinds of medicine:

> Bourgeois medicine [*Heilwesen*] heals the sick, to return them to the factory as quickly as possible; proletarian medicine heals a man, in order to return him to society in general.
>
> Bourgeois medicine reduces a man to a commodity; proletarian medicine raises health to the highest good of society.
>
> Bourgeois medicine treats the sick, isolated from society; proletarian medicine treats a man in terms of his social conditions.[29]

Physicians in the association thus contrasted two great "systems of health" and two corresponding conceptions of medicine. For the capitalist, health is equivalent to capacity to work; medicine in this conception is reduced to maintaining human laborers in working condition. Under socialism, however, health is conceived as a larger social process. For socialists, medicine involves treating the whole man, not just man as adjunct to machine.

In 1926 Ernst Simmel listed five demands of the association: the eight-hour work day; occupational health and safety, not simply as an abstract science, but as a worker's right; maternity leave for pregnant and nursing mothers; laws restricting child labor; and socialization of health care.[30] In 1928 Georg Löwenstein enlarged these demands to include:

> Socialization of the entire field of health and medical care, including hospitalization and all forms of health care delivery; the creation of a separate ministry for health care and social security.
>
> Expansion of the coverage of state-supported health insurance to the entire population, encompassing anyone with a taxable income and including children, wives, and other family members.
>
> Elimination of all institutions that make a profit from any form of medical treatment or health care.

Expansion of the numbers of hospitals, homes for the mentally ill, and mother and infant homes; establishment of a minimum of seven hospital beds per thousand inhabitants.

Socialization of all pharmacies and all firms producing drugs and medical equipment; establishment of pharmacists as employees of the state.

Socialization of midwifery on a nationwide basis.

Medical supervision of the administration of legal punishment.

Establishment of uniform standards for the registration of deaths and the collection of medical statistics.[31]

Socialist medicine was to include a broad range of demands falling outside the traditional bounds of medicine. The association demanded improvements in housing and food; it asked that voters be allowed to decide whether the large feudal (*Junker*) estates of eastern Germany should be confiscated and redistributed among the people. The association fought against the "barbaric" section 218 of the Prussian penal code criminalizing abortion and demanded greater rights for women to control their own fertility.[32]

Socialist Medicine in Exile

In the early 1930s, when the Nazi "revolution" swept through Germany, socialist physicians found themselves shocked and helpless. In January 1933 the Association of Socialist Physicians published a desperate appeal for working-class forces to unite "in this final hour" against the specter of German fascism:

> The deadly enemies of the Proletariat—the Nazis and the magnates of agriculture and industry—have united in support of the government of Hitler, Papen, and Hindenburg . . . We are threatened by complete collapse into barbarism and despotism! There is no longer time for the struggle of brother against brother—that will only destroy us. In this final hour, we appeal to all organizations of the German working class to combine forces for a common defense! Delegates of all socialist parties must meet immediately! Proletarians of all parties unite![33]

By this time, however, such appeals went for nought. The Nazi movement was taking Germany by storm, and opposition forces were in disarray. The *Sozialistische Arzt* would never publish again in Germany.

The political outlook at this time was even worse for physicians than for other sectors of the German populace. In January 1933 the Association of Socialist Physicians claimed a membership of only 1,500. The association remained on the margins of German medicine; at this same time, for example, the Nazi Physicians' League boasted nearly 3,000 members. By the spring of 1933, physicians in the Reichstag were more likely to be Nazi than socialist or even liberal: parties of the Left and center had only one physician among their ranks (Julius Moses); the Nazis, in contrast, had nine.[34] Compared with any of the major left-wing parties, National Socialism was clearly the more popular party among German physicians. In spite of this, the socialist presence could not be entirely ignored: as late as February 1933, German medical journals could still report relatively objectively on both Communist and Nazi medical programs.[35]

One of the first orders issued by the Nazi regime in the early months of 1933 was for SPD and Communist leaders to turn in their arms under penalty of death or imprisonment. On February 27, 1933, the Reichstag burned, and the Nazis used this as a pretext to round up individuals suspected of communist or social democratic sympathies. One month later, on March 24, 1933, the German parliament voted to grant Hitler emergency powers to deal with the supposed communist threat; the majority required for the law was provided by representatives of the Bavarian Volkspartei and the Deutschnationalen. The Social Democrats voted against the measure; the Communists by this time had already been excluded from parliament. With the triumph and consolidation of fascist dictatorship in Germany, socialist and communist political organizations were declared illegal; other parties disbanded voluntarily.

The Association of Socialist Physicians, along with most other socialist organizations, was not allowed to remain in its country of origin. In the spring of 1933, the association was declared illegal, and most of its leading figures were either arrested (for example, Friedrich Geis, head of the VSÄ in Chemnitz) or forced to emigrate (Ewald Fabian, Käte Frankenthal, Ernst Simmel, Ludwig Jaffé, Minna Flake, and many others). The association was forced into exile; toward the end of 1933, several leading members were able to set up offices in Prague, Czechoslovakia. There the exiled socialist doctors continued publishing their journal, now issued as the *Internationales Ärztliches Bulletin*, the "central organ of the International Association of Socialist Physicians."[36]

In its first issue, published in January 1934, the *Bulletin* issued a statement (in both French and German) denouncing the Nazi regime:

> The victory of the fascist counterrevolution in Germany has destroyed the strongest and most active section of our International Association, just as it has destroyed all proletarian organizations. The Hitler government has tortured and massacred thousands of people. Among the imprisoned are to be found many socialist doctors, our comrades. As with the entire socialist press, our central organ, *Der Sozialistische Arzt,* has been outlawed.[37]

The journal announced four urgent goals: (1) "to keep the Hitler regime, the deadly enemy of the proletariat, from moving beyond its present borders"; (2) "to demonstrate to the entire international working class the dangers of fascism"; (3) "to struggle against the dismantling of socialized medical services"; and (4) "to oppose the falsification of medicine by pseudoscientific propaganda."

By 1934, when the International Association began publishing its new journal in Prague, resistance on the part of the association was largely limited to what it could convey by publication in its (now illegal) journal. The journal published lists of colleagues fired or forced into exile; in 1935 it reported on the use of Jewish slave labor to construct the stadium for the 1937 Berlin Olympics. Beginning in 1936, it published reports on medical conditions in Germany's concentration camps.[38] The journal reported on the murders of Jewish and socialist colleagues by the Nazis, and on colleagues sent to prison for providing abortions.[39] It also criticized those who stayed to defend "the revolution"; the most dramatic case was that of Germany's most renowned surgeon, Ferdinand Sauerbruch.

In the summer of 1933 Ferdinand Sauerbruch, director of the Surgical Clinic of Berlin and head of Berlin's prestigious Surgical Society, published an open letter in the *Klinische Wochenschrift* defending the right of the new German government "to develop its national [military] forces," disregarding the terms of the Versailles Treaty. Sauerbruch claimed that the reason so many international conferences had failed to solve Germany's problems was that they had ignored "the historical and biological conditions of peoples." The new German government, in contrast, recognized "the value of sacrifice for one's neighbor, and for the state as a whole." Sauerbruch maintained that the "will to health of a people" fostered confidence in the new government, a government that united the principles of both national self-consciousness and socialism. He thus proclaimed: "The basic world views that have found expression in fascism and in National Socialism embrace all peoples of the world today: to each according to his character, and to each according to his volkish conditions!" Sauerbruch also declared that the present German government believed in peace, and that it was the duty of the physician "to waken the conscience of the world" to the importance of peace, "as long as this is compatible with the honor of one's nation."[40]

In the first issue of the *Internationales Ärztliches Bulletin,* the editors reprinted Sauerbruch's letter and responded with a series of sharply worded accusations against the government Sauerbruch had undertaken to defend. The association charged that, contrary to Sauerbruch's opinion, there was no peace in Germany and that, indeed, those who advocated pacifism had themselves become outlaws in the eyes of the new regime. The "cultural unity" celebrated by Sauerbruch was a farce; in fact, the new regime had shattered German unity by singling out certain groups to be excluded from cultural activities and professional life. Moreover, workers in the new state had been reduced to subordinate, groveling slaves, and Jews had been declared "enemies of the people, worse than Pariahs."[41]

The association further charged that under Hitler, the rule of law had been replaced by the rule of terror, as "armed troops supporting the regime have been vested with the combined powers of arrest, abduction, incarceration, and legal judgment." The new regime was in the process of corrupting intellectual as well as social values: "in Germany, freedom of expression has been suppressed, and the population has been coerced by brute physical force into either silence or collaboration." As a result, "the free pursuit of scientific research . . . has been made impossible," and "biological science, a discipline specially entrusted to the physician, has been corrupted by the most arbitrary and disgusting abuses." The association warned that the new government could by no stretch of the imagination be considered "peace-loving"; indeed, science, medicine, and education had all been geared toward the militaristic goals of the regime. The socialist physicians thus denounced Sauerbruch's letter and issued instead a plea for opposition to the government's "system of lies, intolerance, violence, servitude, injustice, hypocrisy, and restrictions on freedom of expression." In the name of "all of those who have been brutally reduced to silence," the association called for sympathy for those martyred by the Nazi regime. The letter was signed by the Socialist Medical Association and included signatures from representatives of socialist medical bodies in Czechoslovakia, Norway, Austria, Latvia, and Sweden, in addition to physicians from Poland, Hungary, the United States, and France.[42]

The attack on Sauerbruch was only part of a broader attack on the directions taken by Nazi medical policy. The association marveled at the willingness of Nazi physicians to dismantle public medical services—services that had taken decades to construct, and for which Germany was world renowned. It ridiculed suggestions that such measures were designed to serve "the whole, rather than the individual," and deplored the Nazi contempt for the handicapped and the elderly—individuals who, in Nazi medical jargon, were nothing but useless "ballast lives," lives not worth living.[43] It attacked Nazi theories that the "Nordic race" was the source of all culture, and that Jews posed a threat to the health of the German people. It attacked the "medieval character" of Nazi medicine, grounded in "superstition, naiveté, and mysticism." The exiled socialist physicians complained that Nazi politics had so far invaded medicine that "tomorrow, Hitler will throw out the Pythagorean theorem, SA Führers will diagnose diseases, and the sadist will write laws."[44]

(The stereotype of Nazi science as mystical or irrational may have grown in part from reports to this effect issued by emigré physicians attempting to discredit Nazi science and medicine. The Association of Socialist Physicians ridiculed what it called the "orgiastic Byzantism" of the new regime; socialist physicians ridiculed the support offered by Gerhard Wagner for "organic" forms of medicine in the New German Science of Healing.[45] It is probably fair to say that emigré physicians exaggerated the hostility of the new regime to scientific medicine; this may be one reason many scholars have failed, at least until recently, to appreciate the extent to which physicians supported Nazi racial science and policy.)

Before being driven into exile, the Association of Socialist Physicians had allied itself with a number of like-minded medical groups in Europe and the United States. In May 1931 it had organized the first meeting of the International Association of Socialist Physicians (Internationale Vereinigung Sozialistischer Ärzte) in Karlsbad. The result was that in 1933, when socialist physicians were driven from Germany, a number of international groups rallied to their support. The German Medical Society of New York, for example, published a resolution condemning violations of the freedom of science in Germany and denouncing "the exclusion of some of our colleagues in Germany from professional and research activities."[46]

In 1934 the International Association of Socialist Physicians held its second international congress in Brno, Czechoslovakia, where members continued their attack on the regime that claimed to ground itself in "racial socialism." The socialist doctors condemned the persecution of the Jews; using language recalling the persecution of blacks in America, they spoke of Nazi "lynch mobs" and Nazi "lynch justice."[47] In his closing words to the congress, the newly elected chairman of the International Association, Arnold Holitscher, announced that the meeting was proof of the fact that the working class was "not alone in its struggle against barbaric fascism." Holitscher noted that hope sprang from the fact that, "apart from the servile technicians of academic knowledge, there are also women and men for whom science is more than this—namely, a source of critical and revolutionary thinking."[48]

The activities of the association were not entirely limited to publication. In July 1933 it established a fund to help persecuted German physicians. At its 1934 congress at Brno, the association organized an international boycott of German pharmaceuticals and asked members not to purchase German scientific periodicals. The association also received help from member societies in other countries. In 1934 Swiss physicians lodged a complaint with the League of Nations against the mistreatment of Jewish physicians, and in 1936 the Bombay Medical Union voted to boycott German goods as an expression of opposition to German racial persecution. Similar protests were organized in Norway, Austria, Switzerland, Latvia, Sweden, Poland, Hungary, the United States, and Britain. Other medical groups, not necessarily allied with the association, contributed help in other ways. In the spring of 1934, 600 dentists met in the Hotel Astor in New York and resolved to boycott all trade with the Nazi regime.[49] Physicians in New York also established an Emergency Committee in Aid of Displaced Physicians to help exiled physicians regain some form of livelihood.

In the mid-1930s the Spanish Civil War gave socialist physicians another chance to help stem the tide of fascist expansion. While the Nazi Physicians' League (with the support of the German government) organized medical supplies for the Franco forces, the International Association of Socialist Physicians helped to organize support for the Republican cause. In 1936 the association organized in cooperation with Britain's Spanish Medical Assistance Committee an entire field hospital for use by Republican brigades fighting for a democratic Spain. On August 24, 1936, the joint German-British medical expedition set out for Spain with four physicians, six nurses, nine medical students, and medical supplies and equipment to establish a field hospital with thirty beds.[50] In September 1937 there were at least twenty-one (exiled) German physicians in the medical divisions of the International Brigades supporting Republican Spain, joining physicians from the Soviet Union, Argentina, Luxemburg, and other countries.

The Nazis Take Notice

The *Internationales Ärztliches Bulletin* (International physicians' bulletin) was banned in Germany shortly after its first appearance in January 1934. The German medical press responded to attacks from the socialist physicians with a mixture of mockery, counterattack, and apathy. In the *Deutsches Ärzteblatt,* Kurt Klare (responsible for supervising Germany's medical press) reported that the socialist physicians had "thrown up their tents" in Prague, from where they had begun once again to pour forth their "poison" onto the new Germany. Klare maintained that the socialists' attack on him personally only strengthened his conviction that the Nazis were on the right path. He scoffed at the "garbage" (*Dreckkübel*) issued from the *Bulletin,* and accused the journal of treason for having denounced Ferdinand Sauerbruch's support for the new regime. He also wrote, "The anguished cries of these 'emigrants' concerning the supposed 'collapse of German culture' do not bother us at all; these gentlemen may rest assured that we shall keep a close watch on them, even if they shoot their poison arrows from the secure portals of their new asylum."[51]

The *Münchener Medizinische Wochenschrift* also acknowledged the new journal, noting "it is understandable that the journal should attack the new Germany; what is particularly disgusting, however, is that it should do so with the dirtiest weapons of lies, distortions, and slander." It cited as an example the *Bulletin*'s claim that "the Hitler regime has murdered and tortured thousands, and incarcerated many tens of thousands."[52] The editors of the *Bulletin* replied that the Munich journal could hardly be unaware of the fact that thousands had indeed been interned—in SA barracks and concentration camps—and that thousands of people had been physically or morally abused. The Prague journal pointed out that "countless nameless workers" had been murdered, and that in fifty concentration camps, tens of thousands had been tortured and "encouraged" by the SS or SA to undergo a "nationalistic rehabilitation."[53]

Berlin's leading medical publication also responded to the socialist journal in exile. Franz Dörbeck, editor of the *Grossberliner Ärzteblatt*, wrote an article titled "The Insidious Agitation of the Socialist Physicians," accusing the Prague journal of being a Jewish-socialist contrivance (*Machwerk*), whose only purpose was to attack "all that is German." Dörbeck ridiculed the socialists' claim that "certain parts of the German population" had been mistreated. He concluded:

> If the Jewish-socialist physicians want to lie, then they should at least be more clever . . . It is clear that all these smears and slanders are only an expression of the disappointment and anger felt by those unscrupulous individuals who have not been able to achieve their goals of corrupting the German people and destroying national unity. "Journals" such as the *Bulletin* indicate the need to continue cleansing the German medical profession and German literature, with the ultimate goal of eliminating Jews and Marxists.[54]

Apart from the few examples cited here, there is little evidence that the Nazi medical profession ever took serious notice of criticisms raised by socialist physicians. Silence appears to have been an effective method of neutralizing criticism.

Socialists and the Question of Race

In a number of areas the concerns of socialist physicians overlapped those of the Nazis. Both socialist and Nazi doctors stressed the importance of prevention over cure and of treating "the whole man," not just particular diseased organs. Both criticized the assembly-line character of modern health care delivery; both saw the trends of specialization and rationalization as posing dangers to genuine medical practice. Both supported efforts to limit alcohol production and consumption,[55] and conceived personal habits to be a legitimate area of medical critique. Both advocated an increased role of the state in the administration of public health, and viewed the task of medicine as fundamentally a political one.

The differences between these two groups, however, are also significant. Both stressed the importance of prevention over cure, but whereas for the socialist physician the key to prevention was improvements in housing, food, and working conditions, for the Nazi physician it was care for the genetic future of the race. Socialist physicians saw the equality of women and men as a fundamental part of their program; Nazi physicians saw their movement as decidedly masculine. Socialist physicians wanted to legalize abortion; Nazi physicians saw abortion as a feminist plot designed to sap the strength of the nation. Women played an important role in the socialist physicians' movement, and an insignificant role in the Nazi physicians' movement. Georg Löwenstein (a socialist) authored proposals increasing penalties for forcible incest; Fritz Lenz (a Nazi) defended incest as biologically sound. Socialist physicians supported marital counseling, but primarily as part of voluntary family planning; Nazi physicians supported marital counseling, but primarily as part of the administrative apparatus associated with the Sterilization and Nuremberg laws. The socialists supported ambulatory clinics, the expansion of psychiatric facilities, and increased medical care for the handicapped; the Nazis abolished the ambulatory clinics and curtailed support for the handicapped and mentally ill (and eventually exterminated these people). The socialists supported the expansion of socialized medicine; the Nazis (often) equated social insurance with "Marxism, plain and simple" and deplored medical support for the "weak and inferior." Nazi physicians were anti-Semitic; socialist physicians condemned anti-Semitism—indeed most of the leading members of the Association of Socialist Physicians were Jews.[56]

One of the most important issues dividing Nazi and socialist medicine was the question of race—a question tied also to the larger question of the role of nature versus nurture in the development of human character and institutions. According to the Association of Socialist Physicians, all medicine was class medicine. The socialist physician opposed Germany's antiabortion laws on the grounds that such laws worked only against the working classes (wealthier women could always obtain abortions).[57] The association condemned racism and encouraged only those aspects of racial hygiene that could be considered nonracist. *Race,* according to socialist opponents of racial hygiene, was often nothing more than a cover word for *class* ("Die Rasse sagt man, und die Klasse meint man").[58]

For the Nazi physician, in contrast, all medicine was race medicine. Nazi physicians defended the primacy of race over class and saw human biology as governing the structure of human institutions. Physicians writing for the *Münchener Medizinische Wochenschrift* claimed (for example) that "the occupational structure of Germany reflects a racial hierarchy";[59] Gabriele Weymann of Berlin similarly argued that skilled and unskilled workers represent two different genetic stocks (*Erbströme*), maintained by reproductive isolation.[60] This view was shared by Hitler: in a lecture to German students on February 7, 1934, he maintained that the proletariat should be seen not as an economic class, but rather as a natural product of racially determined differences among men.

In hindsight, one is struck by the disturbing fact that, prior to 1930, socialist physicians generally ignored the Nazi movement. Käte Frankenthal points out that socialists regarded the movement as a joke.[61] This changed in 1930, however, as the Nazis swept student elections in several universities and gained their first seats in the German parliament. Criticisms of Nazi racial policies began to appear in the socialist medical press. In April 1930 the socialist medical journal acknowledged the formation of the Nazi Physicians' League; the journal also commented on the centrality of racial hygiene, racial science, and eugenics in the Nazi medical movement.[62] In 1931 criticisms of the Nazi movement began to appear more frequently in the socialist journal. The journal attacked the revival of Gobineau and Chamberlain's "racial conception of history"; it condemned the "reactionary anti-Semitic" publications of Julius F. Lehmann, especially his notorious *Münchener Medizinische Wochenschrift*.[63] On August 8, 1931, when the Nazi newspaper *Völkischer Beobachter* issued an anti-Semitic appeal "to all German physicians," the socialist physicians' journal reported the appeal, but also refused to "stoop to reply" to the arguments of the Nazis.[64]

The socialist physicians more than once stated that Nazi views were so absurd they did not warrant refutation. By 1932, however, they were devoting a substantial portion of their time to criticism of the movement. In 1932 the Association of Socialist Physicians organized a public meeting to attack "National Socialism: Enemy of Public Health." Ernst Simmel delivered a long speech at the meeting, attacking what he called the "medieval mysticism" of the movement. He noted that the Nazi solution to the problem of capitalism was an old one: "Capitalism is the Jews! Disenfranchise the Jews! Banish them! Beat them dead!" The recent popularity of such slogans he compared to the reactions people once had to the plague or other natural disasters: ignorant of true causes, people grasp for straws. In medieval times people blamed the Jews for poisoning the wells. (Today, Simmel claimed, "we laugh at such explanations, but at one time they cost many Jews their lives.") It is not so different, Simmel argued, when the German proletariat of today follows Hitler. Psychologically speaking, they want to return to the war, to lose themselves in an unambiguous struggle with clear villains and heroes. The enemy is once again the outsider—the Jew, the Marxist. Simmel suggested that National Socialism "is an opiate for those who, out of ignorance, have wrongly identified the source of their misery"; those who cry "Germany awake!" he claimed, are actually walking in their sleep.[65]

Others in the association addressed other aspects of Nazi science and policy. In 1932 Georg Benjamin attacked the *Deutsches Ärzteblatt* for publishing Nazi antiabortion propaganda and for refusing to print a rebuttal.[66] In the same year Julian Marcuse condemned Hans F. K. Günther's Nordic supremacy and ridiculed Nazi plans for "racial settlements"—where women would be graded according to their fitness for marriage, marriage between Jews and Germans would be illegal, and children who failed more than two grades would be sterilized.[67]

Some of what Marcuse labeled "racial fanaticism" seems curious today. In early 1932, for example, the Society for Racial Hygiene and the Society for Genetics had issued a joint resolution warning that the increasingly popular use of X-rays to induce temporary sterilization might cause irreparable damage to the genetic material. Hans Luxenburger and Paula Hertwig, leaders in these two societies, repeated this warning at the February 1932 meeting of the Bavarian Society for Gynecology: they argued that experiments on plants and insects had shown that X-rays could produce deleterious mutations that could be transmitted to future generations. Physicians at the meeting rejected this argument. Professors Albert Döderlein of Munich, Carl Gauss of Würzburg, and August Mayer of Tübingen asserted that one could not extrapolate from experiments with animals or plants to humans, and that X-rays had indeed been shown to have *positive* effects on human health. The Munich racial hygienist Kisskalt tried to save the arguments of Luxenburger and Hertwig, but to no avail: the congress resolved to support a motion (authored by Döderlein) rejecting the racial hygienists' warning. This, oddly enough, was one of the events Marcuse applauded as a setback for Germany's growing "racial fanaticism."[68]

Socialist physicians rejected attempts to reduce questions of social policy to narrowly biological or medical elements. Rudolf Elkan, for example, criticized liberal feminists (such as Helene Stöcker in Germany and Margaret Sanger in the United States) for having argued that birth control, by reducing the number of mouths to feed, might help solve the problem of poverty. Elkan noted that socialist physicians supported feminist demands for birth control, but could not go along with the Malthusian notion that birth control alone could solve broader problems of a social or economic nature. He pointed out that poverty or hunger springs not from overpopulation per se, but rather from the social relations governing the means of production. Millions died in the Irish potato famine, not because there were too many mouths to feed, but because the population was divided between the 1 percent who owned land and the 99 percent who owned nothing. Poverty in this sense is not simply the product of shortages: why, after all, are there shortages in the first place? Why, Elkan asked, is coffee burned in Brazil, while millions starve? Why is wheat burned in Canada, while others have none at all? Why is Argentinian beef made into soap, in order not to sell it for less than what it cost to produce? Poverty, according to Elkan, is not the product of too many people, but of a system that allocates goods according to the dictates of profit rather than need. Access to birth control should be supported, not as a means of reducing poverty, but because families should be free and able to plan their future.[69]

After the triumph of the Nazis in 1933, socialist physicians sharpened their attack on Nazi racial legislation. Gertrud Lukas, for example, criticized the Nazi Sterilization Law for assuming "the fixity of genetic material" and minimizing the role of environmental influences in heredity. She objected that "the problem of the inheritance of acquired characters" had not yet been decisively resolved, and that this should be taken into account in judging these laws. Lukas also warned that Nazi sterilization and castration laws might one day be used to support the Nordic "master race"; under the Nazis, problems that could not be solved within the sphere of bourgeois education or legislation were henceforth to be solved "with the knife of the surgeon."[70] She predicted that this situation would only get worse, and that when all of Germany's physicians, surgeons, pathologists, teachers, and nurses had "thrown themselves entirely into this effort," the circle of those brought under the Nazi medical knife would broaden.

Not all of Germany's socialist physicians were hostile to everything that went under the name of racial hygiene. A number of socialists in the Weimar period were enchanted with the prospect of improving society through racial hygiene. Until the early thirties, there was a strong eugenics movement in the Soviet Union; in Britain, also, several Marxists defended the value of eugenics for improving the human species. Some of Germany's most influential advocates of social hygiene (Alfred Grotjahn, Benno Chajes) also defended a qualified form of racial hygiene.

There were several important differences between the Nazis and the socialists in this regard, however. First of all, the eugenic measures supported by socialists were generally conceived as voluntary rather than obligatory state measures. Furthermore, for the socialists racial hygiene was generally of secondary importance compared with social and economic changes. Socialists argued that these larger changes must precede attempts to improve the biological base of the species. Finally, socialist physicians rarely supported the Nordic supremacy central to Nazi ideology. Those few who did tended to view themselves as National Socialists—adherents of what August Bebel once called (referring to anti-Semitism) "the socialism of fools."

After 1933, the attitude of many socialist physicians was that eugenics had been "corrupted" by the Nazis. This was the view, for example, of Ewald Fabian (writing under the alias E. Silva), one of the leading figures in the association. Fabian argued that Galton's eugenics was in principle a good thing that had been abused by Nazi charlatans (*Quacksalber*). Magnus Hirschfeld similarly noted that while sterilization laws might have some value if administered by reasonable physicians, in the hands of "overzealous, fanatical, and prejudiced" Nazis they could become very dangerous.[71] Socialist physicians generally agreed that prevention of human genetic disease was a legitimate goal of medicine, and that the only way to prevent such disease was to prevent carriers of those traits from reproducing. They nevertheless disagreed with their Nazi colleagues on the extent to which various diseases were to be considered genetic in origin. Socialists ridiculed suggestions of Verschuer and others at the Kaiser Wilhelm Institute for Anthropology that crime or tuberculosis or a host of other diseases were genetic.

In the course of the 1930s, however, some socialist physicians accommodated to certain aspects of Nazi racial hygiene. In an article in the socialist doctors' journal in 1937, Jan Belehrádek, dean of the medical faculty at the Czechoslovakian University in Prague and a member of the International Association of Socialist Physicians, argued that one could take a continuum of positions on the question of eugenics, ranging from that of fanatics, who want to breed people like animals, to that of moderates, who feel that education in the laws of genetics is sufficient to improve the human genetic constitution. Belehrádek proposed what he called a middle position, which included the following three demands:

> Obligatory health certification before marriage.
>
> Obligatory sterilization of those suffering from severe genetic disorders, and of those who "for genetic reasons" are chronic criminals.
>
> Material and moral support for mothers of "genetically healthy families."[72]

Such a program, Belehrádek maintained, would have little to do with racial questions (*Rassenfragen*) and nothing to do with Nazi racism or Nordic supremacy. He illustrated the arbitrary nature of racial distinctions by pointing out that distinguishing races not by skin or eye color but by blood type would yield very different racial categories from those of common parlance.

What is also interesting is the judgment Belehrádek rendered on the 1935 Blood Protection Law, disallowing marriage between Jews and non-Jews. He asserted that racial questions should not be *entirely* excluded from eugenics. Indeed, "there are certain racial problems that may be relevant to the goals of eugenics. Certain products of human interbreeding are inferior to others; mixing with another race can also introduce new, diseased genes into the population."[73] Belehrádek pointed out that intermarriage between individuals from closely related races (for example, Germans and Slavs) had never been shown to be harmful, and that indeed the highest levels of culture had been achieved among peoples "who are not pure races, but racial mixtures." He also suggested, however, that the case might be different for races more widely separated—such as blacks and whites. Belehrádek admitted that there were "many great doctors, lawyers, thinkers, and artists among the colored half-breeds of America," and that some of the best-known figures in literature—Dumas, Pushkin, Gobineau—were of "colored" origins. But he also noted that American eugenicists such as Davenport had shown that racial miscegenation could have "undesirable consequences." Belehrádek concluded that races that are distant from one another are best kept separate, if racial degeneration is to be avoided.[74]

The case of Belehrádek demonstrates that several of the important presuppositions motivating Nazi racial policy—including those at the root of Nazi sterilization legislation and the Nuremberg Laws—were sufficiently widespread that even socialist physicians shared them to some degree. These conceptions of race and biology were widely accepted in orthodox biomedical circles; many physicians active in opposing Nazi racial science were unable to isolate themselves entirely from them. Racial science was "normal science," in the sense Thomas Kuhn has used this phrase; even critics of this science found it difficult to see the world through another lens.

The End of Socialist Medicine

The rise of the Nazis to power in January 1933 meant the end of socialist medicine in Germany. Many physicians fled to Palestine, England, or the United States; others tried to remain in German-speaking regions long enough to try to influence the course of events. Prague in this context became a convenient way station for many of those fleeing Nazi persecution. The Czechoslovakian government was not on friendly terms with the Nazi regime, and in Prague many socialists were able to find at least a temporary haven from Nazi persecution. The Czech government was also aware that German medicine had become an important instrument of Nazi racial policy; indeed, the *Münchener Medizinische Wochenschrift,* one of Germany's oldest and most prestigious medical journals, was banned by the Czechoslovakian government as a dangerous political magazine.[75] The exiled Association of Socialist Physicians took advantage of this sympathetic environment by recruiting new members: by April 1936 the Prague branch of the Association of Czechoslovakian Social Democratic Physicians had grown to 180 members; by the summer of 1937 the Czechoslovakian association as a whole had grown to more than 700 members.[76]

The socialist physicians' escape to Prague, however, did not end their troubles. Indeed, the German medical communities of Prague, Vienna, and other regions bordering Germany were in the midst of purges that saw the consolidation of far-right fascist forces in the mid-1930s.

Consider first the case of Austria. The key political transformation in Austrian medicine was not the 1938 *Anschluss,* but rather the 1934 *Umsturz.* In the spring of 1934, a fascist putsch attempt by the Austrian Nazi party was spoiled only after several days of bloody fighting. Although the putsch attempt failed, the net result was that far-right forces gained increasing power in Austrian society. In subsequent months the Austrian medical profession increasingly came under control of conservative clerical (Catholic) forces.[77] In March 1934 the *Internationales Ärztliches Bulletin* reported that Austria's foremost socialist medical journal—the *Sozialärztliche Rundschau,* published by the Austrian Association of Social Democratic Physicians—had fallen victim to moves to suppress socialist institutions; with the closing of the *Rundschau,* there was no longer a voice for socialist medicine in Austria. The duties of the Austrian organization were taken up in part by the Prague journal; yet, as the editors of the *Bulletin* pointed out, this could never fully replace the activities of the Austrian body, which had been the largest organized socialist medical body in the world.[78]

The subordination of the Austrian medical profession to what some called clerical fascist authorities was accompanied by the expulsion of Jewish physicians from government hospitals. In 1937 an Austrian physician writing (anonymously) in the *Internationales Ärztliches Bulletin* claimed that since the 1934 *Umsturz* and the subsequent clericalization (*Verklerikalisierung*) of Austrian medicine, Jewish physicians were no longer able to gain positions in the Austrian medical insurance system (Fonds-Bundes or Gemeindespitälern).[79] In 1936 a meeting of the International Congress of Catholic Physicians in Vienna organized by the St. Luke's Guild was devoted entirely to the question of racial hygiene. Although some papers were critical, Nazi newspapers were still able to report that Austria's Catholic physicians were "surprisingly willing" to embrace the ideals of racial hygiene, despite the hostility of the Vatican to such measures.[80]

In Czechoslovakia the story was in many ways similar. Beginning especially in the mid-thirties, socialist physicians expressed concerns about the growth of right-wing anti-Semitism in the strongly German-oriented medical profession. In 1935, when the conservative opposition won elections in the Bohemian Medical Chamber, Arnold Holitscher, editor of the socialists' *Bulletin,* grimly reported that National Socialism was taking the country by storm:

> The mood across the land is that of the swastika: Hitlerian, anti-Semitic. [Czech] doctors look longingly over their borders to where their Aryan [German] colleagues have been freed from the fatal competition of Jewish colleagues. They still carry in their hearts a hatred for socialized medicine, which they see as the cause of their impoverishment; they yearn for a return to the liberalistic "free choice of the physician,"

where the "communist medical bigshots" [*rote Kassenbonzen*] would no longer call the shots. They don't see—they don't want to see—that *medicine in Germany has been driven into the ground by idiots and barbarians.*[81]

In March of 1936 the Prague government tried to gain some control over the three Czech universities, but failed. On November 14, 1937, Professor Max Gundel of the German University in Prague lectured on diphtheria at a scientific congress in Aussig, in the Sudetenland; the lecture passed without notice, except for the fact that Gundel began and ended his talk with a "Heil Hitler."[82] Toward the end of 1937, the Nazi-oriented Union of German Medical Organizations in Czechoslovakia (Reichsverband der deutschen Ärztevereine) began orchestrating the *Gleichschaltung* of Czechoslovakian medicine; Wilhelm Nonnenbruch, Anton Ghon, Karl Amersbach, and other professors in the medical faculties were central in this effort. Early in 1938 the union began publishing a new journal, *Der deutsche Arzt in der CSR* (successor to the earlier *Ärztliche Nachrichten*). The tone of the journal was nationalistic, optimistic, and openly pro-Nazi; German physicians writing in it were confident that the "volkish spirit" would soon emerge triumphant in Czechoslovakian medicine. Nazi-oriented physicians at this time had good reason for optimism: at the spring 1938 meeting of the Union of German Medical Organizations in Prague, the National Socialist faction of the union announced that 100 new members (mostly hospital physicians) had joined the movement. Nazi physicians entered a motion that all of these physicians be admitted to the union, which would have given the Nazi faction an absolute majority and would have meant the *Gleichschaltung* of German medicine in Czechoslovakia. The chairman of the union (Professor Heinrich Hilgenreiner), however, refused to allow the admission of so many new members at one time, on the grounds that this would upset the organization. The Nazi faction, under the leadership of Professors Nonnenbruch, Amersbach, and Schmidt, walked out in protest, and the formal *Gleichschaltung* of the profession was thereby delayed for several months.[83]

For socialist physicians, the growing nationalism and militarism of many central European nations made political work difficult. Setbacks in Germany, Austria, and Czechoslovakia were compounded by conservative reaction in the Soviet Union. Since World War I and the Russian Revolution, socialist physicians had looked to the Soviet Union as a model for progressive medical policy. Writers in *Der Sozialistische Arzt* envied the "endless rooms" of the Institute for

Workers' Medicine in Charkow; socialist physicians praised the Soviets for having legalized abortion and for implementing many other medical reforms. Soviet medical leaders (for example, the Soviet health minister, N. A. Semashko, in 1925) traveled to Germany to share their ideas with the association; German socialist physicians in turn helped in the construction of medical institutions in the Soviet Union. The image of the Soviet Union as a land of brave new hopes and ideals persisted into the early Nazi period. As late as 1935, Arnold Holitscher contrasted the situation in Germany, where medical care had been "driven into the ground by idiots and barbarians," with the situation in the Soviet Union, where great strides were being taken "to cultivate and promote science as the basis of social development."[84]

In the mid-1930s, however, this image was hurt by two events. The first was the Soviet Union's reinstitution (in 1936) of a ban on abortion and the subsequent arrest of physicians accused of providing abortions. Socialist physicians found it difficult to imagine that the first socialist country in the world could have stooped to such policies: the association's *Bulletin* noted sadly that "the language of the Soviet press [on the abortion question] differs little—it is painful for us to say—from that of the Nazi press in the Third Reich."[85] The second and more important shock came from the show trials of the mid-1930s. In 1936 the association condemned the trials in unambiguous terms:

> While we call upon humanity in the struggle against fascism, we must also raise the sharpest protest against the executions and gruesome persecutions that have occurred in recent weeks in the Soviet Union. Countless early fighters for the liberation of the Russian people, among them, some of the closest colleagues of Lenin—men such as Trotsky, Sinoviev, Kamenev, and many others—have been accused of plotting the assassination of those currently in power in the Soviet Union. No concrete proof or documentation has been brought forth, though the accused have been weakened by long imprisonment and brutal interrogation by the Soviet secret police. It is incredible that Trotsky should be accused of being a fascist, acting as an agent of Germany, as an enemy of the working class . . . In socialist and broader circles the executions are being seen as a blow against the international working class, and correctly so. Such events ride roughshod over the Soviets' own past, against their own flesh and blood [*Man wütet gegen die eigene Vergangenheit, gegen das eigene Fleisch und Blut*].[86]

The association demanded an international inquiry into these events, but by this time the socialists' power base was so severely eroded that protests were essentially impotent.

With the rise of Stalinism in the Soviet Union and fascism in Austria and Czechoslovakia, the socialist physicians remaining in central Europe were increasingly isolated. The final blows to the Association of Socialist Physicians came in the spring and fall of 1938. On March 12, 1938, German armies invaded Austria—thousands of people were arrested, and hundreds committed suicide.[87] Immediately after the invasion, 200 of the country's 2,000 Jewish physicians fled to other countries. Many of those arrested had already once fled from German fascism (such as the cancer specialist Ferdinand Blumenthal). The Austrian press was *gleichgeschaltet* and subjected to the same kinds of transformations Germany had suffered for more than five years.

Several months later, Czechoslovakia suffered a similar fate. In the summer of 1938, German nationals in the Sudetenland began calling for the "return" of ethnic German territories to the Reich. The German government demanded that Czech authorities cede to Germany all territories where ethnic Germans were in the majority; on September 26 Hitler promised to invade Czechoslovakia if these demands were not met. In an effort to avoid war, representatives of Germany, France, Italy, and Britain met in Munich to reach an agreement on German territorial claims. Allied forces ultimately agreed to accept Hitler's claims. The Czech government was forced to cede the Sudetenland to Germany, and over the next several months, under pressure from German authorities, Czech authorities enacted a host of anti-Semitic and antisocialist policies. On October 20 the Czech government outlawed the Communist party; socialist physicians remaining in the country were forced from their jobs or from the country. Finally on March 15, 1939, German armies marched into Prague, declaring Bohemia, Moravia, and Slovakia to be "protectorates" of the German Reich and prompting further repressive measures against Jews and political undesirables. By this time, however, the fate of the association had been sealed. Sometime in October or November of 1938, Arnold Holitscher moved the association's *Bulletin* out of Prague. The November/December 1938 issue was published in Paris. Holitscher was no longer on the editorial board, and most of the articles in the dwindling journal were in French.[88] Barred from political activity and the practice of medicine by virtue of his Jewish ancestry, Holitscher retired in Prague, where he died a natural death on October 21, 1942.

Damage Left Undone

Ian Kershaw has suggested that "the road to Auschwitz was built by hate, but it was paved with indifference."[89] And it is certainly true that acquiescence in Nazi policies was a common feature of the German medical profession. Yet, at least in the case of physicians, indifference may well have been less common than one might imagine. The record of medicine under the Nazis is largely one of eager and active cooperation; and neither resistance nor indifference was able to offset the enthusiasm of the profession for the regime and its policies. The psychoanalyst Carl Jung recognized early in the regime that resistance was useless and indeed laughable, "like protesting against an avalanche."[90] Isolated and pathetic protests continued in certain quarters, but even these were rare. Physicians who remained in Germany rarely spoke out against Nazi racial policies.

Socialist physicians were not indifferent to what was happening in their country. Yet socialists were outnumbered and outmaneuvered. The Nazi revolution succeeded in driving socialist medicine underground, or abroad, or into concentration and death camps. Many of those who struggled against the regime did not survive the war years. Karl Kollwitz, cofounder of the Association of Socialist Physicians, died in 1940 in Berlin at the age of seventy-seven. Benno Chajes emigrated in February 1933 to Switzerland and then (via Turkey) to Palestine, where he founded a medical insurance company and worked as coeditor of the journal *Die Medizin*. He died in Switzerland in 1938.[91]

Others survived the war and managed to establish a practice abroad. Alfred Korach, for example, emigrated in 1933 to Paris and then to Moscow (via Prague), where he worked briefly as a consultant to the Soviet Ministry of Health. In 1937 he emigrated to the United States, where he taught preventive medicine at the University of Cincinnati until 1963. Max Hodann was arrested in 1933 and fled to Switzerland and then to Norway; in 1937–38 he served as a physician for Republican forces in the Spanish Civil War. He survived the war in Sweden and died in Stockholm in 1947. Heinrich Meng, one of the leading figures in the Frankfurt branch of the association, emigrated in 1934 to Switzerland and in 1945 became professor of psychology at Basel. Ernst Simmel, president of the association from 1926 to 1931, was arrested by the Gestapo in 1933 and later emigrated to the United Kingdom. In 1934 he emigrated to the United

States, where he served as president of the San Francisco Psychoanalytic Society (1942–1944) and founded the Los Angeles Psychoanalytic Study Group. He died in Los Angeles in 1947, shortly after the publication of his book *Anti-Semitism: A Social Disease*.[92]

Many of those who were able to leave found it difficult to resume medical practice. Friedrich Friedländer worked as a carpenter in Tel Aviv when he was unable to find work as a physician. Käte Frankenthal became a fortuneteller in the United States until she could rebuild a medical practice. Ewald Fabian, formerly editor of *Der Sozialistische Arzt*, fled from Prague to Paris in 1938 and then to the United States in 1940, where he worked as a packer in one of New York's shipyards. He died in the United States in 1944.[93] Georg Löwenstein was able to remain in Germany until 1938, when he was dismissed from his teaching post and escaped to England and then to the United States. He established a private practice in Chicago, and now lives in Clearwater, Florida.

Others, however, were not so lucky. Georg Benjamin, a member of the Communist party since 1922, was arrested in April 1933 and was forbidden to practice medicine. He was arrested again in 1936 and was killed in 1942 in the concentration camp at Mauthausen. Theodor Plaut, head of the Frankfurt branch of the association, fled to France in 1933 but then returned to Frankfurt in 1935 and took his own life in 1938, shortly after the pogroms of *Kristallnacht*. Ludwig Jaffé and his wife fled to Holland on March 22, 1938; both committed suicide in Amsterdam in early April 1939. Julian Marcuse was murdered at Theresienstadt in December 1942.[94]

National Socialism left its mark on Germany in many ways—not just in the bombed-out buildings or the scars of personal suffering and deprivation. The destruction of socialist medicine and socialist medical institutions was not something that could easily be reversed. When allied authorities worked to reconstruct the West German medical system after the war, they stressed the reprivatization of medical practice. Many of the institutions destroyed under the Nazis (such as the locally controlled ambulatory clinics that flourished during the Weimar period) were never rebuilt in either of the two Germanys;[95] today much of the damage to German medicine (those parts that might at least in principle have been restored) has not yet been undone.

10 | The Politics of Knowledge

> Science is not an end in itself; every science has certain tasks to fulfill.
>
> —Karl Kötschau, 1936

The triumph of National Socialism coincides with the most rapid demise of the scientific culture of a people in recent history. In 1930 Germany led the world in the physical, life, and social sciences. By 1935, however, one in five scientists had been driven from their posts; in some universities (the University of Berlin, for example) this figure approached one in three.[1] National Socialists forced the emigration or imprisonment of some of Germany's most eminent scientists: Einstein, Schrödinger, and Franck in physics; Goldschmidt in biology; Haber and Pauli in chemistry—and these are only some of the better known. In medicine, where Jewish representation was large, the toll was especially great. Between 1933 and 1938, 10,000 German physicians were forced from their jobs; many of these were compelled to flee the country, and others were killed in concentration or death camps.[2] Physicians driven from Germany or Austria included five men who either had won or would eventually win Nobel Prizes: Ernst Boris Chain, Max Delbrück, Hans A. Krebs, Otto Loewi, and Otto Meyerhof. The Nazis forced the dispersal of the world-famous Institute of Physiology headed by Meyerhof, and stripped the famous veterinary college in Berlin of most of its staff. Leading medical figures such as Sigmund Freud, Käte Frankenthal, Rudolf Nissen, Hermann Zondek, Selmer Aschheim, and Friedrich Dessauer were all either fired or forced to emigrate. Other physicians driven from their jobs included von Bayer, Blumenthal, Borschardt, Goldstein, Klemperer, Roesle, and Teleky. The Nazis forced socialist and communist physicians into exile or concentration camps. In countries occupied by German armies, the story was similar. In Poland the medical philosopher Ludwik Fleck was deported to Auschwitz, where he was forced to work on vaccines for the SS.[3] The Nazis destroyed the University of Cracow and forced the majority of its faculty into the camps. In Paris medical scholars such as Langevin were imprisoned.

Charlatans and Quacks or "Normal Science"?

In one sense, the persecution of Jewish, socialist, and communist intellectuals can be seen as part of a larger attack on German intellectual life. Nazi philosophers reoriented schooling from intellectual to manual labor; Education Minister Bernhard Rust shortened the high school week from six to five days and ordered that Saturdays be devoted to sports. Nazi philosophers cultivated the virtues of brawn over those of brain, naming as their first official playwright a man (Hans Johst) whose most memorable phrase appears to have been his boast: "When I hear the word 'culture,' I release the safety catch on my gun."

And yet it is only partially true, and in more than one sense misleading, to characterize the phenomenon of National Socialism as anti-intellectual. The image of the Nazis as irrational, jack-booted fanatics fails to appreciate (1) the extent to which the National Socialist movement appealed to academics and intellectuals; (2) the extent to which the Nazis were able to draw upon the imagery, results, and authority of science; and (3) the extent to which Nazi ideology informed the practice of science.

Academics in every field gave support to the Nazi regime. The Nazis, in return, provided support for various forms of intellectual endeavor, and in some instances quite handsomely. Certain fields, such as psychology, anthropology, and human genetics, actually expanded under the Nazis.[4] The Nazis provided substantial support for research in fields such as criminal biology, genetic pathology, and comparative physical anthropology. The German government provided financial support for twin studies and genealogical research, in an attempt to isolate the effects of nature and nurture, heredity and environment. More than a dozen new medical journals were founded in the Nazi period (see Appendix A), and a host of new scientific institutes and academies were established.[5] The Nazis expanded Germany's public health facilities and state health offices. Health authorities implemented public health reforms with a zeal rarely equaled in modern times; millions of persons were X-rayed as part of a nationwide effort to combat tuberculosis; health authorities initiated a program to provide dental examinations for an entire generation of German youth. One could name many other programs implemented on this scale.

Nazi physicians frequently boasted of the growth of public health and medical science under the Hitler regime. Leonardo Conti, for example, on a trip to Denmark in 1942, maintained that "never before has the importance of science been so recognized as in Germany today," especially in his own area of work: medicine.[6] In 1936, when the first volume of the journal *Öffentlicher Gesundheitsdienst* was published, Hans Rinne of the Nazi party's Office for Public Health claimed that there was no area in which the National Socialist state had undertaken greater efforts of construction than in public health.[7] The same conclusion was reached by Franz Orsós, president of Hungary's National Association of Physicians, after a survey of German medical institutions at the height of Nazi power. Orsós traveled to Germany in 1937 as head of a delegation to evaluate German medical science. On the basis of his visit, he concluded that "no country in the world can compare with German achievements in the field of medicine." Germany, according to Orsós, was "unsurpassed in the health of its people; never before has a nation so thoroughly protected its people from disease; never before has a nation concerned itself to such a degree with the health of 'normal people'— the people who will be useful in the future." He marveled at the new scientific institutions founded in the Nazi period, institutions unique in the extent to which they concentrated on preventive medical care: "Special institutes deal with racial protection and racial care, or with genetics and criminal biology. In genetics institutes, there are special divisions devoted to statistical, etiological, and therapeutic research, and research on genetic diseases . . . There is research on genetic idiocy and mental illness, and all designed to serve the German people."[8]

Nazi racial theory and practice were not the product of a tiny band of marginal or psychotic individuals. Nazi racial hygienists were among the top professionals in their fields and saw themselves in the tradition of Virchow, Semmelweis, Koch, Lister, Pasteur, and Ehrlich. Racial hygienists like Lenz, Fischer, and Verschuer were not men whose scientific or medical credentials were in doubt. Individuals we today remember as men of high ideals and wide learning—like Sauerbruch the surgeon or Diepgen the historian—celebrated Nazi programs and ideals. These were serious and respected scholars and physicians; the same might be said for many others in the Nazi medical apparatus. Rudolf Ramm was not a marginal figure in his profession. Nor was Kurt Blome, or Gerhard Wagner, or Walter Gross. Nazi racial theory was supported not only by cranks and quacks but also by men at the highest levels of German biomedical science. Racial science was "normal science," in the sense that Kuhn has given this expression.[9]

How Could It Happen?

Many of the racial/medical policies of the Nazis were both legal and public—open, that is, to public scrutiny. Legislators codified policies into law; the courts rendered judgments based on these laws, and prisons or hospitals carried out the orders of the courts. The Nazis formed a government only after being elected to power; they were careful to construct racial policies in accordance with the rule of law. By October 30, 1938, the Office of Racial Policy of the NSDAP could publish a list of more than 250 separate "Legal Measures for the Solution of the Jewish Question." Doctors cooperated with lawyers in administrating the new policies. Medical journals reported in a businesslike fashion on the confinement of alcoholics to concentration camps, recommending such measures as a means to prevent "hysterical disorders."[10] In the war years, Germany's leading medical journal carried a regular column on "The Solution of the Jewish Question."

How could such ideas come to dominate a community of scholars and physicians dedicated to serving and preserving life? Each of Germany's doctors had taken the Hippocratic oath; each had sworn never to do harm knowingly. These were men who, in the words of one physician at the Nuremberg trials, were supposed to be "nearer humanity than other men." There are several possible answers to this question, none of which is completely satisfactory, but some of which may help throw light on the matter.

First, it is important to recognize that many elements of racial hygiene were not restricted to Germany. Eugenics movements flourished in England, Norway, Sweden, France, the Soviet Union, the United States, and many other countries.[11] German racial hygienists modeled their science on movements in other countries, imploring their fellow Germans to follow these examples, lest Germany be surpassed in racial purity. Racial hygienists drew upon the examples of American immigration, sterilization, and miscegenation laws to formulate their own policies in these areas. German scholars took notice when American eugenicists helped push through emigration restriction laws; Germany's foremost racial hygiene journal reported on the refusal of the American Medical Association to admit black physicians.[12] German scholars also took notice when British and American journals openly considered the question of euthanasia. Racial hygiene, in short, was an international phenomenon and by no means restricted to Germany.

A second element is of a more philosophical nature. One of the pillars of Nazi medical ideology was the "hereditarian" assumption that nature is more important that nurture in the shaping of human character and institutions. Racial hygienists followed Eugen Fischer's claim that the science of genetics had shown that "all human traits—normal or pathological, physical or mental—are shaped by hereditary factors." They argued that the environment—whether climate, nutrition, or education—played a relatively minor role in the development of human character, and that modern science had "destroyed the theory of the equality of men."[13] This hereditarian bias was part of a broader conception of the place of science in society, one that was shared by eugenics movements in other countries. Common to racial hygiene movements throughout the world was the view that it is to *biology* that we must look to solve social problems. Knowledge of (and control over) the human genetic future was the key to human destiny; racial hygiene would eliminate human disease—not just schizophrenia or flat-feet or epilepsy, but also criminality, alcoholism, and homosexuality. The Nazis took major problems of the day—problems of race, gender, crime, and poverty—and transformed them into medical or biological problems. Nazi philosophers argued that Germany was teetering on the brink of racial collapse, and that racial hygiene was needed to save Germany from "racial suicide." Racial hygiene thus combined a philosophy of biological determinism with a belief that science might provide a technical fix for social problems. Harnessed to a political party mandated to root out all forms of racial, social, or spiritual "disease," the ideology of biological determinism helped drive the kinds of programs for which the Nazis have become infamous.

The Politics of Knowledge 287

The willingness of Nazi authorities to "medicalize" or "biologize" a host of social problems may well be one of the primary reasons National Socialism so appealed to physicians. The Nazis saw their movement as applied biology and conceived their program of "cleansing" in medical terms. Nazi racial programs were seen as public health programs, involving the participation of doctors in state policy on an unprecedented scale. National Socialism promised to place medicine on a new and higher level in society; it may even be true that under the Nazis the medical profession achieved a higher status than at any other time in history.

A further dimension to the question of how such things could come to pass concerns the codes and canons of the profession. Central in the medical code of ethics was (and is) that physicians should stand up for one another, especially in the face of criticism or adversity. Rudolf Ramm, for example, instructed German medical students that a physician should always defend his colleagues against criticisms from outside the profession:

> It often happens that a patient, dissatisfied by the treatment he has received, goes to another doctor and attempts to portray the first doctor as incompetent, ill-willed, or derelict in his duties. It is the duty of the physician, however, to give no credence to such accusations. One should instead attempt to excuse and defend one's colleagues . . . . One should always keep in mind that problems faced by a colleague today, you yourself may one day have to face, and further, that your own reputation, and the reputation of the entire profession may depend on the reputation of one single physician.[14]

One might well wonder whether an ethic that *encouraged* criticism might not have served the profession better.

Why Germany? If eugenics movements flourished outside Germany, then what was special about the German experience? If resistance and antiracialist alternatives existed in Germany, then how did racial science gain the upper hand to a degree not found in other countries? One factor is the relative impoverishment of the German medical profession in the years prior to the rise of the Nazis. The collapse of the German economy in 1929–1932 polarized the profession, driving many from the center to the far Left and Right. (Recall in this context that communism as well as fascism grew in the years before the Nazi rise to power.) Between 1928 and 1932, liberal parties (DVP, Deutsche Demokratische Partei, Wirtschaftspartei) lost nearly 80 percent of their votes, falling from nearly a quarter of the entire vote to fewer than 3 percent. Physicians were among many of those who shifted from the center to the Right because they felt that Germany's other political parties were not addressing their needs. Physicians found it difficult to identify with either proletarian socialism or the interests of Germany's landed, conservative parties. Many found hope in the "third path" of National Socialism.

Professional opportunism also played a role in physicians' support for the Nazis. Overcrowding led to severe competition for jobs, especially among younger physicians. Many entering the job market for the first time saw the elimination of Jews as a way to advance their careers; and in fact, many a Nazi doctor saw his career advance as a direct result of attacks on Jews in the profession. As Jewish physicians fled or were forced from the clinics and the universities, thousands of new positions opened up. Those who stood most to gain from this were younger physicians, and these were the people who were most enthusiastic in their support for National Socialism. Professional opportunism, exacerbated by the reality and threat of unemployment, must be considered one of the chief causes for the attraction of physicians to National Socialism.

There is also a philosophical dimension to this attraction. The decades before the rise of National Socialism saw both the rise of bureaucratic, scientific, and socialized medicine in Germany and an increase in the number of Jews in the profession; many linked the two phenomena as cause and effect. Jews became a scapegoat for all that was wrong with medicine—they were accused of importing abstract science into medicine, of transforming medicine from an art into a business. Jews were blamed for the problems of both capitalist and socialist medicine; Jewish physicians were blamed for the excessive use of drugs or the suppression of natural and folk medicines. Physicians rallied around the Nazis for their promise to return to an earlier, more personal or organic kind of medicine.

Nazi medicine was *authoritarian* medicine. The 1930s–1950s mark a period when medicine achieves unprecedented power and authority in European and Anglo-American culture:[15] the same period that gave us Nazi medicine also witnessed the invention of the lobotomy (in Spain and the United States), the chordotomy (in Germany), electric shock treatment (in the United States), sensory deprivation techniques (in the Soviet Union), and the first use of physicians to administer capital punishment. This is a period when psychiatrists were given increased powers forcibly to confine individuals judged mentally ill or dangerous to the public.

One further element is crucial in understanding medicine under the Nazis, especially those practices we consider criminal. In times of war or economic crisis things can happen that otherwise—in times of peace or economic stability—would never be tolerated. The Nazis gave new meaning to the idea of sacrifice in time of war. Doctors in the Nazi period recalled that nearly 2,000 German physicians lost their lives in World War I. Alfred Hoche, author of the treatise *The Destruction of Lives Not Worth Living,* lost his first and only son in the war, and used this to argue that if the healthy could make such a sacrifice, then why should the sick and inferior not make similar sacrifices? The "euthanasia" of Germany's "less fit elements" was defended as a measure that would balance the counterselective effects of the war and free up beds for the German war effort; the cloak of war also provided the secrecy necessary for the massive programs of human destruction.

There are many different theories on the ultimate causes of the rise of fascism as a whole. Some have argued that fascism is a form of totalitarianism, and that the same forces responsible for the rise of Hitler can be seen at work in the rise of other dictatorships. Others have argued that fascism is a particularly virulent and imperialistic form of monopoly capitalism. Still others have argued that National Socialism was the product of neither capitalism nor totalitarianism but rather of the particular social and economic interests of the distressed middle and lower-middle classes.[16]

Whatever the explanation for the rise of National Socialism, one fact is clear: scientists and physicians were not exempt from the pressures that led to the triumph of the movement. That most of Germany's medical professionals followed Hitler's "revolution" is probably ultimately traceable to the same kinds of forces responsible for the triumph of National Socialism in German society as a whole. This is not to say that physicians blindly followed the political aims of their leaders. Physicians, and the body of intellectuals associated with them, did not follow blindly, but actually helped cast the light and clear the path.

Did the Nazis Depoliticize Science?

It is possible to distinguish different conceptions of what might be called the political philosophy of science. In the liberal view, predominant in twentieth-century liberal democracies, science is political only in its applications. Science in this view is (ideally) neutral or value free, and becomes "tainted" when politics directs the course of intellectual inquiry. This is the view expressed, for example, in the writings of the analytic philosophical tradition that flourished in Britain and the United States in the middle decades of this century; it is also found among philosophers influenced by the so-called Vienna Circle and among many conservative economic theorists such as Ludwig Mises or F. A. von Hayek. The racialist orientation of Nazi science represented (in this view) a violation of the norms of "neutral" and objective science. The Nazis politicized science—twisting it to serve racial or political goals, striking out against the traditional ideal of knowledge for its own sake.[17]

And yet the characterization of Nazi science as an illegitimate "politicization" captures only part of what happened. It is certainly true that, in one important sense, the Nazis sought to politicize the sciences. Nazi doctors sought a National Socialist revolution in medicine; and in this sense Nazi racial science represented a revolt against the liberal ideal of value-free science, against the vision of science and scholarship as ideally detached and apolitical. The Nazis made no secret of their distrust of traditional ideals of academic freedom and expressed scorn for those who remained within the ivory tower in times of political need. Nazi racial theorists attacked the "apathetic equanimity" of parliamentarian, Weimar Republican "liberal-Jewish-Bolshevist science" and contrasted this with the German, volkish science that was to ally itself with the values of nation and race. Jews were accused of attempting to create a state within a state, isolating themselves from the broader community. This accusation extended to art as well as science. In 1938 the in-house journal of the Office of Racial Policy argued that the doctrine of art for art's sake (*l'art pour l'art*) was a characteristically "Jewish and homosexual" philosophy; the office defended this association on the grounds that such groups "shut themselves off" either from the broader community (as in the case of the Jews) or from the reproductive life process (as in the case of homosexuals).[18] Volkish science and medicine were to overcome such "one-sidedness" by rooting science once again in blood and earth.

But the political philosophy of science under the Nazis was by no means consistent in this regard. On the one hand, science was to be brought into accord with certain national (and racial) goals and values; the ideal of "objective science" in this view was simply an excuse to eliminate the "volkish and blood-bound personality" in favor of some mythical thing in itself (*Ding an sich*). Races do not work with the same reality; science therefore cannot be some "value-free and worthless truth"; science must serve the racial spirit of a people. (This concept was articulated by a man who saw the Nazi revolution as completing a process begun not just by Nietzsche but also by Darwin, Mendel, Galton, and Weismann—men whose ideas when properly applied would help put a halt to the decline of the West into "racial chaos, Africanism, and Orientalism.")[19] Nazi philosophers cited Nietzsche's words to the effect that "science, too, is founded upon belief; there is no such thing as a science free of suppositions." Nazi philosophers contrasted this conception of science as assumptive and value laden with what they called a Jewish conception of science—a conception of science as value free and independent of any particular culture or race. Jews were accused of advocating an abstract, neutral, and internationalist (or cosmopolitan) science, in contrast with German earth-rooted science; Nazi racial scientists advocated a "medical-biological revolution" that would reorient science around racial values.[20]

Yet racial philosophers often sought to portray their work as neutral science, standing above all politics. Section 2 of the statutes of the Society for Racial Hygiene announced that the society would "avoid all political and religious tendencies"; the Nordic supremacist *Politisch-anthropologische Revue* similarly claimed to reject any allegiance to particular philosophical doctrines or political parties.[21] When Fritz Lenz attempted to discover the moral and physical qualities of the various races, he saw his work as continuing Darwin's attempts to elucidate the origin of species. Lenz defended his elaborate racial typology as "neutral" with regard to the *value* of the various races; racial science merely described objectively existing racial realities. This was a common argument among racial hygienists prior to 1933. In 1917, for example, Eugen Fischer presented the specter of racial degeneration, not as the product of pessimism on the part of racial hygienists, but as "a binding consequence of naked facts."[22] After 1933, medical societies continued to pledge their allegiance to the ideal of political neutrality at the same time that they proclaimed their willingness to collaborate with the new regime. Germany's leading psychotherapy society, for example, claimed in its 1934 statutes that the society considered itself "neutral in regard to political and religious affairs." The society's journal printed these statutes only two pages after one of its most influential members proclaimed *Mein Kampf* "required reading" for all psychotherapists in the new Germany.[23]

Racial hygienists defended the innocence of their science with respect to politics on other grounds as well. Fritz Lenz, for example, contended that in the broader scale of things, the importance of maintaining racial health far outweighed particular questions of political organization. The maintenance of the genetic quality of the race was "a hundred times more important than the struggle between capitalism and socialism"; indeed, "worse than the political impotence of our Fatherland, worse even than the lost war is the degeneration of our race. The conflict over whether 'republican' or 'monarchical' government is superior fades into insignificance, compared with the problem of maintaining the fitness of the race."[24] Lenz's view was not an uncommon one. *Ziel und Weg*, the journal of the National Socialist Physicians' League, announced in 1932 that "eugenics is a science that has nothing to do with politics, and especially with party politics."[25] A writer for *Die Medizinische Welt* declared in a similar vein that "eugenics dares not become a partisan issue; it cannot. Biological or eugenic value has nothing to do with status, profession, religion, income, financial condition, or any other way in which one discriminates among men: there are inferior, genetically diseased people everywhere and in all classes."[26]

The desire felt by many intellectuals in this period to remain above party politics (*überparteilich*) can be seen in the fact that several of Germany's leading racial hygienists never joined the party or only joined late in the regime. Fritz Lenz edited the most important racial hygiene journal (the *Archiv für Rassen- und Gesellschaftsbiologie*) and helped construct Nazi racial and population policy without becoming a party member until 1937. Eugen Fischer directed Germany's most prestigious eugenics institute until his retirement in 1942 and did not become a member until January 1940. Ernst Rüdin directed one of the most prestigious racial hygiene institutes in the country (the Rüdin Institut at Munich) and helped draft the 1933 Sterilization Law without becoming a member until 1937. Otmar von Verschuer, Mengele's mentor and one of Germany's most influential racial hygienists, did not join until July 1940. Alfred Ploetz, father of racial hygiene and winner of a number of Nazi honors and awards, did not join the party until 1937, when he was seventy-seven years old.

After the war, of course, it became especially important for scholars to be able to claim that their work in science or medicine had remained above party politics. The ideal of science as neutral and apolitical translated into the assumption that, as long as one had concentrated solely on one's science, one was exempt from blame; indeed, in 1945 some German scholars considered it a form of resistance simply to have kept the flame of science alive. The quiet pursuit of science constituted a kind of "inner emigration" that separated one from the culpability of government actions.[27] Even some of those most actively involved in the development of racial science defended their work in these terms. Hans F. K. Günther, author of at least seventeen books on racial science and the period's most widely read racial theorist, reported in his postwar autobiography that he had never mixed science and politics—this despite his widely recognized status as father of German *Rassenkunde* and the Nordic movement.[28]

One might well question the motives of postwar claims to neutrality among Nazi racial theorists. Yet in an important sense the Nazis might indeed be said to have "depoliticized" science (and many other areas of culture). The Nazis depoliticized science by destroying the possibility of political debate and controversy. Authoritarian science based on the "Führer principle" replaced what had been, in the Weimar period, a vigorous spirit of politicized debate in and around the sciences. The Nazis "depoliticized" problems of vital human interest by reducing these to scientific or medical problems, conceived in the narrow, reductionist sense of these terms. The Nazis depoliticized questions of crime, poverty, and sexual or political deviance by casting them in surgical or otherwise medical (and seemingly apolitical) terms. Confronting crime with the knife of the surgeon, justifying genocide on the grounds of quarantine, racial hygienists allowed a reductionist biologism to obscure the political character of social problems.

Politics pursued in the name of science or health provided a powerful weapon in the Nazi ideological arsenal. Important in this was not only a particular conception of science but also a particular conception of *politics*.

Nazi medical philosophers defended their revolution as one in accord with the latest results of science. The appeal to science is not surprising, given the place of science in German society at this time. National Socialism took root in a culture supporting the greatest scientific tradition of the century, one that ranks with the greatest of all times. By 1933 Germany and Austria had been awarded more than one-third of all Nobel Prizes—nearly as many as England, France, and the United States combined. It is not surprising, then, that science should have been drawn upon by any group wishing to stake out its legitimacy. "Politics" by contrast had a bad name, and in this sense the desire of scientists and physicians to appear apolitical represented a desire to move beyond (or avoid) the issues that had divided German society since before World War I. National Socialism was itself supposed to transcend all political differences, to end the squabbles between landlord and peasant, worker and industrialist, and to replace the divisive emphasis on class by a unifying emphasis on race. The Nazi state was supposed to be a *Volksstaat*, and not a *Parteistaat*. The Nazi party was supposed to be not just a party but a movement (*Bewegung*). Nazi medical philosophers praised Hitler for his attempts to address the needs of the German people *as a whole* and to abolish, once and for all, the demands of "special interests."[29] When the Nazis claimed they wanted their philosophy to appear scientific, it was on similar grounds. Science would unite, where politics had divided. Nazi medical periodicals thus cited Hitler's assertion that National Socialism was "no mystical doctrine, but rather a realistic doctrine of a strictly scientific nature."[30] Theobald Lang, we should recall, as early as 1930 declared National Socialist methods strictly scientific (*streng wissenschaftlich*).

Nazi science was also ambivalent on the question of academic freedom. Prior to the rise of National Socialism, the importance of science in Europe had generated a tradition of respect for its freedom. The Prussian Constitution of 1843 declared that the pursuit of science is free; article 142 of the Weimar Constitution reaffirmed this commitment to the freedom of science and of teaching. National Socialism suspended many of the civil liberties won in Weimar and in Wilhelmine Germany, but not without maintaining a certain facade of tolerance. Alfred Rosenberg, in his *Die Freiheit der Wissenschaft*, defended freedom of teaching (*Lehrfreiheit*), but distinguished this from freedom to agitate (*Agitationsfreiheit*), noting that because the universities were *national* institutions, neither treason nor "antisocial" activity could be permitted in the classroom.[31] Absolute freedom of thought or of science was regarded by the Nazis as symptomatic of a society in the midst of chaos and despair. Freedom was to be replaced by the Führer principle, according to which science, like other social activity, was to be hierarchically organized and subordinated to a single, powerful authority.

In 1935 Walter Gross of the Office of Racial Policy said, "National Socialism does not intend to interfere with 'purely scientific matters,' " but qualified this by asserting that tolerance could only go so far and that any attempt on the part of "pseudoscience" to hinder Nazi goals would not be tolerated.[32] In 1937, as calls for "Deutsche Wissenschaft" reached their peak, Alfred Rosenberg issued an order that the Nazi party was not to take sides on questions of cosmology, experimental chemistry, or prehistoric geology; such questions, he proclaimed, must remain free for every individual researcher to decide according to the dictates of "serious scientific investigation."[33]

This same ideological largess did not, of course, apply equally to all sciences or to all scientists. Yet for many—especially those in the vanguard of German racial science—science and National Socialism moved in harmony with each other. Otmar von Verschuer, in a May 1939 speech to the Kaiser Wilhelm Gesellschaft in Breslau, reflected on the fact that

> the parallel development of political and scientific ideas is not by chance but rather by internal necessity.... We geneticists and racial hygienists have been fortunate to have seen our quiet work in the scholar's study and the scientific laboratory find application in the life of the people. Our responsibility has thereby become enormous. We continue quietly with our research, confident that here also, battles will be fought which will be of greatest consequence for the survival of our people.[34]

A Question of Abuse?

In the 1920s American writers on eugenics commonly considered two possible dangers of eugenic sterilization. Some worried that sterilization "might prevent the birth of a genius"; others, that sterilization might allow one to engage in sex with abandon, without fear of pregnancy. Rarely, however, did eugenicists consider the possibility that their science might be used by one group to persecute another. In 1929, for example, Harry H. Laughlin maintained that "the possibility that sterilization might become a political tool that might be used by one race against another, by one religion against another, or by one social class against another, is extremely remote."[35]

In Germany also, physicians dismissed the possibility that their science and skills might be abused. Racial hygienists as late as 1939 mocked warnings of "the Jewish press" that Germany was "once again on the road to barbarism," that Germany was about to "eliminate" persons in political disfavor under the pretense that they were genetically diseased. Germany, like other states, had embarked on a program of racial cleansing. But what made Germany special was that

> in contrast to other states, the German [sterilization] laws have been administered through the large-scale mediation of genetic health courts, with the possibility of appeals to appellate genetic health courts, excluding for all time the possibility of the *abuse* of these laws. Furthermore, criteria for genetic health and sickness have been so thoroughly and clearly formulated that the possibility of error on human grounds has been completely eliminated. Countless safeguards have been built into the law and the procedures for its implementation—safeguards which, taken together, prevent improper diagnosis by a doctor and effectively protect the person to be sterilized.[36]

Carefully administered scientific expertise, in other words, together with the appropriate legal apparatus, would guarantee the execution of the racial task in accord with the rule of law; this was supposed to exclude forever the possibility of abuse.

There is often talk of the "abuse of science" under National Socialism. Yet there may be a problem in conceiving Nazi racial science primarily in such terms. One could well argue that the Nazis were not, properly speaking, abusing the results of science but rather were merely putting into practice what doctors and scientists had themselves already initiated. Nazi racial science in this sense was not an abuse of eugenics but rather an attempt to bring to practical fruition trends already implicit in the structure of this branch of science. Dr. Friedrich Zahn, in his article "Racial Research," intended something of this sort in 1940 when he claimed that "the theory of today becomes the practice of tomorrow."[37]

I do not mean to say that science was *not* abused under the Nazis, or that the quality of science under the Nazis did not suffer, in both a moral and an intellectual sense. There can be no doubt that this was the case. But many scientists of the time did not perceive this to be the case. On the contrary, many—and perhaps most—scientists in the various fields of biomedicine saw no contradiction between the aspirations of science and the goals of the Nazi regime.

There is something missing, then, when we characterize National Socialism as simply "anti-intellectual." The Nazis opposed certain kinds of science and supported others. Many academics and intellectuals found the ideology of Nazism attractive; the Nazis were thereby able to draw upon the imagery, results, and authority of science. Nazi ideology also informed the practice of science; indeed scientists were intimately involved in the construction of racial policy. It is probably as fair to say that Nazi racial policy emerged from *within* the scientific community as to say that it was imposed *upon* the scientific community.

One should not conclude, however, that Nazi medicine rose to power unopposed or that everyone was a Nazi. Alternatives were articulated and institutionalized within the medical profession, and many paid with their lives for expressing or acting upon those alternatives. The fact that these alternatives were ultimately crushed does not lessen the valiancy of their efforts. There *was* resistance—however too little or too late; the example of the Association of Socialist Physicians must not be forgotten. The moral, then, is not just that the Nazis supported science or that science supported the Nazis, but that there was a struggle that led to the triumph of Nazi racial policy, and this struggle was played out, at least in part, in the spheres of science and medicine.

In his 1954 *Destruction of Reason,* Georg Lukács noted that biological determinism (biologism) in the fields of philosophy and sociology has always provided a basis for reactionary world views. Perhaps this has not always been the case—certainly one can find examples in other centuries where appeals to nature or to biology have been used in the service of moral progress or liberation. In the twentieth century, however, the appeal to biology to structure human society has tended to have unfortunate and sometimes tragic consequences. The experience of science and medicine under the Nazis represents an extreme case of the dangers of such a philosophy, but it is by no means the first, and certainly not the last, time intellectuals have hoisted a banner proclaiming that biology is destiny. It is a history, one might say, we have yet to conquer.

Epilogue: Postwar Legacies

The story of racial science no more ends in 1945 than it began in 1933. After the war, organizations associated with the Nazi regime were disbanded or outlawed. Allied powers suspended the genetic health courts on January 8, 1946; the Society for Racial Hygiene ceased to meet. Nazi medical crimes were confronted in the Nuremberg trials, where twenty German doctors were accused of crimes against humanity.[1] Western observers were surprised to find that many of those who had participated in these crimes were leaders in their fields. Karl Brandt, sentenced to death for his part in both the experiments and the euthanasia operation, was responsible for all of German health affairs during the final years of the war. Karl Gebhardt, sentenced to death for his experiments with gas gangrene at Sachsenhausen and Ravensbrück, was chief surgeon at the Hohenlychen Medical Institute and a former president of the German Red Cross. Paul Nitsche, executed in 1947 for his role in the euthanasia operation, was one of Germany's leading psychiatrists. Professor Joachim Mrugowsky, sentenced to death for ordering "terminal" typhus experiments on prisoners at Buchenwald, was editor of a popular book on medical ethics.[2] Gerhard Rose, sentenced to life imprisonment for his role in typhus experimentation, was director of tropical medicine at the Robert Koch Institute. Edwin Katzenellenbogen, sentenced to life imprisonment (not at Nuremberg, but at the Buchenwald trials) for experiments he performed in the Buchenwald concentration camp, was a former Harvard lecturer on abnormal psychology and a fellow for research in logic.[3]

The Arts of Apologia

Those convicted of crimes against humanity were only a handful of those who had participated in the construction of Nazi racial science and policy.[4] Some of those implicated in Nazi crimes were acquitted in courts reluctant to prosecute former Nazis. On January 7, 1956, a West German court ruled that the deportation of 2,500 Gypsies from Hamburg, Bremen, Cologne, Düsseldorf, Stuttgart, and Frankfurt in May 1940 on Himmler's orders did not constitute racial persecution but should be considered "a security measure."[5] Fourteen nurses who administered lethal doses to mental patients at Obrawalde-Muritz were acquitted on grounds that they were following orders. In a separate trial, a Munich court ruled that the killing of the insane constituted manslaughter, not murder. A Cologne court spoke of "burned out human husks" relieved of their misery, in language not unlike that of the Nazis themselves.[6]

Most of those involved in crimes never reached court at all. A number of Germany's leading medical figures took their own lives rather than face prosecution. Ernst Robert Grawitz, vice-president of the German Red Cross, committed suicide in April 1945; Health Führer Leonardo Conti chose this option at Nuremberg not long thereafter. Carl Schneider also chose this path (to avoid facing trial), as did Max de Crinis (when his car was trapped in the Russian encirclement of Berlin). Herbert Linden, the Interior Ministry's man responsible for the euthanasia operation, shot himself on April 27, 1945. Others managed, at least for a time, to survive and evade public scrutiny. Hans Reiter, president of the Reich Health Office, continued as physician in a Kassel clinic from 1949 to 1952. Werner Heyde, one of those responsible for organizing the euthanasia operation, returned to Schleswig-Holstein after the war, and thanks to influential friends was able to land a position as consultant for the State Court of Schleswig. It was not until 1960 that Heyde was brought to trial.[7]

Some of those involved in the euthanasia of Germany's handicapped and mentally ill defended these operations after the war.[8] Nicolai Weiss, for example, in an article in the most important postwar Nazi journal, *Der Weg*, published in Buenos Aires, defended the operation as something natural, based on the "natural instincts" of the healthy vis-à-vis the deformed.[9] One of the most elaborate apologies for the operation was that of Werner Catel, one of the architects of the "T-4" child murders. Shortly after the war, Catel was appointed professor of pediatrics and director of the children's clinic at the University of Kiel. In 1964, after several unsuccessful attempts to bring him to trial, Catel was granted immunity from prosecution on the grounds that he had been convinced of the legality of his actions. Even after his retirement in 1960, Catel published on the issue of euthanasia.[10] He continued publishing into the late 1970s; a 1979 book coedited by Catel was designed to be used as a textbook for nurses in children's hospitals.

There were others for whom the question of guilt was never an issue. Alfred Ploetz died of natural causes in 1940; Ludwig Schmidt-Kehl died on the Russian front in October 1941. Eberhard Geyer, one of Austria's leading racial hygienists, was killed in similar circumstances in February 1942. Among those who survived the war, however, many (especially those who had remained on the plane of theory) continued to enjoy success in German universities. In 1946 Fritz Lenz was reappointed professor of human genetics at the University of Göttingen (his Munich chair for racial hygiene was dissolved); Lenz continued publishing into the 1970s. Otmar Freiherr von Verschuer, successor to Eugen Fischer as head of the Kaiser Wilhelm Institute for Anthropology and mentor of the Auschwitz doctor Josef Mengele, continued as professor of human genetics at the University of Münster. Eugen Fischer himself, though he had retired in 1942, continued after the war to edit various scholarly journals and to lecture on anthropology and other topics.[11] A number of other racial theorists were reappointed to positions at German universities. Günther Just, for example, was appointed professor of "Menschliche Erblehre und Konstitutionslehre (Humangenetik)" at Tübingen in 1948; he was also named director of Tübingen's Anthropological Institute. Egon von Eickstedt was named director of the Institut für Menschenkunde at the University of Mainz; Friedrich Burgdörfer continued to teach statistics at Munich. Some of the less academically inclined racial theorists chose other paths. Ludwig Clauss, editor of the Nordic-supremacist journals *Die Sonne, Odal,* and *Rasse,* emigrated to Saudi Arabia in order to live, as he told his friend Hans F. K. Günther, "as a bedouin among the bedouins" in the freedom of the desert. Günther himself continued to write on racial topics; his 1959 *Begabungschwund in Europa* lamented a host of "counterselective forces" eroding the health of the white races of Europe.

Western occupation forces, eager to get Germany rolling again, took a lenient attitude toward the reconstruction of German industry and academia. In his *Crime and Punishment of I. G. Farben,* Joseph Borkin has documented how Western Allied powers (especially the United States) turned a blind eye to war crimes on the part of certain individuals in order to facilitate the rapid rebuilding of German industry. American officials encouraged the return of Krupp, Bayer, and Höchst executives, despite evidence linking several of these people to war crimes.[12] Similar stories have emerged concerning American attempts to exploit German scientists after the war. In the April 1985 edition of the *Bulletin of the Atomic Scientists,* Linda Hunt presented evidence that, shortly after the war, American officials whitewashed the files of Nazi medical and scientific personnel in order to gain clearance for them to emigrate to the United States. Hunt showed that rocket specialists Arthur Rudolf and Werner von Braun—both former SS officers—had their files laundered to make them appear respectable to immigration authorities; she also showed that four of the defendants in the "Medical Case" at the Nuremberg trials—Hermann Becker-Freysing, Siegfried Ruff, Konrad Schaefer, and Kurt Blome—were hired shortly after the war by the U.S. military as part of a project to see what could be learned from recent German science. Ruff, for example, worked at an army medical center in Heidelberg, where he was asked to report on experiments he had helped conduct at Dachau on human survival capabilities at high altitudes. Becker-Freysing and Schaefer were similarly asked to report on research they had performed on the ingestion of seawater (Schaefer was subsequently recruited into Project Paperclip—the American program designed to exploit German scientific talent after the war). And Blome, the highest-ranking Nazi doctor after the suicide of Conti and the execution of Brandt, was contracted by the Army Chemical Corps to work on chemical and biological warfare. The director of the American Joint Intelligence Objectives Agency justified employing such individuals on the grounds that there was no need to continue "beating a dead Nazi horse."[13]

The German medical profession was not particularly eager to explore the events of the recent past. Medical journals, beginning to publish once again after three or four years of inactivity, rarely attempted to analyze medicine under the Nazis. Some complained of the "isolation" German science had suffered; others spoke of the "terrible years" of the war and how this had forced them to interrupt their publishing. Many complained about the lack of facilities in the postwar period—about shortages, for example, that made publishing difficult or impossible. O. Kneise, for example, in the *Zeitschrift für Urologie*, lamented the damage done by the "unfortunate war" to "our poor fatherland"; he expressed hope that even after the horrible collapse (*grausigen Zusammenbruch*), German medicine might continue to offer spiritual as well as physical aid to the German people.[14]

Many blamed Germany's recent troubles on the intervention of politics into medicine. The *Ärztliche Forschung* warned against "subordinating objective science to utilitarian ends," and pledged to help return German medicine to the time-honored tradition of impersonal objectivity and serious research (*ernsten Forscherfleiss*). Erwin Gohrbandt, in the first issue of the newly revived *Zentralblatt für Chirurgie*, complained that politics and war had forced the field of surgery away from a tradition of democratic research; he expressed his hope that, in the future, surgery would serve not war, but peace. Critique of war and war preparations is a common theme in early postwar medical journals, especially those published under the auspices of Soviet occupation authorities. Editors of the *Zentralblatt für Neurochirurgie*, for example, in the first postwar issue of the journal, warned against the dangers of a new war, one that "would destroy the last remnants of our nation and culture, and bring about unimaginable levels of hunger and suffering."[15]

Rarely, however, do we find any expression of remorse or grief or any of the kind of soul-searching one might have expected after such a history. Journals complained about the state of German science, that "important research institutes and scientific libraries are lying in ruins," and yet failed to mention the role of medicine in bringing about that ruin. They complained that years of armament and war had led to a "hectic and one-sided quality" of the work in medicine; they complained about the spiritual autarchy (*geistige Zwangsautarkie*) imposed by the Nazi regime, but rarely was there any attempt to locate blame within the medical profession itself.[16] Some journals resorted to language redolent of that of the Nazis: one journal blamed the French Revolution for having brought about a triumph of "intellectualism" and "one-sided rationalism" in medicine; this journal cited the recent rediscovery of "holism" as a welcome countermeasure to these excesses.[17]

What is striking about these accounts is that discussion of the recent persecution of Jews, Gypsies, communists, and other "undesirables" was virtually taboo in medical journals published after the war. Individual cases, it is true, are sometimes cited: the *Archiv für experimentelle Pathologie,* for example, brought up the case of Emil Starkenstein, the Prague professor of pharmacology who, as a victim of racial hatred, was forced from his job and eventually died in 1942 in the concentration camp at Mauthausen.[18] But reports such as this one are very rare or are sanitized, as when the editors of the *Archiv für die gesamte Physiologie* expressed their thanks to Rudolf Höber for having worked on the journal's editorial board until 1934, when he "had to leave."[19] Anyone beginning to read German medical journals in 1946 and 1947 would have a confused picture of the past indeed. There is discussion of specialization and holism, war and peace, chaos and destruction, but little sense of who did what to whom, or how, or why.

Postwar Surgeries

The collapse of the German government and the prosecution of Nazi war criminals left German physicians very sensitive to particular topics. It was no longer acceptable or even legal to write about certain issues. Discussions of racial hygiene that had filled medical journals before 1945 disappeared after the collapse. Some of what changed, however, appears on closer examination to be more cosmetic than substantive. A striking example of this can be seen by comparing two editions of Paul Diepgen's *Die Heilkunde und der ärztliche Beruf,* a book published first in 1938 and then reprinted with certain modifications in 1947.[20]

On first glance, the 1938 and 1947 editions of Diepgen's book appear the same. The tables of contents are the same except for the title of one chapter. A reading of the two texts, however, reveals certain more fundamental changes. For one thing, all references to racial hygiene, racial science, and National Socialism have been removed. In some parts of the book, the word *Rassenhygiene* has simply been replaced by the word *Hygiene,* and in at least one instance by the word *Medizin.*[21] In most cases, however, the offending passages have simply been deleted.

Some parts of the book show substantive changes. In 1938 and then again in 1947, there appears the following passage, common to both editions:

> Behind all the affairs of humans, and thus also in the affairs of the physician, there is ultimately a certain world view [*Weltanschauung*]. What do we mean by this? We can perhaps formulate it most simply as follows. By "world view," one means the standpoint from which someone will answer questions about the meaning of Being and Becoming in the world. It is a question of metaphysics. Depending upon what kinds of ideas are expressed in a particular world view, one may speak of a magical, religious, philosophical, political, or social world view, and so forth. And when one examines the history of medicine, one can clearly see that over the course of time, first one and then another of these world views has shaped the thinking of the physician.[22]

Immediately after this, the two editions diverge. The two versions that follow the above passage present diametrically opposing views:

1938	1947
And yet never before has the question of Weltanschauung become of such immediate importance for public and private life, as in our own times. For us in Germany, more immediately than ever before, the most important decisions in recent years have been those in the sphere of Weltanschauung. And this Weltanschauung is the National Socialist Weltanschauung.	And yet one-sidedness has always taken its toll. He who truly wants to help his fellow man must see the world as a physician. His entire world view must be determined by his character as a physician, a position that recognizes no differences in religion, nationality, or race when it comes to help. Science serves the entire world and must be cosmopolitan.

In the 1947 edition, entire passages have been omitted, passages that in the 1938 edition present a clear record of Diepgen's enthusiasm for the Nazi regime. In 1938, for example, shortly after the passage cited above, Diepgen wrote:

> National Socialism means something fundamentally new for medical life. It has overcome an idea that was central to medicine of the recent past: the idea of the right to one's own body. Through this victory, the relationship of the physician to his patient has taken on an entirely new dimension . . .
>
> While formerly, a large part of a physician's work was devoted to care for the sick and the weak, this essentially humanitarian task has not by any means been forgotten. And yet the positive demand for health

stands everywhere in the foreground: it is better to prevent than to cure. It is fortunate for us physicians that our activity at the bedside of our patients can never come in conflict with our duties as National Socialists.[23]

This text is omitted in the 1947 edition; the postwar text resumes the argument with the wording unchanged. Quoting now from the two identical texts:

Certainly, science serves the entire world and must be cosmopolitan. But this does not exclude the fact that every people understands and demands a science in accord with its own distinctive qualities. The historian of medicine—and other, older scholars—have for several hundred years been aware that German medicine has a different character than French, Italian, or English ["Russian" is added in the 1947 edition] medicine. A physician such as the great *Paracelsus von Hohenheim* (died 1541) was only possible in Germany [this sentence is omitted in 1947]. Nobody can jump out of his skin, whether he is looking through his microscope, investigating a chemical reaction, or treating his patients. National character necessarily has an influence on the interests of a people and on how a people's scientists and physicians will formulate their problems. From this, it follows that medicine is nationally conditioned.[24]

In the 1938 text, this passage is followed by a conclusion omitted entirely from the 1947 edition:

It is good that National Socialism has brought this fact into people's consciousness. For only if we have this knowledge can we (a) serve our people in the correct fashion, and (b) search for truth, the highest goal of all science.

The strength of the soldierly spirit which National Socialism demands of us will become a blessing for each person who conceives his calling correctly. I mean by this, that we Germans can have no better foundation for our professional ideals [*Arzttum*] and for our medical studies than that provided by National Socialism in the spirit of Hitler.[25]

Diepgen was the most important historian of medicine in Weimar, Nazi, and early postwar Germany. Although he never joined the Nazi party, he considered the Nazis "to have saved Germany from chaos in the final hour," comparing the final years of the Weimar Republic to the last years of the Roman Empire, with its falling birthrate, corruption, and various forms of degeneration.[26] One does not find such views in his postwar works—these have been excised, and views more in harmony with those of the postwar order have been added.

Postwar "surgeries" were performed on many other texts to remove offending parts. In 1952 the J. F. Lehmann Verlag published a thirteenth edition of Hermann W. Siemens's *Foundations of Genetics, Racial Hygiene, and Population Policy* with a new introduction denouncing "racial fanaticism" and with most politically objectionable passages expunged. Not very long thereafter, Lehmann was able to republish Hans F. K. Günther's *Choosing a Spouse for Marital Happiness and Genetic Fitness*. Critics denounced the Lehmann Verlag as "neo-Nazi" for having published such works; the leading Nazi journal in exile, however, was able to point out that Günther had been cleared by West German courts of any criminal wrongdoing.[27]

Although all traces of explicit Nazi propaganda were removed from these books, certain continuities still remained. The 1952 edition of Siemen's book continued to advocate the forcible sterilization of inferior stocks; Diepgen in 1947 still cited Verschuer's estimates that there were 300,000 genetic defectives in Germany.[28] Many of the problems posed by prewar racial hygienists continued to intrigue postwar scholars; the names for those problems were simply changed to suit the times.

From Racial Hygiene to Human Genetics

In order to appreciate fully the continuities that link racial science before and after the collapse of Germany in 1945, one would have to explore a number of different fields. One would have to examine the legacy of certain specialties after the war—gynecology or psychiatry, for example—and determine how each of these came to grips with the rise and fall of National Socialism. One would want to know how each of the two Germanys struggled (or failed to struggle) with the history of medicine under the Nazis, and how each rebuilt (or failed to rebuild) its medical community. One might want to explore the reemergence of ethology and systems theory, both of which blossomed in the Nazi period. (In the mid-1970s, Theodora Kalikow discovered Konrad Lorenz's 1938 application for membership in the Austrian Nazi party.)[29] One might also want to explore recent attempts to develop a science of human (and animal) "sociobiology" and the revival (especially since the 1960s) of evolutionary, genetic, hormonal, or otherwise hereditarian or biologistic interpretations of social, sexual, and racial inequalities.[30] All these areas need further study.

The transformation of the prewar science of "racial hygiene" into the postwar science of "human genetics" is also a topic that deserves further study. Here I shall simply point to some aspects of the story that touch upon the postwar life of Otmar von Verschuer.

After the war, Soviet occupation forces in what is now East Germany were more persistent in their prosecution of Nazi collaborators than were French, British, or American forces in Allied occupied zones. Anticommunism had been a centerpiece of Nazi ideology, and during the war most of the Nazis' military might had been directed against the Soviet Union. After the war, medical journals resuming publication in the Soviet zone advocated stronger penalties for medical crimes than did their Western counterparts; one journal in the Soviet zone, for example, argued that the Sterilization Law should be considered criminal.[31] Racial hygienists even before the end of the war anticipated this harsher treatment. In February 1945, as the war was drawing to a close, Otmar von Verschuer expressed his fear of the advancing Red Army and transported the files of the Kaiser Wilhelm Institute for Anthropology, Human Genetics, and Eugenics (including especially his twin research data) into the western part of the country, where he expected more sympathetic treatment from the advancing Allied armies.

Verschuer did not fare badly after the war (see Figure 43). In late 1945 or early 1946, he petitioned the mayor of Frankfurt to allow him to reestablish the Kaiser Wilhelm Institute for Anthropology, Human Genetics, and Eugenics. In February 1946 a search was ordered to find appropriate buildings to house the institute. Verschuer had been judged a collaborator (*Mitläufer*) and hence absolved from any major responsibility in the events of the Nazi period; he was fined 600 marks and released from custody. But the commission responsible for rebuilding the Kaiser Wilhelm Gesellschaft, including members sanctioned by the Allied powers, recognized that Verschuer could not be so easily absolved of guilt in this matter. After reviewing Verschuer's publications, the head of the commission wrote:

> Verschuer should be considered not a collaborator, but one of the most dangerous Nazi activists of the Third Reich. An objective judgment of the investigative committee must recognize this, and thereby take actions to guarantee that this man does not come into contact with German youth as a university teacher, or with the broader population as a scientist in the fields of genetics and anthropology.[32]

Verschuer never managed to have the Kaiser Wilhelm Institute for Anthropology reestablished. He did, however, obtain employment in West German universities. In 1951 Verschuer was called to assume the prestigious professorship of human genetics at the University of Münster. Here he built one of the largest centers of genetic research in West Germany. His dominant position in science during the Nazi period became an asset after the war. Already before the war, many of Verschuer's students and co-workers had been appointed to positions teaching human genetics at the universities of Cologne and Rostock. After the war, several of his students were appointed to top positions at the universities of Erlangen, Frankfurt, Düsseldorf, and Münster. Heinrich Schade, who began his career as *Dozent* for genetics and racial hygiene at Frankfurt, was appointed *Dozent* at the Institute for Human Genetics at the University of Münster in 1952. Wolfgang Bauermeister (former director of the Cologne Institute for Genetics and Racial Hygiene) was appointed professor of anthropology at Cologne. Hans Grebe (former director of the University of Rostock Institute for Genetics and Racial Hygiene) was appointed professor of human genetics at the University of Marburg. Even today a number of Verschuer's students occupy important positions in German schools of human genetics. When Verschuer died in 1969 as a result of an automobile accident, obituaries in German scientific journals made no mention of his Nazi involvement.[33] This may have been because at least one of the eulogists was himself a former SS officer.[34]

The story of Verschuer is not unique; many of Germany's racial hygienists were able to continue their careers after the war under the name of "human genetics." I have already noted the postwar appointment of Fritz Lenz as professor of human genetics at the University of Göttingen. Wolfgang Lehmann, professor of racial biology at the University of Strassburg in 1943, was appointed in 1948 to teach human genetics at the University of Kiel. Wolfgang Bauermeister, former director of the Institute for Genetics and Racial Hygiene at the University of Cologne, was named director of the new anthropological institute established in Cologne's medical faculty. Lehmann, Verschuer, Bauermeister, and their students continued publishing in the fields of human genetics, population theory, and various other areas of biology and medicine. The overt ideological trappings of Nazism were purged from these works, yet many of the research interests remain unchanged.[35]

Wrestling with History

In 1946, shortly before the beginning of the Nuremberg trials, a special committee of the West German Physicians' Chambers asked Alexander Mitscherlich and Fred Mielke to prepare a condensed version of the evidence presented before the Nuremberg Tribunal, to inform German physicians about the nature of the crimes of which physicians had been accused. A preliminary version of Mitscherlich and Mielke's report, issued under the title *The Dictates of Inhumanity*, appeared in 1947 in the course of the trial, which lasted from December 9, 1946, to July 19, 1947.[36] But the report, originally intended under the mandate of the fifty-first German Doctors' Congress to provide German physicians with a summary of the proceedings of the trial, was not welcomed by the German medical community. Some of those named in the trial were not eager to have their names publicized; others acted as though Mitscherlich and Mielke had exaggerated medical involvement in Nazi crime, in order to cast aspersions on the "honor" of the German medical profession.

The fate of the first major 1949 edition of Mitscherlich and Mielke's book illustrates the difficulties many in the German medical community had in facing up to the events of the recent past. Ten thousand copies of the book were printed and sent to the West German Physicians' Chambers for distribution among Germany's physicians. It remains today unclear what became of those copies. According to Dr. Mitscherlich, no one he met over the next ten years had ever heard of the book. There was not a single review, nor any mention of the book in professional medical literature. (Walter Wuttke-Groneberg points out that one Göttingen physiologist—F. H. Rein—did in fact review the book; Rein was strongly critical and argued that only "perverts" would read it.)[37] Mitscherlich later complained that it was almost as if the book had never existed. It was from only one source that he knew the book had seen the light of day—and this was from the offices of the International Medical Association, then involved in discussion over whether and under what conditions the German Medical Association would be readmitted to the international body. The publication of Mitscherlich and Mielke's report was to prove instrumental in Germany's reinstatement in the International Medical Association in the early 1950s; the book was taken as evidence that the German medical community had shown itself willing to come to grips with events of the recent past, admitting culpability where it was due. It was not until 1960, however, that the volume was reissued, this time published by Fischer Verlag in an edition of 50,000 copies. Up until this time (and even for some time after), one looks in vain for a discussion of the role of physicians under the Nazis in orthodox German medical journals.[38] The past was buried, and along with this, the moral and political questions raised by the participation of doctors in National Socialist policies.

Outside Germany it is easier to find early analyses of this history. In 1946, barely one year after the collapse of the Nazi regime, Max Weinreich, director of the Yiddish Scientific Institute in New York, published his *Hitler's Professors: The Part of Scholarship in Germany's Crimes against the Jewish People,* a book that remains today one of the best accounts of racialist scholarship in Nazi Germany.[39] A few years later, François Bayle published his *Croix gammée contre caducée,* the first major French analysis of medicine under the Nazis.[40]

In Germany itself, investigation into the history of Nazi racial policy was fostered by offices associated with the West German government's efforts to compensate victims of Nazi persecution (the so-called *Wiedergutmachung*). Beginning immediately after the war, the Institut für Zeitgeschichte in Munich gathered together documents concerning Nazi racial persecution and published these in a series of works under the title *Bibliographie zur Zeitgeschichte und zum zweiten Weltkrieg* (1945–1950).[41] One could name a number of other individual works in this period—works detailing the history of social Darwinism or the euthanasia operation[42]—but the most striking fact about German scholarship during this period is the silence that surrounds this topic, especially on the question of the involvement of the medical profession as a whole. The implicit consensus appears to be that any abuses there may have been were the product of a small and marginal band of fanatics, acting beyond the bounds of orthodox medical practice, because of political corruption, opportunism, and so forth. Leaders in the German medical community warned against exaggerating the actions of what they called a "vanishingly small" portion of that community; according to one commonly cited estimate, out of a total of 90,000 physicians active over this period, only 350 doctors had participated in actual medical crimes, and few others knew about them.[43]

Serious attempts to investigate the involvement of German intellectuals in the events of the 1930s and early 1940s were not undertaken until the mid-1960s, as part of the broader politicization of student consciousness that culminated in protests against German policies in the Middle East and American involvement in the Vietnam war. In the winter semester of 1964–65, the University of Tübingen sponsored a series of lectures (*Ringvorlesungen*) to explore the role of German academics in the Nazi period; shortly after this, students at the Free University of Berlin and the University of Munich organized a similar series. Lectures delivered at these meetings were published in three separate volumes; a fourth volume devoted to this topic was added after the 1966 meeting of the Society for German Language and Literature (*Germanistentag*).[44] These volumes helped break the silence that had settled over the issue; nevertheless, the lectures were criticized by a number of people who regarded them as attempts to minimize the involvement of academics in Nazi activities. Critics in the early German student movement, such as Fritz Haug, ridiculed the lectures as "impotent apologetics" and "helpless antifascism," on the grounds that they left one with the impression that only a tiny fraction of the German professoriate had gone along with the Nazis, and that German academics had been largely helpless in the face of the Nazi onslaught.[45]

Only since the 1970s has serious historical scholarship begun to explore this darker side of history, especially as scholars educated in the turbulent years of the late 1960s have begun to enter positions of power in German universities, and as former National Socialists have begun to retire. Today one of the most exciting movements of West German historical scholarship, relatively unknown in the United States, is the work of Götz Aly, Gerhard Baader, Gisela Bock, Ernst Klee, Fridolf Kudlien, Stephan Leibfried, Georg Lilienthal, Gunter Mann, Benno Müller-Hill, Karl Heinz Roth, Florian Tennstedt, Rolf Winau, and many others involved in documenting the rise of racial hygiene, social Darwinism, and Nazi medical policy (see the Bibliography). In the spring of 1980, more than a thousand medical students and interested others crowded the main auditorium of Berlin's Free University for a two-day *Gesundheitstag*, the first session of which examined the origins and legacy of medicine under the Nazis. The organizers of the conference—Gerhard Baader, Ulrich Schultz, Sepp Graessner, Christof Müller-Busch, and Reinhold Grün—noted that it was a sad comment on the profession that the 9,000 physicians of the West Berlin Medical Association could find no one better to represent them than a man who was once an officer in the Brown Shirts (Dr. Wilhelm Heim, president of the Berliner Ärztekammer and former SA Standartenführer)—this, in a city that saw 60 percent of its practicing physicians forced to emigrate. The conference was intended not only to unearth the past but also to cast light upon alternative paths German medicine might have taken. To this end, conference organizers arranged for several physicians forced from Germany in the 1930s to attend the meeting; Georg Löwenstein, Konrad Hirsch, and other representatives from the exiled Association of Socialist Physicians traveled to Berlin and recounted their experiences for the meeting. The proceedings of the conference were published in seven volumes, the first dealing with medicine under the Nazis,[46] the others with more recent medical politics, including medicine in the third world, the "Valium Age," and problems of authority versus self-help in medicine.

In East Germany scholars have also begun to explore the legacy of medicine under fascism. In 1973 Friedrich Kaul published what up to that time was the most thorough account of the Nazi euthanasia program. In 1982 the Evangelical Academy of Bad Boll published a collection of articles on "Medicine under National Socialism"; and in 1983 the East German Academy for Medical Education organized a symposium devoted entirely to the question of medicine under the Nazis, where more than forty invited speakers presented research on the history of medical experimentation, medical resistance, and the persistence of "medical fascism" in certain parts of the world today.[47]

The strength of these movements to come to grips with the history of science, technology, and medicine under the Nazis can be taken as evidence of a determination on the part of critical German intellectuals to face and overcome the legacies of this past.

Appendixes
Bibliography
Notes
Index

Appendix A
German Medical Journals under the Nazis

The purpose of this appendix is to provide a rough measure of the continuity of German medical publications before and after both the rise of the Nazis and the collapse of the Reich in 1945. This sample of 148 journals is taken from the collections of the Lane Medical Library at Stanford University and should be considered representative rather than exhaustive. I have not included journals that ceased publication prior to the rise of the Nazis; Austrian journals; or, but for a few exceptions (such as the *Ärztliche Rundschau* and the *Ärzteblatt für Berlin*), journals reporting primarily on professional affairs (the so-called *Standespresse*).

The four columns listed after each journal title indicate whether the journal continued to publish regularly after the rise of the Nazis (+ = yes; − = no); whether the journal continued to publish after 1945; the proportion of editors who remained after the *Gleichschaltung;* and the proportion of editors remaining with the journal after the collapse of National Socialism (calculated from the last available pre-1945 issue and first available postwar issue). I have excluded from the statistics editors listed as residing outside Germany. Cases in which editorship changed as a result of natural death are considered "unchanged" here. Several journals list as many as thirty or forty editorial advisers in addition to the primary editors; in these cases the "proportion unchanged" has been calculated from all those names appearing on the title page. For some journals it was standard policy for the board of editors to change regularly; I have listed these as "rotating." In the event that a journal ceased publication during the Nazi period and did not resume publication after the war, I have indicated the last year of publication in parentheses.

Journals	Continued publication		Editorial boards: proportion unchanged	
	1932–1934	Postwar	1932–1934	1942–1947
Ärzteblatt für Berlin	+	−(1941)	?	n.a.
Ärztliche Rundschau	+	−(1936)	3/3	n.a.
Ärztliche Sachverständigen-Zeitung	+	+	5/10	?
Allegemeine Zeitschrift für Psychiatrie	+	+	4/4	3/11
Anatomischer Anzeiger	+	+	1/1	1/1
Anatomischer Bericht	+	−	4/4	n.a.
Anthropologischer Anzeiger	+	+	3/3	1/2
Arbeiten aus dem Reichsgesundheitsamte	+	−	Not listed	n.a.
Arbeiten aus dem Staatsinstitut für Experimentelle Therapie . . . zu Frankfurt	+	+	1/1	1/1
Archiv der Pharmazie	+	+	1/3	0/4
Archiv für Augenheilkunde	+	−(1937)	17/17	n.a.
Archiv für Dermatologie und Syphilis	+	+	34/50	0/8
Archiv für die gesamte Physiologie	+	+	2/3	3/3
Archiv für experimentelle Pathologie	+	+	33/35	0/0
Archiv für Frauenkunde und Konstitutionsforchung	−	−	n.a.	n.a.
Archiv für Gynäkologie	+	+	25/31	2/33
Archiv für Hygiene	+	+	28/30	13/28
Archiv für Kinderheilkunde	+	+	7/8	5/8
Archiv für klinische Chirurgie	+	+	4/4	2/5
Archiv für Kreislaufforschung	n.a.	+	n.a.	0/4

Journals	Continued publication		Editorial boards: proportion unchanged	
	1932–1934	Postwar	1932–1934	1942–1947
Archiv für Ohren- Nasen- und Kehlkopfheilkunde	+	+	32/42	1/3
Archiv für Ophthalmologie	+	+	6/6	2/2
Archiv für orthopädische und Unfall-Chirurgie	+	+	14/15	2/12
Archiv für Psychiatrie und Nervenkrankheiten	+	+	14/16	8/11
Archiv für Schiffs- und Tropenhygiene	+	−(1944)	7/8	n.a.
Archiv für soziale Hygiene und Demographie	+	−(1934)	1/2	n.a.
Archiv für Verdauungs-Krankheiten[a]	+	−(1938)	11/13	n.a.
Der Balneologe	n.a.	−	n.a.	n.a.
Beiträge zur Klinik der Tuberkulose	+	+	36/38	12/30
Beiträge zur pathologischen Anatomie	+	+	1/1	1/1
Berichte über die gesamte Gynäkologie und Geburtshilfe	+	+	3/4	0/3
Berichte über die gesamte Physiologie	+	+	1/1	1/2
Berichte über die gesamte wissenschaftliche Biologie	+	+	?	?
Berliner Medizinische Gesellschaft—Verhandlungen	+	−(1935)	Not listed	n.a.
Berliner Tierärztliche Wochenschrift	+	+	31/35	1/6
Biochemische Zeitschrift	+	+	47/49	0/1
Biologisches Zentralblatt	+	+	2/3	?

318   Appendix A

Journals	Continued publication		Editorial boards: proportion unchanged	
	1932–1934	Postwar	1932–1934	1942–1947
Bruns' Beiträge zur klinischen Chirurgie	+	+	43/47	0/41
Der Chirurg	+	+	16/17	2/4
Dermatologische Wochenschrift	+	+	28/43	5/40
Dermatologische Zeitschrift[b]	+	–(1938)	4/5	n.a.
Deutsche Gesellschaft für Innere Medizin—Verhandlungen	+	+	1/1	0/1
Deutsche Gesellschaft für Kreislaufforschung—Verhandlungen	+	+	Rotating	0/1
Deutsche Medizinische Wochenschrift	+	+	1/2	0/3
Deutsche Ophthalmologische Gesellschaft—Verhandlungen	+	+	1/1	1/1
Deutsche Pathologische Gesellschaft—Verhandlungen	+	+	0/1	1/1
Deutsche tierärztliche Wochenschrift	+	+	12/13	0/31
Deutsche Zeitschrift für Chirurgie	+	–(1944)	34/37	n.a.
Deutsche Zeitschrift für die gesamte gerichtliche Medizin	+	–	4/4	0/3
Deutsche Zeitschrift für Nervenheilkunde	+	+	7/9	3/7
Deutsche Zeitschrift für Verdauungs- und Stoffwechselkrankheiten	n.a.	+	n.a.	1/23
Deutsches Archiv für klinische Medizin	+	+	23/29	3/4
Deutsches Tuberkuloseblatt	+	–(1944)	?	n.a.
Endokrinologie	+	+	1/1	2/2

Appendix A 319

Journals	Continued publication		Editorial boards: proportion unchanged	
	1932–1934	Postwar	1932–1934	1942–1947
Ergebnisse der allgemeine Pathologie	+	+	1/9	0/2
Ergebnisse der Chirurgie und Orthopaedie	+	+	1/1	0/2
Ergebnisse der Enzymforschung	+	+	2/6	2/5
Ergebnisse der gesamten Tuberkuloseforschung	+	+	2/3	?
Ergebnisse der Hygiene, Bakteriologie, Immunitätsforschung, und experimentellen Therapie	+	+	1/1	0/1
Ergebnisse der inneren Medizin und Kinderheilkunde	+	+	4/6	1/2
Ergebnisse der Kreislaufforschung	+	−(1935)	1/1	n.a.
Ergebnisse der Physiologie	+	+	0/14	1/3
Fermentforschung	+	−(1945)	1/1	n.a.
Fortbildungs-Lehrgang im Bad-Nauheim—Verhandlungen	+	+	Not listed	Not listed
Fortschritte auf dem Gebiete der Röntgenstrahlen	+	+	26/31	9/21
Fortschritte der Medizin	+	+	0/1	0/1
Fortschritte der Neurologie, Psychiatrie und ihrer Grenzgebiete	+	+	2/2	0/2
Fortschritte der Therapie	+	−(1944)	3/4	n.a.
Fortschritte der Zahnheilkunde	−	−	n.a.	n.a.
Frankfurter Zeitschrift für Pathologie	+	+	1/1	1/1

Journals	Continued publication		Editorial boards: proportion unchanged	
	1932–1934	Postwar	1932–1934	1942–1947
Gesellschaft für Verdauungs- und Stoffwechselkrankheiten—Verhandlungen	+	+	Not listed	?
Hefte zur Unfallheilkunde	+	+	1/1	1/1
Hoppe-Seyler's Zeitschrift für physiologische Chemie	+	+	24/25	2/3
Jahrbuch für Kinderheilkunde[c]	+	−(1938)	4/4	n.a.
Jahresbericht der Pharmazie	+	+	2/2	?
Jahresbericht Gynäkologie und Geburtshilfe	+	−(1939)	3/3	n.a.
Jahresbericht Ophthalmologie	+	−(1938)	2/2	n.a.
Jahresbericht über die gesamte Physiologie und experimentelle Pharmakologie	+	−(1937)	Not listed	n.a.
Jahreskurse für ärztliche Fortbildung	+	−(1944)	Rotating	n.a.
Journal für Psychologie und Neurologie	+	−(1942)	?	n.a.
Klinische Monatsblätter für Augenheilkunde	+	+	23/24	3/4
Klinische Wochenschrift	+	+	14/16	7/13
Kongresszentralblatt für die gesamte innere Medizin	+	+	4/4	1/3
Krankheitsforschung	−	−	n.a.	n.a.
Medizinische Klinik	+	+	32/35	6/47
Medizinische Welt	+	+	24/34	?
Medizinisches Korrespondenzblatt für Württemberg	+	−(1941)	1/2	n.a.

Journals	Continued publication		Editorial boards: proportion unchanged	
	1932–1934	Postwar	1932–1934	1942–1947
Mitteilungen aus den Grenzgebieten der Medizin und Chirurgie	+	−(1944)	12/13	n.a.
Mitteilungen zur Geschichte der Medizin	+	+	2/2	?
Monatsschrift für Geburtshülfe und Gynäkologie	+	−(1945)	4/6	n.a.
Monatsschrift für Kinderheilkunde	+	+	11/11	6/9
Monatsschrift für Psychiatrie und Neurologie[d]	+	+	3/3	n.a.
Monatsschrift für Unfallheilkunde und Versicherungsmedizin	+	+	3/3	1/1
Münchener Medizinische Wochenschrift	+	+	16/20	12/25
Der Nervenarzt	+	+	4/4	1/3
Passow-Schaefer Beiträge zur praktischen und theoretischen Hals-Nasen- und Ohrenheilkunde[e]	+	−(1935)	13/16	n.a.
Röntgenpraxis	+	+	12/12	?
Sudhoffs Archiv für Geschichte der Medizin	+	+	0/1	2/10
Die Tuberkulose	+	+	1/1	?
Virchows Archiv für Pathologie, Anatomie und Physiologie	+	+	1/1	1/1
Zeitschrift für ärztliche Fortbildung	+	+	4/4	0/1
Zeitschrift für Augenheilkunde	+	+	5/5	?
Zeitschrift für Biologie	+	+	1/1	?
Zeitschrift für die gesamte Anatomie	+	+	1/1	1/1

Journals	Continued publication		Editorial boards: proportion unchanged	
	1932–1934	Postwar	1932–1934	1942–1947
Zeitschrift für die gesamte experimentelle Medizin	+	+	18/19	2/24
Zeitschrift für die gesamte Neurologie und Psychiatrie	+	–	7/7	n.a.
Zeitschrift für die gesamte physikalische Therapie	–	–	n.a.	n.a.
Zeitschrift für Geburtshülfe und Gynäkologie	+	+	28/32	1/32
Zeitschrift für Hals- Nasen- und Ohrenheilkunde	+	+	29/33	?
Zeitschrift für Hygiene und Infektionskrankheiten	+	+	1/2	0/6
Zeitschrift für Immunitätsforschung und experimentelle Therapie[f]	+	+	2/2	2/2
Zeitschrift für Infektionskrankheiten	+	–(1944)	1/1	n.a.
Zeitschrift für Kinderheilkunde	+	+	4/4	8/14
Zeitschrift für klinische Medizin	+	+	9/12	2/13
Zeitschrift für Krebsforschung	+	+	0/2	1/5
Zeitschrift für Kreislaufforschung	+	+	4/6	0/5
Zeitschrift für Laryngologie, Rhinologie, Otologie und ihre Grenzgebiete	+	+	9/15	0/15
Zeitschrift für menschliche Vererbungs- und Konstitutionslehre	n.a.	+	n.a.	3/11
Zeitschrift für mikroskopisch-anatomische Forschung	+	+	5/5	4/6

Appendix A   323

Journals	Continued publication		Editorial boards: proportion unchanged	
	1932–1934	Postwar	1932–1934	1942–1947
Zeitschrift für Morphologie und Anthropologie	+	+	1/1	0/1
Zeitschrift für ophthalmologische Optik	+	−(1944)	12/12	n.a.
Zeitschrift für Orthopädie und ihre Grenzgebiete	+	+	?	3/7
Zeitschrift für orthopädische Chirurgie	+	+	16/20	3/7
Zeitschrift für psychische Hygiene	+	−(1944)	3/5	n.a.
Zeitschrift für Sexualwissenschaft	−	−	n.a.	n.a.
Zeitschrift für Tuberkulose	+	+	28/31	1/26
Zeitschrift für Untersuchung der Lebensmittel	+	+	3/3	1/4
Zeitschrift für Urologie	+	+	19/24	1/22
Zeitschrift für urologische Chirurgie	+	−(1944)	38/43	n.a.
Zeitschrift für wissenschaftliche Mikroskopie	+	+	3/3	2/3
Zeitschrift für Zellforschung und mikroskopische Anatomie	+	+	2/2	0/0
Zentralblatt für allgemeine Pathologie	+	+	2/2	2/2
Zentralblatt für Bakteriologie (Erste Abteilung)	+	+	6/6	1/7
Zentralblatt für Bakteriologie (Zweite Abteilung)	+	+	1/1	?
Zentralblatt für Chirurgie	+	+	4/4	4/11
Zentralblatt für die gesamte Hygiene	+	−(1944)	1/1	n.a.

Journals	Continued publication		Editorial boards: proportion unchanged	
	1932–1934	Postwar	1932–1934	1942–1947
Zentralblatt für die gesamte Kinderheilkunde	+	+	2/4	3/15
Zentralblatt für die gesamte Neurologie und Psychiatrie	+	+	1/4	1/2
Zentralblatt für die gesamte Ophthalmologie	+	+	9/9	2/6
Zentralblatt für die gesamte Radiologie	+	+	2/2	0/2
Zentralblatt für die gesamte Tuberkuloseforschung	+	+	5/5	4/5
Zentralblatt für Gynäkologie	+	+	1/1	1/1
Zentralblatt für Hals- Nasen- und Ohrenheilkunde	+	+	2/2	4/6
Zentralblatt für Haut- und Geschlechtskrankheiten	+	+	1/2	0/3
Zentralblatt für innere Medizin	+	+	4/6	?
Zentralblatt für Psychotherapie	+	−(1944)	0/4	n.a.
Zentralorgan für die gesamte Chirurgie	+	+	6/6	3/6

a. Published in Basel by Samuel Karger after 1938 as *Gastroenterologia*. Karger moved his offices to Basel (and New York) after 1938; Nazi medical leaders cautioned German physicians against buying books and journals from this publisher.

b. Published by Karger in Basel and New York after 1938 as *Dermatologica*.

c. Publication continued by Karger after 1938 in Basel as the *Annales Paediatrici*.

d. Published after 1938 in Basel and New York by Karger.

e. Superseded in 1935 by *Practica Oto- Rhino- Laryngologica*, published by Karger in Basel.

f. The 1932–1934 item refers to main editors only.

Appendix A   325

This display shows that the overwhelming majority of Germany's technical medical journals continued publication during the period of Nazi rule. Most continued without any major change in either format or editorial board. In sheer quantitative terms (numbers of papers published, and so on), one can say that German medical science was hurt more by the *war* than by purges in the early years of the Reich. There is a higher degree of continuity in medical publication from the pre-Nazi to the Nazi period than from the prewar to the postwar period.

Medical journals ceased publication after 1933 for various reasons. Some were discontinued as a result of financial difficulties emerging from the Great Depression; others were reorganized and republished in a new format (for example, the *Zeitschrift für physikalische Therapie*). Some journals merged with others as part of the *Gleichschaltung* of the German medical press (for example, the *Fortschritte der Zahnheilkunde* and the *Zentralblatt für die gesamte Kinderheilkunde*). Few were actually suppressed by the Nazis. Two important exceptions are journals associated with Jewish publishers or editors (for example, journals published by the Samuel Karger Verlag), and journals associated with socialist or other movements politically suspect in the eyes of the Nazis (for example, Magnus Hirschfeld's *Zeitschrift für Sexualwissenschaft*).

The number of *new medical journals* founded in the early years of the Nazi period may well be greater than the number of old journals that ceased publication. Medical journals (or journals published by medical bodies) founded in the Nazi period include the following:

Archiv für die gesamte Virusforschung (1939–)
Archiv für Kreislaufforschung (1937–)
Arzt und Sport (1935–1937)
Balneologe (1934–1944)
Deutscher Militärarzt (1936–1944)
Deutsche Zahn- Mund- und Kieferheilkunde (1934–)
Deutsche Zeitschrift für Verdauungs- und Stoffwechselkrankheiten (1938–)
Erbarzt (1934–1944)
Erbblätter für den Hals- Nasen- und Ohrenarzt (1936–)
Ergebnisse der physikalisch-diätetischen Therapie (1939–1948)
Ernährung (1936–1944)
Fortschritte der Erbpathologie, Rassenhygiene und ihrer Grenzgebiete (1937–1944)
Geburtshilfe und Frauenheilkunde (1939–)
Klinische Fortbildung (1933–1944)
Konstitution, Erbe und Umwelt (1944)
Konstitution und Klinik (1937–)
Luftfahrtmedizin (1936–1944)
Luftfahrtsmedizinische Abhandlungen (1936–1939)
Luftfahrtsmedizinischer Lehrbrief (1944)
Monatsschrift für Krebsbekämpfung (1933–1944)
Öffentlicher Gesundheitsdienst (1935–1944)
Radiologica (1937–1940)
Vertrauensarzt und Krankenkassen (1933–1944)

Volksgesundheit (1936–)
Volksgesundheitswacht (1934–1939)
Zeitschrift für Altersforschung (1938–)
Zeitschrift für Konstitutionslehre (1934–)
Zeitschrift für Rheumaforschung (1938–)
Zentralblatt für die gesamte Zahn- Mund- und Kieferheilkunde (1936–1944)
Zentralblatt für Neurochirurgie (1936–)

From 1930 to 1950 the majority of Germany's technical medical journals (*Fachpresse*) continued publication with no reference whatsoever to broader political affairs. Those most obviously affected by the Nazi "revolution" were *professional* journals (*Standespresse*) that had traditionally concerned themselves not just with technical matters but with the political, social, and economic affairs of the profession. These included publications of local medical societies (the *Ärzteblatt für Bayern,* the *Ärzteblatt für Berlin,* and the like), but also journals such as the *Münchener Medizinische Wochenschrift* or the *Deutsche Medizinische Wochenschrift,* which also discussed the political and economic aspects of medical practice. In a similar category should be placed journals published by government offices, including the *Reichs-Gesundheitsblatt,* the *Blätter für Volksgesundheitspflege,* and journals representing the semiprivate Krankenkassen.

In virtually none of the more than 200 medical journals published from 1933 to 1945 can there be found a criticism of National Socialism during the years of its power. In several cases (the *Münchener Medizinische Wochenschrift,* not to mention official Nazi publications such as *Ziel und Weg*), medical journals expressed sympathy for National Socialism before Hitler's rise to power.

After the war most German medical journals were reestablished with few changes in either format or content. (Journals published under Soviet occupation generally showed more substantial changes in editorial boards than is true for journals republished in areas under American, British, or French control.) Most resumed publication without any reflection on or analysis of recent events. Some journals (for example, *Klinische Medizin*) complained about controls placed on the medical press by occupation forces; few, however, broached the topic of the recent history of medicine under the Nazis.

Appendix B
University and Research Institutes Devoted to Racial Hygiene

Location	Institute and director
Alt-Rehse	Erbbiologisches Forschungsinstitut (Hermann Boehm, 1935–1942)
Berlin	Anstalt für Rassenkunde, Völkerbiologie und ländliche Soziologie der Universität (Hans F. K. Günther, 1935–1940) Erbpathologische Abteilung der I. Medizinischen Poliklinik an der Charité (Friedrich Curtius, 1934–) Institut für Rassenbiologie der Universität (Wolfgang Abel, 1942–1945) Institut für Rassenhygiene an der Universität (Fritz Lenz, 1933–1945) Kaiser Wilhelm Institut für Anthropologie, menschliche Erblehre und Eugenik (Eugen Fischer, 1927–1942; Otmar Freiherr von Verschuer, 1942–1945) Poliklinik für Erb- und Rassenpflege in the Kaiserin Auguste Viktoria-Haus (Eduard Schütt, 1934–)
Bonn	Rheinisches Provinzial-Institut für psychiatrisch-neurologische Erbforschung (Kurt Pohlisch; Chief physician: Friedrich Panse)[a]
Cologne	Institut für Erbbiologie und Rassenhygiene der Universität (Ferdinand Claussen, 1939–1945, assisted by Wolfgang Bauermeister)

328 Appendix B

Location	Institute and director
Danzig	Institut für Erb- und Rassenforschung der Medizinischen Akademie (Erich Grossmann, 1942–1945)
Frankfurt	Institut zur Erforschung der Judenfrage (Wilhelm Grau, 1941–) Universitätsinstitut für Erbbiologie und Rassenhygiene (Otmar von Verschuer, 1935–1942; Heinrich W. Kranz, 1942–1945)
Freiburg	Anstalt für Rassenkunde, Völkerbiologie und ländliche Soziologie der Universität (Hans F. K. Günther, 1940–1945)
Giessen	Institut für Erbgesundheits- und Rassenpflege (Heinrich W. Kranz, 1934–1942; Hermann Boehm, 1943–1945)
Graz	Universitätsinstitut für Erblehre und Rassenhygiene (Rudolf Polland)[a]
Greifswald	Institut für menschliche Erblehre und Eugenik der Universität (Günther Just, 1933–1942; Fritz Steiniger, 1942–1945)
Hamburg	Abteilung für Erb- und Zwillingsforschung an der II. Medizinische Universitätsklinik (Wilhelm Weitz, 1934–1945) Rassenbiologisches Institut der Universität (Walter Scheidt, 1924–1965)
Innsbruck	Erb- und Rassenbiologisches Institut der Universität (Friedrich Stumpfl, 1939–1945)
Jena	Institut für menschliche Erbforschung und Rassenpolitik (Karl Astel, 1934–1945)
Königsberg	Rassenbiologisches Institut der Universität (Lothar Loeffler, 1935–1942)
Leipzig	Institut für Rassen- und Völkerkunde der Universität (Otto Reche, 1927–1945)
Munich	Institut für Erbbiologie und Rassenhygiene der Universität (Fritz Lenz, 1923–1933; Lothar Tirala, 1933–1936; Ernst Rüdin, 1936–1945) Kaiser Wilhelm Institut für Genealogie und Demographie (Ernst Rüdin, 1919–)
Prague	Institut für Rassenbiologie der Deutschen Karls-Universität (Karl Thums, 1940–1945) Institut für Rassenkunde der Deutschen Karls-Universität (Bruno K. Schultz, 1942–1945)

Location	Institute and director
	Institut für Sozialanthropologie und Volksbiologie der Deutschen Karls-Universität (Karl Valentin Müller)[a]
Rostock	Institut für Erbbiologie und Rassenhygiene (Hans Grebe, 1944–1945)
Strassburg	Institut für Rassenbiologie der Reichsuniversität (Wolfgang Lehmann, 1942–1945)
Tübingen	Rassenbiologisches Institut der Universität (Wilhelm Gieseler, 1934–1945)
Vienna	Rassenbiologisches Institut der Universität (Lothar Loeffler, 1942–1945)
Weimar	Thüringisches Landesamt für Rassewesen (President: Karl Astel, 1933–1945)
Würzburg	Institut für Vererbungswissenschaft und Rasseforschung (Ludwig Schmidt-Kehl, 1937–1941; Friedrich Keiter; Günther Just, 1942–1945, 1948–)

a. Data on period of directorship not available.

The Reich Health Office also included the following research divisions devoted to racial hygiene and allied fields:

Abteilung für Erbgesundheits- und Rassenpflege (Division of Genetic Health and Racial Care), headed by Eduard Schütt
Erbwissenschaftliches Forschungsinstitut (Institute for the Scientific Study of Genetics), headed by Günther Just
Kriminalbiologische Forschungsstelle (Criminal Biology Research Station), headed by Ferdinand von Neureiter
Rassenhygienische und bevölkerungsbiologische Forschungsstelle (Racial Hygiene and Population Biology Research Division), headed by Robert Ritter

Bibliography

Archival Sources

Berlin Document Center
  NSDAP Zentralkartei
  Reichsärztekammer
  Parteistatistische Erhebung (1939)
Bundesarchiv Koblenz
  NSDAP Hauptarchiv
  NS 2: Rasse- und Siedlungshauptamt-SS
  NS 19: Reichsführer SS
  NSD: Nationalsozialistischer Dozentenbund
  R18: Reichsgesundheitsführung in the Ministry of the Interior
  R73: Deutsche Forschungsgemeinschaft
  R86: Reichsgesundheitsamt
Harvard University Archives
  Edwin Katzenellenbogen file
Hoover Institution on War, Revolution, and Peace, Stanford
  Deutsche Forschungsgemeinschaft
  Deutsche Kongress-Zentrale
  Himmler files
  U.S. Office of Strategic Services (Research and Analysis Branch), "R and A Reports"
Max Planck Gesellschaft Archives, Berlin
  Kaiser Wilhelm Institut für Anthropologie, menschliche Erblehre, und Eugenik
  Kaiser Wilhelm Institut für Genealogie
Rüdin, Ernst, papers in care of Edith Rüdin, Max Planck Institut für Psychiatrie, Munich

Bibliography 331

National Archives, Washington, D.C.
  T-580: Captured German Documents Filmed at Berlin, Rolls 27, 28
  T-81: Roll 54, "Hauptamt Wissenschaft"
  T-1021: Roll 18
Yiddish Scientific Institute, New York, Archives of the Rosenberg Hauptamt Wissenschaft

Books and Articles

Alexander, Leo. "Medical Science under Dictatorship." *New England Journal of Medicine,* 241(1949): 39–47.
Allen, Garland. "The Eugenics Record Office at Cold Spring Harbor, 1910–40." *Osiris,* 2(1986): 225–264.
Aly, Götz, Angelika Ebbinghaus, Matthias Hamann, Friedemann Pfäfflin, and Gerd Preissler. *Aussonderung und Tod, die klinische Hinrichtung der Unbrauchbaren.* Berlin, 1985. Especially the contribution by Aly, "Medizin gegen Unbrauchbare," pp. 9–74.
Baader, Gerhard. "Politisch motivierte Emigration deutscher Ärzte." *Berichte zur Wissenschaftsgeschichte,* 7(1984): 67–84.
——— and Ulrich Schultz, eds. *Medizin und Nationalsozialismus.* Vol. 1 of series *Dokumentation des Gesundheitstages Berlin.* Berlin (West), 1980.
Baur, Erwin, Eugen Fischer, and Fritz Lenz. *Grundriss der menschlichen Erblichkeitslehre und Rassenhygiene* (1921). Vol. 1, *Menschliche Erblichkeitslehre,* 3rd ed. Munich, 1927. Translated as *Human Heredity.* London, 1931.
Bayle, Francois. *Croix gammée contre caducée.* Neustadt (Palatinat), 1951.
Beyerchen, Alan D. *Scientists under Hitler: Politics and the Physics Community in the Third Reich.* New Haven, 1977.
Bluhm, Agnes. "Zur Frage nach der generativen Tüchtigkeit der deutschen Frauen und der rassenhygienischen Bedeutung der ärztlichen Geburtshilfe." *Archiv für Rassen- und Gesellschaftsbiologie,* 9(1912): 340–346.
———. *Die rassenhygienischen Aufgaben des weiblichen Arztes.* Munich, 1936.
Böttcher, Alfred. "Die Lösung der Judenfrage." *Ziel und Weg,* 5(1935): 225–230.
Bramer, Rainer, ed. *Naturwissenschaft im NS-Staat.* Marburg, 1984.
Bridenthal, Renate, Atina Grossmann, and Marion Kaplan, eds. *When Biology Became Destiny: Women in Weimar and Nazi Germany.* New York, 1985.
Burgdörfer, Friedrich. *Völker am Abgrund.* Vol. 1 of series *Politische Biologie.* Munich, 1937.
Cocks, Geoffrey. *Psychotherapy in the Third Reich: The Göring Institute.* Oxford, 1985.
Comité des Délégations Juives. *Die Lage der Juden in Deutschland 1933.* Frankfurt, 1983. First published in Paris, 1934.
Dawidowicz, Lucy S. *The War against the Jews, 1933–1945.* New York, 1975.
Die deutsche Universität im Dritten Reich, eine Vortragsreihe der Universität München. Munich, 1966.
Diepgen, Paul. *Die Heilkunde und der ärztliche Beruf.* Munich, 1938. Second edition, Berlin, 1947.

Dietl, Hans-Martin, ed. *Eugenik, Entstehung und gesellschaftliche Bedingtheit.* Jena, 1984.
Doeleke, Werner. "Alfred Ploetz (1860–1940), Sozialdarwinist und Gesellschaftsbiologe." Med. diss., University of Frankfurt, 1975.
Dörner, Klaus. "Nationalsozialismus und Lebensvernichtung." *Vierteljahrshefte für Zeitgeschichte,* 15(1967): 121–152.
———. et al., eds. *Der Krieg gegen die psychisch Kranken.* Rehburg-Loccum, 1980.
Fichtmüller, Werner. "Dissertationen in den medizinischen Fakultäten der Universitäten Deutschlands von 1933 bis 1945 zum Thema: 'Gesetz zur Verhütung erbkranken Nachwuchses' von 14. Juli 1933." Med. diss., University of Erlangen-Nuremberg, 1972.
Fischer, Alfons. "Übersicht über die Geschichte der Rassenhygiene in Deutschland." *Sozialhygienische Mitteilungen,* 17(1933): 42–54.
Fischer, Eugen. *Die Rehobother Bastards und das Bastardisierungsproblem beim Menschen.* Jena, 1913.
———. *Der völkische Staat, biologisch gesehen.* Berlin, 1933.
Flitner, Andreas, ed. *Deutsches Geistesleben und Nationalsozialismus, eine Vortragsreihe der Universität Tübingen.* Tübingen, 1965.
Frankenthal, Käte. *Der dreifache Fluch: Jüdin, Intellektuelle, Sozialistin, Lebenserinnerungen einer Ärztin in Deutschland und im Exil.* Frankfurt, 1981.
Frick, Wilhelm. "Bevölkerungs- und Rassenpolitik." Speech of June 28, 1933, printed as a pamphlet at Langensalza, 1933.
Fünfzig Jahre J. F. Lehmanns Verlag 1890–1940. Munich, 1940.
The German New Order in Poland. Published for the Polish Ministry of Information in London, 1942.
Geuter, Ulfried. *Die Professionalisierung der deutschen Psychologie im Nationalsozialismus.* Frankfurt, 1984.
Gildea, Maureen. "Euthanasia: A Review of the American Literature." Senior thesis, Harvard University, 1983.
Gmelin, Walter. "Zur Frage einer erbbiologischen Registrierung der Bevölkerung." *Ärztliche Rundschau,* 43(1933): 197–201.
Graham, Loren R. "Science and Values: The Eugenics Movement in Germany and Russia in the 1920s." *American Historical Review,* 82(1977): 1133–64.
Graml, Hermann. "Die Behandlung 'Deutschblütiger' in 'Rassenschande' Verfahren." In *Gutachten des Instituts für Zeitgeschichte,* Munich, 1957.
Gross, Walter. "Arzt und Judenfrage." *Ziel und Weg,* 3(1933): 186–189.
———. "Rassenpolitische Voraussetzungen einer europäischen Gesamtlösung der Judenfrage." *Rassenpolitische Auslands-Korrespondenz,* March 1941, pp. 1–6.
Günther, Hans F. K. *Rassenkunde des deutschen Volkes.* Munich, 1922.
———. *Rassenkunde des jüdischen Volkes.* Munich, 1929.
———. *Mein Eindruck auf Hitler.* Pähl, 1969.
Gütt, Arthur. *Der Aufbau des Gesundheitswesens im Dritten Reich.* Berlin, 1935.
———. Ernst Rüdin and Falk Ruttke. *Gesetz zur Verhütung erbkranken Nachwuchses.* Munich, 1934.

———. Herbert Linden and Franz Massfeller. *Blutschutz- und Ehegesundheitsgesetz.* Munich, 1936.
Gumpert, Martin. *Heil Hunger! Health under Hitler.* New York, 1940.
Haberer, Joseph. *Politics and the Community of Science.* New York, 1969.
Hadrich, Julius. "Hochschulüberfüllung und wirtschaftliche Lage der Ärzteschaft." *Ärztliche Mitteilungen,* 33(1932): 787–794, special issue devoted to the twenty-ninth meeting of the Hartmannbund.
———. "Einführung in das neue ärztliche Organisationswesen." Published as a supplement to *Reichs-Medizinal-Kalender für Deutschland* (Leipzig, 1936).
———. "Die Ärztekammer Berlin in der Statistik." *Ärzteblatt für Berlin,* 42(1937): 192–194.
Hafner, Karl-Heinz, and Rolf Winau. "Die Freigabe der Vernichtung lebensunwerten Lebens." *Medizinhistorisches Journal,* 9(1974): 227–254.
Hagen, Wilhelm. *Auftrag und Wirklichkeit, Sozialarzt im 20. Jahrhundert.* Munich-Gräfelfing, 1978.
Hartshorne, E. Y. *The German Universities and National Socialism.* London, 1937.
Haug, Alfred. "Die Reichsarbeitsgemeinschaft für eine Neue Deutsche Heilkunde (1935/36)." In *Abhandlungen zur Geschichte der Medizin und der Naturwissenschaften,* 50(1985).
Helmut, Otto. *Volk in Gefahr* (1933), 8th ed. Munich, 1937.
Hoche, Alfred, and Rudolf Binding. *Die Freigabe der Vernichtung lebensunwerten Lebens.* Leipzig, 1920.
Hoffmann, Alfred. "Entwicklung und Aufgaben des Reichsgesundheitsverlages." *Ärzteblatt für den Reichsgau Wartheland,* 1(1940): 24–25.
Hohmann, Joachim S. *Geschichte der Zigeunerfrage in Deutschland.* Frankfurt, 1981.
International Auschwitz Committee. *Nazi Medicine* (1972). New York, 1986.
Just, Günther, ed., with contributions from B. Bavink, H. Muckermann, and K. V. Müller. *Eugenik und Weltanschauung.* Berlin, 1932.
Kater, Michael H. "Die 'Gesundheitsführung' des deutschen Volkes." *Medizinhistorisches Journal,* 18(1983): 349–375.
———. "Medizinische Fakultäten und Medizinstudenten: Eine Skizze." In *Ärzte im Nationalsozialismus,* ed. Fridolf Kudlien. Cologne, 1985.
Kaul, Friedrich. *Ärzte in Auschwitz.* Berlin (East), 1968.
———. *Nazimordaktion T-4; ein Bericht über die erste industriemässig durchgeführte Mordaktion des Naziregimes.* Berlin (East), 1973.
Kaupen-Haas, Heidrun, ed. *Der Griff nach der Bevölkerung, Aktualität und Kontinuität nazistischer Bevölkerungspolitik.* Hamburg, 1986.
Kelting, Kristin. "Das Tuberkuloseproblem im Nationalsozialismus." Med. diss., University of Kiel, 1974.
Kevles, Daniel J. *In the Name of Eugenics.* Berkeley, 1985.
Klee, Ernst. *"Euthanasie" im NS-Staat, Die "Vernichtung lebensunwerten Lebens."* Frankfurt, 1983.
Koch, Gerhard. *Die Gesellschaft für Konstitutionsforschung, Anfang und Ende 1942–1965.* Erlangen, 1985.

Kötschau, Karl. "Die nationalsozialistische Revolution in der Medizin." *Ziel und Weg* (1933–1935). Also published as book, *Zum nationalsozialistischen Umbruch in der Medizin*. Stuttgart, 1936.

Kroll, Jürgen. "Zur Entstehung und Institutionalisierung einer naturwissenschaftlichen und sozialpolitischen Bewegung: Die Entwicklung der Eugenik/Rassenhygiene bis zum Jahre 1933." Ph.D. diss., University of Tübingen, 1983.

Kudlien, Fridolf. *Ärzte im Nationalsozialismus*. Cologne, 1985.

Kühn, Kurt, ed. *Ärzte an der Seite der Arbeiterklasse*, 2nd ed. Berlin (East), 1977.

Labisch, Alfons, and Florian Tennstedt. *Der Weg zum "Gesetz über die Vereinheitlichung des Gesundheitswesens" vom. 3. Juli 1934*. Published as vol. 13 of the *Schriftenreihe der Akademie für Öffentliches Gesundheitswesen in Düsseldorf*. Düsseldorf, 1985.

Lang, Theobald. "Der Nationalsozialismus als politischer Ausdruck unserer biologischen Kenntnis." *Nationalsozialistische Monatshefte*, 1(1930): 393–397.

Lange, Johannes. *Verbrechen als Schicksal, Studien an kriminellen Zwillingen*. Leipzig, 1928.

Lehmann, Ernst. *Irrweg der Biologie*. Stuttgart, 1946.

Lehmann, Melanie. *Verleger J. F. Lehmann, ein Leben im Kampf für Deutschland*. Munich, 1935.

Leibfried, Stephan. "Stationen der Abwehr." *Leo Baeck Institute Bulletin*, 62(1982): 1–39.

——— and Florian Tennstedt. *Berufsverbote und Sozialpolitik 1933: Die Auswirkungen der nationalsozialistischen Machtergreifung auf die Krankenkassenverwaltung und die Kassenärzte* (1979), 3rd ed. Bremen, 1981.

Lenz, Fritz. "Zur Erneuerung der Ethik." *Deutschlands Erneuerung*, 1(1917): 35–56. Reprinted with a new introduction as *Die Rasse als Wertprinzip, Zur Erneuerung der Ethik*. Munich, 1933.

———. *Menschliche Auslese und Rassenhygiene (Eugenik)* (1921), 3rd ed. Munich, 1931. Published as vol. 2 of Baur, Fischer, and Lenz, *Menschliche Erblichkeitslehre und Rassenhygiene*.

———. "Die Stellung des Nationalsozialismus zur Rassenhygiene." *Archiv für Rassen- und Gesellschaftsbiologie*, 25(1931): 300–308.

Lifton, Robert Jay. *The Nazi Doctors*. New York, 1986.

Light, Donald W., Stephan Leibfried, and Florian Tennstedt. "Social Medicine vs. Professional Dominance: The German Experience." *American Journal of Public Health*, 76(1986): 78–83.

Lilienthal, Georg. "Rassenhygiene im Dritten Reich." *Medizinhistorisches Journal*, 14(1979): 114–137.

———. *Der "Lebensborn e.V.," ein Instrument nationalsozialistischer Rassenpolitik*. Stuttgart, 1984.

———. "Der Nationalsozialistische Ärztebund (1929–1943/1945)." In *Ärzte im Nationalsozialismus*, ed. Kudlien. Cologne, 1985.

Loewenstein, Georg. *Kommunale Gesundheitsfürsorge und sozialistische Ärztepolitik zwischen Kaiserreich und Nationalsozialismus*. Bremen, 1980.

Ludwig, Karl-Heinz. *Technik und Ingenieure im Dritten Reich.* Düsseldorf, 1974.
Lukács, Georg. *Die Zerstörung der Vernunft.* Vol. 3, *Irrationalismus und Soziologie* (1954). Darmstadt, 1962.
Lutzhöft, Hans-Jürgen. *Der Nordische Gedanke in Deutschland 1920 bis 1940.* Stuttgart, 1971.
Mangold, Otto. *Die Aufgaben der Biologie im Dritten Reich.* Freiburg in Breslau, 1938.
Mann, Gunter. "Rassenhygiene-Sozialdarwinismus." In *Biologismus im 19. Jahrhundert,* ed. Gunter Mann. Stuttgart, 1973.
Marcuse, Julian. "Nationalsozialistische Rassenexperimente." *Der Sozialistische Arzt,* 8(1932): 76–78.
Medizin im Nationalsozialismus. Published by the Evangelische Akademie Bad Boll as part of their *Protokolldienst,* 23(1982).
Mehrtens, Herbert, and Steffen Richter, eds. *Naturwissenschaft, Technik und NS Ideologie.* Frankfurt, 1980.
Mersmann, I. "Medizinische Ausbildung im Dritten Reich." Med. diss., University of Munich, 1978.
Mitscherlich, Alexander, and Fred Mielke. *Medizin ohne Menschlichkeit* (1949). Frankfurt, 1978. First published in 1947 as *Das Diktat der Menschenverachtung* (Heidelberg); 1947 edition translated into English as *Doctors of Infamy* (New York, 1949); 1949 edition translated as *The Death Doctors* (London, 1962).
Modersohn, Wolf J. "Das Führerprinzip in der deutschen Medizin, 1933–45." Med. diss., University of Kiel, 1982.
Mommsen, Hans. "Die Realisierung des Utopischen: Die 'Endlösung der Judenfrage' im 'Dritten Reich'." *Geschichte und Gesellschaft,* 9(1983): 381–420.
Müller-Hill, Benno. *Tödliche Wissenschaft.* Reinbek bei Hamburg, 1984.
Nationalsozialismus und die deutsche Universität. Published by the Freie Universität. Berlin (West), 1966.
Noakes, Jeremy. "Nazism and Eugenics: The Background to the Nazi Sterilization Law of 14 July 1933." In *Ideas into Politics: Aspects of European History, 1880–1950,* ed. R. J. Bullen, H. Pogge von Strandmann, and A. B. Polonsky. Totowa, N.J., 1984.
Paul, Diane. "Eugenics and the Left." *Journal of the History of Ideas,* 45(1984): 567–590.
Ploetz, Alfred. *Grundlinie einer Rassenhygiene.* Vol. 1, *Die Tüchtigkeit unsrer Rasse und der Schutz der Schwachen.* Berlin, 1895.
Pommerin, Reiner. *Die Sterilisierung der Rheinlandbastarde.* Düsseldorf, 1979.
Provine, William. "Biologists and Race Crossing." *Science,* 182(1973): 790–796.
Ramm, Rudolf. *Ärztliche Rechts- und Standeskunde, der Arzt als Gesundheitserzieher,* 2nd ed. Berlin, 1943.
Reiter, Hans. *Ziele und Wege des Reichsgesundheitsamtes im Dritten Reich.* Leipzig, 1936.
Rissom, Renate. "Fritz Lenz und die Rassenhygiene." *Abhandlungen zur Geschichte der Medizin und der Naturwissenschaften,* 47(1983).

Ritter, Robert. "Kriminalität und Primitivität." *Monatsschrift für Kriminalbiologie und Strafrechtsreform*, 31(1940): 197–210.
Roth, Karl Heinz, ed. *Erfassung zur Vernichtung, von der Sozialhygiene zum "Gesetz über Sterbehilfe."* Berlin (West), 1984.
Saller, Karl. *Die Rassenlehre des Nationalsozialismus in Wissenschaft und Propaganda.* Darmstadt, 1961.
Schaxel, J. "Deutsche Staatsbiologie." *Unter dem Banner des Marxismus*, 9(1935): 261–274.
Scheidt, Walter. *Allgemeine Rassenkunde.* Munich, 1925.
Schütt, Eduard. "Die Bedeutung der wissenschaftlichen Erb- und Rassenforschung für die praktische Gesundheitspflege." *Öffentlicher Gesundheitsdienst*, 4(1938): 472–495.
Schulz, Edgar. "Judentum und Degeneration." *Ziel und Weg*, 5(1935): 349–354.
Seidler, Horst, and Andreas Rett. *Das Reichssippenamt entscheidet: Rassenbiologie im Nationalsozialismus.* Vienna, 1982.
Siemens, Hermann. "Die Proletarisierung unseres Nachwuchses, eine Gefahr unrassenhygienischer Bevölkerungspolitik." *Archiv für Rassen- und Gesellschaftsbiologie*, 12(1916/18): 43–55.
Stähle, Eugen. *Geschichte des NSD-Ärztebundes, e.V., Gau Württemberg-Hohenzollern.* Stuttgart, 1940.
Stämmler, Martin. "Rassenhygiene im Dritten Reich." *Ziel und Weg*, 2(1932): 7–22.
———. *Rassenpflege im völkischen Staat.* Munich, 1934.
Stuckart, Wilhelm. *Rassen- und Erbpflege in der Gesetzgebung des Reiches*, 5th ed. Leipzig, 1944.
Stumpfl, Friedrich. *Erbanlagen und Verbrechen.* Berlin, 1935.
Ternon, Yves, and Socrate Helman. *Histoire de la médecine SS*, 3rd ed. Brussels, 1969.
———. *Les médecins allemands et le nationalsocialisme.* Paris, 1973.
Thom, Achim, and Horst Spaar, eds. *Medizin im Faschismus, Symposium über das Schicksal der Medizin in der Zeit des Faschismus in Deutschland 1933–45.* Berlin (East), 1983.
Trials of War Criminals before the Nuremberg Military Tribunals. 15 vols. Washington, D.C., 1949–1952. Vols. 1 and 2, *The Medical Case.*
Verschuer, Otmar Freiherr von. *Erbpathologie: Ein Lehrbuch für Ärzte und Medizinstudierende* (1934), 2nd ed. Leipzig, 1937.
———. *Leitfaden der Rassenhygiene.* Stuttgart, 1941.
Wagner, Gerhard. "Unser Reichsärzteführer spricht." Speech before the Nuremberg Nazi Party Congress of autumn 1935, printed in *Ziel und Weg*, 5(1935): 431–437.
———. *Reden und Aufrufe*, ed. Leonardo Conti. Berlin, 1943.
Waldinger, Robert. "The High Priests of Nature." Senior thesis, Harvard University, 1973.
Weindling, Paul. "Weimar Eugenics: The Kaiser Wilhelm Institute for Anthropology, Human Heredity, and Eugenics in Social Context." *Annals of Science*, 42(1985): 303–318.

Weinreich, Max. *Hitler's Professors: The Part of Scholarship in Germany's Crimes against the Jewish People.* New York, 1946.
Weiss, Sheila. "Race Hygiene and the Rationalization of National Efficiency: Wilhelm Schallmayer and the Origins of German Eugenics, 1890–1920." Ph.D. diss., Johns Hopkins University, 1983.
Wertham, Fredric. *A Sign for Cain: An Exploration of Human Violence.* New York, 1966.
Wuttke-Groneberg, Walter, ed. *Medizin im Nationalsozialismus: Ein Arbeitsbuch.* Tübingen, 1980.
Zapp, Albert. "Untersuchungen zum Nationalsozialistischen Deutschen Ärztebund." Med. diss., University of Kiel, 1979.
Zmarzlik, Hans-Günter. "Der Sozialdarwinismus in Deutschland als geschichtliches Problem." *Vierteljahrshefte für Zeitgeschichte,* 11(1963): 246–273.

Notes

Abbreviations

ÄfB	*Ärzteblatt für Berlin*
ÄRW	*Ärzteblatt für den Reichsgau Wartheland*
ARGB	*Archiv für Rassen- und Gesellschaftsbiologie*
BA	Bundesarchiv Koblenz
DÄ	*Deutsches Ärzteblatt*
IÄB	*Internationales Ärztliches Bulletin*
MMW	*Münchener Medizinische Wochenschrift*
MPGA	Max Planck Gesellschaft Archives
NSDÄB	Nationalsozialistischer Deutscher Ärztebund
NSDAP	Nationalsozialistische Deutsche Arbeiterpartei
SD	Sicherheitsdienst (State Security Police)
SA	Sturmabteilungen (Storm Troopers)
SPD	Sozialdemokratische Partei Deutschlands
SS	Schutz Staffel (Hitler's personal bodyguard)

Introduction

1. See, for example, Jonathan Rosenhead et al., *The Technology of Political Control* (London, 1977).
2. For recent examples of the use of "biology as a weapon," see Science for the People, ed., *Biology as a Social Weapon* (Ann Arbor, Mich., 1982).
3. Alan Beyerchen, *Scientists under Hitler* (New Haven, 1977).
4. Ibid., p. x.
5. Joseph Needham, *The Nazi Attack on International Science* (Cambridge, 1941).
6. *British Medical Journal,* November 12, 1938, p. 1027.

7. This was the contention of much early Anglo-American sociology of science: see, for example, Robert Merton's "Science and Technology in a Democratic Order" (1942), reprinted as "The Normative Structure of Science," in his *Sociology of Science,* ed. Norman W. Storer (Chicago, 1973), pp. 267–278. Compare also J. D. Bernal's discussion of "Science and Fascism," in his *Social Function of Science* (New York, 1939), pp. 210–221. Bernal suggested: "The destruction of science in Germany, if it can be maintained for many more years, may be one of the major tragedies in the development of civilization . . . What has been done cannot be lost, but it will not be easy to improvise in other countries the mechanisms of a comprehensive and thorough record of scientific advance. Even more than this perhaps is the destruction of the spirit of German science, the appreciation of a patient and exact determination of the structure of the world, the belief in the intrinsic value of pure scientific truth . . . The whole of the claims on which the Nazis' seizure of power was based were so palpably irrational and incapable of standing scientific analysis that if they were to be maintained it could only be by enthroning irrationality over reason and reducing scientific criticism to impotence" (p. 212).
8. I have translated the German term *Rassenhygiene* as "racial hygiene" in order to stress the parallels commonly drawn between "social hygiene" and "racial hygiene." Others have translated this as "race hygiene" or "eugenics"; the meaning should be clear in either case (see also Chapter 1).

1. The Origins of Racial Hygiene

1. Henri Comte de Boulainvilliers, *Histoire de l'ancien gouvernement de la France* (The Hague, 1727).
2. These and other extraordinary tales from early American intellectual history are recounted in William Stanton, *The Leopard's Spots* (Chicago, 1960). See also Thomas Gossett, *Race: The History of an Idea in America* (Dallas, 1963).
3. Marvin Harris, *The Rise of Anthropological Theory* (New York, 1968), p. 16.
4. See James Farr, "So Vile and Miserable an Estate: The Problem of Slavery in John Locke's Political Thought," in *Political Theory,* 14(1986): 263–289.
5. David Hume, "Of National Characters," in his *Essays and Treatises on Several Subjects,* vol. 1 (London, 1768), p. 235.
6. The most important eighteenth-century German racial theorist was Johann Blumenbach, whose 1775 treatise was first published in English as *On the Natural Varieties of Mankind* (London, 1865).
7. Arthur Comte de Gobineau, *Essai sur l'inégalité des races humaines* (Paris, 1853–1855).
8. *Correspondance entre Tocqueville et Gobineau* (Paris, 1909), p. 291.
9. Samuel George Morton, *Crania americana* (Philadelphia, 1839). See also Stephen Jay Gould, *The Mismeasure of Man* (New York, 1981), pp. 30–72.

10. This was the argument put forth by the physician Edward H. Clarke in his *Sex in Education; or, a Fair Chance for the Girls* (Boston, 1873).
11. Samuel A. Cartwright, "Slavery in the Light of Ethnology," in E. N. Elliott, ed., *Cotton Is King, and Pro-Slavery Arguments* (Augusta, Ga., 1860), pp. 689–728.
12. See, for example, Charles Carroll, *The Negro a Beast . . . or . . . in the Image of God* (St. Louis, 1900). Carroll followed in the tradition of the seventeenth-century French pre-Adamite Isaac de la Peyrère, whose *Praeadamitae* was first published in 1655.
13. Carnegie and Rockefeller are cited in Richard Hofstadter, *Social Darwinism in American Thought* (New York, 1944).
14. The expression *Sozialdarwinismus* was first used in Germany in 1906 by S. R. Steinmetz in the *Zeitschrift für Sozialwissenschaft*, 9(1906): 423. The expression appears much earlier in French, as in Emile Gautier's 1880 book *Le Darwinisme sociale*. For the history of social Darwinism in Germany, see Gunter Mann, "Rassenhygiene-Sozialdarwinismus," in *Biologismus im 19. Jahrhundert*, ed. Gunter Mann (Stuttgart, 1973), pp. 73–93.
15. Alfred Ploetz, *Die Tüchtigkeit unsrer Rasse und der Schutz der Schwachen*, published as vol. 1 of his *Grundlinien einer Rassenhygiene* (Berlin, 1895), pp. 116–144.
16. John Haycraft, *Social Darwinism and Race Betterment* (London, 1895), pp. 51–57.
17. Alfred Ploetz, "Sozialpolitik und Rassenhygiene," *Archiv für Soziale Gesetzgebung und Statistik,* 17(1902): 393–425.
18. Ploetz, *Die Tüchtigkeit unsrer Rasse*, pp. 224–232. See also Loren Graham's "Science and Values: The Eugenics Movement in Germany and Russia in the 1920s," *American Historical Review,* 82(1977): 1133–64.
19. In the Nazi period the doctrine of descent (*Dezendenzlehre*) was often associated with the teachings of Ernst Haeckel, which did not meet with favor in Nazi circles. Haeckel was rarely cited by Nazi ideologues; his emphasis on the continuity of ape and human was seen as a source of friction between German scientists and Italian Catholics (see letter from Walter Gross to the Auswärtiges Amt, December 30, 1942, Hauptamt Wissenschaft, Yiddish Scientific Institute [YIVO]). The anthropologist Hans Weinert, for example, was criticized in 1942 as an *eifriger Verfechter Haeckelschen Gedanken* (Erxleben to Bechtold, February 4, 1943, Weinert file, Hauptamt Wissenschaft, YIVO), and for this reason was not considered employable for purposes of political propaganda. Dr. Gross, head of the Rassenpolitisches Amt, advocated maintaining a distance from the doctrine of human evolution (*menschliche Abstammungslehre*), not only because it was controversial but, more important, because it was "often associated in the eyes of the general public . . . with elements of Haeckel's materialist monism" (Gross, "Abschrift," January 1, 1939, Weinert file, Hauptamt Wissenschaft, YIVO). Early in the regime, Haeckel's books (along with those of Einstein, H. G. Wells, H. Mann, representatives of the Bauhaus, and many others) were banned from German bookstores on the

grounds that they represented a holdover of the "democratic-liberalistic spirit." See *Die Bücherei*, 2(1935): 279–280.
20. This oft-quoted passage is from Marx's letter of June 18, 1862, to Engels, reprinted in Ronald L. Meek, *Marx and Engels on the Population Bomb* (Berkeley, 1971), p. 195.
21. Published under the title *Natur und Staat* by Gustav Fischer (Jena, 1903–1907). For a history of the Krupp competition, see Sheila Weiss, "Race Hygiene and the Rational Management of National Efficiency: Wilhelm Schallmayer and the Origins of German Eugenics, 1890–1920," Ph.D. diss., Johns Hopkins University, 1983, pp. 130–175.
22. Heinrich Driesmans, *Die Wahlverwandtschaften der deutschen Blutmischung* (Leipzig, 1901); Wilhelm Jordan, *Zwei Wiegen* (Berlin, 1887). For a discussion of these and other early "utopias of human breeding," see Hedwig Conrad-Martius, *Utopien der Menschenzüchtung. Der Sozialdarwinismus und seine Folgen* (Munich, 1955).
23. *ARGB*, 1(1904): i–iv.
24. Rüdin was the brother of Ploetz's first wife; Nordenholz, who came from a wealthy landowning family in Argentina, was the brother of Ploetz's second wife. Family connections were also important in the associations of publisher J. F. Lehmann: Bruno K. Schultz, editor of Lehmann's journal *Volk und Rasse*, for example, was married to Lehmann's daughter. The early membership of the Society for Racial Hygiene can be found in the "1. und 2. Jahresbericht der Gesellschaft für Rassenhygiene" for June 22, 1905–December 20, 1906, in box 255, Deutsche Kongress-Zentrale, Hoover Institution Archives.
25. R 86/2371, fol. 1, p. 78, BA.
26. See Fritz Lenz, "Alfred Ploetz zum 70. Geburtstag am 22. August," *ARGB*, 24(1930): vii–xv; also *IÄB*, January 1936, p. 18; and Kroll, "Zur Entstehung," pp. 150–203.
27. Agnes Bluhm, "Zur Frage nach der generativen Tüchtigkeit der deutschen Frauen und der rassenhygienischen Bedeutung der ärztlichen Geburtshilfe," *ARGB*, 9(1912): 340–346. Bluhm, one of the earliest members of the Society for Racial Hygiene, first met Ploetz and his circle of friends when she was a medical student at Zurich in the 1880s. In 1905 she proposed that people not be allowed to marry without a medical certificate testifying they were free from venereal disease and what she called "constitutional insanity." In 1919 Bluhm joined the Kaiser Wilhelm Institut für Biologie, where she pursued research on sex roles in mammals, racial hygiene, and the *Rasseprozess der Frau*, for which she eventually became the first (and only?) woman in the Nazi period to win the Goethe Medallion for Art and Science. For a biography of Germany's leading woman racial hygienist, see Günther Just, "Agnes Bluhm und ihr Lebenswerk," in *Die Ärztin*, 17(1941): 516–526.
28. Hermann Siemens, "Die Proletarisierung unseres Nachwuchses, eine Gefahr unrassenhygienischer Bevölkerungspolitik," *ARGB*, 12(1916/18): 43–55.

29. Ploetz, *Die Tüchtigkeit unsrer Rasse*, pp. 202–207.
30. "The Word Eugenics," *Eugenical News*, 19(1934): 143; also Max von Gruber, *Ursachen und Bekämpfung des Geburtenrückgangs im Dritten Reich* (Munich, 1914), pp. 3–11. Nazi medical philosophers continued this attack on Malthus and the popularization of birth control associated with his name. In his remarkable "Der 14. Juli, 1789, deutsch gesehen" (*Ziel und Weg*, 9[1939]: 433), Ludwig Schmidt-Kehl warned that Malthus and his followers had "declared war on the child"; he asserted that the Nazis must struggle against the "Malthusian poison" represented by birth control and the associated *Zweikindersystem*.
31. Otto Bonhard, *Geschichte des Alldeutschen Verbandes* (Leipzig and Berlin, 1920), p. 1.
32. Wilhelm Frick, "Bevölkerungs- und Rassenpolitik," speech of June 28, 1933, printed as a pamphlet at Langensalza, 1933, pp. 1–7.
33. For a discussion of *Entnordung* and *Aufnordung*, see Hans F. K. Günther, *Rassenkunde des deutschen Volkes* (Munich, 1922, and subsequent editions), esp. the chapter on "Die Aufgabe."
34. Grotjahn's remarks are from the *Mitteilungen der Berliner Gesellschaft für Rassenhygiene*, October 1917, p. 2; Baur's remarks can be found in R 86/2371, fol. 1, p. 90, BA.
35. See, for example, "Der Neuaufbau des deutschen Familienlebens nach dem Krieg," *Beilage zur Darmstädter Zeitung*, November 8, 1916; also Emil Abderhalden's "Die Rassenhygienischen Wirkungen des Krieges," *Frankfurter Zeitung*, July 4, 1920.
36. Gunter Mann has made this point in his "Rassenhygiene-Sozialdarwinismus"; see also Georg Lilienthal, "Rassenhygiene im Dritten Reich," *Medizinhistorisches Journal*, 14(1979): 114–132.
37. Ploetz, *Die Tüchtigkeit unsrer Rasse*, pp. 90–176.
38. Hugo Ribbert, *Rassenhygiene, eine gemeinverständliche Darstellung* (Bonn, 1910), p. 6.
39. See, for example, Wilhelm Schallmayer's critique of "Gobineaus Rassenwerk und die moderne Gobineauschule," in *Zeitschrift für Sozialwissenschaft*, n. F., 1(1910): 553–572; also his "Einführung in die Rassenhygiene," in *Ergebnisse der Hygiene*, ed. W. Weichardt, vol. 2 (Berlin, 1917), p. 455. *Rassenhygiene* and *Rassehygiene* were only two of many words proposed to embrace the growing racial hygiene movement in the teens and twenties. Schallmayer described a *Vererbungshygiene*; Eugen Rösle preferred the term *Fortpflanzungshygiene*. Others proposed terms such as *Rassedienst, Rassenpflege, Entartungslehre, Regenerationslehre, Erbguthygiene, Nationalhygiene*, or *Volkshygiene*. These were also sometimes linked with allied sciences of *Anthropologie, Sozialanthropologie*, or *Rassenkunde*. For a bibliography of more than 500 books and articles on racial science prior to 1933, see Achim Gercke and Rudolf Kummer, *Die Rasse im Schrifttum, ein Wegweiser durch das rassenkundliche Schrifttum* (Berlin, 1933); for works up to 1936, see *Rassenkunde, eine Auswahl des wichtigsten Schrifttums*... (Stuttgart, 1937).
40. See Alfred Grotjahn, *Erlebtes und Erstrebtes* (Berlin, 1932), p. 131; also

Karl Heinz Roth, ed., *Erfassung zur Vernichtung* (Hamburg, 1984), pp. 30–56.
41. The British socialist J. B. S. Haldane, in his 1938 *Heredity and Politics*, argued that questions of eugenics "cut right across the usual political divisions"; he pointed out that the sterilization of defectives had been instituted in Denmark under a government considerably to the left of that in England (cited in Diane Paul, "Eugenics and the Left," *Journal of the History of Ideas*, 45[1984]: 570–571).
42. Loren Graham has described the Soviet eugenics movement in his "Science and Values"; see also Mark Adams, "From 'Gene Fund' to 'Gene Pool': On the Evolution of Evolutionary Language," *Studies in the History of Biology*, 3(1979): 241–285.
43. Georg Lilienthal, " 'Rheinlandbastarde,' Rassenhygiene und das Problem der rassenideologischen Kontinuität," *Medizinhistorisches Journal*, 15(1980): p. 432.
44. *Vorwärts—Beilage Frauenstimme*, April 10, 1930; cited in Noakes, "Nazism and Eugenics," pp. 87–88.
45. Jenny Blasbalg, "Ausländische und deutsche Gesetze und Gesetzentwürfe über Unfruchtbarmachung," *Zeitschrift für die gesamte Strafrechtswissenschaft*, 52(1932): 494–496.
46. Paul Weindling, "Weimar Eugenics: The Kaiser Wilhelm Institute for Anthropology, Human Heredity and Eugenics in Social Context," *Annals of Science*, 42(1985): 305.
47. Among historians, the association of eugenics and progressive thought dates back at least to Rudolf Vecoli's "Sterilization: A Progressive Measure?" *Wisconsin Magazine of History*, 43(1960): 190–202; see also Michael Freeden, "Eugenics and Progressive Thought: A Study in Ideological Affinity," *Historical Journal*, 22(1979): 645–671.
48. See Garland Allen, "Genetics, Eugenics and Society: Externalists in Contemporary History of Science," *Social Studies of Science*, 6(1976): 112; also Nils Roll-Hansen, "Eugenics before World War II, the Case of Norway," *History and Philosophy of the Life Sciences*, 2(1980): 296–297.
49. Karl Valentin Müller, "Rasse und Sozialismus," *Süddeutsche Monatshefte*, July 5, 1927, pp. 280–282. See also his *Der Aufstieg des Arbeiters durch Rasse und Meisterschaft* (Munich, 1935), p. 90. One should recall that a number of socialist scholars in America—such as Thorstein Veblen and Ernest Untermann—found a certain sympathy for the "Nordic cause." See, for example, "The Blond Race and the Aryan Culture" and "The Mutation Theory and the Blond Race," in Veblen's *The Place of Science in Modern Civilization* (New York, 1919).
50. It is the thesis of Gunter Mann of Mainz, for example, that the racism we associate with the Nordic movement emerged not among medical professionals, but rather first and foremost among scholars of German culture (*Germanisten*), anthropologists (*Sozialanthropologen*), and nonscientific laymen. Until sometime after World War I, in this view, the two traditions (medical racial hygiene, and nonmedical Nordic racism) remained distinct: racial hygienists warned against the degeneration (*Entartung*) of the human

race as a whole and called for general racial uplifting (*Aufartung*); social anthropologists warned against "de-nordification" (*Entnordung*) and called for "nordification" (*Aufnordung*). See Mann's "Rassenhygiene-Sozialdarwinismus." The most detailed history of the Nordic movement in Germany is Hans-Jürgen Lutzhöft's *Der Nordische Gedanke in Deutschland 1920 bis 1940* (Stuttgart, 1971).

51. Ploetz, *Die Tüchtigkeit unsrer Rasse*, p. 138; also p. 5.
52. Ibid., pp. 91–94.
53. Fritz Lenz, "Zur Erneuerung der Ethik," *Deutschlands Erneuerung*, 1(1917): 56. On the Ring der Norda, see Lutzhöft's *Der Nordische Gedanke*, p. 65.
54. Alfons Labisch and Florian Tennstedt, *Der Weg zum "Gesetz über die Vereinheitlichung des Gesundheitswesens" vom 3. Juli 1934*, published as volume 13 of *Schriftenreihe der Akademie für Öffentliches Gesundheitswesen in Düsseldorf* (Düsseldorf, 1985), p. 157.
55. *Politisch-anthropologische Revue*, 1(1902): 1–2.
56. *Fünfzig Jahre J. F. Lehmanns Verlag 1890–1940* (Munich, 1940), p. 43.
57. Editors of *Deutschlands Erneuerung* included Georg von Below, Houston Stewart Chamberlain, and Max von Gruber. Lehmann began publishing works for the Society for Racial Hygiene before World War I. For a history of the Verlag, see Melanie Lehmann, *Verleger J. F. Lehmann, ein Leben im Kampf für Deutschland* (Munich, 1935). For a postwar analysis, see Gary D. Stark, "Der Verleger als Kulturunternehmer: Der J. F. Lehmanns Verlag und Rassenkunde in der Weimarer Republik," *Archiv für Geschichte des Buchwesens*, 16(1976): 291–318.
58. Karl Saller reports that Lehmann originally approached the anthropologist Rudolf Martin to write a *Rassenkunde des deutschen Volkes;* Martin refused, however, and Lehmann turned to Günther for the book. See Karl Saller, *Die Rassenlehre des Nationalsozialismus in Wissenschaft und Propaganda* (Darmstadt, 1961), p. 27.
59. Racial theorists published by the Lehmann Verlag included L. F. Clauss, Martin Stämmler, Ernst Rüdin, Paul de Lagarde, Houston Stewart Chamberlain, Paul Schultze-Naumburg, Karl Valentin Müller, Ludwig Schemann, and many others. Journals published by Lehmann (apart from those already mentioned) included the *Archiv für Rassenbilder*, the *Zeitschrift für Rassenphysiologie*, the *Monatsschrift für Kriminalbiologie*, and *Die Gesundheitsführung*. After the outbreak of war in 1939, Lehmann published translations of German racial propaganda into Ukrainian and other languages in order to spread the racial gospel to the peoples of the occupied East. In October 1944 Lehmanns Verlag took over publication of the newly created *Medizinische Zeitschrift,* a journal formed from the merger of several of Germany's leading medical publications after they were forced to close "due to the measures of total war." See the *Medizinische Klinik*, 40(1944): 600. After the war the Lehmann Verlag was disbanded as a Nazi-linked organization. The Lehmann name, however, has continued to resonate in the West German medical community: today all official bookstores of the West German Medical Association (the Deutsche Ärzteverein,

with its associated Deutscher Ärzteverlag) bear the name J. F. Lehmann. They no longer belong to the Lehmann/Spatz family, however. I would like to thank Florian Tennstedt for drawing this to my attention.
60. *Ziel und Weg,* 5(1935): 27. Racial hygienists who received the coveted Adlerschild included Ernst Rüdin (in 1944), for his work as a "pathbreaker in the field of human hereditary care," and Eugen Fischer (also in 1944), in recognition of his status as "the founder of human genetics." See *Der Erbarzt,* 11(1944): 54, 83.
61. Hans F. K. Günther, *Mein Eindruck von Hitler* (Pähl, 1969), pp. 17–19. It was Ploetz who suggested to Günther the title for his inaugural lecture: "Die Aufgabe der Sozioanthropologie."
62. Theobald Lang, "Der Nationalsozialismus als politischer Ausdruck unserer biologischen Kenntnis," *Nationalsozialistische Monatshefte,* 1(1930): 417–418.
63. Fritz Lenz, "Alfred Ploetz zum 70. Geburtstag am 22. August," *ARGB,* 24(1930): xiv.
64. *Ziel und Weg,* 6(1936): 125.
65. Unpublished Congress correspondence in the possession of Edith Zerbin-Rüdin, Munich; also *Der Erbarzt,* 1(1934): 94.
66. Alfred Ploetz, "Rassenhygiene und Krieg," *ARGB,* 29(1935): 365.
67. *Ziel und Weg,* 12(1942): 217.
68. In 1936 Eugen Fischer noted in the internal reports of the Kaiser Wilhelm Gesellschaft that Muckermann left the Fischer Institute "for political reasons" (Abschrift Fischer, June 14, 1936, Generalverwaltung 2406, fol. 203, MPGA). Muckermann incurred the wrath of Nazi medical leaders for maintaining, in a lecture of April 1933, that racial intermarriage produced a higher form of culture (*Ziel und Weg,* 3[1933]: 133). In 1934 Muckermann published research purporting to demonstrate that the families of the Prussian police were not breeding at rates sufficient to reproduce themselves. See *Zeitschrift für Morphologie und Anthropologie,* 34(1934): 270–285. One wonders whether Muckermann changed his views concerning the "shortage of Prussian police" after these same police helped to enforce a ban on his books, his travel abroad, and his speaking in public.
69. *Ziel und Weg,* 3(1933): 272.
70. *Fünfzig Jahre J. F. Lehmanns Verlag,* p. 67.
71. Fritz Lenz, *Menschliche Auslese und Rassenhygiene* (Munich, 1921), pp. 112–113. Alfons Fischer's "Über Eugenik," *Klinische Fortbildung,* 1(1933): 377–418, provides a history of the various interpretations of the word *eugenics.*
72. Luxenburger's speech was reported in *Ärztliche Rundschau,* 45(1935): 136.
73. Lang, "Der Nationalsozialismus," p. 393.
74. Eugen Fischer put the matter succinctly in his 1933 inaugural address as rector of the University of Berlin: "What Darwin was not able to do, genetics has achieved. It has destroyed the theory of the equality of man." See his *Der völkische Staat biologisch gesehen* (Berlin, 1933), pp. 11–12.
75. Jean-Baptiste Lamarck, *Philosophie zoologique* (Paris, 1809).

76. See Richard Lewontin and Richard Levins, "The Problem of Lysenkoism," in their *Dialectical Biologist* (Cambridge, Mass., 1985), pp. 163–196.
77. Mendel's experiments were presented to the Natural Sciences Society of Brno (in what is now Czechoslovakia) in February and March 1865; these results were subsequently published under the title "Versuche über Pflanzenhybriden," in *Verhandlungen des Naturforschenden Vereins in Brünn,* 4(1866): 3–22.
78. August Weismann presented his general principles in *Das Keimplasma. Eine Theorie der Vererbung* (Jena, 1892), translated as *The Germ-Plasm: A Theory of Heredity* (New York, 1893).
79. William Bateson, *Problems of Genetics* (New Haven, 1913), p. 190.
80. See, for example, Lothar Löffler, "Die wissenschaftlichen Grundlagen der Rassenhygiene," 4. *Beiheft zum Reichs-Gesundheitsblatt,* December 28, 1938; also "Die Unsterblichkeit des Keimplasmas," *Akademia,* October 4, 1938, p. 1.
81. Eugen Fischer edited the most important biography of Weismann after its author, Ernst Gaupp, died in 1916 (see Ernst Gaupp, *August Weismann, sein Leben und sein Werk* [Jena, 1917]). For recent historical analyses of Weismann's work, see the contributions to the spring 1985 issue of *Freiburger Universitätsblätter,* esp. Frederick Churchill, "Weismanns Vorläufer und die Rezeption seiner Werke," pp. 107–124.
82. Alfred Ploetz expressed his doubts about Lamarckian inheritance in his 1895 *Die Tüchtigkeit unsrer Rasse* (pp. 22–25); Wilhelm Schallmayer rejected the inheritance of acquired characters in his 1903 *Vererbung und Auslese* (Jena, 1903), p. 63. Ploetz noted in his 1895 treatise that "roughly three-quarters" of all contemporary biologists rejected the inheritance of acquired characters (p. 214). Sheila Weiss points out that Schallmayer devoted more than forty pages to Weismann's hereditary theory (Weiss, "Race Hygiene," p. 155).
83. Hermann W. Siemens, "Was ist Rassenhygiene?" *Deutschlands Erneuerung,* 2(1918): 280.
84. For issues touching on this question, see George W. Stocking, "Lamarckianism in American Social Science: 1890–1915," *Journal of the History of Ideas,* 23(1962): 239–256.
85. *Zeitschrift für Volksaufartung und Erbkunde,* 1(1926): 4.
86. The meeting of the Deutsche Gesellschaft für Vererbungswissenschaft at Würzburg, September 24–26, 1938, is reported in *Informationsdienst, Rassenpolitisches Amt der NSDAP,* December 20, 1938. I shall henceforth refer to this journal as *Informationsdienst,* which should not be confused with *Informationsdienst des Hauptamtes für Volksgesundheit der NSDAP.*
87. *Informationsdienst,* October 30, 1938.
88. "Marxismus und Rassengedanke," *Informationsdienst,* February 20, 1937.
89. Socialists who supported Lamarckian inheritance included Paul Kammerer, Benno Chajes, and Gertrud Lukas. For Kammerer's views on this question, see his *Neuvererbung* (Stuttgart, 1925). After his death, Kammerer was eulogized in one Austrian socialist paper as "a comrade in the struggle for a

socialist future" (cited in Arthur Koestler, *The Case of the Midwife Toad* [New York, 1971], p. 18). For the views of the Association of Socialist Physicians on this question, see Chapter 9.
90. There are a number of exceptions to this generalization. Some conservatives supported Lamarckian inheritance, and some socialists supported Mendelian genetics or even racial hygiene. Ludwig Plate, for example, successor to Ernst Haeckel's chair at the University of Jena and one of the early editors of the *Archiv für Rassen- und Gesellschaftsbiologie*, maintained in 1930 that Richard Goldschmidt's heat-induced mutations in *Drosophila* proved the inheritance of acquired characteristics (*ARGB*, 24[1930]: 24). According to Hans F. K. Günther, Hitler believed in the inheritance of acquired characters (*Mein Eindruck von Adolf Hitler* [Pähl, 1968], p. 94). For an example of a systematic Lamarckian eugenics, see V. Slepkov's *Evgenik* (Moscow, 1925).
91. Otmar von Verschuer, in his "Zehn Jahre Rassenpolitisches Amt" (*Der Erbarzt*, 11[1944]: 51), says the ideology of "the omnipotence of the environment" (*Allmacht der Umwelt*) has suffered "shipwreck" under the Nazis.
92. Conrad-Martius, *Utopien der Menschenzüchtung*, p. 167. See also Chapter 2 for Fritz Lenz's extraordinary views on this question.
93. Histories of the "Lysenko affair" include Loren Graham, *Science and Philosophy in the Soviet Union* (New York, 1972), esp. pp. 195–256, and Zhores Medvedev, *The Rise and Fall of T. D. Lysenko* (New York, 1969). Richard Lewontin and Richard Levins' "The Problem of Lysenkoism," in their *Dialectical Biologist* (Cambridge, Mass., 1985), pp. 163–196, is one of the few accounts to stress the importance of hostility to Nazi racial theory in the complex of events that gave rise to Soviet Lysenkoism. See also David Joravsky, *The Lysenko Affair* (Chicago, 1970).
94. Loren Graham points out that the Russian geneticist Filipchenko recognized in the mid-twenties that Lamarckian heredity might have effects *opposite* to those intended by revolutionary Lysenkoists: if acquired characteristics could be inherited, then centuries of impoverishment and deprivation suffered by peasants and workers should have become imprinted on the worker's hereditary constitution. Better that each generation start afresh than bear the scars of previous suffering! See Graham, "Science and Values," pp. 1152–53.
95. Kammerer died in 1926 by his own hand, embroiled in controversy amid charges that he had forged his experiments demonstrating the inheritance of acquired characteristics. Arthur Koestler, in his *Case of the Midwife Toad*, documents the history of the Kammerer controversy.
96. Fritz Lenz, *Menschliche Auslese und Rassenhygiene (Eugenik)*, 3rd ed. (Munich, 1931), p. 403.
97. *Ziel und Weg*, 9(1939): 307–308. The Moscow Museum had sponsored a similar exhibit in 1933 attacking "the lies of bourgeois anthropology"; see *Volk und Rasse*, 9(1934): 126–127.
98. Fritz Brennecke, ed., *Vom deutschen Volk und seinem Lebensraum, Handbuch für die Schulungsarbeit in der Hitler Jugend* (Munich, 1937), pp. 45–

47. The handbook has been translated into English by H. L. Childs as *The Nazi Primer: Official Handbook for Schooling the Hitler Youth* (New York, 1938).
99. Genetics was so important in Nazi ideology that party officials found it "astonishing" that a geneticist such as Hans Stubbe could be so fascinated by the science of genetics without belonging to the party or any of its formations. This was the judgment of a 1938 Nazi party review committee headed by Professors G. Franz and W. Grundig. Stubbe expressed Marxist leanings before 1933; shortly after Hitler's seizure of power, however, he applied to join the SS and the SA but was refused admission. In the early 1940s he was denied a promotion, largely as a result of his left-wing sentiments prior to 1933 (Berlin Document Center).
100. See "Die volkshygienische Bedeutung der Fruchtabtreibung" and Regierungsrat de Bary's "Rassenunterschiede zwischen Deutschen und Juden," both in R 86/2371, fols. 153 and 174, BA. On the formation of the Prussian Landesgesundheitsrat für Rassenhygiene und Bevölkerungswesen, see R 86/2371, fols. 190–191, BA; also Weindling, "Weimar Eugenics," p. 304.
101. R 86/2371, fols. 190–191, BA.
102. The 1922 correspondence of Bumm and Rösle on these matters can be found in R 86/2371, fols. 193–196, BA.
103. "Rassenkreuzung und geistige Leistung," *IÄB*, March/April 1936, p. 35. Fischer's speech was originally published in the *Vossische Zeitung*, February 2, 1933.
104. *Volk und Rasse*, 8(1933): 136.
105. Weindling, "Weimar Eugenics," p. 316.
106. Eugen Fischer, "Die Fortschritte der menschlichen Erblehre als Grundlage eugenischer Bevölkerungspolitik," *Deutsche Medizinische Wochenschrift*, 59(1933): 1069–70. For a bibliography of Fischer's writings on race, see the *Festschrift* for Fischer in the 1934 issue of *Zeitschrift für Morphologie und Anthropologie*.
107. "Tätigkeitsbericht von Prof. Dr. Fischer vom 1.4.35–31.3.36," Generalverwaltung 2406, fol. 211; also 2404, MPGA.
108. Generalverwaltung 2406, fol. 211, and Generalverwaltung 2404, fol. 49, MPGA. The first course for SS physicians at the Kaiser Wilhelm Institute for Anthropology began on October 1, 1934.
109. "Tätigkeitsbericht von Anfang Juli 1933 bis 1. April 1935," Generalverwaltung 2404, fol. 49; also Generalverwaltung 2406, fol. 52b, 74–76, MPGA.
110. Generalverwaltung 363, Finanzielle Sicherstellung 1935 30.7.1934-3.4.1936, MPGA; also Generalverwaltung 2406, fol. 192. Income for the Fischer Institute rose to 176,000 RM in 1937, fell to a low of 144,000 RM in 1940, and then rose again to 183,000 RM in 1941. As late as 1943 the institute was still receiving 161,000 RM, plus 47,000 RM from the Deutsche Industrie Bank (Generalverwaltung 2407-09).
111. See *Journal of the Anthropological Institute*, 5(1875): 391–406. It was eight years after this article, in his *Inquiries into Human Faculty* (New

York, 1883), p. 17, that Galton coined the word *eugenics* to designate the science and art of improving the human race by selective breeding.
112. On Hans F. K. Günther's argument that divorce is a product of "the inheritance of a lack of choice instinct," see his "Gibt es eine 'Vererbung elterlichen Eheschicksals'?" *Rasse,* 11(1944): 1. For an extended review of twin research up through the early Nazi period, see Heinrich Kranz, "Zwillingsforschung," *Klinische Fortbildung,* 4(1937): 134–195.
113. R 73/13816, BA.
114. "Tätigkeitsbericht," July 5, 1933, Generalverwaltung 2404, MPGA. Fischer's assertion is from *Deutsche Medizinische Wochenschrift,* 59(1933): 1068.
115. *Ziel und Weg,* 9(1939): 449. Frick also ordered that all marriages of blood relatives be reported. The Kaiser Wilhelm Institute for Anthropology received monies for twin research from sources outside Germany, even well into the Nazi era: the Rockefeller Foundation, for example, provided funds to the Fischer Institute for twin studies until the mid-1930s, and when the foundation stopped this funding, the philanthropist James Loeb gave $1 million to the institute to continue research in this area.
116. R 73/12756, R 73/13294, and R 73/14120, BA.
117. R 73/14560 and R 73/15195; R 73/13816 and R 73/14398, BA.
118. R 73/15342, fol. 64, BA. Verschuer's project is listed as pursuing the study of *Spezifische Eiweisskörper*. Benno Müller-Hill discovered this document in the Bundesarchiv Koblenz. See his *Tödliche Wissenschaft* (Reinbek bei Hamburg, 1984), p. 23.
119. Müller-Hill, *Tödliche Wissenschaft,* pp. 23–24; see also Miklos Nyiszli, *Auschwitz: A Doctor's Eyewitness Account* (New York, 1960).
120. R 73/13790, BA.
121. Fritz Lenz, "Rassenhygiene und klinische Medizin," *Klinische Wochenschrift,* 12(1933): 1572.

2. "Neutral Racism"

1. Sheila Weiss has discussed the differences between the Munich and Berlin Societies for Racial Hygiene in her "Race Hygiene."
2. "Zehn Grundsätze des Deutschen Bundes für Volksaufartung und Erbkunde" (1925), in R 86/2371, fol. 315, BA.
3. *Zeitschrift für Volksaufartung und Erbkunde,* 1(1926): 2. The *Zeitschrift,* published 1926–1930, was succeeded by the short-lived *Eugenik: Erblehre, Erbpflege* (1930–1931).
4. Hermann Muckermann, "Eugenik und Katholizismus," *Eugenik und Weltanschauung,* ed. Günther Just (Berlin, 1932).
5. Graham, "Science and Values," pp. 1138–40; also Lilienthal, "Rassenhygiene im Dritten Reich," p. 117. Paul Popenoe presents a discussion of these tensions in his "Anthropology and Eugenics," *Journal of Heredity,* 22(1931): 277–280.
6. Fritz Lenz, "Alfred Ploetz zum 70. Geburtstag am 22. Aug. 1930," *ARGB,* 24(1930): xiv. See also his "Die Stellung des Nationalsozialismus zur Ras-

senhygiene," 25(1931): 300–308. In the 1931 edition of his *Menschliche Auslese* (p. 416), Lenz noted that the Nazi party platform authored by Gottfried Feder (*Das Programm der N.S.D.A.P.* [Munich, 1930], p. 32) included racial hygiene as an explicit goal.

7. See Lenz's review of Just's *Eugenik und Weltanschauung* in *MMW*, 80(1933): 392–393.
8. *ARGB*, 27(1933): 419.
9. Fritz Lenz to SS Gruppenführer Pancke, January 5, 1940, "Bemerkungen zur Umsiedlung unter dem Gesichtspunkt der Rassenpflege," now in the Berlin Document Center. Lenz called the resettlement of the occupied East (by Germans to replace Slavs and Jews, especially in Danzig–West Prussia and the Warthegau) "the most weighty task of racial politics. It will determine the racial character of the population in this area for centuries to come." Lenz advised that the selection of settlers for the newly occupied regions be "according to the criteria used by the SS to select racial settlers." This letter is discussed by Renate Rissom in her "Fritz Lenz und die Rassenhygiene," *Abhandlungen zur Geschichte der Medizin und der Naturwissenschaften*, 47(1983): 82–83.
10. For the life of Lenz, see Rissom, "Fritz Lenz und die Rassenhygiene."
11. Fritz Lenz, *Die Rasse als Wertprinzip* (Munich, 1933).
12. Fritz Lenz, "Die sogenannte Vererbung erworbener Eigenschaften," *Medizinische Klinik*, 10(1914): 202–204, 244–247.
13. Fritz Lenz, "Alfred Ploetz zum 70. Geburtstag am 22. August," *ARGB*, 24(1930): xiv.
14. Fritz Lenz, "Über die krankhaften Erbanlagen des Mannes und die Bestimmung des Geschlechts beim Menschen," med. diss., University of Jena, 1912.
15. Baur-Fischer-Lenz, p. 565. The passages cited here and in what follows are from the English translation of Erwin Baur, Eugen Fischer, and Fritz Lenz, *Grundriss der menschlichen Erblichkeitslehre und Rassenhygiene*, vol. 1, 3rd ed. (Munich, 1927), translated by E. Paul and C. Paul as *Human Heredity* (London, 1931). Baur-Fischer-Lenz was originally published in 1921 in two volumes. The first volume, *Menschliche Erblichkeitslehre*, was written by all three authors: Baur provided an overview of the principles of genetics, Fischer described the "racial differences among humans," and Lenz described what he called "human genetic pathologies" and the racial qualities I shall be citing here. The second volume, *Menschliche Auslese und Rassenhygiene (Eugenik)*, was written by Lenz alone and was devoted entirely to the subject of racial hygiene. This volume was never translated.
16. Baur-Fischer-Lenz, pp. 597–598.
17. Ibid., pp. 598–599.
18. Fritz Lenz, "Über die idioplasmatischen Ursachen der physiologischen und pathologischen Sexualcharaktere des Menschen," *ARGB*, 9(1912): 570.
19. Baur-Fischer-Lenz, p. 602.
20. Ibid., pp. 615–626.
21. Ibid., p. 629.
22. Ibid., p. 634.

23. Ibid., p. 636.
24. Ibid., pp. 671–672.
25. Ibid., pp. 644, 668. In 1938, at a meeting of the Gesellschaft Deutscher Naturforscher und Ärzte in Stuttgart, Lenz argued that some European Jews have blond hair not because of racial mixing, but because of local "ecological adaptations." He asserted that Jews were an "ecological race"—adapted, that is, to a particular environmental niche rather than to a particular geographical region. Lenz also elaborated at this meeting his theory that bacteria are responsible for human racial differentiation (for example, malarial plasmodia in blacks, tubercular bacilli in whites). See *Öffentlicher Gesundheitsdienst,* 4(1938): 659–660.
26. Baur-Fischer-Lenz, p. 673.
27. Ibid., p. 674.
28. Ibid., p. 677.
29. Ibid., pp. 674–675.
30. Ibid., p. 648.
31. Ibid., p. 656. Lenz left no doubts about his own racial affiliation: interviewed in the fall of 1933, shortly after Wilhelm Frick named him a member of the Sachverständigenbeirat für Bevölkerungs- und Rassenpolitik, Lenz claimed that "the fate of the Nordic race is our fate" (Köhn-Behrens, *Was Ist Rasse?* p. 95).
32. Baur-Fischer-Lenz, p. 692.
33. Ibid., p. 600.
34. Ibid., pp. 674–677.
35. See the bibliography of Lenz's works in Rissom, "Fritz Lenz und die Rassenhygiene," pp. 111–140.
36. For Stubbe's review, see *Fortschritte der Medizin,* 51(1933): 1143; Verschuer reviewed the 1936 edition in *Zeitschrift für Morphologie und Anthropologie,* 36(1937): 362–363.
37. Baur-Fischer-Lenz, reviewed in *Russkii evgenicheskii zhurnal,* 2(1924): 179–180. This and other Soviet reviews are discussed in Loren Graham's "Science and Values," p. 1147.
38. See, for example, the journal *Volksgezondheid,* 2(1942).
39. *Quadrivio,* October 10, 1937. Translated as "Rassenschutz in Deutschland," in NS 19/3434, BA.
40. Baur-Fischer-Lenz, *Grundriss der menschlichen Erblichkeitslehre und Rassenhygiene,* reviewed by Paul Popenoe in *Journal of Heredity,* 14(1923): 336; reviewed also by Walter Landauer in 19(1928): 122. R. Ruggles Gates gave the work a sympathetic review in *Eugenics Review,* 23(1931): 73–74.
41. L. A. G. Strong, in *New Statesman and Nation,* October 17, 1931, p. 482; S. J. Holmes, in *Journal of Heredity,* 22(1931): 356. Holmes expressed his hope that the high price of the American edition ($8.00) would not "unduly restrict the dissemination of this very valuable work."
42. See *The Spectator,* August 22, 1931, p. 250; also *Sociological Education,* 6(1932–33): 316; and *American Sociological Review,* 3(1938): 147.
43. *Quarterly Review of Biology,* 3(1928): 136; *Sociology and Social Research,* 16(1932): 281.

44. H. J. Muller, review of Baur-Fischer-Lenz, in *Birth Control Review*, 17(1933): 19–21. I would like to thank John Beatty for drawing this review to my attention. For Muller's more general views on eugenics, see his "Dominance of Economics over Eugenics," *Scientific Monthly*, 37(1933): 40–47.
45. *American Sociological Review*, 3(1938): 147–148.
46. Fritz Lenz, "Zur Erneuerung der Ethik," *Deutschlands Erneuerung*, 1(1917), republished as *Die Rasse als Wertprinzip* (Munich, 1933).
47. Rissom, "Fritz Lenz und die Rassenhygiene," p. 19. Max von Gruber, Lenz's mentor and a member of the editorial board of *Deutschlands Erneuerung*, maintained that "nearly everyone" listed as editor of the journal was a member of the Deutsche Vaterlandspartei. See Gruber, "Ziel und Weg der Deutschen Vaterlandspartei," *Deutschlands Erneuerung*, 2(1918): 64.
48. Rissom, "Fritz Lenz und die Rassenhygiene," pp. 38–43.
49. Ibid., pp. 38–39.
50. Lenz, *Die Rasse als Wertprinzip*, p. 7.
51. Hans F. K. Günther, *Mein Eindruck auf Hitler* (Pähl, 1969), p. 93. Lenz's son, Widukind Lenz, reports that his father "learned from Hanfstängels or someone in Lehmanns Verlag" that Hitler had read Baur-Fischer-Lenz while in Landsberg prison (Müller-Hill, *Tödliche Wissenschaft*, p. 123).
52. See Rissom, "Fritz Lenz und die Rassenhygiene," p. 85.
53. Even before his support for Hitler, Lenz saw hope in the rule of Mussolini (ibid., p. 87). See also the enthusiasm expressed by Lenz for Hitler in the interview with Köhn-Behrens, in her *Was Ist Rasse?* pp. 90–95.
54. Lenz, *Menschliche Auslese*, p. 417.
55. Berlin Document Center. Lenz was also a member of the NS Dozentenbund and the NS Volkswohlfahrt; he joined the Nazi Physicians' League in 1940 (no. 31,582). His wife was also a member of the party.
56. Fritz Lenz, "Über Rassen und Rassenbildung," *Unterrichtsblätter für Mathematik und Naturwissenschaften*, 40(1934): 183–187.
57. Baur-Fischer-Lenz, vol. 1, 4th ed., 1936, p. v. The extensive racial characterizations I have cited remained essentially unaltered.
58. Ernst Lehmann, *Biologie im Leben der Gegenwart* (Munich, 1933), p. 5.
59. Lenz, *Menschliche Auslese*, p. 417.

3. Political Biology

1. Hans Weinert, in his 1934 *Biologische Grundlagen für Rassenkunde und Rassenhygiene* (Stuttgart), asserts that biology represents the foundation of the Nazi world view (*Biologie als Kernstück der nationalsozialistischer Weltanschauung*). He repeats this claim in the 1943 enlarged edition of the book (p. 165).
2. Max Weinreich, *Hitler's Professors: The Part of Scholarship in Germany's Crimes against the Jewish People* (New York, 1946), p. 34; see also *Ziel und Weg*, 5(1935): 181.
3. *Nationalsozialistische Monatshefte*, 2(1931): 38.

4. See Fritz Bartels, "Der Arzt als Gesundheitsführer des deutschen Volkes," supplement to *DÄ*, 68(1938): 4–9.
5. "Vom Neuen Aufbau," *Ziel und Weg*, 3(1933): 78; also *Ärztin*, 13(1937): 275.
6. *MMW*, 80(1933): 517.
7. "Satzungen des NSDÄB," reel 83, fol. 1702, NSDAP Hauptarchiv, BA. This first charter of the NSDÄB noted that members of the league need not be members of the Nazi party, as long as they adhered to the goals of the league and the National Socialist world view. Subsequent charters, however, required that one be a member of the party (Hadrich, "Einführung," p. 115). At the first meeting of the league, Ludwig Liebl was elected chairman, Theobald Lang secretary, and Gerhard Wagner treasurer. At the September 1932 meeting in Braunschweig, Wagner was elected chairman; Eugen Stähle and Ernst Wegner were elected to the governing board.
8. Theobald Lang, "Zur Einführung," *Ziel und Weg*, 1(1931): 3; Gregor Strasser, "Geleitwort," *Ziel und Weg*, 1(1931): 2. For the earlier history of the NSDÄB, see Albert Zapp, "Untersuchungen zum Nationalsozialistischen Deutschen Ärztebund (NSDÄB)," med. diss., University of Kiel, 1979, pp. 28–32.
9. Fridolf Kudlien has shown that among 2,525 party members between 1919 and 1921, 64(2.5 percent) were either doctors or medical students. (Among these, only one was a woman.) Given that 290 members at this time were designated either as students or as having some other academic affiliation, this means that medical men comprised about 22 percent of those with academic affiliation. See Kudlien's "Ärzte in der Bewegung," in *Medizin im Nationalsozialismus*, published by the Evangelische Akademie Bad Boll as part of their *Protokolldienst*, 23(1982): 24–28, 50–51.
10. Karl Ludwig, *Technik und Ingenieure im Dritten Reich* (Düsseldorf, 1979), p. 107. Hermann Weinkauf reports that among Prussia's 7,000 judges, only 30 had joined the Nazi party by January 30, 1933 (see his *Die Deutsche Justiz und der Nationalsozialismus* [Stuttgart, 1968], p. 108). Michael Kater points out that from 1925 to 1944, physicians were members of the Nazi party roughly three times as often as the German population as a whole (Kater, *The Nazi Party* [Cambridge, Mass., 1983], pp. 112–113). At the University of Halle, more than 80 percent of the medical faculty were members of the Nazi party; nearly 80 percent of Thüringen's physicians joined the party. See Thom and Spaar, eds., *Medizin im Faschismus*, pp. 64, 322.
11. Georg Lilienthal, "Der Nationalsozialistische Ärztebund (1929–1943/1945)," in *Ärzte im Nationalsozialismus*, ed. Kudlien, p. 116.
12. For an early list of members in the Munich branch of the league, see the "Liste der Mitglieder des NSD-Ärztebundes für München und Vororte, Stand vom 21. Nov. 1932," T-580, roll 28, National Archives, Washington, D.C.
13. Michael H. Kater, "Hitlerjugend und Schule im Dritten Reich," *Historische Zeitschrift*, 228(1979): 609–610.
14. Otmar Freiherr von Verschuer joined the National Socialist Physicians'

League on October 15, 1942 (no. 38,335). He had joined the Nazi party earlier, in July 1940 (no. 8,140,376). These and all subsequent Nazi party records I shall be citing are from the Berlin Document Center, unless otherwise indicated.
15. Lilienthal, "Der Nationalsozialistische Ärztebund," p. 117.
16. Julius Hadrich, "Die Ärztekammer Berlin in der Statistik," *ÄfB*, 42(1937): 192–194.
17. Julius Hadrich, "Zur Statistik der Pommerschen Ärzteschaft," *Ärzteblatt für Pommern, Mecklenburg und Lübeck*, 4(1937): 95–96; compare Lilienthal, "Der Nationalsozialistische Ärztebund," p. 117.
18. "Vertreter der Ärzteschaft beim Reichskanzlei," *DÄ*, 63(1933): 153.
19. *DÄ*, 63(1933): 666.
20. *MMW*, 80(1933): 517. See also Comité des Délégations Juives, *Die Lage der Juden in Deutschland 1933* (Frankfurt, 1983), first published in 1934 in Paris, esp. pp. 195–239.
21. I have translated Deutscher Ärztevereinsbund as "German Medical Association" for the sake of brevity; a more accurate translation would be "Union of German Medical Associations." The Ärztevereinsbund was the umbrella organization for the various local medical societies in Germany. The Hartmannbund (also known as the Verband der Ärzte Deutschlands or the Leipziger Verband), was a separate body organized in 1900 to provide physicians with bargaining power in negotiating with the insurance companies. By the end of 1932, 43,000 of Germany's 49,000 physicians were members of the Hartmannbund.
22. *MMW*, 80(1933): 517. The full text of this announcement, dated March 24, 1933, appeared under the title "Die Säuberungsaktion innerhalb der deutschen Ärzteschaft," *Völkischer Beobachter*, March 27, 1933.
23. *MMW*, 80(1933): 517. See also *DÄ*, 63(1933): 133–134.
24. "Bericht über die Sitzung," *DÄ*, 63(1933): 141–143.
25. "An die Mitglieder des Deutschen Apotheker-Vereins!" *Apotheker Zeitung*, April 1, 1933, reprinted in *Die Lage der Juden in Deutschland 1933*, published by the Comité des Délégations Juives, p. 204.
26. Ramm, *Ärztliche Rechts- und Standeskunde*, pp. 45–52. The "Satzung der Kassenärztliche Vereinigung Deutschlands" (KVD) can be found printed as a supplement to March 15, 1942, issue of the *ÄRW*.
27. "Das Neue Studentenrecht," *MMW*, 80(1933): 633.
28. *Berliner Tierärztliche Wochenschrift*, 50(1934): 95. Weber had joined the Freikorps in 1919 and participated in the "liberation" of Munich; in 1920 he married J. F. Lehmann's daughter. He joined the SS in November 1933 and rose to the rank of Gruppenführer in 1944.
29. Other leaders in German medicine in this period include Richard Liebenow, Chef des Amtes für Gesundheit der Hitler Jugend; Robert Hördemann, Reichsarzt der Hitler Jugend; Fritz Strohschneider, head of the Amt Gesundheit der NS-Volkswohlfahrt; Werner Bockhacker, head of the Amt für Volksgesundheit der Deutschen Arbeits-Front (beginning in 1939, replacing Focke). Leaders were also appointed for occupied territories. Josef Walbaum was head of the Abteilung Gesundheitswesen in occupied Poland;

Harald Waegner was in charge of the Interior Ministry's Abteilung Gesundheit for occupied eastern territories after 1939. Adolf Zimprich was Führer of the *volksdeutsche* physicians in Slovakia; A. Gabriel held an equivalent position for ethnic Slovakian physicians. Several countries occupied by Germany remodeled their medical organizations according to the Nazi *Führerprinzip:* in the (Nazi) Dutch Medisch Front, for example, besides a leader for the profession as a whole (K. Keijer), there were leaders for the separate fields of dentistry, pharmacy, and so on. Lea Thimm headed the *gleichgeschaltete* Bund deutscher Ärztinnen.

30. Schleswig-Holstein had sixteen of these *Kreisamtsleiter*—positions generally filled by the *Kreisobsleute* of the Nazi Physicians' League. For a list of leaders in the Hauptamt für Volksgesundheit in 1936, see the "Liste der politischen Leiter des Hauptamts für Volksgesundheit," T-580, roll 27, National Archives, Washington, D.C.
31. *IÄB,* January 1934, p. 18. See also Werner Bockhacker, "Der deutsche Arzt als Gesundheitsführer," *DÄ,* 68(1938): 115.
32. See, for example, *DÄ,* 63(1933): 658; also *Zeitschrift für Ärztliche Fortbildung,* 34(1937): 144.
33. Gerhard Wagner, son of a surgeon (Wilhelm Wagner), was born in Neu-Heiduk, Upper Silesia, in 1888. He participated in World War I as a physician and in 1919 became a member of the anticommunist Freikorps Eppingen (and later helped found the Freikorps Oberland). He abandoned medical practice after he was elected member of the Reichstag (representing the Nazi party) in 1933. Wagner was a protégé of Rudolf Hess, who was Wagner's patient. Wagner died on March 25, 1939, at the age of fifty-one; his funeral was an elaborate affair, attracting Hitler along with most of the top Nazi military officers. On August 20, 1939, ten days before the invasion of Poland, 1,200 Nazi Storm Troopers of the SA-Standarte 1 were named the Gerhard Wagner Brigade. For the biography of Germany's most important medical man, see *Tilsiter allgemeine Zeitung,* April 30, 1933; also *Völkischer Beobachter,* August 18, 1938. For Wagner's collected speeches, see his *Reden und Aufrufe,* ed. Leonardo Conti (Berlin, 1943).
34. Walder, "Abschied vom alten Ärzteblatt," *DA,* 63(1933): 276; also 263–266. The two journals merged on July 1, 1933. Karl Haedenkamp, longstanding editor of the Hartmannbund's *Ärztliche Mitteilungen,* became editor of the newly "coordinated" journal.
35. Hadrich, "Einführung," pp. 134–135.
36. See Jost Willms, "Vom unausrottbaren Fremdwort," *DÄ,* 63(1933): 177–178; also C. Reinhardt, "Mehr Deutsche in der Fachsprache," *Berliner Tierärztliche Wochenschrift,* 50(1934): 366, and Carl Haeberlin, "Die deutsche Sprache im ärztlichen Schrifttum," *Deutsche Medizinische Wochenschrift,* 65(1939): 1053–55.
37. *Informationsdienst des Hauptamtes für Volksgesundheit der NSDAP,* October/December 1943, p. 122. For an analysis of the Nazi transformation of language, see Claus Müller, *The Politics of Communication* (New York, 1973); also Heinz Paechter, *Nazi Deutsch: A Glossary of Contemporary German Usage* (New York, 1944).

38. Reported in *IÄB*, January 1934, p. 16.
39. On January 21, 1933, the *Ärztliche Mitteilungen* announced a contest on the question, "How can practicing physicians best participate in genetic or eugenic research and data gathering?" offering prizes of 500 RM, 300 RM, and 200 RM for the best answer (p. 55). The July 14, 1933, issue of the *Deutsche Medizinische Wochenschrift* was devoted to "Erbbiologie und Eugenik," as was the April 1, 1934 issue of the *Zeitschrift für Ärztliche Fortbildung*. Both this journal and the *Wiener Klinische Wochenschrift* carried regular columns on racial hygiene. Nazi midwifery journals reported regularly on genetic health and racial care (see, for example, the 1933 *Zeitschrift der Reichsfachschaft Deutscher Hebammen*, pp. 370–372, 393–395). The first (1935/36) volume of the journal *Der Öffentliche Gesundheitsdienst* listed thirty-one separate articles under the rubric of "Practical Genetic and Racial Policy" (*praktische Erb- und Rassenpolitik*). Racial hygiene was the main topic of discussion at the first meeting of the Deutsche Gesellschaft für Hygiene on October 3–6, 1938 (see *4. Beiheft zum Reichs-Gesundheitsblatt*, December 28, 1938).
40. Alfred Hoffmann, "Entwicklung und Aufgaben des Reichsgesundheitsverlages," *ÄRW*, 1(1940): 24.
41. Ibid. Hoffmann is referring only to those journals published by the Reich Publishing House. For a bibliography of medical works published in the first six years of the Nazi regime, see Adolf Jürgens, ed., *Ergebnisse deutscher Wissenschaft 1933–38* (Essen, 1939), esp. pp. 529–608 (on medicine) and pp. 615–646 (on biology). Jürgens points out that between 1933 and 1938, German publishers issued 141,680 new books (including reprints).
42. E. Silva, "Das Sterben der sozialhygienischen Zeitschriften in Deutschland," *IÄB*, November/December 1935, pp. 105–106.
43. See Georg Sticker's contribution to *Sozialhygienische Mitteilungen*, 19(1936).
44. On June 2, 1939, Reich Health Führer Leonardo Conti announced that *Ziel und Weg* would cease publication on August 31, 1939. On October 1, 1939, *Ziel und Weg* merged with the journal *Die Gesundheitsführung* (founded by Gerhard Wagner and Fritz Bartels, with circulation of 7,000 copies) to become *Die Gesundheitsführung des Deutschen Volkes, Ziel und Weg*, edited by Conti's second-in-command, Kurt Blome. Other official Nazi medical journals included the *NS-Gesundheitsdienst* (published in Berlin before the rise of the Nazis); also *Zur Gesundung* and *Ärztliche Mitteilungen aus und für Baden, Gaunachrichtenblatt des National-Sozialistischen-deutschen Ärztebundes*.
45. Walter Gross, "Die Familie," *Informationsdienst*, September 20, 1938. Other journals published by the Office of Racial Policy included *Korrespondenzblatt für Volksaufklärung und Rassenpflege* (1933–1937); *Neues Volk* (1933–1942), and *Rassenpolitische Auslands-Korrespondenz* (1934–1941). This last journal was also distributed abroad in (not always identical) foreign-language editions including Swedish (*Raspolitisk utrikeskorrespondens*); Spanish (*Correspondencia Extranjera sobre Política Racial*);

Portugese (*Correspondência Estranjeira Raço-Política*); and English (*Racio-political Foreign Correspondence*).
46. Stähle, "Blut und Rasse, neue Forschungsergebnisse," in *Die Volksgesundheitswacht*, Gilbhart 1934, pp. 4–6.
47. *DÄ*, 63(1933): 570; "Nazi Manifesto Starts Eugenics Propaganda," *New York Tribune*, September 6, 1933.
48. Eduard Schütt, "Die Bedeutung der wissenschaftliche Erb- und Rassenforschung für die praktische Gesundheitspflege," *Der Öffentliche Gesundheitsdienst*, 4(1938): 475.
49. Fritz Lenz, "Rassenhygiene als Pflichtfach für Mediziner," *MMW*, 80(1933): 849–851; see also H. Roemer, "Der erbbiologisch-rassenhygienische Lehrgang für Psychiater in München," *Zeitschrift für psychische Hygiene*, 7(1934): 2–6.
50. Otmar von Verschuer, *Erbpathologie: Ein Lehrbuch für Ärzte und Medizinstudierende* (1934), 2nd ed. (Dresden, 1937), p. 185.
51. Ibid., p. 188.
52. Michael Kater, "Medizinische Fakultäten und Medizinstudenten: Eine Skizze," in *Ärzte im Nationalsozialismus*, ed. Kudlien, p. 85. Friedrich Keiter's *Kurzes Lehrbuch der Rassenbiologie und Rassenhygiene für Mediziner* (Stuttgart, 1941) describes what medical students were required to learn in order to pass those parts of medical exams dealing with racial hygiene.
53. *ÄRW*, 1(1940): 94.
54. Kater, "Medizinische Fakultäten," p. 85.
55. Ramm, *Ärztliche Rechts- und Standeskunde*, pp. 35–36.
56. Kurt Blome, "Die ärztliche Fortbildung," *Ärzteblatt für Pommern, Mecklenburg und Lübeck*, 2(1935): 283. Documentation on these courses (including photographs) can be found in the file "Ärztliches Fortbildungswesen," box 4, Deutsche Kongress-Zentrale, Hoover Institution Archives.
57. *Die Gesundheitsführung*, 14(1944): 24.
58. Ramm, *Ärztliche Rechts- und Standeskunde*, p. 35.
59. Hadrich, "Einführung," p. 5; also *ÄfB*, 41(1936): 110.
60. Ramm, *Ärztliche Rechts- und Standeskunde*, p. 78; also *ÄfB*, 42(1937): 275.
61. Kurt Stübinger, "7. Jungärztelehrgang an der Ärztlichen Führerschule Alt-Rehse," *DÄ*, 67(1937): 1125; also Gertrud Bambach, "Wie wir Alt-Rehse erlebten," *Ärztin*, 13(1937): 334–337.
62. "Penetranz des Genes 'Hang zur Weiblichkeit' bei Alt-Rehsern." See Kurt Stübinger, "7. Jungärztelehrgang an der Ärztlichen Führerschule Alt-Rehse," *DÄ*, 67(1937): 1125; also Alfred Haug, "Die Führerschule der deutschen Ärzteschaft in Alt-Rehse," in *Ärzte im Nationalsozialismus*, ed. Kudlien, p. 125.
63. Boehm joined the Nazi party on July 2, 1923; he joined again on March 25, 1925 (no. 120). Boehm was a member of the Alldeutsche Verband, the Völkische Rechtsblock, and the Deutschvölkische Offiziersbund (1923–1928). He was *Referent für Rassenhygiene* in the Nazi Physicians' League from October 1931 to June 1933; he was named *SA Sanitätsbrigadeführer*

in 1931 and *Sanitätsgruppenführer* in 1942. Boehm fathered four children: Hartmut, Gudrun, Sigurd, and Sigrid. For his writings, see his "Ausmerzung der geistigen Begabung in vollem Gang," *Zeitschrift für Ärztliche Fortbildung,* 33(1936): 297–299; also his book *Erbkunde* (Berlin, 1936). Boehm published a number of technical articles on the gene as the fundamental unit of heredity; see, for example, his "Vererbungslehre," *Ziel und Weg,* 3(1933): 4–13, 90–96.

64. Hermann Boehm, "Das erbbiologische Forschungsinstitut in Alt-Rehse," *ÄfB,* 42(1937): 415–416.
65. Ibid., p. 416.
66. "Grundsätze nationalsozialistischen Arzttums," *ÄRW,* 2(1941): 83. By the spring of 1942, sixty Dutch physicians had been trained at Alt-Rehse and returned to the Netherlands. See *DÄ,* 72(1942): 115.
67. *ÄRW,* 2(1941): 83.
68. "Die Reichssanitätsschule der SA," *ÄfB,* 42(1937): 312–313; also 43(1938): 771–772. Head of the school was a Dr. Holtgrave.
69. *Zeitschrift der Reichsfachschaft Deutscher Schwestern und Pflegerinnen,* July 15, 1934, p. 131. In the mid-1930s, only 5,000–6,000 from a total of 140,000 nurses were in the Nazi party (Braune Schwestern). See *IÄB,* October 1937, p. 96. On Nazi nurses more generally, see Hermann Jensen, "Sinn, Zweck und Ziel der NS-Schwesternschaft," *Zeitschrift der Reichsfachschaft Deutscher Schwestern und Pflegerinnen,* August 15, 1934, pp. 137–140.
70. *ÄfB,* 44(1939): 178; also "Fachschule für NS-Schwestern," *DÄ,* 68(1938): 903.
71. Sollmann to Himmler, December 23, 1943, NS 19/3382, BA. For the history of the Lebensborn program, see Lilienthal, *Der "Lebensborn e.V."*
72. Ramm, *Ärztliche Rechts- und Standeskunde,* p. 81.
73. *Volk und Rasse,* 12(1937): 209; also *ÄfB,* 42(1937): 571.
74. "Sippenforschung in Schul und Haus," *ÄfB,* 42(1937): 587.
75. *Informationsdienst,* November 20, 1938.
76. "Das Recht," *Deutsche Justiz,* 100(1938): 611.
77. Review of *Der Abstammungsnachweis,* 3rd ed. (Ulmenstein, 1938) in the *Informationsdienst,* December 10, 1938.
78. *Informationsdienst,* November 30, 1938; compare also December 10, 1938.
79. "Filme bringen Aufklärung," *ÄfB,* 44(1939): 141. Films made by the Rassenpolitisches Amt include *Die Sünde der Väter* (1935, silent); *Abseits vom Wege* (1935, silent); *Erbkrank* (1936, silent); *Alles Leben ist Kampf* (1937, silent); and *Was du ererbt . . .* (1939). Herbert Gerdes made several films in this genre for the office. Hitler reportedly liked the film *Erbkrank* so much that he encouraged the production of a full-length feature film, *Victims of the Past: The Sin against Blood and Race (Opfer der Vergangenheit: Die Sünde wider Blut und Rasse),* produced jointly by the Rassenpolitisches Amt and the Reichspropagandaleitung of the NSDAP. For a time in 1937, *Erbkrank* was reportedly showing in nearly all Berlin film theaters. See *Informationsdienst,* December 30, 1938. This film can be found today in

the Bundesarchiv Koblenz (no. 46); the Bundesarchiv also has a copy of *Das Erbe*, a 1935 Nazi propaganda film (with sound) on genetic health (no. 20), and *Wer gehört zu wem?* a 1944 film depicting genetic analysis for the purposes of obtaining "proof of Aryan ancestry" (R 73, no. 1547, BA).
80. *Informationsdienst*, September 20, 1938; also August 30, 1938.
81. Ramm, *Ärztliche Rechts- und Standeskunde*, pp. 45–46.
82. "Bericht über die Sitzung," *DÄ*, 63(1933): 141–143.
83. Ramm, *Ärztliche Rechts- und Standeskunde*, pp. 46–47.
84. Yves Ternon and Socrate Helman, *Les médecins allemands et le national-socialisme* (Paris, 1973), pp. 74–78.
85. *MMW*, 80(1933): 481.
86. Statement signed by Alfons Stauder in the *MMW*, 80(1933): 517. See also the report of Stauder's remarks in *DÄ*, 63(1933): 141–143.
87. *MMW*, 80(1933): 593.
88. Present at this meeting with Hitler were Gerhard Wagner, Alfons Stauder, Hans Deuschl, Walter Schultze, and Bernhard Hörmann. Wagner appointed Gustav Schömig head of the Hartmannbund, and Paul Sperling head of the Deutsche Ärztevereinsbund.
89. Ternon and Helman, *Les médecins allemands*, p. 77; Kater, "Medizinische Fakultäten," p. 83.
90. *IÄB*, January 1, 1936, p. 13. The text of the December 13, 1935, Reichsärzteordnung is reprinted in Rudolf Ramm, *Ärztliche Rechts- und Standeskunde*, p. 223; see also Harm Knüpling, "Untersuchungen zur Vorgeschichte der Deutschen Ärzteordnung von 1935," med. diss., University of Bremen, 1965.
91. See *Illustrierter Beobachter*, September 16, 1937, p. 1365.
92. Wolf J. Modersohn, "Das Führerprinzip in der deutschen Medizin 1933–1945," med. diss., University of Kiel, 1982, p. 25.
93. Ibid., pp. 19–20. The statement declared (among other things): "The Marxist-Bolshevist influences upon the spirit of our people must stop. We therefore declare ourselves ready to work together, with all our powers, in the great work of the [Nazi] Reich government." See *Völkischer Beobachter*, March 4, 1933.
94. Leonardo Conti, "Arzt und Nationalsozialismus," *DÄ*, 73(1943): 33.

4. The Sterilization Law

1. The Nazis' expert committee replaced the previous Reichsausschuss für Bevölkerungsfragen, established by Frick's Weimar predecessor as interior minister, Carl Severing. Only one member of the new committee (*Burgdörfer*) had been also a member of the Weimar committee. See *ARGB*, 27(1933): 419–420. An editorial in the 1936 volume of the *Archiv* noted with regret that the committee was formed too late to influence the first important racial measure of the Reich: the April 7, 1933, Civil Service Law.
2. Wilhelm Frick, "Bevölkerungs- und Rassenpolitik," speech of June 28, 1933, printed as a pamphlet at Langensalza, 1933, p. 7.
3. Georg Lilienthal, in his "Rassenhygiene im Dritten Reich," provides an

analysis of sterilization policy in the context of racial hygiene history; see also Jeremy Noakes, "Nazism and Eugenics: The Background to the Nazi Sterilization Law of 14 July 1933," in *Ideas into Politics*, R. J. Bullen et al. (Totowa, N.J., 1984), pp. 75–94.

4. Lenz, *Menschliche Auslese*, p. 270.
5. Noakes, "Nazism and Eugenics," p. 80.
6. *MMW*, 80(1933): 365. After November 17, 1931, the Swiss law also allowed abortion on "eugenic indications." Paul Popenoe and E. S. Gosney report that in 1907 four persons were castrated in a Swiss asylum for eugenic purposes; see their *Sterilization for Human Betterment* (New York, 1929), p. 18.
7. Finland sterilized only 149 women and 39 men between 1935 and 1938. In 1934 Brazil and Argentina passed laws regulating sterilization. Neither France nor Britain passed sterilization laws in this period; in 1934 the British House of Commons rejected proposals to allow the voluntary sterilization of the mentally ill; see Morris Siegel, *Population, Race and Eugenics* (Ontario, 1939), pp. 161–163. See also Erich Berger's "Das deutsche Beispiel macht Schule," *Ziel und Weg*, 9(1939): 45–47.
8. In 1928 Alberta passed legislation allowing sterilization of patients in mental hospitals before their release; shortly after this, Ontario and British Columbia adopted similar statutes. For the history of the American sterilization movement, see Gosney and Popenoe, *Sterilization for Human Betterment*, esp. chap. 1. Allan Chase's *Legacy of Malthus* (New York, 1976) contains valuable documentation, as does Mark Haller's *Eugenics: Hereditarian Attitudes in American Thought* (New York, 1963). Garland Allen's "The Eugenics Record Office at Cold Spring Harbor, 1910–40," *Osiris* 2(1986): 225–264, provides a history of one of the most important American eugenics institutions.
9. Human Betterment Foundation, *Human Sterilization Today* (Pasadena, Calif., 1939). The foundation subsequently reported that 50,707 Americans had been sterilized by January 1, 1950; it also noted that the pace of sterilization had increased since 1944, after a lull during the early war years. See Robert Dickenson and Clarence Gamble, *Human Sterilization* (n.p., 1950), p. 30. For American sterilization up to 1957, see Samuel Highleyman's *Legal Bibliography on Sterilization* (New York, 1957); for the text of U.S. sterilization laws, see Huston Wendell, *Sterilization Laws* (Des Moines, Iowa, n.d.).
10. *Mitteilungen der Berliner Gesellschaft für Rassenhygiene*, October 1917, p. 1; also Geza von Hoffmann, *Die Rassenhygiene in den Vereinigten Staaten* (Munich, 1913).
11. Gustav Boeters, "Die Unfruchtbarmachung der geistiger Minderwertigen," *Sächsische Staatszeitung*, July 9–11, 1923.
12. Otto Reche, "Die Bedeutung der Rassenpflege für die Zukunft unseres Volkes," *Veröffentlichungen der Wiener Gesellschaft für Rassenpflege*, 1(1925): 6.
13. R. Müller, "Geschichtliches über die Beziehungen von Vererbungslehre und Rassenkunde," *Ziel und Weg*, 2(1932): 24.

14. R 86/2371 vol. 1, fol. 1, pp. 4–6, BA.
15. Lenz, *Menschliche Auslese*, pp. 277–306.
16. Madison Grant, *Der Untergang der grossen Rasse* (Munich, 1925); Lothrop Stoddard, *Der Kulturumsturz, die Drohung des Untermenschen* (Munich, 1925). Both translations were published by J. F. Lehmanns Verlag. In 1910 Otto Neurath translated Francis Galton's *Hereditary Genius* as *Genie und Vererbung*.
17. See H. H. Goddard, *The Kallikak Family: A Study in the Heredity of Feeble-Mindedness* (New York, 1912); also Richard Dugdale, *The Jukes: A Study in Crime, Pauperism, and Heredity* (New York, 1874).
18. See, for example, Martin Stämmler's *Rassenpflege im völkischen Staat* (Munich, 1934), p. 92.
19. See *Zeitschrift für Psychische Hygiene*, 7(1934): 6–9. For statistics on eleven such families in Germany and North America, see E. Dirken, "Asoziale Familien," *Zeitschrift für Volksaufartung und Erbkunde*, 1(1926): 12–16.
20. Dr. Grassl, "Biologische Gedanken," *Ärztliche Rundschau*, 45(1935): 243.
21. On the role of eugenicists in American immigration restriction legislation, see Allen Chase, *Legacy of Malthus* (New York, 1976), pp. 289–301. For German views of American miscegenation laws, see Josef Götz, "Die amtliche Statistik und die Rassenforschung," *Allgemeines Statistisches Archiv*, 27(1938): 415–422.
22. Walter Schultze, "Der nordische Gedanke," *Ziel und Weg*, 2(1932): 4; also his "Grundlagen und Ziele der Rassenpflege," *DÄ*, 63(1933): 567. See also "Sudafrikanische Gesetzentwürfe zur Bekämpfung der Rassenmischung," *Neues Volk*, 4(April 1940): 12–13.
23. *DÄ*, 63(1933): 154.
24. This citation is from a note on the margins of the *New York Times* article "Nazis Open Race Bureau for Eugenic Segregation," published May 4, 1933, and now in the Harry H. Laughlin Papers; I would like to thank Garland Allen for drawing this to my attention.
25. See H. H. Laughlin's "Model Sterilization Law," in *Eugenical Sterilization in the U.S.: A Report of the Psychopathic Laboratory of the Municipal Court of Chicago* (Chicago, 1922), pp. 446–461.
26. NS 2/85, fol. 280, BA.
27. Noakes, "Nazism and Eugenics," pp. 82–85.
28. "Die Eugenik im Dienste der Volkswohlfahrt," *Veröffentlichungen aus dem Gebiet der Medizinalverwaltung*, 38(1932): 3–112.
29. Ramm, *Ärztliche Rechts- und Standeskunde*, p. 141.
30. Ebel, "Jahresbericht des Geschäftsführers," in *Jahrbuch der Gefängnis-Gesellschaft für die Provinz Sachsen und Anhalt 1934: Der Erbkranke und der Asoziale im nationalsozialistischen Staat*, 1934, p. 10.
31. Otto Tolischus, "400,000 Germans to Be Sterilized," *New York Times*, December 20, 1933.
32. Walter Gmelin, "Welche Wirkungen können von dem Sterilizationsgesetz erwartet werden?" *Ärztliche Rundschau*, 43(1933): 238.
33. Although 1,700 genetic health courts were originally envisioned by Nazi

authorities (one in each large city and in each Kreis), the actual number was significantly below this. In 1935 there were 205 *Erbgesundheitsgerichte* and 31 *Erbgesundheitsobergerichte* in Germany (*Der Erbarzt,* 2[1935]: 140); the number of courts probably never rose above these figures.
34. There is at present no adequate historical account of how the genetic health courts functioned. Hanns Schwarz's *Ein Gutachten über die ärztliche Tätigkeit im sogenannten Erbgesundheits-verfahren* (Halle, 1950) is disappointing. Dr. Walter Gmelin reflected on his experience working in a genetic health court in his "Erfahrungen eines Amtsarztes," *Ärztliche Rundschau,* 45(1935): 281–289. For specific genetic health court decisions, see *Die Ärztin,* 15(1939): 31–34. Erich Ristow, in his *Erbgesundheitsrecht* (Berlin, 1935), provides a survey of genetic health law up to 1935; Wolf Bauermeister and Maria Küper, in their "Der erbbiologische Abstammungsprüfung" (in *Fortschritte der Erbpathologie, Rassenhygiene und ihrer Grenzgebiete,* 1937/38), provide some insight into the logic of these rulings.
35. See Ernst Böttger, "Die Grenzen der Schweigepflicht des Arztes," *ÄfB,* 40(1935), p. 76; also Ramm, *Ärztliche Rechts- und Standeskunde,* pp. 108–113, 139.
36. Otmar von Verschuer, "Der Erbarzt—zur Einführung," *Der Erbarzt,* 1(1934): 2. Verschuer became director of the newly founded Institut für Rassenhygiene in Frankfurt on April 1, 1935. His earlier training was at the Kaiser Wilhelm Institut für Anthropologie, menschliche Erblehre und Eugenik in Berlin (the Fischer Institute).
37. Ibid., p. 2. Rudolf Ramm repeated this slogan in his *Ärztliche Rechts- und Standeskunde,* p. 140. Compare also the slogan "Jeder Arzt ein Sportarzt," in *ÄfB,* 43(1938): 377–378.
38. N. V. Timofeev-Ressovsky, "Experimentelle Untersuchungen der erblichen Belastung von Populationen," *Der Erbarzt,* 2(1935): 117–118. In late October 1938, Timofeev-Ressovsky delivered a lecture to the *Gauleiter* of the Office of Racial Policy at a special course on problems of racial policy in Babelsberg. He spoke on "Experimental Mutation Research" after Walter Gross had lectured on "Racial Thinking in Politics" and before Alfred Rosenberg spoke on "Our Philosophical Debate with Opponents of the Racial Idea" (*Informationsdienst,* November 30, 1938).
39. The June 1, 1933, "Gesetz zur Verhinderung der Arbeitslosigkeit" promoted marriage by providing interest-free loans up to 1,000 RM (*Ehestandsdarlehen*) to married couples; the program was financed by increased taxes on unmarried individuals. The law was also designed to encourage women to return to the home by providing financial incentives for employers to hire men instead of women. See *DÄ,* 63(1933): 253. The "Reichserbhofgesetz" of May 15, 1933 was designed to prevent the subdivision of family farms and required that farm heirs be of "German or related blood" dating back to 1800.
40. Otmar von Verschuer, "Der Erbarzt—zur Einführung," *Der Erbarzt,* 1(1934): 2.
41. "Erbärztliche Praxis," *Der Erbarzt,* 1(1934): 13. Article 2 of the law allowed individuals suffering from illnesses specified by the law to request

sterilization for themselves; those judged incompetent to make such requests could have a request submitted by their legal guardian, as long as this was accompanied by a medical certificate affirming that the person was aware of the nature of the operation. Article 3, however, allowed this request to be dispensed with in certain unspecified circumstances; and article 4 provided that medical officials or the directors of psychiatric hospitals or prisons could also issue requests. See *Reichsgesetzblatt,* 1(1933): 529–537; also *Gesetz zur Verhütung erbkranken Nachwuchses* by Gütt, Rüdin, and Ruttke.
42. Bruno Steinwallner, "Zwei Jahre Erbgesundheitsgesetz," *Ärztliche Rundschau,* 45(1935): 221–222.
43. Ibid.
44. Werner Fichtmüller, "Dissertationen in den medizinischen Fakultäten...," med. diss., University of Erlangen-Nuremberg, 1972, pp. 53–55.
45. P. Schneck, "Die Entwicklung der Eugenik als soziale Bewegung in der Epoche des Imperialismus," in *Eugenik,* ed. Dietl, p. 47.
46. "Die Erb- und Rassenpflege in der Praxis," *ÄRW,* 2(1941): 36. Racial hygiene journals also discussed related fears growing among the public that their offspring might be defective. See Alexander Paul, "Ist Erbangst berechtigt?" *Volk und Rasse,* 16(1941): 130–135.
47. Bruman, "Der Schwachsinn im Erbgesundheitsverfahren," *Zeitschrift der Akademie für Deutsches Recht,* 2(1935): 769. Bruman also noted that doctors were not just passive observers (*Beisitzender*) at genetic health court proceedings but were "often the ones ultimately responsible for passing final judgment."
48. *Reichsgesetzblatt,* 1(1935): 773, 1035.
49. See Fritz Lenz, "Über die Grenzen praktischen Eugenik," *Acta genetica,* 6(1956): 13–24; also Gisela Bock, *Zwangssterilisation im Nationalsozialismus* (Opladen, 1986), pp. 230–246.
50. Fichtmüller, "Dissertationen," p. 4.
51. H. W. Schröder, "Die Sterilisierung ein Verbrechen," *Das Deutsche Gesundheitswesen,* February 15, 1947, pp. 113–115.
52. Fichtmüller, "Dissertationen." On the anticipated economic effects of the law, see G. L. Tirala, *Die wirtschaftlichen Folgen des Sterilisierungsgesetzes* (Munich, 1933).
53. *Reichsgesetzblatt,* 1(1936): 122. See also Fichtmüller, "Dissertationen," pp. 152–154. Ramm, in his *Ärztliche Rechts- und Standeskunde,* mentions the sterilization of women by X-rays (p. 143). Experiments were conducted on inducing abortion by X-rays not long after their discovery in 1882. See, for example, *Zentralblatt für Gynäkologie,* 31(1907): 953. In 1933 H. Wintz recommended the use of X-rays to induce abortions in certain situations ("Die Schwangerschaftsunterbrechung durch Röntgenstrahlen," *MMW,* 80[1933]: 172–174). An American survey reported in 1950 that "many thousands of women" had been sterilized by X-rays in the United States (Dickenson and Gamble, *Human Sterilization,* pp. 21–22).
54. In 1934 Professor August Mayer at the Women's Clinic in Tübingen estimated that death rates due to sterilization were about 1 percent and that the

primary causes of death were embolism or peritonitis. See the *Zentralblatt für Gynäkologie,* 58(1934): 1987. In 1974, however, M. Stürzbecher maintained that among 168,989 persons sterilized, only 467 had died as the result of the operation ("Der Vollzug des Gesetzes zur Verhütung erbkranken Nachwuchses . . . ," *Öffentliches Gesundheits-Wesen,* 36[1974]: 356–357).

55. Carl Schroeder, "Über den Ausbau und die Leistung der Hysterioskopie," *Archiv für Gynäkologie,* 156(1934): 404–419.
56. Alexander Mitscherlich and Fred Mielke, *Medizin ohne Menschlichkeit* (1949) (Frankfurt, 1960), p. 246.
57. Ibid. For a discussion of German sterilization efforts after the war, see "Zur Geschichte der Zwangssterilisierung seit der NS-Zeit," *Autonomie,* 7(1981): 43–60.
58. For a list of officially recognized experts on racial ancestry, see *Reichs-Gesundheitsblatt,* 18(1943): 179.
59. See Pearce Kintzing's "On the Persistence of Certain Racial Characteristics," *American Medicine,* July 30, 1904, pp. 204–205.
60. Thordar Quelprud, "Die Ohrmuschel und ihre Bedeutung für die erbbiologische Abstammung," *Der Erbarzt,* 2(1935): 121–124; also H. Hofmann, "Degenerationszeichen im Ohr," *Öffentlicher Gesundheitsdienst,* 6(1940): 573–583.
61. Hans F. K. Günther, *Rassenkunde des jüdischen Volkes* (Munich, 1931), p. 251.
62. For the methods of German intelligence testing, see Gerhard Kloos, *Anleitung zur Intelligenzprüfung und ihrer Auswertung* (1941) (Jena, 1943).
63. Ferdinand Dubitscher, "Die Bewährung Schwachsinniger im täglichen Leben," *Der Erbarzt,* 2(1935): 59.
64. Ibid.
65. Otto Tolischus, "400,000 Germans to be Sterilized," *New York Times,* December 20, 1933.
66. "Erbgesundheitsgesetz und Ermittlung kindlicher Schwachsinnszustände mit den Entwicklungstests von 'Bühler-Hetzer'," *Ärztin,* 13(1937): 116–121.
67. This and much of what follows concerning the sterilization of the *Rheinlandbastarde* is based on the study by Reiner Pommerin, *Die Sterilisierung der Rheinlandbastarde* (Düsseldorf, 1979).
68. "Satzungen des Deutschen Notbundes gegen die schwarze Schmach," March 21, 1921, reel 83, folder 1681, NSDAP Hauptarchiv, BA.
69. Sperr to Reichsgesundheitsamt, July 29, 1927, R 86/2371, fol. 436, BA.
70. Pommerin, *Sterilisierung der Rheinlandbastarde,* p. 102.
71. Ibid., pp. 70–90.
72. Ibid., p. 81.
73. Anordnung 3/37 of the NSDAP: "Betreff: Lockerung der Mitgliedersperre," January 26, 1937, in TS N27 RS35, Hoover Institution Archives.
74. Linden, "Übersicht über die Entscheidungspraxis . . . ," May 14, 1938, NS 19/3434, BA.
75. Wagner to Himmler, January 24, 1938, NS 19/3434, BA.

76. Gütt to Pfundtner and Himmler, August 26, 1937; Gütt to Himmler, May 16, 1938, both in NS 19/3434, BA. Drs. Bartels and Packheiser allied themselves with Wagner in this struggle; Bartels and Packheiser attacked Gütt and Rüdin at public meetings.
77. Albert to the RFSS, May 16, 1938, NS 19/3434, BA.
78. "Vorläufige Begründung," June 11, 1938, NS 19/3434, BA.
79. Heydrich to Himmler, May 20, 1938, NS 19/3434, BA.
80. Klee, *"Euthanasie,"* p. 85.
81. Klaus Dörner et al., *Der Krieg gegen die psychisch Kranken* (Rehburg-Loccum, 1980), p. 20; see also Robert Krieg, "Die nicht vorhersehbare Spätentwicklung des Paul W.," in *Erfassung zur Vernichtung,* ed. Roth, pp. 10–29.
82. After the war some Latin American countries pursued sterilization policies on a wider scale than had Germany (though for different reasons). Bonnie Mass, in her *Population Target: The Political Economy of Population Control in Latin America* (Ontario, 1976), documents the massive sterilization programs of Puerto Rico and Brazil in the 1950s and 1960s.

5. The Control of Women

1. See, for example, Renate Bridenthal et al., eds., *When Biology Became Destiny: Women in Weimar and Nazi Germany* (New York, 1985).
2. David Schoenbaum, *Hitler's Social Revolution* (New York, 1966), p. 179. The SPD attracted far more women: in 1930 approximately 23 percent of the SPD membership were women.
3. Cited in Anna Thüne, *Frauenbilderlesebuch* (Berlin, 1980), p. 9.
4. Cited in "Die Stellung der Frau im Dritten Reich," *Die Gewerkschaftliche Frauenzeitung,* April 15, 1931, p. 30.
5. Eugen Fischer, "Das Preisausschreiben für den besten nordischen Rassenkopf," *Volk und Rasse,* 2(1927): 1–11. The publisher J. F. Lehmann was one of the original forces behind this contest. Even before World War I, Lehmann had offered 3,000 RM in prize money for such a contest; the details, however, were not worked out until after the war. See Lutzhöft, *Der Nordische Gedanke,* pp. 153–154. For a gallery of the ideal Nordic heads produced in the contest, see Eugen Fischer and Hans F. K. Günther, *Deutsche Köpfe nordischer Rasse* (Munich, 1927).
6. For examples of Nazi art and architecture, see *Die Kunst im 3. Reich* (Frankfurt, 1975), edited by the Frankfurter Kunstverein.
7. *Ziel und Weg,* 3(1933): 113.
8. *Mitteilungen der Berliner Gesellschaft für Rassenhygiene,* October 1917, p. 2.
9. "Kinderreichtum ist praktischer Nationalsozialismus." See "Ehrenpass der artreinen Familie," *ÄfB,* 42(1937): 515.
10. *ÄRW,* 2(1941): 101.
11. For the rules governing the award, see "Satzung des Ehrenkreuzes der deutschen Mutter," *Informationsdienst,* January 10, 1939; also February 10, 1939.

12. "Erwerbstätige Ehefrauen in Berlin," *ÄfB*, 42(1937): 654–655.
13. *Die Gesundheitsführung*, 10(1940): 118.
14. Ibid., pp. 159–160.
15. Conti to Himmler, December 9, 1943, Conti file, Berlin Document Center.
16. *Die Gesundheitsführung*, 12(1942): 232.
17. "Das Konzeptionsoptimum," *Informationsdienst des Hauptamtes für Volksgesundheit der NSDAP*, January/March 1944, p. 31.
18. Ramm, *Ärztliche Rechts- und Standeskunde*, pp. 105–106.
19. Hugo Hecht, in *Beiträge zur Ärztliche Fortbildung*, no. 11 (1933).
20. See *Ziel und Weg*, 3(1933): 431.
21. *ÄfB*, 42(1937): 642. In Hamburg in 1936, twenty persons were convicted for violating antiabortion laws; the highest penalty awarded was nine years in prison. In the same year, seven people were convicted in Flensburg (one sentenced to seven years in jail), and seven in Koblenz (for terms up to four years). See *IÄB*, November/December 1936, p. 132.
22. *Informationsdienst des Hauptamtes für Volksgesundheit der NSDAP*, April/June 1944, p. 65.
23. "Grundlagen und Ziele der Rassenpflege," *DÄ*, 63(1933): 566.
24. See, for example, Hans Stadler, *Richtlinien für Schwangerschaftsunterbrechung und Unfruchtbarmachung aus gesundheitliche Gründen* (Munich, 1936); also *Ärzteblatt für Bayern*, 8(1941): 37.
25. Walter Schultze, " 'Euthanasie' und Sterilisation," in *Deutsches Geistesleben und Nationalsozialismus*, p. 79. This emendation allowed abortion only if the woman granted permission, and only if the fetus was not old enough to survive outside the womb. It is unclear whether either of these qualifications was enforced. See M. Küper, "Das Gesetz zur Änderung des Gesetzes zur Verhütung erbkranken Nachwuchses," *Ärztliche Rundschau*, 45(1935): 275.
26. "Sektion 218 gilt nicht für Juden," *Informationsdienst*, December 20, 1938.
27. *Informationsdienst des Hauptamtes für Volksgesundheitsdienst der NSDAP*, January/March 1944, p. 2; also October/December 1943, pp. 96–97.
28. Hitler wrote in *Mein Kampf:* "Das deutsche Mädchen ist Staatsangehörige und wird mit ihrer Verheiratung erst Bürgerin."
29. Mitscherlich and Mielke, *Medizin ohne Menschlichkeit*, p. 42. See also Fritz Lenz, "Die Frage der unehelichen Kinder," *Volk und Rasse*, 12(1937): 91–95.
30. Gerda Guttenberg, "Die fragwürdige Strukturierung des Deutschen Roten Kreuzes," in *Medizin und Nationalsozialismus*, ed. Baader and Schultz, p. 234.
31. Lenz, review of J. Kaup's *Frauenarbeit und Rassenhygiene*, *ARGB*, 11(1914–15): 680.
32. Lenz, review of Felix A. Theilhaber's *Das sterile Berlin*, *ARGB*, 10(1913): 544–545.
33. *ARGB*, 10(1913): 369.
34. Frick, "Bevölkerungs- und Rassenpolitik," pp. 5–7. Racial hygienists' cri-

tique of the *Zwei-Kinder System* dates at least as far back as Ploetz's *Die Tüchtigkeit unsrer Rasse* (p. 205).

35. Otmar von Verschuer, "Erbpflege in der deutschen Gesetzgebung," *Archiv der Julius Klaus-Stiftung,* 10(1935): 59.

36. See *Archiv für Gynäkologie* (1933): 110. Ernst Kahn's widely read *Internationale Geburtenstreik* (Frankfurt, 1930) had raised the specter of a "birth strike" into popular consciousness; debates on this question go back to before World War I. Attempts to draw some kind of link between feminism and the declining birthrate were not, of course, restricted to Germany. At the 1935 International Congress for Population Science in Berlin, K. A. Wieth-Knudsen blamed declining birthrates in Scandinavian countries on what he called "the three great mental distortions and spiritual confusions" of the times: "liberalism, radicalism, and feminism." See the *Ärztliche Rundschau,* 45(1935): 330.

37. Martin Stämmler, "Rassenhygiene im Dritten Reich," *Ziel und Weg,* 2(1932): 9.

38. At the 1935 *Reichsparteitag der Freiheit* in Nuremberg, Hitler declared that "the woman also has her battlefield: with every child she brings into the world, she fights her struggle for the German nation" (cited in *Die Kunst im 3. Reich,* ed. Frankfurter Kunstverein, p. 190).

39. G. A. Wagner, "Die Funktionen und Funktionsstörungen des Ovariums und ihre Bedeutung für die Volksgesundheit," *Archiv für soziale Hygiene und Demographie,* March 1933/34, pp. 394–403. Wagner claimed that a woman "is what she is, both for herself and for the Volk, in large part by virtue of her ovaries and their various functions" (p. 394).

40. Frick, "Bevölkerungs- und Rassenpolitik," p. 15. See also Paula von Groote, *Die Frauenfrage und ihre Lösung durch den Nationalsozialismus* (Berlin, 1933).

41. Friedrich Burgdörfer, *Völker am Abgrund,* published as vol. 1 of the series *Politische Biologie* (Munich, 1937).

42. Ramm, *Ärztliche Rechts- und Standeskunde,* p. 150. These are figures for the "Grossdeutsches Reich," including Germany before 1938 (the "Altreich"), along with Austria and the Sudetenland, but not Bohemia and Moravia, Eupen-Malmedy, or Polish areas then under German control. (In 1940 the population of this Greater Germany was 80.5 million.) According to Nazi statistics, the birthrate in Vienna tripled from the *Anschluss* in March 1938 to January 1941.

43. Friedrich Burgdörfer, "Die unterschiedliche Fortpflanzung," *ARGB,* 36(1942): 420. Burgdörfer's calculation was for Greater Germany. His cherished birthrates were eventually dealt a crushing blow by the war. In the first quarter of 1941, after more than a year and a half of war, births in the Grossdeutsches Reich declined by nearly 25 percent from the previous year (*ARGB,* 35[1941]: 343). After 1941, birthrates rose again, from 15.7/1,000 in 1942 to 17.6/1,000 in 1944. See the *Medizinische Zeitschrift,* 1(1944): 119.

44. The *Ärzteblatt für Berlin* reported that in 1936, German midwives assisted 701,665 women giving birth; 2,353 of these (3.35/1,000) died during child-

birth. See *ÄfB* 42(1937): 604. For home births assisted by midwives in Berlin, maternal mortality rates declined from 0.23 percent in 1923–1933, to 0.16 percent in 1940–1944, to 0.0 percent for 1958–1963. See Felix von Mikulicz-Radecki, *Geburtshilfe in Praxis und Klinik* (Leipzig, 1966), p. 20.

45. "Die Muttersterblichkeit 1932 bis 1936," *Die Gesundheitsführung,* 10(1940): 151–152.
46. "Neue Massnahmen zur Regelung des Arbeitseinsatzes," *Vierteljahresplan,* 2(1938): 143.
47. Alice Rilke, "Die Frauenberufs- und Erwerbstätigkeit . . . ," *Ärztin,* 15(1939): 6. See also "Erwerbstätige Ehefrauen in Berlin," *ÄfB,* 42(1937): 654–655.
48. *Ergebnisse der Arbeitsbuchstatistik, Soziale Praxis,* 18(1938): 492.
49. Ramm, *Ärztliche Rechts- und Standeskunde,* p. 158. For an elaborate list of medical criteria for determining whether women were "fit for work service," see "Richtlinien für die Untersuchung auf Tauglichkeit für den Frauenarbeitsdienst," *Ärzteblatt für Pommern, Mecklenburg und Lübeck,* 2(1935): 151–152.
50. *Informationsdienst,* October 20, 1938.
51. Cited in Annemarie Tröger, "The Creation of a Female Assembly-Line Proletariat," in *When Biology Became Destiny,* ed. Bridenthal et al., p. 256.
52. See, for example, Martha Moers, "Die psychische Einstellung der Frau zur Industriearbeit," *Ärztin,* 18(1942): 260–265.
53. At the beginning of 1939 there were 59,454 physicians in Germany— including physicians in the armed forces as well as in the SS, police, and work services. Later in the year this number was increased by more than 2,000 physicians (and 150 dentists) from the Sudetenland. From September 1939 to the beginning of 1940, another 5,837 physicians were licensed prematurely on an emergency basis to meet war needs. A 1942 count showed 75,960 physicians in the Reich (12 percent women); adding to this 567 physicians in Bohemia and Moravia, plus physicians in Danzig and the Wartheland, plus 1,023 Polish physicians working for the Germans, 100 physicians working for the *Generalgouvernement,* 580 physicians in Alsace, 137 in Lorraine, 180 in Luxemburg, and 90 in the Carpathians, the total comes to 78,637 physicians working for Germany in 1942. See "Die Zahl der Ärzte 1942," *DÄ,* 72(1942): 300–301.
54. See the review of Edith von Lölhöffel's *Das Berufsbild der Ärztin* (1939), *Ärztin,* 15(1939): 128. Lölhöffel was the physician responsible for the German women's teams in the 1936 Berlin Olympics. She took over as editor of *Ärztin* in 1937.
55. *British Medical Journal,* October 30, 1943, p. 554.
56. *DÄ,* 72(1942): 302. In January 1939, only 43 percent of Germany's women physicians were married (compared with about 75 percent for men); nearly half of all married women physicians (47 percent) were married to other doctors. The greatest proportions of women physicians were in East Prussia, Berlin, and Baden; the lowest were in the Sudetenland, Kurhessen, and Lower Saxony.

57. In 1937 more than half of all newly licensed women specialists were pediatricians or gynecologists. See *DÄ,* 67(1937): 906.
58. In 1938 the fields of medicine within which women were least represented were stomach, intestinal, and metabolic medicine (with 0/210); teeth, mouth, and jaw (1/218); surgery (18/2,454) throat, nose, and ears (17/1,590); and urology (3/228). See Udo Tornau, "Der Einsatz im Gesundheitsdienst," *Die Gesundheitsführung,* 10(1940): 22–27. In 1925 only 10 of Germany's 6,250 veterinarians were women. For the proportions of men and women in a wide range of professional occupations for the year 1925, see Lizzie Hoffa, "Das Frauenstudium," *Ärztliche Mitteilungen,* 34(1933): 204.
59. See *Ärztin,* 18(1942): 181–182.
60. *ÄRW,* 1(1940): 220.
61. Gabriele Strecker, "Medical Women in Germany," *Journal of the American Medical Women's Association,* November 1947, pp. 506–508.
62. Ibid.

6. Anti-Semitism in the German Medical Community

1. Walter Schultze, "Grundlagen und Ziele der Rassenpflege," *DÄ,* 63(1933): 567.
2. Personal communication, Edith Zerbin-Rüdin, Summer 1982; see also *Informationsdienst,* October 20, 1938.
3. Hermann Graml, "Die Behandlung 'Deutschblütiger' in 'Rassenschande' Verfahren," *Gutachten des Instituts für Zeitgeschichte* (Munich, 1957), p. 72. There is evidence that racial hygienists were sometimes even more eager than leading Nazi officials to prosecute cases of racial pollution. On October 14, 1937, for example, Justice Minister Franz Gürtner acquitted the defendant in a trial for racial pollution, and Verschuer protested that the decision had been made against his recommendation (Müller-Hill, *Tödliche Wissenschaft,* p. 15).
4. *IÄB,* May 1936, p. 89.
5. Graml, "Die Behandlung 'Deutschblütiger'," pp. 73–75.
6. Ibid., p. 75.
7. See also *ÄfB,* 42(1937): 566.
8. *DÄ,* 65(1935): 895–896, 1010.
9. "Das Judentum in Deutschland," *DÄ,* 63(1933): 75–76.
10. Walter Gmelin, "Zur Frage einer erbbiologischen Registrierung der Bevölkerung," *Ärztliche Rundschau,* 43(1933): 198.
11. Ibid.
12. The best general history of efforts to construct a genetic registry of the German population is Karl Heinz Roth's "Erbbiologische Bestandsaufnahme," in his *Erfassung zur Vernichtung* (Berlin, 1984), pp. 57–100. See also H. Vellguth, "Ziel und Methoden der Erbbestandsaufnahme," *Öffentlicher Gesundheitsdienst,* 4(1938): 495–501.
13. See the review of this proposal in *Ärztliche Rundschau,* 43(1933): 165–

166. See also Ernst Braun, "Zur Frage der erbbiologischen Bestandsaufnahme der deutschen Bevölkerung," *Der Erbarzt,* 2(1935): 17–22; and the booklet (with a foreword by Michael Hesch) *Rasse- und Gesundheits-Pass* (Leipzig, 1934).
14. Bruno Steinwallner, "Die Neuordnung unseres Gesundheitswesens," *Ärztliche Rundschau,* 45(1935): 340.
15. *Ziel und Weg,* 6(1936): 107.
16. See "Dr. Gerhard Wagner 18. August 1888–25. März 1939," *DÄ* 69(1939): 252–253. See also C. Adam, "Was muss der Arzt über die Eheschliessung zwischen Arier und Nichtarier wissen?" *Zeitschrift für Ärztliche Fortbildung,* 33(1936): 114–116; and Schäger, "Der Arzt im Ehegesundheitsgesetz," *Zeitschrift für Ärztliche Fortbildung,* 33(1936): 208.
17. William Provine, "Geneticists and the Biology of Race Crossing," *Science,* 182(1973): 790–796.
18. Lenz, *Menschliche Auslese,* pp. 503–505. Compare Eugen Fischer, *Die Rehobother Bastarde* (Jena, 1913).
19. *Informationsdienst des Hauptamtes für Volksgesundheit der NSDAP,* December 1942, p. 82.
20. R. Müller, "Geschichtliches über die Beziehung von Vererbungslehre und Rassenkunde," *Ziel und Weg,* 2(1932): 27.
21. NS 2/85, fols. 67 and 237-38, BA. Medical records for SS marital engagements in 1942 can be found in the file "Verlobungs- und Heiratsgesuche—Ärztliche Gutachten," NS 2/245, fols. 1-322, BA.
22. See, for example, Ernst Rüdin, "Zehn Jahre nationalsozialistischer Staat," *ARGB,* 36(1942): 322.
23. "Vorbemerkung," Rasse- und Siedlungshauptamt-SS, NS 2, BA.
24. In announcing this change, the Prussian welfare minister pointed out that the Society for Racial Hygiene had long advocated marital counseling. See the *Reichs-Gesundheitsblatt,* June 9, 1926, pp. 542–543.
25. Hermann Muckermann, "Ursprung und Entwicklung der Eheberatung," *Das Kommende Geschlecht,* 6(1931–32): 12.
26. Rainer Fetscher, "Der Stand und die Zukunft der Eheberatung in Deutschland," *Zeitschrift für psychische Hygiene,* 6(1933): 85. The number of visits received by the Dresden Marital Counseling Center grew from 572 in 1927 to 1,285 in 1932. Fetscher notes that in 1930 about 5 percent of Dresden's 4,400 newly wed or engaged couples received marital advice at his center.
27. "Eheberatung," *ÄfB,* 42(1937): 519. See also Otmar von Verschuer, "Aus der Praxis des erbbiologischen Arztes," *ÄfB,* 42(1937): 531, and Heinrich Grote, "Bekanntmachung über Ehetauglichkeitszeugnisse," *ÄfB,* 42(1937): 307–308.
28. "Die Erb- und Rassenpflege in der Praxis," *ÄRW,* 2(1941): 36. Also Herbert Linden, "Schutz der Erbgesundheit des deutschen Volkes," *DÄ,* 65(1935): 1037.
29. "Gefängnisse für Nichtachtung des Ehegesundheitsgesetzes," *ÄRW,* 2(1941): 56.

30. Arthur Gütt, "Die neue ärztliche Aufgabe," *ÄfB*, 43(1938): 328; also "Eheberatung," *ÄfB*, 42(1937): 519.
31. Fritz Cropp, "Was hat der Vierjahresplan auf dem Gebiet der Gesundheitspolitik gebracht?" *Zeitschrift für Ärztliche Fortbildung*, 34(1937): 65–68.
32. L. Conti, "Das städtische Gesundheitswesen in der Geschichte Berlins," *ÄfB*, 42(1937): 415. By June 1938, 23,068 people were employed by the Reich health offices (10,695 full time). Besides 753 health offices, there were also 201 subsidiary offices (*Nebenstellen*) and 95 special Abteilungen für Erb- und Rassenpflege (box 130, Deutsche Kongress-Zentrale, Hoover Institution Archives). By October 1940 there were 850 health offices. A list of these offices can be found in Hans Reiter et al., *Gesundheitsverwaltung des Grossdeutschen Reichs*, published as vol. 2 of *Sammlung deutscher Gesundheitsgesetze* (Leipzig, 1941), pp. 5–33.
33. Franz Orsós, "Ist der Stand der deutschen Wissenschaft gesunken?" *DÄ*, 67(1937): 1119. Orsós (commonly misspelled in Nazi writings as "Orlós") was director of the Institut für gerichtliche Medizin at the University of Budapest.
34. Ibid.
35. Gütt to Himmler, February 7, 1938, NS 19/3434, BA.
36. This does not include retired physicians or physicians not yet practicing; nor does it include medical personnel working exclusively for the government, the military, or the SS. See "Berufstätige Ärzte im alten Reichsgebiet," *ÄRW*, 1(1940): 220.
37. Ramm, *Ärztliche Rechts- und Standeskunde*, p. 162.
38. See, for example, Hans Reiter, Bernhard Möllers, and Wilhelm Hallbauer, *Erb- und Rassenpflege* (Leipzig, 1940), issued as part of *Sammlung deutscher Gesundheitsgesetze*. See also Fritz Cropp, "Was hat der Vierjahresplan auf dem Gebiet der Gesundheitspolitik gebracht?" *Zeitschrift für Ärztliche Fortbildung*, February 1, 1937, pp. 65–68; and Eduard Schütt, *Der Arzt des öffentlichen Gesundheitsdienst* (Dortmund, 1941).
39. Oskar Wiehle, "Rassenkunde des Kreises Oppeln," *Rasse, Volk, Erbgut in Schlesien*, 5(1939): 25.
40. See, for example, Arthur Gütt, "Die neue ärztliche Aufgabe," *ÄfB*, 43(1938): 328.
41. For the history of anti-Semitism in the German medical profession, see J. Lewy, "Antisemitismus und Medizin," *Im deutschen Reich. Zeitschrift des Centralvereins deutscher Staatsbürger jüdischen Glaubens*, 5(1899): 1–19.
42. W. F. Kümmel, "Die Ausschaltung rassisch und politisch missliebiger Ärzte," in *Ärzte im Nationalsozialismus*, ed. Kudlien, pp. 57–58.
43. Jewish racial hygienists included Richard Goldschmidt and Heinrich Poll. Wilhelm Weinberg, founder of the Stuttgart branch of the Society for Racial Hygiene (in 1910), came from a Jewish background on his father's side; he was raised as a Protestant, however, and married a Protestant woman.
44. For the history of anti-Semitism in modern Germany, see Peter G. Pulzer, *The Rise of Political Anti-Semitism in Germany and Austria* (New York, 1964); also Lucy Dawidowicz, *The War against the Jews, 1933–45* (New York, 1975), pp. 29–62.

45. This is a point argued by Donald W. Light, Stephan Leibfried, and Florian Tennstedt in their "Social Medicine vs. Professional Dominance: The German Experience," *American Journal of Public Health*, 76(1986): 78–83.
46. Friedrich Thieding, *Der Arzt in den Fesseln der Sozialpolitik* (Munich, 1966), p. 27.
47. Philalethes Kuhn and Heinrich W. Kranz, *Von deutschen Ahnen für deutsche Enkel* (Munich, 1936).
48. Ternon and Helman, *Les médecins allemands*, pp. 40–42.
49. Holz's words are reported in the article "Blubo-Volksgesundheit," *IÄB*, February/March 1935, pp. 22–23.
50. See Julius Hadrich, "Die nichtarischen Ärzte in Deutschland," *DÄ*, 64(1934): 1242–45. These statistics were widely reported in the foreign medical press. See, for example, *British Medical Journal*, December 19, 1936, p. 1295.
51. *Ziel und Weg*, 5(1935): 435. *Volk und Rasse* reported in 1935 that of 6,261 doctors in Berlin, 2,393 were "non-Aryan," and that the figure of 44 percent was for doctors practicing as part of the social insurance programs (*Kassenärzte*).
52. Reported in *IÄB*, September 1934, p. 146.
53. "Der gelbe Pass," *IÄB*, January 1934, p. 18; see also *MMW*, 80(1933): 633.
54. "Liste von Professoren der Medizin und von medizinischen Forschern, die von der Hitler-Regierung als minderwertig beurlaubt, in den Ruhestand versetzt oder verhaftet wurden," *IÄB*, January 1934, pp. 12–15; see also the additions to this list in the September 1934 issue of the journal, p. 143. The British magazine *Nature* printed lists of German scientists driven from their posts at this time; one article pointed out that among all the professions, physicians had suffered most from racial persecution. See *Nature*, June 18, 1938, pp. 1101–02; also E. Silva, "Der Kampf des Nazis gegen die ärztliche Wissenschaft und die Ärzteschaft," *IÄB*, July/August 1938, pp. 44–46. In the winter of 1937–38, *Nature* was banned from German scientific libraries (*Nature*, January 22, 1938, p. 151).
55. *IÄB*, February/March 1935, p. 41.
56. I would like to thank Kristie Macrakis for bringing this to my attention.
57. Stephan Leibfried, "Stationen der Abwehr," *Leo Baeck Institute Bulletin*, 62(1982): 13.
58. In 1932, among approximately 50,000 physicians in Germany, 32,000 practiced within the insurance companies (as *Kassenärzte*). Another 10,000 were employed in hospitals; 3,000 worked for the government (*Beamtenärzte*); 2,000 operated private practices (*freipraktizierende Ärzte*); and 3,000 were elderly or retired physicians no longer practicing medicine. Nearly three-quarters of Germany's practicing physicians were thus attached to the state-supported insurance programs; see Julius Hadrich, "Hochschulüberfüllung und wirtschaftliche Lage der Ärzteschaft," *Ärztliche Mitteilungen*, 33(1932): 787.
59. *IÄB*, June 1934, p. 107. The *IAB* pointed out that these figures were based on official records, and that the true figures for the numbers dismissed

might be higher. According to government statistics, among the 827 physicians dismissed, 91 were dismissed for "communist activities." Among the 174 dentists dismissed, 16 were accused of being communists; and among the 52 dental technicians (*Zahntechniker*), 3 were listed as communists. The *IÄB* noted, however, that membership in a "Jewish Freemasonry lodge" (for example, B'nai B'rith) was sometimes sufficient to qualify one as a "communist" and that members of the Verein Sozialistischer Ärzte were automatically considered communists, regardless of their actual party affiliation.

60. For the definition of who was a Jew and who was not according to the Nuremberg Laws, see "Verbot von Rassenmischehen," *Öffentlicher Gesundheitsdienst,* 2(1936): 885–887.
61. Ternon and Helman, *Les médecins allemands,* p. 70. The physicist Werner Heisenberg was branded a "white Jew" for his advocacy of quantum mechanics. On the Nazi concept of "white Jews," see "Weisse Juden in der Wissenschaft," *Das Schwarze Korps,* July 15, 1937, p. 2.
62. *IÄB,* February/March 1935, p. 40.
63. Wilhelm Stuckart and Hans Globke, *Kommentar zur deutschen Rassengesetzgebung* (Berlin, 1936).
64. See, for example, Victor Nordmark, "Über Rassenbegutachtung," *Öffentlicher Gesundheitsdienst,* 6(1940): 596–604.
65. Christian von Krogh, "Aus der erbbiologischen und rassenkundlichen Gutachterpraxis," *Ziel und Weg,* 9(1939): 41–44. Objects of interest for Krogh in this regard included "Stirn, Brauen, Oberlidraum, Lidfalte, Lidspalte, Nasenwurzel, Nasenrücken, Nasenspitze, Nasenflügel, Nasenlippenfurche, Hautober- und unterlippe, Schleimhautlippen, Mundkinnfurche, [and] Kinnform."
66. Sefton Delmer, *The Sinister Trail* (New York, 1961), p. 386.
67. In 1925 Reche founded the Wiener Gesellschaft für Rassenpflege; in 1932 he founded the Leipzig branch of the Society for Racial Hygiene. He was director of the Anthropological Institute of the University of Vienna (in 1926) and subsequently held positions as director of the Institut für Rassen- und Völkerkunde and director of the Ethnologisch-Anthropologisches Institut, both at the University of Leipzig. He also directed Leipzig's "Staatliches Forschungsinstitut für Völkerkunde" and served as head of Dresden's Staatsakademie für Rassen- und Gesundheitspflege. Reche's bibliography and curriculum vitae can be found in R 73/13816, BA.
68. Reche, interviewed by Köhn-Behrens in her *Was Ist Rasse?* p. 98.
69. See, for example, R 73/12756, no. 4943, BA.
70. Köhn-Behrens, *Was Ist Rasse?* pp. 98–101.
71. Peter Dahr, "Blutgruppenforschung und Rassenhygiene," *Ziel und Weg,* 9(1939): 98–108.
72. See, for example, Karl Horneck, "Über den Nachweis serologischer Verschiedenheiten der menschlichen Rassen," *Zeitschrift für menschliche Vererbungs- und Konstitutionslehre,* 26(1942): 309–319.
73. Between 1933 and 1939, Jews left Germany at a rate of about 46,000 per year. The two years during which the greatest numbers left were 1933

(when 63,400 left), and 1939 (68,000). According to the May 15, 1939, census, there were 233,973 "Glaubensjuden" and 380,892 "racial Jews" (persons with three or more Jewish grandparents) still in the Altreich. See *DÄ*, 70(1940): 226–227.

74. Ternon, *Les médecins allemands*, p. 96; also *Fortschritte der Medizin*, October 2, 1933, p. 886; and *IÄB*, May/June 1935, p. 79. *IÄB* reported that by the end of 1936, more than 4,000 of Germany's 7,500 Jewish physicians had fled the Reich, and that more than two-thirds of those who remained were over the age of forty-five. See *IÄB*, November/December 1936, p. 132. This figure for the number of emigrés may be slightly exaggerated.

75. *IÄB*, May/June 1935, pp. 79–80. Compare also Gerhard Baader, "Politisch motivierte Emigration deutscher Ärzte," *Berichte zur Wissenschaftsgeschichte*, 7(1984): 75.

76. *IÄB*, April/May 1938, p. 36.

77. "Nichtarischer Rückwanderer," *DÄ*, 65(1935): 521. The Gestapo reported that by 1935, 90,000 Jews and 20,000 non-Jews had fled the country, but also that 10,000 individuals had returned to the Reich, and that 90 percent of these were Jewish (ibid.).

78. The 1937 *Verzeichnis der deutschen Ärzte und Heilanstalten* (Reichsmedizinalkalender) listed the names of 4,220 physicians who were Jewish "in the Nuremberg definition of the term"—that is, with more than one grandparent of Jewish ancestry. Of these, 3,748 were in private practice (*niedergelassene*); 64 were practicing in Jewish hospitals, and 408 were not practicing medicine at all. See *DÄ*, 67(1937): 906.

79. Reported in *DÄ*, 72(1942): 300.

80. The "Vierte Verordnung zum Reichsbürgergesetz" is described in "Bestallungsentziehung der jüdischen Ärzte," *DÄ*, 68(1938): 545–547; see also *IÄB*, November/December 1938, p. 68. Vienna was allowed to keep only 330 Jewish physicians; similar purges were initiated among dentists, pharmacists, and other medical personnel.

81. Gütt to Himmler, NS 19/3434, BA.

82. *British Medical Journal*, August 13, 1938, p. 386.

83. Ramm, *Ärztliche Rechts- und Standeskunde*, p. 47.

84. For a list of 250 such measures, see Edgar Wetzel's "Gesetzliche Massnahmen zur Lösung der Judenfrage," *Informationsdienst*, October 30, 1938.

85. Ramm, *Ärztliche Rechts- und Standeskunde*, pp. 47–48. When the July 25, 1938, ordinance was passed preventing the practice of medicine by Jews (except on other Jews), there were 3,670 Jewish physicians in Germany, representing just under 7 percent of the entire profession. Ramm contrasted the situation in Germany (the "Altreich") with that of Vienna, where 67 percent of all doctors were said to be Jewish. Vienna was commonly cited as the European city where Jews exercised the greatest influence in medicine. *Volk und Rasse* (10[1935]: 331), for example, reported that among 3,100 Viennese doctors in 1935, 2,500 were Jewish.

86. H. H. Meier, "Das Ende des jüdischen Arzttums," *Ziel und Weg*, 9(1939): 110–112.

87. *British Medical Journal,* July 19, 1941, p. 108; also November 29, 1941, p. 794.
88. *British Medical Journal,* November 15, 1941, p. 714. See also "Failure of German Army Medical Service," *Journal of the American Medical Association,* 119(1942): 665.
89. "Um die Arztkosten in der Krankenversicherung," *Ärztliche Mitteilungen,* 27(1926): 270.
90. *ÄfB,* 42(1937): 479. German gross national product (national income) changes as follows (in millions of reichsmarks): 1926, 62,700; 1928, 75,400; 1932, 45,175; 1934, 52,700.
91. Hadrich, "Hochschulüberfüllung," p. 787.
92. Carl Jung wrote of the "boundless misery" of the German doctor (*Neuste Züricher Nachrichten,* March 13, 1934).
93. Wuttke-Groneberg, ed., *Medizin im Nationalsozialismus,* pp. 334–338. Wuttke-Groneberg also notes, however, that this decline was less than that suffered by the economy as a whole. Between 1928 and 1932, physicians' taxable income declined about 25 percent (from 12,600 RM to 9,500 RM); German national income (*Volkseinkommen*) as a whole, however, declined by about 40 percent.
94. *MMW,* 80(1933): 81. The number of persons covered by Germany's health insurance programs (not including family members) evolved as follows:

Year	No. covered
1885	4,700,000
1910	14,000,000
1930	20,300,000
1931	19,000,000
1932	16,650,000
1935	21,000,000
1936	22,000,000

For statistics on the structure and history of the Krankenkassen, see Johannes Scherler, "Zur Jahresende," *ÄfB,* 42(1937): 2–10, 27–33.
95. "Berliner Brief," *MMW,* 80(1933): 225.
96. Hadrich, "Hochschulüberfüllung," p. 787.
97. L. Achner, "Hochschulüberfüllung und akademischer Arbeitsmarkt," *Ärztliche Mitteilungen,* 33(1932): 790. Achner reported that 375,000 academically trained professionals (doctors, lawyers, engineers, and so on) were employed in Germany in 1932.
98. Vollmann, "Die Ärzte im Drang der Zeit," *DÄ,* 63(1933): 2.
99. Heinz Keilhack, "Student und Überfüllung des Medizinstudiums," *Ärztliche Mitteilungen,* 33(1932): 799.
100. Reinhold Stairer described such measures in his *Die akademische Berufsnot* (Jena, 1932).
101. *DÄ,* 63(1933): 2.

102. Fritz Lenz, "Arbeitslosigkeit und Rassenhygiene," *Rasse, Volk und Staat, Rassenhygienisches Beiblatt zum Völkischen Beobachter,* 3(June 1933): 1.
103. The number of women studying medicine grew from 900 in 1913 to 4,919 in the summer semester of 1932 (*MMW*, April 21, 1933, p. 634). For the attack on women studying medicine, see Weller, "Gegen Studium und Beruf der Frau," in *Studentenwerk,* vol. 6, nos. 1 and 2; also Hartnacke's *Bildungswahn—Volkstod* (Munich, 1931).
104. *Praemedicus,* 12(1932): 957–958, 1036–38.
105. *ÄfB,* 42(1937): 649.
106. Ramm, *Ärztliche Rechts- und Standeskunde,* p. 56.
107. *MMW,* 80(1933): 364–365; also *Ärztliche Mitteilungen,* 34(1933): 183–184, where we hear that "finally something is happening. The government is making a serious effort to implement measures to regulate the academic market." In 1934 the president of the Institute for Labor and Unemployment Insurance awarded 500,000 RM to the Deutsche Forschungsgemeinschaft to help academics find jobs. This was the so-called Wissenschaftliche Akademikerhilfe (*Deutscher Wissenschaftsdienst* [Berlin, 1935], p. 9).
108. *DÄ,* 63(1933): 153–155.
109. "Numerus clausus für Medizinstudenten in Bayern," *MMW,* 80(1933): 592.
110. Stephan Leibfried and Florian Tennstedt, *Berufsverbot und Sozialpolitik 1933* (1979), 3rd ed. (Bremen, 1981), p. xv.
111. Ibid.
112. *DÄ,* 63(1933): 154.
113. Wuttke-Groneberg, ed., *Medizin im Nationalsozialismus,* p. 347. These are figures for taxable income—that is, after deducting expenses.
114. See, for example, Georg Lukács, *Geschichte und Klassenbewusstsein* (Vienna, 1922); Otto Bauer, *Das Weltbild des Kapitalismus* (1916), in *Der lebendige Marxismus,* ed. Otto Jennsen (Jena, 1924); Franz Borkenau, *Der Übergang vom feudalen zum bürgerlichen Weltbild* (Paris, 1934); Edgar Zilsel, *Die Entstehung des Geniebegriffs* (Tübingen, 1926); Karl Mannheim, *Ideologie und Utopie* (Bonn, 1929); Boris Hessen, "The Social and Economic Roots of Newton's Principia," in *Science at the Crossroads,* ed. N. I. Bukharin et al. (1931) (London, 1971); and Ludwik Fleck, *Die Entstehung und Entwicklung einer wissenschaftlichen Tatsache* (Basel, 1935).
115. "Zeitgenössisches," *Neuste Züricher Nachrichten,* March 13, 1934. Psychotherapy, like other aspects of German medicine, was *gleichgeschaltet* in the early months of the Nazi regime. Geoffrey Cocks's *Psychotherapy in the Third Reich* (Oxford, 1985) presents a comprehensive history of the Göring Institute, the leading institution in German psychoanalysis during the Nazi period.
116. Hermann Berger, "Auslegung des Begriffs, 'Neue Deutsche Heilkunde'," *Zeitschrift für Ärztliche Fortbildung,* 33(1936): 534.
117. Heinrich Chantraine, "Naturwissenschaft und Raumsichtigkeit," *Ziel und Weg,* 6(1936): 7.

118. Ibid., p. 11. See also his "Die Raumsichtigkeit bei verschiedenen Rassen und Berufen," *Ziel und Weg,* 9(1939): 60–68.
119. Alexander von Senger, "Rasse und Baukunst," *Ziel und Weg,* 5(1935): 249–255, 267–273, 566–569.
120. Wolfgang Uter, "Auswirkungen des Erb- und Rassegedankens in der Geburtshilfe und Gynäkologie," *Ärzteblatt für Pommern,* 3(1936): 210.
121. Karl Kötschau, "Die nationalsozialistische Revolution in der Medizin," *Ziel und Weg* 3(1933): 292–296, 457–463; 4(1934): 11–16, 595–598, 884–889; and 5(1935): 11–14, 132–138.
122. Ibid., 1935, pp. 133–135.
123. Ibid.
124. *Rembrandt als Erzieher,* written in the early years of the twentieth century, became a classic of the Nazi movement in the 1920s and was subsequently cited over and over again by Nazi philosophers. The passage cited here is taken from the frontispiece to *Ziel und Weg,* 5(1935).
125. "Internationale Medizinische Woche in Montreux," *Ziel und Weg,* 5(1935): 379.
126. Alfred Böttcher, "Die Lösung der Judenfrage," *Ziel und Weg,* 5(1935): 226. Professor Böttcher's works also include a book called *Das Scheinglück der Technik* (Weimar, 1932).
127. On Nazi views of Jews and natural medicine, see "Der jüdische Emanationsanalytiker Perls," *Volksgesundheitswacht,* February 1937, pp. 13–14. See also Chapter 8.
128. According to the editors of *Ziel und Weg,* 650 of 1,350 Slovakian physicians at this time were Jewish. See *Ziel und Weg,* 9(1939): 520.
129. Berger, "Das deutsche Beispiel macht Schule," pp. 52–53. In 1942 the *Archiv für Rassen- und Gesellschaftsbiologie* (36[1942]: 82) reported that a Dutch law of May 1, 1941, had forced 367 Jewish doctors, 80 dentists, and 42 pharmacists from their posts.
130. *ÄfB,* 44(1939): 142.
131. *IÄB,* May/June 1937, p. 60. A minority issued a protest against this decision, and indeed the decision did not last. On September 12, 1937, at the annual meeting of Poland's medical organizations, a group of National Socialist physicians were unable to get the Aryan clause written into the permanent statutes of the organization (*IÄB,* October 1937, p. 105).
132. *Volk und Rasse,* 13(1938): 262.
133. Berger, "Das deutsche Beispiel macht Schule," pp. 52–53. See also "Ungarns zweites Judengesetz," *DÄ,* 69(1939): 378–379. On February 15, 1939, Hungarian Premier Imredy was forced to resign because of his Jewish ancestry.
134. *DÄ,* 67(1937): 1106.
135. *Akademia,* April 25, 1940, p. 2; also "Böhmen entlässt jüdische Beamte und Ärzte," *Akademia,* April 22, 1940, p. 2.
136. *Zeitschrift für Ärztliche Fortbildung,* 39(1941): 444. For a discussion of the conditions under which Jewish physicians fleeing Germany would be allowed to practice medicine in France, see "La situation des étudiants en

médecine juifs allemands dans les facultés de médecine," *Le concours médical,* September 2, 1934, pp. 2453–56.
137. *Die Gesundheitsführung,* 14(1944): 88.
138. *DÄ,* 64(1934): 70.
139. *British Medical Journal,* July 16, 1938, p. 155. By 1938 a total of 11,000 German refugees had fled to England. Neville Chamberlain went on record opposing quotas for refugees; in 1938 he proposed resettling refugees in British colonial territories (*British Medical Journal,* December 3, 1938, p. 1183).
140. *British Medical Journal,* July 9, 1938, p. 79.
141. "Massnahmen gegen die jüdischen Ärzte in Österreich," *IÄB,* February/March 1935, p. 42. Austrian racial law before the *Anschluss* was expressed in the "Gesetz zum Schutz des keimenden Lebens."
142. "Nazigeist an den Prager deutschen Hochschulen," *IÄB,* April 1935, pp. 45–46.
143. Ibid., p. 47.
144. Ibid., p. 48.
145. Ibid., pp. 45–47.
146. Report by the Reichsverband der Deutschen Ärztevereine in der Tschechoslowakischen Republik, reprinted in *IÄB,* September 1935, p. 95.
147. On German-Italian relations on the question of racial policy, see Reiner Pommerin, "Rassenpolitische Differenzen in Verhältnisse der Achse Berlin-Rom 1938–43," *Vierteljahrshefte für Zeitgeschichte,* 27(1979): 646–660.
148. *Informationsdienst,* July 30, 1938. The *Informationsdienst* also listed five other Italian periodicals concerned with racial questions: *Il Tevere,* a Rome daily; *Quadrivio,* a Rome bimonthly; *Il Regime Fascista,* a Cremona daily; *Il Giornalissimo,* a Rome monthly; and *La Vita Italiana,* a Rome monthly. Although Italian racial hygiene never reached the dimensions of the movement in Germany, Italy did have a racial hygiene movement. *La Difesa della Razza,* edited by a Mr. Interlandi (publisher of *Il Tevere*), played a role in Italy similar to that of *Rasse* or *Neues Volk* in Germany.
149. *Informationsdienst,* September 10, 1938; also *Ziel und Weg,* 5(1935): 391.
150. "Der Rückzug des Papstes Pius XI," *Informationsdienst,* September 10, 1938.
151. "Mussolini antwortet dem Papst," *Informationsdienst,* September 10, 1938; also Walter Gross, "Italiens Stellung zum Rassengedanken," *Informationsdienst,* July 30, 1938.
152. "Die italienische Erklärung über die Rasse vom 6. October, 1938," *Informationsdienst,* November 30, 1938. See also *Ziel und Weg,* 9(1939): 450–452.
153. *ÄRW,* 1(1940): 201.
154. Lothar Löffler presented this point of view in his "Die Rassenfrage als Brennpunkt des weltanschaulichen Kampfes," *Ziel und Weg,* 6(1936): 101.
155. *IÄB,* January/February 1938, pp. 21–23.
156. See Kenneth M. Ludmerer, *Genetics and American Society* (Baltimore, 1972), pp. 87–119.
157. *Ziel und Weg,* 3(1933): 85–90.

158. *DÄ*, 67(1937): 1108. The German press also reported examples of American hostility toward Nazi policies. On September 25, 1935, for example, *Der Deutsche Weg* reported that the general assembly of the Zentrale Vereinigung Deutscher Katholiker in the United States had rejected "Communism, Nazism and Fascism," and also the "Rassenwahn," nationalism and anti-Semitism of the contemporary German regime.
159. "Jüdische Ärzte in USA," *DÄ*, 69(1939): 379.
160. "Strenge Rassengrundsätze in USA," *Akademia*, November 15, 1939, pp. 2–3; also *DÄ*, 69(1939): 441.
161. *ARGB*, 33(1939): 96, 447.
162. "Jewish Physicians in Berlin," *Eugenical News*, 19(1934): 126.
163. Ramm, *Ärztliche Rechts- und Standeskunde*, pp. 136–137.
164. Ibid., pp. 137–138.
165. Böttcher, "Die Lösung der Judenfrage," p. 226. The metaphor of the Jew as "parasite," "bacillus," "poison," or "vermin" predates the Nazi period: as early as 1895 Hermann Ahlwardt labeled Jews "beasts of prey," and "cholera bacilli" as part of an effort to halt Jewish immigration (Dawidowicz, *The War against the Jews*, p. 54).

7. The Destruction of "Lives Not Worth Living"

1. *Der Prozess gegen die Hauptkriegsverbrecher vor dem internationalen Militärgerichtshof*, vol. 26 (Nuremberg, 1947), p. 169. The language of the command ("*Gnadentod unter Verantwortung . . .*") was taken in part from Helmut Unger's 1936 kitsch novel, *Sendung und Gewissen*.
2. For background on the killings, see the comprehensive study by Ernst Klee, *"Euthanasie" im NS-Staat* (Frankfurt, 1983). A bibliography containing more than 2,000 entries on the question of euthanasia has recently been published by Gerhard Koch: see his *Euthanasie, Sterbehilfe, eine dokumentierte Bibliographie* (Erlangen, 1984).
3. Blasius Szendi, "Selektiv-eugenische Bestrebungen in Ungarn," *Der Erbarzt*, 2(1935): 137; also "How Insanity Is Propagated," *Westminster Review*, 142(1894): 153–163.
4. Alfred Hoche and Rudolf Binding, *Die Freigabe der Vernichtung lebensunwerten Lebens* (Leipzig, 1920).
5. Müller-Hill, *Tödliche Wissenschaft*, p. 12.
6. I. Malbin, "Historische Betrachtungen zur Frage der Vernichtung lebensunwerten Lebens," *Archiv für Frauenkunde und Eugenetik*, 8(1922): 127–141. See also Max Nassauer, *Sterben . . . ich bitte darum* (Munich, 1911); Ewald Meltzer, *Das Problem der Abkürzung "lebensunwerten" Lebens* (Halle, 1925).
7. Ernst Mann, *Die Erlösung der Menschheit vom Elend* (Weimar, 1922).
8. E. Kirchner, "Anfänge rassenhygienischen Denkens in Morus 'Utopie' und Campanellas 'Sonnenstadt'," *ARGB*, 21(1927): 396; also 17(1925): 383–384. For Nietzsche's views on this topic, see his *Twilight of the Idols*, especially the section "Morals for Doctors."
9. *British Medical Journal*, December 21, 1940, p. 881.

10. Bertrand Russell, *Marriage and Morals* (London, 1927), p. 266. The 1929 American Horace Liveright edition was changed to read as follows: "There is no sound reason to regard negroes as on the average inferior to white men, although for work in the tropics they are indispensable, so that their extermination (apart from questions of humanity) would be highly undesirable," a change that rendered the passage nonsensical—especially curious, given the fact that Russell was supposed to be an unexcelled expert on logic and the meanings of words (New York, 1929, p. 180). I would like to thank Jim Adler for drawing this transmogrification to my attention.
11. See Maureen Gildea, "Euthanasia: A Review of the American Literature," senior thesis, Harvard University, 1983. Gildea notes the importance of the Depression in the rise of euthanasia proposals; she also shows that the American discussion largely came to a halt in the early forties, after rumors began to spread of the Nazi program of extermination.
12. W. A. Gould, "Euthanasia," *Journal of the Institute of Homeopathy,* 27(1933): 82.
13. Alexis Carrel, *Man the Unknown* (London, 1936), p. 296.
14. W. G. Lennox, "Should They Live? Certain Economic Aspects of Medicine," *American Scholar,* 7(1938): 454–466. Dr. Abraham Wolbarst, in the 1936 *Forum and Century,* maintained that human society must be protected against "deterioration and ultimate destruction," and that society may have to "painlessly remove those unfortunates who are doomed to constitute a useless burden to themselves and society" (cited in Gildea, "Euthanasia," p. 42).
15. Foster Kennedy, "The Problem of Social Control of the Congenitally Defective: Education, Sterilization, Euthanasia," *American Journal of Psychiatry,* 99(1942): 13–16; compare pp. 141–143. See also Kennedy's article, "Euthanasia: To Be or Not to Be," in *Colliers,* May 20, 1939, p. 15. A "Forster" Kennedy of New York is listed as having delivered a concluding address at the Third International Congress for Medical Postgraduate Study in Berlin in 1937; this may or may not be the same person ("Ärztliches Fortbildungswesen," box 4, Deutsche Kongress-Zentrale, Hoover Institution Archives).
16. Mitscherlich and Mielke, *Medizin ohne Menschlichkeit,* p. 256; also *The Gallup Poll* (New York, 1971), p. 71.
17. Klee, *"Euthanasie,"* pp. 46–47. Paul Wulf, himself a victim of the Nazi sterilization program, recalls that in 1936 a number of patients in psychiatric institutions were killed by injections. See his "Zwangssterilisiert," in *Erfassung zur Vernichtung,* ed. Roth, p. 7.
18. "Unser Reichsärzteführer spricht," *Ziel und Weg,* 5(1935): 431–437.
19. Mitscherlich and Mielke, *Medizin ohne Menschlichkeit,* p. 184.
20. Michael Straight, "Germany Executes Her 'Unfit,' " *New Republic,* May 5, 1941, pp. 627–628. See also W. L. Shirer, "Mercy Deaths in Germany," *Reader's Digest,* July 1941, pp. 55–58.
21. Friedrich Kaul, *Nazimordaktion T-4* (Berlin [East], 1973), p. 58; see also Mitscherlich and Mielke, *Medizin ohne Menschlichkeit,* pp. 191–192.

22. *Frankfurter Zeitung*, March 3, 1937.
23. Helmut Unger, *Sendung und Gewissen* (Berlin, 1936).
24. See the commentary on the film *Ich klage an!* in *ÄRW*, 2(1941): 237.
25. Reported in *IÄB*, October/November 1934, pp. 159–160.
26. Adolf Dorner, *Mathematik im Dienste der nationalpolitischen Erziehung* (Frankfurt, 1935).
27. Kaul, *Nazimordaktion T-4*, pp. 170–173.
28. Klee, *"Euthanasie,"* pp. 340–341.
29. W. Goeze, "Gesundheitsfürsorge in der Invalidenversicherung 1933," *Reichs-Gesundheitsblatt*, 10(1935): 183.
30. *IÄB*, June/July 1936, pp. 82–83.
31. Verschuer, *Erbpathologie*, pp. 38–39.
32. *IÄB*, November/December 1935, pp. 124–125. Georg Sticker, professor of the history of medicine at Würzburg, expressed a similar view when he proclaimed: "The Aryan rejects offspring with signs of retardation, crippling, or inferiority. Children who from birth are malformed, insane, ineducable, or otherwise useless are expelled, or at least tolerated only insofar as they do not disturb the peace and stability of the household and state." See *Sozialhygienische Mitteilungen*, 19(1936).
33. Klee, *"Euthanasie,"* p. 46.
34. Ibid., p. 79.
35. *Informationsdienst des Hauptamtes für Volksgesundheit der NSDAP*, November 1942, p. 75. Kurt Blome issued the 1942 version of these orders. See also *DÄ*, 70(1940): 142. Klee in his *"Euthanasie"* includes a reproduction of this secret *Runderlass* of the Reich Ministry of the Interior (pp. 80–81).
36. Eugen Stähle, "Die Hebammen von Heute," *Wiener Klinische Wochenschrift*, 55(1942): 561–566.
37. Kaul, *Nazimordaktion T-4*, p. 36.
38. Mitscherlich and Mielke, *Medizin ohne Menschlichkeit*, p. 193. See also Pfannmüller's article, "Über das Lebenserwartungsalter unheilbar Geisteskranker in Heil- und Pflegeanstalten," *Öffentlicher Gesundheitsdienst*, 6(1940): 417–432, 449–457, where he noted that the life expectancy of the *Krankenmaterial* under his care in recent years had been "low."
39. Kaul, *Nazimordaktion T-4*, p. 33.
40. Ibid., p. 50.
41. "Der öffentliche Krüppelfürsorge im Reichsgau Wartheland," *ÄRW*, 2(1941): 231.
42. Mitscherlich and Mielke, *Medizin ohne Menschlichkeit*, pp. 211–212.
43. Ibid., pp. 191, 212.
44. These three organizations were the Reichsarbeitsgemeinschaft Heil- und Pflegeanstalten; the Gemeinnützige Stiftung für Anstaltspflege; and the Gemeinnützige Kranken-Transport-G.m.b.H.
45. Müller-Hill, *Tödliche Wissenschaft*, p. 17.
46. Klee, *"Euthanasie,"* pp. 95–98.
47. Cited in Kaul, *Nazimordaktion T-4*, pp. 77–78.

48. Müller-Hill, *Tödliche Wissenschaft*, p. 17. Extermination units later began using the more effective gas Cyclon B, supplied by one of the subsidiaries of the conglomerate IG Farben.
49. Ibid., pp. 17–19.
50. Kaul, *Nazimordaktion T-4*, p. 64.
51. Aly, "Medizin gegen Unbrauchbare," in Aly et al., *Aussonderung und Tod* (Berlin [West], 1985), p. 23. Records for these figures can be found in roll 18, T-1021, National Archives, Washington, D.C.
52. Wertham, *A Sign for Cain*, p. 157.
53. Kaul, *Nazimordaktion T-4*, pp. 106–112.
54. Klee, *"Euthanasie,"* p. 53.
55. Aly, "Medizin gegen Unbrauchbare," pp. 19–31.
56. Peter Breggin, "The Killing of Mental Patients," in *Madness Network News Reader*, ed. Sherry Hirsch et al. (San Francisco, 1974). I would like to thank Jenny Miller for drawing this to my attention.
57. Wertham, *A Sign for Cain*, p. 167.
58. Cited in Aly, "Medizin gegen Unbrauchbare," p. 11. See also Karl Heinz Roth and Götz Aly, "Das 'Gesetz über die Sterbehilfe bei unheilbar Kranken'," in *Erfassung zur Vernichtung*, ed. Roth, pp. 101–120.
59. Mitscherlich and Mielke, *Medizin ohne Menschlichkeit*, pp. 186–188.
60. Götz Aly, paper delivered to the Free University's Institut für Geschichte der Medizin in Berlin, July 1985.
61. Klee, *"Euthanasie,"* p. 48.
62. Aly, "Medizin gegen Unbrauchbare," pp. 14–19.
63. See, for example, Theobald Lang, "Die Belastung des Judentums mit Geistig-Auffälligen," *Nationalsozialistische Monatshefte*, 3(1932): 23–30.
64. Walter Gross, "Die Familie," *Informationsdienst*, September 20, 1938.
65. Peltret, "Der Arzt als Führer und Erzieher," *DÄ*, 65(1935): 565–566.
66. Wagner, "Unser Reichsärzteführer spricht," pp. 432–433.
67. See A. Pilcz, "Die periodischen Geistesstörungen," *Wiener Klinische Rundschau*, 16(1902): 490.
68. Martin Engländer, *Die auffallend häufigen Krankheitserscheinungen der jüdischen Rasse* (Vienna, 1902).
69. See *Jüdisches Volksblatt*, no. 50(1902). In 1919 a Dr. Rafael Becker published evidence that, in 1900–1904, Jews in Switzerland were more than twice as likely to be mentally ill as Protestants or Catholics. See his "Die Geisteserkrankungen bei den Juden in der Schweiz," *Zeitschrift für Demographie und Statistik der Juden*, April 1919, pp. 52–57.
70. Wagner, "Unser Reichsärzteführer spricht," p. 432.
71. Verschuer, *Erbpathologie*, pp. 86–182.
72. Edgar Schulz, "Judentum und Degeneration," *Ziel und Weg*, 5(1935): 349–355.
73. Interestingly, a number of racial hygienists rejected the notion that inbreeding produces a decline in racial fitness. Fritz Lenz, for example, supported marriage between cousins and even siblings, arguing that such inbreeding was dangerous only where deleterious recessive alleles were present. See his *Menschliche Auslese*, p. 506.

74. Pommerin, *Die Rheinlandbastarde*, p. 47.
75. Schulz, "Judentum und Degeneration," pp. 349–355.
76. Wilhelm Hildebrandt, *Rassenmischung und Krankheit* (Leipzig, 1935). These views are not out of line with those among Anglo-American geneticists of the 1920s—see William Provine, "Geneticists and the Biology of Race Crossing," *Science*, 182(1973): 790–796.
77. Franz Goldmann and Georg Wolff, *Tod und Todesursachen unter den Berliner Juden* (Berlin, 1937), published by the Reichsvertretung der Juden in Deutschland and reported in the *British Medical Journal*, October 2, 1937, p. 663. For a contemporary American critique of the idea of racial susceptibility to disease, see Benjamin Malzberg, "The Prevalence of Mental Disease among Jews," *Mental Hygiene*, October 1930, pp. 926–946.
78. M. Stämmler and E. Bieneck, "Statistische Untersuchungen über die Todesursachen der deutschen und jüdischen Bevölkerung von Breslau," *MMW*, 87(1940): 447–450.
79. "German Medicine, Race, and Religion," *British Medical Journal*, August 17, 1940, p. 230.
80. *Krakauer Zeitung*, January 14/15, 1940.
81. Ibid., February 8, 1940. See also *The German New Order in Poland*, published for the Polish Ministry of Information in London, 1942, p. 218.
82. The *Generalgouvernement* was the name given to the provisional government established in Nazi-occupied Poland.
83. *Kölnische Zeitung*, April 5, 1941; see also *The German New Order*, p. 241.
84. Wilhelm Hagen, *Auftrag und Wirklichkeit, Sozialarzt im 20. Jahrhundert* (Munich-Gräfelfing, 1978), p. 166.
85. *Informationsdienst des Hauptamtes für Volksgesundheit der NSDAP*, October/December 1943, p. 110.
86. *Manchester Guardian*, November 3, 1939.
87. Hagen, *Auftrag und Wirklichkeit*, p. 164. Dawidowicz, in *The War against the Jews*, reports that there were 355,000 Jews in prewar Warsaw (p. 265); the discrepancy may lie in the fact that Hagen is counting "racial" rather than religious affiliation.
88. *British Medical Journal*, July 6, 1940, p. 36.
89. Hagen, *Auftrag und Wirklichkeit*, pp. 179, 171. *The German New Order in Poland* reported that by May 1941, the mortality was even higher, at 5,000 per month, representing an annual death rate of 120 per 1,000, or about twelve times the prewar rate (p. 243).
90. Hagen, *Auftrag und Wirklichkeit*, pp. 171–181.
91. *Krakauer Zeitung*, March 12, 1940.
92. On Hamburg attorney Jürgen Rieger's 1978 defense of Arpad Wigand, see "SS und Polizeiführer von Warschau verurteilt," *Frankfurter Allgemeine Zeitung*, December 8, 1981.
93. Robert Ritter, "Kriminalität und Primitivität," *Monatsschrift für Kriminalbiologie*, 31(1940): 197–210. In the Nazi period, leading works in the field of criminal biology include Franz Exner's *Kriminalbiologie in ihren Grundzügen* (Hamburg, 1939); Hans Fickert's *Rassenhygienische Verbrechens-*

bekämpfung (Leipzig, 1938); and Ferdinand von Neureiter's *Kriminalbiologie* (Berlin, 1940). See also the bibliography in Friedrich Stumpfl's *Erbanlagen und Verbrechen* (Berlin, 1935).
94. *Informationsdienst,* October 10, 1938.
95. See, for example, Johannes Lange, *Verbrechen als Schicksal, Studien an kriminellen Zwillingen* (Leipzig, 1928).
96. "Der 4. Kriminal-Biologische Kongress in Hamburg," *Archiv für Bevölkerungswissenschaft und Bevölkerungspolitik,* 4(1936): 51.
97. See Rainer Fetscher's "Aufgaben und Organisation einer Kartei der Minderwertigen," *Mitteilungen der Kriminalbiologischen Gesellschaft,* 1(1928): 55–62.
98. Leading German journals and serials of criminal biology included *Arbeiten aus der bayerischen Kriminalbiologien Sammelstelle (1925–); Mitteilungen der Kriminalbiologischen Gesellschaft* (1927–); and *Monatsschrift für Kriminalbiologie und Strafrechtsreform* (1904–1944). In 1927 a number of scholars in this field banded together to form the Internationale Gesellschaft Kriminalbiologischer Forscher; scholars in Bavaria and Saxony were especially active in organizing this field.
99. For a comprehensive list of course offerings in criminal biology at German universities, see *Monatsschrift für Kriminalbiologie und Strafrechtsreform,* 32(1941): 53–73.
100. *Reichs-Gesundheitsblatt,* 12(1937): 118. See also "Kriminalbiologische Sammelstelle in Berlin," *ÄfB,* 42(1937): 623.
101. *DÄ,* 68(1938): 858.
102. Johannes Schottky, ed., *Rasse und Krankheit* (Munich, 1937).
103. Ibid., p. 681.
104. Ibid.
105. Wagner, "Unser Reichsärzteführer spricht," p. 433.
106. *Die Gesundheitsführung,* 10(1940): 199.
107. See, for example, Rudolf Ramm, "Die Aussiedlung der Juden als europäisches Problem," *Die Gesundheitsführung,* 11(1941): 175–178; also Walter Gross, "Rassenpolitische Voraussetzungen einer europäischen Gesamtlösung der Judenfrage," *Rassenpolitische Auslands-Korrespondenz,* March 1941, pp. 1–6. Wilhelm Stuckart and Hans Globke in 1936 proposed "dissimilation" as the only possible solution to the Jewish question. See their *Kommentar zur deutschen Rassengesetzgebung* (Berlin, 1936), p. 17.
108. W. Bormann, "Grundsätze der deutschen Ostraumpolitik," *ÄRW,* 2(1941): 168.
109. "Die Juden im Generalgouvernement," *DÄ,* 70(1940): 430–431.
110. Ibid.
111. Ibid., p. 432.
112. The deportation of Jews to Madagascar was one of the options Nazi authorities considered in 1939 and 1940. In January 1940 Otto Reche suggested this idea in a letter to SS Gruppenführer Pancke, head of the SS Rasse- und Siedlungsamt; he also proposed that Germany's Jews be deported to Bohemia and Moravia as a "gift" (*Gratisbeigabe*) to these newly

conquered territories (letter to Pancke, January 21, 1940, in the Berlin Document Center, Reche file). The letter is dated 21. Julmonds 1939; from the context, however, it is clear that the letter was written in early 1940.
113. "Gründung der Reichsuniversität Posen," *ÄRW*, 2(1941): 59.
114. Mitscherlich and Mielke, *Medizin ohne Menschlichkeit*, pp. 240–241.
115. Ibid., p. 242.
116. Kaul, *Nazimordaktion T-4*, pp. 90–95.
117. Ibid., pp. 97–99; also Klee, *Euthanasie*, pp. 258–259.
118. Aly, "Medizin gegen Unbrauchbare," p. 28. See also Asmus Finzen, *Auf dem Dienstweg, die Verstrickung einer Anstalt in die Tötung psychisch Kranker* (Rehburg-Loccum, 1984), pp. 23–60.
119. Aly, "Medizin gegen Unbrauchbare," pp. 30–39.
120. The first gassing of Jews who had not been in hospitals took place at the concentration camp at Chelmno on December 9, 1941. (Jews were singled out for destruction among psychiatric patients as early as June 1940.)
121. Mitscherlich and Mielke, *Medizin ohne Menschlichkeit*, pp. 219–220.
122. Ibid., p. 216.
123. *New York Times*, August 21, 1945.
124. See M. Domarus, ed., *Hitler. Reden und Proklamationen 1932–45* (Munich, 1965), vol. 2, pp. 1057–58.
125. See Hans Mommsen, "Die Realisierung des Utopischen: Die 'Endlösung der Judenfrage' im 'Dritten Reich,'" *Geschichte und Gesellschaft*, 9(1983): 394–398, for a discussion of Hitler's role in the final solution.
126. Müller-Hill, *Tödliche Wissenschaft*, p. 20.
127. *Ärztin*, 15(1939): 4.
128. Conti issued these remarks at a meeting of the Wissenschaftlichen Gesellschaft der Deutschen Ärzte des Öffentlichen Dienst. See "Die Erb- und Rassenpflege in den letzten beiden Jahren," *Ärztin*, 15(1939): 28; also *DÄ*, 68(1938): 894–896.
129. Walter Gross, "Die Familie," *Informationsdienst*, September 20, 1938.
130. See, for example, Bernhard Hörmann, "Zur Judenfrage," *Die Volksgesundheitswacht*, Erntin 1933, pp. 3–10.
131. See, for example, "Zur Lösung der Judenfrage," *DÄ*, 72(1942): 16–17; also 72(1942): 33.
132. "Das Ende der jüdischen Kriegsziele," *DÄ*, 70(1940): 312–314; also "Löst Rumanien die Judenfrage?" *DÄ*, 70(1940): 359–360.
133. Otmar von Verschuer, *Leitfaden der Rassenhygiene* (Leipzig, 1941), p. 127; see also his "Rassenbiologie der Juden," *Forschungen zur Judenfrage*, 3(1938): 137–151.
134. Müller-Hill, *Tödliche Wissenschaft*, pp. 18–19.
135. Gross, "Rassenpolitische Voraussetzungen," pp. 1–6. Gross rejected the option of exiling the Jews to an Arab country on the grounds that Jews were also alien to the "Semitic people."
136. Otmar von Verschuer, "Bevölkerungs- und Rassefragen in Europa," *Europäischer Wissenschaftsdienst*, 1(1944): 3.
137. "Vorbereitende Massnahmen zur Endlösung der europäischen Judenfragen," listed as paper no. 881 in the "Vertrauliche Informationen" der Par-

teikanzlei; cited in *Informationsdienst des Hauptamtes für Volksgesundheit der NSDAP,* November 1942, p. 69.
138. NSD 28/8, BA.
139. See Klee, *"Euthanasie,"* pp. 367–379. On the connections of the euthanasia operation and the final solution, see Karl Schleunes, "Nationalsozialistische Entschlussbildung und die Aktion T 4," in *Der Mord an den Juden im zweiten Weltkrieg,* ed. Eberhard Jäckel and Jürgen Rohwer (Stuttgart, 1985), pp. 70–83.
140. *ARGB,* 1(1904): 99–100.
141. Dobrovsky, "Gebissuntersuchungen an homosexuellen Männer," *Zeitschrift für Konstitutionslehre,* 10(1924); Arthur Weil, "Sprechen anatomische Grundlagen für das Angeborensein der Homosexualität?" *Archiv für Frauenkunde,* 10(1924): 23–51.
142. "Bericht über die 11. Versammlung der Internationalen Föderation Eugenischer Organisationen," *Archiv der Julius Klaus-Stiftung,* 10(1935): 40. In 1937 Verschuer presented the concordance of sexual preference among twins as evidence that homosexuality was heritable. See his *Erbpathologie,* p. 90.
143. See, for example, J. Lange, "Die Feststellung und Wertung geistiger Störungen im Ehegesundheitsgesetz," *Öffentlicher Gesundheitsdienst,* 4(1938): 533.
144. "Staatsfeinde sind auszumerzen!" *Informationsdienst,* June 20, 1938.
145. Deussen, "Sexualpathologie," *Fortschritte der Erbpathologie,* 3(1939): 90–99.
146. See Theobald Lang, "Beitrag zur Frage nach der genetischen Bedingtheit der Homosexualität," *Zeitschrift für Neurologie,* 155(1936): 5; 157(1937): 557; and 162(1938): 627. For Goldschmidt's theory, see his *Die sexuelle Zwischenstufen* (Berlin, 1931).
147. "Zum Problem der Homosexualität," *IÄB,* December 1937, p. 114.
148. "Staatsfeinde sind auszumerzen!" *Informationsdienst,* June 20, 1938. This article also contains a discussion of other "natural affinities" between Jews and homosexuals.
149. For the broad outlines of this history, see James Rector, *The Nazi Extermination of Homosexuals* (New York, 1981).
150. For a Nazi perspective on Germany's "Gypsy problem," see A. Würth, "Bemerkungen zur Zigeunerfrage und Zigeunerforschung in Deutschland," *Vehandlungen der Deutschen Gesellschaft für Rassenforschung,* 9(1938): 95–98; for a bibliography of works on Germany's "Gypsy question," see Robert Ritter, "Zeitschriftenartikel über Zigeunerfragen," *Fortschritte der Erbpathologie,* 3(1939): 2–20. For a postwar history of the persecution of Gypsies in the Third Reich, see Joachim S. Hohmann, *Zigeuner und Zigeunerwissenschaft, ein Beitrag zur Grundlagenforschung und Dokumentation des Völkermordes im "Dritten Reich"* (Marburg, 1980).
151. *Öffentlicher Gesundheitsdienst,* 4(1938): 995–996.
152. "Rassische Erfassung der Zigeunern," *DÄ,* 68(1938): 901.
153. Verschuer, *Leitfaden der Rassenhygiene,* p. 130.
154. *Die Gesundheitsführung,* 14(1944): 28.

155. Müller-Hill, *Tödliche Wissenschaft*, p. 20.
156. Ibid., pp. 13–23.
157. See, for example, Kurt Klare, *Tuberkulosefragen* (Leipzig, 1939), p. 51; also F. Koester, "Zeitgemässe Tuberkulosefragen," *Deutsches Tuberkulose-Blatt*, 12(1938): 25–29, 49–53.
158. See Kristin Kelting, "Das Tuberkuloseproblem im Nationalsozialismus," med. diss., University of Kiel, 1974.
159. The most important defense of the heritability of tuberculosis was Otmar von Verschuer and Karl Diehl, *Zwillingstuberkulose, Zwillingsforschung und erbliche Tuberkulosedisposition* (Jena, 1933).
160. F. Redeker, "Tuberkulose und Eugenik," *Zeitschrift für Tuberkulose*, 62(1931): 34. See also Kelting, "Das Tuberkuloseproblem," pp. 10–33.
161. See, for example, K. Schrempf, "Tuberkulosefürsorge und Vererbungsforschung," *Zeitschrift für Gesundheitsverwaltung und Gesundheitsfürsorge*, 6(1935): 25–34.
162. Susanne Hahn, "Ethische Grundlagen der faschistischen Medizin, dargestellt am Beispiel der Tuberkulosebekämpfung," in *Medizin im Faschismus*, ed. Thom and Spaar, pp. 139–140.
163. Mitscherlich and Mielke, *Medizin ohne Menschlichkeit*, pp. 231–236. Approximately 130,000 of the region's Jews had already been eliminated by this time.
164. Gerhard Baader, "Menschenexperimente," in *Ärzte im Nationalsozialismus*, ed. Kudlien, pp. 178–180.
165. Ibid., pp. 186–187.
166. Mitscherlich and Mielke, *Medizin ohne Menschlichkeit*, pp. 160–165.
167. Himmler to Deuschl, n.d.; Deuschl to Himmler, January 24, 1942, NS 19/3382, BA.
168. Documentation of these experiments can be found in Mitscherlich and Mielke, *Medizin ohne Menschlichkeit*, pp. 20–71.
169. Mitscherlich and Mielke, *Medizin ohne Menschlichkeit*, pp. 132–133, 158.
170. Ibid., pp. 26, 33, 253–256.
171. Mitscherlich and Mielke, *Doctors of Infamy*, p. xx.
172. These experiments were begun in August 1942 and lasted into 1943. Gebhardt and Fischer were later sentenced to death and life imprisonment, respectively, for their complicity (Mitscherlich and Mielke, *Medizin ohne Menschlichkeit*, pp. 150–153).
173. In 1943 the neurologist Georg Schaltenbrand published a book describing experiments showing doctor-induced transmission of encephalitis from apes to mental patients. See his *Die multiple Sklerose des Menschen und der übertragbare Markscheidenschwund des Affen* (Leipzig, 1943).
174. Baader, "Menschenexperimente," in *Ärzte im Nationalsozialismus*, ed. Kudlien, pp. 181–182.
175. Alexander, "Medicine under Dictatorship," p. 41.
176. See Kulenkampf, "Die Technik der Tubensterilisation zur Verhütung lebensunwerten Lebens," *Deutsche Medizinische Wochenschrift*, 59(1933): 1294–95.
177. Weinreich, *Hitler's Professors*, pp. 6–7.

8. The "Organic Vision" of Nazi Racial Science

1. Karl Kötschau, "Die nationalsozialistische Revolution in der Medizin," *Ziel und Weg*, 3(1933): 295.
2. Cited in J. Schaxel, "Deutsche Staatsbiologie," *Unter dem Banner des Marxismus*, 9(1935): 261.
3. "Mensch und Technik," *ÄRW*, 2(1941): 155–156.
4. Compare the 1937 statement of Student Führer Gustav Adolf Scheel: "We don't want a scientific National Socialism, but rather a National Socialist science" (cited in Ternon and Helman, *Les médecins allemands*, p. 107).
5. On the Munich-based Kneippärztebund, see Florian Kramer, "Beiträge zur Ausbreitung des Kneipp'schen Heilverfahrens in Deutschland zwischen 1920 und 1933," med. diss., University of Munich, 1981.
6. In 1883 the followers of Priessnitz formed what eventually became known as the Deutsche Bund der Vereine für naturgemässe Lebens- und Heilweise, or Priessnitzbund. See Wolfgang R. Krabbe, *Gesellschaftsveränderung durch Lebensreform* (Göttingen, 1974), p. 162; also Alfred Haug, "Die Reichsarbeitsgemeinschaft für eine Neue Deutsche Heilkunde (1935/36)," in the *Abhandlungen zur Geschichte der Medizin und der Naturwissenschaften*, 50(1985): 20.
7. Eva-Marie Klasen, "Die Diskussion über eine 'Krise' der Medizin in Deutschland zwischen 1925 und 1935," med. diss., University of Mainz, 1984.
8. *DÄ*, 63(1933): 74. In 1936 Germany's leading natural health bodies included the Biochemische Bund (membership 180,000), the Priessnitzbund (120,000), the Hahnemann Bund (48,000), the Kneippärztebund (48,000), and the Schüsslerbund (32,000). See E. G. Schenck, "Naturheilkunde und biologische Medizin seit 1933," *Hippokrates*, 14(1943): 217–221.
9. A comprehensive *Reichsnaturschutzgesetz* providing for the protection of natural habitats was passed on June 26, 1935. See also H. Klose, "Über die Arbeitsgemeinschaft Naturschutz im Reichsbund für Biologie," *Der Biologe*, 10(1941): 140–144.
10. *MMW*, 80(1933): 204.
11. Reported in *Journal of the American Medical Association*, September 30, 1933, p. 1087. On the November 24, 1933, *Reichstierschutzgesetz*, see the *Reichs-Gesundheitsblatt*, 8(1933): 932, and 9(1934): 590.
12. *Ziel und Weg*, 3(1933): 133.
13. *DÄ*, 63(1933): 74. Erwin Liek was the author of *Der Arzt und seine Sendung* (Munich, 1926), one of the most widely cited books among Nazi physicians. As used by Liek, the term *license* means the medical license granted after the completion of university studies.
14. *British Medical Journal*, September 16, 1936, p. 595.
15. IÄB, May/June 1935, p. 77.
16. In the fall of 1934, a German court ruled that one must distinguish carefully between two different senses of the word *Kurpfuscher*. The broader definition of the term refers to someone who practices medicine without a license. The second meaning refers to someone who provides bogus or

worthless medical treatment. See "Das Reichsgericht über den Begriff Kurpfuscher," *Ärzteblatt für Pommern, Mecklenburg und Lübeck,* 2(1935), p. 22.
17. J. Wulf, *Presse und Funk im Dritten Reich* (Reinbek, 1966), pp. 223–224. On Hess and homeopathy, see *ÄfB,* 42(1937): 328. On Himmler's lead poisoning experiments, see the Himmler files, fol. 292, Hoover Institution Archives.
18. The Führer of the short-lived Reichsverband nationalsozialistischer Heilpraktiker Deutschlands was a man by the name of Heinz Philipps. The statutes of this body (dated November 4, 1930) can be found in T-580, roll 27, National Archives, Washington, D.C.
19. Julius Moses, *Der Kampf um die Kurierfreiheit* (Dresden, 1930), pp. 7–9, cited in Haug, "Die Reichsarbeitsgemeinschaft," pp. 33–34. In 1869 the Prussian government ruled that individuals were free to practice medicine without a license as long as they did not call themselves "physicians." This was what was known as *Kurierfreiheit,* roughly translatable as "the freedom to practice medicine." The Nazis did not formally abandon *Kurierfreiheit* until 1939.
20. Rudolf Fincke, "Deutschlands Naturärzte," *Naturärztliche Rundschau,* 7(1935): 126. The body referred to was the Norddeutsche Ärzteverband für physikalische und diätetische Therapie.
21. "Ein Hundert Jahre Volksheilbewegung," *Dresdener Neueste Nachrichten,* June 4, 1936.
22. "Die Aufhebung der Kurierfreiheit," *DÄ,* 63(1933): 650–651.
23. L. R. Grote, "Neue Deutsche Heilkunde," *Zeitschrift für Ärztliche Fortbildung,* 34(1937): 33–36. See also Kurt Blome, "Der Gegensatz: Wissenschaftliche Medizin und Naturheilkunde geht durch die Jahrhunderte," *ÄfB,* 41(1936): 321–324; also Walter Gross, "Populäre Heilkunde und dogmatische Schulmedizin im nationalsozialistischen Staat," *Ärzteblatt für Bayern,* 2(1935): 1–8.
24. "Bericht über die Reichstagung des Reichsverbandes der Naturärzte in Nürnberg," *Ärztliche Rundschau,* 45(1935): 245–246. Väth was also editor of *Hippokrates.* On April 9, 1936, *Hippokrates* was declared the official journal of the New German Science of Healing.
25. Ibid., p. 246.
26. Ibid.
27. Ibid., p. 247.
28. The formal bodies subordinated to the committee included the Deutsche Allgemeine Ärztliche Gesellschaft für Psychotherapie, the Deutsche Gesellschaft für Bäder- und Klimakunde, the Deutsche Zentralverein homöopathischer Ärzte, the Kneippärztebund, the Reichsverband der Naturärzte, the Reichsverband Deutscher Privatkrankenanstalter, and the Vereinigung Anthroposophischer Ärzte. The Anthroposophical Society was banned in November 1935; physicians in this body were absorbed into the Verband für Biologisch-dynamische Heilweise.
29. Hermann Berger, "Auslegung des Begriffs 'Neue Deutsche Heilkunde'," *Zeitschrift für Ärztliche Fortbildung,* 33(1936): 531–535.

30. Karl Eimer, "Die Gemeinschaftstagung der Deutschen Gesellschaft für Heilkunde," *Ärzteblatt für Pommern, Mecklenburg und Lübeck,* 3(1936): 137–139.
31. "Das Gesetz der Ähnlichkeit," *Hamburger Fremdenblatt,* August 17, 1937.
32. *Ärzteblatt für Pommern, Mecklenburg und Lübeck,* 3(1936): 139; see also pp. 153–157.
33. Ibid., p. 140.
34. Some of the leading journals of natural or heterodox health or medicine in this period included *Biochemische Monatsblätter, Demeter, Deutsche Zeitschrift für Homöopathie, Der Heilpraktiker, Die Deutsche Heilpflanze, Hippokrates, Kneipp-Blätter,* and *Naturärztliche Rundschau.* The Hippokrates Verlag, headed by Kurt Klare after the death of Erwin Liek, was the leading publisher of books for the natural health movement in the 1920s and 1930s.
35. *Ärzteblatt für Pommern, Mecklenburg und Lübeck,* 4(1937): 349. See also Alfred Haug, "Der Lehrstuhl für Biologische Medizin in Jena," in *Ärzte im Nationalsozialismus,* ed. Kudlien, pp. 130–138.
36. See Franz Büchner, "Möglichkeiten und Grenzen der natürlichen Heilung in den inneren Organen," *Zeitschrift für Ärztliche Fortbildung,* 33(1936): 121–125; also p. 120.
37. See Gustav Wegner, "Die Aufgaben des biologischen 'Rudolf-Hess-Krankenhaus'," *Die Volksgesundheitswacht,* Erntin 1934, pp. 8–10.
38. Rudolf Tischner, "Stiefkind Homöopathie?—Bemerkungen über Homöopathie und ihrer Stellung in den 'Neuen Deutschen Heilkunde'," *Fortschritte der Medizin,* 55(1937): 41.
39. Paul Diepgen, "Deutsche Medizin und deutsche Kultur," *DÄ,* 63(1933); also *DÄ* 66(1936): 486–490.
40. Box 330, Deutsche Kongress-Zentrale, Hoover Institution Archives; also Wuttke-Groneberg, *Medizin im Nationalsozialismus,* pp. 390–391.
41. *ÄRW,* 2(1941): 251–252, 227–230. See also *Der deutsche Arzt* (Tübingen, 1941), published by the NS-Dozentenbund as part of the *Paracelsusfeier* at the University of Tübingen.
42. *Ärzteblatt für Bayern,* 6(1939): 267.
43. Head of the Reichsarbeitsgemeinschaft der Verbände für naturgemässe Lebens- und Heilweise was SS Hauptsturmführer Georg Gustav Wegener, also a member of the Sachverständigenbeirat für Volksgesundheit of the NSDAP. For the philosophy of this movement, see the talks presented at the second meeting of the Reichsarbeitsgemeinschaft on June 17–18, 1939, published as *Dieses Volk will gesund bleiben* (Stuttgart, 1939).
44. The official organ of this new body was the journal *Volk und Gesundheit, Monatsschrift für naturgemässe Lebens- und Heilweise,* edited by Karl-Heinrich Franke and published 1942–1944.
45. "Die Gesundheitserziehungskurse des DVB," *Volk und Gesundheit,* July/September, 1943, pp. 68–69; also October/December, 1943, pp. 75–76.
46. The most convincing argument for this thesis has been made by Alfred Haug, in his "Die Reichsarbeitsgemeinschaft."

47. "Auflösung der Reichsarbeitsgemeinschaft für eine Neue Deutsche Heilkunde," *Hippokrates,* 8(1937): 1.
48. Franz Wirz, "Die Entfaltung des Vollkornbrotgedankens in und ausser Deutschland," *Die Gesundheitsführung,* 14(1944): 74–78. In 1938 the *Zeitungsdienst des Reichsnährstandes* asked Germans to reduce their consumption of fat by 20–25 percent. The journal asked housewives to prepare fewer eggs and to replace the lost protein with skim milk. Reported in *IÄB,* April/May 1938, p. 36.
49. "Vollkornbrot," *ÄfB,* 42(1937): 13.
50. "Die Stellung des Arztes zur Vollkornbrotfrage," *ÄRW,* 2(1941): 225.
51. "Vollkornbrot," *ÄfB,* 42(1937): 13.
52. See *Kampf ums Brot* (Planegg bei München, 1939), published by the Reichsvollkornbrotausschuss.
53. "Vollkornbrot für Arbeitsdienstmänner," *Akademia,* May 27, 1940, p. 2. See also *ÄRW,* 1(1940): 106.
54. Walter Wegner, "Vollkornbrot-Volksbrot," *Die Gesundheitsführung,* 9(1939): 58–60.
55. "Vollkornbrot für Arbeitsdienstmänner," *Akademia,* May 27, 1940, p. 2.
56. *Ärzteblatt für Bayern,* 8(1941): 47.
57. Franz Wirz, "Die Entfaltung des Vollkornbrotgedankens in und ausser Deutschland," *Die Gesundheitsführung,* 14(1944): 75–77.
58. Cited in *IÄB,* January 1937, p. 26.
59. See *Reichs-Gesundheitsblatt,* 12(1937): 40; also Martin Nordmann, "Der Berufskrebs der Asbestarbeiter," *Archiv für Gewerbepathologie und Gewerbehygiene,* 8(1938): 288–302.
60. *Volksgesundheitswacht,* July 1936, p. 5.
61. Hagen, *Auftrag und Wirklichkeit,* p. 182.
62. See, for example, Hermann Siemens, "Was ist Rassenhygiene?" p. 281. Agnes Bluhm used more than 32,000 mice to try to prove the mutagenicity of alcohol—with negative results. See *Die Gesundheitsführung,* 10(1940): 251. Arthur Gütt complained in 1937 that nearly 6 billion RM were spent on alcohol (3½ billion RM) and tobacco (2½ billion RM) every year in Germany, constituting about 10 percent of the entire national income. See *Öffentlicher Gesundheitsdienst,* 3(1937/38): 211.
63. Lenz, *Menschliche Auslese,* 2nd ed. (Munich, 1923), p. 305.
64. R 73/14560, BA.
65. Rissom, "Fritz Lenz und die Rassenhygiene," p. 50.
66. Hans Reiter, "Alkohol und Nikotinmissbrauch und gesundes Volk," *Ärzteblatt für Pommern, Mecklenburg und Lübeck,* 4(1937): 364.
67. See, for example, Hellmut Haubold, "Die Krebssterblichkeit in einigen deutschen Grossstädten seit der Jahrhundert," *Reichs-Gesundheitsblatt,* 12(1937): 805–815; also Kurt Blome, "Krebsforschung und Krebsbekämpfung," *Die Gesundheitsführung,* 10(1940): 406–412.
68. *Informationsdienst,* September 10, 1938. On Brandt's geopathology, see "Probleme der vergleichenden Völkerpsychologie," *ÄRW,* 2(1941): 18–20.
69. *Informationsdienst,* September 10, 1938.

70. *Ziel und Weg,* 9(1939): 448.
71. P. Bernhard, "Über die Ursachen der Sterilität der Frau," *Zentralblatt für Gynäkologie,* 67(1943): 793. Bernhard also claimed that alcohol and caffeine could be linked to sterility in women. The journal *Die Volksgifte,* edited by Erich Bruns and Theo Paulstich (published by the Reichsgesundheitsverlag), was devoted almost exclusively to the campaign against alcohol and tobacco.
72. *Informationsdienst des Hauptamtes für Volksgesundheit der NSDAP,* April/June 1944, pp. 60–61; also January/February 1943, p. 25. The government also banned the use of the term *Damen-Zigarette* in advertisements. See *ÄRW,* 2(1941): 84.
73. *ÄfB,* 42(1937): 407.
74. *British Medical Journal,* December 18, 1937, p. 1220. In 1940, 5,715 German taxi drivers had their licenses revoked; 1,672 of these were for drunken driving (*British Medical Journal,* July 19, 1941, p. 108).
75. "Hitler's Attitude toward Alcohol," *Scientific Temperance Journal,* Spring 1933, p. 18.
76. E. Georg, *Die wirtschaftlichen Unternehmungen der SS* (Stuttgart, 1963), p. 143; also "Kautschuk aus Löwenzahn," *Der Spiegel,* no. 13 (1981): 103.
77. "Bericht über die erste wissenschaftliche Tagung zur Erforschung der Tabakgefahren am 5. und 6. April (1941) in Weimar," *Ärztin,* 17(1941): 165–166.
78. *ÄfB,* 42(1937): 410.
79. Lenz, *Menschliche Auslese,* pp. 72–73, 453.
80. "Untersuchung zur Frage einer konstitutionellen Bedingtheit für Staubschädigungen der Lunge," in R 73/15342, fol. 58, BA. Verschuer received substantial support from the Deutsche Forschungsgemeinschaft for this research.
81. R 73/15342, fol. 175, BA.
82. The Allgemeine Deutsche Hebammen-Verband and the Vereinigung Deutscher Hebammen were *gleichgeschaltet* in June 1933 into the Reichsfachschaft deutscher Hebammen, headed by Nanna Conti. See "Die Einigung der deutschen Hebammen," *Zeitschrift der Reichsfachschaft Deutscher Hebammen,* 1(1933): 2. For a review of ten years of Nazi midwifery, see Nanna Conti, "Rückblick und Ausblick," in the 1944 *Deutsche Hebammen-Kalender.*
83. Nanna Conti, "Das Hebammenwesen in Deutschland," *Ärztin,* 13(1937): 298. Conti noted that births could not be strictly divided into either "hospital" or "midwife" births, as some births were delivered by midwives in hospitals and may have been counted either twice or not at all in these statistics.
84. *Die Gesundheitsführung,* 14(1944): 51. In 1938 the Reichsfachschaft Deutscher Hebammen was renamed the Reichshebammenschaft. The *Zeitschrift der Reichsfachschaft Deutscher Hebammen* was published after 1938 as *Die Deutsche Hebammen.*
85. "Die Bewährung der deutschen Hebammen im Kriege," *Die Gesundheitsführung,* 15(1945): 11. During the war years some midwives assisted in as many as 200 births per year.

86. Nanna Conti, "Hebammen in Kriegsansatz," *Die Gesundheitsführung,* 14(1944): 80.
87. *Ärzteblatt für Pommern, Mecklenburg und Lübeck,* 1(1934): 42.
88. Nanna Conti, "Das Hebammenwesen in Deutschland," *Ärztin,* 13(1937): 298; also Kurt Pohl, "Entbindungen und Müttersterblichkeit," *Ärztin,* 13(1937): 286–287. In 1941 German midwives attended 1,152,878 births (in Greater Germany) with 35,021 infant deaths (*Fehlgeburten*). This represented an average of 49 live births per midwife, and 1.5 infant deaths per midwife. See *Die Gesundheitsführung,* 14(1944): 51; also 15(1945): 11.
89. See *Reichsgesetzblatt,* vol. 1, 1938, p. 1893 for the text of the midwifery law. See also Eugen Stähle, "Die Hebammen von Heute," *Wiener Klinische Wochenschrift,* 55(1942): 561–566.
90. Nanna Conti, "Hebammen in Kriegsansatz," *Die Gesundheitsführung,* 14(1944): 79.
91. *Die Volksgesundheit,* July 1944, p. 7.
92. *DÄ,* 67(1937): 1106.
93. "Zur Bekämpfung des Kurpfuschertums," *DÄ,* 63(1933): 106.
94. *DÄ,* 63(1933): 183–184.
95. Wagner's and Hess's statements of December 5, 1933, are reprinted in Theodor Gruschka, "Der Aufbau des Primitiven," *IÄB,* March/April 1934, pp. 43–45. The Württemberg Medical Association's accusation can be found in *Medizinisches Korrespondenzblatt für Württemberg,* 14(1933): 256.
96. See, for example, *Volksgesundheitswacht,* June 1936, pp. 1–16; also March 1935, pp. 1–16.
97. *IÄB,* August/September, 1936, p. 95.
98. Hermann Berger, "Eine Frage an die Naturheilkunde," *MMW,* 84(1937): 143–145.
99. *IÄB,* January 1935, pp. 16–17. The original account of this controversy appeared in *Fortschritte der Medizin,* 53(1935): 20.
100. *Fortschritte der Medizin,* 53(1935): 380. See also *Ärztliche Rundschau,* 45(1935): 245–246.
101. *IÄB,* March/April 1934, pp. 43–45.
102. "Kampfansage des Reichsärzteführers an Pg. Streicher?" *Fortschritte der Medizin,* 53(1935): 122.
103. *DÄ,* 67(1937): 749; also *ÄfB,* 42(1937): 383.
104. *Berliner und Münchener Tierärztliche Wochenschrift,* 55(1939): 113. The number of registered nonmedical healers (*nichtbestallte Heilbehandler*) peaked in 1934 at 14,266. By January 1, 1939, this number had declined to only 10,067. See the *Reichs-Gesundheitsblatt,* 15(1940): 593–603. The number of those actually providing folk healing was, of course, greater than the number registered.
105. For the text of the *Heilpraktikergesetz,* see the *Reichsgesetzblatt,* vol. 1, 1939, p. 251.
106. Ramm, *Ärztliche Rechts- und Standeskunde,* pp. 62–63.
107. *Informationsdienst des Hauptamtes für Volksgesundheit der NSDAP,* July 1942, p. 19.
108. Ibid., January/February 1943, p. 26; also November 1942, p. 66.

109. See, for example, *IÄB,* January 1934, p. 17.
110. Ramm, *Ärztliche Rechts- und Standeskunde,* pp. 61, 120.
111. See Schaxel's "Deutsche Staatsbiologie," pp. 261–274. In the early years of the Nazi regime Schaxel, a member of the Soviet Academy of Sciences, circulated a letter among foreign colleagues criticizing German racial hygiene; he directed his attack against the Verband Deutscher Biologen, headed by Ernst Lehmann. On March 17, 1936, the *Völkische Beobachter* published a response to Schaxel's charges.
112. See, for example, Franz Wirz, "Ernährung und Vierjahresplan," *DÄ,* 69(1939): 886. The Hauptamt für Volksgesundheit encouraged physicians to investigate the effects of Coca-Cola on sleep, neural function, addictive patterns, and so forth, as part of a broad campaign to raise the general health of the German people. The office also pointed out, however, that Germany might one day have to do without such drinks; thus it sponsored research into alternative formulas for colas and soft drinks. See *Die Gesundheitsführung,* 10(1940): 162.
113. *Ärztliche Rundschau,* 45(1935): 232. For the statutes of the Reichsarbeitsgemeinschaft für Heilpflanzenkunde und Heilpflanzenbeschaffung, headed by Georg Gustav Wegener, see *Die Deutsche Heilpflanze,* 1(1934/35): 114–116. On medicinal plants more generally, see Walther Ripperger (with Curt Coester), *Grundlagen zur praktischen Pflanzenheilkunde* (Stuttgart, 1937).
114. *ÄRW,* 2(1941): 138; also *Informationsdienst des Hauptamtes für Volksgesundheit der NSDAP,* July 1942, p. 32.
115. *Akademia,* April 23, 1941, p. 2.
116. *Informationsdienst des Hauptamtes für Volksgesundheit der NSDAP,* October 1942, p. 52.
117. Bernhard Hörmann, "Heil- und Nährkräfte aus Wald und Flur," *Die Gesundheitsführung,* 9(1939): 67–68.
118. Walter Wuttke-Groneberg, "Heilkräutergarten und KZ," *Wechselwirkung,* February 1980, pp. 15–18. See also K. O. Bäcker and R. Lucass, *Der Kräutergarten* (Berlin, 1941).
119. G. G. Wegener, "Die Neugestaltung der Volksheilbewegung," *Volksgesundheitswacht,* no. 5(1935): 4–5; see also *Ziel und Weg,* 9(1939): 217–218.
120. "Sechs Jahre Hauptamt für Volksgesundheit der NSDAP. Die Gesundheit als Waffe im Krieg," *ÄRW,* 1(1940): 193; also Conti, "Arbeit für den biologischen Sieg," *ÄRW,* 2(1941): 2.

9. Medical Resistance

1. *Der Kassenarzt,* no. 7/8(1932): 153.
2. Kater, "Medizinische Fakultäten," p. 83.
3. *IÄB,* January 1936, p. 18.
4. Kurt Kühn, "Deutsche Mediziner im Kampf gegen den Faschismus," in his *Ärzte an der Seite der Arbeiterklasse,* 2nd ed. (Berlin [East], 1977), pp. 216–219.

5. Ibid., pp. 208–214.
6. Georg Bonne, "Über Eugenik und Euthanasie im Licht der nationalsozialistischen Ethik," *Ethik,* 11(1935): 130. Parenthetical remarks in original. See also Abderhalden's "Gemeinnutz geht vor Eigennutz" in the same volume, pp. 1–12.
7. Ibid., p. 132. See also the massive tome by Franz Walter, professor of theology at the University of Munich, *Die Euthanasie und die Heiligkeit des Lebens: Die Lebensvernichtung im Dienste der Medizin und Eugenik nach christlicher und monistischer Ethik* (Munich, 1935).
8. Joseph Haberer, *Politics and the Community of Science* (New York, 1969), p. 132.
9. Reported in *MMW,* 81(1934): 1566.
10. See his *Die Rassenlehre des Nationalsozialismus in Wissenschaft und Propaganda* (Darmstadt, 1961).
11. *Zentralblatt für Gynäkologie,* 58(1934): 1986–92.
12. *IÄB,* January 1935, p. 17.
13. Klee, "*Euthanasie,*" pp. 216–219.
14. Aly, "Medizin gegen Unbrauchbare," in Aly et al., *Aussonderung und Tod,* p. 16.
15. Fridolf Kudlien has wrestled with these and related questions in his *Ärzte im Nationalsozialismus,* pp. 210–245. See also K. P. Werle, "Formen des Widerstandes deutscher Ärzte 1933 bis 1945," inaugural diss., University of Kiel, 1974.
16. See Gernot Boehme, "1848 und die Nicht-Entstehung der Sozialmedizin," in his *Alternativen der Wissenschaften* (Frankfurt, 1980), pp. 169–197; also I. Fischer, *Wiens Mediziner und die Freiheitsbewegung des Jahres 1848* (Vienna, 1935).
17. "Der sozialistische Arzt," *Mitteilungsblatt des "Vereins sozialistischer Ärzte,"* March 1925, p. 2.
18. Karl Kautsky, *Ethik und materialistische Geschichtsauffassung* (Stuttgart, 1906), pp. 78–79.
19. See Ignaz Zadek, "Ein sozialdemokratischer Ärzteverein," *Sozialistische Monatshefte,* 20(1914): 158.
20. Leibfried and Tennstedt, *Berufsverbot und Sozialpolitik,* p. 116.
21. "Der sozialistische Arzt," *Mitteilungsblatt des "Vereins sozialistischer Ärzte,"* March 1925, p. 2.
22. Irina Winter, "Ärzte und Arbeiterklasse in der Weimar Republik," in *Ärzte an der Seite der Arbeiterklasse,* ed. Kühn, p. 29.
23. Georg Benjamin was a leader of the Berlin branch of this body. See H. Schwartze, "Zur Geschichte des Arbeiter-Samariter Bundes," in *Ärzte an der Seite der Arbeiterklasse,* ed. Kühn, p. 48.
24. Käte Frankenthal, *Der dreifache Fluch: Jüdin, Intellektuelle, Sozialistin, Lebenserinnerungen einer Ärztin in Deutschland und im Exil* (Frankfurt, 1981), pp. 93–130.
25. "Aus der sozialistischen Ärztebewegung," *Der Sozialististsche Arzt,* March/April 1928, p. 43. On February 12, 1925, the elected members of the VSÄ included Ernst Simmel, chairman; Klauber and Frau Turnau, vice-

chairmen; Ewald Fabian, editor; Minna Flake, assistant editor; and Franz Rosenthal, treasurer. See *Mitteilungsblatt des "Vereins sozialistischer Ärzte,"* March 1925, p. 5.
26. *Mitteilungsblatt des "Vereins Sozialistischer Ärzte,"* July 1925, p. 9.
27. Ernst Simmel, "Zur roten Gesundheitswoche," *Der Sozialistische Arzt,* April 1926, p. 1.
28. Ibid., p. 2.
29. *Der Sozialistische Arzt,* May/June, 1931, p. 158.
30. Ernst Simmel, "Zur roten Gesundheitswoche," *Der Sozialististsche Arzt,* April 1926, p. 3.
31. Georg Löwenstein, "Gesundheitspolitische Forderungen des VSAe," *Der Sozialistische Arzt,* January/February 1928, pp. 29–32.
32. See E. Silva, "Schwangerschaftsunterbrechungen vor deutschen Gerichten," *IÄB,* October/November 1934, p. 150.
33. *Der Sozialistische Arzt,* January/February 1933, pp. 1–2.
34. *MMW,* 80(1933): 517.
35. See, for example, *Ärztliche Mitteilungen,* 34(1933): 105–106.
36. This journal today is extremely difficult to find. It is not listed, for example, in the *Union List of Serials.* The Leo Baeck Institute in New York has some issues; the most complete edition of the journal has been gathered by Stephan Leibfried at the University of Bremen. I would like to thank Professor Leibfried for facilitating my access to this journal.
37. "Was Wir Wollen," *IÄB,* January 1934, p. 2.
38. Valentin, "Die Krankenversorgung im Konzentrationslager," *IÄB,* May 1936, pp. 57–59; see also "Krankenfürsorge im Konzentrationslager," July/August 1937, p. 82.
39. See, for example, *IÄB,* January 1935, p. 127.
40. Ferdinand Sauerbruch, "An die Ärzteschaft der Welt," *Klinische Wochenschrift,* 12(1933): 1551.
41. "Der Appell von Prof. Dr. Sauerbruch," *IÄB,* January 1934, pp. 3–4. German socialists were not the first to attack Sauerbruch's letter. In October 1933, Professor Szymanowski of Poland published a criticism of the letter in the *Warszawskie Czasopismo lekarskie.*
42. "Offene Antwort auf den offenen Brief des Herrn Geheimrat Prof. Dr. E. F. Sauerbruch," *IÄB,* January 1934, pp. 4–6.
43. "Ein Beitrag zur Krankenbehandlung im heutigen Deutschland," *IÄB,* October/November 1934, pp. 159–160.
44. E. Frankl, "Die geistigen Arbeiter und der Kampf gegen den Faschismus," *IÄB,* March/April 1934, p. 52; see also June 1934, p. 97.
45. See, for example, Theodor Gruschka, "Der Aufbruch des Primitiven," *IÄB,* March/April 1934, pp. 43–44.
46. The text of the resolution issued by New York's Deutsche Medizinische Gesellschaft is printed in *IÄB,* January 1934, p. 18.
47. *IÄB,* June 1934, p. 106.
48. Ibid., p. 105.
49. *IÄB,* May 1934, p. 85; also June 1934, p. 104. Support in Britain came from the Socialist Medical Association of Great Britain, founded in Octo-

ber 1930 with Somerville Hastings as president. In France the equivalent body was the Groupe des Médecins Socialistes en France.
50. E. Silva, "Ärztlicher Hilfsdienst für Spanier," *IÄB*, August/September 1936, pp. 93–94; also H. Jentzsch, "Ärztliche Verantwortung und politische Tat," in *Ärzte an der Seite der Arbeiterklasse*, ed. Kühn, pp. 100–108. See also the British journals *Socialist Doctor* and *Medicine Today and Tomorrow* in this period.
51. "Greuelnachrichten," *IÄB*, February 1934, pp. 29–30.
52. Reported in *IÄB*, February 1934, p. 32.
53. *IÄB*, February 1934, p. 32.
54. "So reagieren sie!" ibid., p. 33.
55. The Arbeitsgemeinschaft sozialistischer Alkoholgegner organized efforts to ban all advertising for alcohol, to eliminate alcohol from socialist meetings, to establish alcohol-free sports fields and guest houses, and to prohibit the sale of alcohol between midnight and 8:00 A.M. See *Der Sozialistische Arzt*, March/April 1928, pp. 37–39.
56. August de Bary reported that the Frankfurt branch of the Verein Sozialistischer Ärzte had only three non-Jewish members. See Leibfried and Tennstedt, *Berufsverbot und Sozialpolitik*, pp. 124–125.
57. "Das Sektion 218 Drama," *Der Sozialistische Arzt*, February 1930, p. 84.
58. Professor Kainrath, cited in L. Gschwendtner, "Marxistische Argumentation gegen die Rassenhygiene," *ARGB*, 17(1926): 235.
59. "Die ständische Schichtung in Deutschland [ist] gleichzeitig eine Rassenschichtung." See *IÄB*, March/April 1934, p. 59.
60. Gabriele Weymann, "Zur Erbbiologie des deutschen Arbeiters," *Ärztin*, 13(1937): 158–162. For an elaborate defense of this thesis, see Karl Valentin Müller, *Der Aufstieg des Arbeiters durch Rasse und Meisterschaft* (Munich, 1935).
61. Frankenthal, *Der dreifache Fluch*, pp. 131–152.
62. "Zusammenschluss der Hitler-Aerzte," *Der Sozialistische Arzt*, April 1930, pp. 185–186.
63. "Gegen die politische Hetze der 'Münchener Medizinischen Wochenschrift'," *Der Sozialistische Arzt*, November 1931, p. 313.
64. *Der Sozialistische Arzt*, August/September 1931, p. 245; also February 1931, p. 63.
65. Ernst Simmel, "Nationalsozialismus und Volksgesundheit," *Der Sozialistische Arzt*, September/October 1932, pp. 162–172.
66. Georg Benjamin, "Das 'unpolitische' Deutsche Aerzteblatt," *Der Sozialistische Arzt*, September/October 1932, p. 175.
67. Julian Marcuse, "Nationalsozialistische Rassenexperimente," *Der Sozialistische Arzt*, April/May 1932, pp. 76–77.
68. Julian Marcuse, "Geschlecht gegen Rasse," *Der Sozialistische Arzt*, February/March 1932, pp. 54–55.
69. R. Elkan, "'Birth Control,' ein Weg aus der Wirtschaftskrise?" *Der Sozialistische Arzt*, April/May 1932, pp. 80–82.
70. Gertrud Lukas, "Kritische Gedanken zur Sterilisierungsfrage," *IÄB*, March/April 1934, pp. 57–59.

71. *IÄB*, February 1934, pp. 32; also January 1935, p. 1.
72. Jan Belehrádek, "Eugenik und Rassismus," *IÄB*, May/June 1937, pp. 45–56.
73. Ibid., p. 47.
74. Ibid., pp. 55–57.
75. *IÄB*, September 1935, p. 95.
76. *IÄB*, May/June 1937, p. 63.
77. The leading body organizing the Austrian conservative medical reaction was the St. Luke's Guild of Catholic Physicians (St. Lukas-Gilde katholischer Ärzte), organized as part of the Kulturverband katholischer Verbindungen headed by Viennese Stadtsrat Dr. Ceska.
78. *IÄB*, March/April 1934, pp. 40–41.
79. "Medizinisches aus Österreich," *IÄB*, July/August 1937, p. 74.
80. "Internationale Vereinigung Katholischer Ärzte," box 3, Deutsche Kongress-Zentrale, Hoover Institution Archives. The Austrian St. Lukas-Gilde was headed by R. Höfer.
81. Arnold Holitscher, "Nachwort," *IÄB*, November/December 1935, p. 123. Emphasis in the original.
82. *IÄB*, January/February 1938, pp. 10–15; see also "Schluss mit den Gleichschaltungsbestrebungen im Reichsverbande!" in this issue of the *Bulletin*.
83. *IÄB*, July/August 1938, pp. 48–49.
84. Arnold Holitscher, "Nachwort," *IÄB*, November/December 1935, p. 123.
85. "Nach dem Verbot des Abortus in der Sowetunion," *IÄB*, May/June 1937, p. 59; see also August/September 1936, p. 113. The "Soviet press" referred to in this context was an article that appeared in *Izvestia*, April 3, 1937. The new Soviet law allowed abortion only if the life of the mother was in danger.
86. "Opfer der Gewaltherrschaft," *IÄB*, August/September 1936, pp. 96–97. See also "Pogrom in der Wissenschaft" and "Ärzte im jungsten Moskauer Prozeβ," July/August 1937, p. 83, and April/May 1938, pp. 33–34.
87. Physicians arrested included the Nobel Prize winner Otto Löwi, the surgeon Julius Schnitzler, and the internist Baron Withold Schey. Victims of suicide included Arnold Baumgarten, Bernard Hertz, Wolfgang Denk, Edmund Nobel, and Oskar Frankel—again, only naming some of the better known. See *IÄB*, May 1938, p. 25.
88. In the summer of 1938, the *Internationales Ärztliches Bulletin* was edited by Drs. Oguse (Paris), Holitscher (Prague), Karl Evang (Oslo), and Hans Schneider (Zurich). After Holitscher was lost from the board, Dr. Stark-Murray of London joined as editor.
89. Ian Kershaw, *Popular Opinion and Political Dissent in the Third Reich: Bavaria, 1933–45* (Oxford, 1983), p. 277.
90. "Protestieren ist lächerlich—man protestiere gegen eine Lawine!" See Carl G. Jung, "Zeitgenössisches," *Neuste Züricher Zeitung*, March 13, 1934.
91. Leibfried and Tennstedt, *Berufsverbot und Sozialpolitik*, p. 114.
92. Herbert A. Strauss and Werner Röder, eds., *International Biographical*

Dictionary of Central European Emigrés (Munich, 1983), vol. 1, p. 304, and vol. 2, p. 1083.

93. Leibfried and Tennstedt, *Berufsverbot und Sozialpolitik*, pp. 116, 146.
94. Eckhard Hansen et al., *Seit über einem Jahrhundert . . . Verschüttete Alternativen in der Sozialpolitik* (Cologne, 1981), p. 130. See also Leibfried and Tennstedt, *Berufsverbot und Sozialpolitik*, p. 124, and Winter, "Ärzte und Arbeiterklasse," in *Ärzte an der Seite der Arbeiterklasse*, ed. Kühn, p. 34.
95. See Light et al., "Social Medicine," pp. 78–83.

10. The Politics of Knowledge

1. In 1937 Edward Hartshorne reported that 1,684 scholars had been dismissed from their posts. This included not only professors but also scientists at the Kaiser Wilhelm institutes, assistants, and the like. See his *The German Universities and National Socialism* (London, 1937), p. 93. In 1938 Hartshorne revised the proportion of all scholars dismissed from 14 percent to 20 percent. See his *German Universities and the Government* (Chicago, 1938), pp. 13–14.
2. Leibfried, "Stationen der Abwehr," p. 3.
3. On the life of Ludwik Fleck, see the introduction to his *Die Entstehung und Entwicklung einer wissenschaftlichen Tatsache* (1935) (Frankfurt, 1983).
4. For the case of psychology, see Ulfried Geuter, *Die Professionalisierung der deutschen Psychologie im Nationalsozialismus* (Frankfurt, 1984). For the case of anthropology, see my "From *Anthropologie* to *Rassenkunde* in the German Anthropological Tradition," in *History of Anthropology*, ed. George Stocking, vol. 5 (Madison, Wisc., 1988).
5. Apart from the schools mentioned in Chapter 3, new medical institutions established in the Nazi period include the Academy of Medicine in Munich, the Medical Academy in Danzig, and the Kaiser Wilhelm Institute for Biophysics in Frankfurt (from the older Institut für physikalische Grundlagen der Medizin). The Nazi period saw the establishment of institutes for general medicine at Berlin and Vienna, an institute for colonial medicine at Hamburg, and an institute for rural hygiene in Lichtenheim. The Nazi government funded the establishment of an Institute for Natural Healing (Neue Deutsche Heilkunde) at Dresden and a new Staatsakademie des öffentlichen Gesundheitsdienst in Berlin.
6. Conti rejected as "enemy propaganda" reports that the freedom of science had been restricted under the Nazis. See *DÄ*, 72(1942): 51.
7. Hans Rinne, "Die Aufgaben des Amtes für Volksgesundheit der NSDAP," *Der Öffentliche Gesundheitsdienst*, 2(1936): 857.
8. Franz Orsós, "Ist der Stand der deutschen Wissenschaft gesunken?" *DÄ*, 67(1937): 1119. German medical journals celebrated technical achievements in other fields beside medicine. In 1939 the *Ärzteblatt für Berlin* celebrated the *Wunder des Vierjahresplans*, including synthetic rubber, flexible glass, and prefabricated auto frames (*Presskarosserien*). See *ÄfB*, 44(1939): 94. Other achievements of the Nazi period include the synthesis

of polyvinyl chloride, the fabrication of paper from oil, the harnessing of power from geothermal energy, the production of atomic fission in the laboratory (Hahn and Meitner), the electron microscopy of viruses, ultraviolet irradiation of milk in order to control spoilage, and of course the rocket-powered bombs (V1 and V2) that wreaked havoc over England.

9. See Thomas Kuhn, *The Structure of Scientific Revolutions* (Chicago, 1962).
10. See *Ärzteblatt für Pommern, Mecklenburg und Lübeck*, 1(1934): 107; also *Zeitschrift für die gesamte Neurologie und Psychiatrie* (1935): 177.
11. In 1914 eugenics was taught in 44 American colleges and universities; by 1928 the number had grown to 376—"racial hygiene" was thus taught in nearly three-quarters of all American colleges and universities. See Garland Allen, "A History of Eugenics," in *Biology as Destiny*, ed. Science for the People Sociobiology Study Group (Cambridge, Mass., 1984), p. 14.
12. See "Keine Negerärzte in der amerikanischen Standesorganisation," *ARGB*, 33(1939): 276.
13. Eugen Fischer, *Der völkische Staat biologisch gesehen* (Berlin, 1933), pp. 11–12.
14. Ramm, *Ärztliche Rechts- und Standeskunde*, pp. 88–89.
15. For the American case, see Paul Starr, *The Social Transformation of American Medicine* (New York, 1982); also Elliot S. Valenstein, *Great and Desperate Cures* (New York, 1986), and Barbara Ehrenreich and Deirdre English, *For Her Own Good: 150 Years of the Experts' Advice to Women* (New York, 1978).
16. For a review of theories of fascism, see Richard Saage, *Faschismustheorien*, 2nd ed. (Frankfurt, 1977).
17. For a historical analysis of the ideal of value-free science, see my "Politics of Purity: Origins of the Ideal of Neutral Science," Ph.D. diss., Harvard University, 1984.
18. *Informationsdienst*, June 20, 1938.
19. *Ziel und Weg*, 9(1939): 5.
20. The claim that "Es gibt keine voraussetzungslose Wissenschaft!" was a common one in the Nazi period; the expression was generally traced to Houston Stewart Chamberlain; see his *Natur und Leben*, ed. J. von Uexküll (Munich, 1928).
21. See *Politisch-anthropologische Revue*, 1(1902): 1–2.
22. R 86/2371, fol. 1, p. 94, BA.
23. See *Zentralblatt für Psychotherapie und Ihre Grenzgebiete*, 7(1934): 132–134.
24. Fritz Lenz, "Biologie als staatliche Notwendigkeit der Rassentüchtigkeit," *Der Biologe*, 1(1931/32): 97.
25. *Ziel und Weg*, 2(1932): 8.
26. Struve, "Die Eugenik im Staatsrat," *Die Medizinische Welt*, 6(1932): 1076.
27. See Beyerchen, *Scientists under Hitler*, pp. 68, 208.
28. Hans F. K. Günther, *Mein Eindruck auf Hitler* (Pähl, 1969), p. 19. Günther claimed that since 1919, he had found party politics "tasteless and dirty."
29. "Ausschaltung von Interessengruppen," report of the Verein der Ärzte, Halle, in the July 28, 1934, issue of the *Klinische Wochenschrift*. Ludwig

Liebl, in the first issue of *Ziel und Weg,* denounced "interest-group politics." See *Ziel und Weg,* 1(1931): 4.

30. Compare also Hitler's boast at the 1938 Reichsparteitag that National Socialism was "eine kühle Wirklichkeitslehre schärfster wissenschaftlicher Erkenntnisse," cited in the frontispiece to *Ziel und Weg,* 9(1939): 29.
31. Hauptamt Wissenschaft, file no. 56595 T-81, roll 54, National Archives, Washington, D.C.
32. Walter Gross, "Die Idee bleibt rein," *Ziel und Weg,* 5(1935): 37; also *Ärztin,* 17(1941): 29.
33. "Reichsleiter Rosenbergs parteiamtliche Stellungnahme zur naturwissenschaftlichen Forschung," *Der Biologe* 8(1939). See also *Informationsdienst,* May 20, 1938.
34. Otmar von Verschuer, "Das Erbbild des Menschen," *Der Erbarzt,* 7(1939): 12, cited in Karl Heinz Roth, "Schöner neuer Mensch," in *Der Griff nach der Bevölkerung,* ed. Heidrun Kaupen-Haas (Hamburg, 1986), p. 11.
35. Harry H. Laughlin, "Die Entwicklung der gesetzlichen rassenhygienischen Sterilisierung in den Vereinigten Staaten," *ARGB,* 23(1929): 261. See also *Journal of the American Medical Association,* 101(1933): 866, 877, where the twin dangers of the Sterilization Law are listed as the unwitting destruction of "valuable biologic material" and the fact that a man might have himself sterilized in order "to secure unrestrained sexual gratification without fear of consequences."
36. Erich Berger, "Das deutsche Beispiel macht Schule," *Ziel und Weg,* 9(1939): 44. Otmar von Verschuer, in his "Erbpflege in der deutschen Gesetzgebung," *Archiv der Julius Klaus-Stiftung* (10[1935]: 59), expressed similar views.
37. "Die Theorie von heute wird die Praxis von Morgen." See Friedrich Zahn, "Rassenforschung und Statistik," in *Die Statistik in Deutschland,* ed. Josef Götz (Berlin, 1940).

Epilogue

1. See *Trials of War Criminals before the Nuremberg Military Tribunals,* 15 vols., esp. vols. 1 and 2, *Karl Brandt: The Medical Case* (Washington, D.C., 1951–52).
2. See C. W. Hufeland, *Das ärztliche Ethos,* ed. Joachim Mrugowsky (Munich, 1939).
3. Katzenellenbogen had held this position in 1909–10 (see the Harvard Archives, Edwin Katzenellenbogen file). He had also conducted clinical demonstrations at the Danvers Hospital for the Insane, where he served as an intern.
4. The total number of individuals convicted for crimes associated with the Nazi regime is about 50,000; 6,000 of these trials occurred in West Germany. It is not known what proportion of those tried were physicians.
5. "Die Zigeunerdeportation vom Mai 1940," in the Institut für Zeitgeschichte's *Gutachten des Instituts* (Munich, 1958), p. 51.
6. Wertham, *A Sign for Cain,* pp. 189–191.

7. Ibid.
8. See Kurt Weidner, "Ärztliche Philosophie an der Hochschule," *Medizinische Klinik*, 42(1947): 514–516, for a postwar discussion of euthanasia and "the value of life."
9. Nicolai Weiss, "Euthanasie in der Kinderheilpflege," *Der Weg*, 8(1954): 104–110. *Der Weg* was openly anti-Semitic, publishing regular reports, for example, on the "domination" of the Soviet Union and the United States by Jewish interests. The journal published Alfred Rosenberg's postwar plans for a new German constitution and speculations on whether the Soviet government might become anti-Semitic. See Karl Neck, "Der deutsche 'Rassenwahn'," *Der Weg* 6(1952): 114–117; also G. A. Amaudruz, "Von der Notwendigkeit einer europäischen Rassenpflege," in 6(1952): 329–336.
10. See Werner Catel, *Grenzsituationen des Lebens* (Bayreuth, 1962); also Klee, *"Euthanasie,"* pp. 472–473.
11. Fischer edited *Die Kunde* and the *Zeitschrift für Morphologie und Anthropologie* after the war. Fischer's daughter, Gertrud, reports that her father lectured in Venezuela at the age of eighty, and that the philosopher Martin Heidegger frequently visited the anthropologist at his home into the 1950s (Müller-Hill, *Tödliche Wissenschaft*, p. 120).
12. Joseph Borkin, *The Crime and Punishment of I. G. Farben* (New York, 1978).
13. Bosquest Wev to S. J. Chamberlain, July 2, 1947, cited in Linda Hunt, "U.S. Coverup of Nazi Scientists," *Bulletin of the Atomic Scientists*, April 1985, p. 20.
14. O. Kneise, "Geleitwort," *Zeitschrift für Urologie*, 40 (1947): 1–2.
15. W. Stoeckel and G. Döderlein, in *Zentralblatt für Neurochirurgie*, 9 (1949): 1; also Erwin Gohrbandt, in *Zentralblatt für Chirurgie*, 72(1947): 1.
16. There are, of course, some exceptions. Paul Martini, in a 1947 speech before the German Society for Internal Medicine, noted that the physicians facing charges before the Nuremberg military tribunals were part of "the flesh and spirit of contemporary medicine"—the medicine not just of Germany but of the entire modern world. See his "Eröffnungsansprache des Vorsitzender," in the *Verhandlungen der Deutschen Gesellschaft für Innere Medizin*, 54(1948): 1–11.
17. "Besinnung und Konzentration," *Ärztliche Forschung*, 1(1947).
18. *Archiv für experimentelle Pathologie*, 204(1947): 13.
19. See *Archiv für die gesamte Physiologie*, 249(1948): 1–2.
20. Paul Diepgen, *Die Heilkunde und der ärztliche Beruf* (Munich, 1938); 2nd ed. (Berlin, 1947). A third edition was published in 1949.
21. Ibid., 1938, p. 158; 1947, p. 169.
22. Ibid., 1938, pp. 20–21; 1947, p. 15.
23. Ibid., 1938, pp. 21–22.
24. Ibid., 1938, p. 22; 1947, pp. 15–16.
25. Ibid., 1938, p. 22.
26. See Paul Diepgen, "Der Untergang der antiken Welt und die Medizin," *Jahreskurse für Ärztliche Fortbildung*, 25(1934): 1. See also R. Nabielek,

"Anmerkungen zu Paul Diepgens Selbsteinschätzung seiner Tätigkeit an der Berliner Universität während des NS-Regimes," *Zeitschrift für die gesamte Hygiene,* 31(1985): 309–314.
27. See *Der Weg,* 6(1952): 440. See also Hans F. K. Günther, *Gattenwahl zu ehelichem Glück und erblicher Ertüchtigung* (1941), 3rd rev. ed. (Munich, 1951), and Hermann W. Siemens, *Grundzüge der Vererbungslehre, Rassenhygiene und Bevölkerungspolitik,* 13th ed. (Munich, 1952) (compare the 8th ed., 1937).
28. Diepgen, *Die Heilkunde und der ärztliche Beruf* (1947), p. 137.
29. Theodora J. Kalikow, "Die ethologische Theorie von Konrad Lorenz: Erklärung und Ideologie," in *Naturwissenschaft, Technik und NS—Ideologie,* ed. Herbert Mehrtens and Steffen Richter (Frankfurt, 1980), pp. 189–214.
30. For a recent analysis of biological determinism, see Steven Rose, Leon Kamin, and Richard Lewontin, *Not in Our Genes* (New York, 1983); also Jon Beckwith, "The Political Uses of Sociobiology in the United States and Europe," *Philosophical Forum,* 13(Winter/Spring 1981/82): 311–321.
31. See, for example, H. W. Schröder, "Die Sterilisation ein Verbrechen?" *Das Deutsche Gesundheitswesen,* 2(1947): 113–115.
32. R. Havemann's letter of January 13, 1947, is cited by Klaus-Dieter Thomann in his "Otmar Freiherr von Verschuer—ein Hauptvertreter der faschistischen Rassenhygiene," in *Medizin im Faschismus,* ed. Thom and Spaar, p. 48.
33. H. Schade, "Otmar Freiherr von Verschuer," *Deutsche Medizinische Wochenschrift,* 94(1969): 2407. Verschuer's postwar publications include *Zwillingstuberkulose III* (with Helmut Mitschrich) (Stuttgart, 1956); *Gefährdung des Erbguts—ein genetisches Problem* (Wiesbaden, 1962); and *Eugenik: Kommende Generationen in der Sicht der Genetik* (Witten, 1966).
34. Schade joined the Nazi party in March 1931 and the SS in the final years of the war; he served as *Assistent* at Verschuer's Institute for Genetics and Racial Hygiene beginning in 1935.
35. See Gerhard Koch, *Die Gesellschaft für Konstitutionsforschung, Anfang und Ende 1942–1965* (Erlangen, 1985).
36. Alexander Mitscherlich and Fred Mielke, *Das Diktat der Menschenverachtung* (Heidelberg, 1947).
37. Walter Wuttke-Groneberg, "Leistung, Vernichtung, Verwertung: Überlegungen zur Struktur der nationalsozialistischen Medizin," in *Volk und Gesundheit: Heilen und Vernichten im Nationalsozialismus* (Tübingen, 1982), pp. 10–15.
38. Michael Kater presents an analysis of postwar medical views on Nazi medical crime in his "Burden of the Past: Problems of a Modern Historiography of Physicians and Medicine in Nazi Germany," *German Studies Review,* 10(1987): 31–56.
39. Max Weinreich, *Hitler's Professors: The Part of Scholarship in Germany's Crimes against the Jewish People* (New York, 1946).
40. Francois Bayle, *Croix gammée contre caducée* (Neustadt [Palatinat], 1951).
41. After 1950 these works were attached to the *Vierteljahrshefte für Zeit-*

geschichte. See, for example, the *Gutachten des Instituts für Zeitgeschichte, München,* 2 vols. (Munich, 1958).
42. See, for example, Alice Platen-Hallermund, *Die Tötung Geisteskranker in Deutschland* (Frankfurt, 1948); Hedwig Conrad-Martius, *Utopien der Menschenzüchtung. Der Sozialdarwinismus und seine Folgen* (Munich, 1955); also the somewhat later work by Hans-Günter Zmarzlik, "Der Sozialdarwinismus in Deutschland als geschichtliches Problem," *Vierteljahrshefte für Zeitgeschichte,* 11(1963): 246–273.
43. Rolf Schlögell, "Entschliessung der Westdeutschen Ärztekammern zum Nürnberger Ärzteprozess," in *Hippokrates,* 19(1948); also Mitscherlich and Mielke, *Medizin ohne Menschlichkeit,* p. 13.
44. See Andreas Flitner, ed., *Deutsches Geistesleben und Nationalsozialismus, eine Vortragsreihe der Universität Tübingen* (Tübingen, 1965); also *Die deutsche Universität im Dritten Reich, eine Vortragsreihe der Universität München* (Munich, 1966); *Nationalsozialismus und die deutsche Universität. Universitätstage 1966,* published by the Free University (Berlin, 1966); and *Deutsche Germanistentag 1966* (Frankfurt, 1966).
45. Wolfgang Fritz Haug, *Der hilflose Antifaschismus, zur Kritik der Vorlesungsreihen über Wissenschaft und Nationalsozialismus an deutschen Universitäten* (1967) (Cologne, 1970).
46. Baader and Schultz, *Medizin und Nationalsozialismus.*
47. Thom and Spaar, eds., *Medizin im Faschismus;* also Kaul, *Nazimordaktion T-4,* and *Medizin im Nationalsozialismus,* published by the Evangelische Akademie Bad Boll. East German scholars have also explored the rise of eugenics in Germany: see, for example, Hans-Martin Dietl, ed., *Eugenik, Entstehung und gesellschaftliche Bedingtheit* (Jena, 1984); also Alexander Wernecke, *Biologismus und ideologischer Klassenkampf* (Berlin [East], 1976).

Index

Abderhalden, Emil, 252–253
Abel, Wolfgang, 44, 81, 113, 197
Abortion, 121–123, 263, 366nn21, 25; banned in Soviet Union, 278, 398n85; as feminist plot, 269; legalized for Jews, 123; opposed by Nazis, 121–122, 124; socialist and communist support for, 122, 261, 269, 271; by X-rays, 363n53
Abrams, Robert, 192–193
Alcohol and alcoholism, 228, 239–240, 285–286, 391n62, 392n71, 397n55
Allen, Garland, 23, 360n8
Alt-Rehse, Doctors' Führer School at, 83–86, 218
Aly, Götz, 194, 311
American Medical Association, 174; refusal to admit black physicians, 286
Animals, cruelty toward, 227
Anti-Semitism, 131–176, 269, 402n9; in Austria, 168, 276; ban on use of term, 113; in Bulgaria, 167; condemned by socialist physicians, 263–264, 266, 270, 273; in Czechoslovakia, 166–167, 169–170, 276, 279; in England, 168; in Germany, 89–93, 131–176; in Hungary, 167–168, 377n133; in Italy, 170–172; legislation, 103, 155, 285; Lenz on, 57, 124; Martin Luther's, 88–89; medicalization of, 7, 194–200, 379n165, fig. 34; origins of, 142–146; Ploetz's rejection of, 20–21; in United States, 173–174, 379n158. *See also* Jews
Archiv für Rassen- und Gesellschaftsbiologie, 17, 39
Art for art's sake, 290
Aryan race, Jews considered part of, 24, 142
Association of German Healers, 247
Association of German Health Insurance Physicians (KVD), 71–72, 92, 160
Association of Nature-Physicians, 229–231, 234
Association of Socialist Physicians, 77, 146, 255–281; attack on Sauerbruch, 256, 264–265, 267; collaboration with Soviet physicians, 277–278; collapse and exile of, 261–264, 279; goals of, 260–261, 263; Jews in, 259, 269, 397n56; opposition to Nazis, 261–267, 269–271; postwar return to Berlin, 312; ridicule of organic medicine, 265; in Spanish Civil War, 266–267, 280; views on race, 268–275
Astel, Karl, 22, 182, fig. 9
Auschwitz concentration camp, 217, 221, 283

Baader, Gerhard, 311, 387n164
Bartels, Friedrich (Fritz), 29, 136, 185
Bateson, William, 33, 35

Bauer, Friedrich, 258
Bauermeister, Wolfgang, 110, 308
Baur, Erwin, 20, 25, 35, 50, 57, 132
Baur-Fischer-Lenz, *Grundriss der menschlichen Erblichkeitslehre und Rassenhygiene,* 50–59, 204, 350n15, fig. 10
Bayer Pharmaceutical Company, 221
Becker, August, 189–190
Belehrádek, Jan, 273–275
Benjamin, Georg, 271, 281
Berger, Hermann, 64, 163, 245–246
Bernal, J. D., 2, 339n7
Beyerchen, Alan, 3–4
Binding, Rudolf, 178–179, 182
Biological determinism (biologism), 213, 286, 293, 297, 306, 403n30
Birth control, 19–20, 123
Birthrates: Nazi efforts to increase, 121, 126, 367nn42–43, fig. 25; threat of declining, 19–20, 124–125, figs. 1–4, 24, 26
Blankenburg, Werner, 206–207
Blome, Kurt, 43, 217, 230, 285, 301, 356n44, 381n35
Blood groups, 150–151
Blood Protection Law, 88, 131–132, 175, 274, fig. 29
Bluhm, Agnes, 18, 341n27, 391n62
Bock, Gisela, 108, 311
Boehm, Hermann, 84–85, 357n63
Boeters, Gustav, 98, 178
Böttcher, Alfred, 165–166
Bonne, Georg, 253
Borkin, Joseph, 301
Bormann, Martin, 191
Bouhler, Philipp, 178, 182, 188–189, 206
Boulainvilliers, Henri Comte de, 10
Brack, Viktor, 177, 188–190, 206–208
Brandt, Karl, 68, 178, 181, 186, 189–190, 192, 298
Brauchle, Alfred, 231
Breggin, Peter, 192–193
Buchenwald concentration camp, 208–209, 217–218, 221, 298–299
Bumke, Oswald, 125
Bumm, Franz, 39
Burgdörfer, Friedrich, 95, 126, 300

Caesarean section, 18, 164, 243
Cancer, 238–239, 241
Carnegie, Andrew, 14
Carrel, Alexis, 180

Cartwright, Samuel, 13
Castration Law, 175, 203
Catel, Werner, 186–187, 300
Catholic Church, 47, 171–172, 192, 379n158
Catholic physicians, 276, 398n77
Chain, Boris, 282
Chajes, Benno, 50, 273, 280, 346n89
Chamberlain, Houston Stewart, 270, 344n57, 400n20
Chantraine, Heinrich, 163
Civil Service Law, 88, 91, 93, 105, 134, 148–149, 175, 195, 359n1
Clauberg, Carl, 110, 218
Clauss, Ludwig F., 44, 78, 300
Cocks, Geoffrey, 376n115
Cogni, Giulo, 58
Communist Party of Germany (KPD), 45, 91, 252, 256, 258, 262, 373n59
Comte, Auguste, 11
Concentration camps, 133, 208, 212, 221, 263, 267–268, 281, 285. *See also* Auschwitz; Buchenwald; Dachau; Medical experiments
Conti, Leonardo, 68, 82, 85, 94, 218, 250, 284; on alcohol and tobacco, 239; on childless couples, 121; euthanasia, 182, 188–189; on freedom of science, 399n6; on *Führerprinzip,* 73; on Jewish question, 210; on Paracelsus, 234; on Schüssler's *Biochemie,* 247; suicide, 299; on whole-grain bread, 236–237
Conti, Nanna, 242, 392nn82–83, fig. 41
Copernicus, Nicolaus, 171
Criminal biology, 13, 102, 202–205, 383n93, 384n98

Dachau concentration camp, 208–209, 217–219, 221, 250, 301
Dahr, Peter, 151
Danzer, Paul, fig. 27
Darré, Walther, 27, 72, 95, 137
Darwin, Charles, 13–16, 31–32, 291, 345n74
Davenport, Charles, 100, 274
Dawidowicz, Lucy S., 379n165, 383n87
DDT, Nazi suspicions of, 238
Delbrück, Max, 282
Deuschl, Hans, 161, 218–219, 359n88
Deutsches Ärzteblatt, 70, 74–75, 214
Diepgen, Paul, 234, 285, 303–306
Disease, racial specificity of, 78, 195–198

Döderlein, Albert, 238, 271
Dörbeck, Franz, 268
Dorner, Adolf, 183–184
Dubitscher, Ferdinand, 111

Ehrlich, Paul, 225, 253, 284
Einstein, Albert, 259, 282, 340n19
Ekstein, Albert, 252
Elkan, Rudolf, 271–272
Environmental toxins, 237–238, 241
Epstein, Mieczyslaw, 258
Erbarzt, 104–106
Eugenics: American, 20, 97–101, 173–174, 360n9, 400n11; Soviets on, 22–23, 35–36, 58. *See also* Racial hygiene
Euthanasia, 177–194, 221, 289, 379n2; adult, 188–194; Americans on, 179–180; British on, 179; child-murder operation, 185–188, 300; Committee for the Treatment of Severe, Genetically Determined Illness, 186–187, 189; early experiments with, 189–190; efforts to legalize, 179, 193, 254; "14 f 13," 208–209; ideology behind, 181–185, figs. 36–37; of Jews, 188, 207; methods of, 187, 192, 380n17; as normal hospital routine, 192; popular support for, 193–194; protests against, 191–192, 253; T-4 operation, 189–194, 209, 300; voluntary vs. compulsory, 178
Ewald, Gottfried, 254
Expert Committee on Questions of Population and Racial Policy, 95, 359n1

Fabian, Ewald (alias E. Silva), 262, 273, 281, 396n25
Faith healers, 227
Feder, Gottfried, 350n6
Feminism, blamed for declining birthrates, 20, 125, 367n36
Fetscher, Rainer, 23, 75, 138, 203, 252, 370n26
Fischer, Eugen, 8, 26, 33, 41–44, 94, 106, 113, 119, 136, 211, 284, 286, 291–292, 300, 345nn60, 74, 402n11, fig. 17
Flake, Minna, 262, 396n25
Fleck, Ludwik, 283
Forel, August, 96
Frankenthal, Käte, 257, 262, 270, 281
French Revolution, 11, 14, 65, 302
Freud, Sigmund, 54

Frick, Wilhelm, 20, 43, 72, 95–96, 135, 234
Führer principle, 72–73, 89, 294

Gach, Josef, 170
Galilei, Galileo, 230
Galton, Francis, 19, 29, 42, 98, 273, 291, 349n111
Gebhardt, Karl, 219–221, 298
Geis, Friedrich, 262
Genetic health courts, 41, 101–104, 106–107, 139, 296, 298, 361n33
Genetic pathology, 103, 110, 196, 212–217
Genetic poisons. *See* Alcohol; Tobacco
Genetic police, 107, 139
Genetic registries, 106, 135, 139, 214, 369n12
Genetics: in German medical schools, 81; in Nazi ideology, 45, 84, 86, 348n99; Nazi interpretations of, 30, 37, 101–102, 286; and racial specificity of crime, 203–204; used to determine race, 134, 150; word coined by Fischer, 106. *See also* Human genetics
German Medical Association, 70–71, 92, 146, 170, 309, 354n21
German Research Council (DFG), 43–44, 151, 215, 376n107, 392n80
Gestapo, 114, 133, 252
Geyer, Eberhard, 300
Ghon, Anton, 170, 277
Gildea, Maureen, 380n11
Gleichschaltung. *See* Medical profession
Gmelin, Walter, 102, 134–135
Gobineau, Arthur Comte de, 12, 21, 25, 270
Goebbels, Joseph, 75, 79, 118, 236
Göring, Hermann, 210, 227
Goethe, Johann Wolfgang von, 224
Goethe Medallion, 341n27
Gohrbandt, Erwin, 302
Goldschmidt, Richard, 213, 282, 371n43
Gosney, E. S., 360n6
Gottschaldt, Kurt, 42
Graham, Loren, 22, 343n42, 347n94
Grant, Madison, 99, 173
Grawitz, Ernst, 87, 218, 299
Grebe, Hans, 308
Groscurth, Georg, 252
Gross, Walter, 68, 87, 112, 135, 195, 210–211, 230, 243–244, 285, 295, 340n19, 385

Grote, Louis, 230
Grotjahn, Alfred, 22, 216, 273
Gruber, Max von, 19, 49, 352n47
Gruschka, Theodor, 246
Günther, Hans F. K., 26–27, 44, 53, 78, 110–111, 119, 150, 211, 271, 293, 300–301, 306, 400n28
Gürtner, Franz, 27, 116, 203, 369n3
Gütt, Arthur, 44, 77, 95, 115, 117, 135, 141, 153–154, fig. 18
Gundel, Max, 277
Gypsies, 140, 211, 214–215, 220

Hadrich, Julius, 66, 157, fig. 31
Haeckel, Ernst, 8, 33, 146, 256, 340n19
Haedenkamp, Karl, 355n34
Hagen, Wilhelm, 201
Haldane, J. B. S., 343n41
Hartmannbund, 71–74, 92, 144, 156, 159, 161, 256, 354n21
Hartshorne, Edward, 399n1
Haug, Alfred, 390n46
Haug, Fritz, 311
Haycraft, John, 15
Hefelmann, Hans, 186–188, 193, 206
Hegel, G. W. F., 11
Heidegger, Martin, 402n11, fig. 17
Heim, Wilhelm, 312
Heinze, Hans, 186–187
Helman, Socrate, 149
Helmut, Otto, figs. 1–4, 26
Hertwig, Paula, 271
Hess, Rudolf, 228–229, 233, 245, 252
Heyde, Werner, 208, 299
Heydrich, Reinhard, 117, 133, 210, 216–217, 219
Hildebrandt, R. H., 189
Hildebrandt, Wilhelm, 197
Hilgenreiner, Heinrich, 277
Himmler, Heinrich, 91, 95, 109–110, 115–116, 123, 137, 191, 193, 203, 208, 210, 216–219, 228, 299
Hirschfeld, Magnus, 273
Hitler, Adolf, 92, 122, 206, 265, 401n30, fig. 35; admired by Eugenics Record Office, 101; committed to peace, 28–29; "doctor of German people," 64, fig. 11; in euthanasia operation, 177, 181, 191–194; on inheritance of acquired characters, 347n90; on Jews, 210; praised by Lenz, 47–48; read Baur-Fischer-Lenz, 60, 352n51; on Stalin's racial ancestry, 150; on proletariat, 270; territorial claims on Czechoslovakia, 279; vegetarian, 228, 240
Hitler Youth, 73
Hoche, Alfred, 178–179, 182, 289
Hodann, Max, 280
Hörmann, Bernhard, 247–248
Hoffmann, Alfred, 76
Hoffmann, Philip, 210
Holitscher, Arnold, 266, 276–277, 279, 398n88
Holmes, S. J., 58
Holz, Kurt, 147
Homeopathy, 218, 225, 228–229, 231–232, 234, 245–246; Robert Bosch Homeopathic Hospital, 233
Homosexuality, 196; as heritable pathology, 212–214, 386n142; linked with Jews, 213, 290, 386n148
Honor Cross of German Motherhood, 120, fig. 23
Human genetics, 283, 306–308, 345n60
Hume, David, 11
Hunt, Linda, 301

Institutes for racial hygiene, 39–44, 139, 327–329, fig. 9
Insurance companies, 128, 143–146, 148–149, 157, 245, 257–258, 276, 372n58, 375n94
International Association of Socialist Physicians, 265–267, 273
Internationales Ärztliches Bulletin, 133, 148, 213, 262–264, 267
IQ tests, 111–112, 115

Jaffé, Ludwig, 262, 281
Jaspersen, Karsten, 254
"Jewish art," 163
"Jewish psychology," 162–163
"Jewish question," 7, 198, 205–212, 221, 285, 384nn107, 112, 385nn120, 135
Jews: accused of stealing German jobs, 146, 159; Aryan ancestry of, 24, 142; in Association of Socialist Physicians, 259, 269, 397n56; barred from civil service, 91, 148; barred from practicing medicine, 75, 90, 92–93, 129–130, 148, 151–153, 268; blamed for suppressing organic medicine, 227, fig. 38; "disease incarnate," 198–199; diseases of, 195–

196; emigration of, 152, 373n73, 374nn74, 77; "hybrid" of Negro and Oriental, 114, 197; Lenz on, 53–55; in natural health movement, 229; "natural Lamarckians," 55; Nazi definitions of, 149–150; proportion in German medicine, 66, 90, 92–93, 147, 153, 374n85, fig. 31; in racial hygiene movement, 142, 371n43; scapegoat for Germany's problems, 143, 166, 288. *See also* Anti-Semitism
Johst, Hans, 283
Jukes family, 99
Jung, Carl, 162–163, 280, 375n92
Just, Günther, 47, 300

Kaiser Wilhelm Institute for Anthropology, Human Genetics, and Eugenics, 39–43, 106, 273, 307–308, 348n110, 349n115
Kallikak family, 99–100
Kammerer, Paul, 35–36, 55, 346n89, 347n95
Kant, Immanuel, 59
Karstedt, Oskar, 148
Kater, Michael, 66, 353n10, 403n38
Katzenellenbogen, Edwin, 298–299, 401n3
Kaul, Friedrich, 312
Kautsky, 256
Kees, Ernst, 72, 229
Keiter, Friedrich, 357n52
Kennedy, Foster, 180, 380n15
Kirschner, E., 179
Klare, Kurt, 75, 267, 390n34
Klee, Ernst, 254, 311, 379n2
Kneise, O., 302
Koch, Gerhard, 379n2
Koch, Robert, 225, 284
Kötschau, Karl, 164–165, 223, 231–232, 235, 237
Kollwitz, Käte, 259
Kollwitz, Karl, 280
Korach, Alfred, 280
Krankenkassen. *See* Insurance companies
Kranz, Heinrich Wilhelm, 41, 349n112
Krebs, Hans A., 282
Kretschmer, Ernst, 162, 216
Krupp, Friedrich Alfred, 17
Kudlien, Fridolf, 311, 353n9, 395n15
Kürten, Heinz, 173
Kuhn, Philalethes, 18

Kuhn, Thomas, 275, 285
Kurierfreiheit, 229, 244, 389n19

Lamarck, Jean-Baptiste, 31
Lamarckian inheritance (inheritance of acquired characters), 31–38, 49, 346n82, 347nn90, 94–95; Nazi hostility toward, 31–38; rejected by Fritz Lenz, 48–49; socialists on, 33–37, 272; Soviet support for, 35, 49; "typically Jewish," 55
Lammers, Hans-Heinrich, 116, 193
Lang, Theobald, 30, 213, 294, 353n7, fig. 6
Lapouge, Georges Vacher de, 17
Laughlin, Harry H., 99–101, 173, 295
Law against Overcrowding at German Schools and Colleges, 148, 160
Law for the Prevention of Genetically Diseased Offspring, 96–117, fig. 18. *See also* Sterilization
Lebensborn, 87, 358n71
Lehmann, Ernst, 394n111
Lehmann, Julius Friedrich, 26–27, 29, 59, 119, 169, 203, 270, 306, 341n24, 344nn57–59, 354n28, 361n16, 365n5, figs. 5, 21, 33
Lehmann, Wolfgang, 308
Leibfried, Stephan, 256, 311, 396n36
Lenin, V. I., 278
Lennox, W. G., 180
Lenz, Fritz, 8, 22, 33, 41, 45–63, 79, 95, 112, 159, 181, 269, 284, 300; concern about environmental toxins, 238, 241; and euthanasia law, 193; on Galton's eugenics, 29; on Gobineau, 25; on Hitler and Nazi world view, 45, 47, 292, 352n53; on incest, 269, 382n73; on inheritance of acquired characters, 37, 49; on Jews, 53–55, 57, 204, 351n25; on maintaining racial fitness, 292; on Nordic race, 28, 55–56, 216, 351n31; on women's rights, 124; postwar university appointment, 300, 308; on racial miscegenation, 136; on racial specificity of crime, 204; on resettlement of occupied East, 350n9; on "value problem," 48, 291
Levins, Richard, 347n93
Lewontin, Richard, 347n93
Ley, Robert, 247, 250
Liek, Erwin, 227, 239, 388n13, 390n34
Lilienthal, Georg, 66, 311, 358n71, 359n3

Linden, Herbert, 188, 299
"Lives not worth living," 73, 178–222, 265
Locke, John, 11
Lodz (Litzmannstadt) ghetto, 199–200
Loeb, James, 349n115
Loeffler, Lothar, 43, 87, 378n154
Lölhöffel, Edith von, 210, 368n54
Löwenstein, Georg, 260–261, 269, 281, 312
Loewi, Otto, 282, 398n87
Lombroso, Cesare, 13, 202
Lorenz, Konrad, 306
Lukács, Georg, 162, 297
Lukas, Gertrud, 272, 346n89
Lundborg, H., 34
Luther, Martin, 88–89
Luxenburger, Hans, 29, 216, 271

Malthus and neo-Malthusians, 19, 342n30
Mann, Gunter, 311, 343n50
Marcuse, Julian, 271, 281
Marital counseling, 49, 136–139, 370n26
Marital fitness, 138–141
Marital Health Law, 132, 175
Marital loans, 120, 362n39
Martin, Rudolf, 344n58
Martini, Paul, 402n16
Marx, Karl, 16, 21
Marxism: Nazi attacks on, 35, 92, 268–269, 271, 359n93; Fischer on, 40–41; Lenz's critique of, 49
Mass, Bonnie, 365n82
Maternity leave, 127, 260
Mauz, Friedrich, 189
Mayer, August, 253–254, 271, 363n54
Medical experiments, 6, 217–221, 228
Medical profession: ethical standards of, 287; *Gleichschaltung* of, 7, 70–74, 90, 228, 242, 277, 279; Hitler's reliance on, 64; impoverishment of, 69, 143, 257, 287; opposition to natural healing, 244–248; overcrowding and unemployment in, 157–161, 376n107; polarization of, 257, 287–288; reluctance to examine Nazi past, 301–303; support for Hitler, 70–71. *See also* Physicians
Medicalization: of anti-Semitism, 7, 194–199, 379n165; of social deviance, 7, fig. 34
Medicine: authoritarian, 288; bourgeois vs. proletarian, 258–261; bureaucratization of, 69, 144; crisis in, 69; "Jewish," 166; National Socialist revolution in, 290; preventive vs. curative, 73, 84, 231, 240–241, 268–269, 284; proletarization of, 157. *See also* Natural healing
Meier, H. H., 154
Meltzer, Ewald, 179, 194
Mendel, Gregor, 31, 291, 346n77
Mengele, Josef, 44, 211, 292
Mennecke, Friedrich, 208–209
Meyerhof, Otto, 282
Midwifery, 241–243, 261, 356n39, 367n44, 392nn82–85, 393n88, fig. 41
Mielke, Fred, 309
Mikulicz-Radecki, Felix, 109–110
Mitscherlich, Alexander, 309
Morell, Theodor, 194, 238
Moses, Julius, 229, 262
Muckermann, Hermann, 29, 46–47, 345n68
Müller, Karl Valentin, 23–24, 43
Müller, Reinhold, 98, 137
Müller-Hill, Benno, 311, 349n118
Münchener Medizinische Wochenschrift, 26, 160, 169, 267, 269–270, 275, fig. 33
Muller, Hermann J., 59
Mussolini, Benito, 172, 352n53

National Socialism: as "applied biology," 30, 62, 64, 287; doctors' support for, 280, 288, 305; in Holland (Medisch Front), 58, 66; Lenz on, 60; and the occult, 247–248; and progressive thought, 23; view of science in, 294–297
National Socialist German Workers' Party (NSDAP): physicians in, 65–70, 353nn9–10; racial hygienists in, 292; women in, 118
National Socialist Nurses' Association, 86, 358n69
National Socialist Physicians' League, 64–66, 83, 92, 173, 227, 228–229, 292, fig. 14; early leadership of, 353n7; foreign branches, 66; Hitler's speech before, 64; rule over German medical profession, 71, 92; support for Franco, 266; and whole-grain bread, 236
National Socialist Student Association, 68
National Socialist Teachers' Association, 87
Natural Healers' Law, 247

Natural healing, 83, 164, 223–250, 393n104; in German universities, 233; Healers' League of Germany, 229–230; Kneipp physicians, 225, 231, 234; medicinal plants, 249–250; opposition to, 245; Priessnitz physicians, 225–226; Rosehip-Gathering Operation, 249; Rudolf Hess Hospital (Dresden), 84, 86, 229, 231, 233; SS experimental gardens, 250; Whole-Grain Bread Committee, 236–237. *See also* Homeopathy
"Nature" vs. "nurture" controversy, 30–38, 286
Naturopathic medicine. *See* Natural healing
Needham, Joseph, 5
Negroes: "beasts of the field," 13; Hume on, 11; diseases of, 13, 196; Lenz on, 52–53; Ploetz on, 24–25; "racial smell," 78; refused admission to AMA, 286
Neue Anthropologie, 48
Neurath, Otto, 361n16
New German Science of Healing, 230–235, 237, 245, 265, fig. 39
Newton, Isaac, 224
Nietzsche, Friedrich, 56, 179
Nitsche, Paul, 189, 208, 298
Nobel Prize, 28, 294
Nonnenbruch, Wilhelm, 170, 277
Nordic supremacy, 24, 55–56, 265, 271–274, 293, fig. 20
Nuremberg Laws, 87, 131–141, 172; applauded by medical journals, 133–134; marital counseling in, 138; penalties for violating, 133; as public health measures, 141–142; socialist physicians on, 133, 275. *See also* Blood Protection Law; Marital Health Law
Nuremberg Trials, 6, 206, 217, 219–220, 285, 298–299, 301, 309, 402n16
Nyiszli, Miklos, 44

Occult, Nazi attack on, 247–248
Office for Public Health of the NSDAP, 73, 154, 249–250, 284
Office of Racial Policy, 68, 77, 87–89, 107, 172, 197, 210, 212, 285, 290; campaign of enlightenment, 87; films made by, 358n79; *Informationsdienst, Rassenpolitisches Amt der NSDAP,* 77, 88, 346n86; publications of, 88, 356n45; refutation of environmentalism, 35; Reich school, 87
Organic medicine. *See* Natural healing
Orsós, Franz, 140–142, 284, 371n33
Ostermann, Arthur, 29, 46

Pan-German League, 20, 143
Panse, Friedrich, 189
Paracelsus von Hohenheim, 183, 233–234, 305
Pfanmüller, Hermann, 187, 381n38
Pharmacy, 72, 152, 249, 261
Physicians: leadership of, 70–72, 354n29; in Nazi movement, 65–70, 94, 353nn9–10; number in Germany, 128, 368n53; power and prestige of, 93–94, 287. *See also* Medical profession
Planck, Max, 253
Plate, Ludwig, 146, 347n90
Ploetz, Alfred, 8, 14–17, 95, 300, 345n61, 346n82, fig. 6; on anti-Semitism, 21; honored by Nazis, 27; Nazi party member, 292; Nobel Peace Prize nomination, 28; Nordic supremacy of, 24–25, 27–28; opposition to birth control, 19; on racial degeneration, 15–16; in United States, 98
Pohlisch, Kurt, 189
Politisch-anthropologische Revue, 26, 39, 142, 291
Pommerin, Reiner, 364n67, 378n147
Popenoe, Paul, 349n5, 360n6
Pratje, Andreas, 18
Pre-Adamites, 13
Proletarian Health Service, 257–258
Provine, William, 383n76
Publishing House of the German Medical Profession, 75–76

Quacks and Quackery, Nazi attack on, 244–245, 247–248, 253, 388n16
Quelprud, Thordar, 110

Racial ancestry, methods of determining, 110, 134, 150
Racial degeneration, origins of, 15, 18, 137
Racial diagnosis, 141–142, 208
Racial hygiene: conflicts with religion, 47; continuities with postwar human genetics, 306–308; controversies in definition of, 21, 46–47, 61; in German univer-

412 Index

Racial hygiene (*continued*)
sities, 38, 49–50, 80–81, fig. 7; in Italy, 378n148; journals devoted to, 38–39; Nazi support for, 47, 269; origins of, 10–45; in orthodox medical journals, 75, 356n39; positive and negative, 134; as social policy, 286; socialists on, 271, 273–275; vs. eugenics, 29
Racial intermarriage, 141, 172, 197, 274; black-white, 174; German-African, 136; German-Jewish, 134–136, 196, 271, fig. 30; Gypsy-German, 140
Racial Manifesto, Italian, 171–172
Radiation, 237–238
Ramm, Rudolf, 82, 89–90, 102, 154, 174–175, 247–248, 285, 287
Rascher, Sigmund, 219, 221
Reche, Otto, 43, 98, 150–151, 373n67, 384–385
Red Cross, 73, 87, 123, 156, 187, 298
Reich Health Office, 99, 138, 140–141, 214, 239, 299, 371n32
Reich Physicians' Chambers, 67
Reich Physicians' Ordinance, 82, 93
Reiter, Hans, 218, 238, 249, 299
Renthe, Barbara von, 129
Resistance. *See* Association of Socialist Physicians
Rheinlandbastarde, 87, 112–114, 197
Ribbert, Hugo, 21
Rieger, Jürgen, 383n92
Rinne, Hans, 284
Ritter, Robert, 202, 215
Rockefeller Foundation, 349n115
Rockefeller, John D., 14
Röhm, Ernst, 213–214
Rösle, Emil, 39
Roll-Hansen, Nils, 23
Romanova, Galina, 252
Rose, Gerhard, 218, 298
Rosenberg, Alfred, 210, 224, 294, 402n9
Rosenthal, Franz, 396n25
Roth, Karl Heinz, 311
Rüdin, Ernst, 17, 26, 40, 95, 112, 212, 292, 341n24, 345n60, fig. 18
Ruff, Siegfried, 301
Russell, Bertrand, 179, 380n10
Russian prisoners of war, 218–219, 221
Rust, Bernhard, 283
Ruttke, Falk, 43, 115, fig. 18

Saller, Karl, 29, 253, 344n58

Sauerbruch, Ferdinand, 94, 221, 224, 245, 263–265, 267, 285, fig. 17
Schade, Heinrich, 308, 403n34
Schaefer, Konrad, 301
Schäuble, Johann, 41
Schallmayer, Wilhelm, 8, 14, 18, 21, 26, 33, 37, 46, 342n39
Schaltenbrand, Georg, 387n173
Schaxel, Julius, 394n111
Scheel, Gustav Adolf, 388n4
Schemann, Ludwig, 25
Scheunert, Arthur, 235
Schloffer, Karl, 170
Schmidt-Kehl, Ludwig, 43, 300, 342n30
Schmierer, Albert, 72, 249, 257
Schneider, Carl, 189
Schömig, Gustav, 359n88
Schottky, Johannes, 203
Schultz, Bruno K., 40, 341n24
Schultze, Walter, 22, 72, 79, 100, 122, 131
Schulz, Edgar, 197
SA (Storm Troopers), 69, 72; Reichssanitätsschule, 86, fig. 16
SS (Schutz-Staffel), 66, 67, 69, 88, 123, 254; ideology of selection in, fig. 12; Medical Academy, 86; production of fruit juices, 240; Race and Settlement Office, 210; research on herbal medicines, 250
Schwenkenbecher, Alfred, 232
Science: depoliticization of, 293; destruction of, 5, 282–284; functions of, 1–3, 62–63; hereditarian bias in, 286; politics and objectivity of, 56, 289–295; and solution to "Jewish question," 204–205; "value-free," 165, 290, 291
Semashko, N. A., 278
Senger, Alexander von, 163
Siemens, Hermann W., 19–20, 34, 306
Simmel, Ernst, 256, 259–260, 262, 270–271, 280–281, 395n25
Smith, Samuel Stanhope, 10
Social Darwinism, 13–17, 159–160, 226
Social Democratic party (SPD), 23, 45, 144–145, 255, 365n2
Socialism: evolutionary theory in, 16; hereditary theory in, 35–37; racial hygienists on, 15, 60–61; suppressed, in Czechoslovakia, 276. *See also* Association of Socialist Physicians
Society for Racial Hygiene, 17–18, 25, 33, 79, 120, 271, 291, 298

Sociobiology, 306, 403n30
Soviet Union, 307; critique of nordic supremacy, 37; Lamarckian thought in, 36–37; Stalinism in, 277–279; medical support for Republican Spain, 267
Sozialistische Arzt, 24, 77, 259–261, 263, 270, 277
Sperling, Paul, 359n88
Stähle, Eugen, 65, 78–79, 353n7
Stämmler, Martin, 87, 125, 198
Stalin, Joseph, 150
Stanton, William, 339n2
Stauder, Alfons, 70–71, 359n88
Sterilization, 95–117, 123, 134, 175, 221, 296, 362n41, fig. 18; by X-rays, 109–110, 113, 206–207, 238, 271, 363n53; classified not as war crime, 117; dangers of, 401n35; early advocacy of, 96–97; methods of, 109; "operationless," 109; outside Germany, 23, 97–98, 360nn6–9, 365n82, fig. 19; popular fear of, 107, 253–254, 363n46; punitive vs. eugenic, 102; of *Rheinlandbastarde*, 87, 112–114; socialists on, 273; slowdown, 114–116; in United States, 97–98, 100. *See also* Genetic health courts
Sticker, Georg, 381n32
Stoddard, Lothrop, 99, 173
Streicher, Julius, 30, 61, 228, 230, 234, 246, fig. 39
Stubbe, Hans, 57, 85, 348n99
Stuck, Ernest, 68
Stuckart, Wilhelm, 135, 150
Stumpfl, Friedrich, 44

Tennstedt, Florian, 256, 311
Ternon, Yves, 149
Thums, Karl, 18
Thurnwald, Richard, 17
Tille, Alexander, 60
Timofeev-Ressovsky, N. V., 34–35, 85, 105, 362n38
Tirala, Lothar, 212
Tischner, Rudolf, 233
Tobacco and smoking, 228, 239–240, 391n62, 392n62, fig. 40; banned on city trains, 240
Trotsky, Leon, 278
Tuberculosis, 138, 195, 197–198, 200, 215–217, 273, 284
Twin studies, 42–44, 202, 307, 349n115, fig. 8

Unger, Helmut, 182–183, 186, 379n1
United States: sterilization laws, 97; immigration restriction laws, 100, 173; Jewish question, 100

Väth, Oskar, 229, 231
Veblen, Thorstein, 343n49
Venereal disease, 49
Verschuer, Otmar Freiherr von, 42–44, 81, 104–106, 125, 196, 257, 273, 284, 292, 353n14, 369n3, 386n142, figs. 8, 43; on Baur-Fischer-Lenz, 57–58; collaboration with Mengele, 44; on Gypsies, 215; on harmony of science and National Socialism, 295; postwar scientific career, 300, 307–308, 403n33; on racial specificity of disease, 196–197, 241; on socialized medicine, 185; on "solution of the Jewish question," 211
Virchow, Rudolf, 224, 255

Wagner, G. A., 125, 367n39
Wagner, Gerhard, 27, 45, 70–74, 91–92, 95, 135, 165, 204, 234, 257, 285, 355n33, figs. 13, 18, 35, 39; on alcohol and tobacco, 239; praise for American immigration restrictions, 173; controversy with Vatican, 171; and Nuremberg Laws, 136; on Führer principle, 73; on Jewish disease, 195–196; on "lives not worth living," 181, 183, 188; on mandatory vaccination, 246; objections to sterilization, 115–116; opposition to abortion, 122; on unifying academic and natural medicine, 229–230, 245–246, 265; on whole-grain bread question, 235–236
War: Lenz on, 59; medicine in the service of, 248–250; opposed by racial hygienists, 28; as opportunity for euthanasia, 181–182, 289
Warsaw ghetto, 199–202
Weber, Friedrich, 68, 72, 257, 354n28
Wegener, Georg Gustav, 234, 250, 390n43, 394n113
Weinberg, Wilhelm, 8, 371n43
Weindling, Paul, 23
Weinert, Hans, 340n19, 352n1
Weinreich, Max, 222, 310
Weismann, August, 8, 30–38, 291
Weiss, Nicolai, 299–300

Weiss, Sheila, 346n82, 349n1
Wentzler, Ernst, 186–187
Whole-grain bread operation, 235–237
Wigand, Arpad, 383n92
Winau, Rolf, 311
Wirz, Franz, 235–236, 249
Wolbarst, Abraham, 380n14
Wolff, Albert, 246
Woltmann, Ludwig, 18, 21, 26
Women: accused of stealing German jobs, 159; birth strike by, 20, 367n36; in German universities, 123, 129, 376n103; Lenz on, 51; motherhood duty of, 123–125, 367n39; practicing as physicians, 128–129, 368n56, 369n58; working outside home, 120, 126–127
Wulf, Paul, 380n17
Wuttke-Groneberg, Walter, 157, 309, 375n93

Zadek, Ignaz, 256, 258–259, fig. 42
Ziegler, Heinrich Ernst, 33
Ziel und Weg, 77, 119–120, 356n44, fig. 15